Feminist Anthropo

Blackwell Anthologies in Social & Cultural Anthropology

Series Editor: Parker Shipton, Boston University

Drawing from some of the most significant scholarly work of the nineteenth and twentieth centuries, the *Blackwell Anthologies in Social and Cultural Anthropology* series offers a comprehensive and unique perspective on the ever-changing field of anthropology. It represents both a collection of classic readers and an exciting challenge to the norms that have shaped this discipline over the past century.

Each edited volume is devoted to a traditional subdiscipline of the field such as the anthropology of religion, linguistic anthropology, or medical anthropology; and provides a foundation in the canonical readings of the selected area. Aware that such subdisciplinary definitions are still widely recognized and useful – but increasingly problematic – these volumes are crafted to include a rare and invaluable perspective on social and cultural anthropology at the onset of the 21st century. Each text provides a selection of classic readings together with contemporary works that underscore the artificiality of subdisciplinary definitions and point students, researchers, and general readers in the new directions in which anthropology is moving.

Published Volumes:
1 *Linguistic Anthropology: A Reader*
   Edited by Alessandro Duranti
2 *A Reader in the Anthropology of Religion*
   Edited by Michael Lambek
3 *The Anthropology of Politics: A Reader in Ethnography, Theory, and Critique*
   Edited by Joan Vincent
4 *Kinship and Family: An Anthropological Reader*
   Edited by Robert Parkin and Linda Stone
5 *Law and Anthropology: A Reader*
   Edited by Sally Falk Moore
6 *The Anthropology of Development and Globalization:*
   From Classical Political Economy to Contemporary Neoliberalism
   Edited by Marc Edelman and Angelique Haugerud
7 *The Anthropology of Art: A Reader*
   Edited by Howard Morphy and Morgan Perkins
8 *Feminist Anthropology: A Reader*
   Edited by Ellen Lewin

Feminist Anthropology

A Reader

Edited by
Ellen Lewin

Blackwell Publishing

BLACKWELL PUBLISHING
350 Main Street, Malden, MA 02148-5020, USA
9600 Garsington Road, Oxford OX4 2DQ, UK
550 Swanston Street, Carlton, Victoria 3053, Australia

First published 2006 by Blackwell Publishing Ltd

1 2006

Library of Congress Cataloging-in-Publication Data

Feminist anthropology : a reader / edited by Ellen Lewin.
p. cm. — (Blackwell anthologies in social & cultural anthropology; 8)
Includes bibliographical references and index.
ISBN-13: 978-1-4051-0195-0 (hardcover : alk. paper)
ISBN-10: 1-4051-0195-4 (hardcover : alk. paper)
ISBN-13: 978-1-4051-0196-7 (pbk. : alk. paper)
ISBN-10: 1-4051-0196-2 (pbk. : alk. paper) 1. Feminist anthropology. I. Lewin, Ellen.
II. Series: Blackwell anthologies in social and cultural anthropology ; 8.

GN33.8.F44 2006
301—dc22

2005013797

A catalogue record for this title is available from the British Library.

Set in 10/12pt Sabon
by SPI Publisher Services, Pondicherry, India
Printed and bound in the United Kingdom
by TJ International Ltd, Padstow, Cornwall

The publisher's policy is to use permanent paper from mills that operate a sustainable forestry policy, and
which has been manufactured from pulp processed using acid-free and elementary chlorine-free practices.
Furthermore, the publisher ensures that the text paper and cover board used have met acceptable
environmental accreditation standards.

For further information on
Blackwell Publishing, visit our website:
www.blackwellpublishing.com

Contents

Acknowledgments

The task of representing the field of feminist anthropology for this reader has been enormously challenging. Not only is the field growing before one's eyes – a truly moving target – but it has broadened over the years in ways that make a succinct statement of its contributions all but impossible. It has been exciting to revisit many of the writings that inspired me over the years and to get acquainted with newer work that has gone further than could have been imagined thirty years ago.

I want to thank the editorial staff at Blackwell who made this volume come to fruition. Jane Huber suggested the volume after looking at the syllabus of a course I was teaching on the history of feminist anthropology. Throughout the revisions and rethinkings that followed, she encouraged me when I wondered whether I could satisfy all the competing demands a project like this made, spurring me on with unfailing good humor. Her assistant, Emily Martin, has been a miracle of organization throughout. The series adviser, Parker Shipton, offered many provocative and wise comments and kept me on my toes. And the meticulous attention given the manuscript by the copy editor, Veronica Ions, was truly awe-inspiring. At last, I had encountered someone whose passion for correct punctuation and citation rivaled my own!

During the planning of the volume, I benefited from the advice of a number of colleagues. Carole Browner, Meena Khandelwal, Lynn Bolles, and Evelyn Blackwood had particularly useful comments, and I also appreciated the suggestions offered by the anonymous readers for Blackwell. My research assistants Natalia Chernyayeva and Jill Moffett helped with the details of assembling the manuscript at various stages and I appreciate their attention to consistency and accuracy under sometimes trying circumstances. I also am thankful for the resources made available to me at the Obermann Center for Advanced Studies at the University of Iowa, where I was in residence during the final preparations of the volume.

My location in the Anthropology Department at the University of Iowa has been a special source of inspiration to me as I worked on this volume. As the only anthropology department offering an organized graduate specialization in feminist anthropology, it has been an exciting place to teach, a place where the field is accorded the respect it deserves. My colleagues in the feminist track, past and present, have set consistently high standards for what feminist anthropology can be and have kept me informed about aspects of the field I couldn't have grasped on my own. So I want to give particular thanks to all of them: Florence Babb, Virginia Dominguez, Laura Graham, Meena Khandelwal, Mac Marshall, Beth Pauls, Erica Prussing, Mary Whelan, and most importantly Margery Wolf, who was on the scene when I discovered feminist anthropology and helped me to find my way in it many years later.

The editor and publisher gratefully acknowledge the permission granted to reproduce the copyright material in this book:

1 Edwin Ardener, "Belief and the Problem of Women" and "The 'Problem' Revisted," pp. 1–27 from Shirley Ardener, *Perceiving Women*. London: Malaby Press, 1975 [1968]. Reprinted with permission of Shirley Ardener.

2 Judith K. Brown, "A Note on the Division of Labor by Sex," pp. 1073–8 from *American Anthropologist*, 72 (1970). © 1970 by University of California Press. Reproduced with permission of University of California Press via Copyright Clearance Center.

3 Sherry B. Ortner, "Is Female to Male as Nature Is to Culture?," from Michelle Z. Rosaldo and Louise Lamphere, *Women, Culture, and Society*. Stanford, CA: Stanford University Press, 1974. © 1974 by the Board of Trustees of the Leland Stanford Jr. University. Reprinted with permission of the publisher and author.

4 Gayle Rubin, "The Traffic in Women: Notes on the 'Political Economy' of Sex," pp. 157–210 from Rayna R. Reiter, *Toward an Anthropology of Women*. New York: Monthly Review Press, 1975. © Gayle Rubin. Reprinted with the kind permission of the author.

5 Michelle Z. Rosaldo, "The Use and Abuse of Anthropology: Reflections on Feminism and Cross-Cultural Understanding," pp. 389–417 from *Signs*, 5/3 (1980). Reprinted by permission of the University of Chicago Press.

6 Karen Brodkin Sacks, "Toward a Unified Theory of Class, Race, and Gender," pp. 534–50 from *American Ethnologist*, 16/3 (1989). © 1989 by University of California Press. Reprinted by permission of University of California Press via Copyright Clearance Center, and the author, now Karen Brodkin.

7 Lila Abu-Lughod, "Writing against Culture," pp. 137–62 from Richard G. Fox, ed. *Recapturing Anthropology: Working in the Present*. Santa Fe, NM: School of American Research Press, 1991. © 1991 by the School of American Research, Santa Fe. Reprinted by permission of School of American Research, Santa Fe.

8 Esther Newton, "My Best Informant's Dress: The Erotic Equation in Fieldwork," pp. 212–35 from Ellen Lewin and William L. Leap, *Out in the Field: Reflections of Lesbian and Gay Anthropologists*. Urbana, IL: University of Illinois Press, 1996. © 1993 by University of California Press. Reproduced with permission of University of California Press via Copyright Clearance Center, and the author.

9 Patricia Zavella, "Feminist Insider Dilemmas: Constructing Ethnic Identity with Chicana Informants," pp. 138–59 from Diane L. Wolf, *Feminist Dilemmas in Fieldwork*. Boulder, CO: Westview, 1996. Reprinted with permission of University of Nebraska Press, Lincoln, and the author.

10 Paulla A. Ebron, "Contingent Stories of Anthropology, Race, and Feminism," pp. 211–32 from Irma McClaurin, *Black Feminist Anthropology: Theory, Politics, Praxis, and Poetics*. New Brunswick, NJ: Rutgers University Press, 2001. © Paulla A. Ebron. Reprinted with the kind permission of the author.

11 Louise Lamphere, "Bringing the Family to Work: Women's Culture on the Shop Floor," pp. 519–40 from *Feminist Studies*, 11 (1985). Reprinted by permission of the publisher, Feminist Studies Inc.

12 Faye Ginsburg, "Procreation Stories: Reproduction, Nurturance, and Procreation in Life Narratives of Abortion Activists," pp. 623–36 from *American Ethnologist*, 14/4 (1987). © 1999 by University of California Press. Reprinted by permission of University of California Press via Copyright Clearance Center, and the author.

13 Elizabeth Chin, "Ethnically Correct Dolls: Toying with the Race Industry," pp. 305–21 from *American Anthropologist*, 101/2 (1999). © 1999 by University of California Press. Reproduced with permission of University of California Press via Copyright Clearance Center, and the author.

14 Charis Thompson, "Strategic Naturalizing: Kinship in an Infertility Clinic," pp. 175–202 from Sarah Franklin and Susan McKinnon, *Relative Values: Reconfiguring Kinship Studies*. Durham, NC: Duke University Press, 2001. © 2001 by Duke University Press. All rights reserved. Used by permission of the publisher and the author.

15 Begoña Aretxaga, "Dirty Protest: Symbolic Overdetermination and Gender in Northern Ireland Ethnic Violence," pp. 123–48 from *Ethos*, 23/2 (1995). © 1995 by University of California Press. Reproduced with permission of University of California Press via Copyright Clearance Center, and the author.

16 Lynn Stephen, "Women's Rights Are Human Rights: The Merging of Feminine and Feminist Interests among El Salvador's Mothers of the Disappeared (CO-MADRES)," pp. 807–27 from *American Ethnologist*, 22/4 (1995). © 1995 by University of California Press. Reproduced with permission of University of California Press via Copyright Clearance Center, and the author.

17 Christine J. Walley, "Searching for 'Voices': Feminism, Anthropology, and the Global Debates over Female Genital Operations," pp. 405–38 from *Cultural Anthropology*, 12/3 (1997). © 1997 by University of California Press. Reproduced with permission of University of California Press via Copyright Clearance Center, and the author.

18 Lynn M. Morgan, "Imagining the Unborn in the Ecuadoran Andes," pp. 323–50 from *Feminist Studies*, 23/2 (1997). Reprinted by permission of the publisher, Feminist Studies, Inc.

19 Shellee Colen, " 'Like a Mother to Them': Stratified Reproduction and West Indian Childcare Workers and Employers in New York," pp. 78–102 from Faye D. Ginsburg and Rayna Rapp, *Conceiving the New World Order: The Global Politics of Reproduction*. Berkeley, CA: University of California Press, 1995. © Shellee Colen. Reprinted with the kind permission of the author.

20 Carla Freeman, "Femininity and Flexible Labor: Fashioning Class through Gender on the Global Assembly Line," pp. 245–62 from *Critique of Anthropology*, 18/3 (1998). © 1998 by Sage Publications. Reproduced with the kind permission of the author and Sage Publications Ltd, UK.

21 Evelyn Blackwood, "*Tombois* in West Sumatra: Constructing Masculinity and Erotic Desire," pp. 491–521 from *Cultural Anthropology*, 13/4 (1998). © 1998 by

University of California Press. Reproduced with permission of University of California Press via Copyright Clearance Center, and the author.

22 Gloria Wekker, " 'What's Identity Got to Do with It?': Rethinking Identity in Light of the *Mati* Work in Suriname," pp. 119–38 from Evelyn Blackwood and Saskia E. Wieringa, *Female Desires: Same-Sex and Transgender Practices across Cultures*. New York: Columbia University Press, 1999. © 1999 by Columbia University Press. Reprinted with permission of the publisher.

Introduction
Feminist Anthropology: A Reader

Ellen Lewin

Feminist anthropology first burst onto the scene only about 30 years ago, in the early to mid-1970s. Along with similar efforts taking hold throughout the academy in this period, it was inspired and shaped by the women's liberation movement of the late 1960s and early 1970s, with scholar-activists asking questions that they thought might help them to formulate strategies for addressing persistent social injustices. Departing from anthropological conventions of the time, their concern was not only focused on the parts of the world traditionally studied by anthropologists – small-scale, exotic, technologically primitive cultures, or populations defined as "others" close at hand – but with relating the insights yielded in cross-cultural study to the societies in which they lived. Curiosity about "the other" was filtered through a sense that the problems facing women in Western societies were urgent and that the more banal versions of cultural relativism could no longer be used to disguise their significance. Furthermore, in insisting on what was then a very unpopular interrogation of taken-for-granted assumptions about women and men, many of these early feminist anthropologists felt themselves to be outsiders in their own cultures.

At the same time, however, in line with a strong belief in the common humanness of all the peoples anthropologists studied and the existence of fundamental commonalities between women across cultural boundaries, the originators of feminist anthropology were convinced that lessons relevant to their own concerns could be drawn from the study of women in other cultures. The notion that there were cultural regularities awaiting discovery was implicit in this venture, as was an as yet unexamined reliance on sexual categories as real and cross-culturally valid. In moving toward originating a new field, these scholars were moved, as well, by the desire to do justice to women in various cultures, a group they saw as having been ethnographically disenfranchised. Drawing on their perception that women, including themselves, had been silenced and subordinated in many cultural domains but, especially the realm of the public, early feminist anthropologists sought to make women visible in the ethnographic record and in their own worlds. Since that time, however, as this volume will demonstrate, the field has moved from being an anthropology of women to an anthropology of gender, and finally, in its present form, primarily a feminist anthropology.

Not only has the field matured intellectually, but its place in anthropology has changed enormously. The graduate students and junior faculty who launched the field in the early 1970s have moved through their careers (and in some cases, even retired), and their work is no longer thought to challenge the boundaries of the discipline. The early excitement of being involved in an insurgent enterprise, one that continued the legacy of the civil rights and anti-war movements, shifted into the security of respectability; many of the radical leaders of the early anthropology of women have become the *éminences grises* of anthropology – the presidents of the associations, recipients of awards, honors, and endowed professorships. The bitter struggles of the early years, for example, to force anthropology departments to be accountable for patterns of discrimination against women faculty, have resulted in at least formal measures meant to promote equity, and now (along with some other causes, like a renewed focus on race, a critique of colonialism and the abuses of globalization, and a concern with lesbian and gay rights) have become assumed elements of anthropology's political face.[1] This doesn't mean, of course, that all inequalities have been addressed adequately, but it does mean that (open) controversy no longer surrounds efforts to consider them. In short, feminist anthropology has become respectable and no longer connotes radical opposition to the powers that be.

It is difficult to offer an account of the period when feminist anthropology was born without reflecting on some of the personal dynamics that drove its emergence. Those of us who were there for its gestation were passionate about what we were doing, even as we were struggling to define how it would ultimately fit into anthropology. Many of us were active in various feminist organizations, particularly in consciousness-raising groups whose politics stretched from liberal to radical to socialist (Boxer 1998; Echols 1989; Freedman 2002; Rosen 2000). We understood our commitment to craft a solution to the subordination of women less as an intellectual challenge than as a calling that both self-interest and altruism demanded that we fulfill. Our non-anthropologist political allies – our "sisters" – had charged us with the weighty task of situating women's oppression cross-culturally. Had women always been oppressed? Were there factors – economic, cultural, historical – that could be shown to influence women's status? How could we go about assessing the status of women cross-culturally; in other words, what were the indicators that we should look for in the ethnographic record and in our own research? I don't think most of us gave a second thought to the idea that we female anthropologists and the women we might encounter in other cultures were in some way "the same," all linked by a shared experience of male dominance.

When a group of us at Stanford University – four graduate students and two faculty wives, members of a department consciousness-raising group that also included clerical staff – planned an experimental course called "Women in Cross-Cultural Perspective" in 1971, we had to search diligently for almost a year to uncover readings we could use for the class. The options were so limited, in fact, that we also included the women's liberation collection *Sisterhood is Powerful* (Morgan 1970) among our texts. But as we prepared to teach the course, a process through which we essentially taught ourselves "the anthropology of women," we uncovered some texts that demonstrated that some of our predecessors, mainly women, had in fact given the status of women some thought. We found the work of Ruth Landes, Phyllis Kaberry, Denise Paulme, Ester Boserup, and of course, Margaret Mead.

At around the same time, I was planning to take one of my doctoral comprehensive exams in something the department and I called, for lack of a better designation, "Women and Sex Roles" and neither I nor my committee members had any clear sense of what sorts of works should be included on the reading list or what topics would need to be covered. In fact, the faculty struggled over whether I should be permitted to proceed in this uncharted area, and only because of the general permissiveness of the 1970s – this was the era, after all, of almost constant student strikes and protests – was I permitted to go forward in what they all saw as an extremely strange and quixotic venture. To say the least, the emergent anthropology of women lacked not only a canon but even the most minimal institutional legitimacy. Nonetheless, that first course on "Women in Cross-Cultural Perspective" was a huge success, enrolling about 100 students, and despite its unevenness one of the organizers, the late Michelle Z. Rosaldo, used some of the basic ideas we had developed as the foundation of *Women, Culture, and Society,* co-edited with Louise Lamphere in 1974 (see below).

From these fragile and inauspicious beginnings, feminist anthropology has exploded over the past three decades, now consisting in a large and diverse literature of books, articles in feminist journals, and articles in mainstream anthropological publications. The exponential growth of the literature is probably the single most challenging problem I have faced in trying to assemble this collection of "classic" readings. Not only does the sheer volume of this literature prevent one from achieving a clear sense of mastery of the field, but its ramification into a broader set of issues and questions also presents substantial difficulties for an editor trying to "make sense" of a very broad field. To keep the scope of the volume somewhat more manageable, I've excluded essays that deal with topics outside social-cultural anthropology; readers should be aware that major contributions have been made by scholars whose focus is in linguistics and archaeology, as well as biological and applied anthropology. For the same practical reasons, contributors from outside North America are conspicuously absent; major contributions to feminist anthropology have been made by scholars from Great Britain and Europe, and from elsewhere in the world, but giving them a presence appropriate to their significance is simply not possible in a work of this scope. Similarly, I have been unable to include works in the important areas of ethnographic film, development studies and applied anthropology, and child development. Coverage of ethnographic areas is, at best, uneven: some culture areas make an appearance in more than one selection, while others are not represented; my choices in this regard have nothing to do with the scope of work in feminist anthropology, which has emerged from virtually every field setting imaginable. And despite the fascinating depictions of anthropologists and ethnographic ventures in many works of fiction and in non-scholarly nonfiction, all the articles included here are drawn from academic anthropological sources. All of these limitations are reflected in the overview of the field I offer in this introduction and at the beginning of each of the book's five parts.

One final caveat. While I have struggled mightily to provide the most even-handed treatment of feminist anthropology that I could under the particular constraints that framed this project, the account of the field that follows cannot be described as other than "Feminist Anthropology According to Ellen Lewin." As much as feminist and postmodernist realizations have taught us to be self-conscious about the constructed and positional nature of all scholarship, collections are as vulnerable to the skewed vision of their editors as are other sorts of representations. Others charged with editing this volume would undoubtedly have told a different story, shaped, as mine has been, by generation, personal interests, social and academic location, theoretical preferences, political inclinations, and by indefinable matters of taste and esthetics. Beyond this, the feminist anthropological writings that have made their way into this volume are, in a sense, the winners of the struggle for legitimacy that took place when the field was first forming. Doing feminist work, studying gender, and particularly studying marginal populations such as sexual minorities, was not a popular undertaking in the early years, and some courageous innovators weren't able to reap the rewards of the field's eventual institutionalization. Although it finally became respectable – even status-enhancing – to study gender, it was not always so, and many early scholars never saw their work gain prestigious publication outlets. In like fashion, there were many among the early feminist anthropologists who paid for their commitment with their careers, and who have no platform from which to pass on a legacy. This volume is dedicated to them, with gratitude.

Foremothers and Other Genealogies

Feminist anthropology may be said to have its roots in the work of a number of earlier scholars, including many who would have been surprised to know that their writings had inspired this particular disciplinary turn. Who may be counted as ancestors varies, of course, but I would argue that they should include both stylistic and intellectual predecessors, as well as individuals whose professional contributions stood as beacons to women anthropologists who followed after them. There were actually many women active in US anthropology as early as the late nineteenth century (Lurie 1999 [1966]; Parezo 1993), some of them self-taught, but their accomplishments have tended to fade with time, partly because, in some cases they produced few publications, but also because their heritage was erased by the professionalization of the discipline at the turn of the twentieth century. Of the earlier figures, only Elsie Clews Parsons has achieved a significant place in the history of the field. Lurie's account of the accomplishments of some of the others – Erminnie Platt Smith, Alice Fletcher, Matilda Stevenson, Zelia Nuttall, and Frances Densmore – raise questions that have yet to be fully answered.

Prominent among these unsung heroines have been the wives of anthropologists, some of whom facilitated their husbands' research, and others of whom arguably created their own genre of anthropological writing (Tedlock 1995). As Barbara Tedlock details, the genres these "wives" employed varied, as a number of them struggled over whether or not to define themselves as anthropologists. Elizabeth Fernea (Fernea 1965) called her early work, *Guests of the Sheik,* an ethnography, but wrote it in the style of a memoir. Her time among the women of a southern Iraqi village only came to pass, as she explained, because she had married an anthropologist, accompanied him to the field, and gamely taken on the task of learning about the women. Similarly, Margery Wolf called her classic ethnography, *The House of Lim,* a study, but opens the book with a disclaimer, "Because my husband is an anthropologist who specializes in Chinese studies, I came in 1959 to live in a small country village in Northern Taiwan" (Wolf 1968: vii). In later years, even after the book had achieved enormous success, particularly as a textbook in anthropology classes, some of her husband's colleagues referred to it as "her little novel" (Wolf, personal communication). Even among women anthropologists who were more thoroughly professionalized, efforts to write about their experiences as women seemed to demand a form that would distinguish those works from "real" scholarship (cf. Bowen 1954).

Other works produced by anthropologists' wives have also had a lasting impact on the field, often because of their innovative, i.e., not classically ethnographic, expository styles. A number of these were life histories that adopted the "as told to" framework in order to make the words and the ideas of native women accessible. *Baba of Karo,* by Mary F. Smith, M. G. Smith's wife, was one such early effort (Smith 1954). Marjorie Shostak's later *Nisa,* which presents the life history of a !Kung woman, has long been a staple of anthropology classrooms, despite the fact that its author, the wife of Melvin Konner, had no professional credentials as an anthropologist (Shostak 1981, 1989).

For those (mostly young) women anthropologists who brought the women's movement and anthropology into conversation, there was limited knowledge of the ways that women had already made their mark in the discipline. Of course, we all knew about Margaret Mead and Ruth Benedict – who could possibly not know about them? – but our understanding of the degree to which their work shaped our own development was slim. Margaret Mead was often derided as a popularizer, and by the time I became aware of Ruth Benedict's work, her emphasis on characterizing cultures as totalized psychological types had already begun to drift out of fashion. Mead and Benedict stood, in a sense, as exceptions that proved the rule: we had come to understand that women were discriminated against in anthropology as in other academic disciplines, and the fact that the two most famous American anthropologists of the period were women was just the sort of curious fact that made the larger pattern more convincing.

That both Mead's and Benedict's intellectual projects depended upon implicit and often explicit comparison between the United States and non-Western cultures was less well known to us, surprising now since our own objectives drew on the same impulses. Benedict, we now know, was both an ardent feminist and relatively open (for her time) as a lesbian; Mead shared some of her interests, but drew far less on personal or political commitments for inspiration. Their visibility, perhaps more than the content of their writing, gave a feminine face to anthropology as a discipline that made it seem a possible destination for women who came after them (Babcock 1995; Lapsley 1999; Lutkehaus 1995; Mead 1974).

Less widely known by the 1970s, however, were a number of early women anthropologists whose professional lives and intellectual output could both have offered paradigms for our generation (see above). Probably the most noteworthy of these was Elsie Clews Parsons, who was a political radical and an outspoken feminist, while her personal wealth also enabled her to offer financial support to younger scholars in the era before public funding for field research had been institutionalized. Louise Lamphere's account makes clear that her feminism, pacifism, and commitment to other progressive movements were important catalysts for her scholarship, anchored in the experience of radical politics after World War I. Parsons focused her work on a search for cultural universals, an emphasis that would be echoed by the (more explicitly feminist) anthropology of the 1970s, which had been shaped in part by the movement against the Vietnam War and the Civil Rights Movement. The later feminist anthropologists were influenced, as well, by thinkers who had written during the intervening years, so the parallel ought not be overstated. Nonetheless, as Lamphere demonstrates, Parsons was concerned with ways in which women were limited by "taboos, constraints, and exclusionary practices – often centering on women's bodies, their sexuality, and their reproductive roles as mothers" (Lamphere 1995: 98), issues that were vigorously taken up by contributors to *Women, Culture, and Society* (see below).

The work of some other early to mid-twentieth-century women anthropologists prefigure the later concerns of feminist anthropology more directly. Ruth Landes, for example, early on made women an explicit object of study (Landes 1971 [1938]; Landes 1994 [1947]) and her essay in the first edition of *Women in the Field* speaks directly of the personal difficulties she encountered as a single woman doing fieldwork in Brazil in the 1930s. Hortense Powdermaker, a contemporary of Mead's who studied with Malinowski, was a political activist before becoming an anthropologist. After her fieldwork in Melanesia (Powdermaker 1933), she conducted research in a number of then-atypical settings: urban anthropology in the African Copper Belt (Powdermaker 1962), a project on race in the American South (Powdermaker 1939), and an innovative study of Hollywood (Powdermaker 1950), prefiguring later work by feminists who sought to address contemporary social problems through their anthropology.

Zora Neale Hurston, whose work on African American culture took her back to the Florida town where she was raised, has now been recognized to have experimented with a number of narrative forms and to have moved audaciously between academic and creative writing modes. As a young African American woman studying at Columbia University under Boas, however, her ability to develop as a professional was impeded by her value to some scholars as an informant as well as by her difficulties affording study for the doctorate (Boyd 2003; Hernandez 1995; Hurston 1969 [1942], 1935; Mikell 1988, 1999). But Hurston was not the only African American woman to make significant contributions to anthropology, though the others have received even less general attention than Hurston. Among these were Caroline Bond Day, a physical anthropologist (Ross, Adams, and Williams 1999), Irene Ellen Diggs, who worked closely with W. E. B. DuBois (Bolles 1999; McClaurin 2001), Katherine Dunham and Pearl Primus, both of whom worked at the intersection of dance and anthropology in the 1940s (Aschenbrenner 1999; McClaurin 2001), and somewhat later Vera Green, a founding member of the Association of Black Anthropologists (McClaurin 2001).

There are also figures like Daisy Bates, an Irish expatriate who for decades lived in the Australian bush close to aboriginal peoples. Some accounts of her life suggest that she provided Radcliffe-Brown with data that he subsequently claimed as his own, though her life story is filled with contradictions and the story is far from clear (Blackburn 1994; Salter 1971). Although she published some ethnographic materials (Bates 1939), she never achieved a scholarly reputation. The women's movement resurrected her memory, chiefly in connection to the mistreatment she claimed to have suffered at the hands of Radcliffe-Brown, and since that time she has enjoyed some fame as an archetype of exploited womanhood.

Some other women had already produced useful ethnographic works that focused on the lives of women long before the rise of feminist anthropology. Phyllis Kaberry, an Australian scholar, wrote *Aboriginal Woman: Sacred and Profane* in 1939, a study that focused on the rich but separate ritual lives enjoyed by women. In 1952 she published a study called *Women of the Grassfields,* that detailed the economic position of women in British Cameroon (Kaberry 1939, 1952). Another early contributor was the French anthropologist Denise Paulme, who edited the collection *Women of Tropical Africa,* one of the only scholarly collections available to new feminist anthropologists in the early 1970s (Paulme 1963).

Why did we know so little about the figures who might have provided us with an intellectual anchor as we sought to understand more about the lives of women in other cultures and in our own society, and to found a new subdiscipline? How did the names of these scholars slip into obscurity, sometimes within a few short years of the time they made their contributions? Catherine Lutz and Lynn Bolles have both argued persuasively that citation practices in the discipline have tended to remove the names of women anthropologists, and particularly of those who are African American or members of other minority groups, from disciplinary memory. These citation practices not only consign the contributions of women scholars to obscurity but suggest that their work is neither reputable nor significant. Regular citations of a scholar's work, in other words, construct that individual's intellectual stature. When work is not cited, the scholar will be perceived as peripheral and eventually forgotten, even when she has been successful in getting her work published (Bolles 2001; Lutz 1990).

Also fueling the development of feminist anthropology in the early 1970s were intellectual developments in anthropology not explicitly tied to the women's movement or even to questions of gender. One of these was the critique of assumed links between biology and culture put forward by David Schneider in his slender 1968 volume, *American Kinship: A Cultural Account.* Schneider argued that kinship was far less rooted in biological essences than was usually claimed; rather, he contended that the shared biological substance, blood, was constituted by culture to account for and make sense of kinship bonds. In American kinship, according to Schneider, *blood* and *law* offer symbolic resources by which ideas about kinship relationships are constituted (Schneider 1968).

In their preface to *Naturalizing Power,* a 1995 volume explicitly inspired by Schneider's contribution to feminist anthropology, Sylvia Yanagisako and Carol Delaney explain his importance:

> In his cultural analysis of American kinship, Schneider demonstrated that a particular folk model of heterosexual reproduction lies behind assumptions of the genealogical grid. In a more graphic vein, he tried to explain that the thin red fluid we call blood does not make ties strong; the ties that bind are in culture, not nature. That is, blood *symbolizes* kinship rather than constitutes it. By explicating the symbolic system through which Americans

construct seemingly natural relationships of shared bio-genetic substance, Schneider opened up the possibility for anthropologists to explore other areas in which social relations are naturalized. (Yanagisako and Delaney 1995: ix; emphasis in original)

By questioning that kinship was simply the automatic attribute of biologically grounded connections, Schneider could be read as suggesting that other cultural categories thought to be rooted in biology – most notably gender – also were culturally, rather than biologically, constituted, that they were ideas framed in particular cultural contexts and as such far more flexible than anyone had previously thought. While Schneider didn't take up matters of differential power that have preoccupied feminist anthropologists, and certainly didn't envision the impact his writings on kinship would have (Schneider 1995), the fact that many pioneers of feminist (and lesbian/gay) anthropology had been mentored by him at the University of Chicago is hardly incidental.

Some early statements by mainstream anthropologists, not inspired by the women's movement, were discovered by feminist scholars in the early years of their study of women. Edwin Ardener's article "Belief and the Problem of Women" (this volume, chapter 1) was first presented in 1968 at a seminar taught by Phyllis Kaberry at University College London. Its later inclusion in the 1975 volume *Perceiving Women*, brought it to the attention of feminist anthropologists and it remains a compelling statement on how women come to be a "muted group." Ardener argues that it is not the inherent importance (or lack thereof) of women's activities that determine how they are represented in anthropological texts, but their use of models of society that offer less satisfying accounts than those typically provided by men, that is, less global and inclusive than in male discourse.

To use the terminology that would become prominent in the work of Rosaldo and other contributors to *Women, Culture, and Society*, women's location in the seemingly limited arena of domesticity makes them less apt to generate explanations that meet the (male) ethnographer's requirements, in effect, they seem "inarticulate." Ardener calls this the "hot stove" argument: that women are too busy with "the realities of childbirth and child-rearing" and thus "have less time for or less propensity towards the making of models of society, for each other, for men, or for ethnographers" (Ardener 1975). That this constitutes a kind of collusion between male (or male-identified) anthropologists and male informants does not escape Ardener's attention, and he clearly situates the resultant muteness or invisibility of women in ethnographic texts to the shared power of males. He also assumes a sort of sameness in the interests and structural position of men, whether they be ethnographers or informants, an essentializing of gender that will come to be questioned later on.

Emergence

As an academic field, feminist anthropology began modestly, with some papers and panels offered at conferences, almost exclusively the work of graduate students and very junior faculty, initially presented with great trepidation. In 1970, for example, Sally Linton (later Slocum) presented a paper at the American Anthropological Association annual meeting entitled "Woman the Gatherer: The Male Bias in Anthropology." Later published in Rayna Reiter's collection *Toward an Anthropology of Women,* the paper long stood as one of the classics of the approach that characterized the early anthropology of women: a careful rethinking of the male-centered thinking that shaped the development of anthropology as a field. But at the time that the paper was presented, it represented a daring challenge to business as usual in the academy, particularly as it criticized the virtually sacred trope of "Man the Hunter," a mainstay of anthropological theory at the time. At that same 1970 annual meeting, some young anthropologists involved in the women's movement made tentative efforts to form some sort of collectivity, though they nervously dispersed after only a few women appeared at the appointed time.

Also in 1970, Peggy Golde edited what would become a path breaking volume of essays by women anthropologists, *Women in the Field* (Golde 1986 [1970]). Though Golde denied that she was inspired by the new feminist movement, her volume raised the important question of how being a woman might affect the experience of anthropologists as they conducted their research in different sorts of settings and in different historical times. The contributors represented a wide swath of professional accomplishment, from well-known scholars like Margaret Mead and Cora DuBois to younger anthropologists like Rena Lederman. These essays added to some recent autobiographies by women anthropologists, including an influential book by Hortense Powdermaker, *Stranger and Friend* (1966), that feminist anthropologists trying to find their way had looked to for inspiration.

But from these tentative beginnings the field virtually exploded, and within a very few years two key volumes had been published, both edited by younger scholars, that sought to bring visibility and voice to those who had been long overlooked. In retrospect, these efforts can be described as establishing an *anthropology of women* in that they sought to recuperate women as distinct cultural actors and to question the assumptions that had rendered the discipline as androcentric as they argued it was. They also depended on assumptions about "woman" as an easily defined and recognized category that exhibited significant cross-cultural regularities.

Both of these volumes shared a commitment to making women's voices audible, and both were self-consciously oriented toward delineating a new field of specialization. As Michelle Zimbalist Rosaldo and Louise Lamphere put it in the introduction to *Women, Culture, and Society* their investigation of whether women are universally "the second sex" was inspired "not simply out of some sort of abstract, intellectual curiosity, but because we are searching for ways to think about ourselves" (Rosaldo and Lamphere 1974: 1). They also mention, in the preface, that the impetus for the volume grew out of an experimental course taught at Stanford in 1971; Rosaldo was one of the six instructors who collaborated in that venture. From the outset, Rosaldo and Lamphere's approach focused on the premise that asymmetry between women and men was universal. Even as they acknowledged that societies in which "women have achieved considerable social recognition and power" exist, they were more concerned with the fact that "none has observed a society in which women have publicly recognized power and authority surpassing that of men." They went on:

Everywhere we find that women are excluded from certain crucial economic or political activities, that their roles as wives and mothers are associated with fewer powers and prerogatives than are the roles of men. It seems fair to say then, that all contemporary societies are to some extent male-dominated, and although the degree and expression of female subordination vary greatly, sexual asymmetry is presently a universal fact of human social life. (Rosaldo and Lamphere 1974: 1)

The essays in the volume all framed women's status as universally devalued, though the mechanism through which the authors sought to explain this phenomenon varied. Rosaldo set the tone for the volume in her essay "Woman, Culture, and Society: A Theoretical Overview" by advancing the argument that women are everywhere subordinated because in all societies their maternal obligations confine them to the domestic or private domain. In contrast, men predominate in the public domain and are thus better positioned to form extra-familial alliances, to dominate in political and religious activities, and to control valuable economic resources. She concluded that "universal asymmetries in the actual activities and cultural evaluations of men and women" are related to "a universal, structural opposition between domestic and public spheres" (Rosaldo 1974: 41). Consistent with her stated commitment to use anthropological evidence as a basis for political strategies, Rosaldo linked improvements in women's status to their ability to "transcend domestic limits" and suggested that "the most egalitarian societies would not be those in which male and female are opposed or are even competitors, but those in which men value and participate in the domestic life of the home" (1974: 41).

Other essays in the volume expanded on this theme, but interpreted the origins of these universals somewhat differently. Nancy Chodorow, drawing on a cross-cultural survey of masculine and feminine personality characteristics and using a psychoanalytic framework, argued that the psychological differentiation between males and females "arises out of the fact that women, universally, are largely responsible for early child care and for (at least) later female socialization. . . . Specifically . . . in any given society, feminine personality comes to define itself in relation and connection to other people more than masculine personality does" (Chodorow 1974: 43–4. Thus Chodorow located sexual asymmetry in what she saw as the universality of direct affective links between mothers and daughters and the corresponding indirectness of male socialization. Like Rosaldo, she saw a way out of the recapitulation of these patterns from generation to generation in somehow encouraging men's involvement in the domestic. "Boys," she argued, "need to grow up around men who take a major role in child care, and girls around women who, in addition to their child-care responsibilities, have a valued role and recognized spheres of legitimate control" (Chodorow 1974: 66).

The other major theoretical piece in the Rosaldo and Lamphere volume, Sherry B. Ortner's "Is Female to Male as Nature is to Culture?" (this volume, chapter 3), also used the assumption of women's universal secondary status as its foundation, but looked to diverse symbolic constructions of women as the way to explain this pattern. Like Rosaldo and Chodorow, Ortner's concerns were political as well as academic.

My interest in the problem is of course more than academic: I wish to see genuine change come about, the emergence of a social and cultural order in which as much of the range of human potential is open to women as is open to men. The universality of female subordination, the fact that it exists within every type of social and economic arrangement and in societies of every degree of complexity, indicates to me that we are up against something very profound, very stubborn, something we cannot rout out simply by rearranging a few tasks and roles in the social system, or even by reordering the whole economic structure. In this paper I try to expose the underlying logic of cultural thinking that assumes the inferiority of women; I try to show the highly persuasive nature of the logic, for if it were not so persuasive, people would not keep subscribing to it. But I also try to show the social and cultural sources of that logic, to indicate wherein lies the potential for change. (Ortner 1974: 67–8; p. 72 below)

Other contributors to the volume offered a range of ethnographic illustrations of the basic principles put forward in the three theoretical chapters. These papers drew on various schools of anthropological thought and were set in a wide variety of cultural locations, but all elaborated the ways in which, on the one hand, women's status was everywhere compromised and secondary, but on the other hand, women proved capable of acting strategically on their own behalf. The image of the universally oppressed woman that emerged from the volume was not that of a helpless victim, though the forces arrayed to challenge her were deeply entrenched and seemingly unmovable.[2]

The following year, in 1975, a second major collection made its appearance. *Toward an Anthropology of Women,* edited by Rayna R. Reiter (now Rapp) was also frankly inspired by the emergent feminist movement. Reiter started the introduction with a simple declaration: "This book has its roots in the women's movement" (Reiter 1975: 11). She explained that the movement has asked anthropology for explanations about women's inequality, and that "these questions are more than academic: the answers will help feminists in the struggle against sexism in our own society (1975: 11). As Rosaldo and Lamphere had done the previous year, Reiter used the introduction to chronicle her own engagement with the issue, describing a student-initiated course on women that she had helped to organize and the re-examination that teaching experience had forced her to make of her training and the assumptions on which it rested.

Like Rosaldo and Lamphere, she outlined the basic problem of male bias in anthropology and the dearth of ethnographic works that give full attention to the cultural and social contributions of women, but also noted a number of works that had appeared prior to the women's movement, such as those by Margaret Mead and Ruth Landes, in which women's lives were carefully examined. She also cautioned against the perils of what she called "double male bias," that emanating from the scholar's own culture which conditions our ability to understand what we see in our research and that which leads us to accede to male dominance in the cultures we study. But she also questioned common understandings of what "male dominance" is – whether its assertion by men necessarily reflects the experience of women, whether a reading of dominance draws more on "our own experience in a class-stratified society" or are actually features of other cultures. Unlike Rosaldo and Lamphere, Reiter questioned notions of universal sexual asymmetry, urging feminists to resist the impulse to impose their own dichotomized world view on other cultures.

Reiter's volume thus framed the exploration of women's roles in cultures somewhat differently than Rosaldo and Lamphere's. Rather than opening with essays that explore a particular theoretical orientation about universal sexual asymmetry, the first three essays in the volume considered the ways in which male bias has influenced anthropological knowledge, particularly as it relates to theories of cultural evolution. Lila Leibowitz's essay used primate data to question widely held beliefs about sexual dimorphism as the source of social differentiation between men and women (Leibowitz 1975). Sally Slocum's paper, mentioned above, put forward a radical critique of the notion that male hunting was the engine that drove cultural evolution, suggesting a different interpretation of the fossil record (Slocum 1975). And Kathleen Gough's paper on families among hunter-gatherers reassessed the view that these societies were male dominated (Gough 1975). Other essays in the volume made extensive use of Marxist theory to approach questions of sexual inequality, with several contributors making use of Engels's ideas about the relationship between male dominance and the development of private property, while others questioned the accuracy of accounts of female inferiority in some cultures. The volume also included essays that explored the importance of public and private domains among contemporary European peasants and several that examined changes in the roles of women in the Third World and in socialist countries, with special attention being given to the impact of capitalism on the status of women.

The essay in Reiter's volume that has had the most lasting impact on the development of feminist anthropology was Gayle Rubin's "The Traffic in Women: Notes on the 'Political Economy' of Sex" (this volume, chapter 4). Rubin's intellectual *tour de force* used the work of Marx, Engels, Freud, Lévi-Strauss, and other theorists from across the disciplines to propose a process by which a biological category, females, is transformed into a social and cultural category, woman, what she called the "sex/gender system." From the start, Rubin rejected some of the circulating explanations for gender differences, at least partly because they lead to political dead-ends:

> Thus, if innate male aggression and dominance are at the root of female oppression, then the feminist program would logically require either the extermination of the offending sex, or else a eugenics project to modify its character. If sexism is a by-product of capitalism's relentless appetite for profit, then sexism would wither away in the advent of a successful socialist revolution. If the world historical defeat of women occurred at the hands of an armed patriarchal revolt, then it is time for Amazon guerrillas to start training in the Adirondacks. (Rubin 1975: 157–8; p. 87 below)

Since none of those explanations could be verified in the historical or ethnographic record, and none of them could be made to yield viable strategies for change, Rubin reasoned that only a general theory of sex and gender could produce an understanding of pervasive women's oppression. By pointing to a mechanism through which sex, which she understood as some sort of universal biological attribute of the person, was transformed into gender, she identified a considerably more flexible and relative, as well as constructed, quality. Gender was the site where the rudimentary bodily characteristics of sex were framed in cultural terms, endowed with meaning, and where females were turned into women, much as phonological systems and grammars turn physical speech sounds into the meaningful systems we know as languages. Rubin's scheme rested on an assumption that a more or less universal system could be teased out of the varied cultures of the world, explaining the pervasive inequalities that were widely observable.

These two edited volumes set the tone for the anthropology of women through the 1970s, giving rise to two somewhat distinctive styles of scholarship. What might be called the "universal asymmetry" approach that predominated in Rosaldo and Lamphere continued to map the ways that inequalities between the sexes played out in different cultural contexts, with scholars framing scenarios that would explain particular kinds of variations in the degree and type of subordination women experienced. In contrast, an approach more grounded in Marxist explanations, particularly in the work of Engels, also proliferated following on Reiter's volume. In 1972, for example, Leacock wrote the introduction to a new edition of Friedrich Engels's *Origin of the Family, Private Property and the State*, claiming the historic text for the anthropology of women (Engels 1972). Other contributions that exemplify this approach include studies by June Nash (1983), Christine Ward Gailey (1980), and Karen Sacks (now Brodkin) (Sacks 1979; Sacks and Remy 1984). These works and others that originated in socialist feminism framed their analyses in terms of the struggles of impoverished women around the world and also explicitly employed a Marxist-inspired evolutionist paradigm to understand the role of women across cultural boundaries. The status of women in capitalist societies like the United States was often either implicitly or directly compared with the situation of women in cultures with more egalitarian structures and simpler economic and political systems.

Regardless of specific approaches and overall philosophy, mostly female anthropologists during this period produced a diverse set of ethnographies that put into action the mandate that formerly invisible women across the world's cultures be recognized and allowed to speak. These works demonstrated how placing women at the heart of analysis yielded results very different from what one would find in a traditional, male-centered ethnography. Margery Wolf's *Women and the Family in Rural Taiwan*, for example, proposed that a focus on women revealed a hitherto invisible kinship form she called the "uterine family" (Wolf 1972). Although the Chinese patriarchal family gave no name to any such form, Wolf documented the ways in which Chinese peasant women elaborated their bonds with children, using those bonds to achieve various sorts of material and cultural goals. Women gave no name to this activity, but its configuration was sufficiently stable for Wolf to argue persuasively that it was, in fact, part of the kinship system.

Carol Stack's classic ethnographic study of low-income black women in a US city also led to new recognition for women as agentive social actors (Stack 1974). Stack argued that social patterns that had been interpreted as deviant from the perspective of mainstream (white) American families, particularly the widely practiced institution of "child keeping," were in fact rational adaptations to life under conditions of chronic economic hardship. Women in the community she studied were poor, often dependent on public assistance, and never actually had sufficient resources to manage on their own. If, however, they traded and exchanged goods on a regular basis, including taking turns caring for their children, it was possible to manage. Her careful documentation of the system that sustained urban life for poor black women not only revealed its underlying logic, but also demonstrated how difficult it was for individuals in the community to achieve upward mobility. Any effort to catapult oneself into a better economic position, including gaining the advantages that might result from marriage, would also mean disengaging from complex ties of reciprocity and affect, a wrenching task that few could see through to its conclusion. Stack's work highlighted the benefits of focusing on women's accounts of their lives, but also served as a model for some of the politically engaged work that would follow in feminist anthropology, particularly in the context of the United States. Situated in the context of the then-raging debate over "culture of poverty" research on the poor in the US and elsewhere, Stack specifically spoke to authors who sought to locate the causes of poverty in the cultures of poor people themselves. She also defied a long-standing taboo on working in the US as not sufficiently "other" to qualify as anthropology.

These were only two of the large corpus of writings published during the first decade of the anthropology of women. Works that focused on the status of women in some part of the world – often with a phrase like "women of . . . " in their titles – began to appear with increasing frequency, gradually addressing the problem of women's visibility that launched the field. While these ethnographies, articles, and collections were not re-studies *per se*, they drew on many of the same impulses in that they sought to situate women in the ethnographic record, perhaps for the first time. These scholars argued forcefully that the "important" information in fieldwork was not the exclusive province of male informants, that women's voices would not only offer different perspectives on how culture worked, but might point to inter-pretations not accessible if they continued to be silent.

Among the works that typify this recuperative movement are *Women of the Andes* by Susan C. Bourque and Kay Barbara Warren. The book started from an assumption that women were subordinated by patriarchal authority, but emphasized the diversity that characterized women's lives in the Andes, using an economics-based comparison of two villages to clarify those factors that contributed to or modified women's subordination. Like Stack and Wolf, Bourque and Warren focused on the strategies mounted by women to empower themselves, even in the face of pervasive poverty and entrenched masculine authority, particularly noting the ways that women themselves perceive their contributions, even those that are devalued by others. Importantly, they situated the local circumstances of the two villages in the context of wider national agendas, paying close attention to the ways in which economic development schemes would, or would not, bring greater autonomy to women.

Other ethnographies that appeared during this period lent more texture to images of non-Western women, tending to either celebrate situations where women's status was comparatively high or to lament the abuse that women suffered in some cultures. Many of these works sought in particular to examine symbols of subor-dination and to understand the way in which these cultural elements were experi-enced by women who lived with them. In other instances, they examined some of the issues raised by Ester Boserup in her 1970 classic, *Woman's Role in Economic Development*, focusing on the impact of economic growth and urbanization, much of it the product of colonialism, and noting that changes in women's economic activities incidental to such developments could sometimes offer them resources for autonomy, but could also undermine traditional sources of power. The literature returned often to the conundrums of women's status: the seeming salutary effects of modernization balanced against the traditional resources that women could mobil-ize to enhance their own positions. As a counterbalance to the ethnocentrism of their peers outside the discipline, feminist anthropologists often sought to destabilize congenial notions of what were "good" and "bad" conditions for women. Fernea, as mentioned above, questioned the degree to which the veil and other restrictions on women's movements in public truly constituted forms of oppression. Wolf suggested that even in patriarchal Chinese peasant culture women could carve out a form of influence that benefited them and their children. Daisy Dwyer (1978) argued that women do not necessarily share the same symbolic systems or cognitive models employed by men and thus may escape damage from negative views promulgated by men.

The new attention to women and gender inspired some anthropologists to return to sites where they had conducted fieldwork before they were alerted to the importance of women's roles. For example, Robert and Yolanda Murphy published a restudy of their earlier work in the Amazon, returning to their earlier fieldwork to comment on the position of women in what had been described in distinctly androcentric terms (Murphy and Murphy 1974). Other ethnographers launched projects that explicitly sought to reconsider earlier studies. Jane Goodale's re-study of the Tiwi, an aboriginal people of Australia, offered an interpretation that turned the study by Arnold Pilling and C. W. M. Hart on its head. While the two male ethnographers had described a culture in which women were traded like commodities and had virtually no agency or voice, Goodale's account presented women who actively strategized on their own behalf and saw the marriage system as something they orchestrated and controlled (Goodale 1971; Hart and Pilling 1960). In a similar vein, Annette Weiner audaciously undertook research in the Trobriand Islands, revisiting the site of Bronislaw Malinowski's classic work, and offering new interpretations based on paying close attention to the voices of women (Weiner 1976).

The re-studies had a multifaceted effect on work to come in feminist anthropology. Most palpably, they demonstrated that the ethnographic record had failed to pay sufficient attention to the activities of women and to their perspectives on their cultures, showing that when women were the center of analysis – or at least fully present – the accounts that emerged would be significantly different. On another level, they raised the question of positionality and stance, a matter that would prove to be of ongoing importance as the new field developed. That is, they provided evidence that ethnographic accounts were not just presentations of facts, composed from material that was waiting to be discovered by whatever anthropologist might enter a culture. Rather, the differences between work by male and female ethnographers, or between ethnographers who depended on men's voices for their data and those who recognized the importance of hearing from women, produced different realities, either of which could be "true" in different ways. This perspective on the nature of ethnographic knowledge has become even more influential in recent years, and has been further elaborated under the influence of postmodernism. But the impact of this view began to be felt in the early 1970s as feminist anthropology moved through its formative years, and as we shall see in Part II of this volume, has continued to be central to the feminist anthropological enterprise.

The early years of feminist anthropology also saw the publication of a varied series of books that mobilized cross-cultural comparisons to propose definitions of and explanations for sexual inequality. Karen Sacks, a leading opponent of the universal subordination model, published *Sisters and Wives* in 1979, an effort to

understand the relative status of women in terms of their roles in economic production, particularly in terms of their ability to contribute to basic productive activities
and to control the products of their labor (Sacks 1979). Peggy Reeves Sanday looked
to the cultural resources that chartered either female power or male dominance,
paying close attention to myths and to the kinds of symbols that are attached to
gender in particular cultures (Sanday 1981). Alice Schlegel's study of matrilineal
societies looked to statistically rarer social forms to understand the conditions under
which women might achieve autonomy, even as they appeared to be subject to male
authority (Schlegel 1972).

A number of edited collections also promoted cross-cultural comparison as a way
to comprehend the sources of male dominance and also to identify ways to undermine and defeat it. Alice Schlegel's *Sexual Stratification*, for example, framed sexual
stratification as consisting of three elements of rank – rewards, prestige, and power –
which can operate somewhat independently of one another. She carefully selected
essays that represented the two divergent theories of the time: those that traced
sexual inequality to universal characteristics ultimately traceable to biology, and
those that saw inequality as incident to specific economic relations (Schlegel 1977).
In contrast, Mona Etienne and Eleanor Leacock's edited volume, *Women and
Colonization*, drew on case studies from a wide range of cultures to illustrate how
historically produced economic conditions shaped women's relative power and
authority (Etienne and Leacock 1980). Patricia Caplan and Janet M. Bujra's
Women United, Women Divided, also drew on an evolutionary perspective of
inequality, but included essays particularly concerned with the conditions under
which women were able to constitute themselves as political forces (Caplan and
Bujra 1979). Similarly, another influential collection published in Great Britain, *Of
Marriage and the Market*, traced women's subordination to their lack of control
over resources and production (Young, Wolkowitz, and McCullagh 1981). With still
another approach, *Women in Ritual and Symbolic Roles*, edited by Judith Hoch-
Smith and Anita Spring (1978), turned attention to ways through which women
could overcome or derail subordination through their access to particularly valued
or feared ritual specializations.

Collections published in the 1970s also sought to describe women's status from a
cross-cultural perspective, sometimes offering a kind of atlas of women's oppression
and empowerment defined along geographical, sociological or cultural lines. These
volumes reflected two major sensibilities: one, a commitment to demonstrate that
taking a cross-cultural view would reveal an almost limitless diversity in women's
lives and the degree to which they were subordinated by patriarchal forces. Carolyn
J. Mattiasson, for example, edited *Many Sisters*, a volume that categorized cultures
according to a continuum from those where women had to resort to manipulation
and subterfuge to gain power, to those described as "complementary," presumably
unequal but in a relatively benign way, to still others where women were said to have
achieved political or economic ascendancy (Mattiasson 1974). Other collections
that appeared in this period pointed to factors such as religion, economic complexity, and political organization as ways of understanding cross-cultural variations in
women's status. All of these collections struggled with defining the particular dimensions of social and cultural life that should be examined for evidence of subordination or equality. Should anthropologists look to women's views of their

circumstances to offer a reliable measure of their relative status? Can assessments be made on the basis of material resources, access to valued roles, the extent to which particular arrangements made methods of subterfuge more accessible to women? Some collections, like Ruby Rohrlich-Leavitt's *Women Cross-Culturally,* cut a wide swath, with essays on women in Islam, Africa, and across Latin America contrasting with papers on the status of women in the United States and in planned societies, though overall political economic explanations predominated. In other instances, like Dana Raphael's volume *Being Female: Reproduction, Power, and Change*, essays directed attention to features of kinship organization and reproduction that yielded both social impediments and resources to women.

The 1970s also saw the development of what would later coalesce into feminist medical anthropology, with a central focus on reproduction and related women's health issues. These works found their inspiration in the women's health movement, which had mounted vocal critiques of the delivery of reproductive health care to women in the US, particularly focusing on contraception, abortion, and birth (Arms 1977; Rothman 1982; Shaw 1974). A crucial article by Carol McClain established the idea that birth was a cultural system; the term she coined to designate this domain was *ethno-obstetrics* (McClain 1975).

The figure who would come to have the broadest influence on this emergent field was Brigitte Jordan, who had trained as a midwife and worked with a variety of feminist health projects during her graduate school years. Her early article on women's knowledge of their own pregnancy status and her comparative ethnographic study of childbirth practices have continued to influence the direction of feminist scholarship and activism in this area (Jordan 1977, 1978). In line with feminist demands for more humane standards of obstetrical care, and particularly for practices that would empower women and validate their self-knowledge, Jordan argued that women's knowledge of their own bodily states had been systematically erased and devalued in the West. Paradoxically perhaps, many non-Western cultures, despite the unequal treatment their women received in matters of politics and economics, emerged as the heroes of the story, as they tended to make childbirth a women's domain, with little or no interference by men. Women depended on traditional birth attendants (TBAs), their kinswomen, and on their knowledge of their own bodies to maintain control over reproduction in a way that appeared to be markedly different from their experience in the West, where (mostly male) physicians controlled birth and access to other kinds of reproductive health care. Jordan coined the term *authoritative knowledge* as a way to think about the process whereby some kinds of knowledge come to carry more weight than others, either because they are judged to be more efficacious or because their adherents are more powerful. She argued that this can happen even when differing kinds of knowledge are equally legitimate, and that "a consequence of the legitimation of one kind of knowing as authoritative is the devaluation, often the dismissal, of all other kinds of knowing" (Jordan 1997: 56). A common consequence of one kind of knowledge achieving this status is that competing systems are judged to be inherently incorrect and their advocates labeled as a defective or deluded.

Jordan's work echoed scholarly and popular statements about male medical domination that had a prominent place in the 1970s women's movement (see, for instance, Arms 1977; Ehrenreich and English 1972; Kaplan 1997; Morgen 2002;

Rothman 1982; Ruzek 1979; Shaw 1974). It gave rise to a rich and varied literature on women and reproduction, beginning with studies anchored in particular culture areas that sought to understand childbirth practices as indexical of other features of society (Laderman 1983; Sargent 1981). Work by feminist anthropologists contributed significantly to increasingly vocal denunciations of male-dominated obstetrical care, later emerging in the work of such influential figures as Robbie Davis-Floyd and Emily Martin (Davis-Floyd 1992; Martin 1989). That this critique of Western medical practices reflected orientalized images of "primitive" women's birth practices being somehow more pure and authentic – perhaps even animal-like – than the mediated, medicalized conventions of the West has only recently begun to receive attention (Bobel 2002; Klassen 2001).

A theme that underlay all of this work was the question of how to define and recognize the status of men and women. Do economic factors constitute the most significant determinants of dominance and subordination? Do symbolic expressions of value shape the psyches of both women and men in ways that alter their ability to act on their own behalf? Do all the members of a society need to share the same beliefs for a particular gender configuration to have general applicability? Are covert expressions of autonomy as meaningful as named positions of authority and power? How do people's own assessments of their welfare fit into an anthropological evaluation of their society, particularly in relation to questions of inequality and stratification? Should we look to embodied, biologically defined processes for a more "authentic" configuration of gender than can be found elsewhere in cultures? By extension, of course, all of these issues were persistent problems for feminists in examining their own experiences of oppression, as they struggled to understand how women in their own culture experienced the strictures of gender.

An Anthropology of Gender and Beyond

At the same time that scholars heeded the call for women to become visible and vocal, the notion that sex and gender were not interchangeable, and that knowing about women alone would not illuminate the workings of what Gayle Rubin had called "the sex/gender system" began to have an impact on the field. As work in the new field progressed, scholars came more fully to understand the use of gender as a set of meanings and relationships related to but not isomorphic with biological sex and broadened their inquiries to use these approaches to look at all sorts of cultural phenomena. The anthropology of women morphed into the *anthropology of gender*.

Central to this approach was recognition that "women" could not be classified categorically as constituents of a population whose membership was simply self-evident, an insight that was also beginning to have an impact in women's studies more generally and in feminist activism (Brenner 2000; Caraway 1991; Spelman 1988). Thus the mission of women anthropologists to study other women could no longer sustain congenial assumptions that all women were in some ineffable way "sisters" with common objectives and embodied experiences, or that these objectives and experiences, when they existed, were indeed at the heart of identity formation. Instead, scholars had to be cognizant of the complexity of factors that determined how women lived, including taking into account intersectional analyses that considered not only gender (or sex), but other features of identity and status. Feminist anthropologists were compelled to think about these issues not only by the increasing ambiguity of some of the expressions of gender their research yielded, but by the pressures that were assailing the early women's movement and its facile definition of "women" – and "men." In the world of feminist politics, women of color, members of sexual minorities, and representatives of impoverished and otherwise disadvantaged groups all came to exercise more visible influence on the shape of future organizing, or at least to have their long-standing concerns acknowledged. Some of these pressures reflected the perception that some of the goals of early feminists were too closely tied to bourgeois social ambitions to be universally desirable; in particular, the question of how to imagine equality, and to whom one might wish to be equal, came to be central questions across feminism.

By the late 1980s and early 1990s anthropologists of gender broadened their concerns from women's experiences *per se* to the ways in which gender and other analytical categories meet and complicate one another under varying material and cultural conditions. Much of the impetus for this realignment came from the parallel emergence of women's studies during the same years that feminist anthropology was developing. Women's studies began with many of the same assumptions that early anthropologists of gender held: that the definition of "woman" was stable and knowable, ultimately connected (somehow) to interpretations or actualizations of biological sex; but by the mid-1980s scholars had begun rigorously to examine such notions and to imagine the proper subject matter of the field much more broadly (Butler 1990; Riley 1988; Roth 2004).

For many, this shift demanded that they fully engage with a consideration of the varied sources of privilege and disempowerment that not only affect the lives of women in various settings, but shape the ways in which gender offers a set of symbols and meanings for interpreting inequality. From early on, there were contributors to feminist anthropology who demanded that we consider the ways that determinants of social status – caste, class, race, and sexuality – also inflect the differential experiences of women and men. Ethel Albert's early essay in *Women of Tropical Africa,* for example, presented the seeming conundrum of women from the ruling Tutsi ethnic group who dominated men and women alike who were members of the less powerful Hutu (Albert 1963). Increasingly, the work published in feminist anthropology came to echo some early essays that documented the ability of elite women to maintain positions of privilege in highly stratified societies (Caplan 1979; Cohen 1979). Thus a growing concern with the degree to which dominant feminist preoccupations reflected the priorities of a particular group of women – middle-class, educated, and white – sparked a rethinking of how gender and other sources of stratification intersected, and also led feminist scholars in anthropology and other fields to interrogate earlier assumptions about definitions upon which gender systems depended. These interrogations were furthered by the growing corpus of writing that concerned the specific ethical issues facing feminist scholars in particular and anthropologists more generally (Abu-Lughod 1990a; Stacey 1988).

As Henrietta Moore explains, feminist anthropology has gone beyond an anthropology of women in many ways, not the least of which is its emphasis on understanding difference broadly construed. Its accomplishments are far-reaching, ranging from its reconsideration of the conflation of womanhood and motherhood, its challenge to established concepts of the individual and society, and, perhaps most of all, its rethinking of the concept of the self (Moore 1989: 187). In reorganizing itself as the anthropology of gender, feminist anthropology resisted the hegemony of Western cultural assumptions and opened up a conversation between the West and "other women." As a result of the work done by feminists in anthropology and other disciplines, "the contemporary social sciences now take it as axiomatic that gender is a cultural construct, that, far from being natural objects, women and men are fundamentally cultural constructions" (Moore 1994: 71).

At the same time that scholars were rethinking sex and gender, they were also becoming increasingly aware that anthropological (or any other) knowledge had to be considered situational and grounded in the particular dynamics of the research situation. Further, feminist consideration of academic ethics mandated that anthropologists give careful consideration to the extent to which their (relatively) greater power shaped the fieldwork encounter and ethnographic representation. These concerns were taken up by the profession as a whole some years after they began to be extensively explored in feminist scholarship, though feminists rarely were credited with the importance of their insights to what came to be called the postmodernist turn (Mascia-Lees, Sharpe, and Cohen 1989).

Thus the field moved from being concerned with documenting the experience of particular populations – namely women – to interpreting the place of gender in broader patterns of meaning, interaction, and power, not only among those people who are the objects of investigation, but among anthropologists themselves. Like other fields in social and cultural anthropology, the study of gender has been influenced by the many intellectual movements that have shaped the larger discipline during the three decades of its existence, particularly the move from structural/functionalist approaches, from studying cultures strictly as bounded entities that were inherently stable and marked by structural harmony, and the growing discomfort of some anthropologists with positivistic narratives more generally. Considering these shifts and taking the political origins of the field into account, the designation that has most aptly described this body of work is now *feminist anthropology*.

Feminist anthropology has virtually exploded since the mid-1980s, propelling an almost dizzying diversity of topics and approaches into its broad embrace. I would like to offer an overview of the trends I see as most influential and innovative, partly to convey just how powerful the paradigm of gender has proven to be, but also to demonstrate how daunting the task of assembling a reader of "classic" works has become. Some of the directions the field has taken are coterminous with those elsewhere in cultural anthropology, such as the pervasive concern with resistance and agency, sparked by such scholars as James Scott (Abu-Lughod 1990b; Scott 1987), though some others raised a cautionary note about feminists' desire to see resistance everywhere (Abu-Lughod 1990b). But others reveal the particular strength of a gender-centered analysis to raise new and compelling research agendas.

Continuities

As feminist anthropology has continued to develop into the present, it has maintained some of the commitments that inspired it, but has also changed enormously, largely because of its meteoric growth and the complexity that it has brought to the field. Most notably, feminist anthropology has had considerable success in the academic institutions of the discipline and in many respects has been absorbed into mainstream academic sites. Scholars now openly claim "gender" as among their specialized interests, and advertisements for new positions, as well, recruit for faculty with expertise in this field. Journals across the subdisciplines routinely publish articles with gender-related topics; such authoritative publications as the *Annual Review of Anthropology* regularly survey the field and its subfields. Many leaders in feminist anthropology have achieved positions of considerable esteem in the profession, serving as officers of the organizations that represent the subfields, and also as leaders of the American Anthropological Association (for instance, Louise Lamphere's recent tenure as President of the AAA). Books on feminist topics are published in such large numbers that keeping up with the field is no longer a reasonable ambition; indeed, feminist anthropology has ceased to be a single field, but can be classified into a number of subfields defined according to ethnographic areas, theoretical approach, genre, and other variations.

The process of institutionalization and normalization has also meant that scholars no longer are necessarily drawn to feminist anthropology (or feminist scholarship in any other discipline, for that matter) primarily by their commitment to effect social change or by their concern with and loyalty to other women. Doing feminist anthropology doesn't require the outlaw sensibility that permitted its early adherents to withstand powerful opposition; one can become engaged with questions of gender as little more than compelling intellectual problems, no more personal than any other area of anthropological inquiry.

At the same time, however, the desire to understand the problems women face or the impact of gender on the welfare of real people has not disappeared by any means. This bifurcation, between those whose interest is primarily abstractly intellectual and those for whom feminist anthropology is a calling, generates perhaps the sharpest division in the field. Where particular scholars stand is sometimes readily discernible in their prose. Some feminist anthropology is written in a way that makes it accessible to diverse audiences and that takes care to keep close to the lived experience of the "natives" under study. Other work that has emerged since the mid-1980s is increasingly dense and inaccessible, marked by expository mannerisms and obscure allusions (Abu-Lughod, this volume, chapter 7).

Social Commitment and Social Change

Feminist anthropologists have been energetic contributors to a body of work that explores questions of social justice and the impact of economic and political processes on the welfare of populations, both in the traditional anthropological bailiwick of non-Western cultures, and closer to home. Indeed, as scholars have become increasingly concerned with the flexibility and permeability of cultural boundaries and their irregular overlap with spatial entities, the notion that anthropologists cannot work in the West has become increasingly irrelevant. Feminist anthropologists have studied the ways in which gender inflects economic development, migration, nationalisms, and how state policies and priorities shape the lived experience of women and men (Gailey 1987; Silverblatt 1991; B. Williams 1996). They have asked how such processes as the transnational circulation of people and information reflect established gender patterns or initiate new ones. At their most powerful, they have avoided unilinear accounts of social change that might cast the people they study as unwitting victims of forces beyond their control, seeking instead to identify elements of agency in the thoughts and behavior of actors (Freeman 2000; Wilson 2004).

Accordingly, feminist anthropologists have been active in the study of the ways in which the movements of workers into the global marketplaces generated by multi-national commerce, both as this plays out at the local level and as it produces migration, are deeply gendered and productive of new gender configurations (Constable 2003; Freeman 2000). They have examined some of the cultural responses generated by changing political and economic terrains, for example, as they emerge in shaping spiritual and religious phenomena, in behavioral patterns (Ong 1987) and in the formation of social movements and political alliances (Stephen 1997). They have interrogated the assumptions that drive international development projects (Warren and Bourque 1991), and have produced influential analyses of women's behavior as economic actors (Babb 1989, 2001; Weismantel 1988, 2001).

Feminist anthropologists have also sought to intervene in discussions of persistently controversial social issues in the West, applying ethnographic methods and a cross-cultural sensibility to understand phenomena that are close at hand. Peggy Sanday has studied patterns of sexual assault, particularly as rape is institutionalized in college fraternities (Sanday 1990, 1996). Others have focused on questions of race and class, examining the ways in which poverty and labor conditions play out in the lives of women in the US (Anglin 2002; Brodkin 1988; Morgen and Weigt 2001; Susser 1982; Zavella 2001).

Motherhood and the Body

The early interest of feminist anthropologists in women's reproductive health has expanded in recent years into a diverse field allied variously with medical and applied anthropology. Perhaps the most contentious issue currently under discussion is the set of practices known by terms such as "female circumcision" and "female genital mutilation," depending on one's position. Some feminist anthropologists have been active in campaigns to eradicate these procedures, viewing them as serious public health hazards that are inherently harmful to women. Others have sought to context-ualize the surgery, examining the diverse ways that these procedures intersect with both men's and women's interests and beliefs (Boddy 1998; Gruenbaum 2001; Hayes 1975; Inhorn and Buss 1993; Walley this volume, chapter 17). These are debates in which the anthropological tradition of cultural relativism is most painfully confronted. Questions of how to approach these practices have been complicated by accusations that such efforts represent the paternalistic imposition of Western values on other groups. If female circumcision is to be eliminated, many argue, the impetus for change should come from the groups most affected by the procedures.

Other health-related issues have also loomed large in feminist anthropological scholarship. As new diagnostic and procreative technologies have proliferated both in the West and around the world, anthropologists have been particularly active in research on their utilization, the ways in which they intersect with local customs and medical systems (Handwerker 1995; Inhorn 1994; Inhorn and Van Balen 2002; Kahn 2000; Taylor 2004). They have also contributed broadly to the process of understanding rapidly shifting procreative and diagnostic technologies in the West, noting how they have been naturalized by both medical professionals and consumers, and their implications for new imaginings of systems of kinship and family (Davis-Floyd 1992; Davis-Floyd and Dumit 1998; Franklin and Ragoné 1998; Rapp 1999; Strathern 1992).

In other words, the body – and particularly the female body – as it intersects with or is acted upon by cultural, medical, economic, and other forces has become central to feminist anthropological thought. Boundaries between reproduction, health and illness, use of medical resources, and clusters of meanings that surround motherhood, family, and the nation are flexible, as feminist anthropologists examine the various ways that they are mutually constitutive across time and space (Lock and Kaufert 1998). Much of this work looks at women as patients or objects of medical attention; a smaller body of literature, however, has focused on women's experiences as health-care providers, including examinations of how such expertise may allow them to claim mystical skills and elevate their status (McClain 1989).

Health and illness including pain, spirit possession, sexually transmitted diseases (particularly AIDS since the emergence of the pandemic), and the uses made of women's bodies by family members, nations, and enemies of those nations have been at the center of these analyses (Das 1995; Finkler 1994; Sered 2000). For example, various scholars have looked at the ramifications of fertility in various sites. Gail Kligman's work on Communist Romania has explored the use of women's reproductive capacities in the service of national agendas (Kligman 1998). Susan Kahn has studied the meanings associated with various procreative technologies when used by Jewish women in Israel, where demographic politics must be interpreted through Jewish religious law (Kahn 2000). Also focusing on the Middle East, Rhoda Kanaaneh has analyzed the contradictory meanings of reproduction among Israeli Palestinian women. On the one hand, high fertility represents resistance to Jewish domination, but on the other hand, only low fertility can signal modernity, ironically defined along the lines that predominate among European-origin Jews in Israel (Kanaaneh 2002)

In related projects, a number of scholars have studied the particularly compelling cultural logic of such diagnostic techniques as amniocentesis and ultrasonography, both of which are employed in the context of interactions with medical professionals, but also are interpreted in frameworks that may be remote from their scientific rationale. Rapp has looked at amniocentesis as it is employed among various ethnic populations in New York City; Taylor has looked at how ultrasonography is embedded in wider cultural matrices of consumption and value, as well as how the seemingly neutral action of science is inflected by the politics of its practitioners (Taylor 1992, 2004). Sandelowski and Franklin have both undertaken studies of women undergoing fertility treatment, offering complex accounts of the strategies these women undertake to accommodate the outcomes within existing notions of nature (Franklin 1997; Sandelowski 1993). Helena Ragoné (1994) has focused on the complex logic of surrogacy.

Moving from medically based examinations of women's bodies to their experience as mothers, feminist anthropologists have continued to explore the complexities of maternal experience. Essays in Ginsburg and Rapp's important collection *Conceiving the New World Order* employ the concept of *stratified reproduction* developed by Shellee Colen (this volume, chapter 19):

> By *stratified reproduction* I mean that physical and social reproductive tasks are accomplished differentially according to inequalities that are based on hierarchies, of class, race, ethnicity, gender, place in a global economy, and migration status and that are structured by social, economic, and political forces. The reproductive labor – physical, mental, and emotional – of bearing, raising, and socializing children and of creating and maintaining households and people (from infancy to old age) is differentially experienced, valued, and rewarded according to inequalities of access to material and social resources in particular historical and cultural contexts. Stratified reproduction, particularly with the increasing commodification of reproductive labor, itself reproduces stratification by reflecting, reinforcing, and intensifying the inequalities on which it is based. (Colen 1995: 78; p. 380 below)

Colen's approach represented a particularly significant advance in that it conceptualizes motherhood as pertaining to all the activities and labor that result in the reproduction and care of children. Some of this work is centered in the bodies of biological mothers, but Colen allows us to consider these in conjunction with the work done by nannies and potentially others (surrogates, co-mothers) who engage in these essential activities. Other scholars have focused on how maternal narratives offer critical insights into broader cultural practices and priorities, offering strategies for identity formation and for making claims to valued moral attributes (Ginsburg 1989; Inhorn 1996; Lewin 1993; Modell 1994; Ragoné and Twine 2000; Wozniak 2002).

Nancy Scheper-Hughes's well-known volume (1992) on motherhood in an impoverished region of Northeast Brazil firmly situates the presumably natural domain of the maternal in the political economy of extreme deprivation. In this context, women's understandings of their bodies and their children's health cannot be detached from the precarious hold all have on survival. But even in a situation where mothers may strategically prepare to lose some children, attachments between mothers and children continue to be anchored in a universalized sentimental discourse. Along related lines, examinations of the nature of emotion itself have become one of the most interesting new areas in feminist anthropology. As in much of the work on motherhood, scholars who attempt to understand the seemingly ineffable world of love and romance show how these feelings and their enactment in marriage, infidelity, and emotional anxiety cannot be separated from the socioeconomic context in which they are grounded (Constable 2003; Hirsch 2003; Rebhun 1999).

Knowledge and Representation

Feminist anthropologists have maintained their long-term interest in questions of positionality, knowledge, and the impact of these factors on ethnographic writing and the nature of anthropological knowledge. Some have pulled apart the difficult questions of insider and outsider, interrogating the notion that there can be true insider researchers in anthropology (Abu-Lughod 1995; Altorki and El-Solh 1989;

Lewin 1995; Narayan 1993). Others have used experimental narrative strategies to convey the complex intersection of ethnographer and informant (Behar 1993, 1996; Chin 1999; Frank 2000; Kondo 1990; Lepowsky 1993; Tsing 1993). Other feminist scholars have engaged directly with questions of anthropological epistemology, questioning the nature of data and the ways in which an ethnography makes its object (Krasniewicz 1992; Wolf 1992).

A central insight that emerges from all of this new work is the recognition of the instability of objects of long-standing anthropological interest, including social boundaries, national boundaries, and racial and sexual definitions. Physical perceptions, illness, sexuality, and other embodied conditions, once easily assumed to be primal, take on a sometimes strategic and sometimes reactive position. Even more decentering, new work in feminist anthropology has forced us to consider the contingent nature of such deeply mystified forces as romantic and maternal love.

On another level, the field has reinforced ongoing discussions in cultural anthropology over the fragility of the ethnographic product, the inescapably political nature of various forms of representation, and the ways in which the anthropologist is implicated in the diverse machinations that yield these works. At the same time as anthropologists have been struggling over the nature of culture and ethnographic representation (Clifford and Marcus 1986; Geertz 1988; Rosaldo 1989), feminist anthropologists have brought their early concern with positionality to the debate. Feminist politics had long been preoccupied with the power of the observer's stance and had long understood moments of creativity as grounded in the history of the creator. Feminist anthropology has come to accommodate more diverse sorts of cultural expression, including the observer as part of the story, absorbing various expressive genres, and urging more experimentation in form. Demanding visibility for women across cultures also meant demanding that the author be visible. Feminists' profound discomfort with the position of omniscient observer reflects not only the professional anxieties one might expect from the recently disenfranchised, but is enriched by our understanding of how we inflect and shape our topics, our data, and particular forms of representation.

New Questions

As feminist anthropology becomes firmly anchored in the twenty-first-century development of the field, it is important to note some further directions that have come to characterize its intellectual stance, and particularly some of the newer areas of inquiry that owe their existence to feminist anthropology. In some cases, scholars working with feminist paradigms have extended their insights to the study of men and masculinities, reconsidering the ways in which male dominance is enacted and sometimes questioning well-established assumptions about gender stratification (Gutmann 1996; Passaro 1996; Townsend 2002).

The recent emergence of what has variously been called lesbian and gay or queer anthropology drew its life breath directly from feminist scholarship, and indeed, from many feminist scholars. The foundational work in this field, Esther Newton's *Mother Camp* (1972), drew on research conducted in the 1960s. A study of female impersonators who performed in nightclubs, Newton's study was informed both by a personal commitment to explore a gay cultural form and by her involvement in the women's movement of the 1960s and 1970s. In swift succession, other ethnographic studies of "gay" phenomena followed, including work by Gilbert Herdt (1981) and Walter Williams (1986). These projects paralleled research on lesbian and gay lives underway in other disciplines, much in the same way that feminist anthropology was in constant conversation with feminist scholarship in other fields. Studies of lesbian, gay, bisexual, and transgender phenomena depend on questions and knowledge about sex, gender, embodiment, and identity that were at the heart of the feminist project in anthropology, and they continue to parallel the work done in feminist anthropology (Lewin and Leap 2002). Lesbian and gay anthropologists have also concerned themselves with problems of knowledge, ethics, and representation, interrogating their own positionality as have feminist scholars (Lewin and Leap 1996; Valentine 2003).

Lesbian and gay anthropologists have generated a large corpus of ethnographic works, particularly since the early 1990s, most drawing intellectual energy from earlier developments in feminist anthropology. The genres represented in this body of work are diverse, from ethnohistories (Kennedy and Davis 1993; Newton 1993), to studies of kinship and family (Lewin 1993, 1998; Weston 1991). Some authors have focused on sexual discourse, typically responding to the urgency that surrounds the AIDS pandemic (Carrillo 2002) and others have examined lesbians, gay men, and other members of sexual minorities through the lens of transnational population flows (Manalansan 2003). Still other work in this rapidly growing field has used cross-cultural comparison to understand the dynamics underlying patterns of sexual diversity (Blackwood and Wieringa 1999).

Overview of the Volume

Despite the intellectual currents that have buffeted and reconfigured feminist anthropology over the years, the readings in this volume will show that some central concerns have continued to characterize the work and to justify its designation as a distinct field. Feminist anthropology remains an embattled terrain, partly because, as Marilyn Strathern (1987) has noted, the two domains that constitute the field – feminism and anthropology – are to some extent fated to have an "awkward relationship." Anthropology, she points out, understands itself in terms of its concern with the Other, while feminism constantly questions the viability of the alienation and exploitation such an approach would seem to mandate. Feminist anthropologists have devised varied solutions to this seeming conundrum, sometimes interrogating the very foundations of the discipline, at other times defending cross-cultural strategies and relativism from attack.

Above all, feminist anthropologists maintain a concern with the issues of social justice that inspired the field's creation; their work reveals a desire to account for patterns of inequality that obtain in specific cultural locations and at least imply (and sometimes specify outright) ways in which anthropological scholarship might contribute to the fashioning of meaningful interventions. At the same time, however, the selections also reveal a diversification and complexity that extend far beyond the original objectives of the field that first showed its face as a protest against male domination of an academic discipline.

This collection is arranged to highlight a number of themes from the past and present. Because the literature is so substantial, I begin each section with a bibliographic essay that sets forth the contribution of the writers, but that also offers an overview of the many other sorts of work a reader interested in the area might pursue. A number of other volumes have made important contributions to my understanding of feminist anthropology, and to avoid recapitulating the excellent overviews of the field they offer, I've focused here on substantive and ethnographic writings.[3]

In the first section, I've been concerned to trace the route that scholars followed in first becoming conscious of the importance of women and gender in culture and society, essentially discovering women as an anthropological subject. In planning this section, I recall the intellectual odyssey I undertook in the early 1970s. The articles I have chosen for this section were ones that had a particularly direct impact on the thinking of the first scholars to attempt an anthropology of women. Ardener's now classic article opened doors, perhaps unwittingly, that could not be closed again. Brown framed early questions which resonate repeatedly across the discipline, particularly in the early years. From here, I present articles that illustrate a number of different approaches taken early in the 1970s to understanding women, approaches that have continued to influence the work that has been done thereafter. Ortner, Rubin, Sacks (now Brodkin), and Rosaldo were all concerned with tracing large-scale patterns of sexual oppression and with ascertaining what, if anything, about the devaluation of women was specific to Western cultures. A number of these essays appeared in the two most influential collections of the period, *Woman, Culture, and Society,* edited by Michelle Zimbalist Rosaldo and Louise Lamphere, and *Toward an Anthropology of Women,* edited by Rayna Reiter (now Rapp).

The second section focuses on questions about ethnographic stance, method, and ethics that have been prominent in feminist anthropology and that often overlap with other fields of feminist scholarship, some focusing on the way in which anthropologists choose their questions and research sites, and others looking more at matters of reflexivity and knowledge. These discussions, of course, have not been unique to feminist anthropology; indeed, they parallel passionate debates over objectivity, domination, and exoticization that have emerged at various points over the past three decades.[4] But feminist anthropologists consistently have situated these topics in a central position, particularly as they intersect with the original political objectives of the field, and they have returned as themes repeatedly over the last three decades. They have also constituted the fulcrum of debate over the stability of the category "woman," both as this has made problematic notions of insider and/ or engaged research and as anthropologists have taken their cues from scholars in other disciplines.[5] Essays in this section also address questions of inclusion and citation, that is, visibility of work by women and work by women of color.

The third section examines the ways in which feminist anthropology moved decisively to study the West and more specifically for Americans, the US, moves that in part reflected feminist anthropologists' commitment to understand their own culture and to intervene to improve it. The large body of work done by feminist anthropologists on North American and Western European cultures has helped to move such inquiry to a newly respectable position in anthropology. In line with the reflexive moves being made by feminist anthropology, this work has often focused on topics in anthropologists' own experience; thus the family and reproduction have been the target of particularly pointed ethnographic work. In many instances, these topics have emerged directly from the personal lives of anthropologists, reflecting their experiences in obtaining medical care, working in political movements, or interacting with their own communities. Again, this focus on the West is hardly unique, being paralleled by – and often overlapping with – similar efforts by black and other ethnic minority anthropologists, but feminist anthropologists' commitment to interpolate the personal and the scholarly has given such work particular urgency.

The fourth section includes readings that demonstrate the continuing commitment of feminist anthropology to promoting movements for social change that can improve women's lives. Here I draw both on work that addresses specific contentious issues (such as female genital surgery) and on studies of women's political organizing in various contexts. We shall see that this body of work, some of it concerning the West and some anchored in non-Western areas of traditional anthropological concern, has been influenced by the rethinking of "us" and "them" covered in the previous section. These writings also reflect the continuing commitment of feminist anthropologists to addressing questions of social justice and to understanding how both power and agency shape the status of women and broader conditions of inequality in various contexts. Many of these readings engage explicitly with the ambiguities of cultural relativism and its sometimes problematic relationship with political and social change agendas anthropologists may want to further.

The fifth section focuses on some of the kinds of rethinking that have come to be central to feminist anthropology in recent years, particularly in relation to studies of transnational and global concerns, and gender in relation to nation, race, and class. These readings engage with questions about the boundaries of sex and gender, and other examinations of power that draw on cultural studies and ethnic studies models. In these articles, feminist anthropology's object of study loses much of the stability it had in the early days of the field; studies of non-Western cultures are acknowledged to be embedded in global systems of inequality, and the object of feminist anthropology – woman – also becomes much less stable and certain than it was in the early days. Dichotomized distinctions based on economic development, cultural boundaries, sexuality, and gender itself all become subjects of investigation rather than assumptions that organize basic questions.

Feminist anthropology's fate seems to be to deconstruct itself: its object is no longer as firmly female as it was thirty years ago, nor are its practitioners any longer willing to make facile assumptions about how to understand sex and gender. Its frame of reference is no longer clearly culture, its understanding of the body where it all starts no longer confident. And it has been profoundly changed as a field by the processes of institutionalization that have moved it from a vanguard movement of outsiders to a respected field of inquiry that merits publication of a volume of its "classic" works. Yet throughout these shifts and realignments, feminist anthropological inquiry has been able to sustain its commitment to social justice. Scholars in the field continue to be inspired by contemporary social movements and by the needs of real people all over the world to have their problems addressed from the humanistic perspective anthropology can offer. We continue to work on issues of sex, gender, sexuality, and the inequalities that intersect them because we must. We can best measure our success by our ability to convey the stories people share with us, making their motives, feelings, and hopes real to the audiences we address through our writings and in the classroom.

NOTES

1   During this period, the American Anthropological Association formed the Commission on the Status of Women in Anthropology (COSWA) which was charged with assessing discrimination in the profession. Its efforts to survey the progress of women in anthropology departments generated a series of bitter controversies in the 1970s. But the formation of COSWA arguably set the stage for the solidification of a number of identity-based AAA sections, including the Association for Feminist Anthropology (AFA), the Association of Black Anthropologists (ABA), the Society for Lesbian and Gay Anthropology (SOLGA) and others, groups whose existence is no longer particularly controversial.

2   Ortner's article was enormously controversial. In 1980, a volume edited by Carol Mac-Cormack and Marilyn Strathern, *Nature, Culture and Gender,* with mainly British contributors, offered a major critique of Ortner's argument. In a later volume, *Making Gender: The Politics and Erotics of Culture*, Ortner herself revisits her paper and presents an updated version (Ortner 1997).

3   The most important of these volumes are *Women Writing Culture,* edited by Ruth Behar and Deborah Gordon, and *Gender at the Crossroads of Knowledge,* edited by Micaela di Leonardo. Sandra Morgen's edited volume *Anthropology and Gender,* published in 1990, was intended as a resource to assist faculty who wanted to incorporate more material about women and gender into anthropology classes in various specialized areas.

4   e.g. *Writing Culture,* edited by James Clifford and George Marcus (1986) and *Reinventing Anthropology,* edited by Dell Hymes (1974).

5   e.g. Judith Butler, *Gender Trouble* (1990), Denise Riley, *"Am I That Name?": Feminism and the Category of "Women" in History* (1988).

REFERENCES

Abu-Lughod, Lila. 1990a. Can There Be a Feminist Ethnography? *Women and Performance,* 5/1: 7–27.
—— 1990b. The Romance of Resistance: Tracing Transformations of Power through Bedouin Women. *American Ethnologist,* 17/1: 41–55.
—— 1995. A Tale of Two Pregnancies. In *Women Writing Culture.* R. Behar and D. A. Gordon, eds. pp. 339–349 Berkeley: University of California Press.
Albert, Ethel. 1963. Women of Burundi: A Study of Society Values. In *Women of Tropical Africa.* D. Paulme, ed. pp. 179–215. Berkeley: University of California Press.
Altorki, Soraya, and Camillia El-Solh. 1989. *Arab Women in the Field: Studying Your Own Society.* Syracuse, NY: Syracuse University Press.
Anglin, Mary K. 2002. *Women, Power, and Dissent in the Hills of Carolina.* Urbana: University of Illinois Press.
Ardener, Edwin. 1975. Belief and the Problem of Women. In *Perceiving Women.* S. Ardener, ed. pp. 1–17. London: Malaby Press. [This volume, ch. 1.]
Arms, Suzanne. 1977. *Immaculate Deception: A New Look at Women and Childbirth in America.* New York: Bantam Books.

Aschenbrenner, Joyce. 1999. Katherine Dunham: Anthropologist, Artist, Humanist. In *African-American Pioneers in Anthropology*. I. E. Harrison and F. V. Harrison, eds. pp. 137–53. Urbana: University of Illinois Press.

Babb, Florence E. 1989. *Between Field and Cooking Pot: The Political Economy of Market-women in Peru*. Austin: University of Texas Press.

——2001. *After Revolution: Mapping Gender and Cultural Politics in Neoliberal Nicaragua*. Austin: University of Texas Press.

Babcock, Barbara A. 1995. "Not in the Absolute Singular": Rereading Ruth Benedict. In *Women Writing Culture*. R. Behar and D. A. Gordon, eds. pp. 104–30. Berkeley: University of California Press.

Bates, Daisy. 1939. *The Passing of the Aborigines: A Lifetime Spent among the Natives of Australia*. New York: Putnam.

Behar, Ruth. 1993. *Translated Woman: Crossing the Border with Esperanza's Story*. Boston: Beacon Press.

——1996. *The Vulnerable Observer: Anthropology that Breaks your Heart*. Boston: Beacon Press.

Behar, Ruth, and Deborah A. Gordon, eds. 1995. *Women Writing Culture*. Berkeley: University of California Press.

Blackburn, Julia. 1994. *Daisy Bates in the Desert*. New York: Pantheon.

Blackwood, Evelyn, and Saskia E. Wieringa, eds. 1999. *Female Desires: Same-Sex Relations and Transgender Practices across Cultures*. New York: Columbia University Press.

Bobel, Chris. 2002. *The Paradox of Natural Mothering*. Philadelphia: Temple University Press.

Boddy, Janice. 1998. Violence Embodied? Female Circumcision, Gender Politics, and Cultural Aesthetics. In *Rethinking Violence against Women*. R. E. Dobash and R. P. Dobash, eds. pp. 77–110. Thousand Oaks, CA: Sage.

Bolles, A. Lynn. 1999. Ellen Irene Diggs: Coming of Age in Atlanta, Havana, and Baltimore. In *African-American Pioneers in Anthropology*. I. E. Harrison and F. V. Harrison, eds. pp. 154–67. Urbana: University of Illinois Press.

——2001. Seeking the Ancestors: Forging a Black Feminist Tradition in Anthropology. In *Black Feminist Anthropology: Theory, Politics, Praxis, and Poetics*. I. McClaurin, ed. pp. 24–48. New Brunswick, NJ: Rutgers University Press.

Boserup, Ester. 1970. *Woman's Role in Economic Development*. London: George Allen and Unwin.

Bourque, Susan C., and Kay Barbara Warren. 1981. *Women of the Andes: Patriarchy and Social Change in Two Peruvian Towns*. Ann Arbor, MI: University of Michigan Press.

Bowen, Elenore Smith [Laura Bohannan]. 1954. *Return to Laughter: An Anthropological Novel*. New York: Harper.

Boxer, Marilyn Jacoby. 1998. *When Women Ask the Questions: Creating Women's Studies in America*. Baltimore: Johns Hopkins University Press.

Boyd, Valerie. 2003. *Wrapped in Rainbows: The Life of Zora Neale Hurston*. New York: Scribner.

Brenner, Johanna. 2000. *Women and the Politics of Class*. New York: Monthly Review Press.

Brodkin, Karen. 1988. *Caring by the Hour: Women, Work, and Organizing at Duke Medical Center*. Urbana: University of Illinois Press.

Butler, Judith. 1990. *Gender Trouble: Feminism and the Subversion of Identity*. New York: Routledge.

Caplan, Patricia. 1979. Women's Organizations in Madras City, India. In *Women United, Women Divided: Comparative Studies of Ten Contemporary Cultures*. P. Caplan and J. M. Bujra, eds. pp. 99–128. Bloomington: Indiana University Press.

Caplan, Patricia, and Janet M. Bujra, eds. 1979. *Women United, Women Divided: Comparative Studies of Ten Contemporary Cultures*. Bloomington: Indiana University Press.

Caraway, Nancie. 1991. *Racism and the Politics of American Feminism*. Knoxville: University of Tennessee Press.

Carrillo, Héctor. 2002. *The Night is Young: Sexuality in Mexico in the Time of AIDS*. Chicago: University of Chicago Press.

Chin, Soo-Young. 1999. *Doing What Had to be Done: The Life Narrative of Dora Yum Kim*. Philadelphia: Temple University Press.

Chodorow, Nancy. 1974. Family Structure and Feminine Personality. In *Woman, Culture, and Society*. M. Z. Rosaldo and L. Lamphere, eds. pp. 43–66. Stanford, CA: Stanford University Press.

Clifford, James, and George E. Marcus. 1986. *Writing Culture: The Poetics and Politics of Ethnography*. Berkeley: University of California Press.

Cohen, Gaynor. 1979. Women's Solidarity and the Preservation of Privilege. In *Women United, Women Divided: Comparative Studies of Ten Contemporary Cultures*. P. Caplan and J. M. Bujra, eds. pp. 129–56. Bloomington: Indiana University Press.

Colen, Shellee. 1995. "Like a Mother to Them": Stratified Reproduction and West Indian Childcare Workers and Employers in New York. In *Conceiving the New World Order: The Global Politics of Reproduction*. F. D. Ginsburg and R. R. Rapp, eds. pp. 78–102. Berkeley: University of California Press. [This volume, ch. 19.]

Constable, Nicole. 2003. *Romance on a Global Stage: Pen Pals, Virtual Ethnography, and "Mail-Order" Marriages*. Berkeley: University of California Press.

Das, Veena. 1995. National Honor and Practical Kinship: Unwanted Women and Children. In *Conceiving the New World Order: The Global Politics of Reproduction*. F. D. Ginsburg and R. R. Rapp, eds. pp. 212–33. Berkeley: University of California Press.

Davis-Floyd, Robbie. 1992. *Birth as an American Rite of Passage*. Berkeley: University of California Press.

Davis-Floyd, Robbie, and Joseph Dumit. 1998. *Cyborg Babies: From Techno-Sex to Techno-Tots*. New York: Routledge.

Di Leonardo, Micaela, ed. 1991. *Gender at the Crossroads of Knowledge: Feminist Anthropology in the Postmodern Era*. Berkeley: University of California Press.

Dwyer, Daisy Hilse. 1978. *Images and Self Images: Male and Female in Morocco*. New York: Columbia University Press.

Echols, Alice. 1989. *Daring to be Bad: Radical Feminism in America, 1967–1975*. Minneapolis: University of Minnesota Press.

Ehrenreich, Barbara, and Deirdre English. 1972. *Witches, Midwives, and Nurses: A History of Women Healers*. New York: Feminist Press.

Engels, Friedrich. 1972. *The Origin of the Family, Private Property and the State, in Light of the Researches of Lewis H. Morgan*. New York: International Publishers.

Etienne, Mona, and Eleanor Leacock, eds. 1980. *Women and Colonization: Anthropological Perspectives*. New York: Praeger.

Fernea, Elizabeth Warnock. 1965. *Guests of the Sheik: An Ethnography of an Iraqi Village*. Garden City, NY: Doubleday.

Finkler, Kaja. 1994. *Women in Pain: Gender and Morbidity in Mexico*. Philadelphia: University of Pennsylvania Press.

Frank, Gelya. 2000. *Venus on Wheels: Two Decades of Dialogue on Disability, Biography, and Being Female in America*. Berkeley: University of California Press.

Franklin, Sarah. 1997. *Embodied Progress: A Cultural Account of Assisted Conception*. New York: Routledge.

Franklin, Sarah, and Helena Ragoné. 1998. *Reproducing Reproduction: Kinship, Power, and Technological Innovation*. Philadelphia: University of Pennsylvania Press.

Freedman, Estelle B. 2002. *No Turning Back: The History of Feminism and the Future of Women*. New York: Ballantine.

Freeman, Carla. 2000. *High Tech and High Heels in the Global Economy: Women, Work, and Pink-Collar Identities in the Caribbean*. Durham, NC: Duke University Press.

Gailey, Christine Ward. 1980. Putting Down Sisters and Wives: Tongan Women and Colonization. In *Women and Colonization: Anthropological Perspectives*. M. Etienne and E. Leacock, eds. pp. 294–322. New York: Praeger.

—— 1987. *From Kinship to Kingship: Gender Hierarchy and State Formation in the Tongan Islands*. Austin: University of Texas Press.

Geertz, Clifford. 1988. *Works and Lives: The Anthropologist as Author*. Stanford, CA: Stanford University Press.

Ginsburg, Faye D. 1989. *Contested Lives: The Abortion Debate in an American Community*. Berkeley: University of California Press.

Golde, Peggy, ed. 1986 [1970]. *Women in the Field: Anthropological Experiences*. Berkeley: University of California Press.

Goodale, Jane C. 1971. *Tiwi Wives: A Study of the Women of Melville Island, North Australia*. Seattle: University of Washington Press.

Gough, Kathleen. 1975. The Origin of the Family. In *Toward an Anthropology of Women*. R. R. Reiter, ed. pp. 51–76. New York: Monthly Review Press.

Gruenbaum, Ellen. 2001. *The Female Circumcision Controversy*. Philadelphia: University of Pennsylvania Press.

Gutmann, Matthew C. 1996. *The Meanings of Macho: Being a Man in Mexico City*. Berkeley: University of California Press.

Handwerker, Lisa. 1995. The Hen that Can't Lay an Egg (*Bu Xia Dan de Mu Ji*): Conceptions of Female Infertility in Modern China. In *Deviant Bodies*. J. Terry and J. Urla, eds. Bloomington: Indiana University Press.

Hart, C. W. M., and Arnold R. Pilling. 1960. *The Tiwi of North Australia*. New York: Holt.

Hayes, Rose Oldfield. 1975. Female Genital Mutilation, Fertility Control, Women's Roles, and the Patrilineage in Modern Sudan. *American Ethnologist*, 2: 617–33.

Herdt, Gilbert H. 1981. *Guardians of the Flutes: Idioms of Masculinity*. New York: McGraw Hill.

Hernandez, Graciela. 1995. Multiple Subjectivities and Strategic Positionality: Zora Neale Hurston's Experimental Ethnographies. In *Women Writing Culture*. R. Behar and D. A. Gordon, eds. pp. 148–65. Berkeley: University of California Press.

Hirsch, Jennifer S. 2003. *A Courtship after Marriage: Sexuality and Love in Mexican Transnational Families*. Berkeley: University of California Press.

Hoch-Smith, Judith, and Anita Spring, eds. 1978. *Women in Ritual and Symbolic Roles*. New York: Plenum.

Hurston, Zora Neale. 1935. *Mules and Men*. New York: J. B. Lippincott.

—— 1969 [1942]. *Dust Tracks on a Road*. New York: Arno Press.

Hymes, Dell, ed. 1972. *Reinventing Anthropology*. New York: Pantheon.

Inhorn, Marcia C. 1994. *Quest for Conception: Gender, Infertility, and Egyptian Medical Traditions*. University of Pennsylvania Press.

—— 1996. *Infertility and Patriarchy: The Cultural Politics of Gender and Family Life in Egypt*. Philadelphia: University of Pennsylvania Press.

Inhorn, Marcia C., and Kimberly Buss. 1993. Infertility, Infection, and Iatrogenesis in Egypt: The Anthropological Epidemiology of Blocked Tubes. *Medical Anthropology*, 15/1: 1–28.

Inhorn, Marcia C., and Frank Van Balen, eds. 2002. *Infertility around the Globe: New Thinking on Childlessness, Gender, and Reproductive Technologies*. Berkeley: University of California Press.

Jordan, Brigitte. 1977. The Self-Diagnosis of Early Pregnancy: An Investigation of Lay Competence. *Medical Anthropology*, 1/2: 1–38.

—— 1978. *Birth in Four Cultures: A Crosscultural Investigation of Childbirth in Yucatan, Holland, Sweden, and the United States*. Montreal: Eden Press Women's Publications.

—— 1997. Authoritative Knowledge and its Construction. In *Childbirth and Authoritative Knowledge: Cross-Cultural Perspectives*. R. Davis-Floyd and C. F. Sargent, eds. pp. 55–79. Berkeley: University of California Press.

Kaberry, Phyllis. 1939. *Aboriginal Woman: Sacred and Profane*. Philadelphia: Blakiston.

—— 1952. *Women of the Grassfields: A Study of the Economic Position of Women in Bamenda, British Cameroons*. London: Her Majesty's Stationery Office.

Kahn, Susan Martha. 2000. *Reproducing Jews: A Cultural Account of Assisted Conception in Israel*. Durham, NC: Duke University Press.

Kanaaneh, Rhoda Ann. 2002. *Birthing the Nation: Strategies of Palestinian Women in Israel*. Berkeley: University of California Press.

Kaplan, Laura. 1997. *The Story of Jane: The Legendary Underground Feminist Abortion Service*. Chicago: University of Chicago Press.

Kennedy, Elizabeth Lapovsky, and Madeline D. Davis. 1993. *Boots of Leather, Slippers of Gold: The History of a Lesbian Community*. New York: Routledge.

Klassen, Pamela E. 2001. *Blessed Events: Religion and Home Birth in America*. Princeton: Princeton University Press.

Kligman, Gail. 1998. *The Politics of Duplicity: Controlling Reproduction in Ceausescu's Romania*. Berkeley: University of California Press.

Kondo, Dorinne K. 1990. *Crafting Selves: Power, Gender, and Discourses of Identity in a Japanese Workplace*. Chicago: University of Chicago Press.

Krasniewicz, Louise. 1992. *Nuclear Summer: The Clash of Communities at the Seneca Women's Peace Encampment*. Ithaca, NY: Cornell University Press.

Laderman, Carol. 1983. *Wives and Midwives: Childbirth and Nutrition in Rural Malaysia*. Berkeley: University of California Press.

Lamphere, Louise. 1995. Feminist Anthropology: The Legacy of Elsie Clews Parsons. In *Women Writing Culture*. R. Behar and D. A. Gordon, eds. pp. 85–103. Berkeley: University of California Press.

Landes, Ruth. 1971 [1938]. *The Ojibwa Woman*. New York: W. W. Norton.

—— 1994 [1947]. *The City of Women*. Albuquerque: University of New Mexico Press.

Lapsley, Hilary. 1999. *Margaret Mead and Ruth Benedict: The Kinship of Women*. Amherst: University of Massachusetts Press.

Leibowitz, Lila. 1975. Perspectives on the Evolution of Sex Differences. In *Toward an Anthropology of Women*. R. R. Reiter, ed. pp. 20–35. New York: Monthly Review Press.

Lepowsky, Maria. 1993. *Fruit of the Motherland: Gender in an Egalitarian Society*. New York: Columbia University Press.

Lewin, Ellen. 1993. *Lesbian Mothers: Accounts of Gender in American Culture*. Ithaca, NY: Cornell University Press.

—— 1995. Writing Lesbian Ethnography. In *Women Writing Culture*. R. Behar and D. A. Gordon, eds. pp. 322–35. Berkeley: University of California Press.

—— 1998. *Recognizing Ourselves: Ceremonies of Lesbian and Gay Commitment*. New York: Columbia University Press.

Lewin, Ellen, and William L. Leap, eds. 1996. *Out in the Field: Reflections of Lesbian and Gay Anthropologists*. Urbana: University of Illinois Press.

—— —— 2002. *Out in Theory: The Emergence of Lesbian and Gay Anthropology*. Urbana: University of Illinois Press.

Lock, Margaret, and Patricia A. Kaufert, eds. 1998. *Pragmatic Women and Body Politics*. New York: Cambridge University Press.

Lurie, Nancy Oestreich. 1999 [1966]. *Women and the Invention of American Anthropology.* Prospect Heights, IL: Waveland.

Lutkehaus, Nancy C. 1995. Margaret Mead and the "Rustling-of-the-Wind-in-the-Palm-Trees School" of Ethnographic Writing. In *Women Writing Culture.* R. Behar and D. A. Gordon, eds. pp. 186–206. Berkeley: University of California Press.

Lutz, Catherine. 1990. The Erasure of Women's Writing in Sociocultural Anthropology. *American Ethnologist,* 17/4: 611–27.

McClain, Carol Shepherd. 1975. Ethno-Obstetrics in Ajijic. *Anthropological Quarterly,* 40/1: 38–56.

—— 1989. *Women as Healers.* New Brunswick, NJ: Rutgers University Press.

McClaurin, Irma. 2001. *Black Feminist Anthropology: Theory, Politics, Praxis, and Poetics.* New Brunswick, NJ: Rutgers University Press.

Manalansan, Martin F. IV. 2003. *Global Divas: Filipino Gay Men in the Diaspora.* Durham, NC: Duke University Press.

Martin, Emily. 1989. *The Woman in the Body: A Cultural Analysis of Reproduction.* Boston: Beacon Press.

Mascia-Lees, Frances E., Patricia Sharpe, and Colleen Ballerino Cohen. 1989. The Postmodernist Turn in Anthropology: Cautions from a Feminist Perspective. *Signs,* 15/1: 7–33.

Mattiasson, Carolyn J. 1974. *Many Sisters: Women in Cross-Cultural Perspective.* New York: Free Press.

Mead, Margaret. 1974. *Ruth Benedict.* New York: Columbia University Press.

Mikell, Gwendolyn. 1988. Zora Neale Hurston (1903–1960). In *Women Anthropologists: A Biographical Dictionary.* U. Gacs, A. Kahn, J. McIntyre, and R. Weinberg, eds. pp. 160–6. New York: Greenwood Press.

—— 1999. Feminism and Black Culture in the Ethnography of Zora Neale Hurston. In *African-American Pioneers in Anthropology.* I. E. Harrison and F. V. Harrison, eds. pp. 51–69. Urbana: University of Illinois Press.

Modell, Judith S. 1994. *Kinship with Strangers: Adoption and Interpretations of Kinship in American Culture.* Berkeley: University of California Press.

Moore, Henrietta. 1989. *Feminism and Anthropology.* Minneapolis: University of Minnesota Press.

—— 1994. *A Passion for Difference: Essays in Anthropology and Gender.* Bloomington, IN: Indiana University Press.

Morgan, Robin, ed. 1970. *Sisterhood is Powerful: An Anthology of Writings from the Women's Liberation Movement.* New York: Vintage.

Morgen, Sandra, ed. 1990. *Anthropology and Gender: Critical Reviews for Research and Teaching.* Washington, DC: American Anthropological Association.

—— 2002. *Into Our Own Hands: The Women's Health Movement in the United States, 1969–1990.* New Brunswick, NJ: Rutgers University Press.

Morgen, Sandra, and Jill Weigt. 2001. Poor Women, Fair Work, and Welfare-to-Work That Works. In *The New Poverty Studies: The Ethnography of Power, Politics, and Impoverished People in the United States.* J. Goode and J. Maskovsky, eds. pp. 152–78. New York: New York University Press.

Murphy, Yolanda, and Robert F. Murphy. 1974. *Women of the Forest.* New York: Columbia University Press.

Narayan, Kirin. 1993. How Native is a "Native" Anthropologist? *American Anthropologist,* 95/3: 671–86.

Nash, June. 1983. *Women, Men, and the International Division of Labor.* Albany, NY: State University of New York Press.

Newton, Esther. 1972. *Mother Camp: Female Impersonators in America.* Englewood Cliffs, NJ: Prentice-Hall.

—— 1993. *Cherry Grove, Fire Island: Sixty Years in America's First Lesbian and Gay Town.* Boston: Beacon Press.

Ong, Aihwa. 1987. *Spirits of Resistance and Capitalist Discipline: Factory Women in Malaysia.* Albany, NY: State University of New York Press.

Ortner, Sherry B. 1974. Is Female to Male as Nature is to Culture? In *Woman, Culture, and Society.* M. Z. Rosaldo and L. Lamphere, eds. pp. 67–87. Stanford, CA: Stanford University Press. [This volume, ch. 3.]

—— 1997. *Making Gender: The Politics and Erotics of Culture.* Boston: Beacon Press.

Parezo, Nancy J. 1993. *Hidden Scholars: Women Anthropologists and the Native American Southwest.* Albuquerque: University of New Mexico Press.

Passaro, Joanne. 1996. *The Unequal Homeless: Men on the Streets, Women in their Place.* New York: Routledge.

Paulme, Denise. 1963. *Women of Tropical Africa.* Berkeley: University of California Press.

Powdermaker, Hortense. 1933. *Life in Lesu: The Study of a Melanesian Society in New Ireland.* New York: W. W. Norton.

—— 1939. *After Freedom: A Cultural Study in the Deep South.* New York: Viking.

—— 1950. *Hollywood: The Dream Factory.* Boston: Little Brown.

—— 1962. *Copper Town: Changing Africa: The Human Situation on the Rhodesian Copper Belt.* New York: Harper and Row.

—— 1966. *Stranger and Friend: The Way of an Anthropologist.* New York: W. W. Norton.

Ragoné, Helena. 1994. *Surrogate Motherhood: Conception in the Heart.* Boulder, CO: Westview.

Ragoné, Helena, and France Winddance Twine, eds. 2000. *Ideologies and Technologies of Motherhood: Race, Class, Sexuality, Nationalism.* New York: Routledge.

Raphael, Dana, ed. 1975. *Being Female: Reproduction, Power, and Change.* The Hague: Mouton.

Rapp, Rayna R. 1999. *Testing Women, Testing the Fetus: The Social Impact of Amniocentesis in America.* New York: Routledge.

Rebhun, L. A. 1999. *The Heart is Unknown Country: Love in the Changing Economy of Northeast Brazil.* Stanford, CA: Stanford University Press.

Reiter, Rayna R. 1975. Introduction. In *Toward an Anthropology of Women.* R. R. Reiter, ed. pp. 11–19. New York: Monthly Review Press.

Riley, Denise. 1988. *"Am I that Name?": Feminism and the Category of "Women" in History.* Minneapolis: University of Minnesota Press.

Rohrlich-Leavitt, Ruby, ed. 1975. *Women Cross-Culturally: Change and Challenge.* The Hague: Mouton.

Rosaldo, Michelle Zimbalist. 1974. Woman, Culture, and Society: A Theoretical Overview. In *Woman, Culture, and Society.* M. Z. Rosaldo and L. Lamphere, eds. pp. 17–42. Stanford, CA: Stanford University Press.

Rosaldo, Michelle Zimbalist, and Louise Lamphere. 1974. Introduction. In *Woman, Culture, and Society.* M. Z. Rosaldo and L. Lamphere, eds. pp. 1–15. Stanford, CA: Stanford University Press.

Rosaldo, Renato. 1989. *Culture and Truth: The Remaking of Social Analysis.* Boston: Beacon Press.

Rosen, Ruth. 2000. *The World Split Open: How the Modern Women's Movement Changed America.* New York: Viking.

Ross, Hubert B., Amelia Marie Adams, and Lynne Mallory Williams. 1999. Caroline Bond Day: Pioneer Black Physical Anthropologist. In *African-American Pioneers in Anthropology.* I. E. Harrison and F. V. Harrison, eds. pp. 37–50. Urbana: University of Illinois Press.

Roth, Benita. 2004. *Separate Roads to Feminism: Black, Chicana, and White Feminist Movements in America's Second Wave.* Cambridge: Cambridge University Press.

Rothman, Barbara Katz. 1982. *In Labor: Women and Power in the Birthplace*. New York: W. W. Norton.

Rubin, Gayle. 1975. The Traffic in Women: Notes on the "Political Economy" of Sex. In *Toward an Anthropology of Women*. R. R. Reiter, ed. pp. 157–210. New York: Monthly Review Press. [This volume, ch. 4.]

Ruzek, Sheryl Burt. 1979. *The Women's Health Movement: Feminist Alternatives to Medical Control*. New York: Praeger.

Sacks, Karen. 1979. *Sisters and Wives: The Past and Future of Sexual Equality*. Westport, CT: Greenwood Press.

Sacks, Karen Brodkin, and Dorothy Remy, eds. 1984. *My Troubles Are Going to Have Trouble With Me: Everyday Trials and Triumphs of Women Workers*. New Brunswick, NJ: Rutgers University Press.

Salter, Elizabeth. 1971. *Daisy Bates: "The Great White Queen of the Never Never"*. Melbourne: Angus and Robertson.

Sanday, Peggy Reeves. 1981. *Female Power and Male Dominance: On the Origins of Sexual Inequality*. Cambridge: Cambridge University Press.

—— 1990. *Fraternity Gang Rape: Sex, Brotherhood, and Privilege on Campus*. New York: New York University Press.

—— 1996. *A Woman Scorned: Acquaintance Rape on Trial*. New York: Doubleday.

Sandelowski, Margarete. 1993. *With Child in Mind: Studies of the Personal Encounter with Infertility*. Philadelphia: University of Pennsylvania Press.

Sargent, Carolyn Fishel. 1981. *The Cultural Context of Therapeutic Choice: Obstetrical Care Decisions among the Bariba of Benin*. Dordrecht: Reidel.

Scheper-Hughes, Nancy. 1992. *Death without Weeping: The Violence of Everyday Life in Brazil*. Berkeley: University of California Press.

Schlegel, Alice. 1972. *Male Dominance and Female Autonomy: Domestic Authority in Matrilineal Societies*. New Haven: HRAF Press.

—— 1977. *Sexual Stratification: A Cross-Cultural View*. New York: Columbia University Press.

Schneider, David M. 1968. *American Kinship: A Cultural Account*. Englewood Cliffs, NJ: Prentice-Hall.

—— 1995. *Schneider on Schneider: The Conversion of the Jews and Other Anthropological Stories*. Durham, NC: Duke University Press.

Scott, James C. 1987. *Weapons of the Weak: Everyday Forms of Peasant Resistance*. New Haven: Yale University Press.

Sered, Susan. 2000. *What Makes Women Sick? Maternity, Modesty, and Militarism in Israeli Society*. Hanover, NH: Brandeis University Press.

Shaw, Nancy Stoller. 1974. *Forced Labor: Maternity Care in the United States*. New York: Pergamon Press.

Shostak, Marjorie. 1981. *Nisa: The Life and Words of a !Kung Woman*. New York: Random House.

—— 1989. "What the Wind Won't Take Away": The Genesis of *Nisa – The Life and Words of a !Kung Woman*. In *Interpreting Women's Lives: Feminist Theory and Personal Narratives*. Personal Narratives Group, ed. Bloomington: Indiana University Press.

Silverblatt, Irene. 1991. Interpreting Women in States: New Feminist Ethnohistories. In *Gender at the Crossroads of Knowledge: Feminist Anthropology in the Postmodern Era*. M. di Leonardo, ed. pp. 140–71. Berkeley: University of California Press.

Slocum, Sally. 1975. Woman the Gatherer: Male Bias in Anthropology. In *Toward an Anthropology of Women*. R. R. Reiter, ed. pp. 36–50. New York: Monthly Review Press.

Smith, Mary F. 1954. *Baba of Karo: A Woman of the Muslim Hausa*. London: Faber & Faber.

Spelman, Elizabeth V. 1988. *Inessential Woman: Problems of Exclusion in Feminist Thought*. Boston: Beacon Press.

Stacey, Judith. 1988. Can There Be a Feminist Ethnography? *Women's Studies International Forum*, 11/1: 21–7.

Stack, Carol B. 1974. *All our Kin: Strategies for Survival in a Black Community*. New York: Harper and Row.

Stephen, Lynn. 1997. *Women and Social Movements in Latin America: Power from Below*. Austin: University of Texas Press.

Strathern, Marilyn. 1987. An Awkward Relationship: The Case of Anthropology and Feminism. *Signs*, 12/2: 276–92.

—— 1992. *Reproducing the Future: Essays on Anthropology, Kinship, and the New Reproductive Technologies*. New York: Routledge.

Susser, Ida. 1982. *Norman Street: Poverty and Politics in an Urban Neighborhood*. New York: Oxford University Press.

Taylor, Janelle S. 1992. The Public Fetus and the Family Car: From Abortion Politics to a Volvo Advertisement. *Public Culture*, 4/2: 67–80.

—— 2004. A Fetish is Born: Sonographers and the Making of the Public Fetus. In *Consuming Motherhood*. J. S. Taylor, L. L. Layne, and D. F. Wozniak, eds. New Brunswick, NJ: Rutgers University Press.

Tedlock, Barbara. 1995. Works and Wives: On the Sexual Division of Textual Labor. In *Women Writing Culture*. R. Behar and D. A. Gordon, eds. pp. 267–86. Berkeley: University of California Press.

Townsend, Nicholas W. 2002. *The Package Deal: Marriage, Work, and Fatherhood in Men's Lives*. Philadelphia: Temple University Press.

Tsing, Anna Lowenhaupt. 1993. *In the Realm of the Diamond Queen*. Princeton: Princeton University Press.

Valentine, David. 2003. "The Calculus of Pain": Violence, Anthropological Ethics, and the Category Transgender. *Ethnos*, 68: 27–48.

Warren, Kay Barbara, and Susan C. Bourque. 1991. Women, Technology, and International Development Ideologies: Analyzing Feminist Voices. In *Gender at the Crossroads of Knowledge: Feminist Anthropology in the Postmodern Era*. M. di Leonardo, ed. pp. 278–311. Berkeley: University of California Press.

Weiner, Annette B. 1976. *Women of Value, Men of Renown: New Perspectives in Trobriand Exchange*. Austin: University of Texas Press.

Weismantel, Mary. 1988. *Food, Gender, and Poverty in the Ecuadorian Andes*. Philadelphia: University of Pennsylvania Press.

—— 2001. *Cholas and Pishtacos: Stories of Race and Sex in the Andes*. Chicago: University of Chicago Press.

Weston, Kath. 1991. *Families We Choose: Lesbians, Gays, Kinship*. New York: Columbia University Press.

Williams, Brackette. 1996. *Women Out of Place: The Gender of Agency and the Race of Nationality*. New York: Routledge.

Williams, Walter L. 1986. *The Spirit and the Flesh: Sexual Diversity in American Indian Culture*. Boston: Beacon Press.

Wilson, Ara. 2004. *The Intimate Economies of Bangkok: Tomboys, Tycoons, and Avon Ladies in the Global City*. Berkeley: University of California Press.

Wolf, Margery. 1968. *The House of Lim: A Study of a Chinese Family*. New York: Appleton-Century-Crofts.

—— 1972. *Women and the Family in Rural Taiwan*. Stanford, CA: Stanford University Press.

—— 1992. *A Thrice-Told Tale: Feminism, Postmodernism, and Ethnographic Responsibility*. Stanford, CA: Stanford University Press.

Wozniak, Danielle F. 2002. *They're All My Children: Foster Mothering in America*. New York: New York University Press.

Yanagisako, Sylvia, and Carol Delaney. 1995. *Naturalizing Power: Essays in Feminist Cultural Analysis*. New York: Routledge.

Young, Kate, Carol Wolkowitz, and Roslyn McCullagh, eds. 1981. *Of Marriage and the Market: Women's Subordination Internationally and its Lessons*. London: Routledge & Kegan Paul.

Zavella, Patricia. 2001. The Tables Are Turned: Immigration, Poverty, and Social Conflict in California Communities. In *The New Poverty Studies: The Ethnography of Power, Politics, and Impoverished People in the United States*. J. Goode and J. Maskovsky, eds. pp. 103–31. New York: New York University Press.

Part I
Discovering Women across Cultures

Introduction

The essays in this section represent some of the early efforts to carve out a basis for understanding what gender is and how it affects men and women. The notion that women awaited "discovery" by anthropologists may seem odd, but there is little question that while the presence of women was recognized, few anthropologists had given serious consideration to what cultural contributions they might make. While most scholars simply assumed that reproduction was the business of women, attempts to find regularities in these spheres, or to evaluate the status of women as a group in relation to men rarely inspired the interest of researchers. In this context, the first two articles reprinted here were written prior to the formation of the new field, and were among the few writings available in the early 1970s that suggested that putting women on center stage was appropriate and could be productive.

Edwin Ardener's paper "Belief and the Problem of Women" was originally presented in a seminar at University College London and was then included as part of a festschrift assembled to honor Audrey Richards, who had been one of his teachers. The essay, with the later commentary titled "The 'Problem' Revisited," was published in Shirley Ardener's 1975 collection, *Perceiving Women*, and thus found its way to feminist anthropologists in the US. Edwin Ardener sought to explain the minimal attention women received in anthropological research by looking to the ways that they express and represent themselves, proposing that social groups can be distinguished as "articulate" or "muted," a characteristic linked to forms of dominance or subordination. While not asserting that women were unique as a muted group, Ardener likened their situation to other groups that have little ability to make themselves heard, such as children. While attempting to avoid reducing men and women to absolutely opposing groups, he argued that women fall outside the definitions of social systems made by men and thus tend to be invisible and thus unreadable by anthropologists. A crucial point here is that the male domination that characterizes most cultures also applies to anthropology. Thus the questions anthropologists (regardless of their individual gender) ask, and the answers they recognize as responsive to their questions and relevant to their research "just happen" to be those that are articulated by men and decipherable by men. Women's voices are either discounted because they don't respond to interviewing or other research inquiries in a form that meets the anthropologist's criteria as "data," or are simply assumed to have nothing to offer because they are marginal to visible markers of political and economic status.

Ardener's argument struck a nerve in the early 1970s. The anthropologists who had begun to produce work on women were critically aware of their own blind spots; many, including women anthropologists, had gone off to do fieldwork assuming that success would depend on the degree to which they could gain acceptance among the men. Being relegated to working with women, which sometimes happened to female anthropologists, was not unlike being sent to the kitchen at a cocktail party where conversations could be expected to revolve around children and cooking, and thus being cut off from the "important" topics of conversation seemingly pursued by the men in the living room. At the same time, Ardener had put into intellectually respectable language the crucial questions of voice and visibility with which the women's movement was preoccupied at the time. His article thus offered a way to think about the erasure of women's voices without reference to the political texts that were situated well outside the academy. It made an argument that prefigured later discussions of standpoint and positionality and reminded readers that the anthropologist is not a neutral interpreter of cultural information, but a kind of lens that shapes whatever light traverses it. This was a startling assertion at the time.[1]

The second article, by Judith K. Brown, was published just ahead of the first work to systematically study women that I outlined in the Introduction to this volume. Like some other efforts that preceded and followed it (Chodorow 1974, 1978; D'Andrade 1967), Brown was grappling with the question of whether there was something universal about women's role in economic activities. To approach the question, she surveyed ethnographic materials from a wide range of cultures in search of regularities and patterns in men's and women's participation in the division of labor. It's a short article, but its conclusions live on into the present. Brown proposed that women's primary responsibility for young children – not only their biological role in reproduction, but the obligations that role placed on them afterwards – offered an explanation for the division of labor by sex. She argued that it was simply not conducive to the survival of young children for women to undertake work that was dangerous, that could not be interrupted for childcare duties, or that took them away from their homes for protracted periods of time. Brown's article thus codifies a classic statement of the relationship between sex and gender: women's reproductive roles are, in this view, a biological given; the social expectations that arise from them are cultural, but fundamentally linked to that biological foundation in ways that admit few variations. Sex and gender, then, are imagined as theoretically divisible, but empirically intertwined, tied together by evolutionary pressures as much as by convention.

Brown's reading of the division of labor set the tone for much of the theorizing that would follow in feminist anthropology, but also is in sync with theories of gender that have predominated across the disciplines. The crucial component in these approaches is the conviction that women's reproductive roles and the parental obligations that seem to spring directly from them – namely motherhood – are at the heart of gender as a system that is found in all of the world's cultures. Regardless of the level of technological sophistication or the complexity of the political and economic systems that characterize any particular society, women will be charged with a predictable and biologically grounded set of reproductive responsibilities. These activities in turn will dictate the terms of their participation in other kinds of activities, particularly those that obtain outside the confines of the domestic arena. That this division of labor is interpreted as being "natural," and that it would carry with it ideological baggage – such as ideas about women's activities being less culturally significant – is not surprising, and was taken up famously by Sherry Ortner (this section, chapter 3), but also by other anthropologists who sought to account for cross-cultural regularities in gender systems. Importantly, Brown's findings indicated considerable variation in the specific content of women's and men's roles, but confirmed that even with these variations, the division of labor by sex still exhibited a number of marked consistencies.

Nancy Chodorow's influential essay in *Woman, Culture, and Society* (Chodorow 1974) typifies one of the approaches to the study of cross-cultural gender regularities that goes beyond Brown's approach. Looking at various kinds of cultures, Chodorow explored the formation of what she called "gender personality," by which she referred to "nearly universal differences that characterize masculine and feminine personality and roles" (1974: 43). Seeking to avoid reducing these patterns to simple biology, Chodorow looked to psychological processes, arguing that since women are universally responsible for early childcare, both male and female children must respond to having their most crucial early relationship with their mothers. "The fact that males and females experience this social environment differently as they grow up accounts for the development of basic sex differences in personality" (1974: 44), with feminine ego structure being directly grounded in the dynamics of the mother–daughter relationship. Feminine personality, according to Chodorow, is more based in connectedness and relationality than masculinity, with dependency being far less problematic for female children, whose growth into adult women involves continuity. In contrast, male children must separate themselves from their mothers at a critical point in their development, a step Chodorow calls "individuation," and maintain their distance from all that is feminine in order to grow successfully into adult men. Since men's economic activities are extra-domestic and not readily observable by very young boys, their socialization is characterized by disjuncture and sometimes by hostile repudiation of everything associated with femininity. Adult personalities and sex roles, in this reading, are complementary and mutually constitutive.

Chodorow later developed this argument in greater detail, using psychoanalytic materials from Western cultures to craft a theory on "the reproduction of mothering" (Chodorow 1978). In response to the widely accepted view that women's reproductive roles were universally the engine of their subordination, Chodorow asked why women, in fact, became mothers at all. How could women be convinced to assume a role that imposed such dire consequences? Rejecting notions that childhood socialization or other conscious forms of indoctrination or role-modeling could explain such a pervasive and resilient pattern, Chodorow sought a more psychodynamic explanation rooted in fundamental patterns of mother–child interaction. She argued that females are never required to jettison their close relationships with their mothers, as their development into adult women proceeds relatively organically from the earliest mother–child bonds. Males, on the other hand, must forcibly wrench themselves away from their mothers, a factor that, among other things, is reflected in some patterns of hostility toward women and femininity. For both males and females, this system entails some dilemmas, as both must eventually form family units and become parents. For women, this is particularly problematic because men's personalities tend toward distance from the feminine; in search of an experience of connectedness commensurate with that they had with their mothers, they reproduce. In becoming mothers themselves, they start the process over again.

Chodorow's position has sparked considerable debate both in feminist anthropology and in feminist theory more generally, with scholars taking issue with the subjective nature of psychoanalytic "data," its lack of resonance cross-culturally, and more generally with the effort to construct a universal theory of "gender personality." Her theory does, however, offer a particularly pointed application of the search for cross-cultural gender regularities, one that posits agency and motivation as aspects of gender that demand explanation. Motherhood, in her hands, is not just automatic or "natural," it comes from a particular psychodynamic configuration and thus its dynamics can be imagined as being subject to change. Her approach also connects to a large body of feminist literature (mainly from outside anthropology) that focuses on the specificity and universality of maternal behaviors (see, for example, Belenky, Clinchy, Goldberger, and Tarule 1986; Gilligan 1982; Ruddick 1989). These and other works that focus on traits posited as maternally based – altruism, cooperation, emotional accessibility – are often linked to a politics of difference sometimes labeled "cultural feminism," a stance that views women as different from men in ways that should be valued and celebrated.

Ortner's essay (this volume, chapter 3) is one of the most widely cited and controversial contributions to early feminist anthropology. Assailed for its reliance on Lévi-Straussian structuralism and particularly for its assertion of a universal binary opposition between "nature" and "culture," the article has prompted numerous reconsiderations, including one by Ortner herself (1997) about the degree to which anthropologists are apt to impose the categories that prevail in their own culture on those they study and interpret. The ambiguity of "nature" and "culture" have been noted by various critics, of course, as discussed in the Introduction to this volume, but probably the primary angle of attack has been on the project of creating universal explanations that will serve to neatly wrap up gender (or anything else) in a tidy bundle with no loose ends.

Gayle Rubin's article, which appeared in the 1975 volume *Toward an Anthropology of Women*, is arguably the single most influential essay produced during the early period of feminist anthropology, and continues to be widely cited today. As discussed in the Introduction to this volume, Rubin's goals were similar to those of other feminists who hoped to find a dynamic that would account for cross-cultural regularities in the status of women. Her theory of the "sex/gender system," which drew on Marx, Engels, Freud, Lacan, and Lévi-Strauss, avoided some of the hazards of other efforts to define universal features of gender in that she was more concerned with a process than with a specific arrangement. Most centrally, her essay posited a dynamic system through which the biological specificities of "sex" were transformed into the social particularities of "gender." Societies depended on gender as a way to render persons eligible for particular kinds of manipulation in the social exchanges that occurred through marriages. Because societies "needed" men and women, she explained, they are everywhere created.

While Rubin participated in an intellectual project that sought to define universal structural attributes to account for gender, the scope of her argument depended less than had Ortner's on rigid binaries or on specific attributes that could be claimed to be cross-culturally constant. Instead, by specifying the operation of a general system, albeit one that she imagined as universal, she allowed for wide applications far beyond the original reach of the essay, and provided a satisfying way to understand both universal features of gender and its simultaneous properties of flexibility and variability.

The theoretical essay by Michelle Z. Rosaldo reprinted here stands as a first major rethinking of the categories she had posited in her chapter in *Woman, Culture, and Society*. The earlier paper had argued strongly for viewing women's roles as stemming from universal social structural arrangements that divided "public" from "domestic" space. In many ways, her argument offered a social structural analogue to Ortner's symbolic claims and Chodorow's psychodynamic argument which appeared in the same 1974 volume. But feminist anthropology had moved rapidly, and by 1980, in response to writings that had criticized the assumptions that shaped *Woman, Culture, and Society*, Rosaldo had begun to rethink many of the assertions she made in her earlier writing. In particular she wished to interrogate the validity of viewing "domestic" and "public" as dichotomous categories that provide universal explanations for gender inequalities, and suggested that reliance on such categories might, in fact, be more a reflex of models drawn from anthropologists' own cultures than an accurate reflection of the reality experienced by the people they studied. Probably most importantly, Rosaldo questioned the entire quest for origins as one that propelled researchers into relying on dichotomous explanations of gender asymmetry. While motherhood and reproduction shape such inequalities, she now argued, regarding them as invariably yielding gender stratification would erase the specific logic of each system. Further, the search for universal explanations and for origins would further solidify claims to inevitability that frustrate efforts to create change. Gender hierarchies arise in relation to a wide range of social conditions that inflect them in many ways; searching for processes rather than irrefutable patterns would move anthropology toward more sensitive ethnographic representations.

Rosaldo's questions about the search both for universal sexual asymmetry and for universally applicable explanations of that asymmetry reflected debates that were pervasive in feminist anthropology by the late 1970s and early 1980s. But her approach was not the only critique of efforts to frame universally applicable theories. Karen Brodkin Sack's 1987 review article (reprinted here, chapter 6) offers an entirely different take on the project of seeking universal origins than did Rosaldo's. Brodkin speaks from the perspective of a large body of Marxist-influenced work that has sought to situate gender as an element of broader patterns of political economic organization. Importantly, Brodkin questions the organizing principles of much feminist theory, both in anthropology and elsewhere, particularly criticizing the tendency to define gender as something that is played out in the privacy of domestic units, somehow insulated from wider currents of class and race that are shaped by relations of production. Her quest is also processual, but her interpretation of the engine that drives the gender inequalities resists the notion that the personal domain is a more compelling site for locating such inequalities than the wider economy. She is particularly concerned that capitalism and patriarchy be understood as mutually reinforcing systems, both of which demand stratification, rather than as distinctive domains that can be addressed by separate social change agendas. Brodkin's approach is shared by a large cohort of feminist anthropologists, such as Eleanor Leacock, June Nash, Lynn Stephen, and Sandra Morgen, whose political foundations could be located in socialist feminism rather than in radical feminism. These scholars have focused their attention on the interplay between broad political-economic systems and gender inequalities out of a conviction that these two domains cannot be analytically separated without concealing the ways in which gender emerges within particular economic arrangements. For Brodkin, the proper unit of analysis ought not to be the private domain, but the community within which personal relationships are enacted. She questions the notion that individual strategies can yield satisfying solutions to systemic inequalities, and argues that the liberation of women can only be achieved in concert with other sorts of social change. The debate, then, while grounded in anthropology, resonates across the diversity of perspectives that characterize the feminist movement.

The body of work that Brodkin reviews has produced many fine ethnographies of workplace settings and of the experience of women workers in specific economic systems (see e.g. Anglin 2002; Brodkin 1988; Lamphere 1987; Nash 1983). Other work influenced by this approach has been concerned with the conditions under which women are empowered to organize as workers or as community members, the interplay between women's domestic roles and their activities in the public sphere, and more recently, the many-layered impact of globalization and transnational economic processes on the shape of gender inequalities (Freeman 2000; Ong 1987; Stephen 1997; Susser 1982).

NOTE

1 Ardener's paper also prefigured a large literature in anthropological linguistics that has examined the nature of men's and women's speech and use of language as basic kinds of cultural miscommunication, akin in some ways to members of different cultures trying to make themselves understood to one another. Such prominent linguists as Deborah Tannen have produced numerous works that detail these miscommunications, though considerable controversy surrounds this approach.

REFERENCES

Anglin, Mary K. 2002. *Women, Power, and Dissent in the Hills of Carolina*. Urbana: University of Illinois Press.

Belenky, Mary Field, Blythe Clinchy, Nancy Goldberger, and Jill Tarule. 1986. *Women's Ways of Knowing: The Development of Self, Voice, and Mind*. New York: Basic Books.

Brodkin, Karen. 1988. *Caring by the Hour: Women, Work, and Organizing at Duke Medical Center*. Urbana: University of Illinois Press.

Chodorow, Nancy. 1974. Family Structure and Feminine Personality. In *Woman, Culture, and Society*. M. Z. Rosaldo and L. Lamphere, eds. pp. 43–66. Stanford, CA: Stanford University Press.

—— 1978. *The Reproduction of Mothering: Psychoanalysis and the Sociology of Gender*. Berkeley: University of California Press.

D'Andrade, Roy G. 1967. Sex Differences and Cultural Institutions. In *The Development of Sex Differences*. E. Maccoby, ed. pp. 174–204. Stanford, CA: Stanford University Press.

Freeman, Carla. 2000. *High Tech and High Heels in the Global Economy: Women, Work, and Pink-Collar Identities in the Caribbean*. Durham, NC: Duke University Press.

Gilligan, Carol. 1982. *In a Different Voice: Psychological Theory and Women's Development*. Cambridge, MA: Harvard University Press.

Lamphere, Louise. 1987. *From Working Daughters to Working Mothers: Immigrant Women in a New England Industrial Community*. Ithaca, NY: Cornell University Press.

Nash, June. 1983. *Women, Men, and the International Division of Labor*. Albany, NY: State University of New York Press.

Ong, Aihwa. 1987. *Spirits of Resistance and Capitalist Discipline: Factory Women in Malaysia*. Albany, NY: State University of New York Press.

Ortner, Sherry B. 1997. *Making Gender: The Politics and Erotics of Culture*. Boston: Beacon Press.

Ruddick, Sara. 1989. *Maternal Thinking: Toward a Politics of Peace*. Boston: Beacon Press.

Stephen, Lynn. 1997. *Women and Social Movements in Latin America: Power from Below*. Austin: University of Texas Press.

Susser, Ida. 1982. *Norman Street: Poverty and Politics in an Urban Neighborhood*. Oxford: Oxford University Press.

1

Belief and the Problem of Women and the 'Problem' Revisited

Edwin Ardener

The Problem

The problem of women has not been solved by social anthropologists. Indeed the problem itself has been often examined only to be put aside again for want of a solution, for its intractability is genuine. The problem of women is not the problem of 'the position of women', although valuable attention has been paid to this subject by Professor Evans-Pritchard (1965). I refer to the problem that women present to social anthropologists. It falls into (1) a technical and (2) an analytical part. Here is a human group that forms about half of any population and is even in a majority at certain ages: particularly at those which for so many societies are the 'ruling' ages – the years after forty. Yet however apparently competently the female population has been studied in any particular society, the results in understanding are surprisingly slight, and even tedious. With rare exceptions, women anthropologists, of whom so much was hoped, have been among the first to retire from the problem. Dr Richards was one of the few to return to it at the height of her powers. In *Chisungu* (1956) she produced a study of a girls' rite that raised and anticipated many of the problems with which this

paper will deal.[1] While I shall illustrate my central point by reference to a parallel set of rites among the Bakweri of Cameroon, through which women and girls join the world of the mermaid spirits, this paper is less about ethnography than about the interpretation of such rites through the symbolism of the relations between men and women.

The methods of social anthropology as generally illustrated in the classical monographs of the last forty years have purported to 'crack the code' of a vast range of societies, without any direct reference to the female group. At the level of 'observation' in fieldwork, the behaviour of women has, of course, like that of men, been exhaustively plotted: their marriages, their economic activity, their rites, and the rest. When we come to that second or 'meta' level of fieldwork, the vast body of debate, discussion, question and answer, that social anthropologists really depend upon to give conviction to their interpretations, there is a real imbalance. We are, for practical purposes, in a male world. The study of women is on a level little higher than the study of the ducks and fowls they commonly own – a mere bird-watching indeed. It is equally revealing and ironical that Lévi-Strauss (1963: 61) should

From Edwin Ardener, "Belief and the Problem of Women" and "The 'Problem' Revisited," pp. 1–27 in Shirley Ardener, *Perceiving Women*. London: Malaby Press, 1975 [1968]. Reprinted with permission of Shirley Ardener.

write: 'For words do not speak, while women do.' For the truth is that women rarely speak in social anthropology in any but that male sense so well exemplified by Lévi-Strauss's own remark: in the sense of merely uttering or giving tongue. It is the very inarticulateness of women that is the technical part of the problem they present. In most societies the ethnographer shares this problem with its male members. The brave failure (with rare exceptions) of even women anthropologists to surmount it really convincingly (and their evident relief when they leave the subject of women) suggests an obvious conclusion. Those trained in ethnography evidently have a bias towards the kinds of model that men are ready to provide (or to concur in) rather than towards any that women might provide. If the men appear 'articulate' compared with the women, it is a case of like speaking to like. To pursue the logic where it leads us: if ethnographers (male and female) want only what the men can give, I suggest it is because the men consistently tend, when pressed, to give a bounded model of society such as ethnographers are attracted to. But the awareness that women appear as lay figures in the men's drama (or like the photographic cut-outs in filmed crowd-scenes) is always dimly present in the ethnographer's mind. Lévi-Strauss, with his perennial ability to experience ethnographic models, thus expressed no more than the truth of all those models when he saw women as items of exchange inexplicably and inappropriately giving tongue.

The technical treatment of the problem is as follows. It is commonly said, with truth, that ethnographers with linguistic difficulties of any kind will find that the men of a society are generally more experienced in bridging this kind of gap than are the women. Thus, as a matter of ordinary experience, interpreters, partial bilinguals, or speakers of a vehicular language are more likely to be found among men than among women. For an explanation of this we are referred to statements about the political dominance of men, and their greater mobility. These statements, in their turn, are referred ultimately to the different biological roles of the two sexes. The cumulative effect of these explanations is then: to the degree that communication between ethnographer and people is imperfect, that imperfection drives the ethnographer in greater measure towards men.

This argument while stressing the technical aspect does not dispose of the problem even in its own terms, although we may agree that much ethnography (more than is generally admitted) is affected by factors of this type. It is, however, a common experience that women still 'do not speak' even when linguistic aspects are constant. Ethnographers report that women cannot be reached so easily as men: they giggle when young, snort when old, reject the question, laugh at the topic, and the like. The male members of a society frequently see the ethnographer's difficulties as simply a caricature of their own daily case. The technical argument about the incidence of interpreters and so on is therefore really only a confirmation of the importance of the analytical part of the problem. The 'articulateness' of men and of ethnographers is alike, it would appear, in more ways than one. In the same way we may regard as inadequate the more refined explanation that ethnographers 'feed' their own models to their male informants, who are more susceptible for the same technical reasons, and who then feed them back to the ethnographer. That something of this sort does happen is again not to be doubted, but once again the susceptibility of the men is precisely the point. Nor is it an answer to the problem to discuss what might happen if biological facts were different; arguments like 'women through concern with the realities of childbirth and child-rearing have less time for or less propensity towards the making of models of society, for each other, for men, or for ethnographers' (the 'Hot Stove' argument) are again only an expression of the situation they try to explain.

We have here, then, what looked like a technical problem: the difficulty of dealing ethnographically with women. We have, rather, an analytical problem of this sort: if the models of a society made by most ethnographers tend to be models derived from the male portion of that society, how does the symbolic weight of that other mass of persons – half or more of a normal human population, as we have accepted – express itself? Some will maintain that the problem as it is stated here is exaggerated, although only an extremist will deny its existence completely. It may be that individual ethnographers have received from women a picture of a society very similar to the picture given by men. This possibility is conceded, but the female evidence provides in such cases confirmation of a male model which requires no confirmation of this type. The fact is that no one could come back from an ethnographic study of 'the X', having talked only *to* women, and *about* men, without professional comment and some self-doubt. The reverse can and does happen constantly. It is not enough to see this merely as another example of 'injustice to women'. I prefer to suggest that the models of society that women can provide are not of the kind acceptable at first sight to men or to ethnographers, and specifically that, unlike either of these sets of professionals, they do not so readily see society bounded from nature. They lack the metalanguage for its discussion. To put it more simply: they will not necessarily provide a model for society as a unit that will contain both men and themselves. They may indeed provide a model in which women and nature are outside men and society.

I have now deliberately exaggerated, in order to close the gap in a different way. The dominance of men's models of a society in traditional ethnography I take to be accepted. However, men and women do communicate with each other, and are at least aware of each other's models. It has been furthermore the study by ethnographers of myth and belief, collected no doubt, as formerly, largely from men, that has provided the kinds of insights that now make it possible to reopen the problem of women. Much of this material still discusses women from a male viewpoint. Women

are classed as inauspicious, dangerous, and the like. But models of society as a symbolic system made from this kind of data are (it is no surprise to note) of a rather different type from the ethnographic (male) models deriving from the older type of fieldwork (e.g. Needham 1958, 1960, 1967). So much so that many social anthropologists are unable to accept them as 'true' models, that is 'true to reality', where 'reality' is a term of art for what fieldwork reveals. I suggest, on the contrary, that a fieldwork problem of the first magnitude is illuminated. Indeed the astounding deficiency of a method, supposedly objective, is starkly revealed: the failure to include half the people in the total analysis.

Statement and Observation

At the risk of labouring the obvious, but to avoid being buried in a righteous avalanche of fieldnotes, I say this yet again with a diagram (figure 1.1).

Because of an interesting failing in the functionalist observational model, statements *about* observation were always added to the ethnographer's own observations. To take a simple case: typically an ethnographer 'observed' a number of marriages and divorces, and heard a number of statements about the frequency of divorce, and then cumulated these quasi-quantitatively into a general statement about divorce frequency. So he did in other less easily detectable ways, and in some of those ways he may still do so today. This confusion had many serious consequences; in particular the difficulty of dealing with statements that were not about 'observation' at all (relegated to 'belief' or the like). For our purposes here, it is enough to note that statements

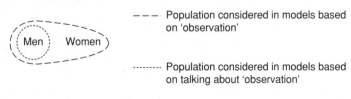

--- Population considered in models based on 'observation'

.... Population considered in models based on talking about 'observation'

Figure 1.1 *Observation and statements about observation.*

made by the male segment were *about* both males and females. The functionalist confusion of the two levels at any time obscured the inadequacy of the total analysis as far as women were concerned. Since the analysis was always thought to represent observation, or to be checked by observation, it was hard for anyone with field-notes on women to see that they were effectively missing in the total analysis or, more precisely, they were there in the same way as were the Nuer's cows, who were observed but also did not speak.

The students of symbolism cannot be accused of any functionalist bias towards the primacy of observation. Functionalist fieldwork was unhappy with myths precisely because they made statements that conflicted with, could not be cumulated to, objective measures of economic or political status. Not being faced with this mistaken necessity, the symbolists, almost incidentally, rediscovered women, who loom rather large in their material. In view of the absence of conscient women from the older models, this gains further significance, and suggests a further step, which is taken here. The study of symbolism uncovers certain valuations of women – some of which make more sense if women, not men, had made them (they conflict with the social models of men). Old women ('old wives' tales') or mothers (we may extend this analysis even to the lore and language of children) acquire in the world of symbolism something more like their demographic conspicuity. Furthermore, in a field situation poor communication with women in this area is not so often complained of. I here contend that much of this symbolism in fact enacts that female model of the world which has been lacking, and which is different from the models of men in a particular dimension: the placing of the boundary between society and nature.

I suppose in Lévi-Strauss's terms this would place women in an ideologically more primitive position than men. It is not a necessary conclusion. It means something like this: the notion of themselves in society is imposed by its members upon a relatively unbounded continuum in ways which involve the setting up of a multitude of bounded categories, the bounds being marked by taboo, ridicule, pollution,

category inversion and the rest, so ably documented of late by social anthropologists (Douglas 1966; Leach 1961, 1964). The tension between 'culture' and 'nature' (the 'wild') is to be understood as an outcome of this struggle, from which no human beings are free. The appreciation of the symbolic stress on the division between society and nature derives from Lévi-Strauss (1949), and lies behind much of his later work, including the three volumes of *Mythologiques* (1964, 1966, 1968). Lévi-Strauss now prefers the terminology 'nature' and 'culture' (1967: 3; trans. 1969: 3). Of late he has also been concerned to state that the distinction lacks objective criteria (1967: 12). This concern seems surprising since it is easily resolved as Lévi-Strauss himself shows:

> [T]he contrast of nature and culture would be neither a primeval fact, nor a concrete aspect of universal order. Rather it should be seen as an artificial creation of culture, a protective rampart thrown up around it because it only felt able to assert its existence and uniqueness by destroying all the links that led back to its original association with the other manifestations of life. (1967: xvii; trans. 1969: xxix)

Within this wider task men have to bound themselves in relation both to women and to nature.

Since women are biologically not men, it would be surprising if they bounded themselves against nature in the same way as men do. Yet we have seen that the men's models are characteristically dominant in ethnography. If men are the ones who become aware of 'other cultures' more frequently than do women, it may well be that they are likely to develop metalevels of categorization that enable them at least to consider the necessity to bound themselves-and-their-women from other-men-and-their-women. Thus all such ways of bounding society against society, including our own, may have an inherent maleness. The first level is still recognizable, however, in the tendency to slip back to it from the metalevel: that is, to class other men and their wives with nature; as the Germans say, as *Naturmensch* (cf. Lévi-Strauss 1967: xvi). If men, because of their political dominance, may tend purely pragmatically to 'need' total bounding models of either type, women may tend to take over men's models when they share the same definitional problems as men. But the models set up by women bounding themselves are not encompassed in those men's models. They still subsist, and both sexes through their common humanity are aware of the contradictions. In the social anthropologist's data the process can be more clearly viewed.

Man, Mouse, Ape, and Water Spirit

According to a story of the Bakweri of Cameroon (in a male recension): 'Moto, Ewaki, Eto, and Mojili were always quarrelling and agreed to decide by a test which of them was to remain in the town and which should go into the bush. All were to light fires in their houses in the morning and the person whose fire was still burning on their return from the farms in the evening was to be the favoured one. Moto being more cunning than the others built a fire with big sticks properly arranged, whereas they only built with small dry sticks, and so his was the only fire that was still alight on their return in the evening. Thus Moto remained in the town and became Man. Ewaki and Eto went into the bush and became the Ape and the Mouse. Mojili was driven into the water and became a water spirit.'[2] *Moto* (Common Bantu **muntu*) is the ordinary Bakweri word for 'human being of either sex', and thus includes 'woman'. Ewaki, Eto, and Mojili, who are opposed to Moto by reason of his special skill with fire, lack of which relegates them to the bush, are in Bakweri belief all associated with women and their children, whom they attract into their domain. Mojili is responsible for young girls becoming mermaids (*liengu*, plural *maengu*) who are dangerous to men, and whose husbands are *eto* (pl. *veto*), the rats; while the attraction of human children to the apes of the forest is so great that the word *ewaki* must not be mentioned in front of children under seven, in case they fall sick and die. Mojili's name has the same effect. Rites exist to control these manifestations (E. Ardener 1956).[3]

The possible marginality of women when men are defining 'the wild' is evident. Thus

the idea of the denizens of the wild, outside Moto's village, being a danger or attraction to women and their offspring is comprehensible in a male model of the universe, in which female reproductive powers do not fall under male control. This is, however, inadequate. Bakweri women themselves bound their world as including the wild that Moto excluded. They go through rites by which they become *liengu* mermaid spirits, or spirits of the forest, generally in adolescence, and retain this feature of womanhood throughout their lives. The story of Moto gives the clue, for the three excluded 'animal' brothers all have the human gift of fire. Although the men bound off 'mankind' from nature, the women persist in overlapping into nature again. For men among the Bakweri this overlapping symbolic area is clearly related to women's reproductive powers. Since these powers are for women far from being marginal, but are of their essence as women, it would seem that a woman's model of the world would also treat them as central. When we speak of Bakweri belief we must therefore recognize a man's sector and a woman's sector, which have to be reconciled. Thus the myth of Moto states the problem of woman for Bakweri men: she insists on living in what is for them the wild.

Mermaids and the Wild

The wild for the male Bakweri is particularly well differentiated, because of the many striking forms in which it expresses itself. This people occupies the southeastern face of the 13,000 foot Cameroon Mountain, on the West African coast of Cameroon – an environment of romantic contrasts. The mountain rises straight from a rocky sea coast through zones of forest, grass, and bare lava to the active volcanic craters of the peak. The Bakweri proper occupy the forest, and hunt in the grass zones. A deity or hero, Efasamote, occupies the peak. Congeners of the Bakweri (Mboko, Isubu, and Wovea Islanders) occupy the rocky strand, and fish. The Bakweri proper are agriculturists; the staple crop was traditionally the male-cultivated plantain banana, although since the introduction of the

Xanthosoma cocoyam in the last century, this female crop has become the staple (Ardener 1970). It should be added that the whole area is now greatly fragmented by plantations and a large migrant population now lives in the Bakweri area (Ardener, Ardener, and Warmington 1960). The mountain is an extremely wet place, and visibility is often reduced to a few yards because of the clouds that cover it for much of the time.

The villages are traditionally fenced – people and livestock living inside the fence, the farms being outside the fence. This way of looking at it is not inaccurate. In the light of the subject of this paper it is, however, just as true to say: the men live inside the fence with their livestock (goats, cows, and pigs) and most of their plaintains; the women go outside the fence for their two main activities – firewood-collecting and farming the Xanthosoma. The men and their livestock are so closely associated that the animals have characteristically lived in the houses themselves. I have myself visited in his hut an elderly man on his bed, so hemmed in by dwarf cows (still the size of ponies) that it was difficult to reach him. The women are all day in the forest outside the fence, returning at evening with their back-breaking loads of wood and cocoyams, streaming with rain, odds and ends tied up with bark strips and fronds, and screaming with fatigue at their husbands, with the constant reiteration in their complaints of the word *wanga* 'bush', 'the forest'. The Bakweri men wait in their leaking huts for the evening meal. It is no wonder that the women seem to be forest creatures, who might vanish one day for ever.

At the coast, the 'wild' *par excellence* is the sea, and its symbolism is expressed through the *liengu* water-spirits. The Cameroon coast provides a kaleidoscope of beliefs about *liengu*. They are found among the Kole, the Duala, the Wovea, the Oli, the Tanga, the Yasa, and many other peoples. Ittmann (1957) gathers together material from numbers of such sources.[4] The common theme is, however, used in the different belief systems of the various peoples in different ways. As I have tried to demonstrate elsewhere (1970), from a consideration of the Bakweri zombie belief, the *content* of a belief system can be analysed as a

specific problem, by methods of the type used by Lévi-Strauss in *Mythologiques* (1964, 1966, 1968), as well as through those of more humdrum ethnographic aim. Among the latter, it is possible to discuss the geographical distribution of parts of the content of the belief, and consider, in the *liengu* case, questions such as whether the mermaids 'are' manatees or dugongs, which will not concern us here. The *realien* of the belief for each people are the elements plundered by the *bricoleur*: dugongs, mermaids are all to hand, but what dictates the particular disposition of elements in each system, the 'template' of the belief?

The Bakweri incorporate the *liengu* mermaids into a damp tree-ridden environment in which the sea is not visible, or is seen only far off on clear days, and in which the forest is the dominant external embodiment of the wild. The *liengu* beliefs and rites are in detail marked as a result by the inconsistency of a marine iconography with a non-marine environment. We have various different combinations producing a patchwork of several women's rites all of which are linked by the name *liengu*, some of which have content that links them with certain other West African rites. They are all enacted, however, as a response to a fit or seizure that comes mainly upon adolescent girls but also upon older women. For those men who participate in the rites, the stress is laid upon the 'curing' of the women. For, as we shall see, the men have their own view of the rites. *Liengu la ndiva* (*ndiva*: 'deep water') appears to retain the closest connection with the water spirits.[5] The sickness attacks a girl or woman, characteristically, by causing her to faint over the fireplace, so that she knocks out one of the three stones that are used to support the cooking pots. A woman versed in this form of *liengu* then comes and addresses her in the secret *liengu* language. If she shows any signs of comprehension, a *liengu* doctor (male or female) is called and given a black cock, on which he spits alligator pepper; he then kills it and sprinkles its blood in the hole made when the girl knocked out the hearth-stone, and replaces the stone. The patient then enters a period of seclusion. Drummers are called on a fixed evening, the girl herself staying in an inner room, dressed only in a skirt made of strips of bark of roots of the *iroko* tree, hung over a waist string. The doctor then makes her a medicine which she vomits, bringing up the black seeds of the wild banana; these are then threaded on a string and worn like a bandolier. The drummers stay all night and they and the doctor receive a fee. There are usually a number of visitors, especially *liengu* women, and these are given food.

During the period of seclusion which then follows, the girl has a woman sponsor who teaches her the secret *liengu* language, and gives her a *liengu* name. She is subject to a number of conventions and taboos during this period, which will be summarized later. After several months, the *liengu* doctor is called again, and, in the darkness before dawn, she is picked up and carried in turn, one by one, by men chosen for their strength, until they reach the deep part of a stream where the doctor pushes her in. Women who accompany them sing *liengu* songs, and the company try to catch a crab, representing the water spirit. After this rite, the girl is regarded as being a familiar of the water spirits and one of the *liengu* women. On the return of the party, the *liengu* drummers play and food is provided for the guests. After the visit to the stream the girl stays in her house for a further period. On the occasion when she finally comes out the doctor and the drummers, and other women and visitors, come to the house, where she is dressed in new clothing. Traditionally she was rubbed with camwood. There is another feast, and she is regarded by the men as finally immune from any attack by the water spirits.

Liengu la mongbango differs from *ndiva* in several respects. For example, the first symptom is sometimes said to be the girl disappearing into the bush as if attracted by spirits. She is then sought by a group of female relatives singing to her in *liengu* language, and when she is found, is taken to the seclusion room. There the doctor makes the vomiting medicine as in *Liengu la ndiva*. Details of the seclusion show little difference, but in this case it does not last the whole period of the rite. After a few months, a feast is made which is traditionally all eaten on the ground, after which the girl is

allowed to go out, although still subject to taboos. After a further period of about nine months, a sheep is killed and a similar feast made, the girl and her *liengu* woman sponsor being secluded in an enclosure in the bush. She is now dressed in fern-fronds (*senge or njombi*) rubbed with camwood, and led through the village tied to the middle of a long rope held by her companions in front and behind. Outside her house, both sets of people pull the rope, as in a tug of war, until the rope comes apart, when the girl falls down, as if dead. She is revived by being called nine times in the *liengu* language, after which she gets up, and is dressed in new clothing. A few weeks later, she is washed in a stream by the doctor to show that she is free from the taboos she observed during the rites. Both with *ndiva* and *mongbango* the rites extend over about a year.

A third version of the rite, *liengu la vefea*, reduces the procedure essentially to the killing of a goat and a young cock, and the drinking of the vomiting medicine followed by food taboos. The medicine is the same in all three rites. Among the upper Bakweri who live furthest from the sea, an even more generalized *liengu* rite seems to have existed in which the simple *rite de passage* aspect is very noticeable. It is said that formerly every daughter was put through *liengu* at about 8 to 10 years of age so that she would be fertile. She would wear fern-fronds and be secluded for a period, apparently shorter than in the above examples. Other variations in detail appear to have existed in different places and at different times.[6]

The reduced rites were, at the time of my first acquaintance with the Bakweri (in 1953), the commonest. The people had, during the previous generation, been overwhelmed by their belief that they were 'dying out' – a belief not without some slight demographic justification. Their economy was stagnant. Public rites of all kinds had gone into decline. The people blamed the general conditions of their country on witch-craft. The decline of the *liengu* rites was further blamed by many for the fertility problems of Bakweri women. Nevertheless, a celebration of the *mongbango* ceremony occurred in that same year. In 1958 a Bakweri *liengu* girl was even brought, with a *liengu* mother, to grace a Cameroon Trade Fair.

Since then there has been a revival of all kinds of *liengu* rites (I was asked to contribute to the expenses of one in 1970). However, the great rites of *mongbango* and *ndiva*, because of their expense, were probably always relatively rare, compared with *vefea* and other reduced rites. The latter are also common now, because so many *liengu* celebrations are 'remedial', for women who did not pass through them in their adolescence – during the long period of decline. Nevertheless, even such women are told the ideology of the great rites: the immersion (of *ndiva*), the tug-of-war (of *mongbango*), the seclusion, and the secret language. Since we are concerned here with the dimension of belief, it may be added that the image of the *liengu* is a powerful one even for the many Christian, educated, and urban Bakweri women. Scraps of the secret language are common currency. It is as if the *liengu* rites are always 'there' as a possibility of fulfilment; and also as if the rites are themselves less important than the vision of women's place in nature that appears in them: the template of the belief.

Despite the fact that *liengu* is a woman's rite, men are not immune to the precipitating sickness, especially if there are no women left in a man's extended family, and rare cases are cited in which men have gone through at least part of the rite. The fertility associations of the rite are uppermost in such cases, and the *liengu* mermaids have had to work through a male in the absence of viable females. *Liengu* doctors may be men or women. As we shall see, the participation of men does not obscure the symbolism of the rites for women. It does assist their symbolism for men. Thus the men who carry the *ndiva* girl have to be strong. Although men from her matrilineage (in practice, perhaps, her full brothers) would be favoured, a man from her patrilineage, or just a fellow-villager would be acceptable. Men see themselves as helping out with the treatment of morbidity (social and physical) in women. The domination of men as doctors in Bakweri medical rites means that the specialization as *liengu* doctors by men presents few problems. The major rites (*ndiva* and *mongbango*) have a public aspect, because of their relative expense, and a male doctor is likely to be involved. The female *liengu* doctors are associated with the less expensive, reduced rites. The 'medical' aspects of the rite have thus a somewhat 'male' aspect.

The female significance of the rites lies in the girl's acceptance by her fellow *liengu* women. In the fuller *ndiva* and *mongbango* forms, as already noted, it is customary for her to have a sponsor (*nyangb'a liengu*, 'liengu mother') to teach her the mysteries. For the periods of seclusion, in both rites, the girl is not allowed to plait her hair but must must let it grow uncontrolled, and rub it, as well as her whole body, with charcoal mixed with palm-kernel oil, so that she is completely black. This is supposed to make her resemble a spirit. She is forbidden to talk to visitors, but greets them with a rattle, of different types in *liengu la ndiva* (*njola*, made of wicker-work) and in *mongbango* (*lisonjo*, made of certain tree-seed shells). This is also used night and morning, when she has to recite certain formulae in the *liengu* language. While in the house, the *liengu*, as the girl herself is now called, treats rats (*veto*) with special respect as they are regarded as her husbands (compare the story of Moto above). If a rat is killed she must cry all day and wash it and bury it in a cloth; killing rats in her compound is forbidden. No man or boy can enter the *liengu* house wearing a hat or shoes, or carrying a book (all introduced by Europeans) or she will seize them, and return them only on the payment of a fine. If a person dies in the village the *liengu* must not eat all day. In *liengu la mongbango*, after her period of seclusion, and before the completion of the rite, the girl may go out only with her rattle, and should turn away if she sees any person not a Bakweri. If anyone wishes to stop her he has only to say the word *yowo* ('magical rite') and she must do whatever he says. However, the *liengu* has an effective retaliation if molested, as any male whom she knocks with her rattle is thought to become permanently impotent. The *liengu* may not go into any room but her own and dogs must not go near her. She should always be addressed by her special *liengu* name. Truncated forms of these requirements are also followed by women in the *vefea* rite. After all rites the participant is henceforth known by one of a standard series of *liengu* names.

Symbolism of the Mermaid Cult

It has been the intention here merely to indicate those aspects of the symbolism that are
peculiar to the *liengu* corpus. This is not the
place for an extended analysis, which I hope to
attempt elsewhere. The male interpretation is
that the *liengu* rites cure a spiritual illness.
That is why male doctors take part. The
women nod at this sort of interpretation in
male Bakweri company, but there is a heady
excitement when the *liengu* subject is raised in
the absence of Bakweri men. It is accepted that
the *liengu* mermaid spirits do 'trouble' the
women, and cause them physical symptoms.
The trouble is solved when a woman becomes
a *liengu*. The mermaid world is one of Alice
through the looking-glass – no manmade objects, garments only of forest products; no
imported goods, traded through men.[7] For
the edible plantain banana, a male crop and
consciously seen as clearly phallic, we find the
inedible seed-filled, wild banana – a total symbolic reversal whose effect is a 'feminization'
of the male symbol. The male doctor, who is
perhaps only a half-aware participant in this,
makes the medicine in an integument of (male)
plantain leaves to him in its harmful effects.
The rites see the women as attracted away into
the wild. The domestic hearth-stone (*lio*) is the
popular symbol of the household (a unit in the
essentially patrilineal residence pattern). It is
dislodged. In *mongbango* food is eaten on the
earth, and not on the customary (male) plantain leaves. The mermaid's rattle destroys the
potency of males. The men are reduced to the
scale of little rats, her 'husbands'. She returns
to the world through the symbolic tug-of-war
at which she is in the middle. She falls sense-
less. The men assume the world has won. Yet
she is revived by nine calls in the *liengu* language. There is surely little reassuring to men
in her final incorporation in the wild outside
the fence of the village.[8]

The interpretation of the Bakweri *liengu*
rites as 'nubility rites', because they often (but
not always) precede marriage, is not exactly an
error, since it does not say anything. It merely
draws attention to the question 'what after all
is a nubility rite?' Passage through *liengu* rites

shows that a girl is a woman; her fellow-
women vouch for it. The men feel a danger
has been averted; she has been rescued from
the wild and is fitted for marriage with men.
But she still continues to bear a spirit name,
and converses with fellow-women in the mermaid language. The term 'nubility rite' implies
for some that the rites have a social 'function';
the girl takes her place in the system of relations between corporate kin-groups. The rites
no doubt can be shown to 'validate' this and
that aspect of the structure in the normal 'functionalist' manner. Alternatively they prepare
the girl for the role of exchangeable unit in a
system of alliance. These are good partial
statements, but we are left asking questions
like 'why did she vomit the seeds of the wild
banana?' The terms 'puberty rite' and 'fertility
rite' would be just as useful and just as partial.
'Puberty' stresses the biological basis that 'nubility' obscures, but of course even when the
rites are not delayed until after marriage, they
may take place some years after the onset of
puberty – the rigid association of puberty with
the menarche is a result of our mania for precision. 'Fertility' at least takes account of the
association of the rites with a whole period of
the woman's life. They are also 'medical rites'
because they 'cure' sickness, and share features
in common with Bakweri medical rites for men
and women. A set of overlapping analyses such
as Richards makes for *Chisungu* (1956) would
clearly be equally fruitful here.

The rites are open to analysis in the manner
of Van Gennep as classical rites of passage.
They fall like all such rites into stages of separation, transition, and incorporation, but the
notion of passage is either self-evident
(through the rite) or inadequately defined. An
analysis in the manner of Turner (1967) could
also be attempted, and it is evident that there is
the material for such an analysis. The Turn-
erian method assumes that symbolism is generated by society as a whole. This is of course
in a sense true: the very contradiction of symbolic systems, their 'multivalency', 'polysemy',
'condensation', and the like, derive from the
totalitarian nature of symbolism. But as the
Moto story shows, its surface structure may
express the male view of the world, obscuring the existence at deeper levels of an

autonomous female view. I feel also that Turner does not perceive the 'bounding' problem that male/female symbolism is about, and which introduces an element of ordering into the symbolic sets.

I have argued that Bakweri women define the boundary of their world in such a way that they live as women in the men's wild, as well as partly within the men's world inside the village fence. In modern times the world outside the fence has included the 'strangers', migrants who are allowed to settle there. Sometimes the strangers' quarter is larger than the Bakweri settlement. Bakweri women have long travelled from stranger-quarter to stranger-quarter, entering into casual liaisons, while the men have complained (Ardener et al. 1960: 294–308; Ardener 1962). This fortuitous overlap of the old wild with the new urban jungle may well account for the peculiar sense of defeat the Bakweri showed for so many years, which made them come to believe that zombies were killing them off (Ardener 1956 and 1970). For the women's part, it is possibly not sufficient to account for their notable conjugal freedom, as I have argued elsewhere (1962), merely on the grounds that there are nearly three males to every woman in the plantation area. The Bakweri system of double descent similarly expresses the basic dichotomy. The patrilineage controls residence (the village), the inheritance of land and cattle, succession to political office – the men's world. The matrilineage controls fertility, and its symbolic fertility bangle is found on a woman's farm outside the village fence (Ardener 1956).

Mankind and Womankind

The Bakweri illustration can only briefly document my theme. Men's models of society are expressed at a metalevel which purports to define women. Only at the level of the analysis of belief can the voiceless masses be restored to speech. Not only women, but (a task to be attempted later) inarticulate classes of men, young people, and children. We are all lay figures in someone else's play.

The objective basis of the symbolic distinction between nature and society, which Lévi-Strauss recently prematurely retreated from, is a result of the problem of accommodating the two logical sets which classify human beings by different bodily structures: 'male'/'female'; with the two other sets: 'human'/'non-human'. It is, I have suggested, men who usually come to face this problem, and, because their model for *mankind* is based on that for *man*, their opposites, *woman* and *non-mankind* (the wild), tend to be ambiguously placed. Hence, in Douglas's terms (1966), come their sacred and polluting aspects. Women accept the implied symbolic content, by equating *womankind* with the men's wild.

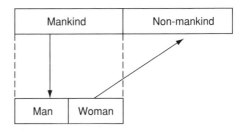

Figure 1.2 *Symbolic distinction between nature and society.*

The topic of this paper is 'the problem of women'. Women, of course, have 'a problem of men', who may indeed live in a part of the wild that women bound off from themselves. With that world of hunting and war, both sexes are familiar. The men's wild is, of course, a threat to women. The *liengu* taboos of the Bakweri express some of this. The secluded mermaids hate European goods, which have increased male power. The tabooed 'male' animal, the dog (used in the chase), is an added danger because it can see the spirit world. Dogs walk purposefully on their own, although they have nowhere to go, and they frequently stare attentively into space. Bakweri men have their own symbolic zone of adventure and hunting beyond that of the women, on the mountain-top away from all villages and farms. This is ritually expressed in the men's elephant dance (Ardener 1959). Elephants sometimes emerge from the remote parts of the mountain and destroy the women's farms. Men and boys in many villages belong to an elephant society, a closed association that claims responsibility for the work of elephants, through the elephant-doubles (*naguals*) of its more powerful members. In their annual dance they enact their control over the elephant world. Women on such occasions form the audience, who clap out the rhythm for the men's virtuoso dancer. Some women rather half-heartedly claim the role of bush-pigs, but like Dames in an order of chivalry or girls at Roedean, they are performing a male scenario.[9]

It is a tragedy of the male life-position that, in the modern age, the men's wild is not now so easily accessible to them. For modern Bakweri as for American males the hunting fantasy at least is no longer plausible. For if women still symbolically live in their wild, men have tried to ignore their own in the official symbolism of civilization. It will have emerged that the argument of this paper as it applies to women is a special but submerged case of the mode whereby self-identification is made. Obviously the different classes of men and of women, and individuals of all ages and both sexes contribute to that totality of symbolism – which merely appears a 'forest' when one fails to look at the trees.

To return, then, to the limited problem of my title, we need not doubt that the societies from which ethnographers come share the problem of all societies. If, as I suggest is the case, men's models of society accommodate women only by making certain assumptions that ignore or hold constant elements that would contradict these models, then the process may be traced further back into the ethnographer's own thinking and his own society. Our women ethnographers may then be expressing the 'maleness' of their subject when they approach the women of other societies.[10] It may well be, too, that their positive reluctance to deal with the problem of women is the greater because they sense that its consideration would split apart the very framework in which they conduct their studies.

NOTES

1 This paper was read at Dr Kaberry's seminar in University College London in late

1968. In presenting it for Dr Audrey Richards's festschrift, I acknowledged my debt to her for the main part of my early anthropological training. Her astringent humour and basic open-mindedness are qualities that I have respected ever since. I also thanked Dr Jean La Fontaine for her appreciative remarks on the paper, and for entering into the spirit of the analysis in her comments as editor.

2 This version was given in 1929 by Charles Steane, a Bakweri scholar, to B. G. Stone (MS, 1929).

3 *Moto*, *eto*, and *ewaki* are the ordinary words for 'person', 'rat', and 'ape'. *Mojili* or *Mojele* is to the coastal Bakweri a spirit. For inland Bakweri his name is a euphemism for 'ape'. It is likely that the term belongs to the animal world, but is borrowed from the fishing peoples. Possibly it is the manatee.

4 When the term is used *in isolation* the spelling *liengu* will be used (not, that is, the 'Africa' alphabet spelling *liɛngu*, nor the occasional spelling with orthographic subscript *lięngu*). The belief appears to be of coastal origin. There it is concerned with men, fishing, and the dangers of the deep. This paper is concerned with the *liengu* belief as utilized by the Bakweri. Elements of content are differently combined even between the coast and the mountain. Ittmann's rich material (1957) is to be used with caution because it combines several different systems. The pidgin English translation for water spirit is 'mammy water'. The 'mammy water' myth has wide currency in West Africa in urban contexts. The ambiguity of the position of women in African towns makes this secondary elaboration of the belief very appropriate.

5 See also Ardener (1956).

6 Various forms cited by myself (1956) and Ittmann (1957) are closer to 'fattening room' seclusion rites of the Cross River area in form and content. Their assimilation to the *liengu* belief is explicable because the latter belief most clearly organizes the women's world-view for the Bakweri.

7 Here is a subtle case of identical content yielding different meaning. The Duala

mer-people hate European objects, but the *maengu* are often male. There they symbolize men's domination of the deep; they particularly detest paper (conceived of as the bible).

8   For the *liengu* language, see Ardener (1956) and Ittmann (1957). It is a code calqued upon Bakweri with vocabulary from various sources.

9   Dr La Fontaine commented on this paper that men plus wild = death, destruction; women plus wild = agriculture, fertility. She, a woman, thus expresses that faith in the female civilizing mission shared by so many reflective members of her sex!

10 For some unresolved puzzles of a new woman fieldworker see Bovin (1966). For a resolution through literature see Bowen (1954).

The 'Problem' Revisited

The paper reprinted above is now somewhat old, and as composed just antedated the main impact of the new feminist literature. It is important to stress therefore that it was not seen as a contribution to that literature. Most of what it says seems quite commonplace at the present. In its rather long unpublished existence it was orally delivered in various places in the context of a discussion of the nature of dominant structures. It is not exactly the paper I would now write, if indeed I would write it at all. It has been a genuine pleasure to me, as a result, that it has not been rejected in its entirety by women social anthropologists concerned with the social differentiation of men and women. There have, however, been questions, and one or two misunderstandings, most of which occur in a critique by Nicole-Claude Mathieu called 'Homme-Culture et Femme-Nature?' (1973).

First of all, it should not be necessary for a social anthropologist, male or female, to offer any particular explanation for writing on 'the problem of women' as I presented it. One of the greatest statements of it was made by Virginia Woolf in 1928. She noted the great gulf between the saliency of women in symbolism and literature and their position until recently in the official structure. 'Imaginatively she is of the highest importance; practically she is completely insignificant. She pervades poetry from cover to cover; she is all but absent from history' (Woolf 1928: 45). Perhaps there were certain coincidences, for what they are worth, that at least did not place any obstacles of experience to my attempt on the question. My first fieldwork was among the Ibo, in the area in which the Women's Uprising of 1929 occurred. This was followed by studies among the Bakweri of Cameroon, who were portrayed, and who portrayed themselves, as riven by marital conflict. Among the latter, studies from the male point of view (Part III of Ardener et al. 1960) were followed by a study from the women's side (Ardener 1962).[1] The difference in atmosphere was extremely striking. For the men, society was in chaos, even breaking down. For the women,

life was a periplus of adventures, in which the role of independent 'harlot' was often viewed as objectively a proud one. I admit that the paper may be affected by ethnographic experiences that particularly highlight the 'separate realities' of men and women. There will be societies in which the gap is greater or smaller, confined to one area of life or another. Alternatively the gap should be seen as an exemplification of all discontinuities in the experience of groups in society, however defined.

Still, the necessity to interview women in such numbers as is required in a fertility and marital survey provides a considerable body of data for an anthropologist, which it has not always been fashionable to see in other than statistical terms. In the general social-anthropological world, I do not think it an exaggeration to say that by 1960 studies of women had declined to a fairly low theoretical status. Temporarily even the standard books by Margaret Mead had receded into the background. No doubt my recollection can be contested. Nevertheless, I recall the remark then being made (by a woman): 'No anthropological book with "women" in the title sells.' The writings were there, as some critics point out, but (to modify the pre-nineteenth-century motto of the Russians about their literature): 'De mulieribus – sunt, non leguntur.'

I have been asked whether women anthropologists 'raised my consciousness'. Although this hints at a characteristic modern paradox,[2] the question is relevant and deserves a careful answer. Because in both Eastern Nigeria and Cameroon, women had caused 'trouble' to the male population and to the administration, there had already been women anthropologists in these areas. In Iboland Sylvia Leith-Ross and M. M. Green had been deliberately invited to make studies in the aftermath of the Women's Riots, or what Caroline Ifeka terms the Women's War. It was Miss Green who in later years taught me the first elements of Ibo. In Cameroon, Phyllis Kaberry at one time nearly studied the Bakweri but eventually studied 'women' on the inland Plateau. She had already written *Aboriginal Woman*, and was to write *Women of the Grassfields*. Then through all phases of both the Nigerian and Cameroon studies, the last of which are still not finally completed, I worked with Shirley Ardener who must be the female anthropologist of the most continuous and subtle influence on me. Later she and Phyllis Kaberry and I collaborated on studies in Cameroon history with Sally Chilver – now one of the most distinguished ethno-historians in the study of the region. If in retrospect I note that my first teacher was Audrey Richards, and that the paper appeared in her festschrift, edited in its turn by Jean La Fontaine, there is a galaxy of female talent enough here to reassure any who might view with regret and suspicion the presence of a male anthropologist in this field.

Yet what was the precise nature of their influence on this paper? None of them, certainly of the senior ones, were particularly of a 'feminist' turn of mind. None appeared to be then students of 'women' except fortuitously, as part of their general anthropological work. Thus arose the paradox that a 'problem of women anthropologists' began to present itself unbidden to my mind. It had two components: (1) That they did not seem to be in a much more privileged position in interpreting the women of their fields than was a male anthropologist. (2) That the women anthropologists themselves, although they were loth to differentiate themselves from male anthropologists, did have significantly different academic pasts, presents, and (it looked likely) futures, in the anthropological profession itself.

It is easy nowadays to criticize me for needing these insights. A critic (Mathieu 1973) has stated that only one who believes in 'women' as a universal category could have fallen into the error of entertaining such an expectation as is implied in the first point. That reading is not quite exact: the problem was that women anthropologists did not themselves then reject the expectation, even though uncomfortable with it. Of course, in the last few years all this has changed – or begun to change. My second point is also a mere commonplace among militant women. Nevertheless, an independent perspective is not without its value. During the 'sixties it did sometimes look as if women anthropologists had even more academic vitality

in relation to their numbers than had their male colleagues. At long anthropological conferences their contributions frequently threw brave, short-lived beams of light into the gloom before being overwhelmed by it. Nevertheless no woman became until recently a Professor of Anthropology in a British University.[3] It was quite apparent, however, that women formed only an easily recognizable part of a class of social anthropologists in the same condition. Yet while male anthropologists of a 'destructured' tendency were generally conscious of the nature of the situation which enveloped them, the women anthropologists seemed 'muted' on their own position. Publicly, at least, they did not 'see' or 'perceive' themselves within the structure of academic anthropology; so, inevitably, they did not 'see' other women clearly in their own fields. That is the reason why 'Belief and the Problem of Women' ends with the challenge to women anthropologists 'to split apart the very framework in which they conduct their studies'. Nicole-Claude Mathieu asks, should not men do likewise? Precisely. No one who knows my general position will imagine that this conclusion was to be seen as an achievement of male complacency. I have taken the 'woman' case in order to *de*sexualize it. When I say that it is a special case of a situation applying to other social classes and individuals, both men and women, this is not a casual aside as Mathieu again seems to think – it is the intended conclusion of the paper, which has been merely illustrated by the case of women.

In the light of the foregoing it may be worth noting for the chronological record that in July 1973 at the Session on Marxism of the ASA Decennial Conference I made an oral contribution to the discussion of class:

> If we look at those classes which are usually considered to be the exploiting or dominant classes, and then we consider those others which are supposedly the exploited or suppressed classes, there is this dimension that hasn't been mentioned yet: which is [that] of relative articulateness. One of the problems that women presented was that they were rendered 'inarticulate' by the male structure; that the dominant structure was articulated in terms of a male world-position. Those who

were not in the male world-position, were, as it were, 'muted'.

I repeated my suggestion that this applied to other social groups and also to individuals, and stated its relevance to the question of the universality or otherwise of the concept of class:

We may speak of 'muted groups' and 'articulate groups' along this dimension. There are many kinds of muted groups. We would then go on to ask: 'What is it that makes a group muted?' We then become aware that it is muted simply because it does not form part of the dominant communicative system of the society – expressed as it must be through the dominant ideology, and that 'mode of production', if you wish, which is articulated with it. (From transcript of discussion 7 July 1973.)

Nevertheless, the point must be made that not all phenomena of mutedness can be linked simply and directly to a 'mode of production'. Dominant/muted alternations, as we shall see, occur at too many levels to actualize themselves always in these terms. The definition of 'mode of production' itself would suffer extraordinary transfigurations if it were so. Nevertheless, those alternations which are tied to a mode of production certainly acquire a special kind of salience or stability – an institutionalization – that will be familiar to marxist analysts.

The approach is already being provisionally applied to other muted groups, such as children (Hardman 1973) and criminals (Maguire 1974). We owe the convenient term 'muted' itself to Charlotte Hardman. But the phenomenon of 'mutedness' (it must be warned) is a technically defined condition of structures – not some condition of linguistic silence.[4] There is also an ambiguity about the term 'muted' in this connection – for in English we mean by it both 'dumb' and 'of a reduced level of perceptibility'. The muted structures are 'there' but cannot be 'realized' in the language of the dominant structure.

The operation of a dominant structure from the point of view of a subdominant may be likened to a pin-table in which the very operation of the spring, to propel the ball, itself moves the scoring holes some centimetres to the side. The more skill the operator uses in directing the ball, the more carefully he ensures that the scoring hole will not be there to receive it. The ultimate negativity of attempts to modify dominant structures by their own 'rules' derives from the totally reality-defining nature of such structures. Because of this essential element the manifold of experience through the social may be usefully termed a 'world-structure', for it is an organization both of *people and of their reality*. It is not my intention to appear to confuse the apparently practical aspects of the perception of woman, and of perceiving by women, by alluding in too much detail to these questions, some of which are at early stage of analysis. But a 'world-structure', in these clearly defined terms, is the nearest congener to the 'society' or (and?) 'culture' of traditional anthropology. The characteristic bounding problem that those terms imply ('Where does a society begin or end?', 'When are cultures the "same", or "different"? In space or in time?') is solved by its resolution in the chief criterion of a 'world-structure': it is a *self*-defining system.

We are now able to examine an unfortunate misunderstanding of my previous paper. I find it difficult to see how any careful reader can deduce that for me it is a simple case of 'man=culture' and 'women=nature'. The fault lies, no doubt, in my citation of Lévi-Strauss. My readers should concentrate upon the 'defining' or 'bounding' problem presented by women in a situation in which the 'bounds' of 'society' are themselves defined by men. In the conceptual act of bounding 'society' there is a fortuitous homology between the purely ideational field or background against which 'society' is defined as a *concept*, and that part of the actual, territorial world which is not socially organized – the 'wild'. The 'wild' = the 'non-social'. It is a mere confusion that it may also be walkable into, and be found to contain sounding cataracts and unusual beasts. A 'society', because it has a geographical *situs*, in one of its defining spaces, or along one of its dimensions, therefore projects an equivalent geographical aspect on to its counter-concept – the 'non-social'. If the world were geographically a uniformly barren surface, the self-defining human entities upon it would thereby merely lack a useful set of topographical differentia for the 'non-social'. Conceptually these differentiae would not cease to exist. In rural societies the equation: non-social = non-human = the wild = 'nature' is easily concretized. There is a powerful metaphor, with a key into experience. This is the source of the triviality as well as the power of the binary opposition 'nature/culture' in Lévi-Strauss's own analyses. Its 'universality' is indeed a powerful triviality. It is 'self/not-self' raised to the level of society's own self-definition, and clothed in 'totemic' and botanical imagery.

My argument was: where society is defined by men, some features of women do not fit that definition. In rural societies the anomaly is experienced as a feature of the 'wild', for the 'wild' is a metaphor of the non-social which in confusing ways is vouched for by the senses.

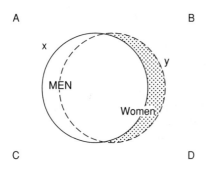

A   B

x

MEN

y

Women

C   D

Figure 1.3 *Male and female perceptions.*

In figure 1.3 A B C D is an unbounded field against which the two intersecting circles *x, y* are defined. From the perspective of circle *x* the shaded portion of *y* is part of the field A B C D. The circle *x, plus* the unshaded overlap of circle *y*, is the model of society where the male model is dominant (heavy outline and capital letters). In metaphorical terms, A B C D is 'the wild'. In the diagram, the shaded area of *y*, which is classified by men with the 'wild', is not confused by women themselves with the 'wild' (save when they speak in the dominant 'language'). Rather, for them there is a zone in circle *x* which is ambiguously male and 'wild', a zone which men do not perceive.[5]

This confusion of self-definition with geographical reality is avoided when we think not of 'society', but of a world-structure

which defines human reality – if you like 'relevant' reality. In these terms if the male perception yields a dominant structure, the female one is a muted structure. It is an empirical contingency that the immanent realizations of muted structures are so often equated in this way with the nullity of the background, of 'nature'; and also that 'nature' itself should thus contain at its core a common metaphorical conceptualization, appearing in Rousseau and Lévi-Strauss, on the one hand, and the Bororo or the Bakweri, on the other.

Mathieu appears to take my own argument to its extreme when she chides me for mentioning the female biology as one of the features males find difficult to tidy away into the perceptions of the dominant structure. Yes, of course, we can say that the very concept of female biology is a product of the dominant structure. But once more I reply that the undoubted anatomical and functional differences become a powerful and convenient metaphor for this, possibly the most ancient and surely the most nearly universal, structural dominance. Hertz similarly showed that a possibly slight anatomical ('biological') discrepancy between a right- and a left-handed tendency became a powerful metaphor for all binary discriminations, including this very one between the sexes; and, as Needham's comprehensive volume on the subject also illustrates (1973), it is also no surprise that spatial concepts (inside–outside, village–wild) should be lined up with these pairs. Mathieu thus is quite mistaken in asserting that I am a 'biological essentialist' and that my analysis demands a theory of biological causation.

Some of her mistakes rest upon subtle difficulties of translation from English into French, and I accept part of the blame for this, as even for an English-speaking reader there are a number of levels of irony and ambiguous nuance in the style of the paper. Still, when I write of 'women overlapping into [the men's view of] nature again' I do not mean 'refaire le saut dans la nature' (Mathieu 1973: 107–8). Women do not 'leap back' into nature: they overlap, protrude beyond the limits set for them by men. When I write of a 'propensity' of males to make models of society of a particular bounded type, I do not mean *une capa-*

cité (1973: 107) but 'a structural readiness'; nor do I refer to *des modèles bien délimités, modèles discrets de la société* (1973: 102), but to models of a society bounded (*délimités*) *in a particular way*. Furthermore, when I say that 'all such ways of bounding society against society...may have an inherent maleness', the term 'maleness' is of course not here a biological term, a function of male gonads. We cannot draw from it the conclusion that: 'La "dominance politique" des hommes est ainsi conçue comme une charactéristique fixe d'une catégorie biologique fixe: le politique est à l'homme ce que la vertu dormitive est au pavot, une propriété' (1973: 107). It is strange to be suspected of an ethologistic determinism, even greater than Professors Fox and Tiger are normally accused of.

Lastly, nothing but some basic stereotypical error can account for the sternness of Mathieu's response to my interchange with Jean La Fontaine (note 9 above). She detects an irony on my part. There is indeed one: I certainly do not reject (as she suggests) the validity of a female equation of the wild of 'maleness' with death, destruction, and 'non-culture'. I was gently deprecating, however, any hint of a simple 'female utopianism' that would define death and destruction as incompatible with *itself*. But in the end I suspect that 'culture' is for Mathieu an *a priori* category with a high positive marking – whereas, for many of us, a position 'in the wild' (were that actually in question) still has no negative connotations. I am quite prepared to be defined as 'nature' by Mathieu for I detect in her paper the salutary symptoms of one who has begun to 'split apart the very framework of her studies'.[6]

In conclusion I would state my position so: The woman case is only a relatively prominent example of muting: one that has clear political, biological, and social symbols. The real problem is that all world-structures are totalitarian in tendency. The Gypsy world-structure, for example, englobes that of the sedentary community just as avidly as that of the sedentary community englobes that of the Gypsies. The englobed structure is totally 'muted' in terms of the englobing one. There is then an absolute equality of world-structures in this principle,

for we are talking of their self-defining and reality-reducing features. *Dominance* occurs when one structure blocks the power of actualization of the other, so that it has no 'freedom of action'. That this approach is not simply a marxist one lies in our recognition that the articulation of world-structures does not rest only in their production base but at all levels of communication: that a structure is also a kind of language of many semiological elements, which specify all actions by its power of definition.

My intervention in the discussion as far as it concerns women was a product of concern with the technical features of socio-intellectual structures which regularly assign contending viewpoints to a non-real status; making them 'overlooked', 'muted', 'invisible': mere black holes in someone else's universe.

NOTES

1 See References below, p. 64.
2 The paradox is that studies of the cultural relativity of ideas of 'women' should seem to increase rather than reduce the tendency to see this as a 'women's' subject.
3 I think the date was 1966.
4 For those familiar with this terminology, the following diagram will suffice: The 'reality' configurations (s-structures) are generated from p-structures. Dominant p-structures generate s-structures relatively directly. Sub-dominant p-structures generate only indirectly – through the mode of specification of the dominant structure.

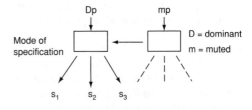

Figure 1.4 *Dominant and muted p-structures.*

5 Since the 'wild' is always 'symbolic' it is not surprising that women do sometimes

see *themselves* as part of it (cf. Ortner 1973). Her approach, by a greatly different route, complements mine.

6   I should like to add here that I find myself in general agreement with much of Mathieu's own position. In misreading mine she has really done my paper too great an honour: she has judged it by the standards of length of a monograph. To push through an argument in a short paper one begins with certain common-sense categories in order to dissolve them. The terms are redefined between the beginning and the end. I accept then that there are 'generalizations'. But I do not think that the many examples of ethnographers to whom the women *have* 'spoken' (among whom I am after all one!) touch the central point that within social anthropology 'no one could come back from an ethnographic study… having talked only *to* women and about men, without professional comment and some self-doubt. The reverse can and does happen constantly.' I have not replied to all points, not because they are without interest or are too compelling, but because the central charge of biologism is so improbable that it distorts all her presentation. As a final exemplification of it I quote from her last words: 'Vouloir rendre la parole aux classes inarticulées en allant rechercher "aux niveaux les plus profonds" du symbolisme ce que, tels des schizophrènes, ils tenteraient d'exprimer, présente le même danger en ethnologie que l'explication constitutionnaliste de la schizophrénie en psychiatric. …' It is astonishing that here the Laingian approaches to the 'meaning' of schizophrenia, with which my approach is most comparable, are interpreted as 'constitutionalist' psychiatry.

REFERENCES

Ardener, E. W. 1956. *Coastal Bantu of the Cameroons*. London: Oxford University Press for International African Institute.
—— 1959. The Bakweri Elephant Dance. *Nigeria*, 60: 31–8.
—— 1962. *Divorce and Fertility*. London: Oxford University Press.
—— 1970. Witchcraft, Economics, and the Continuity of Belief. In M. Douglas ed., *Witchcraft Confessions and Accusations*. ASA Monograph 9. London: Tavistock.
Ardener, E. W., S. G. Ardener, and W. A. Warmington. 1960. *Plantation and Village in the Cameroons*. London: Oxford University Press.
Bovin, M. 1966. The Significance of the Sex of the Field Worker for Insights into the Male and Female Worlds. *Ethnos*, 31 (supp.): 24–7. Stockholm.
Bowen, E. S. 1954. *Return to Laughter*. London: Gollancz.
Douglas, M. 1966. *Purity and Danger*. London: Routledge & Kegan Paul.
—— ed. 1970. *Witchcraft Confessions and Accusations*. ASA Monograph 9. London: Tavistock.
Evans-Pritchard, E. E. 1965. The Position of Women in Primitive Societies and in Our Own. In *The Position of Women and Other Essays in Social Anthropology*. London: Faber & Faber.
Hardman, C. 1973. Can there be an Anthropology of Children? *Journal of the Anthropological Society of Oxford* 4: 85–99.
Hertz, R. 1909. The Pre-eminence of the Right Hand: a Study in Religious Polarity. Translated and reprinted in R. Needham, *Right and Left: Essays on Dual Symbolic Classification*. Chicago and London: University of Chicago Press, 1973.
Ittmann, J. 1957. Der kultische Geheimbund djĕngú an der Kameruner Küste. *Anthropos*, 52: 135–76.
Kaberry, P. M. 1939. *Aboriginal Woman: Sacred and Profane*. London: Routledge & Kegan Paul (reprinted Gregg International, 1970).
—— 1952. *Women of the Grassfields*. London: HMSO (reprinted Gregg International, 1970).
Leach, E. R. 1961. Two Essays concerning the Symbolic Representation of Time. In *Rethinking Anthropology*. London: Athlone Press.
—— 1964. Animal Categories and Verbal Abuse. In E. H. Lenneberg, ed., *New Directions in Language*. Cambridge, Mass.: MIT Press.

Lenneberg, E. H., ed. 1964. *New Directions in Language*. Cambridge, Mass.: MIT Press.

Lévi-Strauss, C. 1949. *Les Structures élémentaires de la parenté*. Paris: Presses Universitaires de France (2nd edn 1967).

—— 1963. *Structural Anthropology*. New York: Basic Books.

—— 1964. *Mythologiques: Le Cru et le cuit*. Paris: Plon.

—— 1966. *Mythologiques: Du miel aux cendres*. Paris: Plon.

—— 1967. *Les Structures élémentaires de la parenté*. Paris: Mouton.

—— 1968. *Mythologiques: L'Origine des manières du table*. Paris: Plon.

—— 1969. *The Elementary Structures of Kinship*. London: Eyre & Spottiswoode.

Maguire, M. 1974. Criminology and Social Anthropology, *Journal of the Anthropological Society of Oxford*, 5(2): 109–17.

Mathieu, N. C. 1973. Homme-Culture, Femme-Nature? *L'Homme*, July–Sept.: 101–113.

Needham, R. 1958. A Structural Analysis of Purum Society. *American Anthropologist*, 60: 75–101.

—— 1960. The Left Hand of the Mugwe. *Africa*, 30: 20–33.

—— 1967. Right and Left in Nyoro Symbolic Classification. *Africa*, 37: 425–52.

—— 1973. *Right and Left: Essays on Dual Symbolic Classification*. Chicago and London: University of Chicago Press.

Ortner, S. B. 1973. Is Female to Male as Nature Is to Culture? *Feminist Studies*, 1(2). Also in M. Z. Rosaldo and M. Lamphere eds., *Woman, Culture, and Society*. Stanford, Calif.: Stanford University Press, 1974.

Richards, A. I. 1956. *Chisungu: A Girls' Initiation Ceremony among the Bemba of Northern Rhodesia*. London: Faber & Faber.

Stone, B. G. 1929. Assessment Report of Buea District. MS. Victoria Divisional Office, Cameroons.

Turner, V. W. 1967. *The Forest of Symbols*. Ithaca, NY: Cornell University Press.

Woolf, V. 1928. *A Room of One's Own*. London: Hogarth Press (cited from Penguin edition).

2

A Note on the Division of Labor by Sex

Judith K. Brown

In spite of the current interest in the economic aspect of tribal and peasant societies, the division of labor by sex continues to elicit only the most perfunctory consideration. This paper attempts to reassess the scant theoretical literature dealing with this division of labor and to suggest a reinterpretation based on some of the available ethnographic evidence.

I will begin with Durkheim. According to his theory, among the very primitive (both in the distant past and today) men and women are fairly similar in strength and intelligence. Under these circumstances the sexes are economically independent, and therefore "sexual relations [are] preeminently ephemeral" (1893: 61). With the "progress of morality," women became weaker and their brains became smaller. Their dependence on men increased, and division of labor by sex cemented the conjugal bond. Indeed, Durkheim asserts that the Parisienne of his day probably had the smallest human brain on record. Presumably she was able to console herself with the stability of her marriage, which was the direct result of her underendowment and consequent dependence.

Unlike Durkheim, Murdock does not attempt to reconstruct history, but his explanatory principle is also naïvely physiological. He writes:

By virtue of their primary sex differences, a man and a woman make an exceptionally efficient cooperating unit. Man, with his superior physical strength, can better undertake the more strenuous tasks.... Not handicapped, as is woman, by the physiological burdens of pregnancy and nursing, he can range farther afield to hunt, to fish, to herd and to trade. Woman is at no disadvantage however, in the lighter tasks which can be performed in or near home.... All known human societies have developed specialization and cooperation between the sexes roughly along this biologically determined line of cleavage. (1949: 7)

This overly simple explanation is contradicted by numerous ethnographic accounts of heavy physical labor performed by women. The greater spatial range of male subsistence activities may also not be based on physiology as Murdock suggests. Recently, Munroe and

Munroe (1967) have reported sex differences in environmental exploration among Logoli children. According to the authors, the greater geographical range of boys' activities in this society may result from learning, although innate sex linked factors are suggested as a possible alternative explanation.

Lévi-Strauss also suggests the economic interdependence of the sexes as the basis for the conjugal (or nuclear) family. This interdependence does not so much arise from actual sex differences as from culturally imposed prohibitions that make it impossible for one sex to do the tasks assigned to the other. He writes of the division of labor by sex as "a device to make the sexes mutually dependent on social and economic grounds thus establishing clearly that marriage is better than celibacy" (1956: 277).

Taking their cue from ethnographic descriptions that suggest that women often perform the dull and monotonous subsistence activities (for example, Pospisil 1963), other authors have offered "psychologizing" theories concerning the division of labor by sex. Malinowski suggested that women, owing to their docility, are forced to do such work: "Division of labor is rooted in the brutalization of the weaker sex by the stronger" (1913: 287). Others have suggested that women are psychologically better fitted for dull work. Mead summarizes this view, stating "Women have a capacity for continuous monotonous work that men do not share, while men have a capacity for the mobilization of sudden spurts of energy, followed by a need for rest and reassemblage of resources" (1949: 164).

What facts have these theories tried to explain? First, division of labor by sex is a universal. Planned societies such as Israel and Communist China have attempted to implement an ideology that views men and women as interchangeable parts within the economy, but have done so with only mixed success (Spiro 1956; Huang 1961, 1963). Second, in spite of the physiological constants and the possible, but less well-substantiated, psychological ones, women may contribute nothing to subsistence – as among the Rajputs (Minturn and Hitchcock 1963); or they may support the society almost completely – as among

the Nsaw (Kaberry 1952). This variation, briefly noted by Mead (1949), has never been fully explained.

I would like to suggest that the degree to which women contribute to the subsistence of a particular society can be predicted with considerable accuracy from a knowledge of the major subsistence activity. It is determined by the compatibility of this pursuit with the demands of child care. (Female physiology and psychology are only peripheral to this explanation.) This fact has been noted repeatedly by ethnographers, but it has never been articulated in the theoretical literature dealing with the division of labor by sex.

Nowhere in the world is the rearing of children primarily the responsibility of men, and in only a few societies are women exempted from participation in subsistence activities. If the economic role of women is to be maximized, their responsibilities in child care must be reduced or the economic activity must be such that it can be carried out concurrently with child care.

The former is the method familiar to us among industrial or industrializing societies. Whether in the United States or in Communist China, the working mother is separated from her child, who is in the care of specialists in the school or the residential nursery while the mother is in her place of employment. In our society, controversy over the presence of mothers in the labor force inevitably centers on the desirability and quality of this substitute care (Maccoby 1960).

Tribal societies also resort to substitute care so that mothers may work. Among the Gusii, women are responsible for the cultivation on which the society depends, and young child nurses (usually girls) are in charge of younger children and infants. However, the mother must periodically supervise the young caretakers. Minturn and Lambert write:

This does not mean that the Nyasongo [Gusii] mothers spend a great deal of time actually interacting with their children. They have domestic and agricultural duties that take up most of their time....Older children are often left with no one to look after them directly, but are kept close to home and within earshot of their mothers....The burden of such supervision is clear, for instance, with respect to infant care. Older children chiefly care for infants but mothers must, in turn supervise older children. (1964: 244, 252)

Among the Yoruba (Marshall 1964) an intricate system of reciprocity makes possible the trade activities of the women. During the early years of marriage, when her children are very young, a woman carries on only limited commercial activities. At this time she is likely to take into her home an older child as a helper. When her children are older, they in turn are placed in the homes of women who are still in the previous stage, and the mother's market activities increase in scope.

I have greatly oversimplified both examples. They illustrate two contrasts with the substitute care patterns of our own society. First, the women are not freed as completely for their economic pursuits. Second, the ethnographic accounts suggest that such substitute care is viewed not only as desirable but as an absolute necessity. Finally, the two cases are similar to the cases that are the focus of this paper, in that the work the women perform is not incompatible with child watching, even though the supervision of children may be only sporadic. My main concern is with those societies that, without the intercession of schools, child-care centers, or child nurses, nevertheless depend on the subsistence activities of working mothers. These societies are able to draw on womanpower because their subsistence activities are compatible with simultaneous child watching. Such activities have the following characteristics: they do not require rapt concentration and are relatively dull and repetitive; they are easily interruptible and easily resumed once interrupted; they do not place the child in potential danger; and they do not require the participant to range very far from home.

Anthropologists have long noted the narrow range of subsistence activities in which women make a substantial contribution: gathering, hoe agriculture, and trade (Lippert 1886/7; Schmidt 1955; Murdock 1957; Aberle 1961). Although men do gather, carry on hoe cultivation, and trade, no society depends on its women for the herding of large animals, the hunting of large game, deep-sea fishing, or plow agriculture. That women can be proficient at these activities (Jenness [1923] reports women seal hunters among the Copper Eskimo; Forde [1934] reports that women herd reindeer for parts of the year among the Tungus) is evidence that the division of labor by sex is not based entirely on immutable physiological facts of greater male strength and endurance. However, it is easy to see that all these activities are incompatible with simultaneous child watching. They require rapt concentration, cannot be interrupted and resumed, are potentially dangerous, and require that the participant range far from home.

Bogoras' report of the summer herding of the reindeer Chukchee provides an especially appropriate illustration of a subsistence activity that is incompatible with child watching. Bogoras suggests that the division of labor is not sexually determined; instead the population is divided according to child-watching and non-child-watching members. He writes:

> With the beginning of summer, when sledges become useless and tents cannot be moved around the country, the Chukchee herdsmen usually leave their families in camp, and move with the herd about twenty miles away, to the summer pastures. Boys and girls of more than ten years, and young women having no small children, usually go along for a time. While moving about with the herd, the herdsmen have to carry on their backs all necessaries, such as extra clothing, rifle and ammunition, kettles, and provisions....The burdens are carried by girls and by men who are not very agile; while the best herds-men must remain unencumbered for moving swiftly around the herd. (1904: 83)

The reindeer Chukchee lived by herding and hunting, both very incompatible with simultaneous child care, and the women of the society made a negligible contribution to subsistence. In contrast, the Azande, as described by De Schlippe, are hoe cultivators, and the contribution of women to subsistence is considerable. De Schlippe offers a very detailed description of the division of labor by sex. Only a portion will be cited here because it illustrates the compatibility of the women's activities with simultaneous child watching:

In all those field types which are grouped around the homestead and to which the common name of garden has been applied, as a rule women work alone or with their children. This may be explained by the proximity to the homestead and accordingly by the nature of this work. It consists of a great variety of different small tasks, many of which can be packed into one single day. A woman, trained in household work, is capable of doing a great deal of minor independent tasks without losing the order of her day's work. (1956: 140)

Another account that demonstrates the compatibility of hoe agriculture with simultaneous child watching is offered in the early nineteenth-century biography of the adopted Indian captive Mary Jemison (Seaver 1823). It is the only description of Iroquois agricultural activity given from the point of view of a participant. It runs as follows:

Our labor was not severe; and that of one year was exactly similar, in almost every respect, to that of the others.... Notwithstanding the Indian women have all the fuel and bread to procure ... their cares certainly are not half as numerous, nor as great [as those of white women]. In the summer season, we planted, tended and harvested our corn, and generally had all our children with us ... we could work as leisurely as we pleased. (Seaver 1823: 55)

The carefree tone of this account is deceptive. The agricultural activities of the Iroquois women were highly productive. Not only was the tribe well provided with food, but the harvested surplus was carefully preserved and constituted a considerable part of the tribe's wealth. Morgan (1851) had high praise for the industry of the Iroquois women. It is all the more remarkable that such high productivity was possible with simultaneous childcare responsibilities.

The relaxed atmosphere that characterized the agricultural–child-watching activities of the Iroquois women also characterized the gathering–child-watching activities of the Lunga women, inhabitants of the Kimberley District of Western Australia. Phyllis Kaberry

writes of the Aborigine women, "If livelihood is sometimes precarious, it is belied by the absence of any feverish haste" (1939: 18). Children accompanied the small groups of women gatherers on their daily forays into the bush. Kaberry describes one of these forays in great detail, ending her account as follows:

They lie for a while in the shade, gossip, eat some of the fish and roots, sleep, and about three o'clock move homeward. For all their desultory searching, there is little that they miss, or fail to note for a future occasion.... In actual quantity, the woman probably provides more over a fixed period than the man, since hunting is not always successful. She always manages to bring home something, and hence the family is dependent on her efforts to a greater extent than on those of the husband. (1939: 22, 25)

A more recent study, that by Rose of the Angus Downs Aborigines, focuses on the effects of White contact on Aborigine economic activity and kinship structure. Under precontact conditions, according to Rose, when women gathered nuts and seeds for grinding, they formed themselves into "collectives of co-wives for the purpose of sharing the burdens of caring for children" (1965: 99). With the introduction of white flour, the women's economic role became what Rose considers a passive one, "collectives" were no longer necessary, and polygyny decreased markedly.

The final ethnographic example I will offer is that of the Yahgan as described by Gusinde. This tribe was rated by Murdock (1957) as being supported mostly by the subsistence activities of its women. It was the only tribe that depended on fishing, marine hunting, and marine gathering that was so rated in the world sample of 565 societies. Gusinde writes:

Far beyond the limited participation of the man in procuring food, she makes a considerable, altogether independent contribution to the support of her family by means of an activity that she alone can carry out. This is gathering, for which she is equipped by nature and to which she can devote herself without jeopardizing her more important duties as mother and wife. (1937: 538)

His description of subsistence activities is extremely detailed. Only a small portion will be cited here:

Assuming that low tide sets in during the day, one woman will make a date with another.... Each of them brings along her baby clinging to her back, and little girls run ahead, each with her own little basket. Sometimes a boy or two will run along out of curiosity and sheer pleasure, and they will watch for a while, but it would never occur to them to help because that is not their work. These women are only short distances apart. Walking slowly, they go from one spot to another, for the entire ocean floor is usually densely strewn with mussels.... They stop working only when their little baskets are full. (1937: 541–2)

The ethnographers cited here have all addressed themselves to the relationship between women's economic activities and their child-rearing responsibilities. It is obvious that certain subsistence activities are extremely compatible with simultaneous child care and that societies depending on such subsistence bases invite considerable economic contribution by women. In the past, theoretical considerations of the division of labor by sex have suggested that women do only certain kinds of work for physiological and psychological reasons. On the basis of the ethnographic evidence I have presented here, I would like to suggest a further explanation: in tribal and peasant societies that do not have schools and child-care centers, only certain economic pursuits can accommodate women's simultaneous child-care responsibilities. Repetitive, interruptible, non-dangerous tasks that do not require extensive excursions are more appropriate for women when the exigencies of child care are taken into account.

REFERENCES

ABERLE, DAVID. 1961. Matrilineal Descent in Cross-cultural Perspective. In *Matrilineal Kinship*. David M. Schneider and Kathleen Gough, eds. Berkeley: University of California Press.

BOGORAS, WALDEMAR. 1904. *The Chukchee: The Jesup North Pacific Expedition*. American Museum of Natural History Memoir 7(1). New York: Stechert.

DE SCHLIPPE, PIERRE. 1956. *Shifting Cultivation in Africa: The Zande System of Agriculture*. London: Routledge & Kegan Paul.

DURKHEIM, ÉMILE. 1893. De la division du travail social. [Reference here is to the 1933 edition: *The Division of Labor in Society*. George Simpson, trans. Glencoe, Ill.: Free Press.]

FORDE, C. DARYLL. 1934. *Habitat, Economy and Society*. [Reprinted New York: Dutton, 1963.]

GUSINDE, MARTIN. 1937. Die Yamana, vom Leben und Denken der Wassernomaden am Kap Horn. [English translation: *The Yamana: The Life and Thought of the Water Nomads of Cape Horn* (1937). Frieda Schütze, trans. New Haven: Human Relations Area Files, 1961.]

HUANG, JEN LUCY. 1961. Some Changing Patterns in the Communist Chinese Family. *Marriage and Family Living*, 23: 137–46.

——1963. A Re-evaluation of the Primary Role of the Communist Chinese Woman: The Homemaker or the Worker. *Marriage and Family Living*, 25: 162–6.

JENNESS, D. 1923. *The Copper Eskimo. Report of the Canadian Arctic Expedition, 1913–18*, p. 12. Ottawa: Acland.

KABERRY, PHYLLIS. 1939. *Aboriginal Woman: Sacred and Profane*. London: Routledge.

——1952. *Women of the Grass Fields: A Study of the Economic Position of Women in Bamenda, British Cameroons*. Colonial Research Publication 14. London: Her Majesty's Stationery Office.

LÉVI-STRAUSS, CLAUDE. 1956. The Family. In *Man, Culture, and Society*. Harry L. Shapiro, ed. New York: Oxford University Press.

LIPPERT, JULIUS. 1886/7. *The Evolution of Culture*. [English translation: G. P. Murdock, trans. and ed. New York: Macmillan, 1931.]

MACCOBY, ELEANOR E. 1960. Effects upon Children of their Mothers' Outside Employment. In *A Modern Introduction to the Family*. Norman W. Bell and Ezra F. Vogel, eds. Glencoe, Ill.: Free Press.

MALINOWSKI, BRONISLAW. 1913. *The Family among the Australian Aborigines: A Sociological Study*. London: University of London Press.

MARSHALL, GLORIA. 1964. Women, Trade and the Yoruba Family. PhD dissertation, Columbia University.

MEAD, MARGARET. 1949. *Male and Female: A Study of the Sexes, in a Changing World*. New York: William Morrow.

MINTURN, LEIGH, and JOHN T. HITCHCOCK. 1963. The Rājpūts of Khalapur, India. In *Six Cultures: Studies of Child Rearing*. Beatrice B. Whiting, ed. New York: Wiley.

MINTURN, LEIGH, and WILLIAM LAMBERT. 1964. *Mothers of Six Cultures: Antecedents of Child Rearing*. New York: Wiley.

MORGAN, LEWIS HENRY. 1851. *League of the Iroquois*. [*Reprinted* New York: Corinth Books, 1962.]

MUNROE, ROBERT L., and RUTH H. MUNROE 1967. Maintenance-system Determinants of Child Development among the Logoli of Kenya. Paper presented at the American Anthropological Association meetings, Washington, DC.

MURDOCK, GEORGE PETER. 1949. *Social Structure*. New York: Macmillan.

—— 1957 World Ethnographic Sample. *American Anthropologist*, 59: 664–87.

POSPISIL, LEOPOLD. 1963. *Kapauku Papuan Economy*. Yale University Publications in Anthropology 67. New Haven: Department of Anthropology, Yale University.

ROSE, FREDERICK G. G. 1965. *The Wind of Change in Central Australia: The Aborigines at Angas Downs, 1962*. Berlin: Akademie Verlag.

SCHMIDT, WILHELM S. V. D. 1955. *Das Mutterrecht*. Studia Instituti Anthropos 10. Vienna-Mödlingen: Missions-druckerei St. Gabriel.

SEAVER, JAMES E. 1823. A Narrative of the Life of Mrs. Mary Jemison. [*Reprinted* New York: Corinth Books, 1961.]

SPIRO, M. E. 1956. *Kibbutz: Venture in Utopia*. Cambridge, Mass.: Harvard University Press.

3

Is Female to Male as Nature Is to Culture?

Sherry B. Ortner

Much of the creativity of anthropology derives from the tension between two sets of demands: that we explain human universals, and that we explain cultural particulars. By this canon, woman provides us with one of the more challenging problems to be dealt with. The secondary status of woman in society is one of the true universals, a pan-cultural fact. Yet within that universal fact, the specific cultural conceptions and symbolizations of woman are extraordinarily diverse and even mutually contradictory. Further, the actual treatment of women and their relative power and contribution vary enormously from culture to culture, and over different periods in the history of particular cultural traditions. Both of these points – the universal fact and the cultural variation – constitute problems to be explained.

My interest in the problem is of course more than academic: I wish to see genuine change come about, the emergence of a social and cultural order in which as much of the range of human potential is open to women as is open to men. The universality of female sub-ordination, the fact that it exists within every type of social and economic arrangement and in societies of every degree of complexity, indicates to me that we are up against something very profound, very stubborn, something we cannot rout out simply by rearranging a few tasks and roles in the social system, or even by reordering the whole economic structure. In this paper I try to expose the underlying logic of cultural thinking that assumes the inferiority of women; I try to show the highly persuasive nature of the logic, for if it were not so persuasive, people would not keep subscribing to it. But I also try to show the social and cultural sources of that logic, to indicate wherein lies the potential for change.

It is important to sort out the levels of the problem. The confusion can be staggering. For example, depending on which aspect of Chinese culture we look at, we might extrapolate any of several entirely different guesses concerning the status of women in China. In the ideology of Taoism, *yin*, the female principle, and *yang*, the male principle, are given equal weight; "the opposition, alternation, and inter-

social change

action of these two forces give rise to all phenomena in the universe" (Siu 1968: 2). Hence we might guess that maleness and femaleness are equally valued in the general ideology of Chinese culture.[1] Looking at the social structure, however, we see the strongly emphasized patrilineal descent principle, the importance of sons, and the absolute authority of the father in the family. Thus we might conclude that China is the archetypal patriarchal society. Next, looking at the actual roles played, power and influence wielded, and material contributions made by women in Chinese society – all of which are, upon observation, quite substantial – we would have to say that women are allotted a great deal of (unspoken) status in the system. Or again, we might focus on the fact that a goddess, Kuan Yin, is the central (most worshiped, most depicted) deity in Chinese Buddhism, and we might be tempted to say, as many have tried to say about goddess-worshiping cultures in prehistoric and early historical societies, that China is actually a sort of matriarchy. In short, we must be absolutely clear about *what* we are trying to explain before explaining it.

We may differentiate three levels of the problem:

1. The universal fact of culturally attributed second-class status of woman in every society. Two questions are important here. First, what do we mean by this; what is our evidence that this is a universal fact? And second, how are we to explain this fact, once having established it?

2. Specific ideologies, symbolizations, and socio-structural arrangements pertaining to women that vary widely from culture to culture. The problem at this level is to account for any particular cultural complex in terms of factors specific to that group – the standard level of anthropological analysis.

3. Observable on-the-ground details of women's activities, contributions, powers, influence, etc., often at variance with cultural ideology (although always constrained within the assumption that women may never be officially preeminent in the total system). This is the level of direct observation, often adopted now by feminist-oriented anthropologists.

This paper is primarily concerned with the first of these levels, the problem of the universal devaluation of women. The analysis thus depends not upon specific cultural data but rather upon an analysis of "culture" taken generically as a special sort of process in the world. A discussion of the second level, the problem of cross-cultural variation in conceptions and relative valuations of women, will entail a great deal of cross-cultural research and must be postponed to another time. As for the third level, it will be obvious from my approach that I would consider it a misguided endeavor to focus only upon women's actual though culturally unrecognized and unvalued powers in any given society, without first understanding the overarching ideology and deeper assumptions of the culture that render such powers trivial.

The Universality of Female Subordination

What do I mean when I say that everywhere, in every known culture, women are considered in some degree inferior to men? First of all, I must stress that I am talking about *cultural* evaluations; I am saying that each culture, in its own way and on its own terms, makes this evaluation. But what would constitute evidence that a particular culture considers women inferior?

Three types of data would suffice: (1) elements of cultural ideology and informants' statements that *explicitly* devalue women, according them, their roles, their tasks, their products, and their social milieux less prestige than are accorded men and the male correlates; (2) symbolic devices, such as the attribution of defilement, which may be interpreted as *implicitly* making a statement of inferior valuation; and (3) social-structural arrangements that exclude women from participation in or contact with some realm in which the highest powers of the society are felt to reside.[2] These three types of data may all of course be interrelated in any particular system, though they need not necessarily be. Further, any one of them will usually be sufficient to make the point of female inferiority in a given culture. Certainly, female exclusion from the most sacred rite or the highest political council is sufficient evidence. Certainly, explicit cultural ideology devaluing women (and their tasks, roles, products, etc.) is sufficient evidence. Symbolic indicators such as defilement are usually sufficient, although in a few cases in which, say, men and women are equally polluting to one another, a further indicator is required – and is, as far as my investigations have ascertained, always available.

On any or all of these counts, then, I would flatly assert that we find women subordinated to men in every known society. The search for a genuinely egalitarian, let alone matriarchal, culture has proved fruitless. An example from one society that has traditionally been on the credit side of this ledger will suffice. Among the matrilineal Crow, as Lowie (1956) points out, "Women . . . had highly honorific offices in the Sun Dance; they could become directors of the Tobacco Ceremony and played, if anything, a more conspicuous part in it than the men; they sometimes played the hostess in the Cooked Meat Festival; they were not debarred from sweating or doctoring or from seeking a vision" (p. 61). Nonetheless, "Women [during menstruation] formerly rode inferior horses and evidently this loomed as a source of contamination, for they were not allowed to approach either a wounded man or men starting on a war party. A taboo still lingers against their coming near sacred objects at these times" (p. 44). Further, just before enumerating women's rights of participation in the various rituals noted above, Lowie mentions one particular Sun Dance Doll bundle that was not supposed to be unwrapped by a woman (p. 60). Pursuing this trail we find: "According to all Lodge Grass informants and most others, the doll owned by Wrinkled-face took precedence not only of other dolls but of all other Crow medicines whatsoever. . . . This particular doll was not supposed to be handled by a woman" (p. 229).[3]

In sum, the Crow are probably a fairly typical case. Yes, women have certain powers and rights, in this case some that place them in fairly high positions. Yet ultimately the line is drawn: menstruation is a threat to warfare, one of the most valued institutions of the tribe, one that is central to their self-definition;

and the most sacred object of the tribe is taboo to the direct sight and touch of women.

Similar examples could be multiplied ad infinitum, but I think the onus is no longer upon us to demonstrate that female subordination is a cultural universal; it is up to those who would argue against the point to bring forth counterexamples. I shall take the universal secondary status of women as a given, and proceed from there.

Nature and Culture[4]

How are we to explain the universal devaluation of women? We could of course rest the case on biological determinism. There is something genetically inherent in the male of the species, so the biological determinists would argue, that makes them the naturally dominant sex; that "something" is lacking in females, and as a result women are not only naturally subordinate but in general quite satisfied with their position, since it affords them protection and the opportunity to maximize maternal pleasures, which to them are the most satisfying experiences of life. Without going into a detailed refutation of this position, I think it fair to say that it has failed to be established to the satisfaction of almost anyone in academic anthropology. This is to say, not that biological facts are irrelevant, or that men and women are not different, but that these facts and differences only take on significance of superior/inferior within the framework of culturally defined value systems.

If we are unwilling to rest the case on genetic determinism, it seems to me that we have only one way to proceed. We must attempt to interpret female subordination in light of other universals, factors built into the structure of the most generalized situation in which all human beings, in whatever culture, find themselves. For example, every human being has a physical body and a sense of nonphysical mind, is part of a society of other individuals and an inheritor of a cultural tradition, and must engage in some relationship, however mediated, with "nature," or the nonhuman realm, in order to survive. Every human being is born (to a mother) and ultimately dies, all are assumed to have an interest in personal survival, and society/culture has its own interest in (or at least momentum toward) continuity and survival, which transcends the lives and deaths of particular individuals. And so forth. It is in the realm of such universals of the human condition that we must seek an explanation for the universal fact of female devaluation.

I translate the problem, in other words, into the following simple question. What could there be in the generalized structure and conditions of existence, common to every culture, that would lead every culture to place a lower value upon women? Specifically, my thesis is that woman is being identified with – or, if you will, seems to be a symbol of – something that every culture devalues, something that every culture defines as being of a lower order of existence than itself. Now it seems that there is only one thing that would fit that description, and that is "nature" in the most generalized sense. Every culture, or, generically, "culture," is engaged in the process of generating and sustaining systems of meaningful forms (symbols, artifacts, etc.) by means of which humanity transcends the givens of natural existence, bends them to its purposes, controls them in its interest. We may thus broadly equate culture with the notion of human consciousness, or with the products of human consciousness (i.e., systems of thought and technology), by means of which humanity attempts to assert control over nature.

Now the categories of "nature" and "culture" are of course conceptual categories – one can find no boundary out in the actual world between the two states or realms of being. And there is no question that some cultures articulate a much stronger opposition between the two categories than others – it has even been argued that primitive peoples (some or all) do not see or intuit any distinction between the human cultural state and the state of nature at all. Yet I would maintain that the universality of ritual betokens an assertion in all human cultures of the specifically human ability to act upon and regulate, rather than passively move with and be moved by, the givens of natural existence. In ritual, the purposive manipulation of given forms toward

regulating and sustaining order, every culture asserts that proper relations between human existence and natural forces depend upon culture's employing its special powers to regulate the overall processes of the world and life.

One realm of cultural thought in which these points are often articulated is that of concepts of purity and pollution. Virtually every culture has some such beliefs, which seem in large part (though not, of course, entirely) to be concerned with the relationship between culture and nature (see Ortner 1973). A well-known aspect of purity/pollution beliefs cross-culturally is that of the natural "contagion" of pollution; left to its own devices, pollution (for these purposes grossly equated with the unregulated operation of natural energies) spreads and overpowers all that it comes in contact with. Thus a puzzle – if pollution is so strong, how can anything be purified? Why is the purifying agent not itself polluted? The answer, in keeping with the present line of argument, is that purification is effected in a ritual context; purification ritual, as a purposive activity that pits self-conscious (symbolic) action against natural energies, is more powerful than those energies.

In any case, my point is simply that every culture implicitly recognizes and asserts a distinction between the operation of nature and the operation of culture (human consciousness and its products); and further, that the distinctiveness of culture rests precisely on the fact that it can under most circumstances transcend natural conditions and turn them to its purposes. Thus culture (i.e., every culture) at some level of awareness asserts itself to be not only distinct from but superior to nature, and that sense of distinctiveness and superiority rests precisely on the ability to transform – to "socialize" and "culturalize" – nature.

Returning now to the issue of women, their pan-cultural second-class status could be accounted for, quite simply, by postulating that women are being identified or symbolically associated with nature, as opposed to men, who are identified with culture. Since it is always culture's project to subsume and transcend nature, if women were considered part of nature, then culture would find it "natural" to subordinate, not to say oppress, them. Yet although this argument can be shown to have considerable force, it seems to oversimplify the case. The formulation I would like to defend and elaborate on in the following section, then, is that women are seen "merely" as being *closer* to nature than men. That is, culture (still equated relatively unambiguously with men) recognizes that women are active participants in its special processes, but at the same time sees them as being more rooted in, or having more direct affinity with, nature.

The revision may seem minor or even trivial, but I think it is a more accurate rendering of cultural assumptions. Further, the argument cast in these terms has several analytic advantages over the simpler formulation; I shall discuss these later. It might simply be stressed here that the revised argument would still account for the pan-cultural devaluation of women, for even if women are not equated with nature, they are nonetheless seen as representing a lower order of being, as being less transcendental of nature than men are. The next task of the paper, then, is to consider why they might be viewed in that way.

Why is Woman Seen as Closer to Nature?

It all begins of course with the body and the natural procreative functions specific to women alone. We can sort out for discussion three levels at which this absolute physiological fact has significance: (1) woman's *body and its functions*, more involved more of the time with "species life," seem to place her closer to nature, in contrast to man's physiology, which frees him more completely to take up the projects of culture; (2) woman's body and its functions place her in *social roles* that in turn are considered to be at a lower order of the cultural process than man's; and (3) woman's traditional social roles, imposed because of her body and its functions, in turn give her a different *psychic structure*, which, like her physiological nature and her social roles, is seen as being closer to nature. I shall discuss each of these points in turn, showing first how in each instance certain factors

strongly tend to align woman with nature, then indicating other factors that demonstrate her full alignment with culture, the combined factors thus placing her in a problematic intermediate position. It will become clear in the course of the discussion why men seem by contrast less intermediate, more purely "cultural" than women. And I reiterate that I am dealing only at the level of cultural and human universals. These arguments are intended to apply to generalized humanity; they grow out of the human condition, as humanity has experienced and confronted it up to the present day.

Ⓘ *Woman's physiology seen as closer to nature.*

This part of my argument has been anticipated, with subtlety, cogency, and a great deal of hard data, by de Beauvoir (1953). De Beauvoir reviews the physiological structure, development, and functions of the human female and concludes that "the female, to a greater extent than the male, is the prey of the species" (p. 60). She points out that many major areas and processes of the woman's body serve no apparent function for the health and stability of the individual; on the contrary, as they perform their specific organic functions, they are often sources of discomfort, pain, and danger. The breasts are irrelevant to personal health; they may be excised at any time of a woman's life. "Many of the ovarian secretions function for the benefit of the egg, promoting its maturation and adapting the uterus to its requirements; in respect to the organism as a whole, they make for disequilibrium rather than for regulation – the woman is adapted to the needs of the egg rather than to her own requirements" (p. 24). Menstruation is often uncomfortable, sometimes painful; it frequently has negative emotional correlates and in any case involves bothersome tasks of cleansing and waste disposal; and – a point that de Beauvoir does not mention – in many cultures it interrupts a woman's routine, putting her in a stigmatized state involving various restrictions on her activities and social contacts. In pregnancy many of the woman's vitamin and mineral resources are channeled into nourishing the fetus, depleting her own strength and energies. And finally, childbirth itself is painful and dangerous (pp. 24–7 *passim*). In sum, de Beauvoir concludes that the female "is more enslaved to the species than the male, her animality is more manifest" (p. 239).

While de Beauvoir's book is ideological, her survey of woman's physiological situation seems fair and accurate. It is simply a fact that proportionately more of woman's body space, for a greater percentage of her lifetime, and at some – sometimes great – cost to her personal health, strength, and general stability, is taken up with the natural processes surrounding the reproduction of the species.

De Beauvoir goes on to discuss the negative implications of woman's "enslavement to the species" in relation to the projects in which humans engage, projects through which culture is generated and defined. She arrives thus at the crux of her argument (pp. 58–9):

Here we have the key to the whole mystery. On the biological level a species is maintained only by creating itself anew; but this creation results only in repeating the same Life in more individuals. But man assures the repetition of Life while transcending Life through Existence [i.e. goal-oriented, meaningful action]; by this transcendence he creates values that deprive pure repetition of all value. In the animal, the freedom and variety of male activities are vain because no project is involved. Except for his services to the species, what he does is immaterial. Whereas in serving the species, the human male also remodels the face of the earth, he creates new instruments, he invents, he shapes the future.

In other words, woman's body seems to doom her to mere reproduction of life; the male, in contrast, lacking natural creative functions, must (or has the opportunity to) assert his creativity externally, "artificially," through the medium of technology and symbols. In so doing, he creates relatively lasting, eternal, transcendent objects, while the woman creates only perishables – human beings.

This formulation opens up a number of important insights. It speaks, for example, to the great puzzle of why male activities involving the destruction of life (hunting and warfare) are often given more prestige than the female's ability to give birth, to create life. Within de Beauvoir's framework, we realize it is not the killing that is the relevant and valued aspect of hunting and warfare; rather, it is the transcendental (social, cultural) nature of these activities, as opposed to the naturalness of the process of birth: "For it is not in giving life but in risking life that man is raised above the animal; that is why superiority has been accorded in humanity not to the sex that brings forth but to that which kills" (ibid.).

Thus if male is, as I am suggesting, everywhere (unconsciously) associated with culture and female seems closer to nature, the rationale for these associations is not very difficult to grasp, merely from considering the implications of the physiological contrast between male and female. At the same time, however, woman cannot be consigned fully to the category of nature, for it is perfectly obvious that she is a full-fledged human being endowed with human consciousness just as a man is; she is half of the human race, without whose cooperation the whole enterprise would collapse. She may seem more in the possession of nature than man, but having consciousness, she thinks and speaks; she generates, communicates, and manipulates symbols, categories, and values. She participates in human dialogues not only with other women but also with men. As Lévi-Strauss says, "Woman could never become just a sign and nothing more, since even in a man's world she is still a person, and since insofar as she is defined as a sign she must [still] be recognized as a generator of signs" (1969a: 496).

Indeed, the fact of woman's full human consciousness, her full involvement in and commitment to culture's project of transcendence over nature, may ironically explain another of the great puzzles of "the woman problem" – woman's nearly universal unquestioning acceptance of her own devaluation. For it would seem that, as a conscious human and member of culture, she has followed out the logic of culture's arguments and has reached culture's conclusions along with the men. As de Beauvoir puts it (p. 59):

For she, too, is an existent, she feels the urge to surpass, and her project is not mere repetition but transcendence towards a different future – in her heart of hearts she finds confirmation of the masculine pretensions. She joins the men in the festivals that celebrate the successes and victories of the males. Her misfortune is to have been biologically destined for the repetition of Life, when even in her own view Life does not carry within itself its reasons for being, reasons that are more important than life itself.

In other words, woman's consciousness – her membership, as it were, in culture – is evidenced in part by the very fact that she accepts her own devaluation and takes culture's point of view.

I have tried here to show one part of the logic of that view, the part that grows directly from the physiological differences between men and women. Because of woman's greater bodily involvement with the natural functions surrounding reproduction, she is seen as more a part of nature than man is. Yet in part because of her consciousness and participation in human social dialogue, she is recognized as a participant in culture. Thus she appears as something intermediate between culture and nature, lower on the scale of transcendence than man.

2 Woman's social role seen as closer to nature.

Woman's physiological functions, I have just argued, may tend in themselves to motivate[5] a view of woman as closer to nature, a view she herself, as an observer of herself and the world, would tend to agree with. Woman creates naturally from within her own being, whereas man is free to, or forced to, create artificially, that is, through cultural means, and in such a way as to sustain culture. In addition, I now wish to show how woman's physiological functions have tended universally to limit her social movement, and to confine her universally to certain social contexts which *in turn* are seen as closer to nature. That is, not only her bodily processes but the social situation in which her bodily processes locate her may carry this significance. And insofar as she is permanently associated (in the eyes of culture)

with these social milieux, they add weight (perhaps the decisive part of the burden) to the view of woman as closer to nature. I refer here of course to woman's confinement to the domestic family context, a confinement motivated, no doubt, by her lactation processes.

Woman's body, like that of all female mammals, generates milk during and after pregnancy for the feeding of the newborn baby. The baby cannot survive without breast milk or some similar formula at this stage of life. Since the mother's body goes through its lactation processes in direct relation to a pregnancy with a particular child, the relationship of nursing between mother and child is seen as a natural bond, other feeding arrangements being seen in most cases as unnatural and make-shift. Mothers and their children, according to cultural reasoning, belong together. Further, children beyond infancy are not strong enough to engage in major work, yet are mobile and unruly and not capable of understanding various dangers; they thus require supervision and constant care. Mother is the obvious person for this task, as an extension of her natural nursing bond with the children, or because she has a new infant and is already involved with child-oriented activities. Her own activities are thus circumscribed by the limitations and low levels of her children's strengths and skills:[6] she is confined to the domestic family group; "woman's place is in the home."

Woman's association with the domestic circle would contribute to the view of her as closer to nature in several ways. In the first place, the sheer fact of constant association with children plays a role in the issue; one can easily see how infants and children might themselves be considered part of nature. Infants are barely human and utterly unsocialized; like animals they are unable to walk upright, they excrete without control, they do not speak. Even slightly older children are clearly not yet fully under the sway of culture. They do not yet understand social duties, responsibilities, and morals; their vocabulary and their range of learned skills are small. One finds implicit recognition of an association between children and nature in many cultural practices. For example, most cultures have initiation rites for adolescents (primarily for boys; I shall return to this point below), the point of which is to move the child ritually from a less than fully human state into full participation is society and culture; many cultures do not hold funeral rites for children who die at early ages, explicitly because they are not yet fully social beings. Thus children are likely to be categorized with nature, and woman's close association with children may compound her potential for being seen as closer to nature herself. It is ironic that the rationale for boys' initiation rites in many cultures is that the boys must be purged of the defilement accrued from being around mother and other women so much of the time, when in fact much of the woman's defilement may derive from her being around children so much of the time.

The second major problematic implication of women's close association with the domestic context derives from certain structural conflicts between the family and society at large in any social system. The implications of the "domestic/public opposition" in relation to the position of women have been cogently developed by Rosaldo (1974), and I simply wish to show its relevance to the present argument. The notion that the domestic unit – the biological family charged with reproducing and socializing new members of the society – is opposed to the public entity – the superimposed network of alliances and relationships that *is* the society – is also the basis of Lévi-Strauss's argument in the *Elementary Structures of Kinship* (1969a). Lévi-Strauss argues not only that this opposition is present in every social system, but further that it has the significance of the opposition between nature and culture. The universal incest prohibition[7] and its ally, the rule of exogamy (marriage outside the group), ensure that "the risk of seeing a biological family become established as a closed system is definitely eliminated; the biological group can no longer stand apart, and the bond of alliance with another family ensures the dominance of the social over the biological, and of the cultural over the natural" (p. 479). And although not every culture articulates a radical opposition between the domestic and the public as such, it is hardly contestable that the domestic is always sub-

sumed by the public; domestic units are allied with one another through the enactment of rules that are logically at a higher level than the units themselves; this creates an emergent unit – society – that is logically at a higher level than the domestic units of which it is composed.

Now, since women are associated with, and indeed are more or less confined to, the domestic context, they are identified with this lower order of social/cultural organization. What are the implications of this for the way they are viewed? First, if the specifically biological (reproductive) function of the family is stressed, as in Lévi-Strauss's formulation, then the family (and hence woman) is identified with nature pure and simple, as opposed to culture. But this is obviously too simple; the point seems more adequately formulated as follows: the family (and hence woman) represents lower-level, socially fragmenting, particularistic sort of concerns, as opposed to interfamilial relations representing higher-level, integrative, universalistic sorts of concerns. Since men lack a "natural" basis (nursing, generalized to child care) for a familial orientation, their sphere of activity is defined at the level of interfamilial relations. And hence, so the cultural reasoning seems to go, men are the "natural" proprietors of religion, ritual, politics, and other realms of cultural thought and action in which universalistic statements of spiritual and social synthesis are made. Thus men are identified not only with culture, in the sense of all human creativity, as opposed to nature; they are identified in particular with culture in the old-fashioned sense of the finer and higher aspects of human thought – art, religion, law, etc.

Here again, the logic of cultural reasoning aligning woman with a lower order of culture than man is clear and, on the surface, quite compelling. At the same time, woman cannot be fully consigned to nature, for there are aspects of her situation, even within the domestic context, that undeniably demonstrate her participation in the cultural process. It goes without saying, of course, that except for nursing newborn infants (and artificial nursing devices can cut even this biological tie), there is no reason why it has to be mother – as opposed to father, or anyone else – who remains identified with child care. But even assuming that other practical and emotional reasons conspire to keep woman in this sphere, it is possible to show that her activities in the domestic context could as logically put her squarely in the category of culture.

In the first place, one must point out that woman not only feeds and cleans up after children in a simple caretaker operation; she in fact is the primary agent of their early socialization. It is she who transforms newborn infants from mere organisms into cultured humans, teaching them manners and the proper ways to behave in order to become full-fledged members of the culture. On the basis of her socializing functions alone, she could not be more a representative of culture. Yet in virtually every society there is a point at which the socialization of boys is transferred to the hands of men. The boys are considered, in one set of terms or another, not yet "really" socialized; their entrée into the realm of fully human (social, cultural) status can be accomplished only by men. We still see this in our own schools, where there is a gradual inversion in the proportion of female to male teachers up through the grades: most kindergarten teachers are female; most university professors are male.[8]

Or again, take cooking. In the overwhelming majority of societies cooking is the woman's work. No doubt this stems from practical considerations – since the woman has to stay home with the baby, it is convenient for her to perform the chores centered in the home. But if it is true, as Lévi-Strauss has argued (1969b), that transforming the raw into the cooked may represent, in many systems of thought, the transition from nature to culture, then here we have woman aligned with this important culturalizing process, which could easily place her in the category of culture, triumphing over nature. Yet it is also interesting to note that when a culture (e.g. France or China) develops a tradition of *haute cuisine* – "real" cooking, as opposed to trivial ordinary domestic cooking – the high chefs are almost always men. Thus the pattern replicates that in the area of socialization – women perform lower-level conversions from nature to culture, but when the culture distinguishes a higher level of the same functions, the higher level is restricted to men.

In short, we see once again some sources of woman's appearing more intermediate than man with respect to the nature/culture dichotomy. Her "natural" association with the domestic context (motivated by her natural lactation functions) tends to compound her potential for being viewed as closer to nature, because of the animal-like nature of children, and because of the infrasocial connotation of the domestic group as against the rest of society. Yet at the same time her socializing and cooking functions within the domestic context show her to be a powerful agent of the cultural process, constantly transforming raw natural resources into cultural products. Belonging to culture, yet appearing to have stronger and more direct connections with nature, she is once again seen as situated between the two realms.

3 Woman's psyche seen as closer to nature.

The suggestion that woman has not only a different body and a different social locus from man but also a different psychic structure is most controversial. I will argue that she probably *does* have a different psychic structure, but I will draw on Chodorow's paper (1974) to establish first that her psychic structure need not be assumed to be innate; it can be accounted for, as Chodorow convincingly shows, by the facts of the probably universal female socialization experience. Nonetheless, if we grant the empirical near universality of a "feminine psyche" with certain specific characteristics, these characteristics would add weight to the cultural view of woman as closer to nature.

It is important to specify what we see as the dominant and universal aspects of the feminine psyche. If we postulate emotionality or irrationality, we are confronted with those traditions in various parts of the world in which women functionally are, and are seen as, more practical, pragmatic, and this-worldly than men. One relevant dimension that does seem pan-culturally applicable is that of relative concreteness vs. relative abstractness: the feminine personality tends to be involved with concrete feelings, things, and people, rather than with abstract entities; it tends toward personalism and particularism. A second, closely related, dimension seems to be that of relative subjectivity vs. relative objectivity: Chodorow cites Carlson's study (1971: 270), which concludes that "males represent experiences of self, others, space, and time in individualistic, objective, and distant ways, while females represent experiences in relatively interpersonal, subjective, immediate ways" (Chodorow 1974: 56). Although this and other studies were done in Western societies, Chodorow sees their findings on the differences between male and female personality – roughly, that men are more objective and inclined to relate in terms of relatively abstract categories, women more subjective and inclined to relate in terms of relatively concrete phenomena – as "general and nearly universal differences" (p. 43).

But the thrust of Chodorow's elegantly argued paper is that these differences are not innate or genetically programmed; they arise from nearly universal features of family structure, namely that "women, universally, are largely responsible for early child care and for (at least) later female socialization" (p. 43) and that "the structural situation of child rearing, reinforced by female and male role training, produces these differences, which are replicated and reproduced in the sexual sociology of adult life" (p. 44). Chodorow argues that, because mother is the early socializer of both boys and girls, both develop "personal identification" with her, i.e. diffuse identification with her general personality, behavior traits, values, and attitudes (p. 51). A son, however, must ultimately shift to a masculine role identity, which involves building an identification with the father. Since father is almost always more remote than mother (he is rarely involved in child care, and perhaps works away from home much of the day), building an identification with father involves a "positional identification," i.e. identification with father's male role as a collection of abstract elements, rather than a personal identification with father as a real individual (p. 49). Further, as the boy enters the larger social world, he finds it in

fact organized around more abstract and universalistic criteria (see Rosaldo 1974: 28–9; Chodorow 1974: p. 58), as I have indicated in the previous section; thus his earlier socialization prepares him for, and is reinforced by, the type of adult social experience he will have.

For a young girl, in contrast, the personal identification with mother, which was created in early infancy, can persist into the process of learning female role identity. Because mother is immediate and present when the daughter is learning role identity, learning to be a woman involves the continuity and development of a girl's relationship to her mother, and sustains the identification with her as an individual; it does not involve the learning of externally defined role characteristics (Chodorow, 1974: 51). This pattern prepares the girl for, and is fully reinforced by, her social situation in later life; she will become involved in the world of women, which is characterized by few formal role differences (Rosaldo 1974: 29), and which involves again, in motherhood, "personal identification" with *her* children. And so the cycle begins anew.

Chodorow demonstrates to my satisfaction at least that the feminine personality, characterized by personalism and particularism, can be explained as having been generated by social-structural arrangements rather than by innate biological factors. The point need not be belabored further. But insofar as the "feminine personality" has been a nearly universal fact, it can be argued that its characteristics may have contributed further to the view of women as being somehow less cultural than men. That is, women would tend to enter into relationships with the world that culture might see as being more "like nature" – immanent and embedded in things as given – than "like culture" – transcending and transforming things through the superimposition of abstract categories and transpersonal values. Woman's relationships tend to be, like nature, relatively unmediated, more direct, whereas man not only tends to relate in a more mediated way, but in fact ultimately often relates more consistently and strongly to the mediating categories and forms than to the persons or objects themselves.

It is thus not difficult to see how the feminine personality would lend weight to a view of women as being "closer to nature." Yet at the same time, the modes of relating characteristics of women undeniably play a powerful and important role in the cultural process. For just as relatively unmediated relating is in some sense at the lower end of the spectrum of human spiritual functions, embedded and particularizing rather than transcending and synthesizing, yet that mode of relating also stands at the upper end of that spectrum. Consider the mother-child relationship. Mothers tend to be committed to their children as individuals, regardless of sex, age, beauty, clan affiliation, or other categories in which the child might participate. Now any relationship with this quality – not just mother and child but any sort of highly personal, relatively unmediated commitment – may be seen as a challenge to culture and society "from below," insofar as it represents the fragmentary potential of individual loyalties vis-à-vis the solidarity of the group. But it may also be seen as embodying the synthesizing agent for culture and society "from above," in that it represents generalized human values above and beyond loyalties to particular social categories. Every society must have social categories that transcend personal loyalties, but every society must also generate a sense of ultimate moral unity for all its members above and beyond those social categories. Thus that psychic mode seemingly typical of women, which tends to disregard categories and to seek "communion" (Chodorow 1974: 55, following Bakan, 1966) directly and personally with others, although it may appear infracultural from one point of view, is at the same time associated with the highest levels of the cultural process.

The Implications of Intermediacy

My primary purpose in this paper has been to attempt to explain the universal secondary status of women. Intellectually and personally, I felt strongly challenged by this problem; I felt compelled to deal with it before undertaking an analysis of woman's position in any particular society. Local variables of economy, ecology, history, political and social structure, values, and world view – these could explain

variations within this universal, but they could not explain the universal itself. And if we were not to accept the ideology of biological determinism, then explanation, it seemed to me, could only proceed by reference to other universals of the human cultural situation. Thus the general outlines of the approach – although not of course the particular solution offered – were determined by the problem itself, and not by any predilection on my part for global abstract structural analysis.

I argued that the universal devaluation of women could be explained by postulating that women are seen as closer to nature than men, men being seen as more unequivocally occupying the high ground of culture. The culture/nature distinction is itself a product of culture, culture being minimally defined as the transcendence, by means of systems of thought and technology, of the natural givens of existence. This of course is an analytic definition, but I argued that at some level every culture incorporates this notion in one form or other, if only through the performance of ritual as an assertion of the human ability to manipulate those givens. In any case, the core of the paper was concerned with showing why women might tend to be assumed, over and over, in the most diverse sorts of world views and in cultures of every degree of complexity, to be closer to nature than men. Woman's physiology, more involved more of the time with "species of life"; woman's association with the structurally subordinate domestic context, charged with the crucial function of transforming animal-like infants into cultured beings; "woman's psyche," appropriately molded to mothering functions by her own socialization and tending toward greater personalism and less mediated modes of relating – all these factors make woman appear to be rooted more directly and deeply in nature. At the same time, however, her "membership" and fully necessary participation in culture are recognized by culture and cannot be denied. Thus she is seen to occupy an intermediate position between culture and nature.

This intermediacy has several implications for analysis, depending upon how it is interpreted. First, of course, it answers my primary question of why woman is everywhere seen as lower than man, for even if she is not seen as nature pure and simple, she is still seen as achieving less transcendence of nature than man. Here intermediate simply means "middle status" on a hierarchy of being from culture to nature.

Second, intermediate may have the significance of "mediating," i.e. performing some sort of synthesizing or converting function between nature and culture, here seen (by culture) not as two ends of a continuum but as two radically different sorts of processes in the world. The domestic unit – and hence woman, who in virtually every case appears as its primary representative – is one of culture's crucial agencies for the conversion of nature into culture, especially with reference to the socialization of children. Any culture's continued viability depends upon properly socialized individuals who will see the world in that culture's terms and adhere more or less unquestioningly to its moral precepts. The functions of the domestic unit must be closely controlled in order to ensure this outcome; the stability of the domestic unit as an institution must be placed as far as possible beyond question. (We see some aspects of the protection of the integrity and stability of the domestic group in the powerful taboos against incest, matricide, patricide, and fratricide.[9]) Insofar as woman is universally the primary agent of early socialization and is seen as virtually the embodiment of the functions of the domestic group, she will tend to come under the heavier restrictions and circumscriptions surrounding that unit. Her (culturally defined) intermediate position between nature and culture, here having the significance of her *mediation* (i.e. performing conversion functions) between nature and culture, would thus account not only for her lower status but for the greater restrictions placed upon her activities. In virtually every culture her permissible sexual activities are more closely circumscribed than man's, she is offered a much smaller range of role choices, and she is afforded direct access to a far more limited range of its social institutions. Further, she is almost universally socialized to have a narrower and generally more conservative set of attitudes and views than man, and the limited social contexts of her adult life reinforce

this situation. This socially engendered conservatism and traditionalism of woman's thinking is another – perhaps the worst, certainly the most insidious – mode of social restriction, and would clearly be related to her traditional function of producing well-socialized members of the group.

Finally, woman's intermediate position may have the implication of greater symbolic ambiguity (see also Rosaldo, 1974). Shifting our image of the culture/nature relationship once again, we may envision culture in this case as a small clearing within the forest of the larger natural system. From this point of view, that which is intermediate between culture and nature is located on the continuous periphery of culture's clearing; and though it may thus appear to stand both above and below (and beside) culture, it is simply outside and around it. We can begin to understand then how a single system of cultural thought can often assign to woman completely polarized and apparently contradictory meanings, since extremes, as we say, meet. That she often represents both life and death is only the simplest example one could mention.

For another perspective on the same point, it will be recalled that the psychic mode associated with women seems to stand at both the bottom and the top of the scale of human modes of relating. The tendency in that mode is to get involved more directly with people as individuals and not as representatives of one social category or another; this mode can be seen as either "ignoring" (and thus subverting) or "transcending" (and thus achieving a higher synthesis of) those social categories, depending upon the cultural view for any given purpose. Thus we can account easily for both the subversive feminine symbols (witches, evil eye, menstrual pollution, castrating mothers) and the feminine symbols of transcendence (mother goddesses, merciful dispensers of salvation, female symbols of justice, and the strong presence of feminine symbolism in the realms of art, religion, ritual, and law). Feminine symbolism, far more often than masculine symbolism, manifests this propensity toward polarized ambiguity – sometimes utterly exalted, sometimes utterly debased, rarely within the normal range of human possibilities.

If woman's (culturally viewed) intermediacy between culture and nature has this implication of generalized ambiguity of meaning characteristic of marginal phenomena, then we are also in a better position to account for those cultural and historical "inversions" in which women are in some way or other symbolically aligned with culture and men with nature. A number of cases come to mind: the Sirionó of Brazil, among whom, according to Ingham (1971: 1098), "nature, the raw, and maleness" are opposed to "culture, the cooked, and femaleness";[10] Nazi Germany, in which women were said to be the guardians of culture and morals; European courtly love, in which man considered himself the beast and woman the pristine exalted object – a pattern of thinking that persists, for example, among modern Spanish peasants (see Pitt-Rivers, 1961; Rosaldo 1974). And there are no doubt other cases of this sort, including some aspects of our own culture's view of women. Each such instance of an alignment of women with culture rather than nature requires detailed analysis of specific historical and ethnographic data. But in indicating how nature in general, and the feminine mode of interpersonal relations in particular, can appear from certain points of view to stand both under and over (but really simply outside of) the sphere of culture's hegemony, we have at least laid the groundwork for such analyses.

In short, the postulate that woman is viewed as closer to nature than man has several implications for further analysis, and can be interpreted in several different ways. If it is viewed simply as a *middle* position on a scale from culture down to nature, then it is still seen as lower than culture and thus accounts for the pan-cultural assumption that woman is lower than man in the order of things. If it is read as a *mediating* element in the culture-nature relationship, then it may account in part for the cultural tendency not merely to devalue woman but to circumscribe and restrict her functions, since culture must maintain control over its (pragmatic and symbolic) mechanisms for the conversion of nature into culture. And if it is read as an *ambiguous* status between culture and nature, it may help account for the fact that, in specific cultural ideologies and symbolizations, woman can occasionally be aligned with culture, and in any event is often assigned polarized and contradictory meanings within a single symbolic system. Middle status, mediating functions, ambiguous meaning – all are different readings, for different contextual purposes, of woman's being seen as intermediate between nature and culture.

Conclusions

Ultimately, it must be stressed again that the whole scheme is a construct of culture rather than a fact of nature. Woman is not "in reality" any closer to (or further from) nature than man – both have consciousness, both are mortal. But there are certainly reasons why she appears that way, which is what I have tried to show in this paper. The result is a (sadly) efficient feedback system: various aspects of woman's situation (physical, social, psychological) contribute to her being seen as closer to nature, while the view of her as closer to nature is in turn embodied in institutional forms that reproduce her situation. The implications for social change are similarly circular: a different cultural view can only grow out of a different social actuality; a different social actuality can only grow out of a different cultural view.

It is clear, then, that the situation must be attacked from both sides. Efforts directed solely at changing the social institutions – through setting quotas on hiring, for example, or through passing equal-pay-for-equal-work laws – cannot have for-reaching effects if cultural language and imagery continue to purvey a relatively devalued view of women. But at the same time efforts directed solely at changing cultural assumptions – through male and female consciousness-raising groups, for example, or through revision of educational materials and mass-media imagery – cannot be successful unless the institutional base of the society is changed to support and reinforce the changed cultural view. Ultimately, both men and women can and must be equally involved in projects of creativity and transcendence. Only then will women be seen as aligned with culture, in culture's ongoing dialectic with nature.

NOTES

The first version of this paper was presented in October 1972 as a lecture in the course "Women: Myth and Reality" at Sarah Lawrence College. I received helpful comments from the students and from my co-teachers in the course and the present version of the paper, in which the thrust of the argument has been rather significantly changed, was written in response to those comments. The paper is dedicated to Simone de Beauvoir, whose book *The Second Sex* (1953), first published in French in 1949, remains in my opinion the best single comprehensive understanding of "the woman problem."

1 It is true of course that *yin*, the female principle, has a negative valence. Nonetheless, there is an absolute complementarity of *yin* and *yang* in Taoism, a recognition that the world requires the equal operation and interaction of both principles for its survival.

2 Some anthropologists might consider this type of evidence (social-structural arrangements that exclude women, explicitly or de facto, from certain groups, roles, or statuses) to be a subtype of the second type of evidence (symbolic formulations of inferiority). I would not disagree with this view, although most social anthropologists would probably separate the two types.

3 While we are on the subject of injustices of various kinds, we might note that Lowie secretly bought this doll, the most sacred object in the tribal repertoire, from its custodian, the widow of Wrinkled-face. She asked $400 for it, but this price was "far beyond [Lowie's] means," and he finally got it for $80 (p. 300).

4 With all due respect to Lévi-Strauss (1969a, b, and *passim*).

5 Semantic theory uses the concept of motivation of meaning, which encompasses various ways in which a meaning may be assigned to a symbol because of certain objective properties of that symbol, rather than by arbitrary association. In a sense, this entire paper is an inquiry into the motivation of the meaning of woman as a symbol, asking why woman may be unconsciously assigned the significance of being closer to nature. For a concise statement on the various types of motivation of meaning, see Ullman (1963).

6 A situation that often serves to make her more childlike herself.

7 David M. Schneider (personal communication) is prepared to argue that the incest taboo is not universal, on the basis of material from Oceania. Let us say at this point, then, that it is virtually universal.

8 I remember having my first male teacher in the fifth grade, and I remember being excited about that – it was somehow more grown-up.

9 Nobody seems to care much about sororicide – a point that ought to be investigated.

10 Ingham's discussion is rather ambiguous itself, since women are also associated with animals: "The contrasts man/animal and man/woman are evidently similar... hunting is the means of acquiring women as well as animals" (p. 1095). A careful reading of the data suggests that both women and animals are mediators between nature and culture in this tradition.

REFERENCES

Bakan, David. 1966. *The Duality of Human Existence*. Boston.

Carlson, Rae. 1971. Sex Differences in Ego Functioning: Exploratory Studies of Agency and Communion. *Journal of Consulting and Clinical Psychology*, 37: 267–77.

Chodorow, Nancy. 1974. Family Structure and Feminine Personality. In *Woman, Culture, and Society*. M. Z. Rosaldo and L. Lamphere, eds. pp. 43–66. Stanford, Calif.

De Beauvoir, Simone. 1953. *The Second Sex*. New York. Originally published in French in 1949.

Ingham, John M. 1971. Are the Sirionó Raw or Cooked? *American Anthropologist*, 73: 1092–9.

Lévi-Strauss, Claude. 1969a. *The Elementary Structures of Kinship*. Trans. J. H. Bell and J. R. von Sturmer; ed. R. Needham. Boston.
—— 1969b. *The Raw and the Cooked*. Trans. J. and D. Weightman. New York.

Lowie, Robert. 1956. *The Crow Indians.* New York. Originally published in 1935.

Ortner, Sherry B. 1973. Sherpa Purity, *American Anthropologist,* 75: 49–63.

Pitt-Rivers, Julian. 1961. *People of the Sierra.* Chicago.

Rosaldo, Michelle. 1974. Woman, Culture, and Society: A Theoretical Overview. In *Woman, Culture, and Society.* M. Z. Rosaldo and L. Lamphere, eds. Stanford, Calif.

Siu, R. G. H. 1968. *The Man of Many Qualities.* Cambridge, Mass.

Ullman, Stephen. 1963. Semantic Universals, in Joseph H. Greenberg, ed., *Universals of Language.* Cambridge, Mass.

4

The Traffic in Women: Notes on the "Political Economy" of Sex

Gayle Rubin

The literature on women – both feminist and anti-feminist – is a long rumination on the question of the nature and genesis of women's oppression and social subordination. The question is not a trivial one, since the answers given it determine our visions of the future, and our evaluation of whether or not it is realistic to hope for a sexually egalitarian society. More importantly, the analysis of the causes of women's oppression forms the basis for any assessment of just what would have to be changed in order to achieve a society without gender hierarchy. Thus, if innate male aggression and dominance are at the root of female oppression, then the feminist program would logically require either the extermination of the offending sex, or else a eugenics project to modify its character. If sexism is a by-product of capitalism's relentless appetite for profit, then sexism would wither away in the advent of a successful socialist revolution. If the world historical defeat of women occurred at the hands of an armed patriarchal revolt, then it is time for Amazon guerrillas to start training in the Adirondacks.

It lies outside the scope of this paper to conduct a sustained critique of some of the currently popular explanations of the genesis of sexual inequality – theories such as the popular evolution exemplified by *The Imperial Animal*, the alleged overthrow of prehistoric matriarchies, or the attempt to extract all of the phenomena of social subordination from the first volume of *Capital*. Instead, I want to sketch some elements of an alternate explanation of the problem.

Marx once asked: "What is a Negro slave? A man of the black race. The one explanation is as good as the other. A Negro is a Negro. He only becomes a slave in certain relations. A cotton spinning jenny is a machine for spinning cotton. It becomes *capital* only in certain relations. Torn from these relationships it is no more capital than gold in itself is money or sugar is the price of sugar" (Marx 1971: 28). One might paraphrase: What is a domesticated woman? A female of the species. The one explanation is as good as the other. A woman is a woman. She only becomes a domestic, a wife, a chattel, a playboy bunny, a prostitute, or a human dictaphone in certain relations. Torn from these relationships, she is no more the helpmate of man than gold in itself is money... etc. What then are these relationships

From Gayle Rubin, "The Traffic in Women: Notes on the 'Political Economy' of Sex," pp. 157–210 in Rayna R. Reiter, *Toward an Anthropology of Women*. New York: Monthly Review Press, 1975. © Gayle Rubin. Reprinted with kind permission of the author.

by which a female becomes an oppressed woman? The place to begin to unravel the system of relationships by which women become the prey of men is in the overlapping works of Claude Lévi-Strauss and Sigmund Freud. The domestication of women, under other names, is discussed at length in both of their *oeuvres*. In reading through these works, one begins to have a sense of a systematic social apparatus which takes up females as raw materials and fashions domesticated women as products. Neither Freud nor Lévi-Strauss sees his work in this light, and certainly neither turns a critical glance upon the processes he describes. Their analyses and descriptions must be read, therefore, in something like the way in which Marx read the classical political economists who preceded him (on this, see Althusser and Balibar 1970: 11–69). Freud and Lévi-Strauss are in some sense analogous to Ricardo and Smith: They see neither the implications of what they are saying, nor the implicit critique which their work can generate when subjected to a feminist eye. Nevertheless, they provide conceptual tools with which one can build descriptions of the part of social life which is the locus of the oppression of women, of sexual minorities, and of certain aspects of human personality within individuals. I call that part of social life the "sex/gender system," for lack of a more elegant term. As a preliminary definition, a "sex/gender system" is the set of arrangements by which a society transforms biological sexuality into products of human activity, and in which these transformed sexual needs are satisfied.

The purpose of this essay is to arrive at a more fully developed definition of the sex/gender system, by way of a somewhat idiosyncratic and exegetical reading of Lévi-Strauss and Freud. I use the word "exegetical" deliberately. The dictionary defines "exegesis" as a "critical explanation or analysis; especially, interpretation of the Scriptures." At times, my reading of Lévi-Strauss and Freud is freely interpretive, moving from the explicit content of a text to its presuppositions and implications. My reading of certain psychoanalytic texts is filtered through a lens provided by Jacques Lacan, whose own interpretation of the Freudian scripture has been heavily influenced by Lévi-Strauss.[1]

I will return later to a refinement of the definition of a sex/gender system. First, however, I will try to demonstrate the need for such a concept by discussing the failure of classical Marxism to fully express or conceptualize sex oppression. This failure results from the fact that Marxism, as a theory of social life, is relatively unconcerned with sex. In Marx's map of the social world, human beings are workers, peasants, or capitalists; that they are also men and women is not seen as very significant. By contrast, in the maps of social reality drawn by Freud and Lévi-Strauss, there is a deep recognition of the place of sexuality in society, and of the profound differences between the social experience of men and women.

Marx

There is no theory which accounts for the oppression of women – in its endless variety and monotonous similarity, cross-culturally and throughout history – with anything like the explanatory power of the Marxist theory of class oppression. Therefore, it is not surprising that there have been numerous attempts to apply Marxist analysis to the question of women. There are many ways of doing this. It has been argued that women are a reserve labor force for capitalism, that women's generally lower wages provide extra surplus to a capitalist employer, that women serve the ends of capitalist consumerism in their roles as administrators of family consumption, and so forth.

[...]

Briefly; Marx argued that capitalism is distinguished from all other modes of production by its unique aim: the creation and expansion of capital. [...] Capitalism is a set of social relations – forms of property, and so forth – in which production takes the form of turning money, things, and people into capital. And capital is a quantity of goods or money which, when exchanged for labor, reproduces and augments itself by extracting unpaid labor, or surplus value, from labor and into itself. [...] The exchange between capital and labor which produces surplus value, and hence capital, is highly specific. The worker gets a wage; the capitalist gets the things the worker has made during his or her time of employment. If the total value of the things the worker has made exceeds the value of his or her wage, the aim of capitalism has been achieved. The capitalist gets back the cost of the wage, plus an increment – surplus value. This can occur because the wage is determined not by the value of what the laborer makes, but by the value of what it takes to keep him or her going – to reproduce him or her from day to day, and to reproduce the entire work force from one generation to the next. Thus, surplus value is the difference between what the laboring class produces as a whole, and the amount of that total which is recycled into maintaining the laboring class. [. . .]

The amount of the difference between the reproduction of labor power and its products depends, therefore, on the determination of what it takes to reproduce that labor power. Marx tends to make that determination on the basis of the quantity of commodities – food, clothing, housing, fuel – which would be necessary to maintain the health, life, and strength of a worker. But these commodities must be consumed before they can be sustenance, and they are not immediately in consumable form when they are purchased by the wage. Additional labor must be performed upon these things before they can be turned into people. Food must be cooked, clothes cleaned, beds made, wood chopped, etc. Housework is therefore a key element in the process of the reproduction of the laborer from whom surplus value is taken. Since it is usually women who do housework, it has been observed that it is through the reproduction of labor power that women are articulated into the surplus value nexus which is the *sine qua non* of capitalism.[2] It can be further argued that since no wage is paid for housework, the labor of women in the home contributes to the ultimate quantity of surplus value realized by the capitalist. But to explain women's usefulness to capitalism is one thing. To argue that this usefulness explains the genesis of the oppression of women is quite another. It is precisely at this point that the analysis of capitalism ceases to explain very much about women and the oppression of women.

Women are oppressed in societies which can by no stretch of the imagination be described as capitalist. In the Amazon valley and the New Guinea highlands, women are frequently kept in their place by gang rape when the ordinary mechanisms of masculine intimidation prove insufficient. "We tame our women with the banana," said one Mundurucu man (Murphy 1959: 195). The ethnographic record is littered with practices whose effect is to keep women "in their place" – men's cults, secret initiations, arcane male knowledge, etc. And pre-capitalist, feudal Europe was hardly a society in which there was no sexism. Capitalism has taken over, and rewired, notions of male and female which predate it by centuries. No analysis of the reproduction of labor power under capitalism can explain foot-binding, chastity belts, or any of the incredible array of Byzantine, fetishized indignities, let alone the more ordinary ones, which have been inflicted upon women in various times and places. The analysis of the reproduction of labor power does not even explain why it is usually women who do domestic work in the home, rather than men.

[. . .]

Engels

In *The Origin of the Family, Private Property, and the State*, Engels sees sex oppression as part of capitalism's heritage from prior social forms. Moreover, Engels integrates sex and sexuality into his theory of society. [. . .] The idea that the "relations of sexuality" can and should be distinguished from the "relations of production" is not the least of Engels' intuitions:

According to the materialistic conception, the determining factor in history is, in the final instance, the production and reproduction of immediate life. *This again, is of a twofold character: on the one hand, the production of the means of existence, of food, clothing, and shelter and the tools necessary for that production; on the other side, the production of human beings themselves*, the propagation of the species. The social organization under which the people of a particular historical epoch and a particular country live is determined by both kinds of production: by the stage of development of labor on the one hand, and of the family on the other... (Engels 1972: 71–2; my italics)

This passage indicates an important recognition – that a human group must do more than apply its activity to reshaping the natural world in order to clothe, feed, and warm itself. We usually call the system by which elements of the natural world are transformed into objects of human consumption the "economy." But the needs which are satisfied by economic activity even in the richest, Marxian sense, do not exhaust fundamental human requirements. A human group must also reproduce itself from generation to generation. The needs of sexuality and procreation must be satisfied as much as the need to eat, and one of the most obvious deductions which can be made from the data of anthropology is that these needs are hardly ever satisfied in any "natural" form, any more than are the needs for food. Hunger is hunger, but what counts as food is culturally determined and obtained. Every society has some form of organized economic activity. Sex is sex, but what counts as sex is equally culturally determined and obtained. Every society also has a sex/gender system – a set of arrangements by which the biological raw material of human sex and procreation is shaped by human, social intervention and satisfied in a conventional manner, no matter how bizarre some of the conventions may be.[3]

The realm of human sex, gender, and procreation has been subjected to, and changed by, relentless social activity for millennia. Sex as we know it – gender identity, sexual desire and fantasy, concepts of childhood – is itself a social product. [...] In most Marxist tradition, and even in Engels' book, the concept of the "second aspect of material life" has tended to fade into the background, or to be incorporated into the usual notions of "material life." Engels' suggestion has never been followed up and subjected to the refinement which it needs. But he does indicate the existence and importance of the domain of social life which I want to call the sex/gender system.

Other names have been proposed for the sex/gender system. The most common alternatives are "mode of reproduction" and "patriarchy." It may be foolish to quibble about terms, but both of these can lead to confusion. All three proposals have been made in order to introduce a distinction between "economic" systems and "sexual" systems, and to indicate that sexual systems have a certain autonomy and cannot always be explained in terms of economic forces. "Mode of reproduction," for instance, has been proposed in opposition to the more familiar "mode of production." But this terminology links the "economy" to production, and the sexual system to "reproduction." It reduces the richness of either system, since "productions" and "reproductions" take place in both. Every mode of production involves reproduction – of tools, labor, and social relations. We cannot relegate all of the multi-faceted aspects of social reproduction to the sex system. Replacement of machinery is an example of reproduction in the economy. On the other hand, we cannot limit the sex system to "reproduction" in either the social or biological sense of the term. A sex/gender system is not simply the reproductive moment of a "mode of production." The formation of gender identity is an example of production in the realm of the sexual system. And a sex/gender system involves more than the "relations of procreation," reproduction in the biological sense.

The term "patriarchy" was introduced to distinguish the forces maintaining sexism from other social forces, such as capitalism. But the use of "patriarchy" obscures other distinctions. Its use is analogous to using capitalism to refer to all modes of production, whereas the usefulness of the term "capitalism" lies precisely in that it distinguishes between the different systems by which societies are provisioned and organized. [...] The power of the term lies in its implication that, in fact, there are alternatives to capitalism.

Similarly, any society will have some systematic ways to deal with sex, gender, and babies. Such a system may be sexually egalitarian, at least in theory, or it may be "gender stratified," as seems to be the case for most or all of the known examples. But it is important – even in the face of a depressing history – to maintain a distinction between the human capacity and necessity to create a sexual world, and the empirically oppressive ways in which sexual worlds have been organized. Patriarchy subsumes both meanings into the same term. Sex/gender system, on the other hand, is a neutral term which refers to the domain and indicates that oppression is not inevitable in that domain, but is the product of the specific social relations which organize it.

Finally, there are gender-stratified systems which are not adequately described as patriarchal. Many New Guinea societies (Enga, Maring, Bena Bena, Huli, Melpa, Kuma, Gahuku-Gama, Fore, Marind Anim, ad nauseum; see Berndt 1962; Langness 1967; Rappaport and Buchbinder 1976; Read 1952; Meggitt 1964; Glasse 1971; Strathern 1972; Reay 1959; Van Baal 1966; Lindenbaum 1973) are viciously oppressive to women. But the power of males in these groups is not founded on their roles as fathers or patriarchs, but on their collective adult maleness, embodied in secret cults, men's houses, warfare, exchange networks, ritual knowledge, and various initiation procedures. Patriarchy is a specific form of male dominance, and the use of the term ought to be confined to the Old Testament-type pastoral nomads from whom the term comes, or groups like them. [...]

Whichever term we use, what is important is to develop concepts to adequately describe the social organization of sexuality and the reproduction of the conventions of sex and gender. We need to pursue the project Engels abandoned when he located the subordination of women in a development within the mode of production.[4] To do this, we can imitate Engels in his method rather than in his results. Engels approached the task of analyzing the "second aspect of material life" by way of an examination of a theory of kinship systems. Kinship systems are and do many things. But they are made up of, and reproduce, concrete forms of socially organized sexuality. Kinship systems are observable and empirical forms of sex/gender systems.

Kinship (On the part played by sexuality in the transition from ape to "man")

To an anthropologist, a kinship system is not a list of biological relatives. It is a system of categories and statuses which often contradict actual genetic relationships. There are dozens of examples in which socially defined kinship statuses take precedence over biology. [...]

In pre-state societies, kinship is the idiom of social interaction, organizing economic, political, and ceremonial, as well as sexual, activity. One's duties, responsibilities, and privileges vis-à-vis others are defined in terms of mutual kinship or lack thereof. The exchange of goods and services, production and distribution, hostility and solidarity, ritual and ceremony, all take place within the organizational structure of kinship. The ubiquity and adaptive effectiveness of kinship has led many anthropologists to consider its invention, along with the invention of language, to have been the developments which decisively marked the discontinuity between semi-human hominids and human beings (Sahlins 1960; Livingstone 1969; Lévi-Strauss 1969).

While the idea of the importance of kinship enjoys the status of a first principle in anthropology, the internal workings of kinship systems have long been a focus for intense controversy. Kinship systems vary wildly from one culture to the next. They contain all sorts of bewildering rules which govern whom one may or may not marry. Their internal complexity is dazzling. Kinship systems have for decades provoked the anthropological imagination into trying to explain incest taboos, cross-cousin marriage, terms of descent, relationships of avoidance or forced intimacy, clans and sections, taboos on names – the diverse array of items found in descriptions of actual kinship systems. [...]

In taking up Engels' project of extracting a theory of sex oppression from the study of kinship, we have the advantage of the maturation of ethnology since the nineteenth century. We also have the advantage of a peculiar and particularly appropriate book, Lévi-Strauss's *The Elementary Structures of*

Kinship. [...] It is a book in which kinship is explicitly conceived of as an imposition of cultural organization upon the facts of biological procreation. It is permeated with an awareness of the importance of sexuality in human society. It is a description of society which does not assume an abstract, genderless human subject. On the contrary, the human subject in Lévi-Strauss's work is always either male or female, and the divergent social destinies of the two sexes can therefore be traced. Since Lévi-Strauss sees the essence of kinship systems to lie in an exchange of women between men, he constructs an implicit theory of sex oppression. [...]

"Vile and precious merchandise" – Monique Wittig

The Elementary Structures of Kinship is a grand statement on the origin and nature of human society. It is a treatise on the kinship systems of approximately one-third of the ethnographic globe. Most fundamentally, it is an attempt to discern the structural principles of kinship. Lévi-Strauss argues that the application of these principles (summarized in the last chapter of *Elementary Structures*) to kinship data reveals an intelligible logic to the taboos and marriage rules which have perplexed and mystified Western anthropologists. He constructs a chess game of such complexity that it cannot be recapitulated here. But two of his chess pieces are particularly relevant to women – the "gift" and the incest taboo, whose dual articulation adds up to his concept of the exchange of women.

The Elementary Structures is in part a radical gloss on another famous theory of primitive social organization, Mauss's essay on *The Gift* (see also Sahlins 1972: ch. 4). It was Mauss who first theorized as to the significance of one of the most striking features of primitive societies: the extent to which giving, receiving, and reciprocating gifts dominates social intercourse. In such societies, all sorts of things circulate in exchange – food, spells, rituals, words, names, ornaments, tools, and powers.

[...]

Although both Mauss and Lévi-Strauss emphasize the solidary aspects of gift exchange, the other purposes served by gift giving only strengthen the point that it is an ubiquitous means of social commerce. Mauss proposed that gifts were the threads of social discourse, the means by which such societies were held together in the absence of specialized governmental institutions. [...]

Lévi-Strauss adds to the theory of primitive reciprocity the idea that marriages are a most basic form of gift exchange, in which it is women who are the most precious of gifts. He argues that the incest taboo should best be understood as a mechanism to insure that such exchanges take place between families and between groups. Since the existence of incest taboos is universal, but the content of their prohibitions variable, they cannot be explained as having the aim of preventing the occurrence of genetically close matings. Rather, the incest taboo imposes the social aim of exogamy and alliance upon the biological events of sex and procreation. The incest taboo divides the universe of sexual choice into categories of permitted and prohibited sexual partners. Specifically, by forbidding unions within a group it enjoins marital exchange between groups. [...]

The result of a gift of women is more profound than the result of other gift transactions, because the relationship thus established is not just one of reciprocity, but one of kinship. The exchange partners have become affines, and their descendents will be related by blood. [...] As is the case with other gift giving, marriages are not always so simply activities to make peace. Marriages may be highly competitive, and there are plenty of affines who fight each other. Nevertheless, in a general sense the argument is that the taboo on incest results in a wide network of relations, a set of people whose connections with one another are a kinship structure. All other levels, amounts, and directions of exchange – including hostile ones – are ordered by this structure. The marriage ceremonies recorded in the ethnographic literature are moments in a ceaseless and ordered procession in which women, children, shells, words, cattle names, fish, ancestors, whale's teeth, pigs, yams, spells, dances, mats, etc., pass from hand to hand, leaving as their tracks the ties that bind. Kinship is organization, and organization gives power. But who is organized?

If it is women who are being transacted, then it is the men who give and take them who are linked, the woman being a conduit of a relationship rather than a partner to it. The exchange of women does not necessarily imply that women are objectified, in the modern sense, since objects in the primitive world are imbued with highly personal qualities. But it does imply a distinction between gift and giver. If women are the gifts, then it is men who are the exchange partners. And it is the partners, not the presents, upon whom reciprocal exchange confers its quasi-mystical power of social linkage. The relations of such a system are such that women are in no position to realize the benefits of their own circulation. As long as the relations specify that men exchange women, it is men who are the beneficiaries of the product of such exchanges – social organization.

[...]

The "exchange of women" is a seductive and powerful concept. It is attractive in that it places the oppression of women within social systems, rather than in biology. Moreover, it suggests that we look for the ultimate locus of women's oppression within the traffic in women, rather than within the traffic in merchandise. It is certainly not difficult to find ethnographic and historical examples of trafficking in women. Women are given in marriage, taken in battle, exchanged for favors, sent as tribute, traded, bought, and sold. Far from being confined to the "primitive" world, these practices seem only to become more pronounced and commercialized in more "civilized" societies. Men are of course also trafficked – but as slaves, hustlers, athletic stars, serfs, or as some other catastrophic social status, rather than as men. Women are transacted as slaves, serfs, and prostitutes, but also simply as women. And if men have been sexual subjects – exchangers – and women sexual semi-objects – gifts – for much of human history, then many customs, clichés, and personality traits seem to make a great deal of sense (among others, the curious custom by which a father gives away the bride).

The "exchange of women" is also a problematic concept. Since Lévi-Strauss argues that the incest taboo and the results of its application constitute the origin of culture, it can be deduced that the world historical defeat of women occurred with the origin of culture, and is a prerequisite of culture. If his analysis is adopted in its pure form, the feminist program must include a task even more onerous than the extermination of men; it must attempt to get rid of culture and substitute some entirely new phenomena on the face of the earth. However, it would be a dubious proposition at best to argue that if there were no exchange of women there would be no culture, if for no other reason than that culture is, by definition, inventive. It is even debatable that "exchange of women" adequately describes all of the empirical evidence of kinship systems. Some cultures, such as the Lele and the Luma, exchange women explicitly and overtly. In other cultures, the exchange of women can be inferred. In some – particularly those hunters and gatherers excluded from Lévi-Strauss's sample – the efficacy of the concept becomes altogether questionable. What are we to make of a concept which seems so useful and yet so difficult?

The "exchange of women" is neither a definition of culture nor a system in and of itself. The concept is an acute, but condensed, apprehension of certain aspects of the social relations of sex and gender. A kinship system is an imposition of social ends upon a part of the natural world. [...] It has its own relations of production, distribution, and exchange, which include certain "property" forms in people. These forms are not exclusive, private property rights, but rather different sorts of rights that various people have in other people. Marriage transactions – the gifts and material which circulate in the ceremonies marking a marriage – are a rich source of data for determining exactly who has which rights in whom. It is not difficult to deduce from such transactions that in most cases women's rights are considerably more residual than those of men.

Kinship systems do not merely exchange women. They exchange sexual access, genealogical statuses, lineage names and ancestors, rights and *people* – men, women, and children – in concrete systems of social relationships.

These relationships always include certain rights for men, others for women. "Exchange of women" is a shorthand for expressing that he social relations of a kinship system specify that men have certain rights in their female kin, and that women do not have the same rights either to themselves or to their male kin. In this sense, the exchange of women is a profound perception of a system in which women do not have full rights to themselves. [...]

If Lévi-Strauss is correct in seeing the exchange of women as a fundamental principle of kinship, the subordination of women can be seen as a product of the relationships by which sex and gender are organized and produced. The economic oppression of women is derivative and secondary. But there is an "economics" of sex and gender, and what we need is a political economy of sexual systems. We need to study each society to determine the exact mechanisms by which particular conventions of sexuality are produced and maintained. The "exchange of women" is an initial step toward building an arsenal of concepts with which sexual systems can be described.

Deeper into the Labyrinth

More concepts can be derived from an essay by Lévi-Strauss, "The Family," in which he introduces other considerations into his analysis of kinship (1971). In *The Elementary Structures of Kinship*, he describes rules and systems of sexual combination. In "The Family," he raises the issue of the preconditions necessary for marriage systems to operate. He asks what sort of "people" are required by kinship systems, by way of an analysis of the sexual division of labor.

Although every society has some sort of division of tasks by sex, the assignment of any particular task to one sex or the other varies enormously. In some groups, agriculture is the work of women, in others, the work of men. Women carry the heavy burdens in some societies, men in others. There are even examples of female hunters and warriors, and of men performing child-care tasks. Lévi-Strauss concludes from a survey of the division of labor by sex that it is not a biological specialization, but

must have some other purpose. This purpose, he argues, is to insure the union of men and women by making the smallest viable economic unit contain at least one man and one woman. [...] The division of labor by sex can therefore be seen as a "taboo": a taboo against the sameness of men and women, a taboo dividing the sexes into two mutually exclusive categories, a taboo which exacerbates the biological differences between the sexes and thereby *creates* gender. The division of labor can also be seen as a taboo against sexual arrangements other than those containing at least one man and one woman, thereby enjoining heterosexual marriage.

[...]

It is of interest to carry this kind of deductive enterprise even further than Lévi-Strauss does, and to explicate the logical structure which underlies his entire analysis of kinship. At the most general level, the social organization of sex rests upon gender, obligatory heterosexuality, and the constraint of female sexuality.

Gender is a socially imposed division of the sexes. It is a product of the social relations of sexuality. Kinship systems rest upon marriage. They therefore transform males and females into "men" and "women," each an incomplete half which can only find wholeness when united with the other. Men and women are, of course, different. But they are not as different as day and night, earth and sky, yin and yang, life and death. In fact, from the standpoint of nature, men and women are closer to each other than either is to anything else – for instance, mountains, kangaroos, or coconut palms. The idea that men and women are more different from one another than either is from anything else must come from somewhere other than nature. Furthermore, although there is an average difference between males and females on a variety of traits, the range of variation of those traits shows considerable overlap. There will always be some women who are taller than some men, for instance, even though men are on the average taller than women. But the idea that men and women are two mutually exclusive categories must arise out of something other than a non-existent "natural" opposition. Far from being an expression of natural differences, exclusive gender identity is the suppression of natural similarities. It requires repression: in men, of whatever is the local version of "feminine" traits; in women, of the local definition of "masculine" traits. [. . .]

Furthermore, individuals are engendered in order that marriage be guaranteed. Lévi-Strauss comes dangerously close to saying that heterosexuality is an instituted process. If biological and hormonal imperatives were as overwhelming as popular mythology would have them, it would hardly be necessary to insure heterosexual unions by means of economic interdependency. Moreover, the incest taboo presupposes a prior, less articulate taboo on homosexuality. A prohibition against *some* heterosexual unions assumes a taboo against *non-* heterosexual unions. Gender is not only an identification with one sex; it also entails that sexual desire be directed toward the other sex. The sexual division of labor is implicated in both aspects of gender – male and female it creates them, and it creates them heterosexual. The suppression of the homosexual component of human sexuality, and by corollary, the oppression of homosexuals, is therefore a product of the same system whose rules and relations oppress women.

In fact, the situation is not so simple, as is obvious when we move from the level of generalities to the analysis of specific sexual systems. Kinship systems do not merely encourage heterosexuality to the detriment of homosexuality. In the first place, specific forms of heterosexuality may be required. For instance, some marriage systems have a rule of obligatory cross-cousin marriage. A person in such a system is not only heterosexual, but "cross-cousin-sexual." If the rule of marriage further specifies matrilateral cross-cousin marriage, then a man will be "mother's-brother's-daughter-sexual" and a woman will be "father's-sister's-son-sexual."

On the other hand, the very complexities of a kinship system may result in particular forms of institutionalized homosexuality.

[. . .]

The rules of gender division and obligatory heterosexuality are present even in their transformations. These two rules apply equally to the constraint of both male and female behavior and personality. Kinship systems dictate some sculpting of the sexuality of both sexes. But it can be deduced from *The Elementary Structures of Kinship* that more constraint is applied to females when they are pressed into the service of kinship than to males. If women are exchanged, in whatever sense we take the term, marital debts are reckoned in female flesh. A woman must become the sexual partner of some man to whom she is owed as return on a previous marriage. [. . .] From the standpoint of the system, the preferred female sexuality would be one which responded to the desire of others, rather than one which actively desired and sought a response.

This generality, like the ones about gender and heterosexuality, is also subject to considerable variation and free play in actual systems. The Lele and the Kuma provide two of the clearest ethnographic examples of the exchange of women. Men in both cultures are perpetually engaged in schemes which necessitate that they have full control over the sexual destinies of their female kinswomen. Much of the drama in both societies consists in female attempts to evade the sexual control of their kinsmen. [. . .]

One last generality could be predicted as a consequence of the exchange of women under a system in which rights to women are held by men. What would happen if our hypothetical woman not only refused the man to whom she was promised, but asked for a woman instead? If a single refusal were disruptive, a double refusal would be insurrectionary. [. . .]

In summary, some basic generalities about the organization of human sexuality can be derived from an exegesis of Lévi-Strauss's theories of kinship. These are the incest taboo, obligatory heterosexuality, and an asymmetric division of the sexes. The asymmetry of gender – the difference between exchanger and exchanged – entails the constraint of female sexuality. Concrete kinship systems will have more specific conventions, and these conventions vary a great deal. While particular sociosexual systems vary, each one is specific, and individuals within it will have to conform to a finite set of possibilities. Each new generation must learn and become its sexual destiny, each person must be encoded with its appropriate status within the system. It would be extraordinary for one of us to calmly assume that we would conventionally marry a mother's brother's daughter, or a father's sister's son. Yet there are groups in which such a marital future is taken for granted.

Anthropology, and descriptions of kinship systems, do not explain the mechanisms by which children are engraved with the conventions of sex and gender. Psychoanalysis, on the other hand, is a theory about the reproduction of kinship. Psychoanalysis describes the residue left within individuals by their confrontation with the rules and regulations of sexuality of the societies to which they are born.

Psychoanalysis and its Discontents

The battle between psychoanalysis and the women's and gay movements has become legendary. In part, this confrontation between sexual revolutionaries and the clinical establishment has been due to the evolution of psychoanalysis in the United States, where clinical tradition has fetishized anatomy. The child is thought to travel through its organismic stages until it reaches its anatomical destiny and the missionary position. Clinical practice has often seen its mission as the repair of individuals who somehow have become derailed en route to their "biological" aim. Transforming moral law into scientific law, clinical practice has acted to enforce sexual convention upon unruly participants. In this sense, psychoanalysis has often become more than a theory of the mechanisms of the reproduction of sexual arrangements; it has been one of those mechanisms. Since the aim of the feminist and gay revolts is to dismantle the apparatus of sexual enforcement, a critique of psychoanalysis has been in order.

But the rejection of Freud by the women's and gay movements has deeper roots in the rejection by psychoanalysis of its own insights. Nowhere are the effects on women of male-dominated social systems better documented than within the clinical literature. [...] Psycho-analysis contains a unique set of concepts for understanding men, women, and sexuality. It is a theory of sexuality in human society.

Most importantly, psychoanalysis provides a description of the mechanisms by which the sexes are divided and deformed, of how bisexual, androgynous infants are transformed into boys and girls. Psychoanalysis is a feminist theory *manqué*.

The Oedipus Hex

Until the late 1920s, the psychoanalytic movement did not have a distinctive theory of feminine development. Instead, variants of an "Electra" complex in women had been proposed, in which female experience was thought to be a mirror image of the Oedipal complex described for males. The boy loved his mother, but gave her up out of fear of the father's threat of castration. The girl, it was thought, loved her father, and gave him up out of fear of maternal vengeance. This formulation assumed that both children were subject to a biological imperative toward heterosexuality. It also assumed that the children were already, before the Oedipal phase, "little" men and women.

Freud had voiced reservations about jumping to conclusions about women on the basis of data gathered from men. But his objections remained general until the discovery of the pre-Oedipal phase in women. [...] In the pre-Oedipal phase, children of both sexes were psychically indistinguishable, which meant that their differentiation into masculine and feminine children had to be explained, rather than assumed. Pre-Oedipal children were described as bisexual. Both sexes exhibited the full range of libidinal attitudes, active and passive. And for children of both sexes, the mother was the object of desire.

In particular, the characteristics of the pre-Oedipal female challenged the ideas of a primordial heterosexuality and gender identity. Since the girl's libidinal activity was directed toward the mother, her adult heterosexuality had to be explained:

> It would be a solution of ideal simplicity if we could suppose that from a particular age onwards the elementary influence of the mutual attraction between the sexes makes itself felt and impels the small woman towards men. . . .

But we are not going to find things so easy; we scarcely know whether we are to believe seriously in the power of which poets talk so much and with such enthusiasm but which cannot be further dissected analytically. (Freud 1965: 119)

Moreover, the girl did not manifest a "feminine" libidinal attitude. Since her desire for the mother was active and aggressive, her ultimate accession to "femininity" had also to be explained. [...] In short, feminine development could no longer be taken for granted as a reflex of biology. Rather, it had become immensely problematic. It is in explaining the acquisition of "femininity" that Freud employs the concepts of penis envy and castration which have infuriated feminists since he first introduced them. The girl turns from the mother and represses the "masculine" elements of her libido as a result of her recognition that she is castrated. She compares her tiny clitoris to the larger penis, and in the face of its evident superior ability to satisfy the mother, falls prey to penis envy and a sense of inferiority. She gives up her struggle for the mother and assumes a passive feminine position vis-à-vis the father. Freud's account can be read as claiming that femininity is a consequence of the anatomical differences between the sexes. He has therefore been accused of biological determinism. Nevertheless, even in his most anatomically stated versions of the female castration complex, the "inferiority" of the woman's genitals is a product of the situational context: the girl feels less "equipped" to possess and satisfy the mother. If the pre-Oedipal lesbian were not confronted by the heterosexuality of the mother, she might draw different conclusions about the relative status of her genitals.

Freud was never as much of a biological determinist as some would have him. He repeatedly stressed that all adult sexuality resulted from psychic, not biologic, development. But his writing is often ambiguous, and his wording leaves plenty of room for the biological interpretations which have been so popular in American psychoanalysis. In France, on the other hand, the trend in psychoanalytic theory has been to de-biologize Freud, and to conceive of psychoanalysis as a theory of information rather than organs. Jacques

Lacan, the instigator of this line of thinking, insists that Freud never meant to say anything about anatomy, and that Freud's theory was instead about language and the cultural meanings imposed upon anatomy. [...]

Kinship, Lacan, and the Phallus

Lacan suggests that psychoanalysis is the study of the traces left in the psyches of individuals as a result of their conscription into systems of kinship. [...] Kinship is the culturalization of biological sexuality on the societal level; psychoanalysis describes the transformation of the biological sexuality of individuals as they are enculturated.

Kinship terminology contains information about the system. Kin terms demarcate statuses, and indicate some of the attributes of those statuses. For instance, in the Trobriand Islands a man calls the women of his clan by the term for "sister." He calls the women of clans into which he can marry by a term indicating their marriageability. When the young Trobriand male learns these terms, he learns which women he can safely desire. In Lacan's scheme, the Oedipal crisis occurs when a child learns of the sexual rules embedded in the terms for family and relatives. [...]

The Oedipal complex is an apparatus for the production of sexual personality. It is a truism to say that societies will inculcate in their young the character traits appropriate to carrying on the business of society. For instance, E. P. Thompson (1963) speaks of the transformation of the personality structure of the English working class, as artisans were changed into good industrial workers. Just as the social forms of labor demand certain kinds of personality, the social forms of sex and gender demand certain kinds of people. In the most general terms, the Oedipal complex is a machine which fashions the appropriate forms of sexual individuals (see also the discussion of different forms of "historical individuality" in Althusser and Balibar 1970: 112, 251–3).

[...]

The differentiation between phallus and penis in contemporary French psychoanalytic terminology emphasizes the idea that the penis could not and does not play the role attributed to it in the classical terminology of the castration complex.

In Freud's terminology, the Oedipal complex presents two alternatives to a child: to have a penis or to be castrated. In contrast, the Lacanian theory of the castration complex leaves behind all reference to anatomical reality. [...] The alternative presented to the child may be rephrased as an alternative between having, or not having, the phallus. Castration is not having the (symbolic) phallus. Castration is not a real "lack," but a meaning conferred upon the genitals of a woman. [...]
The phallus is, as it were, a distinctive feature differentiating "castrated" and "noncastrated." The presence or absence of the phallus carries the differences between two sexual statuses, "man" and "woman" (see Jakobson and Halle 1971, on distinctive features). Since these are not equal, the phallus also carries a meaning of the dominance of men over women, and it may be inferred that "penis envy" is a recognition thereof. [...]

Lacan also speaks of the phallus as a symbolic object which is exchanged within and between families (see also Wilden 1968: 303–5). It is interesting to think about this observation in terms of primitive marriage transactions and exchange networks. In those transactions, the exchange of women is usually one of many cycles of exchange. Usually, there are other objects circulating as well as women. Women move in one direction, cattle, shells, or mats in the other. In one sense, the Oedipal complex is an expression of the circulation of the phallus in intrafamily exchange, an inversion of the circulation of women in interfamily exchange. In the cycle of exchange manifested by the Oedipal complex, the phallus passes through the medium of women from one man to another – from father to son, from mother's brother to sister's son, and so forth. In this family *Kula* ring, women go one way, the phallus the other. It is where we aren't. In this sense, the phallus is more than a feature which distinguishes the sexes: it is the embodiment of the male status, to which men accede, and in which certain rights inhere – among them, the right to a woman. It is an expression

of the transmission of male dominance. It passes through women and settles upon men. The tracks which it leaves include gender identity, the division of the sexes. But it leaves more than this. It leaves "penis envy," which acquires a rich meaning of the disquietude of women in a phallic culture.

Oedipus Revisited

We return now to the two pre-Oedipal androgynes, sitting on the border between biology and culture. Lévi-Strauss places the incest taboo on that border, arguing that its initiation of the exchange of women constitutes the origin of society. In this sense, the incest taboo and the exchange of women are the content of the original social contract (see Sahlins 1972: ch. 4). For individuals, the Oedipal crisis occurs at the same divide, when the incest taboo initiates the exchange of the phallus.

The Oedipal crisis is precipitated by certain items of information. The children discover the differences between the sexes, and that each child must become one or the other gender. They also discover the incest taboo, and that some sexuality is prohibited – in this case, the mother is unavailable to either child because she "belongs" to the father. Lastly, they discover that the two genders do not have the same sexual "rights" or futures.

In the normal course of events, the boy renounces his mother for fear that otherwise his father would castrate him (refuse to give him the phallus and make him a girl). But by this act of renunciation, the boy affirms the relationships which have given mother to father and which will give him, if he becomes a man, a woman of his own. In exchange for the boy's affirmation of his father's right to his mother, the father affirms the phallus in his son (does not castrate him). The boy exchanges his mother for the phallus, the symbolic token which can later be exchanged for a woman. The only thing required of him is a little patience. He retains his initial libidinal organization and the sex of his original love object. The social contract to which he has agreed will eventually recognize his own rights and provide him with a woman of his own.

What happens to the girl is more complex. She, like the boy, discovers the taboo against incest and the division of the sexes. She also discovers some unpleasant information about the gender to which she is being assigned. For the boy, the taboo on incest is a taboo on certain women. For the girl, it is a taboo on all women. Since she is in a homosexual position vis-à-vis the mother, the rule of heterosexuality which dominates the scenario makes her position excruciatingly untenable. The mother, and all women by extension, can only be properly beloved by someone "with a penis" (phallus). Since the girl has no "phallus," she has no "right" to love her mother or another woman, since she is herself destined to some man. She does not have the symbolic token which can be exchanged for a woman. [. . .]

She turns from the mother because she does not have the phallus to give her. She turns from the mother also in anger and disappointment, because the mother did not give her a "penis" (phallus). But the mother, a woman in a phallic culture, does not have the phallus to give away (having gone through the Oedipal crisis herself a generation earlier). The girl then turns to the father because only he can "give her the phallus," and it is only through him that she can enter into the symbolic exchange system in which the phallus circulates. But the father does not give her the phallus in the same way that he gives it to the boy. The phallus is affirmed in the boy, who then has it to give away. The girl never gets the phallus. It passes through her, and in its passage is transformed into a child. When she "recognizes her castration," she accedes to the place of a woman in a phallic exchange network. She can "get" the phallus – in intercourse, or as a child – but only as a gift from a man. She never gets to give it away.

[. . .]

The ascendance of passivity in the girl is due to her recognition of the futility of realizing her active desire, and of the unequal terms of the struggle. Freud locates active desire in the clitoris and passive desire in the vagina, and thus describes the repression of active desire as the repression of clitoral eroticism in favor of passive vaginal eroticism. In this scheme, cultural stereotypes have been mapped onto the genitals. Since the work of Masters and Johnson, it is evident that this genital division is a false one. Any organ – penis, clitoris, vagina – can be the locus of either active or passive eroticism. What is important in Freud's scheme, however, is not the geography of desire, but its self-confidence. It is not an organ which is repressed, but a segment of erotic possibility. Freud notes that "more constraint has been applied to the libido when it is pressed into the service of the feminine function . . . " (Freud 1965: 131). The girl has been robbed.

If the Oedipal phase proceeds normally and the girl "accepts her castration," her libidinal structure and object choice are now congruent with the female gender role. She has become a little woman – feminine, passive, heterosexual. Actually, Freud suggests that there are three alternate routes out of the Oedipal catastrophe. The girl may simply freak out, repress sexuality altogether, and become asexual. She may protest, cling to her narcissism and desire, and become either "masculine" or homosexual. Or she may accept the situation, sign the social contract, and attain "normality."

[. . .]

There is an additional element in the classic discussions of the attainment of womanhood. The girl first turns to the father because she must, because she is "castrated" (a woman, helpless, etc.). She then discovers that "castration" is a prerequisite to the father's love, that she must be a woman for him to love her. She therefore begins to desire "castration," and what had previously been a disaster becomes a wish. [. . .]

The psychoanalytic theory of femininity is one that sees female development based largely on pain and humiliation, and it takes some fancy footwork to explain why anyone ought to enjoy being a woman. At this point in the classic discussions biology makes a triumphant return. The fancy footwork consists in arguing that finding joy in pain is adaptive to the role of women in reproduction, since childbirth and defloration are "painful." Would it not make more sense to question the entire procedure? If women, in finding their place in a sexual system, are robbed of libido and forced into a masochistic eroticism, why did the analysts not argue for novel arrangements, instead of rationalizing the old ones?

Freud's theory of femininity has been subjected to feminist critique since it was first
published. To the extent that it is a rationalization of female subordination, this critique
has been justified. To the extent that it is a
description of a process which subordinates
women, this critique is a mistake. As a description of how phallic culture domesticates
women, and the effects on women of their
domestication, psychoanalytic theory has no
parallel (see also Mitchell 1971 and 1974;
Lasch 1974). And since psychoanalysis is a
theory of gender, dismissing it would be sui-
cidal for a political movement dedicated to
eradicating gender hierarchy (or gender itself).
We cannot dismantle something that we under-
estimate or do not understand. The oppression
of women is deep; equal pay, equal work, and
all of the female politicians in the world will
not extirpate the roots of sexism. Lévi-Strauss
and Freud elucidate what would otherwise be
poorly perceived parts of the deep structures of
sex oppression. They serve as reminders of the
intractability and magnitude of what we fight,
and their analyses provide preliminary charts
of the social machinery we must rearrange.

Women Unite to Off the Oedipal Residue of Culture

The precision of the fit between Freud and
Lévi-Strauss is striking. Kinship systems require a division of the sexes. The Oedipal
phase divides the sexes. Kinship systems include sets of rules governing sexuality. The
Oedipal crisis is the assimilation of these rules
and taboos. Compulsory heterosexuality is the
product of kinship. The Oedipal phase constitutes heterosexual desire. Kinship rests on a
radical difference between the rights of men
and women. The Oedipal complex confers
male rights upon the boy, and forces the girl
to accommodate herself to her lesser rights.

This fit between Lévi-Strauss and Freud is by
implication an argument that our sex/gender
system is still organized by the principles outlined by Lévi-Strauss, despite the entirely non-
modern character of his data base. The more
recent data on which Freud bases his theories
testifies to the endurance of these sexual struc-

tures. If my reading of Freud and Lévi-Strauss
is accurate, it suggests that the feminist movement must attempt to resolve the Oedipal crisis
of culture by reorganizing the domain of sex
and gender in such a way that each individual's
Oedipal experience would be less destructive.
The dimensions of such a task are difficult to
imagine, but at least certain conditions would
have to be met.

Several elements of the Oedipal crisis would
have to be altered in order that the phase not
have such disastrous effects on the young female ego. The Oedipal phase institutes a contradiction in the girl by placing irreconcilable
demands upon her. On the one hand, the girl's
love for the mother is induced by the mother's
job of child care. The girl is then forced to
abandon this love because of the female sex
role – to belong to a man. If the sexual division
of labor were such that adults of both sexes
cared for children equally, primary object
choice would be bisexual. If heterosexuality
were not obligatory, this early love would not
have to be suppressed, and the penis would not
be overvalued. If the sexual property system
were reorganized in such a way that men did
not have overriding rights in women (if there
was no exchange of women) and if there were
no gender, the entire Oedipal drama would be
a relic. In short, feminism must call for a revolution in kinship.

The organization of sex and gender once
had functions other than itself – it organized
society. Now, it only organizes and reproduces
itself. The kinds of relationships of sexuality
established in the dim human past still dominate our sexual lives, our ideas about men
and women, and the ways we raise our children. But they lack the functional load they
once carried. One of the most conspicuous
features of kinship is that it has been systematically stripped of its functions – political,
economic, educational, and organizational. It
has been reduced to its barest bones – *sex and
gender*.

Human sexual life will always be subject to
convention and human intervention. It will
never be completely "natural," if only because
our species is social, cultural, and articulate.
The wild profusion of infantile sexuality will
always be tamed. The confrontation between

immature and helpless infants and the developed social life of their elders will probably always leave some residue of disturbance. But the mechanisms and aims of this process need not be largely independent of conscious choice. Cultural evolution provides us with the opportunity to seize control of the means of sexuality, reproduction, and socialization, and to make conscious decisions to liberate human sexual life from the archaic relationships which deform it. Ultimately, a thoroughgoing feminist revolution would liberate more than women. It would liberate forms of sexual expression, and it would liberate human personality from the straightjacket of gender.

"Daddy, daddy, you bastard, I'm through." – Sylvia Plath

In the course of this essay I have tried to construct a theory of women's oppression by borrowing concepts from anthropology and psychoanalysis. But Lévi-Strauss and Freud write within an intellectual tradition produced by a culture in which women are oppressed. The danger in my enterprise is that the sexism in the tradition of which they are a part tends to be dragged in with each borrowing. "We cannot utter a single destructive proposition which has not already slipped into the form, the logic, and the implicit postulations of precisely what it seeks to contest" (Derrida 1972: 250). And what slips in is formidable. Both psychoanalysis and structural anthropology are, in one sense, the most sophisticated ideologies of sexism around.

For instance, Lévi-Strauss sees women as being like words, which are misused when they are not "communicated" and exchanged. On the last page of a very long book, he observes that this creates something of a contradiction in women, since women are at the same time "speakers" and "spoken." His only comment on this contradiction is this:

> But woman could never become just a sign and nothing more, since even in a man's world she is still a person, and since insofar as she is defined as a sign she must be recognized as a generator of signs. [...] In contrast

to words, which have wholly become signs, woman has remained at once a sign and a value. *This explains why the relations between the sexes have preserved that affective richness, ardour and mystery which doubtless originally permeated the entire universe of human communications.* (Lévi-Strauss 1969: 496; my italics)

This is an extraordinary statement. Why is he not, at this point, denouncing what kinship systems do to women, instead of presenting one of the greatest rip-offs of all time as the root of romance?

A similar insensitivity is revealed within psychoanalysis by the inconsistency with which it assimilates the critical implications of its own theory. [...]

When psychoanalysis demonstrates with equal facility that the ordinary components of feminine personality are masochism, self-hatred, and passivity, a similar judgment is *not* made. Instead, a double standard of interpretation is employed. Masochism is bad for men, essential to women. Adequate narcissism is necessary for men, impossible for women. Passivity is tragic in man, while lack of passivity is tragic in a woman.

It is this double standard which enables clinicians to try to accommodate women to a role whose destructiveness is so lucidly detailed in their own theories. It is the same inconsistent attitude which permits therapists to consider lesbianism as a problem to be cured, rather than as the resistance to a bad situation that their own theory suggests.

There are points within the analytic discussions of femininity where one might say, "This is oppression of women," or "We can demonstrate with ease that what the world calls femininity demands more sacrifices than it is worth." It is precisely at such points that the implications of the theory are ignored, and are replaced with formulations whose purpose is to keep those implications firmly lodged in the theoretical unconscious. It is at these points that all sorts of mysterious chemical substances, joys in pain, and biological aims are substituted for a critical assessment of the costs of femininity. These substitutions are the symptoms of theoretical repression, in that they are not consistent with the usual canons

of psychoanalytic argument. The extent to
which these rationalizations of femininity go
against the grain of psychoanalytic logic is
strong evidence for the extent of the need to
suppress the radical and feminist implications
of the theory of femininity. [...]

The argument which must be woven in order
to assimilate Lévi-Strauss and Freud into feminist theory is somewhat tortuous. I have
engaged it for several reasons. First, while
neither Lévi-Strauss nor Freud questions the undoubted sexism endemic to the systems they
describe, the questions which ought to be
posed are blindingly obvious. Secondly, their
work enables us to isolate sex and gender from
"mode of production," and to counter a certain
tendency to explain sex oppression as a reflex of
economic forces. Their work provides a framework in which the full weight of sexuality and
marriage can be incorporated into an analysis of
sex oppression. It suggests a conception of the
women's movement as analogous to, rather than
isomorphic with, the working-class movement,
each addressing a different source of human
discontent. In Marx's vision, the working-class
movement would do more than throw off the
burden of its own exploitation. It also had the
potential to change society, to liberate humanity,
to create a classless society. Perhaps the women's
movement has the task of effecting the same kind
of social change for a system of which Marx had
only an imperfect apperception. Something of
this sort is implicit in Wittig (1973) – the dicta-
torship of the Amazon *guérillères* is a temporary
means for achieving a genderless society.

The sex/gender system is not immutably oppressive and has lost much of its traditional
function. Nevertheless, it will not wither
away in the absence of opposition. It still carries the social burden of sex and gender, of
socializing the young, and of providing ultimate propositions about the nature of human
beings themselves. And it serves economic and
political ends other than those it was originally
designed to further (cf. Scott 1965). The sex/
gender system must be reorganized through
political action.

Finally, the exegesis of Lévi-Strauss and
Freud suggests a certain vision of feminist politics and the feminist utopia. It suggests that we
should not aim for the elimination of men, but

for the elimination of the social system which
creates sexism and gender. I personally find a
vision of an Amazon matriarchate, in which
men are reduced to servitude or oblivion (depending on the possibilities for parthenogenetic
reproduction), distasteful and inadequate. Such
a vision maintains gender and the division of
the sexes. It is a vision which simply inverts the
arguments of those who base their case for
inevitable male dominance on ineradicable
and *significant* biological differences between
the sexes. But we are not only oppressed *as*
women, we are oppressed by having to *be*
women, or men as the case may be. I personally
feel that the feminist movement must dream of
even more than the elimination of the oppression of women. It must dream of the elimination of obligatory sexualities and sex roles.
The dream I find most compelling is one of an
androgynous and genderless (though not sex-
less) society, in which one's sexual anatomy is
irrelevant to who one is, what one does, and
with whom one makes love.

The Political Economy of Sex

It would be nice to be able to conclude here
with the implications for feminism and gay
liberation of the overlap between Freud and
Lévi-Strauss. But I must suggest, tentatively, a
next step on the agenda: a Marxian analysis of
sex/gender systems. Sex/gender systems are not
ahistorical emanations of the human mind;
they are products of historical human activity.

We need, for instance, an analysis of the
evolution of sexual exchange along the lines
of Marx's discussion in *Capital* of the evolution of money and commodities. There is an
economics and a politics to sex/gender systems
which is obscured by the concept of "exchange
of women." For instance, a system in which
women are exchangeable only for one another
has different effects on women than one in
which there is a commodity equivalent for
women. [...] There are systems in which
there is no equivalent for a woman. To get a
wife, a man must have a daughter, a sister, or
other female kinswoman in whom he has a
right of bestowal. He must have control over
some female flesh. [...]

In other societies, there is an equivalent for women. A woman can be converted into bridewealth, and bridewealth can be in turn converted into a woman. The dynamics of such systems vary accordingly, as does the specific kind of pressure exerted upon women. [. . .]

In some societies, like the Nuer, bridewealth can only be converted into brides. In others, bridewealth can be converted into something else, like political prestige. In this case, a woman's marriage is implicated in a political system. [. . .]

In short, there are other questions to ask of a marriage system than whether or not it exchanges women. Is the woman traded for a woman, or is there an equivalent? Is this equivalent only for women, or can it be turned into something else? If it can be turned into something else, is it turned into political power or wealth? On the other hand, can bridewealth be obtained only in marital exchange, or can it be obtained from elsewhere? Can women be accumulated through amassing wealth? Can wealth be accumulated by disposing of women? Is a marriage system part of a system of stratification?

These last questions point to another task for a political economy of sex. Kinship and marriage are always parts of total social systems, and are always tied into economic and political arrangements.

> Lévi-Strauss . . . rightly argues that the structural implications of a marriage can only be understood if we think of it as one item in a whole series of transactions between kin groups. So far, so good. But in none of the examples which he provides in his book does he carry this principle far enough. The reciprocities of kinship obligation are not merely symbols of alliance, they are also economic transactions, political transactions, charters to rights of domicile and land use. No useful picture of "how a kinship system works" can be provided unless these several aspects or implications of the kinship organization are considered simultaneously. (Leach 1971: 90)

Among the Kachin, the relationship of a tenant to a landlord is also a relationship between a son-in-law and a father-in-law. "The procedure for acquiring land rights of any kind is in almost all cases tantamount to marrying a woman from the lineage of the lord" (1971: 88). In the Kachin system, bridewealth moves from commoners to aristocrats, women moving in the opposite direction.

> From an economic aspect the effect of matrilateral cross-cousin marriage is that, on balance, the headman's lineage constantly pays wealth to the chief's lineage in the form of bridewealth. The payment can also, from an analytical point of view, be regarded as a rent paid to the senior landlord by the tenant. The most important part of this payment is in the form of consumer goods – namely cattle. The chief converts this perishable wealth into imperishable prestige through the medium of spectacular feasting. The ultimate consumers of the goods are in this way the original producers, namely, the commoners who attend the feast. (1971: 89)

In another example, it is traditional in the Trobriands for a man to send a harvest gift – *urigubu* – of yams to his sister's household. For the commoners, this amounts to a simple circulation of yams. But the chief is polygamous, and marries a woman from each subdistrict within his domain. Each of these subdistricts therefore sends *urigubu* to the chief, providing him with a bulging storehouse out of which he finances feasts, craft production, and *kula* expeditions. This "fund of power" underwrites the political system and forms the basis for chiefly power (Malinowski 1970).

In some systems, position in a political hierarchy and position in a marriage system are intimately linked. In traditional Tonga, women married up in rank. Thus, low-ranking lineages would send women to higher ranking lineages. Women of the highest lineage were married into the "house of Fiji," a lineage defined as outside the political system. If the highest ranking chief gave his sister to a lineage other than one which had no part in the ranking system, he would no longer be the highest ranking chief. Rather, the lineage of his sister's son would outrank his own. In times of political rearrangement, the demotion of the previous high-ranking lineage was formalized when it gave a wife to a lineage which it had formerly outranked. In traditional Hawaii, the situation was the reverse. Women married down, and the dominant lineage gave wives to junior lines.

A paramount would either marry a sister or obtain a wife from Tonga. When a junior lineage usurped rank, it formalized its position by giving a wife to its former senior line. [...]

These examples – like the Kachin and the Trobriand ones – indicate that sexual systems cannot, in the final analysis, be understood in complete isolation. A full-bodied analysis of women in a single society, or throughout history, must take *everything* into account: the evolution of commodity forms in women, systems of land tenure, political arrangements, subsistence technology, etc. Equally important, economic and political analyses are incomplete if they do not consider women, marriage, and sexuality. Traditional concerns of anthropology and social science – such as the evolution of social stratification and the origin of the state – must be reworked to include the implications of matrilateral cross-cousin marriage, surplus extracted in the form of daughters, the conversion of female labor into male wealth, the conversion of female lives into marriage alliances, the contribution of marriage to political power, and the transformations which all of these varied aspects of society have undergone in the course of time.

This sort of endeavor is, in the final analysis, exactly what Engels tried to do in his effort to weave a coherent analysis of so many of the diverse aspects of social life. He tried to relate men and women, town and country, kinship and state, forms of property, systems of land tenure, convertibility of wealth, forms of exchange, the technology of food production, and forms of trade, to name a few, into a systematic historical account. Eventually, someone will have to write a new version of *The Origin of the Family, Private Property, and the State*, recognizing the mutual interdependence of sexuality, economics, and politics without underestimating the full significance of each in human society.

NOTES

1 Moving between Marxism, structuralism, and psychoanalysis produces a certain clash of epistemologies. In particular, structuralism is a can from which worms crawl out all over the epistemological map. Rather than trying to cope with this problem, I have more or less ignored the fact that Lacan and Lévi-Strauss are among the foremost living ancestors of the contemporary French intellectual revolution (see Foucault 1970). It would be fun, interesting, and, if this were France, essential, to start my argument from the center of the structuralist maze and work my way out from there, along the lines of a "dialectical theory of signifying practices" (see Hefner 1974).

2 A lot of the debate on women and housework has centered around the question of whether or not housework is "productive" labor. Strictly speaking, housework is not ordinarily "productive" in the technical sense of the term (I. Gough 1972; Marx 1969: 387–413). But this distinction is irrelevant to the main line of the argument. Housework may not be "productive," in the sense of directly producing surplus value and capital, and yet be a crucial element in the production of surplus value and capital.

3 That some of them are pretty bizarre, from our point of view, only demonstrates the point that sexuality is expressed through the intervention of culture (see Ford and Beach 1972). [...]

4 Engels thought that men acquired wealth in the form of herds and, wanting to pass this wealth to their own children, overthrew "mother right" in favor of patrilineal inheritance. "The overthrow of mother right was the *world historical defeat of the female sex*. The man took command in the home also; the woman was degraded and reduced to servitude; she became the slave of his lust and a mere instrument for the production of children" (Engels 1972: 120–1; italics in original). As has been often pointed out, women do not necessarily have significant social authority in societies practicing matrilineal inheritance (Schneider and Gough 1961).

REFERENCES

Althusser, Louis, and Étienne Balibar. 1970. *Reading Capital*. London: New Left Books.

Berndt, Ronald. 1962. *Excess and Restraint.* Chicago: University of Chicago Press.

Chasseguet-Smirgel, J. 1970. *Female Sexuality.* Ann Arbor: University of Michigan Press.

Derrida, Jacques. 1972. Structure, Sign, and Play in the Discourse of the Human Sciences. In *The Structuralist Controversy*, edited by R. Macksey and E. Donato. Baltimore: Johns Hopkins University Press.

Engels, Frederick. 1972. *The Origin of the Family, Private Property, and the State*, edited by Eleanor Leacock. New York: International Publishers.

Ford, Clellan, and Frank Beach. 1972. *Patterns of Sexual Behavior.* New York: Harper.

Foucault, Michel. 1970. *The Order of Things.* New York: Pantheon.

Freud, Sigmund. 1965. Femininity. In *New Introductory Lectures in Psychoanalysis*, edited by J. Strachey. New York: W. W. Norton.

Glasse, R. M. 1971. The Mask of Venery. Paper read at the 70th Annual Meeting of the American Anthropological Association, New York City, December 1971.

Gough, Ian. 1972. Marx and Productive Labour. *New Left Review* 76: 47–72.

Hefner, Robert. 1974. The *Tel Quel* Ideology: Material Practice upon Material Practice. *Substance*, 8: 127–38.

Jakobson, Roman, and Morris Halle. 1971. *Fundamentals of Language.* The Hague: Mouton.

Jones, Ernest. 1933. The Phallic Phase. *International Journal of Psychoanalysis*, 14: 1–33.

Lacan, Jacques. 1970. The Insistence of the Letter in the Unconscious. In *Structuralism*, edited by J. Ehrmann. Garden City, N.Y.: Doubleday Anchor.

Langness, L. L. 1967. Sexual Antagonism in the New Guinea Highlands: A Bena Bena Example. *Oceania*, 37/3: 161–77.

Lasch, Christopher. 1974. Freud and Women. *New York Review of Books*, 21/15: 12–17.

Leach, Edmund. 1971. *Rethinking Anthropology.* New York: Humanities Press.

Lévi-Strauss, Claude. 1969. *The Elementary Structures of Kinship.* Boston: Beacon Press.

—— 1971, 'The Family'. In Man, Culture and Society, edited by H. Shapiro, London: Oxford University Press.

Lindenbaum, Shirley. 1973. A Wife Is the Hand of Man. Paper read at the 72nd Annual Meeting of the American Anthropological Association.

Livingstone, Frank. 1969. Genetics, Ecology, and the Origins of Incest and Exogamy. *Current Anthropology*, 10/1: 45–9.

Malinowski, Bronislaw, 1929. *The Sexual Life of Savages.* London: Routledge and Kegan Paul.

—— 1970. The Primitive Economics of the Trobriand Islanders. In *Cultures of the Pacific*, edited by T. Harding and B. Wallace. New York: Free Press.

Marx. Karl. 1969. *Theories of Surplus Value*, Part I. Moscow: Progress Publishers.

—— 1971. *Wage-Labor and Capital.* New York: International Publishers.

Mauss, Marcel. 1967. The Gift. New York: W.W. Norton.

Meggitt, M. J. 1964. Male–Female Relationships in the Highlands of Australian New Guinea. *American Anthropologist*, 66/4, pt. 2: 204–24.

Mitchell, Juliet. 1971. *Women's Estate.* New York: Vintage.

—— 1974. *Psychoanalysis and Feminism.* New York: Pantheon.

Murphy, Robert. 1959. Social Structure and Sex Antagonism. *South-western Journal of Anthropology*, 15/1: 81–96.

Rappaport, Roy, and Buchbinder, Georgeda, 1976. Fertility and Death among the Maring. In *Sex Roles in the New Guinea Highlands*, edited by Paula Brown and G. Buchbinder. Washington, DC: American Anthropological Association, special publication, no. 8.

Read, Kenneth. 1952. The Nama Cult of the Central Highlands, New Guinea. *Oceania*, 23/1: 1–25.

Reay, Marie. 1959. *The Kuma.* London: Cambridge University Press.

Sahlins, Marshall. 1960. The Origin of Society. *Scientific American*, 203/3: 76–86.

—— 1972. *Stone Age Economics.* Chicago: Aldine-Atherton.

Schneider, David, and Kathleen Gough, eds. 1961. *Matrilineal Kinship.* Berkeley: University of California Press.

Scott, John Finley. 1965. The Role of Collegi-
    ate Sororities in Maintaining Class and
    Ethnic Endogamy. *American Sociological
    Review*, 30/4: 415–26.
Strathern, Marilyn. 1972. *Women in Between*.
    New York: Seminar.
Thompson, E. P. 1963. *The Making of the
    English Working Class*. New York: Vintage.

Van Baal, J. 1966. *Dema*. The Hague:
    Nijhoff.
Wilden, Anthony. 1968. *The Language of the
    Self*. Baltimore: Johns Hopkins University
    Press.
Wittig, Monique. 1973. *Les Guérillères*. New
    York: Avon.

5

The Use and Abuse of Anthropology: Reflections on Feminism and Cross-cultural Understanding

Michelle Z. Rosaldo

This is an article about questions. Feminists have managed, in recent years, to impress a matter of undeniable importance on both academic and popular audiences alike. Previously blinded by bias, we have begun a "discovery" of women and have reported a good deal of data on women's lives, needs, and interests that earlier scholars ignored. Sexist traditions have, of course, made our records uneven. Now more than ever we see just how little is known about women. And the urgency experienced by current researchers is fueled by a recognition that invaluable records of women's arts, work, and politics are irretrievably lost. Our theories are – the saying goes – only as good as our data. As was suggested in a recent review of anthropological writings on sex roles, "What is clearest in the literature reviewed is the need for further investigation.... What is most impressive about this literature is the overwhelming number of specific researchable questions it has produced.

Hopefully the social force which inspired anthropological interest in women's status will sustain this interest through the long second stage of research fashioned to explore these hypotheses."[1]

But whatever we do or do not know, my sense is that feminist thinking – in anthropology at least – faces yet a more serious problem. Many a fieldworker has spent her months in the hills with predominantly female companions. These women spoke of their homes and children and husbands. They told us about men who fed, loved, or beat them; and they shared with us their experiences both of triumph and disappointment, their sense of their own strengths and powers, and the burden of their workaday chores. Female informants have told us about ties among kin and the politics surrounding marriage; they probably labeled each pot and each knife in their homes with a tale about work, obligation, and structurally significant bonds. Contrary

From Michelle Z. Rosaldo, "The Use and Abuse of Anthropology: Reflections on Feminism and Cross-Cultural Understanding," pp. 389–417 in *Signs*, 5/3 (1980). Reprinted by permission of the University of Chicago Press.

to those anthropologists who have suggested that our problems lie in incomplete reports or, even worse, in inarticulate and "silent" female voices,[2] I would suggest that we hear women speak in almost all anthropological descriptions. We have, in fact, plenty of data "on women"; but when it comes to writing about them, all too few of us know what to say. What is needed, I will suggest, is not so much data as questions. The feminist discovery of women has begun to sensitize us to the ways in which gender pervades social life and experience; but the sociological significance of feminist insight is potentially a good deal deeper than anything realized as yet. What we know is constrained by interpretive frameworks which, of course, limit our thinking; what we *can* know will be determined by the kinds of questions we learn to ask.[3]

The Search for Origins

The significance of these all too general remarks for anthropology becomes clear when we consider the following observation. Few historians, sociologists, or social philosophers writing today feel called upon – as was common practice in the nineteenth century – to begin their tales "at the beginning" and probe the anthropological record for the origins of doctors in shamans or of, say, Catholic ritual in the cannibalism of an imagined past. Where turn-of-the-century thinkers (one thinks here of persons as diverse as Spencer, Maine, Durkheim, Engels, and Freud) considered it necessary to look at evidence from "simple" cultures as a means of understanding both the origins and the significance of contemporary social forms, most modern social scientists have rejected both their methods and their biases. Rather than probe origins, contemporary theorists will use anthropology, if at all, for the comparative insight that it offers; having decided, with good cause, to question evolutionary approaches, most would – I fear – go on to claim that data on premodern and traditional forms of social life have virtually no relevance to the understanding of contemporary society.

Yet it seems to me that quite the opposite is true of the vast majority of recent feminist writing. If anthropology has been too much ignored by most contemporary social thinkers, it has achieved a marked – though problematic – pride of place in classics like *Sexual Politics* and *The Second Sex*. Simone de Beauvoir, Kate Millett, Susan Brownmiller, Adrienne Rich, all introduce their texts with what seems to anthropologists a most old-fashioned evocation of the human record. On the assumption that preparing meals, making demands of sons, enjoying talks with women friends, or celebrating their fertility and sexual vitality will mean the same thing to women independent of their time and place, these writers catalog the customs of the past in order to decide if womankind can claim, through time, to have acquired or lost such rightful "goods" as power, self-esteem, autonomy, and status. Though these writers differ in conclusions, methods, and particulars of theoretical approach, all move from some version of Beauvoir's question, "What is woman?" to a diagnosis of contemporary subordination and from that on to the queries: "Were things always as they are today?" and then, "When did 'it' start?"

Much like the nineteenth-century writers who first argued whether mother-right preceded patriarchal social forms, or whether women's difficult primeval lot has been significantly improved in civilized society, feminists differ in their diagnoses of our prehistoric lives, their sense of suffering, of conflict, and of change. Some, like Rich, romanticize what they imagine was a better past, while others find in history an endless tale of female subjugation and male triumph. But most, I think, would find no cause to question a desire to ferret out our origins and roots. Nor would they challenge Shulamith Firestone, who, in her important book, *The Dialectic of Sex*, cites Engels to assert our need first to "examine the historic succession of events from which the antagonism has sprung in order to discover in the conditions thus created the means of ending the conflict."[4] Firestone suggests, in fact, that we seek out the roots of present suffering in a past which moves from history back to "primitive man" and thence to animal biology. And most recently, Linda Gordon, in her splendid account of birth control as it has related to developments in American political life,[5] attempted in less than thirty pages to summarize the history of birth control throughout the premodern world, providing her readers with a catalog of premodern practices and beliefs that is disappointing both as history and as anthropology. In a book concerned to show how birth control agitation has fit into a history of leftist politics in the modern United States (its meaning bound to changes in the nature and organization of our families and our economy), I was surprised to find that anthropology was used to universalize contemporary political demands and undermine our present sense of singularity. There is something wrong – indeed, morally disturbing – in an argument which claims that the practitioners of infanticide in the past are ultimately our predecessors in an endless and essentially unchanging fight to keep men from making claims to female bodies.

By using anthropology as precedent for modern arguments and claims, the "primitive" emerges in accounts like these as the bearer of primordial human need. Women elsewhere are, it seems, the image of ourselves undressed, and the historical specificity of their lives and of our own becomes obscured. Their strengths prove that we can be strong. But ironically, and at the same time that we fight to see ourselves as cultural beings who lead socially determined lives, the movement back in evolutionary time brings in inevitable appeal to biological givens and the determining impact of such "crude" facts as demography and technology. One gets the feeling that birth control today is available to human *choice*, while in the past women's abilities to shape their reproductive fates were either nonexistent or constrained by such mechanical facts as a nomadic need to move, the need for helpers on the farm, or an imbalance between food supply and demography. We want to claim our sisters' triumphs as a proof of our worth, but at the same time their oppression can be artfully dissociated from our own, because we live with choice, while they are victims of biology.

My point here is not to criticize these texts. Feminists (and I include myself) have with good reason probed the anthropological record for evidence which appears to tell us whether "human nature" is the sexist and constraining thing that many of us were taught. Anthropology is, for most of us, a monument to human possibilities and constraints, a hall of mirrors wherein what Anthony Wallace called the "anecdotal exception" seems to challenge every would-be law; while at the same time, lurking in the oddest shapes and forms, we find a still familiar picture of ourselves, a promise that, by meditating on New Guinea menstrual huts, West African female traders, ritualists, or queens, we can begin to grasp just what – in universal terms – we "really" are.

But I would like to think that anthropology is more than that. Or, rather, I would claim that anthropology asked to answer ideologies and give voice to universal human truth is ultimately an anthropology limited by the assumptions with which it first began and so unable to transcend the biases its questions presuppose. To look for origins is, in the end, to think that what we are today is something other than the product of our history and our present social world, and, more particularly, that our gender systems are primordial, transhistorical, and essentially unchanging in their roots. Quests for origins sustain (since they are predicated upon) a discourse cast in universal terms; and universalism permits us all too quickly to assume – for everyone but ourselves perhaps – the *sociological* significance of what individual people *do* or, even worse, of what, in biological terms, they are.[6]

Stated otherwise, our search for origins reveals a faith in ultimate and essential truths, a faith sustained in part by cross-cultural evidence of widespread sexual inequality. But an analysis which assumes that sexual asymmetry is the first subject we should attempt to question or explain tends almost inevitably to reproduce the biases of the male social science to which it is, quite reasonably, opposed. These biases have their bases in a pervasive, individualistic school of thought that holds that social forms proceed from what particular persons need or do, activities which – where gender is concerned – are seen to follow from the "givens" of our reproductive physiology. And so, for feminists and traditionalists alike, there is a tendency to think of gender as, above all else, the creation of biologically

NO
↑

based differences which oppose women and men, instead of as the product of social relationships in concrete (and changeable) societies.

The Problem of Universals

It would be nice to overthrow convention at this point and find myself entitled to proclaim that anthropological fact definitively belies sexist assumptions. Were anthropological evidence available that denied the universal place of gender in the organization of human social life, the association of women with reproduction and care for infant young, or the relevance of women's reproductive role to the construction of women's public status, much of the difficulty in what I have to say could be avoided. More narrowly, could I cite a single instance of a truly matriarchal – or, for that matter, sexually egalitarian – social form, I could go on to claim that all appeals to universal "nature" in explaining women's place are, simply, wrong. But instead, I must begin by making clear that, unlike many anthropologists who argue for the privileged place of women here or there, my reading of the anthropological record leads me to conclude that human cultural and social forms have always been male dominated. By this, I mean not that men rule by right or even that men rule at all and certainly not that women everywhere are passive victims of a world that men define. Rather, I would point to a collection of related facts which seem to argue that in all known human groups – and no matter the prerogatives that women may in fact enjoy – the vast majority of opportunities for public influence and prestige, the ability to forge relationships, determine enmities, speak up in public, use or forswear the use of force are all recognized as men's privilege and right.[7]

But I have moved, intentionally, too fast. In order to evaluate the conclusion just put forth, it seems important first to pause and ask what, substantively, has been claimed. Male dominance, though apparently universal, does not in actual behavioral terms assume a universal content or a universal shape. On the contrary, women typically have power and influence in political and economic life, display autonomy from men in their pursuits, and rarely find themselves confronted or constrained by what might seem the brute fact of male strength. For every case in which we see women confined, by powerful men or by the responsibilities of child care and the home, one can cite others which display female capacities to fight back, speak out in public, perform physically demanding tasks, and even to subordinate the needs of infant children (in their homes or on their backs) to their desires for travel, labor, politics, love, or trade. For every cultural belief in female weakness, irrationality, or polluting menstrual blood, one can discover others which suggest the tenuousness of male claims and celebrate women for their productive roles, their sexuality or purity, their fertility or perhaps maternal strength. Male dominance, in short, does not inhere in any isolated and measurable set of omnipresent facts. Rather, it seems to be an aspect of the organization of collective life, a patterning of expectations and beliefs which gives rise to imbalance in the ways people interpret, evaluate, and respond to particular forms of male and female action. We see it not in physical constraints on things that men or women can or cannot do but, rather, in the ways they think about their lives, the kinds of opportunities they enjoy, and in their ways of making claims.

Male dominance is evidenced, I believe, when we observe that women almost everywhere have daily responsibilities to feed and care for children, spouse, and kin, while men's economic obligations tend to be less regular and more bound up with extrafamilial sorts of ties; certainly, men's work within the home is not likely to be sanctioned by a spouse's use of force. Even in those groups in which the use of physical violence is avoided, a man can say, "She is a good wife, I don't have to beat her," whereas no woman evokes violent threats when speaking of her husband's work. Women will, in many societies, discover lovers and enforce their will to marry as they choose, but, again, we find in almost every case that the formal initiation and arrangement of permanent heterosexual bonds is something organized by men. Women may have ritual powers of considerable significance to themselves as well as men, but women never dominate in rites requiring the participation of the community as a whole. And even though men everywhere are apt to listen to and be influenced by their wives, I know of no case where men are required to serve as an obligatory audience to female ritual or political performance. Finally, women often form organizations of real and recognized political and economic strength; at times they rule as queens, acquire followings of men, beat husbands who prefer strange women to their wives, or perhaps enjoy a sacred status in their role as mothers. But, again, I know of no political system in which women individually or as a group are expected to hold more offices or have more political clout than their male counterparts.

Thus, while women in every human group will have forms of influence and ways of pursuing culturally acknowledged goals, it seems beside the point to argue – as many anthropologists in fact have – that observations such as mine are relatively trivial from the woman's point of view or that male claims are often balanced by some equally important set of female strengths.[8] Some women, certainly, are strong. But at the same time that women often happily and successfully pursue their ends, and manage quite significantly to constrain men in the process, it seems to me quite clear that women's goals themselves are shaped by social systems which deny them ready access to the social privilege, authority, and esteem enjoyed by a majority of men.

Admittedly, we are dealing with a very problematic sort of universal fact. Every social system uses facts of biological sex to organize and explain the roles and opportunities men and women may enjoy, just as all known human social groups appeal to biologically based ties in the construction of "familial" groups and kinship bonds. And much as "marriage," "family," and "kinship" have, for anthropologists, been troubling but, it seems, quite unavoidable universal terms, so I would claim the same thing holds for something like "male dominance." Sexual asymmetry, much like kinship, seems to exist everywhere, yet not without perpetual challenge or almost infinite variation in its contents and its forms. In short, if the universalizing questions are the ones

with which we start, the anthropological record seems to feed our fear that sexual asymmetry is (again, like kinship, and the two, of course, are linked) a deep, primordial sort of truth, in some way bound to functional requirements associated with our sexual physiology. Though various, our gender systems *do* appear more basic than our ways of organizing our economies, religious faiths, or courts of law. And so, at much the same time that the evidence of behavioral variation suggests that gender is less a product of our bodies than of social forms and modes of thought, it seems quite difficult to believe that sexual inequalities are not rooted in the dictates of a natural order. Minimally, it would appear that certain biological facts – women's role in reproduction and, perhaps, male strength – have operated in a nonnecessary but universal way to shape and reproduce male dominance.

Domestic/Public as Explanation

A common feminist response to the facts that I have outlined here has been, essentially, to deny their weight and argue that the evidence we have itself reflects male bias. By focusing on women's lives, researchers have begun to reinterpret more conventional accounts and school us to be sensitive to female values, goals, and strengths. If formal authority is not something women enjoy, so this research claims, we ought to learn to understand informal female powers; if women operate in "domestic" or "familial" spheres, then we must focus our attention on arenas like these, wherein women can make claims.[9] The value of scholarship of this sort is that it shows that when we measure women against men we fail to grasp important structural facts which may, in fact, give rise to female power. But while this point is an important one – to which I will return – the tendency to ignore imbalances in order to permit a grasp of women's lives has led too many scholars to forget that men and women ultimately live together in the world and, so, that we will never understand the lives that women lead without relating them to men. Ignoring sexual asymmetry strikes me as an essentially romantic move, which only blinds us to the sorts of facts we must attempt to understand and change.

An alternative approach,[10] elaborated in a set of essays by Chodorow, Ortner, and myself,[11] has been to argue that even universal facts are not reducible to biology. Our essays tried to show how what appears a "natural" fact must yet be understood in social terms – a by-product, as it were, of nonnecessary institutional arrangements that could be addressed through political struggle and, with effort, undermined. Our argument was, in essence, that in all human societies sexual asymmetry might be seen to correspond to a rough institutional division between domestic and public spheres of activity, the one built around reproduction, affective, and familial bonds, and particularly constraining to women; the other, providing for collectivity, jural order, and social cooperation, organized primarily by men. The domestic/public division as it appeared in any given society was not a necessary, but an "intelligible," product of the mutual accommodation of human history and human biology; although human societies have differed, all reflected in their organization a characteristic accommodation to the fact that women bear children and lactate and, because of this, find themselves readily designated as "mothers," who nurture and care for the young.

From these observations, we argued, one could then trace the roots of a pervasive gender inequality: Given an empirical division between domestic and public spheres of activity, a number of factors would interact to enhance both the cultural evaluations and social power and authority available to men. First, it appeared that the psychological effects of being raised by a woman would produce very different emotional dispositions in adults of both sexes; because of the diverging nature of preoedipal ties with *their* mothers, young girls would grow up to be nurturant "mothers" and boys would achieve an identity that denigrates and rejects women's roles.[12] In cultural terms, a domestic/public division corresponded to Ortner's discussion of "natural" versus "cultural" valuations,[13] wherein such factors as a woman's involvement with young and disorderly children would tend to give her the appearance of less composure, and, therefore, of

less "culture" than men. Finally, sociologically, the views prevalent in our analytical tradition (and at least as old as Plato) that public activities are valued, that authority involves group recognition, and that consciousness and personality are apt to develop most fully through a stance of civic responsibility and an orientation to the collective whole – all argued that men's ability to engage in public activities would give them privileged access to such resources, persons, and symbols as would sustain their claims to precedence, grant them power and disproportionate rewards.

Whatever its difficulties, the account, as it stands, seems suggestive. Certainly, one can find in all human societies some sort of hierarchy of mutually embedded units. Although varying in structure, function, and societal significance, "domestic groups" which incorporate women and infant children, aspects of child care, commensality, and the preparation of food can always be identified as segments of a larger, overarching social whole. While we know that men are often centrally involved in domestic life and women will, at times, range far beyond it, one can, I think, assert that women, unlike men, lead lives that they themselves construe with reference to responsibilities of a recognizably domestic kind.

Thus, even such apparently "egalitarian" and communally oriented peoples as the Mbuti Pygmy gatherer-hunters of southern Africa require that women sleep in individual huts with infant children.[14] And women hide with children in these huts while men collectively enjoin the blessings and support of their forest god. Mbuti women do have a role in men's religious rites, but only to observe and then disrupt them. As if defined by their domestic and individual concerns, these women are entitled only to break up the sacred fire which joins all Pygmies to men's god; their power does not permit them to light the fires that soothe the forest and give collective shape to social bonds.

Examples like this are not hard to find, nor would they seem to pose real difficulties of interpretation. The evidence of peasant societies abounds with celebrated public men who are constrained by "honor" to defend their families' claims to "face," while the women seem to lack authority beyond the households where they live. But although denigrated in public "myth," these women "in reality" may use the powers of their "sphere" in order to attain considerable influence and control.[15] Domestic women in such peasant groups have powers which the analyst can hardly minimize or dismiss, and yet they are constrained in spatial range and lack the cultural recognition associated with male activities in the public realm.

In short, domestic/public as a general account seems to fit well with some of what we know of sex-linked action systems and of cultural rationales for male prestige, suggesting how "brute" biological facts have everywhere been shaped by social logics. Reproduction and lactation have provided a functional basis for the definition of a domestic sphere, and sexual asymmetry appears as its intelligible, though nonnecessary, consequence. Much as, in very simple human groups, the constraints of pregnancy and child care seem easily related to women's exclusion from big-game hunting – and thus from the prestige which comes of bringing in a product requiring extrahousehold distribution[16] – so, in more general terms, domestic obligations and demands appear to help us understand why women everywhere are limited in their access to prestigious male pursuits. Finally, our sense of sexual hierarchy as a deep and primary sort of truth appears compatible with a theory that asserts that mother–child bonds have lasting social and psychological ramifications; sociological constraints appear consistent with psychological orientations that arise through female-dominated patterns of child care.[17]

As should be clear by now, I find much that is compelling in this universalist account; but at the same time I am troubled by some of what appear to be its analytical consequences. In probing universal questions, domestic/public is as telling as any explanation yet put forth. Certainly, it seems more than reasonable to assume that marriage and reproduction shape the organization of domestic spheres and link them to more public institutional forms in ways that are particularly consequential for the shape of women's lives. Specifically, if women care for children and child care takes

place within the home, and, furthermore, if political life, by definition, extends beyond it, then domestic/public seems to capture in a rough, but telling, set of terms the determinants of women's secondary place in all human societies.

But if this account "makes sense" in universal terms, I would go on to claim that when we turn to concrete cases, a model based upon the opposition of two spheres assumes – where it should rather help illuminate and explain – too much about how gender really works. Just as "kinship systems" vary far too widely to be viewed as mere reflections of established biological constraints (and anthropologists have argued endlessly as to whether kinship should be understood as something built upon the biologically "given" facts of human genealogy), so the alignments of the sexes seem at once too similar to deny a universal common base and yet too various to be understood adequately in terms of any universal cause. Pygmy women do not hide in huts because of the requirements of domestic life; rather, their assignment to small huts appears a consequence of their lack of power. American women may experience child care as something that confines them to the home, but I am quite sure that child care is *not* what many American households are about.[18] By linking gender, and in particular female lives, to the existence of domestic spheres, we have inclined, I fear, to think we know the "core" of what quite different gender systems share, to think of sexual hierarchies primarily in functional and psychological terms, and, thus, to minimize such sociological considerations as inequality and power. We think too readily of sexual identities as primordial acquisitions, bound up with the dynamics of the home, forgetting that the "selves" children become include a sense, not just of gender, but of cultural identity and social class.

What this means ultimately is that we fail to school ourselves in all the different ways that gender figures in the organization of social groups, to learn from the concrete things that men and women do and think and from their socially determined variations. It now appears to me that woman's place in human social life is not in any direct sense a product of the things she does (or even less a function of what, biologically, she is) but of the meaning her activities acquire through concrete social interactions. And the significances women assign to the activities of their lives are things that we can only grasp through an analysis of the relationships that women forge, the social contexts they (along with men) create – and within which they are defined. Gender in all human groups must, then, be understood in political and social terms, with reference not to biological constraints but instead to local and specific forms of social relationship and, in particular, of social inequality. Just as we have no apparent cause to look for physiological facts when we attempt to understand the more familiar inequalities in human social life – such things as leadership, racial prejudice, prestige, or social class – so it seems that we would do well to think of biological sex, like biological race, as an excuse rather than a cause for any sexism we observe.

Stated otherwise, I now believe that gender is not a unitary fact determined everywhere by the same sorts of concerns but, instead, the complex product of a variety of social forces. The most serious objections to my 1974 account have demonstrated – with good cause, I think – that "women's status" is itself not one but many things, that various measures of women's place do not appear to correlate among themselves, and, furthermore, that few of them appear to be consistently related to an isolable "cause."[19] The failure of attempts to rank societies in terms of "women's place" or to explain apparent variations in the amounts of privilege women elsewhere may enjoy (in terms consistent with cross-cultural data) suggests that we have been pursuing something of a ghost – or, rather, that an investigator who asks if women's status here or there ought to be reckoned high or low is probably conceptually misguided.

To talk of women's status is to think about a social world in ultimately dichotomous terms, wherein "woman" is universally opposed to "man" in the same ways in all contexts. Thus, we tend repeatedly to contrast and stress presumably given differences between women and men, instead of asking how such differences are themselves created by gender relations. In so doing, we find ourselves the victims of a conceptual tradition that discovers "essence" in the natural characteristics which distinguish us from men and then declares that women's present lot derives from what, "in essence," women are, portraying social roles and rules as products not of action and relation in a truly human world, but of self-serving individuals who perform by rote.

The Victorian Precedent

The notion that all human societies can be analyzed in terms of opposed domestic and public spheres – and that this opposition fits, in some way, with the social fact of male dominance – is not limited to feminist researchers. Indeed, one finds it more or less explicitly elaborated in a good deal of traditional social scientific thought. The turn-of-the-century social theorists whose writings are the basis of most modern social thinking tended without exception to assume that women's place was in the home. In fact, the Victorian doctrine of separate male and female spheres was, I would suggest, quite central to their sociology.[20] Some of these thinkers recognized that modern women suffered from their association with domestic life, but none questioned the pervasiveness (or necessity) of a split between the family and society. Most never bothered to ask just why two spheres exist; rather, all assumed their fundamental differences in sociological and moral terms and linked these to their views of the normal roles of men and women in human societies.

Most obviously, perhaps, Herbert Spencer, commonly cited as the founder both of "functionalist" and "evolutionary" social thought, disparaged feminist claims to political liberties and rights by arguing that women's "natural" place within the home proves a necessary complement to the more competitive world of men. And while some of his contemporaries feared that women's entry into public life would rob society of its stores of altruism and love, Spencer claimed that women's softer hearts would undermine all shows of selfish interest in the public world, therefore inhibiting the realization (through competition) of new forms of social excellence and strength.[21] The socialist Friedrich Engels never argued that women should, by nature, stay within the home, but he – like Spencer – tended to assume that women never were engaged in public action or in socially productive work and, correspondingly, that women everywhere had been concerned primarily with the activities dictated by a maternal role.[22] Similarly, Georg Simmel and Émile Durkheim, both acutely conscious of feminine oppression within familial realms, described the sexes in terms suggesting an analysis based on complementary spheres:

Up to now the sociological position of the individual woman has certain peculiar elements. The most general of her qualities, the fact that she was a woman and as such served the functions proper to her sex, caused her to be classified with other women under one general concept. It was exactly this circumstance which removed her from the processes of group-formation in their strict sense, as well as from actual solidarity with other women. Because of her peculiar functions she was relegated to activities within the limits of her home, confined to devote herself to a single individual, and prevented from transcending the group-relations established by marriage, family, social life, and perhaps charity and religion.[23]

...the interests of husband and wife in marriage are...obviously opposed....It originates in the fact that the two sexes do not share equally in social life. Man is actively involved in it, while woman does little more than look on from a distance. Consequently, man is much more highly socialized than woman.[24]

And though both of these theorists spoke in favor of women's increased role in "social" life, they thought as well that women were and would remain distinguishable from men; their woman of the future was, it seems, designed to make her mark not in the masculine sphere of politics, but – the now predictable answer came – in the more feminine arts.[25]

Finally, the evolutionary social history with which turn-of-the-century feminists (like Gilman and Stanton), as well as more conventional social theorists, were concerned was rooted equally in an opposition between maternal or domestic spheres and a more public world of men. Though many of these thinkers wrote of matriarchies in the past, what they meant was not that women ruled in public life but, rather, that humanity's first social forms gave women an important place because public society was not yet differentiated from domestic realms. Using data they were ill equipped to understand, these theorists assumed a time of promiscuity and incest in the past when men had no occasion to lay claim to individual women as their own and so enjoyed undifferentiated sexual freedom in a maternal home. They claimed – in imagery that still abounds in psychological accounts of individual growth – that social evolution waited on male efforts to compete, stake private claims, and forge a differentiated and interest-governed public sphere while leaving "mother" in the more "natural" world where she belonged.

Modern thinkers have found cause to challenge many of these nineteenth-century claims, and I have scarcely given them the scrutiny they deserve. But social scientists who would now proclaim that prior cultures knew no more of incest than we know today continue in more subtle ways to reproduce the sexist imagery and assumptions we discern in nineteenth-century accounts. Victorian theory cast the sexes in dichotomous and contrastive terms, describing home and woman not primarily as they were but as they had to be, given an ideology that opposed natural, moral, and essentially unchanging private realms to the vagaries of a progressive masculine society. And, similarly, I would suggest that when modern theorists write that paternity is a variable and social fact whereas maternity is a relatively constant and unchanging one, constrained by nature;[26] when they contrast expressive with more instrumental roles;[27] or, perhaps, when they distinguish moral kinship from the bonds of selfish interest forged in economic life;[28] or, then again, when they describe the differences between apparently formal and informal social roles and forms of power – they are the nineteenth century's unwitting heirs. Indeed, contemporary thinkers reproduce what many recognize as outdated contrasts and conceptually misleading terms,[29] at least in part because we still believe that social being is derived from essences that stand outside of social process. Life in a social world that differentiates our more natural from our constructed social bonds is then interpreted in terms of stereotyped views of what in essence men and women are, views linking women to maternity and the home in opposition to what anthropologists now would call the political-jural sphere of public society.

Within the social sciences, the early twentieth century saw a rejection of earlier schools of evolutionary thought in favor of a search for functionally grounded universals. Biological families, through the researches of Malinowski and Radcliffe-Brown, came to be seen as necessary and virtually presocial facts, born out of our most basic human needs instead of evolutionary progress.[30] But, casting needs as universal, anthropologists had still to think of change, and in order to account for the diversity and complexity of reported kinship forms, they found themselves required to reinstate – although in somewhat less gendered and considerably more sophisticated terms – the nineteenth-century opposition between a female sphere of family and an inherently masculine society. Kinship, anthropologists came to see, is not a natural, biological, or genealogical fact but, instead, a molding of presumed ties of blood in terms of jural norms and rules constructed by human societies. But at the same time that they recognized that kinship always has a public, jural sense, they still insisted that the various and political uses of kinship to articulate bonds of lineage, clan, or caste were to be distinguished from a more universal kinship essence, with, of course, a bit of nature – most particularly a family, genealogy, or maternal grouping – at its source.[31]

In its most fully articulated contemporary form, domestic and jural-political now contrast in terms of normative premises that divide those inner realms defined by the prescriptive altruism we think belongs within the home from the outer spheres subjected to external rule by contract, law, and force.[32] And though most writers now would claim that this division carries no assumptions about sex, their actual characterizations of the opposed spheres in fact reflect stereotyped nineteenth-century views of necessary sexual dichotomy. Thus, domestic spheres are not defined as women's nor are women seen as necessarily limited to the home; but most theorizing about domestic spheres presumes first of all their normative opposition to (male) jural realms and, second, their basis in the universal, and inherently altruistic, bonds associated with the mother-infant dyad.[33] Anthropologists have carefully distinguished the term "family" (a group of kinsfolk) from that of "household" (a space), and these, in turn, from claims concerning gender roles with reference to domestic functions.[34] But in actual fact, we find that what domestic means is the locale where kinfolk share a living space and mothers do the day-by-day providing. In complementary fashion, no contemporary anthropologist would claim that the political-jural sphere is always, or exclusively, the concern of men, but available accounts of the political relationships that organize, link, and divide domestic groups assume that men shape public (and so, ultimately, private) life because they have both selfish interests and public authority.

Our analytical tradition, in short, has preserved the nineteenth-century division into inherently gendered spheres and, in doing so, has cast one presumably basic social fact not in moral or relational terms but, rather, in individualistic ones, wherein the shape of social institutions is implicitly understood as a reflection of individual needs, resources, or biology. Thus, we contrast family with political-jural realms but do not speak of "opposition" when distinguishing, for instance, the sphere of law from that of work, religious faith, or school, because we see the latter as the product of real human history and work. In contrast, home versus public life appears to have a transhistoric sense, at least in part, because it corresponds to our long-standing ideological terms contrasting inner and outer, love and interest, natural and constructed bonds, and men's and women's natural activities and styles. As we have seen, there is some cause to think that our acceptance of these dichotomous terms makes sense; but at the same time, it would now appear that understandings shaped by oppositional modes of thought have been – and will most likely prove themselves to be – inherently problematic for those of us who hope to understand the lives that women lead within human societies.[35]

Having conceptualized the family as something other than the world, we are then led to think that things like love and altruism, gender, the organization of kinship, and the texture of familial life cannot be adequately understood in terms that we would use to analyze society as a whole. Thus, anthropologists will argue that kinship must be understood as a phenomenon in and of itself,[36] much as many feminists proclaim that sociology is not enough to understand sex/gender orders.[37] That conventional sociology (including much of Marxist social thought) is as yet ill equipped to understand the way all human social life depends upon our forms of feeling and belief is an observation that these theorists pass by.[38]

A related point is that – not only for anthropologists but for sociologists and social historians as well – most studies of domestic groupings tend to presuppose their universal deep familial core; and so, while asking how and why domestic spheres expanded or collapsed, few analysts probe the various *contents* of familial bonds or ask how varying relationships within the home might influence relationships outside it. The fact that people elsewhere do not view domestic groupings as the closed familial groups we know, that warmth and altruism are rarely the unique prerogatives of close coresident kin – in short, that we cannot presume to know just what, in any given case, it means to be a parent, sibling, spouse, or child – are things too rarely probed because we start by thinking that we know just what the answers are. Our studies of domestic groups report their demographic flux and demonstrate how authority in public life can shape such things as residential choice and aspects of familial politics. But it remains the case that anthropological accounts, at least, have more to say about the organization of the public sphere (and so of male pursuits) than of real variations in domestic life because we think that social process works "from outside in."[39] The contents of what we view as women's

world is something all too readily conceptualized as shaped either by natural constraints or by the dynamism associated with men, their public dealings, and authority.

My point in citing precedents like these is not, however, to proclaim that people now should look inside the home; certainly many sociologists have done this. Nor do I think that in recognizing women's ties to the domestic sphere we would do well to work from inside out in trying to rethink the nature of the family or to reconceptualize women's lives. Rather, I would suggest that the typically flat and unilluminating picture of women that appears in most conventional accounts is bound up with theoretical difficulties that emerge whenever we assume that feminine or domestic spheres can be distinguished from the larger world of men because of their presumably panhuman functions. And insofar as feminists are willing to accept this kind of virtually presocial and unchanging base for women's lives, their explorations of the worlds of women will remain a mere addition – and not a fundamental challenge – to traditional ways of understanding social forms as the creation of the lives and needs of men.

The most serious deficiency of a model based upon two opposed spheres appears, in short, in its alliance with the dualisms of the past, dichotomies which teach that women must be understood not in terms of relationship – with other women and with men – but of difference and apartness.[40] "Tied down" by functions we imagine to belong to mothers and the home, our sisters are conceptualized as beings who presently *are*, and have at all times been, the same, not actors but mere subjects of male action and female biology. And feminists reveal themselves the victims of this past when their accounts attempt to focus our attention on the important things that women do, by adding variables that concern domestic roles, maternity, and reproductive life.[41]

The Example of Simple Societies

Feminist research began – to borrow Marx's phrase – by turning sociology "on its head" and using relatively conventional sorts of tools to forge new kinds of arguments. Much as I argued in 1974 for the importance of attention to domestic spheres in order to understand the place of women in human social life, so the 1970s saw a number of essentially comparable attempts to "turn the tables" by a wide range of feminist social scientists. For some, discovering women's world[42] or sphere[43] was an analytical first step. An emphasis on informal roles[44] or muted expressive forms[45] provided a critical starting point for others. One of the most important developments in anthropology was the challenge by a number of feminist writers of a traditional account that celebrated the evolutionary first steps achieved by Man the Hunter.[46] In order to clarify my arguments above, I want to comment briefly on the process by which Woman the Gatherer came to undermine what had been Man the Hunter's pride of place and then go on to argue that our newfound gathering women are, in fact, the direct heirs of hunting men, in that each is cast within a sexually stereotyped sphere that is – empirically – problematic and – conceptually – one more instance of our tendency to think within the individualizing and biologistic terms that underlie Victorian dichotomies.

Briefly, the 1960s saw a flowering of anthropological interest concerning three related themes: human evolution, the nature of primate social life, and the organization of simple (and so, it was inferred, ancestral) hunter-gatherer societies. The research, overwhelmingly informed by ecological and adaptationist concerns, led on the one hand to the recognition that in most of the world's hunting groups, women in fact supplied most of humanity's food as gatherers and collectors of small game. But at the same time, scholars argued that it was not gathering but the hunting of large game that moved our primate ancestors over the abyss that separates humanity from the brute natural world. Hunters, it was argued, needed language – and therefore large brains – in order to communicate and plan; and in designing weapons they made further strides, providing man with his first skills in artistry and making tools.[47]

Not surprisingly, the feminist response to this account began by arguing that our schol-

arly tradition had unduly slighted women's central place. Writings through the 1970s traced a complex set of links connecting the decline in human groups of large carnivorous pointy teeth, the emergence of opposable thumbs, the rise in skill requiring larger brains in order to coordinate eye and hand, and, finally, the fact that human females needed larger pelvises in order to accommodate and bear their large-brained young. These females, in the new account, adopted upright postures which ultimately permitted them to exploit the environment within new ways. The feminist account points out as well that human infants must be born with brains still relatively immature, requiring prolonged periods of dependency and adult care. Thus, it must have been for females a necessity, of sorts, to forge at once the social and productive skills that would permit them to provide for both dependent offspring and themselves. Furthermore, females are thought to have been concerned to find not violent but cooperative males as mates, in hopes of winning males to serve as their assistants and providers. So it was, the story goes, that females managed to create our basic social skills (like language) and our first basketry and digging tools; also – because of their concern for the infant young – they managed, through selection, to create an Adam who would understand and help.

With good reason, this new account has won considerable esteem. Using forms of argument and data that had fueled an obviously deficient and male-biased traditional account, it not only made good sense but corresponded well with what ethnographers had observed of women's action in contemporary hunting groups – in particular, their very real autonomy and self-regard. Hardly passive stay-at-homes dependent on the will of men who bring them game, women in hunter-gatherer groups appear, in general, to enjoy a life as flexible and relatively egalitarian as any yet reported.

But at the same time that Woman the Gatherer has, in fact, begun to set the record straight, it seems to me that this revised account is far from adequate, if what we seek is not simply an appreciation of the contribution women make but instead an understanding of how these women organized their lives and claims in any actual society. The account insists, with reason, that our gathering sisters did important things; but it cannot explain why hunting peoples never celebrated women's deeds so necessary to human survival. Indeed, if we appeal to the contemporary evidence for what it might say about the past, hunting peoples celebrate – both in all male and in collective rites – not gathering or childbirth but rather the transcendent role of hunters. Man the Hunter boasts about his catch, and women choose as lovers able hunters; but in no report are we informed of women celebrated for their gathering skill or granted special recognition because of their success as mothers.

Yet more serious, perhaps, Woman the Gatherer as presently portrayed is overwhelmingly a biological being whose concerns are dictated by her reproductive role. She seeks a male who will impregnate and, perhaps, provide; but she has no cause to forge – or to resist – ongoing adult bonds, or to create and use a jural order made of regular expectations, norms, and rules. If anything, Woman the Gatherer seems a being who is content unto herself; absorbed in what in fact appear as relatively domestic chores, she frees her male associates to engage in risky hunts, forge wider bonds, and so, again, she allows Man the upper hand, permitting him to make the social whole.[48] That youthful men in actual hunter-gatherer groups appear much more concerned than women both to marry and to have new offspring of their own; that women do not look either to husbands or sons for meat (but rather, through their early married years, are likely to depend on fathers, lovers, or brothers); that mother-child bonds are fragile because women urge sons to leave the natal sphere and celebrate not female fertility but sexuality; that men in almost every hunting group will say they "exchange" sisters in order to get wives; and finally, that women typically find their autonomy constrained by threats of masculine rape and violence – are systematic and recurrent features of the social life in hunter-gatherer groups that an account that dwells either on men's or women's roles (or starts by studying families without attending to the links between familial

groups and overarching social process) cannot begin to understand.

I cannot detail here the contours of an alternative approach, but I would like to suggest briefly some possible directions. In recent research by Jane Collier and myself, we have been concerned to stress not the activities of women – or of men – alone; instead, we are attempting to convey the ways in which a sexual division of labor in all human social groups is bound up with extremely complex forms of interdependence, politics, and hierarchy.[49] In particular, we note that in most hunter-gatherer groups, women feed husbands but men do not necessarily feed their wives, nor do sexually mature unmarried men spend bachelor years displaying their potential as providers. Instead, what seems to happen is that women tend the hearth, feeding children and adult men who are associated with them as brothers, fathers, or husbands. And what this means for men is that they either eat at the hearths of women who enjoy a primary, marital tie to someone other than themselves – and so experience their subordination to a nonwife's husband – or else they have a wife and fire of their own and so consider themselves as social adults.

A social hierarchy is thus created which ranks married over unmarried men and so makes men want to marry. And men get married not by winning maidens' hearts but, rather, by giving game and labor to the in-laws who alone can then persuade young women to assume the wifely role. Happy to win immediate gifts both of affection and of game from lovers whom they do not have to feed, most women have small cause to seek a spouse, because they rest assured of the protection and support of fathers and brothers. Women may use their sexual appeal to undermine, support, or stimulate initiatives by men. But in a world where men – and not women – have good cause to win and make claims in a spouse, only men are recognized and described as persons who actively create the deep affinal bonds that organize society. Thus whereas men in making love make claims that stand to forge alliances – or perhaps cause conflict by disputing claims of equal men – female sexuality is seen more as a stimulant (demanding celebration) or an irritant (requiring control by rape) than as an active force in organizing social life. In fact, the reason Man the Hunter is so often celebrated in these groups is that young suitors give their in-laws game in order to dramatize affinal claims *and* to win their support in an endeavor to secure much-needed loyalty and services from a (quite reasonably) unwilling wife.

To speak of sexual asymmetry in these groups is not, therefore, to claim that all "men . . . exercise control,"[50] or that all women, unlike men, are apt to be excluded from the public world because of care required by young families. Children constrain women, not from speaking out, but instead from dabbling in the pleasant politics of sex. And sexual politics, much more than child care itself, appears to be the center of most of these women's lives. Services expected of women in the home make sense not as extensions of maternal chores but, rather, as concomitants of male hierarchies; and women celebrate their sexual selves because it is in terms of sexual claims that people of both sexes at once organize and challenge their enduring social bonds. In the end, the preeminence enjoyed by men in groups like these appears to have as much to do with the significance of marriage for relationships among the men themselves – relationships that make wives something to achieve – as it does with sexual opposition or a more brute male dominance. Though male threats of force may check such women as might see fit to rebel, the fact remains that women rarely seem oppressed, but at best limited, by the simple fact that they cannot enjoy the highest prize of male political life: the status of a hunter who enjoys a wife and private hearth.

Woman the Gatherer was discovered in an attempt to clarify our accounts of "how it all began" and to challenge those accounts which presuppose a necessary and natural foundation for male dominance. But I have sketched the outlines of an alternative approach because it seemed to me that Woman the Gatherer failed (much like her more silent sisters of the past), in sociological and ethnographic terms, to help us understand just what, in simple hunter-gatherer groups, a woman's life is all about. The problem, I suggested, lay in an attempt to understand the forms of female action and the

woman's role by asking, "What did early woman do?" and not, "What kinds of bonds and expectations shaped her life?" Assuming that brute reproductive, or productive, facts (the food they bring, the children they give life) define what women are and mean, this view casts all women, initially, as mothers. Thus, much as with domestic/public and related analytic frames, women are conceptualized as biological beings, differentiated from men, instead of as men's partners and/or competitors in an ongoing and constraining social process.[51]

My alternative is to insist that sexual asymmetry is a political and social fact, much less concerned with individual resources and skills than with relationships and claims that guide the ways that people act and shape their understandings. Thus, it appears to me that if we are to grasp just what it is that women lack or men enjoy – and with what sorts of consequences – what we require are not accounts of how it all began, but theoretical perspectives, like that sketched above, which analyze the relationships of women and men as aspects of a wider social context. If men, in making marriages, appear to be the actors who create the social world, our task is neither to accept this fact as adequate in sociological terms nor to attempt, by stressing female action, to deny it. Instead, we must begin to analyze the social processes that give appearances like these their sense, to ask just how it comes about – in a world where people of both sexes make choices that count – that men come to be seen as the creators of collective good and the preeminent force in local politics. Finally, I would suggest, if these become the questions that guide our research, we will discover answers not in biological constraints or in a morphology of functionally differentiated spheres but, rather, in specific social facts – forms of relationship and thought – concerning inequality and hierarchy.

Conclusion

I began this paper by suggesting that the time has come for us to pause and reflect critically upon the sorts of questions feminist research has posed for anthropology. Rather than quarrel with the blatantly inaccurate accounts in texts like *Women's Evolution* or *The First Sex*, I argued that our most serious problem lies, not in the futile quest for matriarchies in the past, but in our very tendency to cast questions first in universalizing terms and to look for universal truths and origins.

It seems likely to me that sexual asymmetry can be discovered in all human social groups, just as can kinship systems, marriages, and mothers. But asking "Why?" or "How did it begin?" appears inevitably to turn our thoughts from an account of the significance of gender for the organization of all human institutional forms (and, reciprocally, of the significance of all social facts to gender) toward dichotomous assumptions that link the roles of men and women to the different things that they, as individuals, are apt to do – things which for women, in particular, are all too readily explained by the apparently primordial and unchanging facts of sexual physiology.[52] My earlier account of sexual asymmetry in terms of the inevitable ranking of opposed domestic and public spheres is not, then, one that I am willing to reject for being wrong. Rather, I have suggested that the reasons that account made sense are to be found not in empirical detail, but in the categories, biases, and limitations of a traditionally individualistic and male-oriented sociology. In fact, I now would claim that our desire to think of women in terms of a presumed "first cause" is itself rooted in our failure to understand adequately that the individuals who create social relationships and bonds are themselves social creations. Because we tend to think of human social forms as a reflection of the individuals who give them life, we then find cause to fear that women's social roles as presently observed are based upon what some might claim all women are: not human actors – social adults – but reproducing mothers. At much the same time, the traditional assumptions which inform a mode of thought that sees in all domestic groupings an unchanging nurturant and altruistic core – in opposition to the more contingent bonds that make for more encompassing social orders – lead us repeatedly to reinstate the things we fear by casting women's roles in particular as something other than the product of human action in concrete, historical societies.

Thus, without denying that biological facts like reproduction leave their mark on women's lives, I would insist that facts of this sort do not themselves explain or help us to describe sexual hierarchies in relation to either domestic or public life. To claim that family shapes women is, ultimately, to forget that families themselves are things that men and women actively create and that these vary with particulars of social context. And just as families (in social and cultural terms) are far more various (and less ubiquitous) than most scholars have assumed, so gender inequalities are hardly universal in their implications or their contents. The roles the sexes play contribute to and are in turn shaped by all other inequalities in their social world, be these the split between a hunting husband and dependent bachelor youth or the relationship of capitalist to worker in our own society. In every case, the shapes that gender takes – and so, the possibilities and implications of a sexual politics – are things to be interpreted in political and social terms, that speak initially of the relationships and opportunities men and women may enjoy, in order then to comprehend how they may come to be opposed in terms of interests, images, or styles.

I cannot begin here to add to the fast-growing literature on women's place in our contemporary social form. It seems relevant to my argument, however, to observe that one way gender is bound up with modern capitalist social life is that a central quality we believe that women lack, aggression, figures overwhelmingly in popular accounts of how it is that some men fail and some succeed. I do not for one moment think that hormones make for the success of businessmen or the failings of the poor, nor that they help us understand the social fact of female subordination. But what I would suggest is that in our society talk of natural aggressive and assertive drives is one way that sexism and other forms of social inequality are interlinked. It seems no accident, for instance, that the author of *The Inevitability of Patriarchy* cites hormonal data in order to proclaim that women, lacking aggression, are destined never to succeed.

No reader of the ethnography on contemporary hunting groups would claim that capitalist competitive drives are very closely tied to the quite different qualities and skills that make for a successful husband/hunter. But having recognized that inequalities in political and economic terms are, though universal, intelligible only in their locally specific forms, we must now come to understand how much the same is true of inequalities we naturalize by talking about sex. Questions of origins may find their answers in a story based on functional oppositions between spheres. But both the question and response teach us to locate women's "problem" in a domain apart – and so to leave men happily in their traditional preserve, enjoying power and creating social rules, while, of course, ignoring women in the process. So doing, they fail to help us understand how men and women both participate in and help to reproduce the institutional forms that may oppress, liberate, join, or divide them.

 What traditional social scientists have failed to grasp is not that sexual asymmetries exist but that they are as fully social as the hunter's or the capitalist's role, and that they figure in the very facts, like racism and social class, that social science claims to understand. A crucial task for feminist scholars emerges, then, not as the relatively limited one of documenting pervasive sexism as a social fact – or showing how we can now hope to change or have in the past been able to survive it. Instead, it seems that we are challenged to provide new ways of linking the particulars of women's lives, activities, and goals to inequalities wherever they exist.

NOTES

This paper, previously known as "Thoughts on Domestic/Public," was first presented to a Rockefeller Conference on Women, Work and Family in September 1977.

1 Naomi Quinn, Anthropological Studies on Women's Status, *Annual Review of Anthropology*, 6 (1977): 181–222, esp. p. 222.

2 Edwin Ardener, Belief and the Problem of Women, in *The Interpretation of Ritual*, ed. J. LaFontaine (London: Tavistock Publications, 1972); Shirley Ardener, *Perceiving Women* (New York: John Wiley & Sons, 1975).

3 See Annette G. Weiner, Sexuality among the Anthropologists: Reproduction among the Natives, in *Sexual Antagonism, Gender, and Social change in Papua New Guinea*, ed. J. P. Poole and G. Herdt, *Social Analysis* special issue, 1982, and Trobriand Kinship from Another View: The Reproductive Power of Women and Men, *Man*, 14/2 (1979): 328–48, for probably the most articulate of anthropologists writing about the need for us to radically reconceptualize traditional perspectives on society and social structure if we are to do more than "add" data on women to what remain, in structural terms, essentially male biased accounts. At the same time, however, her "reproductive model" strikes me as dangerously close to much of the nonrelational thinking criticized below.

4 Shulamith Firestone, *The Dialectic of Sex: The Case for Feminist Revolution* (New York: Bantam Books, 1975), p. 2.

5 Linda Gordon, *Woman's Body, Woman's Right* (New York: Penguin Books, 1975).

6 N. C. Mathieu, Homme–Culture, Femme–Nature? *L'Homme*, 13/3 (1973): 101–13.

7 See Louise Lamphere, Review Essay: Anthropology, *Signs: Journal of Women in Culture and Society*, 2/3 (1977): 612–27.

8 See Elsie B. Begler, Sex, Status and Authority in Egalitarian Society, *American Anthropologist*, 80/3 (1978): 571–88; or Ruby Rohrlich-Leavitt, Barbara Sykes, and Elizabeth Weatherford, Aboriginal Women: Male and Female Anthropological Perspectives, in *Towards an Anthropology of Women*, ed. R. Reiter (New York: Monthly Review Press, 1975), for reasonable attempts to tilt the balance. A juxtaposition of these two articles – which come to radically opposed characterizations of women's lot in Australian aboriginal societies – is informative for what it says about the difficulty of deciding what is, ultimately, an evaluative argument in empirical terms.

9 See e.g. Susan Carol Rogers, Female Forms of Power and the Myth of Male Dominance: A Model of Female/Male Interaction in Peasant Society, *American Ethnologist*, 2 (1975): 727–56; Yolanda Murphy and Robert Murphy, *Women of the Forest* (New York: Columbia University Press, 1974); and Margery Wolf, *Women and the Family in Rural Taiwan* (Stanford, Calif.: Stanford University Press, 1972).

10 There is a third alternative, which situates itself somewhere between the two extremes cited here, namely, that of stressing variation and trying to characterize the factors that make for more or less "male dominance" or "female status." Karen Sacks (Engels Revisited, in *Woman, Culture, and Society*, ed. M. Rosaldo and L. Lamphere [Stanford, Calif.: Stanford University Press, 1974]) and Peggy Sanday (Women's Status in the Public Domain, ibid.) provide examples, though it is interesting to note that while forswearing universalism both in fact make use of an analytical separation between domestic and public in organizing their variables. Martin King Whyte, in *The Status of Women in Preindustrial Societies* (Princeton, NJ: Princeton University Press, 1978), argues (most cogently, I think) that only by studying variation will we begin to understand any of the processes relevant to the formation or reproduction of sexual inequalities, and therefore that methodological and political wisdom both require us to disaggregate summary characterizations concerning sexual status into their component parts. I agree with him and, further, was pleased to see that his empirical study led toward the recognition that it is virtually impossible to "rank" societies in terms of women's place. His conclusions agree with mine in that he comes to see more promise in a comparative approach that looks for social structural *configurations* than one concerned with summary evaluations. Because he is able to show that particular variables mean different things in different social contexts, his re-sults call into question all attempts to talk, cross culturally, about the components of women's status or their ever-present causes.

11 Nancy Chodorow, Family Structure and Feminine Personality; Sherry Ortner, Is Female to Male as Nature Is to Culture? [ch. 3 above]; and Michelle Rosaldo, Woman, Culture, and Society: A Theoretical Overview, in Rosaldo and Lamphere.

12 Nancy Chodorow, Being and Doing, in *Woman in Sexist Society: Studies in Power and Powerlessness*, ed. V. Gornick and B. K. Moran (New York: Basic Books, 1971); and Chodorow, Family Structure and Feminine Personality.

13 Ortner, Is Female to Male as Nature Is to Culture?

14 Colin M. Turnbull, *The Forest People* (New York: Simon & Schuster, 1961).

15 Louise Sweet, ed., Appearance and Reality: Status and Roles of Women in Mediterranean Societies, *Anthropological Quarterly*, 40 (1967); and Rogers (n. 9).

16 Ernestine Friedl, *Women and Men: An Anthropologist's View* (New York: Holt, Rinehart & Winston, 1975), p. 21.

17 Nancy Chodorow, *The Reproduction of Mothering* (Berkeley: University of California Press, 1978); and Juliet Mitchell, *Psychoanalysis and Feminism* (New York: Random House, 1974).

18 The issue is complex. A number of recent analysts have pointed to the way in which modern American family ideology leads us to think about the roles of women as defined by a necessary association of certain functions (e.g. nurturance, altruism, "diffuse enduring solidarity"; see David M. Schneider, *American Kinship: A Cultural Account* [Englewood Cliffs, NJ: Prentice-Hall, 1968]) with certain persons (close kin) and in particular with mothers (Sylvia Junko Yanagisako, Women-centered Kin Networks in Urban Bilateral Kinship, *American Ethnologist*, 4/2 [1977]: 207–26). R. Rapp (Family and Class in Contemporary America: Notes Toward an Understanding of Ideology, *Science and Society*, 42/3 [1978]: 278–300) makes it particularly clear,

however, that the ways in which this ideology of "familial bonding" maps onto groups of coresidents is problematic and varies with social class. Furthermore, Diane K. Lewis (A Response to Inequality: Black Women, Racism, and Sexism, *Signs: Journal of Women in Culture and Society*, 3/2 [1977]: 339–61) makes the cogent point that our belief in the necessary association of women and domestic functions often blinds us to the fact that, in our society, marginalization ("domestication") is more a consequence than a cause for lack of power.

19 These points are developed with reference to empirical data most fully in recent writings by Quinn (n. 1) and Whyte (n. 10). Whyte's findings make it clear, in particular, that male dominance is not something that lends itself to ranking in cross-culturally significant terms (see n. 10). That this conclusion undermines *all* arguments concerning women's status as analytically problematic – and requires that we look instead for pattern in the social structuring of gender (a conclusion very close to that of this paper) – is, however, something even Whyte has barely realized.

20 Of course, the correlated oppositions, male/female, public/domestic, do not begin with the Victorian era; one finds them more or less explicitly elaborated in political philosophy since the time of the Greeks (Nannerl Keohane, Female Citizenship: The Monstrous Regiment of Women, a paper presented at the Conference for the Study of Political Thought, April 1979). My stress on the Victorians derives, first of all, from a conviction that they are our most relevant predecessors in this regard, and, second, from an intuition that the Victorian dichotomies – in their appeal to maternity and biology – were, in fact, significantly different from those that came before. Once it is realized that domestic/public constitutes an ideological rather than an objective and necessary set of terms, we can, of course, begin to explore the differences in formulations which may appear initially to be "more of the same."

21 Herbert Spencer's assumptions about women run throughout volume 1, *Domestic Institutions*, of his multivolume *Principles of Sociology* (New York: D. Appleton & Co., 1893), in which the wedding of these simple assumptions to biology and nascent functionalism is clear. John Haller and Robin Haller (*The Physician and Sexuality in Victorian America* [Urbana: University of Illinois Press, 1974]) provide a rather devastating statement of some of the historical implications of Spencerian misogyny, and the relationship of sexist attitudes to his general theory is explored as well in Elizabeth Fee (The Sexual Politics of Victorian Social Anthropology, in *Clio's Consciousness Raised*, ed. M. Hartman and L. C. Banner [New York: Harper & Row, 1974]). My own reading of Spencer is, if anything, a bit more sympathetic: Of Victorian evolutionists, he paid some of the closest attention to available anthropological data, and his sexist assumptions emerge, in only slightly less offensive form, in much of his contemporaries' work.

22 For useful critical readings of Friedrich Engels's now classic *The Origins of the Family, Private Property, and the State* (in *Karl Marx and Frederick Engels: Selected Works*, vol. 2 [Moscow: Foreign Languages Publishing House, 1962]), see Sacks, Engels Revisited (n. 10), Ann Lane (Women in Society: A Critique of Frederick Engels, in *Liberating Women's History*, ed. B. Carroll [Urbana: University of Illinois Press, 1976]), and Eleanor Leacock (Introduction to Frederick Engels, in *The Origin of the Family, Private Property, and the State* [New York: International Publishers Co., 1972]). Contemporary interest in Engels's materialism and his sense of variation tends to excuse his "Victorian" biases as trivial; I would argue, by contrast, that his much quoted dictum – "According to the materialist conception, the determining factor in history is, in the last resort, the production and reproduction of immediate life" (Engels, pp. 170–1) – fits squarely with the individualizing and dichotomous

tradition criticized here and is, in very deep ways, problematic for a Marxist understanding of women's lives. That the banner of reproduction has been assumed by a number of neo-Marxist and Marxist-feminist social scientists (e.g., Claude Meillassoux, *Femmes, greniers et capitaux* [Paris: Françoise Maspero Librairie, 1975]; Renate Bridenthal, The Dialectics of Production and Reproduction in History, *Radical America*, 10/2 (1976): 3–11; and Felicity Edholm, Olivia Harris, and Kate Young, Conceptualizing Women. *Critique of Anthropology*, 3/9 and 10 [1977]: 101–30) only underlines the difficulties we all face in conceptualizing the kinds of issues with which this paper is concerned.

23 Georg Simmel, *Conflict and the Web of Group Affiliations* (New York: Macmillan Publishing Co., 1955), p. 180.

24 Émile Durkheim, *Suicide* (Glencoe, Ill.: Free Press, 1951), pp. 384–5.

25 Ibid., and Lewis A. Coser, Georg Simmel's Neglected Contributions to the Sociology of Women, *Signs: Journal of Women in Culture and Society*, 2/4 (1977): 869–76.

26 J. A. Barnes, Genetrix: Genitor: Nature: Culture? in *The Character of Kinship*, ed. J. Goody (London: Cambridge University Press, 1973).

27 Talcott Parsons, *Social Structure and Personality* (New York: Free Press, 1964); and Morris Zelditch, Role Differentiation in the Nuclear Family, in *Family, Socialization and Interaction Process*, ed. T. Parsons and R. Bales (Glencoe, Ill.: Free Press, 1955).

28 Maurice Bloch, The Long Term and the Short Term: The Economic and Political Significance of the Morality of Kinship, in Goody.

29 That the classic Parsonian assumptions about inherently differentiated instrumental and expressive "functions" (e.g. Parsons, p. 59) in interaction may, in large part, be the product of an ideological evaluation of the activities appropriate to different (and implicitly gendered) "spheres" is suggested in Rosaldo, *Women, Culture, and Society*

(n. 10). For a useful critique of the analytical opposition between instrumental and expressive and, more generally, of assumptions about differentiation within functionalist sociology, see Veronica Beechy, Women and Production: A Critical Analysis of Some Sociological Theories of Women's Work, in *Feminism and Materialism*, ed. Annette Kuhn and Ann-Marie Wolpe (London: Routledge & Kegan Paul, 1978). Judith Irvine's recent critique, Formality and Informality in Communicative Events (*American Anthropologist*, 81/4 [1979]: 773–90), of the concepts of formality and informality comes from a different but relevant perspective. What is interesting for our purposes is that she shows at once that the empirical referents of the formal/informal distinction are problematic at best and, further (as with domestic/public), that the intuitive appeal of this distinction is rooted in the way it promises to connect aspects of social "function" with observed interactional "styles." This functional linkage is then called into question.

30 My characterization here follows closely on Meyer Fortes (*Kinship and the Social Order* [Chicago: Aldine Publishing Co., 1969]), who points out that a commitment to "the familial origins of . . . kinship systems" (p. 49) was important to Malinowski, whose *The Family among the Australian Aborigines* (New York: Schocken Books, 1963) was specifically intended as an argument for universals, and to A. R. Radcliffe-Brown (The Social Organization of Australian Tribes, *Oceania*, 1 [1930]: 34–63, 206–46, 322–41, 426–56), who assumed a familial, or genealogical, "core" to kinship, although Radcliffe-Brown himself was interested in more variable jural realms. The Australian aborigines have for a long time enjoyed the questionable status of "prototypical primitive" (they figure centrally, e.g., in Durkheim's *The Elementary Forms of the Religious Life* and Freud's *Totem and Taboo*), and so the "discovery" that they too have "families" was crucial for universalist thought. Fortes is

concerned to dissociate himself from genealogism but not absolutely: "I regard the political jural aspect as complementary to the familial aspect of kinship relations" (p. 73): in a world of two spheres, nature and culture remain of equal analytical status, complementary and distinct.

31 David Schneider (What Is Kinship All About? in *Kinship Studies in the Morgen Centennial Year*, ed. Priscilla Reining [Washington, DC: Anthropological Society of Washington, 1972]) discusses the genealogizing tendency in most anthropological treatments of kinship by relating it to yet another piece of our modern, dichotomizing ideology, a tendency to discriminate and see as necessarily complementary the orders of nature and of law. Sylvia Yanagisako's review of studies of family and kinship (Family and Household: The Analysis of Domestic Groups, *Annual Review of Anthropology*, 8 [1979]: 161–205) traces the relationship between assumptions about genealogy and domestic spheres. The particular conundrums we confront when trying to think about apparently universal "facts" like kinship – especially once we recognize that would-be analytical terms are rooted in ideology – is discussed, from different points of view, by Andrew Strathern ("Kinship, Descent and Locality: Some New Guinea Examples," in Goody [n. 26]) and Steve Barnett and Martin Silverman (*Ideology and Everyday Life* [Ann Arbor: University of Michigan Press, 1979]).

32 My characterization here leans heavily on Yanagisako, Family and Household: The Analysis of Domestic Groups, which is a critical discussion of Fortes's analytical framework (see n. 30).

33 Fortes speaks, e.g. about the "matricentral cell," in his introduction to *The Developmental Cycle in Domestic Groups*, ed. J. Goody (London: Cambridge University Press, 1958), p. 8, and argues that "the domestic domain is the system of social relations through which the reproductive nucleus is integrated with the environment and with the structure of the total society" (p. 9). In characterizing the familial, as opposed to the political-jural, component of meaning in kinship relations, he contrasts "the affection and trust parents and children have for one another" with the "authority of the parents and the subordination of the children" (Fortes, p. 64). My suggestion, of course, is that this contrast does not necessarily derive from actual social relationships "out there" but, rather, that its "sense" is located in a particular, Western, highly gendered ideology.

34 For one of the clearest discussions of these distinctions, see Donald R. Bender, A Refinement of the Concept of Household: Families, Co-Residence and Domestic Functions, *American Anthropologist*, 69/5 (1967): 493–504; and Yanagisako, Family and Household: The Analysis of Domestic Groups. Lila Leibowitz's recent book, *Females, Males, Families* (North Scituate, Mass.: Duxbury Press, 1978), does a first-rate job of documenting variation in structure and function in both primate and human familial groups and, in doing so, challenges all attempts to give a unitary, functionalist account of either gender roles or families. Unfortunately, she seems to forget her own best advice when she then attempts (unsuccessfully, I think) to come up with a cross-cultural definition of the family that lacks functionalist presuppositions. In addition, she diverges from my own approach in trying to account for the emergence of familial groups in a manner that casts families as the creations of individual needs, which in some sense "precede" society.

35 For a closely related statement, see Patricia Caplan and Janet M. Burge, eds. *Women United, Women Divided* (London: Tavistock Publications, 1978). There the authors argue that the problem with domestic/public as a formulation is that it fails to help us conceptualize the nature of the "articulation" among spheres, and they suggest that this articulation should be understood with reference to relations of production. See also Bridget O'Laughlin, Production and

Reproduction: Meillassoux's Femmes, greniers and capitaux, *Critique of Anthropology* 2/8 (1977): 3–32, for a critique of a related set of oppositions as inherently incompatible with the study of relationships.

36 Fortes, pp. 219–49.

37 This issue runs through contemporary Marxist-feminist discussion (see, e.g. Kuhn and Wolpe, n. 29 above); for a deep and telling statement of this position (one with which I find myself in sympathy, if not agreement), see Gayle Rubin, The Traffic in Women [ch. 4 above]; also Heidi Hartmann, Capitalism, Patriarchy, and Job Segregation by Sex, *Signs: Journal of Women in Culture and Society*, 1/3, pt. 2 (1975): 137–69.

38 My characterization is not entirely fair, since concerns for attitudes, culture, consciousness, or, in Marxist terms, the reproduction of ideology are long-standing issues in social science. Still, one gets the feeling that feminist distress with the failure of social science to address issues of gender in the past feeds a sense that gender as a sociological issue is inherently different from other aspects of social organization with implications for personal identity, demanding some sort of nonconventional (and, usually, psychologically oriented) account. My own sense, by contrast, is that our frustration stems, first, from the failure of sociological theory to relate gender in systematic ways to other kinds of inequality and, second, from the inadequacies of a utilitarian tradition that has made it extremely difficult to conceptualize the sociological significance of human consciousness, culture, or thought.

39 Yanagisako documented this point in Family and Household (n. 31) with a number of ethnographic examples. Again and again she found that variation in domestic spheres is not deemed deeply interesting nor is it given the descriptive or conceptual attention associated with more public or jural realms.

40 June Nash, The Aztecs and the Ideology of Male Dominance, (*Signs: Journal of

Women in Culture and Society*, 4/2 [1978]: 349–62), and June Nash and Eleanor Leacock, Ideologies of Sex: Archetypes and Stereotypes (*Annals of the New York Academy of Science* 285 [1977]: 618–45) have suggested that such dualisms as nature/culture and domestic public are rooted less in other cultures' "reality" than in our modern Western ideology. Unfortunately, their critique stops at the level of debunking Western Capitalism Bias, without, I think, formulating an alternative adequate both to our intuitions and to the problem (understanding gender) at hand.

41 Again, it seems to me that this is the inclination in a good deal of Marxist-feminist writing and research (see nn. 21, 34, and 35).

42 Carroll Smith-Rosenberg, The Female World of Love and Ritual: Relations between Women in Nineteenth-Century America, *Signs: Journal of Women in Culture and Society*, 1/1 (1975): 1–30.

43 Nancy F. Cott, *The Bonds of Womanhood: "Woman's Sphere" in New England, 1780–1835* (New Haven, Conn.: Yale University Press, 1977).

44 Susan Rogers, Female Forms of Power (n. 9); Susan Rogers, Woman's Place: A Critical Review of Anthropological Theory, *Comparative Studies in Society and History*, 20/1 (1978): 123–62; and Beverly L. Chiñas, *The Isthmus Zapotecs: Women's Roles in Cultural Context* (New York: Holt, Rinehart & Winston, 1973).

45 E. Ardener (n. 2 above).

46 Sally Slocum, Woman the Gatherer: Male Bias in Anthropology, in Reiter (n. 8 above); Nancy Tanner and Adrienne Zihlman, Women in Evolution. Part I: Innovation and Selection in Human Origins, *Signs: Journal of Women in Culture and Society*, 1/3, pt. 1 (1976): 585–608; and Adrienne Zihlman, Women in Evolution. Part II: Subsistence and Social Organization among Early Hominids, *Signs: Journal of Women in Culture and Society*, 4/1 (1978): 4–20.

47 E.g. Sherwood L. Washburn and C. S. Lancaster, The Evolution of Hunting, in

Man the Hunter, ed. R. Lee and I. DeVore (Chicago: Aldine Publishing Co. 1968).

48 Amusingly (if distressingly), this view is most explicit in Charlotte Perkins Gilman, *Women and Economics* (New York: Harper & Row, 1966), in which she argues that women, once dominant, gave the business of "building society" over to men in order to win their cooperation.

49 The research referred to is explicated in M. Z. Rosaldo and Jane Collier, Politics and Gender in Simple Societies, in *Sexual Meanings: The Cultural Construction of Gender and Sexuality*, ed. S. Ortner and H. Whitehead (Cambridge: Cambridge University Press, 1981). In addition, Jane Collier's *Marriage and Inequality in Classless Societies* (Stanford, Calif.: Stanford University Press) provides, I think, the fullest theoretical and descriptive explication of the perspective advocated here.

50 Robin Fox, *Kinship and Marriage* (Harmondsworth, Middlesex: Penguin Books, 1967), p. 31.

51 Donna Haraway's Animal Sociology and a Natural Economy of the Body Politic, Parts I and II (*Signs: Journal of Women in Culture and Society*, 4/1 [1978]: 21–60) on ideology in recent primatology and evolutionary thought shows how Tanner and Zihlman, in particular, are using the analytical presuppositions of sociobiology to make a most unsociobiological argument. Haraway does not claim that this approach is wrong, but she does urge caution. My argument here develops what I take to be Haraway's intention. In particular, I have suggested at a number of points that an approach that assumes or postulates "opposed spheres" and/or the "obvious" significance of biological reproduction (and motherhood) is wedded in fairly deep ways to the biases associated with "methodological individualism" in sociology. "Two spheres" tend, we have seen, to reflect what are taken as (biologically given) individual needs and capacities; therefore, it is only on the assumption that society *is* the simple product of the individuals who compose it that an analysis in terms of two spheres makes sense. Sociobiology makes this assumption. My point has been to call it into question by stressing that it is only by understanding social relationships that we will grasp the significance, in any given case, of individual capacities and constraints.

52 My argument with biologism operates on two levels. Men and women both, of course, have bodies, and in some sense our biological nature does constrain what we can be (we cannot live under water or fly in the sky). More deeply, I would not question that there are important "interactions" between such things as hormones and behavioral dispositions, like aggression. What I do object to, first, in theoretical terms, is a tendency to think that social relationships "reflect" and ultimately are "built upon" presumed biological givens (a tendency associated with methodological individualism [see n. 48]). And second, strategically, I am disturbed that when we look to find a biological first base we tend to think of women's lives as shaped by biological "constraints," whereas the "in-born" characteristic most usually associated with men – aggression – tends to be seen, if anything, as a source of freedom and a ground for the creation of constructive social bonds.

6

Toward a Unified Theory of Class, Race, and Gender

Karen Brodkin

Two contradictory missions lie at the heart of anthropological practice. The first is to understand, appreciate, and interpret cultural uniqueness in its own terms, a mission in which ethnographic case studies have been central. The second mission is to generalize, to discover similarities amid diversity, and to develop cross-cultural explanations and theories that proceed in practice from a much more restricted range of Western cultural frameworks. Just as anthropologists grapple with tensions over how much attentiveness to accord sameness and difference, so too marxists and socialist feminists struggle with this same tension in theorizing the interrelations of class, race, and gender. This effort has been in explicit dialogue and struggle with nonfeminist marxism over how to conceptualize class. Do race and gender "reduce" to class? Are they separable and secondary dimensions of being in the context of theorizing social transformation? Like anthropologists, both marxists and socialist feminists rely heavily on case studies and comparisons of attempted social transformations to answer these questions. While anthropology has considerable sophistication in dealing with tensions between specificity and generalization in cross-cultural comparison, it can benefit from feminist scholars' growing fund of experience in dealing with similar tensions in conceptualizing the interrelations of these three central dimensions of social being in the twentieth-century world. This paper reviews those efforts – in dialogue with nonfeminist marxism – to develop such a theoretical framework. There has been an extraordinary florescence of work in this area, much more than can be adequately discussed in a single paper. Consequently, this essay is selective in its focus on the United States, and does not pretend to do justice to the wealth of literature worldwide.

More important, it is also selective in an interpretive sense, in that I want to explore the ways that feminist theories and case studies are, or can be read as sustaining the centrality of class and class struggle as key forces for social transformation. I am seeking both to retain Marx's notion of class and to modify it very significantly so that it becomes both a

From Karen Brodkin Sacks, "Toward a Unified Theory of Class, Race, and Gender," pp. 534–50 in *American Ethnologist*, 16/3 (1989). © 1989 by University of California Press. Reprinted by permission of University of California Press via Copyright Clearance Center, and the author, now Karen Brodkin.

gendered and racially specific concept, one that has no race-neutral or gender-neutral "essence." This may be controversial to some marxists and some feminists, but it seems to be a way to move toward that unified understanding sought by both, of how racial, class, and gender oppression are part of a single, specifiable, and historically created system.

The plan of the paper is as follows: A brief first part suggests that second-wave socialist feminists came to focus so intensely on theorizing women's domestic and community-based experiences in response to a marxist and labor union practice that almost equated class struggle with shop-floor struggle. One of the most striking differences between the first and second wave of feminist thought is the amount of attention the latter has devoted to analyzing "the private sphere." Indeed, analysis of women's unwaged labor in all its diversity has become the center of feminist attempts to understand the links between class and gender analysis.

The second part shows how feminist debates about domestic labor led to theoretical understandings of the ways in which women experienced class differently from men, and led as well to the beginnings of a theoretical recognition that so too did white and racial/ethnic women. In the American context at least, the working class historically has been created in racially/ethnically specific ways such that one's race was and continues to be a relation to the means of production, with respect to labor and reproduction.

The third part explores both the parallels and the racial diversity of working-class women's experiences and struggles, and the ways in which these shape the directions of an emerging, unified theory. Although class and class struggle are key forces for social transformation, recent feminist case studies considerably modify Marx's vision of class and class struggle in two ways. First, instead of focusing on the wage nexus as that which defines an individual's class membership, they look through working-class women's eyes to focus on class reproduction, the unities of women's work and family lives, and the community of working-class membership. Second, they theorize racial/ethnic and regional work-ing-class diversity stemming both from the funds of experience crystallized in racial/ethnic cultural traditions, and from the political and economic differences in relation to the means of capitalist production.

Social Context of Feminism

The more radical streams of second-wave feminism were born from the milieu of post-World War II grassroots and freedom movements among people of color around the world. These movements challenged socialist and community practice and theory about the relations of race and class, and the relations of anti-racist struggle to class struggle. Marxist theories as well as less articulated notions about class consciousness and class struggles have come largely from analyses of exemplary cases. In this respect, marxist praxis and "proof" is not that different from anthropological praxis and "proof." In the United States, the Communist party's successes during the 1930s – following on some 40 years of industrial class warfare between 1876 and 1918 – in building the CIO and creating powerful industrial trade unions shaped a generation of radical American understandings of the nature of working-class struggle as centered at the "point of production" in heavy industry (Brecher 1972). Shop-floor issues and battles were some of the most dramatic and vital struggles of that era, and subsequently came to be seen as the only ones that had revolutionary potential. Because those shop floors were mainly white and male, both in the United States and in Europe, the class analysis that developed from this practice was race and gender biased: neither people of color nor women were seen as being at the center of the working class, nor were the issues that affected them most directly seen as class issues or as politically central ones – even in cases where black and women workers were thrown out of their unionized wartime jobs.

By the early 1960s, the center of grassroots activism in the United States shifted away from factories partly as a result of earlier union gains and postwar industrial prosperity. In this milieu, it was harder to persuade people that trade union issues were the stuff of real struggle when major changes and mobilization were being made from black, Latino, and Native American community bases around a wide range of issues that in the course of the decade came increasingly clearly to link class and racial oppression. The vitality and successes of these movements' community-based mobilization around housing, voting, welfare, and education issues drew old and young activists to them, and made them new models for popular and working-class movements.[1] In the last decade, work by Sara Evans (1980), Paula Giddings (1984), Jo Ann Robinson (1987), and Ellen Cantarow and Sharon O'Malley (1980), as well as the first conference devoted exclusively to black women's contributions to the civil rights movement (Atlanta, 12–13 October, 1988) have begun to reveal the ways in which the more radical currents of feminism developed from and were fundamentally shaped by the civil rights movement, and more specifically, by black women's centrality in it. Many early feminists got their political education from the women who led the day-to-day work of the local SNCC, CORE, and NAACP chapters. There were also the national leaders, some deliberately not so visible, like Ella Baker, while others like Daisy Bates, Gloria Richardson, Rosa Parks, and Fanny Lou Hamer were more visible.

As the issues and actors of American grassroots politics shifted in the course of the 1950s and 60s, so too did the ways scholars and activists conceptualize the nature of the social and interpersonal relations that might emerge from their efforts. An older vision of these relationships had been associated with the theory and practice of pre-World War II shop-floor left politics, of working-class uprisings by people of diverse races and genders, but based on their being oppressed in the same way by the same source – a revolution of likes. A newer set of visions was being born from attempts to make sense out of the diverse history of postwar anti-racist and anti-colonialist movements, of the same people rising against a wider range of oppressions faced by all of the people some of the time and some of the people all of the time. The first vision saw racism and sexism as inextricably bound

up with race and gender as important aspects of social being. It seemed to imply that race and gender were salient social categories and categories of meaningful cultural existence only to the degree that people were stigmatized on those bases, and that they would therefore wither away as necessary parts of the process of eliminating racism and sexism.

The visions born of the anti-colonial, freedom, and feminist movements were just the opposite. They celebrated race and gender-based cultures, stressing them (albeit variously and selectively) as repositories of strength and resistance as well as providing alternative models for constructing social relationships and social identity. These movements envisioned maintaining their diversities while somehow sharing their strengths more widely. Or, as George C. Wolfe put it, "So yes, America is getting more colored, or maybe we're beginning to realize just how colored we've always been. But let's not stop there. Let's get busy coloring it brown and yellow and lots of really interesting off-shades of white. And even if somebody wanted to stop it, it's too late" (Wolfe 1988: 40).

It was this second set of visions that animated marxist-feminists and brought them into conflict with the majority of active marxists, at least through the 1960s. For Marx, and for many on the left who were inspired by the first vision, what defined workers as a class was that each of them individually sold their labor power to capital, and from their similar relationship they developed common interests, perspectives, and interdependence in opposition to capital. It is obvious that the industrial working class once away from the factory floor was not a sack of individual proletarians, each in independent relation to capital. But this was the model developed from Marx's labor theory of value, and it prevailed as well in a great deal of non-marxist labor politics prevalent through most of the 60s.

The hegemony of the shop-floor perspective meant that post-World War II would-be feminists tended to work within an analytic tradition that went back to Engels, but which was also quite widely shared across the left political spectrum from people like Charlotte Perkins Gilman to Lenin. Its received wisdom was that incorporation into wage labor was key to ending women's oppression, because only wage labor would give them the necessary class experience from which to develop a working-class consciousness. I do not wish to deny the progressive role this perspective played at particular points in its history. Nevertheless, it did not regard family and domestic relations as class relations. Instead, they were most often seen (flattening the complexities of Marx's formulations) as somehow natural rather than social, sometimes peripheral, or personal. But in any event "real" class struggle would be both necessary and sufficient conditions for creating egalitarian gender relations. So long as attention focused on "point of production" issues and militance, there was no room to explore the social relations by which the working class made itself a class able to reproduce itself daily and over the generations. Consequently, the social relations of domestic labor remained outside class analysis, as did household, community, racial, and quality-of-life issues.

One consequence of such a perspective was that women had no class identity as women, or as Verena Stolcke so elegantly put it:

If women's subordination is attributed to women's exclusion from production, then equality between men and women will depend on women's incorporation into production. But this reasoning is based on the idea that only by making accessible to women the defining attribute of men within class society, i.e., their non-involvement in procreation and involvement in so-called productive labour, only by converting women into men, will equality be achieved.... To propose that women have first to become like men in order to become free is almost like suggesting that class exploitation might be ended by making it possible for workers to become capitalists. (Stolcke 1981: 46)

How are Gender, Class, and Racial Oppression Related?

When early North American second-wave feminists first claimed "the personal is political," they probably did not realize the theoretical depth and breadth that later theorists would discover in so simple a slogan. Initially, "the personal" meant the politics of experience, of interpersonal and sexual relations with men, but it was not long before it expanded to encompass lesbian sexualities, reproductive rights, heterosexism, "private" violence against women and public complicity in making it an institution, as well as the economic exploitation of women's unwaged labor. Indeed, Maria Mies argues that this sequence of widening awareness is being repeated throughout the Third World as feminist movements spring up on all continents (Mies 1986: 6–44). How are we to understand this complex of things that is most commonly referred to as patriarchy or the subordination of women? More specifically, how is it related to capitalism and the class system? Although there are many approaches, I want to focus on debates over the meaning of domestic labor and its relation to class oppression. White socialist feminists have focused on unwaged domestic labor (including childbearing and -rearing) as the defining center of women's subordination. A number of black, Latina, and Asian feminists argued that women of color also have experienced domestic labor as waged labor, and that this has entailed forms of subordination that are at once different from white women's, and that pit them against white women.

In this section I will summarize the major debates about domestic labor by which socialist-feminist theory has developed a historical understanding of the relationship between class and gender, and the beginnings of such an understanding with respect to race. In brief, the dialectics of debate have been as follows: Early recognition of domestic exploitation in capitalism led to arguments that this was a universal and precapitalist condition of social existence and at the root of women's subordination under capitalism ("domestic labor as primary"). Counter arguments suggested that capitalism's organization of waged labor kept women out, and hence was what devalued domestic labor, and hence women as a gender ("capitalism as primary"). Neither of these arguments stood for very long in the face of new anthropological and social historical studies of women's life circumstances.

A second line of argument suggested that women's subordination lay in an interaction of a precapitalist patriarchal mode of production with a capitalist mode of production ("dual systems theory"). Dual systems theorists argued that both capitalism and patriarchy shared responsibility for the particular shape of women's oppression in the contemporary world, and that working-class men joined capital in benefiting from women's domestic subordination even as they suffered from wage exploitation. Dual systems theorists faced critiques that their concept of patriarchy was ahistorical and culture-bound.

A third stream of argument that struggled to relate race to gender and class challenged the notion of domestic labor and problematized its meanings for women and men of color. In the United States black, Asian, and Latina feminists argued that for women of color, domestic labor was often both waged work and unwaged labor. Because domestic labor had different shapes, it was likely to have a different historical significance for domestic relations in the social structures of minority communities. Some European feminists worked toward theories that stressed the similarities between the racially defined unwaged labor of colonized peoples and the gender-defined unwaged labor of women. These theorists expanded the notion of a potentially revolutionary class to include the unwaged as well as waged workers whose continued existence is crucial to capital.

Women's domestic labor as primary

To conceptualize women's subordination in political and economic terms was the first task early feminists theorists took on. At its center was a gendered reconceptualization of domestic labor under capitalism. By the late 1960s marxist-feminists began to analyze the family as a unit of production, hence as embedding a set of political and economic relations. By doing this, they challenged notions that domestic relations were only about consumption and emotion, and were somehow "natural" rather than political (Mainardi 1970). Juliet Mitchell made the first major effort to develop a marxist-feminist analysis of women's domestic oppression. She distin-

guished four aspects, or "structures" of oppression: production, reproduction, sexuality, and the socialization of children (1966, 1971).

Margaret Benston (1969) argued that women are defined under capitalism as the group responsible for creating use-values in a domestic setting, that the family is a production unit key to the existence of capitalism, and that women's oppression hangs on their position as uncompensated domestic workers whose free labor benefits capital in two ways: freeing capital from having to pay for the full cost of working-class maintenance and reproduction, and maintaining women as a reserve army of wage laborers, while Rayna Rapp (1978) suggested in turn that family as a concept was the ideology by which domestic units reproduced themselves. In any event, this early theory provided a class analysis in which women were directly exploited by capital through their social responsibility for unwaged domestic labor.

Capitalism as primary

While the dominant current in marxist-feminist analysis was to see women's relations to the means of capitalist production as unwaged laborers, and exploitable primarily in this capacity, a smaller current suggested that its origin lay in capitalism's organization of *waged* work combined with women's precapitalist domestic responsibilities, which made them less exploitable in the waged labor sector, excluded from it, and hence subordinated to men under capitalism (Brenner and Ramas 1984; Sacks 1974; Vogel 1983). In these interpretations, because women were responsible in agrarian culture for raising children, early capitalists could not recruit them to work as long and hard as men, nor persuade them to work for such low wages (because their wages had to support child as well as mother). This made women less reliably and intensively exploitable than men as workers, and therefore less attractive and valuable to capitalists. Economically disadvantaged in wage relations, as these came to be key means to subsistence, women became dependent on men and subordinate to them in the family.

Although I made this argument in 1974, today I think it is wrong because it confuses gender, social status, and kinship. In one or another way, these arguments assume that early capitalists operated in a cultural system in which motherhood and marriage were attributes of the gender woman. In such a cultural system capitalists would not have distinguished single from married women, or actual mothers from childless women or women in pre-childbearing years, would have rejected them all categorically, and simply sought men as reliable and exploitable workers. It is precisely because the cultural systems from which capitalism developed had already made linkages among gender, status, and labor that capitalists did not develop an anti-parent bias rather than a gender bias (and employ *both* single, childless women and men equally). We know that did not happen. The capitalism-as-primary argument presumes that gender was already socially constructed as it came to be constructed in the nineteenth century, a fundamental and dichotomous division, more so than age, condition of parenthood, or generation. Moreover, it presumes that the essence of defining the gender "woman" is the social status "mother," and that potential mothers are in the same category as actual ones. We will see later that capitalists in the past and present have had no difficulty in recognizing that youth and lack of socially defined financial responsibility for others make young women ideal workers precisely because these conditions allow them to work for very low wages. Indeed, this is the main attraction for the proliferation of garment and microelectronic plants in Asia and Mexico. Recent case studies show that offshore monopolies specifically target young single women, fire them when they get pregnant, and often refuse to hire mothers, and that reliance on a workforce of young, single women has been characteristic of the garment and textile industries since their beginnings (Frankel 1984; Hall et al. 1987; Lamphere 1987; Nash and Fernandez-Kelly 1983; Ong 1983). This suggests that however incompatible motherhood may be with waged labor, it was not a likely first cause of lower wages for women, nor, following from this, is it likely that capitalist wage relations are first causes of women's domestic oppression under capitalism.

Jane Humphries (1977) took a different tack to explain unequal wages. She saw demands for a male family wage and consequent maintenance of women as nonwaged workers as a historical working-class strategy to limit capital's control over working-class life, both by protecting women and children from wage labor itself, and by freeing women to do the work that preserves a working-class infrastructure to handle child care, welfare, health care, and education free from dependence on capitalists. This followed similar arguments that began to be made in the mid-1970s by social scientists and historians who saw family relations as "cultures of resistance" to capitalist exploitation (Caulfield 1974; MacLean 1982; Tax 1980), and by ethnographic work on domestic and working-class kinship networks as organizations for coping with economic adversity (Eisenstein 1983; Sacks 1984, 1988b; Stack 1974). This point as well as important critiques of this position will be taken up later.

Universal patriarchy and dual systems

Even as some theorists were locating the central dynamic for the perpetuation of race and gender oppression in capitalism, others were discussing the origins of "patriarchy," conceived as a universal system of oppression preceding and coexisting with capitalism (and socialism). Among others, Meillassoux (1981) stressed that male domination and control of women's sexuality in marriage were at the root of women's subordination from the beginning. Edholm, Harris, and Young (1977) and Stolcke (1981) both criticized assumptions that the oppression of women could have been kept going without any historical signs of resistance, that it is a universal pillar on which precapitalist social orders are built, and that it is neither something that needs explaining nor changing.

Other theorists were less concerned with origins of patriarchy than with its persistence as a precapitalist system of domination separate from but in symbiosis with capitalism. They explained the relations between gender and class subordination as a product of two mutually reinforcing systems of domination – capitalism and patriarchy – such that both the capitalists and the working-class men who benefited from women's domestic labor acted in concert to maintain women's subordination (Beneria 1982; Eisenstein 1979; Hartmann 1976; Jaggar 1983). By extension, the concept of "public patriarchy" was developed to describe an alleged shift from individual male control over women to state control via family and reproductive policies of capitalist states (Boris and Bardaglio 1983). Such views were criticized for the lack of historical specificity in the concept of patriarchy (Edholm, Harris, and Young 1977), and for not being able to specify exactly how patriarchy and capitalism were related historically or conceptually (Sargent 1981). Maria Mies argued further that such dual system explanations replicate and reinforce capitalism's separation of public and private by assigning patriarchy to a private sphere: "women's oppression in the private sphere of the family or in 'reproduction' is assigned to 'patriarchy,' patriarchy being seen as part of the superstructure, and their exploitation as workers in the office and factory is assigned to capitalism" (1986: 38).

Race, gender, and class

All these theories spoke inadequately or not at all to racial domination, and efforts to comprehend all three systems of domination expanded efforts already begun mainly by feminists of color to develop voices and theoretical frameworks built from their experiences. One important theoretical strand emerged from black feminist analyses of women's lives in Afro-American culture. Another came from analyses of black, Latina, and Asian women's experiences with domestic labor as waged work (Dill 1979; Glenn 1985, 1986; Palmer 1983, 1984; Rollins 1985; Romero 1987).

Bonnie Dill bridged the two in her study of the ways in which black women domestic workers constructed social identity based on their contributions to their families and communities. Patricia Hill Collins (1989) and Elsa Barkley-Brown (1989) emphasize the complementarity and mutual reinforcement that exists in Afro-American culture between individual identity and expressiveness on the one hand, and group membership and responsibility on the other. This is very different from the opposition between group and individual in domin-

ant white American cultural constructs. Collins argues that Afro-American women – and the Afro-American feminism that derives from their experiences as everyday black women – are central to culture and community-building by virtue of their places in families and churches. Dill, Collins, and Barkley-Brown join Paula Giddings (1984) and Cheryl Gilkes (1980, 1988) in arguing that community and family-based social identity construction, and rejection of occupational bases for status are part of Afro-American patterns of resistance to the negative ways that white society defines black women and men based on the low-status occupations – and hence class position – to which it confines them.

Analyses of black, Latino, and Asian women's experiences of domestic work by feminists of color gives them a distinctly different perspective on and critique of domestic labor from that developed by white feminists. Domestic waged workers have struggled to define their jobs as work with concrete job descriptions, regular, adequate wages and benefits, and, not least, to be allowed to work free of denigrating close supervision. This should be consistent with white feminist efforts, and supported by them, yet the adversaries of domestic workers are the middle-class (usually but not always white) women for whom they work. In perhaps the sharpest analysis, Rollins (1985) argues that the "madams" who act as "matronizing" employers are acting as if domestic laborers were objects of charity (and their employers were dispensers of it), and their maids' work was not real work worthy of real wages. This certainly undercuts feminist efforts. Phyllis Palmer argues that white feminists have a history of "cutting off their nose to spite their face" – in the sense of denying support to black women's struggles that would also benefit white women. She locates this in fear of being identified with black women, who have been stereotyped in the dominant culture as bad women. Rollins argues that madams "matronize" their domestic workers because it enhances the madams' class/race relationship and position at the expense of maids'. Palmer suggests that the feminist movement has historically bought into such stereotypes even though it undermines women's demands for gender equality, largely from fear of confronting the fact that their class/race status is contingent on and mediated by a subordinate domestic relationship to white men.

A number of European feminists have worked to encompass race as well as class by analyzing capitalism as a worldwide imperialist system. Mariarosa Dalla Costa and Selma James (1972) began this line of development by explicitly linking their efforts to black marxist attempts to redefine class in such a way as to make racism and sexism class issues. In a pamphlet that sparked the infamous "productive/unproductive labor" debate that held up Marx's labor theory of value to feminist critique, Dalla Costa and James argued that housework had exchange value, and thus that working-class women could organize on a class basis around demanding wages for housework. I see the force of their argument in insisting – against male marxists – that working-class women's issues were "real," or economic, that they, like black and Third World people of both genders faced specific and particular exploitations beyond factory-centered wage relations that were nevertheless, somehow, class-based. It is striking that the relations between sexism and racism, which are central to Dalla Costa and James, are totally ignored by all the other participants in the domestic labor debate. Their opponents were arguing (variously) that housewives could not "unite and fight," or that if they could, it was not a class struggle. The significant question to emerge from that debate was whether class is a relationship of individuals with capital through the wage nexus, or whether it was something more complex, a something which would give women, Third World people, and their struggles working-class standing.

Bennholdt-Thomsen (1981, 1984) and Mies (1986) directly confronted the ideology embedded in the labor theory of value, which, as Bennholdt-Thomsen put it, "starts from an ideological assumption, namely that the separation of subsistence production from social production is something real." Instead, capitalism continuously creates "non-capitalist forms of production as its surroundings" for its "existence and future development." It does

so indirectly by creating a reserve army of labor, which itself creates nonwaged forms of surviving that involve a variety of forms of subsistence and petty commodity production (Bennholdt-Thomsen 1981: 23). It is super-exploitable in that it can be forced to sell its labor power below the cost of its own reproduction. Her description applies to "housewife production" and to peasant workers and peasant/artisan producers of both genders. But whatever the histories of peasant, artisan, or domestic production, once in relation to capital, these cease to be modes of production in the sense of retaining independent dynamics, and become noncapitalist forms of production subordinated to and part of the capitalist mode of production. This model challenged the functionalist fiction that capitalism is a closed, self-reproducing system of workers and capitalists in order to stress similarities between domestic labor and other forms of noncapitalist production, and presents cogent arguments for reformulating the labor theory of value to incorporate them. It also resonates with feminist analyses of the economic centrality of household and community relations to social change processes by suggesting that capitalism's economic dynamic continually creates and recreates "housewife-like" forms of nonwaged work and petty commodity production upon which the wage system itself depends.

The logic of these arguments is to expand the meaning of working class, and to take seriously domestic relations and issues around which people mobilize. In so doing feminists have raised fundamental questions about the meaning of class: How has the working class reproduced itself both daily and generationally? Certainly not as individuals. And, growing from this question, what do working-class structures for daily maintenance and reproduction suggest about class-based structures for resistance? And what do both tell us about the internal structure of the working class internationally?

Racial/Ethnic and Gender Diversity

After a decade of research on women and wage labor, it is becoming clear that capitalism has specifically recruited workers on the basis of race, and of gender and family relations within specific racial-ethnic communities. But this is part of a historical dialectic whose other pole was the age/marital status and gender of those who were "expendable" in a particular culture's division of labor – as for example, the contrast between male-centered farming systems in Euroamerica with "expendable" farm daughters, and female-centered farming in Africa with "expendable" sons. The "value" of such expendable laborers seems to have been set by an interaction of the social relations and expectations of domestic production with employers' demands for cheap labor, where sons' and daughters' wages were not expected to support them. Recognizing the influence of peasant or agrarian family organization on the age, race, and gender makeup of wage labor forces further highlights continuities among family, community, and workplace for the experience and interpretation of class (Sacks 1984).

The long-term workings out of this dialectic throughout the capitalist world – begun with capitalists' eternal search for cheap labor and nonproletarian communities' turning loose only their less "valuable" laborers – has been a major contributor to racial/ethnic segregation of working-class communities and racial/ethnic and sex segregation. This dialectic operated historically when industrialists sought out specifically white, Yankee daughters in nineteenth-century New England textiles and twentieth-century Southeast Asian daughters in apparel (Dublin 1979; Ong 1983); pre-married African boys and men in colonial East and Southern Africa in domestic work as well as mining (Hansen 1989); white mothers in contemporary front office work, and young black women for back offices (Glenn and Feldberg 1977; Machung 1984); black families in pre-World War II agriculture (Jones 1985); white rural daughters in Appalachian textiles before World War II, and black southerners more recently (Frankel 1984; Hall et al. 1987); European young women as live-in maids and then black women in pre-WWII domestic day work (Katzman 1978; Rollins 1985); teenagers in today's fast food shops; European immigrants in mining and heavy

industry, and so on (see Glenn 1985 for a summary of the changing historical patterns of job segregation for black, Latina, and Chinese-American women in the United States).

It is important not to lose sight of women's history of struggles to break through race and gender occupational patterns, but even victories have been eroded through new forms of occupational segregation. Recent work has documented women's gains in the auto industry (Milkman 1987), in the pre-deregulation phone company (Hacker 1982); hospitals (Sacks 1988a); heavy industry during World War II (Anderson 1981; Gluck 1987). However, even when women do win battles, they may still face an "up the down escalator" phenomenon – when women and minorities gain access to a job it is redefined as less skilled, becomes intensely supervised, and, at the same time typed as women's/minority's. Thus Carter and Carter (1981) show that women's recent progress in professions like medicine and law are largely into an emergent second-class track characterized by lower pay, less professional autonomy, and fewer opportunities for advancement. The subtitle of their article, "Women Get a Ticket to Ride After the Gravy Train Has Left the Station" is especially apt for the professions, but Hacker (1982) documents a similar down side for women's victory in access to skilled craft jobs in the Bell phone system – except here those jobs were eliminated by more advanced technology shortly after women entered them. Remy (1984) shows the ways in which company and union in meatpacking have manipulated new technologies and job design to eliminate high-seniority women workers. Sacks (1988a), Glenn (1985), and Glenn and Feldberg (1977) deal with minority women's progress in clerical work in the 1960s, but show them also being simultaneously tracked into an emergent factory-like back office sector.

There has been considerable recent attention devoted to women's work culture in workplaces where women predominate, such as department stores, offices, hospitals, and garment factories (Benson 1978, 1986; Feldberg and Glenn 1983; Glenn and Feldberg 1977; Machung 1984; Sacks 1988a; Westwood 1985). It is becoming clear that occupational segregation results in different experiences and consciousness of class for women and men, racial-ethnic and white workers. The concomitant is that "working class-consciousness" has multiple shapes (Eisenstein 1983; Goldberg 1983; Sacks 1988b). It would also appear that women's ways of expressing class consciousness are as often as not drawn from their community and family-based experiences of being working class. And, because working-class communities in the United States have been segregated, the experience and expressions of class consciousness have also been embedded in ethnically specific forms (Collins 1989; Davis 1981). To some degree, women have used family-based metaphors and values to share these consciousnesses across racial/ethnic lines (see especially Bookman and Morgen 1988; Lamphere 1984; Westwood 1985).

The point of all this is that one should not expect to find any generic worker or essential worker, or for that matter, working-class consciousness; that not only is class experienced in historically specific ways, but it is also experienced in racially specific, gender-specific, and kinship-specific ways.

The big issue is how to go about finding the unities and commonalities of class and class consciousness while being attentive to specificity. Critiques of white feminism by women of color and critiques by socialist feminists of male marxist views of class offer parallel solutions about how to conceptualize unity in diversity. Both criticize implicit and privileged norms against which "others" are measured, and urge instead taking "the other," as the subject in conceptualizing womanhood, and class.

For example, bell hooks (1984) urges placing women of color at the center of feminist analysis, while Bettina Aptheker (1982) suggests "pivoting the center." Along with Deborah King (1988) they argue for theory that stems directly from the experiences of women of color – in contrast to theory that is generated from comparisons that interpret those experiences with reference to a norm or modal woman, who, in feminist theory, has been white and middle class. As Bonnie Dill (1979) suggested in indicating the importance of understanding the "dialectics of black womanhood," doing so offers the possibility of a more inclusive sisterhood for all American women. Such statements about *how* to construct theory underlie the concrete analyses cited earlier about racially specific conceptualizations of domestic labor, women's economic dependence, and the sexual stereotypes. In these analyses commonalities emerged from the process of resolving conflicts. I will return to the issue of commonalities underlying racial and class-specific gender stereotypes later.

We have seen parallel socialist feminist critiques of traditional, white, male-centered notions of class, which have asked how women relate to a wage-based class structure. Socialist feminists have answered that women's unwaged domestic labor is a necessary condition for the existence of waged labor. When working-class women are the subjects and narrative voices of case studies, class membership, gender and kinship organization, class-based mobilization, and class consciousness look very different from the way they have been portrayed in nonfeminist marxist analyses. Feminist theorists, as Martha Acklesberg put it so trenchantly, "talk of the need to unite workplace and community. But women's lives have done that – and do it – on a daily basis, although perhaps without the consciousness that that is what they are about!" (1984: 256).

Feminist theory applied to the study of working-class women's lives has birthed questions like: What are the social relations by which the working class sustains and reproduces itself? How do women conceptualize their unwaged labor and community-building activities? How – and where – do working-class women organize to struggle against capital? What are the issues women find worth fighting about? What are we learning about the persistence of unwaged labor and the ways it changes forms? What are the experiential sources and metaphors by which working-class women express class consciousness? How do women's constructions of their sexuality relate to issues of class and kinship?

Embedded in these questions, I would suggest, is a definition of the working class in which membership is not determinable on an individual basis, but rather as *membership in a community that is dependent upon waged labor, but that is unable to subsist or reproduce by such labor alone.* This then is the economic basis of class as a relationship to the means of capitalist production. Following on this, it is not surprising that women of many ethnicities, times, and regions share a broader conception of class struggle than men. In part this results from women's socially assigned responsibility for unwaged domestic labor and their consequent centrality in confrontations with the state over family and community welfare issues (Bookman and Morgen 1988; Hall et al. 1987; Susser 1982; Zavella 1987a). This has led to suggestions that working-class women in general, and women of color in particular are likely to develop the most radical demands for social change (Giddings 1984; Hooks 1984; Kaplan 1982; Kessler-Harris and Sacks 1987).

Many new case studies describe the ways in which women's unwaged work creates community-based and class-based social ties of interdependence that are key to neighborhood and household survival. Many of these build on older understandings that working-class kin networks are important resources for coping with economic adversity (Bott 1957; Young and Willmott 1962). Some show women as central economic and political actors in these kinship networks, and suggest that these networks create and carry parts of what tends to be called working-class culture in European literature (Humphries 1977; Scott and Tilly 1978; Tilly 1981; but see Eisenstein 1983 for an early feminist class analysis in the United States); black culture in Afro-American communities (Day 1982; Gilkes 1980; Jones 1985; Reagon 1986; Stack 1974); Chicana or Latina culture (Zavella 1987a, 1987b); Third World (Caulfield 1974); or southern working class among southern whites (Hall et al. 1987). Others show ways women use languages and values of kinship to create unity and community in the waged workplace (Lamphere 1984, 1987; Sacks 1988a, 1988b; Westwood 1985).

Although the bulk of these studies focus on the social history of daily life (Westwood 1985; Zavella 1987a), some show the way these ties become the infrastructure of large-scale class protest, whether classic strikes (Cameron 1985; Frankel 1984; Hall et al. 1987; Milkman 1985; Tax 1980) or community-based movements, which make demands on the state for civil rights, housing, health care, education, or welfare (Bookman and Morgen 1988; Kaplan 1982; West 1981). They analyze women's centrality in organizing and sustaining labor unions, civil rights, and community-based movements (Giddings 1984; Gilkes 1980; MacLean 1982; Robinson 1987; Ruiz 1987).

Two "findings" regarding social structure and working-class culture are embedded in this new literature. One is the contributions made by working-class women through household economies and community-based cultures to notions of social justice and entitlement (Acklesberg 1984; Bookman and Morgen 1988). The other is the prevalence of institutions, networks, and cultures that women generate outside family life, in public space in working-class communities (see Zagarell 1988 for an analysis of "novels of community" as a women's literary genre). In short, this literature does more than counter theories of the workplace as the sole source for generating political mobilization around economic issues. It provides the beginnings of a gender-based construction of class that is somewhat attentive to racial/ethnic diversity.

A third set of "findings" about working-class women's conceptions of womanhood is emerging from some very diverse studies that explore long-hidden histories of (mainly) working-class women's challenges to bourgeois ideals of domesticity, femininity, compulsory heterosexuality, motherhood, and reproduction. For example, Emily Martin's (1987) wonderful exploration of how American women understand menstruation, birth, and menopause shows middle-class women tending to accept the dominant, medicalized views of women as ruled by their reproductive organs, while working-class, especially black working-class women, do not see these as ruling events, nor does the medical view of their bodies have much hegemony in their consciousnesses.

In a similar vein, studies of conflicts between Progressive-era reformers' notions of proper domesticity and those of working-class women (Ehrenreich and English 1978; Kessler-Harris 1982) have shown overt and covert resistance to submissive domesticity on the latter's part. They resonate with theoretical suggestions by Mies (1986) that "housewifization" is historically a relatively new and middle-class-specific organization of women's unwaged labor. Mies argues that the privatization of women's work, and the cult of domesticity surrounding and sustaining it were and are resisted by working-class women (though not by working-class men, who benefited from it), who struggle to keep their work "socialized," or collectively organized. Bennholdt-Thomsen (1988) illustrates one such form this takes in the Isthmus of Tehuantepec, Mexico, where women sustain a regional marketing and food preparation system with an elaborate division of labor, interdependence among women, and no subordination to men. Similar arguments are implicit in discussions about women's marketing and subsistence production in Africa (Leis 1974; Mbilinyi 1988), and in the economies of taking in boarders, laundry, and so on, widely described for European-American working-class pre-World War II urban neighborhoods, although the power dynamics of gender need to be explored further (Cott and Pleck 1979; Ewen 1985; Kessler-Harris 1982; see also Kessler-Harris and Sacks 1987; Sacks 1984).

We are also beginning to learn some of the ways in which young working-class women, past and present, white and black, have independently appropriated and refashioned some of the conventional images of sexiness to convey the sense of themselves as autonomous, independent, and assertive adult women, and to challenge – often at high risk to themselves – our culture's insistence on submissive femininity for women (Hall 1986; Ladner 1970; Myerowitz 1988; Peiss 1985; Petchesky 1985; Stansell 1986; Westwood 1985; see also Vance 1984 and Snitow, Stansell, and Thompson 1983). Hall's study, "Disorderly Women," is perhaps the most dramatic discussion of how women used their sexuality as a metaphor of class strength and confrontation, how it was understood in that way by other men and women of their working-class Appalachian community, but was seen in conventional "bad women" terms by both employers and outside union representatives.[2]

Just as heterosexuality has been a language of working-class women's resistance to a combined class and gender subordination, so too has lesbian sexual identity and community provided a historically specific tradition of resistance to submissive domesticity. Following Adrienne Rich's (1983) insights on the politics of homophobia and Carol Smith-Rosenberg's work on 19th-century women's worlds of love and ritual (1985), D'Emilio and Freedman (1988), as well as Rapp and Ross (1983) argue that stigmatization of homosexuality and its complement, celebration of companionate marriages (or compulsory heterosexuality), developed about the same time that it became possible for a significant number of women to be able to live on their own earnings, without domestic dependence on men. Davis and Kennedy's (1986) oral history of Buffalo's working-class lesbian community, as well as D'Emilio and Freedman's (1988), Katz's (1976) and D'Emilio's (1983) analyses of the creation of specifically gay and lesbian social identities in the mid-twentieth century show some of these forms of resistance as well as the creation of alternate institutions, roles, and identities.

Summary

As Martha Acklesberg has noted, when "we take seriously the 'relatedness' that seems to characterize the lives of many women," we also challenge "the assumption central to the Marxist paradigm that the development of a truly radical consciousness requires the transcendence, or abandonment, of all sources of community feeling other than class (in particular, those feelings based in racial, ethnic, national, or – we might add – sexual identity). ...In fact, rather than acting as a 'drag' on radical consciousness, communities – and the network of relationships that they nurture and on which they are based – have been, and can be, important contexts for politicization" (Acklesberg 1988: 306).

This essay has reviewed some of the theoretical consequences of socialist feminist critiques of the political economy of "personal life." Its focus has been on efforts to comprehend class, race, and gender oppression as parts of a unitary system, as opposed to analyses that envision capitalism and patriarchy as separate systems. More specifically, I have interpreted analyses of the relations of waged and unwaged labor, work and family in such a way as to expand the meaning of working class to encompass both waged and unwaged workers who are members of a *community* that is dependent upon waged labor but that is unable to reproduce itself on those wages alone. The implications of such a reading are fairly radical, and each one requires a great deal of further exploration. First and most apparent, it significantly alters conventional marxist understandings of class and of contemporary social movements. Second, it does so in such a way as to make visible the centrality of people of color and white working-class women to the direction of world history. Third, for feminist theory, it suggests the fruitfulness of recognizing that women's gender identities are not analytically separable from their racial and class identities. Fourth, class emerges as a relation to the means of production that is collective rather than individual, a relation of communities to the capitalist state more than of employees to employers. Fifth, this embeds a critique of the ideology of liberal individualism, and links it to the shapes of post-World War II resistance to capitalism, which have generated the pluralistic visions behind efforts to develop a unified feminist theory that encompasses race and class as well as gender and sexuality.

NOTES

1   The issues of political debate, sometimes taking the form of battles between the "old left" and the "new left," sometimes between Stalinism and Eurocommunism, are extremely complex and beyond the scope of this review, but it is important to locate both these debates and second-wave left feminism in the challenges posed by the black freedom movement in the United States, as well as by anti-colonial struggles worldwide. It is also important to recognize that industrial working-class struggle in the

United States has always been based in and shaped by ethnic immigrant communities.

2   This converges with critiques of compulsory heterosexuality and analyses of domesticity (Rich; Rapp and Ross), which argue that fear of being labeled "bad girls" has made white feminist practice and analysis more of a loyal opposition to patriarchy than a full-blown attack on it.

REFERENCES

Acklesberg, Martha. 1984. Women's Collaborative Activities and City Life: Politics and Policy. In *Political Women: Current Roles in State and Local Government*. J. Flammang, ed. pp. 242–59. Beverly Hills: Sage Publications.

——1988 Communities, Resistance, and Women's Activism: Some Implications for a Democratic Polity. In *Women and the Politics of Empowerment*. A. Bookman and S. Morgen, eds. pp. 297–313. Philadelphia: Temple University Press.

Anderson, Karen. 1981. *Wartime Women*. Westport, CT: Greenwood.

Aptheker, Bettina. 1982. *Women's Legacy: Essays in Race, Sex and Class in American History*. Amherst: University of Massachusetts Press.

Barkley-Brown, Elsa. 1989. African-American Women's Quilting: A Framework for Conceptualizing and Teaching African-American Women's History. *Signs*, 14/4: 921–9.

Benería, Lourdes, ed. 1982. *Women and Development*. New York: Praeger.

Bennholdt-Thomsen, Veronika. 1981. Subsistence Production and Extended Reproduction. In *Of Marriage and the Market*. K. Young, C. Wolkowitz, and R. McCullagh, eds. pp. 16–29. London: CSE Books.

——1984. Towards a Theory of the Sexual Division of Labor. In *Households and the World Economy*. J. Smith, I. Wallerstein, and H.-D. Evers, eds. pp. 252–71. Beverly Hills: Sage.

——1988. Women's Dignity Is the Wealth of Juchitan (Oax., Mexico). Paper presented at 12th International Congress of Anthropological and Ethnological Sciences, Zagreb, 24–31 July.

Benson, Susan Porter. 1978. The Clerking Sisterhood: Rationalization and the Work Culture of Saleswomen. *Radical America*, 12: 41–55.

——1986. *Counter Cultures: Saleswomen, Managers, and Customers in American Department Stores 1890–1940*. Urbana: University of Illinois Press.

Benston, Margaret. 1969. The Political Economy of Women's Liberation. *Monthly Review*, 21/4: 13–27.

Bookman, Ann, and Sandra Morgen, eds. 1988. *Women and the Politics of Empowerment*. Philadelphia: Temple University Press.

Boris, Eileen, and Peter Bardaglio. 1983. The Transformation of Patriarchy: The Historic Role of the State. In *Families, Politics and Public Policy: A Feminist Dialogue on Women and the State*. I. Diamond and M. L. Shanley, eds. pp. 70–93. New York: Longman.

Bott, Elizabeth. 1957. *Family and Social Network*. London: Tavistock Publications.

Brecher, Jeremy. 1972. *Strike: The True History of Mass Insurgency from 1877 to the Present*. San Francisco: Straight Arrow.

Brenner, Johanna, and Maria Ramas. 1984. Rethinking Women's Oppression. *New Left Review*, 144: 33–71.

Cameron, Ardis. 1985. Bread and Roses Revisited: Women's Culture and Working-Class Activism in the Lawrence Strike of 1912. In *Women, Work and Protest*. R. Milkman, ed. pp. 42–61. Boston: Routledge and Kegan Paul.

Cantarow, Ellen, and Sharon O'Malley. 1980. Ella Baker: Organizing for Civil Rights. In *Moving the Mountain: Women Working for Social Change*. E. Cantarow, ed. pp. 52–93. Old Westbury, NY: Feminist Press.

Carter, Susan B., and Michael Carter. 1981. Women's Recent Progress in the Professions, or Women Get a Ticket to Ride after the Gravy Train Has Left the Station. *Feminist Studies*, 7: 477–504.

Caulfield, Mina Davis. 1974. Imperialism, the Family and Cultures of Resistance. *Socialist Revolution*, 20: 76–85.

Collins, Patricia Hill. 1989. The Social Construction of Black Feminist Thought. *Signs*, 14/4: 745–73.

Cott, Nancy, and Elizabeth Pleck, eds. 1979. *A Heritage of Her Own: Toward a New Social History of American Women*. New York: Simon and Schuster.

Dalla Costa, Mariarosa, and Selma James. 1972. *The Power of Women and the Subversion of the Community*. Montpelier, England: Falling Wall Press.

Davis, Angela Y. 1981. *Women, Race and Class*. New York: Random House.

Davis, Madeline, and Elizabeth L. Kennedy. 1986. Oral History and the Study of Sexuality in the Lesbian Community: Buffalo, New York, 1940–1960. *Feminist Studies*, 12 (spring): 7–26.

Day, Kay. 1982. Kinship in a Changing Economy: A View from the Sea Islands. In *Holding onto the Land and the Lord*. C. Stack and R. Hall, eds. Athens: University of Georgia Press.

D'Emilio, John. 1983. *Sexual Politics, Sexual Communities: The Making of a Homosexual Minority in the United States, 1940–1970*. Chicago: University of Chicago Press.

D'Emilio, John, and Estelle B. Freedman. 1988. *Intimate Matters. A History of Sexuality in America*. New York: Harper and Row.

Dill, Bonnie Thornton. 1979. The Dialectics of Black Womanhood. *Signs*, 4: 543–55.

Dublin, Thomas. 1979. *Women at Work: The Transformation of Class and Community in Lowell, Massachusetts 1826–1860*. New York: Columbia University Press.

Edholm, Felicity, Olivia Harris, and Kate Young. 1977. Conceptualising Women. *Critique of Anthropology*, 3/9–10: 101–30.

Ehrenreich, Barbara, and Dierdre English. 1978. *For Her Own Good*. New York: Pantheon.

Eisenstein, Sarah. 1983. *Give Us Bread, but Give Us Roses Too*. Boston: Routledge and Kegan Paul.

Eisenstein, Zillah, ed. 1979. *Capitalist Patriarchy and the Case for Socialist Feminism*. New York: Monthly Review Press.

Evans, Sara. 1980. *Personal Politics: The Roots of Women's Liberation in the Civil Rights Movement*. New York: Random House.

Ewen, Elizabeth. 1985. *Immigrant Women in the Land of Dollars.* New York: Monthly Review Press.

Feldberg, Roslyn, and Evelyn Nakano Glenn. 1983. Technology and Work Degradation: Effects of Office Automation on Women Clerical Workers. In *Machina ex Dea: Feminist Perspectives on Technology.* J. Rothschild, ed. pp. 59–78. New York: Pergamon.

Frankel, Linda. 1984. Southern Textile Women: Generations of Struggle and Survival. In *My Troubles Are Going to Have Trouble with Me.* K. Sacks and D. Remy, eds. pp. 39–60. New Brunswick, NJ: Rutgers University Press.

Giddings, Paula. 1984. *When and Where I Enter.* New York: Bantam.

Gilkes, Cheryl. 1980. "Holding Back the Ocean with a Broom": Black Women and Community Work. In *The Black Woman.* La Rodgers-Rose, ed. pp. 217–31. Beverly Hills: Sage Publications.

—— 1988. Building in Many Places: Multiple Commitments and Ideologies in Black Women's Community Work. In *Women and the Politics of Empowerment.* A. Bookman and S. Morgen, eds. pp. 53–76. Philadelphia: Temple University Press.

Glenn, Evelyn Nakano. 1985. Racial Ethnic Women's Labor: The Intersection of Race, Gender and Class Oppression. Review in *Radical Political Economics,* 17(3): 86–108.

—— 1986. *Issei, Nissei, War Bride: Three Generations of Japanese American Women in Domestic Service.* Philadelphia: Temple University Press.

Glenn, Evelyn Nakano, and Roslyn Feldberg. 1977. Degraded and Deskilled: The Proletarianization of Clerical Work. *Social Problems,* 25/1: 2–64.

Gluck, Sherna B. 1987. *Rosie the Riveter Revisited: Women, the War, and Social Change.* Boston: Twayne Publishers.

Goldberg, Roberta. 1983. *Organizing Women Office Workers: Dissatisfaction, Consciousness and Action.* New York: Praeger.

Hacker, Sally. 1982. Sex Stratification, Technology and Organizational Change: A Longitudinal Case Study of AT&T. In *Women and Work.* R. Kahn-Hut, A. Daniels, and R. Colvard, eds. pp. 248–66. New York: Oxford University Press.

Hall, Jacqueline D. 1986. Disorderly Women: Gender and Labor Militancy in the Appalachian South. *Journal of American History,* 73/2: 354–82.

Hall, Jacqueline D., J. Leloudis, R. Korstad, M. Murphy, L. Jones, and C. Daly, 1987. *Like a Family: The Making of a Southern Mill World.* Chapel Hill: University of North Carolina Press.

Hansen, Karen T. 1989. *Distant Companions: Servants and Employers in Zambia, 1900–1985.* Ithaca, NY: Cornell University Press.

Hartmann, Heidi I. 1976. Capitalism, Patriarchy and Job Segregation by Sex. *Signs,* 1/3 pt. 2: 137–70.

hooks, bell. 1984. *Feminist Theory from Margin to Center.* Boston: South End Press.

Humphries, Jane. 1977. Class Struggle and the Persistence of the Working Class Family. *Cambridge Journal of Economics,* 1: 241–8.

Jaggar, Alison. 1983. *Feminist Politics and Human Nature.* Sussex: Rowman and Allenheld.

Jones, Jacqueline. 1985. *Labor of Love, Labor of Sorrow.* New York: Basic Books.

Kaplan, Temma. 1982. Female Consciousness and Collective Action: The Case of Barcelona, 1910–1918. *Signs,* 7/3: 545–67.

Katz, Jonathan, ed. 1976. *Gay American History: Lesbians and Gay Men in the U.S.A.* New York: Thomas Crowell.

Katzman, David. 1978. *Seven Days a Week: Women and Domestic Service in Industrializing America.* New York: Oxford University Press.

Kessler-Harris, Alice. 1982. *Out to Work.* New York: Oxford University Press.

Kessler-Harris, Alice, and Karen Brodkin Sacks. 1987. The Demise of Domesticity. In *Women, Households and the Economy.* L. Benería and C. Stimpson, eds. pp. 65–84. New Brunswick, NJ: Rutgers University Press.

King, Deborah. 1988. Multiple Jeopardy, Multiple Consciousness: The Context of a Black Feminist Ideology. *Signs,* 14/1: 42–72.

Ladner, Joyce. 1970. *Tomorrow's Tomorrow.* New York: Doubleday Anchor.

Lamphere, Louise. 1984. On the Shop Floor: Multi-Ethnic Unity against the Conglomerate. In *My Troubles Are Going to Have Trouble with Me*. K. Sacks and D. Remy, eds. pp. 247–63. New Brunswick, NJ: Rutgers University Press.

—— 1987. *From Working Daughters to Working Mothers: Immigrant Women in a New England Industrial Community*. Ithaca, NY: Cornell University Press.

Leis, Nancy. 1974. Women in Groups: Ijaw Women's Associations. In *Woman, Culture, and Society*. M. Rosaldo and L. Lamphere, eds. pp. 223–42. Stanford: Stanford University Press.

Machung, Anne. 1984. Word Processing: Forward for Business, Backward for Women. In *My Troubles Are Going to Have Trouble with Me*. K. Sacks and D. Remy, eds. pp. 124–39. New Brunswick, NJ: Rutgers University Press.

MacLean, Nancy. 1982. *The Culture of Resistance: Female Institution-Building in the Ladies Garment Workers' Union 1905–1925*. Occasional Papers in Women's Studies, University of Michigan.

Mainardi, Pat. 1970. The Politics of Housework. In *Sisterhood Is Powerful*. R. Morgan, ed. pp. 447–54. New York: Random House.

Martin, Emily. 1987. *The Woman in the Body*. Boston: Beacon.

Mbilinyi, Marjorie. 1988. Runaway Wives in Colonial Tanganyika: Forced Labour and Forced Marriage in Rungwe District 1919–1961. *International Journal of the Sociology of Law*, 16: 1–29.

Meillassoux, Claude. 1981. *Maidens, Meal and Money: Capitalism and the Domestic Community*. Cambridge: Cambridge University Press.

Mies, Maria. 1986. *Patriarchy and Accumulation on a World Scale: Women and the International Division of Labour*. London: Zed Books.

Milkman, Ruth, ed. 1985. *Women, Work and Protest*. Boston: Routledge and Kegan Paul.

—— 1987. *Gender at Work: The Dynamics of Job Segregation by Sex During World War II*. Urbana: University of Illinois Press.

Mitchell, Juliet. 1966. Women – The Longest Revolution. *New Left Review*, 40: 11–37.

—— 1971. *Woman's Estate*. Baltimore: Penguin Books.

Meyerowitz, Joanne J. 1988. *Women Adrift: Independent Wage Earners in Chicago: 1880–1930*. Chicago: Chicago University Press.

Nash, June, and Maria Patricia Fernandez-Kelly, eds. 1983. *Women, Men and the International Division of Labor*. Albany, NY: SUNY Press.

Ong, Aihwa. 1983. Global Industries and Malay Peasants in Peninsular Malaysia. In *Women, Men and the International Division of Labor*. J. Nash and M. Fernandez-Kelly, eds. pp. 426–39. Albany, NY: SUNY Press.

Palmer, Phyllis M. 1983. White Women/Black Women: The Dualism of Female Identity and Experience in the United States. *Feminist Studies*, 9: 151–70.

—— 1984. Housework and Domestic Labor: Racial and Technological Change. In *My Troubles Are Going to Have Trouble with Me*. K. Sacks and D. Remy, eds. pp. 80–94. New Brunswick, NJ: Rutgers University Press.

Peiss, Kathy. 1985. *Cheap Amusements: Working Women and Leisure in Turn-of-the-Century New York*. Philadelphia: Temple University Press.

Petchesky, Rosalind P. 1985. *Abortion and Woman's Choice*. Boston: Northeastern University Press.

Rapp, Rayna. 1978. Family and Class in Contemporary America: Notes Toward an Understanding of Ideology. *Science and Society*, 42/3: 278–300.

Rapp, Rayna, and Ellen Ross. 1983. The Twenties' Backlash: Compulsory Heterosexuality, the Consumer Family and the Waning of Feminism. In *Class, Race and Sex*. A. Swerdlow and H. Lessinger, eds. pp. 93–107. Boston: G. K. Hall.

Reagon, Bernice Johnson. 1986. African Diaspora Women: The Making of Cultural Workers. *Feminist Studies*, 12/1: 77–90.

Remy, Dorothy, and Larry Sawers. 1984. Economic Stagnation and Discrimination. In *My Troubles Are Going to Have Trouble with Me*. K. Sacks and D. Remy, eds.

pp. 95–112. New Brunswick, NJ: Rutgers University Press.

Rich, Adrienne. 1983. Compulsory Heterosexuality and Lesbian Existence. In *Powers of Desire: The Politics of Sexuality.* A. Snitow, C. Stansell, and S. Thompson, eds. pp. 177–205. New York: Monthly Review Press.

Robinson, Jo Ann Gibson. 1987. *The Montgomery Bus Boycott and the Women Who Started It.* David J. Garrow, ed. Knoxville: University of Tennessee Press.

Rollins, Judith. 1985. *Between Women.* Philadelphia: Temple University Press.

Romero, Mary. 1987. Domestic Service in the Transition from Rural to Urban Life: The Case of La Chicana. *Women's Studies,* 13/3: 199–222. (Special issue, "As the World Turns," K. B. Sacks and N. Scheper-Hughes, eds.)

Ruiz, Vicki L. 1987. *Cannery Women Cannery Lives: Mexican Women, Unionization and the California Food Processing Industry, 1930–1950.* Albuquerque: University of New Mexico Press.

Sacks, Karen Brodkin. 1974. Engels Revisited. In *Woman, Culture, and Society.* M. Rosaldo and L. Lamphere, eds. pp. 207–22. Stanford: Stanford University Press.

—— 1979. *Sisters and Wives.* Westport, CT: Greenwood Press.

—— 1984. Generations of Working Class Families. In *My Troubles Are Going to Have Trouble with Me.* K. Sacks and D. Remy, eds. New Brunswick, NJ: Rutgers University Press.

—— 1988a. *Caring by the Hour.* Urbana: University of Illinois Press.

—— 1988b. Gender and Grassroots Leadership. In *Women and the Politics of Empowerment.* A. Bookman and S. Morgen, eds. pp. 77–96. Philadelphia: Temple University Press.

Sargent, Lydia, ed. 1981. *Women and Revolution: A Discussion of the Unhappy Marriage of Marxism and Feminism.* Boston: South End Press.

Scott, Joan W., and Louise Tilly. 1978. *Women, Work and Family.* New York: Holt, Rinehart and Winston.

Smith-Rosenberg, Carol. 1985. The Female World of Love and Ritual: Relations Between Women in Nineteenth-Century America. Reprinted in *Disorderly Conduct: Visions of Gender in Victorian America.* C. Smith-Rosenberg, ed. New York: Oxford University Press.

Snitow, Ann, Christine Stansell, and Sharon Thompson, eds. 1983. *Powers of Desire: The Politics of Sexuality.* New York: Monthly Review Press.

Stack, Carol. 1974. *All Our Kin.* New York: Harper Colophon.

Stansell, Christine. 1986. *City of Women: Sex and Class in New York, 1789–1860.* New York: Knopf.

Stolcke, Verena. 1981. Women's Labours: The Naturalisation of Social Inequality and Women's Subordination. In *Of Marriage and the Market.* K. Young, C. Wolkowitz, and R. McCullagh, eds. pp. 30–48. London: CSE Books.

Susser, Ida. 1982. *Norman Street.* New York: Oxford University Press.

Tax, Meredith. 1980. *The Rising of the Women: Feminist Solidarity and Class Conflict 1880–1917.* New York: Monthly Review Press.

Tilly, Louise A. 1981. Paths of Proletarianization: Organization of Production, Sexual Division of Labor, and Women's Collective Action. *Signs,* 7(2): 400–17.

Vance, Carole, ed. 1984. *Pleasure and Danger.* Boston: Routledge and Kegan Paul.

Vogel, Lise. 1983. *Marxism and the Oppression of Women: Toward a Unitary Theory.* New Brunswick, NJ: Rutgers University Press.

West, Guida. 1981. *The National Welfare Rights Movement: The Social Protest of Poor Women.* New York: Praeger.

Westwood, Sallie. 1985. *All Day Every Day.* Urbana: University of Illinois Press.

Wolfe, George C. 1988. *The Colorization of American Culture, or, One playwright (of color)'s not-so-humble opinion.* Performing Arts Westwood Playhouse, Los Angeles.

Young, Michael, and Peter Willmott. 1962. *Family and Kinship in East London.* Baltimore: Penguin Books.

Zagarell, Sandra. 1988. The Narrative of Community: The Identification of a Genre. *Signs,* 13/3: 498–527.

Zavella, Patricia. 1987a. "Abnormal Intimacy": The Varying Work Networks of Chicana Cannery Workers. *Feminist Studies*, 11/3: 541–58.

——1987b. *Women's Work and Chicano Families: Cannery Workers of the Santa Clara Valley*. Ithaca, NY: Cornell University Press.

Part II

Questioning Positionality

Introduction

Feminist anthropology has made its mark in a number of domains, but its impact on the discipline has been perhaps nowhere as distinctive as in the emphasis it has placed on reflexivity. Other scholars have also interrogated their status as researchers and the impact of their particular attributes and social positions on their research (Rabinow 1978; Ruby 1982), but their approaches largely have been inspired by the postmodern call to destabilize the authority of the text (Clifford and Marcus 1986). While these intellectual currents have also influenced feminist anthropology, the demand that scholars always consider how their individuality shapes the work that they do has far more political roots for feminists. Of course, such self-examination has also been a hallmark of feminist scholarship more generally, as questions of autobiography have taken center stage and the personal narrative has achieved near iconic centrality (Personal Narratives Group 1989). These developments directly echoed the consciousness-raising methods of the Second Wave which used the mantra "the personal is political" to frame accounts of individual experience as the only reliable route to more general social and political awareness. Each story or personal narrative was viewed as inviolable and authoritative in these contexts, yielding a sometimes intractable form of identity politics that still troubles feminist organizing (Jones 1993).

Some feminist scholars and activists severely criticized writings about women that objectified or exploited them, and concern about the ethical dimensions of anthropological research loomed large from the beginning of the new field. An early article by British sociologist Ann Oakley, for example, was titled "Interviewing Women: A Contradiction in Terms" (Oakley 1981) and at least two articles have appeared over the years with the provocative title "Can There Be a Feminist Ethnography?" (Abu-Lughod 1990; Stacey 1988). Chapters in a 1999 book on ethical dilemmas in feminist research (Kirsch 1999) bear such titles as "What Do You Know about My Life Anyway? Ethical Dilemmas in Researcher–Participant Relations" and "Whose Words? Whose Reality? The Politics of Representation and Interpretation." Feminist scholarship in all fields has been accompanied by a prolific interdisciplinary literature on research methods, ethics, and pedagogy, much of it centered on questions of power, professionalism, and profit. Parallel to these discussions have been debates over the possibility of "insider" research in anthropology and elsewhere, in which scholars sometimes painfully examine their own positions during research and their discovery that the simple fact of studying people quickly erases the possibility of true "insider" status (Lewin 1995; Narayan 1993). Although feminists are not the only scholars who have confronted issues of power and difference in defining their own positionality (Limón 1991), feminists have been particularly energetic in efforts to sort out the intellectual and ethical issues that beset politically committed research.

The papers in this section address the matter of location through a number of lenses. Abu-Lughod's article takes on the volume *Writing Culture* (Clifford and Marcus 1986), chiding its editors for failing fully to confront how positionality shapes anthropological representations and knowledge. She considers the glaring omission of feminist anthropological contributions from the scope of Clifford and Marcus's approach, in the process suggesting that intellectual posturing and efforts to assert authority undermine their efforts to consider the representational strategies that characterize ethnographic writing. Feminist anthropologists and "halfies" (persons who share some identity attributes with the populations they study) destabilize "the boundary between self and other" (p. 153), virtually a seismic shift for a discipline that has long taken such boundaries for granted. Culture, Abu-Lughod asserts, itself reinforces hierarchical arrangements, and thus the task politically conscious anthropologists much undertake is to question its ability to naturalize separations that instantiate power.

Esther Newton approaches the long-taboo topic of sexuality in field research in "My Best Informant's Dress," a reflection on her relationship with an informant in Cherry Grove, the gay and lesbian summer resort that was the subject of her 1993 ethnohistorical study *Cherry Grove, Fire Island* (Newton 1993). Newton notes that nearly all references to sexual activity with "natives" in the field have dealt with male conquest, usually heterosexual, though more recently occasionally homosexual. Such accounts have typically engendered discomfort, most notably in the case of Malinowski's diaries which revealed his eroticized but also demeaning views of the native women. In nearly all cases Newton recounts, sexual behavior in the field is understood to be unprofessional, and those who write about their sexual experiences typically use non-academic venues such as memoirs to make their confessions. Sexual adventures are even more clearly frowned upon for women; Manda Cesara (Karla Poewe), for example, published a rather romanticized narrative under a pseudonym that reports on sexual liaisons she formed with men in her African field site (Cesara 1982).

In questioning the conventions that have relegated sexual feelings to the margins of the anthropological enterprise, Newton analyzes the erotic edge that animated her interactions with Kay, a key informant who had lived through most of the historical events Newton was investigating. Although this relationship never became physical, she argues that the "passion" we feel for the people and community we study cannot properly be cleansed of their erotic dimensions. If distance between anthropologist and informant is to be questioned, ought we not interrogate the sources of our fascination? Newton argues that an erotic dimension is deeply imbedded in our desire to know, and that rather than regarding such realizations as anomalous, we ought to consider their implications for dissolving some of the boundaries that have been erected between researcher and "native." Her question is central to the larger quest to destabilize the power that inheres in objectivity, a key quest for feminist scholars across the disciplines.

The essays reprinted here by Patricia Zavella and Paulla Ebron confront some of the ambiguities of attempting to undertake "insider" research. Zavella describes her fieldwork with Chicana cannery workers, a project that was inspired and informed by her view of herself as a Chicana feminist. But her work in the factory disrupted her assumptions not only about the extent to which she and her informants shared an identity, but whether ethnicity as she understood it was even a meaningful category to the women. Her privileges as an educated woman loomed larger for the women workers than her Chicana identity, and even the questions she had formulated about the intersection between that identity and their management of workplace challenges relied more on preconceptions derived from feminism than on the actual, alarmingly "traditional" categories the women used to organize their lives. Zavella came to realize that her attachment to a particular construction of Chicana in thinking about who she was had more salience in an academic environment than in the world inhabited by her informants. Even more disturbing, categories the women she studied had insisted on using sometimes offended politically engaged colleagues, while at other times the refusal of the women to subscribe to any of the ethnic designations in current use also left her with no "correct" way to discuss her findings. Zavella argues persuasively that feminist anthropologists of any ethnicity must acknowledge the degree to which they may impose categories and identities on their informants in service of their own agendas. Full accountability demands distinguishing between the interests of informants and those of colleagues, understanding that the representations that make sense in one or the other domain may not be the same.

Ebron's essay interrogates a different set of connections, those between African peoples and herself as an African American. How were her interests in anthropology sparked by her awareness of herself as an African American? How have particular representations of Africa been situated in her research, and what are the meanings of these images in the construction of African American identity? Ebron uses an innovative narrative technique that tacks back and forth between a theoretical consideration of race and the personal memories that constitute race in her own life. She argues that doing research in Africa forced her to re-evaluate the Pan-African ideas that had drawn her into the academy, while she also struggled to situate her feminism in the nationalist consciousness that had inspired her. Her awareness of the African diaspora had been framed largely through experience, while her feminism was drawn from books and thus a more self-conscious element of the intellectual apparatus with which she encountered Africa. On her return, she made a further realization: how writing would demand a further renegotiation of the African American and feminist aspects of her identity. The process is ongoing, established in a dynamic dialogue between her personal and intellectual selves and the works of other scholars.

REFERENCES

Abu-Lughod, Lila. 1990. Can There Be a Feminist Ethnography? *Women and Performance*, 5/1: 7–27.
Cesara, Manda [Karla O. Poewe]. 1982. *Reflections of a Woman Anthropologist: No Hiding Place*. London: Academic Press.
Clifford, James, and George E. Marcus. 1986. *Writing Culture: The Poetics and Politics of Ethnography*. Berkeley: University of California Press.
Jones, Kathleen B. 1993. *Compassionate Authority: Democracy and the Representation of Women*. New York: Routledge.
Kirsch, Gesa E. 1999. *Ethical Dilemmas in Feminist Research*. Albany, NY: State University of New York Press.
Lewin, Ellen. 1995. Writing Lesbian Ethnography. In *Women Writing Culture*. R. Behar and D. A. Gordon, eds. pp. 322–35. Berkeley: University of California Press.

Limón, José E. 1991. Representation, Ethnicity, and the Precursory Ethnography: Notes of a Native Anthropologist. In *Recapturing Anthropology: Working in the Present*. R. G. Fox, ed. pp. 115–35. Santa Fe: School of American Research.

Narayan, Kirin. 1993. How Native is a "Native" Anthropologist? *American Anthropologist*, 95/3: 671–86.

Newton, Esther. 1993. *Cherry Grove, Fire Island: Sixty Years in America's First Lesbian and Gay Town*. Boston: Beacon Press.

Oakley, Ann. 1981. Interviewing Women: A Contradiction in Terms. In *Doing Feminist Research*. H. Roberts, ed. pp. 30–61. London: Routledge and Kegan Paul.

Personal Narratives Group. 1989. *Interpreting Women's Lives: Feminist Theory and Personal Narratives*. Bloomington: Indiana University Press.

Rabinow, Paul. 1978. *Reflections on Fieldwork in Morocco*. Berkeley: University of California Press.

Ruby, Jay. 1982. *Crack in the Mirror: Reflexive Perspectives in Anthropology*. Philadelphia: University of Pennsylvania Press.

Stacey, Judith. 1988. Can There Be a Feminist Ethnography? *Women's Studies International Forum*, 11/1: 21–7.

7

Writing against Culture

Lila Abu-Lughod

Writing Culture (Clifford and Marcus 1986), the collection that marked a major new form of critique of cultural anthropology's premises, more or less excluded two critical groups whose situations neatly expose and challenge the most basic of those premises: feminists and "halfies" – people whose national or cultural identity is mixed by virtue of migration, overseas education, or parentage.[1] In his introduction, Clifford (1986) apologizes for the feminist absence; no one mentions halfies or the indigenous anthropologists to whom they are related. Perhaps they are not yet numerous enough or sufficiently self-defined as a group.[2] The importance of these two groups lies not in any superior moral claim or advantage they might have in doing anthropology, but in the special dilemmas they face, dilemmas that reveal starkly the problems with cultural anthropology's assumption of a fundamental distinction between self and other. In this essay I explore how feminists and halfies, by the way their anthropological practice unsettles the boundary between self and other, enable us to reflect on the conventional nature and political effects of this distinction

and ultimately to reconsider the value of the concept of culture on which it depends. I will argue that "culture" operates in anthropological discourse to enforce separations that inevitably carry a sense of hierarchy. Therefore, anthropologists should now pursue, without exaggerated hopes for the power of their texts to change the world, a variety of strategies for writing *against* culture. For those interested in textual strategies, I explore the advantages of what I call "ethnographies of the particular" as instruments of a tactical humanism.

Selves and Others

The notion of culture (especially as it functions to distinguish "cultures"), despite a long usefulness, may now have become something anthropologists would want to work against in their theories, their ethnographic practice, and their ethnographic writing. A helpful way to begin to grasp why is to consider what the shared elements of feminist and halfie anthropology clarify about the self/other distinction

From Lila Abu-Lughod, "Writing against Culture," pp. 137–62 in Richard G. Fox, ed. *Recapturing Anthropology: Working in the Present*. Santa Fe, NM: School of American Research Press, 1991. © 1991 by School of American Research, Santa Fe. Reprinted by permission of School of American Research, Santa Fe.

central to the paradigm of anthropology. Marilyn Strathern (1985, 1987) raises some of the issues regarding feminism in essays that both Clifford and Rabinow cited in *Writing Culture*. Her thesis is that the relationship between anthropology and feminism is awkward. This thesis leads her to try to understand why feminist scholarship, in spite of its rhetoric of radicalism, has failed to fundamentally alter anthropology, and why feminism has gained even less from anthropology than vice versa.

The awkwardness, she argues, arises from the fact that despite a common interest in differences, the scholarly practices of feminists and anthropologists are "differently structured in the way they organize knowledge and draw boundaries" (Strathern 1987: 289) and especially in "the nature of the investigators' *relationship to* their subject matter" (1987: 284). Feminist scholars, united by their common opposition to men or to patriarchy, produce a discourse composed of many voices; they "discover the self by becoming conscious of oppression from the Other" (1987: 289). Anthropologists, whose goal is "to make sense of differences" (1987: 286), also constitute their "selves" in relation to an other, but do not view this other as "under attack" (1987: 289).

In highlighting the self/other relationship, Strathern takes us to the heart of the problem. Yet she retreats from the problematic of power (granted as formative in feminism) in her strangely uncritical depiction of anthropology. When she defines anthropology as a discipline that "continues to know itself as the study of social behavior or society in terms of systems and collective representations" (1987: 281), she underplays the self/other distinction. In characterizing the relationship between anthropological self and other as nonadversarial, she ignores its most fundamental aspect. Anthropology's avowed goal may be "the study of man [sic]," but it is a discipline built on the historically constructed divide between the West and the non-West. It has been and continues to be primarily the study of the non-Western other by the Western self, even if in its new guise it seeks explicitly to give voice to the Other or to present a dialogue between the self and other, either textually or through an expli-

cation of the fieldwork encounter (as in such works as Crapanzano 1980, Dumont 1978, Dwyer 1982, Rabinow 1977, Riesman 1977, Tedlock 1983, and Tyler 1986). And the relationship between the West and the non-West, at least since the birth of anthropology, has been constituted by Western domination. This suggests that the awkwardness Strathern senses in the relationship between feminism and anthropology might better be understood as the result of diametrically opposed processes of self-construction through opposition to others – processes that begin from different sides of a power divide.

The enduring strength of what Morsy (1988: 70) has called "the hegemony of the distinctive-other tradition" in anthropology is betrayed by the defensiveness of partial exceptions. Anthropologists conducting fieldwork in the United States or Europe wonder whether they have not blurred the disciplinary boundaries between anthropology and other fields such as sociology or history. One way to retain their identities as anthropologists is to make the communities they study seem "other." Studying ethnic communities and the powerless assures this.[3] So does concentrating on "culture" (or on the method of holism based on it, as Appadurai [1988] has argued), for reasons I will discuss later. There are two issues here. One is the conviction that one cannot be objective about one's own society, something that affects indigenous anthropologists (Western or non-Western). The second is a tacit understanding that anthropologists study the non-West; halfies who study their own or related non-Western communities are still more easily recognizable as anthropologists than Americans who study Americans.

If anthropology continues to be practiced as the study by an unproblematic and unmarked Western self of found "others" out there, feminist theory, an academic practice that also traffics in selves and others, has in its relatively short history come to realize the danger of treating selves and others as givens. It is instructive for the development of a critique of anthropology to consider the trajectory that has led, within two decades, to what some might call a crisis in feminist theory, and others, the development of postfeminism.

From Simone de Beauvoir on, it has been accepted that, at least in the modern West, women have been the other to men's self. Feminism has been a movement devoted to helping women become selves and subjects rather than objects and men's others.[4] The crisis in feminist theory (related to a crisis in the women's movement) that followed on the heels of feminist attempts to turn those who had been constituted as other into selves – or, to use the popular metaphor, to let women speak – was the problem of "difference." For whom did feminists speak? Within the women's movement, the objections of lesbians, African-American women, and other "women of color" that their experiences as women were different from those of white, middle-class, heterosexual women problematized the identity of women as selves. Cross-cultural work on women also made it clear that masculine and feminine did not have, as we say, the same meanings in other cultures, nor did Third World women's lives resemble Western women's lives. As Harding (1986: 246) puts it, the problem is that "once 'woman' is deconstructed into 'women' and 'gender' is recognized to have no fixed referents, feminism itself dissolves as a theory that can reflect the voice of a naturalized or essentialized speaker."[5]

From its experience with this crisis of selfhood or subjecthood, feminist theory can offer anthropology two useful reminders. First, the self is always a construction, never a natural or found entity, even if it has that appearance. Second, the process of creating a self through opposition to an other always entails the violence of repressing or ignoring other forms of difference. Feminist theorists have been forced to explore the implications for the formation of identity and the possibilities for political action of the ways in which gender as a system of difference is intersected by other systems of difference, including, in the modern capitalist world, race and class.

Where does this leave the feminist anthropologist? Strathern (1987: 286) characterizes her as experiencing a tension – "caught between structures...faced with two different ways of relating to her or his subject matter." The more interesting aspect of the feminist's

situation, though, is what she shares with the halfie: a blocked ability to comfortably assume the self of anthropology. For both, although in different ways, the self is split, caught at the intersection of systems of difference. I am less concerned with the existential consequences of this split (these have been eloquently explored elsewhere [e.g., Joseph 1988, Kondo 1986, Narayan 1989]) than with the awareness such splits generate about three crucial issues: positionality, audience, and the power inherent in distinctions of self and other. What happens when the "other" that the anthropologist is studying is simultaneously constructed as, at least partially, a self?

Feminists and halfie anthropologists cannot easily avoid the issue of positionality. Standing on shifting ground makes it clear that every view is a view from somewhere and every act of speaking a speaking from somewhere. Cultural anthropologists have never been fully convinced of the ideology of science and have long questioned the value, possibility, and definition of objectivity.[6] But they still seem reluctant to examine the implications of the actual situatedness of their knowledge.[7]

Two common, intertwined objections to the work of feminist or native or semi-native anthropologists, both related to partiality, betray the persistence of ideals of objectivity. The first has to do with the partiality (as bias or position) of the observer. The second has to do with the partial (incomplete) nature of the picture presented. Halfies are more associated with the first problem, feminists the second. The problem with studying one's own society is alleged to be the problem of gaining enough distance. Since for halfies, the Other is in certain ways the self, there is said to be the danger shared with indigenous anthropologists of identification and the easy slide into subjectivity.[8] These worries suggest that the anthropologist is still defined as a being who must stand apart from the Other, even when he or she seeks explicitly to bridge the gap. Even Bourdieu (1977: 1–2), who perceptively analyzed the effects this outsider stance has on the anthropologist's (mis)understanding of social life, fails to break with this doxa. The obvious point he misses is that the outsider self never simply stands outside. He or she stands in a definite relation with the Other of the study, not just as a Westerner, but as a Frenchman in Algeria during the war of independence, an American in Morocco during the 1967 Arab-Israeli war, or an Englishwoman in postcolonial India. What we call the outside is a position *within* a larger political-historical complex. No less than the halfie, the "wholie" is in a specific position vis-à-vis the community being studied.

The debates about feminist anthropologists suggest a second source of uneasiness about positionality. Even when they present themselves as studying gender, feminist anthropologists are dismissed as presenting only a partial picture of the societies they study because they are assumed to be studying only women. Anthropologists study society, the unmarked form. The study of women is the marked form, too readily sectioned off, as Strathern (1985) notes.[9] Yet it could easily be argued that most studies of society have been equally partial. As restudies like Weiner's (1976) of Malinowski's Trobriand Islanders or Bell's (1983) of the well-studied Australian aborigines indicate, they have been the study of men.[10] This does not make such studies any less valuable; it merely reminds us that we must constantly attend to the positionality of the anthropological self and its representations of others. James Clifford (1986: 6), among others, has convincingly argued that ethnographic representations are always "partial truths." What is needed is a recognition that they are also positioned truths.

Split selfhood creates for the two groups being discussed a second problem that is illuminating for anthropology generally: multiple audiences. Although all anthropologists are beginning to feel what might be called the Rushdie effect – the effects of living in a global age when the subjects of their studies begin to read their works and the governments of the countries they work in ban books and deny visas – feminist and halfie anthropologists struggle in poignant ways with multiple accountability. Rather than having one primary audience, that of other anthropologists, feminist anthropologists write for anthropologists and for feminists, two groups whose relationship to their subject matter is at odds and who

hold ethnographers accountable in different ways.[11] Furthermore, feminist circles include non-Western feminists, often from the societies feminist anthropologists have studied, who call them to account in new ways.[12]

Halfies' dilemmas are even more extreme. As anthropologists, they write for other anthropologists, mostly Western. Identified also with communities outside the West, or subcultures within it, they are called to account by educated members of those communities. More importantly, not just because they position themselves with reference to two communities but because when they present the Other they are presenting themselves, they speak with a complex awareness of and investment in reception. Both halfie and feminist anthropologists are forced to confront squarely the politics and ethics of their representations. There are no easy solutions to their dilemmas.

The third issue that feminist and halfie anthropologists, unlike anthropologists who work in Western societies (another group for whom self and other are somewhat tangled), force us to confront is the dubiousness of maintaining that relationships between self and other are innocent of power. Because of sexism and racial or ethnic discrimination, they may have experienced – as women, as individuals of mixed parentage, or as foreigners – being other to a dominant self, whether in everyday life in the U.S., Britain, or France, or in the Western academy. This is not simply an experience of difference, but of inequality. My argument, however, is structural, not experiential. Women, blacks, and people of most of the non-West have been historically constituted as others in the major political systems of difference on which the unequal world of modern capitalism has depended. Feminist studies and black studies have made sufficient progress within the academy to have exposed the way that being studied by "white men" (to use a shorthand for a complex and historically constituted subject-position) turns into being spoken for by them. It becomes a sign and instrument of their power.

Within anthropology, despite a long history of self-conscious opposition to racism, a fast-growing, self-critical literature on anthropology's links to colonialism (for example, Asad

1973, Clifford 1983a, Fabian 1983, Hymes 1969, Kuper 1988), and experimentation with techniques of ethnography to relieve a discomfort with the power of anthropologist over anthropological subject, the fundamental issues of domination keep being skirted. Even attempts to refigure informants as consultants and to "let the other speak" in dialogic (Tedlock 1987) or polyvocal texts – decolonizations on the level of the text – leave intact the basic configuration of global power on which anthropology, as linked to other institutions of the world, is based. To see the strangeness of this enterprise, all that is needed is to consider an analogous case. What would our reaction be if male scholars stated their desire to "let women speak" in their texts while they continued to dominate all knowledge about them by controlling writing and other academic practices, supported in their positions by a particular organization of economic, social, and political life?

Because of their split selves, feminist and halfie anthropologists travel uneasily between speaking "for" and speaking "from." Their situation enables us to see more clearly that dividing practices, whether they naturalize differences, as in gender or race, or simply elaborate them, as I will argue the concept of culture does, are fundamental methods of enforcing inequality.

Culture and Difference

The concept of culture is the hidden term in all that has just been said about anthropology. Most American anthropologists believe or act as if "culture," notoriously resistant to definition and ambiguous of referent, is nevertheless the true object of anthropological inquiry. Yet it could also be argued that culture is important to anthropology because the anthropological distinction between self and other rests on it. Culture is the essential tool for making other. As a professional discourse that elaborates on the meaning of culture in order to account for, explain, and understand cultural difference, anthropology also helps construct, produce, and maintain it. Anthropological discourse gives cultural difference

(and the separation between groups of people it implies) the air of the self-evident.

In this regard, the concept of culture operates much like its predecessor – race – even though in its twentieth-century form it has some important political advantages. Unlike race, and unlike even the nineteenth-century sense of culture as a synonym for civilization (contrasted to barbarism), the current concept allows for multiple rather than binary differences. This immediately checks the easy move to hierarchizing; the shift to "culture" ("lower case *c* with the possibility of a final *s*," as Clifford [1988a: 234] puts it) has a relativizing effect. The most important of culture's advantages, however, is that it removes difference from the realm of the natural and the innate. Whether conceived of as a set of behaviors, customs, traditions, rules, plans, recipes, instructions, or programs (to list the range of definitions Geertz [1973: 44] furnishes), culture is learned and can change.

Despite its anti-essentialist intent, however, the culture concept retains some of the tendencies to freeze difference possessed by concepts like race. This is easier to see if we consider a field in which there has been a shift from one to the other. Orientalism as a scholarly discourse (among other things) is, according to Said (1978: 2), "a style of thought based upon an ontological and epistemological distinction made between 'the Orient' and (most of the time) 'the Occident'." What he shows is that in mapping geography, race, and culture onto one another, Orientalism fixes differences between people of "the West" and people of "the East" in ways so rigid that they might as well be considered innate. In the twentieth century, cultural difference, not race, has been the basic subject of Orientalist scholarship devoted now to interpreting the "culture" phenomena (primarily religion and language) to which basic differences in development, economic performance, government, character, and so forth are attributed.

Some anticolonial movements and present-day struggles have worked by what could be labelled reverse Orientalism, where attempts to reverse the power relationship proceed by seeking to valorize for the self what in the former system had been devalued as other. [. . .]

A parallel can be drawn with feminism. It is a basic tenet of feminism that "women are made, not born." It has been important for most feminists to locate sex differences in culture, not biology or nature. While this has inspired some feminist theorists to attend to the social and personal effects of gender as a system of difference, for many others it has led to explorations of and strategies built on the notion of a women's culture. Cultural feminism (cf. Echols 1984) takes many forms, but it has many of the qualities of reverse Orientalism just discussed. [...] These proposals nearly always build on values traditionally associated in the West with women – a sense of care and connectedness, maternal nurturing, immediacy of experience, involvement in the bodily (versus the abstract), and so forth.

This valorization by cultural feminists, like reverse Orientalists, of the previously devalued qualities attributed to them may be provisionally useful in forging a sense of unity and in waging struggles of empowerment. Yet because it leaves in place the divide that structured the experiences of selfhood and oppression on which it builds, it perpetuates some dangerous tendencies. First, cultural feminists overlook the connections between those on each side of the divide, and the ways in which they define each other. Second, they overlook differences within each category constructed by the dividing practices, differences like those of class, race, and sexuality (to repeat the feminist litany of problematically abstract categories), but also ethnic origin, personal experience, age, mode of livelihood, health, living situation (rural or urban), and historical experience. Third, and perhaps most important, they ignore the ways in which experiences have been constructed historically and have changed over time. Both cultural feminism and revivalist movements tend to rely on notions of authenticity and the return to positive values not represented by the dominant other. As becomes obvious in the most extreme cases, these moves erase history. Invocations of Cretan goddesses in some cultural-feminist circles and, in a more complex and serious way, the powerful invocation of the seventh-century community of the Prophet in some Islamic movements are good examples.

The point is that the notion of culture which both types of movements use does not seem to guarantee an escape from the tendency toward essentialism. It could be argued that anthropologists use "culture" in more sophisticated and consistent ways and that their commitment to it as an analytical tool is firmer. Yet even many of them are now concerned about the ways it tends to freeze differences. [...]

Others, including myself (1990b), have argued that cultural theories also tend to overemphasize coherence. Clifford notes both that "the discipline of fieldwork-based anthropology, in constituting its authority, constructs and reconstructs coherent cultural others and interpreting selves" (Clifford 1988b: 112) and that ethnography is a form of culture collecting (like art collecting) in which "diverse experiences and facts are selected, gathered, detached from their original temporal occasions, and given enduring value in a new arrangement" (Clifford 1988a: 231). Organic metaphors of wholeness and the methodology of holism that characterizes anthropology both favor coherence, which in turn contributes to the perception of communities as bounded and discrete.

Certainly discreteness does not have to imply value; the hallmark of twentieth-century anthropology has been its promotion of cultural relativism over evaluation and judgment. If anthropology has always to some extent been a form of cultural (self-) critique (Marcus and Fischer, 1986), that too was an aspect of a refusal to hierarchize difference. Yet neither position would be possible without difference. It would be worth thinking about the implications of the high stakes anthropology has in sustaining and perpetuating a belief in the existence of cultures that are identifiable as discrete, different, and separate from our own.[13] Does difference always smuggle in hierarchy?

In *Orientalism*, Said (1978: 28) argues for the elimination of "the Orient" and "the Occident" altogether. By this he means not the erasure of all differences but the recognition of more of them and of the complex ways in which they crosscut. More important; his analysis of one field seeks to show how and when certain differences, in this case of places and the people attached to them, become implicated in the domination of one by the other.

Should anthropologists treat with similar suspicion "culture" and "cultures" as the key terms in a discourse in which otherness and difference have come to have, as Said (1989: 213) points out, "talismanic qualities"?

Three Modes of Writing against Culture

If "culture," shadowed by coherence, timelessness, and discreteness, is the prime anthropological tool for making "other," and difference, as feminists and halfies reveal, tends to be a relationship of power, then perhaps anthropologists should consider strategies for writing against culture. I will discuss three that I find promising. Although they by no means exhaust the possibilities, the sorts of projects I will describe – theoretical, substantive, and textual – make sense for anthropologists sensitive to issues of positionality and accountability and interested in making anthropological practice something that does not simply shore up global inequalities. I will conclude, however, by considering the limitations of all anthropological reform.

Discourse and practice

Theoretical discussion, because it is one of the modes in which anthropologists engage each other, provides an important site for contesting "culture." It seems to me that current discussions and deployments of two increasingly popular terms – practice and discourse – do signal a shift away from culture. Although there is always the danger that these terms will come to be used simply as synonyms for culture, they were intended to enable us to analyze social life without presuming the degree of coherence that the culture concept has come to carry.

Practice is associated, in anthropology, with Bourdieu (1977; also see Ortner 1984), whose theoretical approach is built around problems of contradiction, misunderstanding, and misrecognition, and favors strategies, interests, and improvisations over the more static and homogenizing cultural tropes of rules, models, and texts. Discourse (whose uses I discuss in

L. Abu-Lughod 1989 and Abu-Lughod and Lutz 1990) has more diverse sources and meanings in anthropology. In its Foucauldian derivation, as it relates to notions of discursive formations, apparatuses, and technologies, it is meant to refuse the distinction between ideas and practices or text and world that the culture concept too readily encourages. In its more sociolinguistic sense, it draws attention to the social uses by individuals of verbal resources. In either case, it allows for the possibility of recognizing within a social group the play of multiple, shifting, and competing statements with practical effects. Both practice and discourse are useful because they work against the assumption of boundedness, not to mention the idealism (Asad 1983), of the culture concept.[14]

Connections

Another strategy of writing against culture is to reorient the problems or subject matter anthropologists address. An important focus should be the various connections and interconnections, historical and contemporary, between a community and the anthropologist working there and writing about it, not to mention the world to which he or she belongs and which enables him or her to be in that particular place studying that group. This is more of a political project than an existential one, although the reflexive anthropologists who have taught us to focus on the fieldwork encounter as a site for the construction of the ethnographic "facts" have alerted us to one important dimension of the connection. Other significant sorts of connections have received less attention. [...] We need to ask questions about the historical processes by which it came to pass that people like ourselves could be engaged in anthropological studies of people like those, about the current world situation that enables us to engage in this sort of work in this particular place, and about who has preceded us and is even now there with us (tourists, travelers, missionaries, AID consultants, Peace Corps workers). We need to ask what this "will to knowledge" about the Other is connected to in the world.

[...]

Not all projects about connections need be historical. Anthropologists are increasingly concerned with national and transnational connections of people, cultural forms, media, techniques, and commodities.[15] They study the articulation of world capitalism and international politics with the situations of people living in particular communities. All these projects, which involve a shift in gaze to include phenomena of connection, expose the inadequacies of the concept of culture and the elusiveness of the entities designated by the term *cultures*. Although there may be a tendency in the new work merely to widen the object, shifting from culture to nation as locus, ideally there would be attention to the shifting groupings, identities, and interactions within and across such borders as well. If there was ever a time when anthropologists could consider without too much violence at least some communities as isolated units, certainly the nature of global interactions in the present makes that now impossible.[16]

Ethnographies of the particular

The third strategy for writing against culture depends on accepting the one insight of Geertz's about anthropology that has been built upon by everyone in this "experimental moment" (Marcus and Fischer 1986) who takes textuality seriously. Geertz (1975, 1988) has argued that one of the main things anthropologists do is write, and what they write are fictions (which does not mean they are fictitious).[17] Certainly the practice of ethnographic writing has received an inordinate amount of attention from those involved in *Writing Culture* and an increasing number of others who were not involved. Much of the hostility toward their project arises from the suspicion that in their literary leanings they have too readily collapsed the politics of ethnography into its poetics. And yet they have raised an issue that cannot be ignored. Insofar as anthropologists are in the business of representing others through their ethnographic writing, then surely the degree to which people in the communities they study appear "other" must also be partly a function of how anthro-

pologists write about them. Are there ways to write about lives so as to constitute others as less other?

I would argue that one powerful tool for unsettling the culture concept and subverting the process of "othering" it entails is to write "ethnographies of the particular." Generalization, the characteristic mode of operation and style of writing of the social sciences, can no longer be regarded as neutral description (Foucault 1978; Said 1978; Smith 1987). It has two unfortunate effects in anthropology that make it worth eschewing. I will explore these before presenting some examples from my own work of what one could hope to accomplish through ethnographies of the particular.

[...]

I also want to make clear what the argument for particularity is not: it is not to be mistaken for arguments for privileging micro over macro processes. Ethnomethodologists and other students of everyday life seek ways to generalize about microinteractions, while historians might be said to be tracing the particulars of macroprocesses. Nor need a concern with the particulars of individuals' lives imply disregard for forces and dynamics that are not locally based. On the contrary, the effects of extralocal and long-term processes are only manifested locally and specifically, produced in the actions of individuals living their particular lives, inscribed in their bodies and their words. What I am arguing for is a form of writing that might better convey that.

There are two reasons for anthropologists to be wary of generalization. The first is that, as part of a professional discourse of "objectivity" and expertise, it is inevitably a language of power. On the one hand, it is the language of those who seem to stand apart from and outside of what they are describing. [...]

On the other hand, even if we withhold judgment on how closely the social sciences can be associated with the apparatuses of management, we have to recognize how all professionalized discourses by nature assert hierarchy. The very gap between the professional and authoritative discourses of generalization and the languages of everyday life (our own and others') establishes a fundamental separation between the anthropologist and the people being written about that facilitates the construction of anthropological objects as simultaneously different and inferior.

Thus, to the degree that anthropologists can bring closer the language of everyday life and the language of the text, this mode of making other is reversed. The problem is, as a reflection on the situation of feminist anthropologists suggest, that there may be professional risks for ethnographers who want to pursue this strategy. I have argued elsewhere (1990a) that Rabinow's refreshingly sensible observation about the politics of ethnographic writing – that they are to be found closer to home, in academia, than in the colonial and neocolonial world – helps us understand a few things about feminist anthropology and the uneasiness about it that even someone like Clifford betrays in his introductory essay for *Writing Culture*.[18] His excuse for excluding feminist anthropologists was that they were not involved in textual innovation. If we were to grant the dubious distinction he presumes between textual innovation and transformations of content and theory, we might concede that feminist anthropologists have contributed little to the new wave of experimentation in form.

But then a moment's thought would provide us with clues about why. Without even asking the basic questions about individuals, institutions, patrons, and tenure, we can turn to the politics of the feminist project itself. Dedicated to making sure that women's lives are represented in descriptions of societies and women's experiences and gender itself theorized in accounts of how societies work, feminist scholars have been interested in the old political sense of representation. Conservatism of form may have been helpful because the goal was to persuade colleagues that an anthropology taking gender into account was not just good anthropology but better anthropology.

The second pressure on feminist anthropology is the need to assert professionalism. Contrary to what Clifford writes (1986: 21), women *have* produced "unconventional forms of writing." He just ignored them, neglecting a few professional anthropologists like Bowen (Bohannon) (1954), Briggs (1970), and Cesara (Poewe) (1982) who have experimented with form.[19] More significantly, there is also what

might be considered a separate "woman's tradition" within ethnographic writing. Because it is not professional, however, it might only reluctantly be claimed and explored by feminist anthropologists uncertain of their standing. I am referring to the often excellent and popular ethnographies written by the "untrained" wives of anthropologists, books like Elizabeth Fernea's *Guests of the Sheik* (1965), Marjorie Shostak's *Nisa* (1981), Edith Turner's *The Spirit of the Drum* (1987), and Margery Wolf's *The House of Lim* (1968). Directing their works to audiences slightly different from those of the professional writers of standard ethnographies, they have also followed different conventions: they are more open about their positionality, less assertive of their scientific authority, and more focused on particular individuals and families.

Why does this other tradition not qualify as a form of textual innovation? A partial answer can be found in *Writing Culture* itself. The proponents of the current experiments and critiques of ethnographic writing tend to break with humdrum anthropology by borrowing from elite disciplines like philosophy and literary theory rather than looking to more prosaic sources like ordinary experience or the terms in which their anthropological subjects operate.[20] They reject the rhetoric of social science not for ordinary language but for a rarefied discourse so packed with jargon that a press editor was provoked to compose a mocking jargon poem playing with their vocabulary of tropes, thaumasmus, metonymy, pathopoeia, phenomenology, ecphonesis, epistemology, deictics, and hypotyposis – a poem ironically included as an invocation in the preface to the book (Clifford and Marcus 1986: ix). Whatever the merits of their contributions, the message of hyperprofessionalism is hard to miss. Despite a sensitivity to questions of otherness and power and the relevance of textuality to these issues, they use a discourse even more exclusive, and thus more reinforcing of hierarchical distinctions between themselves and anthropological others, than that of the ordinary anthropology they criticize.

The second problem with generalization derives not from its participation in the authoritative discourses of professionalism but from the effects of homogeneity, coherence, and timelessness it tends to produce. When one generalizes from experiences and conversations with a number of specific people in a community, one tends to flatten out differences among them and to homogenize them. The appearance of an absence of internal differentiation makes it easier to conceive of a group of people as a discrete, bounded entity, like the "the Nuer," "the Balinese," and "the Awlad 'Ali Bedouin" who do this or that and believe such-and-such. The effort to produce general ethnographic descriptions of people's beliefs or actions tends to smooth over contradictions, conflicts of interest, and doubts and arguments, not to mention changing motivations and circumstances. The erasure of time and conflict make what is inside the boundary set up by homogenization something essential and fixed. These effects are of special moment to anthropologists because they contribute to the fiction of essentially different and discrete others who can be separated from some sort of equally essential self. Insofar as difference is, as I have argued, hierarchical, and assertions of separation a way of denying responsibility, generalization itself must be treated with suspicion.

For these reasons I propose that we experiment with narrative ethnographies of the particular in a continuing tradition of fieldwork-based writing.[21] In telling stories about particular individuals in time and place, such ethnographies would share elements with the alternative "women's tradition" discussed above. I would expect them to complement rather than replace a range of other types of anthropological projects, from theoretical discussions to the exploration of new topics within anthropology, a range well represented by the contributors to this volume. I will take up in the final section the reason ethnographies are still important to write. Before that I want to give some sense of the potential value of such ethnographies.

Anthropologists commonly generalize about communities by saying that they are characterized by certain institutions, rules, or ways of doing things. For example, we can and often do say things like "The Bongo-Bongo are polygynous." Yet one could refuse to generalize in this way, instead asking how a particular set of individuals – for instance, a man and his three wives in a Bedouin community in Egypt whom I have known for a decade – live the "institution" that we call polygyny. Stressing the particularity of this marriage and building a picture of it through the participants' discussions, recollections, disagreements, and actions would make several theoretical points.

First, refusing to generalize would highlight the constructed quality of that typicality so regularly produced in conventional social scientific accounts. Second, showing the actual circumstances and detailed histories of individuals and their relationships would suggest that such particulars, which are always present (as we know from our own personal experiences), are also always crucial to the constitution of experience. Third, reconstructing people's arguments about, justifications for, and interpretations of what they and others are doing would explain how social life proceeds. It would show that although the terms of their discourses may be set (and, as in any society, include several sometimes contradictory and often historically changing discourses), within these limits, people contest interpretations of what is happening, strategize, feel pain, and live their lives [...] seeking textual means of representing how this happens rather than simply making theoretical assertions that it does.

By focusing closely on particular individuals and their changing relationships, one would necessarily subvert the most problematic connotations of culture: homogeneity, coherence, and timelessness. Individuals are confronted with choices, struggle with others, make conflicting statements, argue about points of view on the same events, undergo ups and downs in various relationships and changes in their circumstances and desires, face new pressures, and fail to predict what will happen to them or those around them. So, for example, it becomes difficult to think that the term "Bedouin culture" makes sense when one tries to piece together and convey what life is like for one old Bedouin matriarch.

[...]

[...] How does her nostalgia for the past – when the area was empty and she could see for miles around; when she used to play as a little girl digging up the occasional potsherd or glass bottle in the area now fenced and guarded by the government Antiquities Organization; when her family migrated with the sheep herds and milked and made butter in desert pastures – go with her fierce defense of her favorite grandson, whose father was furious with him because the young man was rumored to have drunk liquor at a local wedding? People do not drink in the community, and drinking is, of course, religiously proscribed. What can "culture" mean, given this old woman's complex responses?

Time is the other important dimension that gets built in if one takes seriously the narrative of people's everyday lives. When the young man's father hits him, the son who has been accused of drinking at the wedding sells his cassette player to a neighbor to raise cash and then disappears. His grandmother cries over him, his aunts discuss it. His father says nothing. It is days before a distant in-law comes to reassure his grandmother that the young man is fine and to indicate that they know his whereabouts (he is working at a construction site about 100 kilometers away). No one knows what the consequences of this event will be. Will he return? What will his father do? Family honor is at stake, reputations for piety, paternal authority. When the young man returns several weeks later, accompanied by a maternal uncle from 50 kilometers west who intervenes to forestall any further punishments, his grandmother weeps in relief. It could easily have turned out differently. Since his disappearance, her days had been taken up with worrying, discussing, waiting, and not knowing what would happen next. That beating and that running away, events that happened in time, become part of the history of that family, the individuals involved, and their relationships. In this sequence of events in a particular family in 1987, we can read what we call the "larger forces" that made it possible, things like growing opportunities for wage labor, the commercialization of Bedouin weddings, and the influx of goods from the cities. Yet because these "forces" are only embodied in the actions of individuals living in time and place, ethnographies of the particular capture them best.

Even ritual, that communal practice for which time seems to have such a different, perhaps cyclical, meaning, that kind of practice which in anthropological discourse so perfectly marks the (exotic, primitive) cultural other as different, turns out to be particular and anything but timeless. If looked at closely in terms of the actual participants and ritual event, it involves unpredictability. Even in ritual the unfolding of what cannot be known beforehand generates great drama and tension. Let me give an example, again from my work. Within the first week of my arrival in the Bedouin community in Egypt where I was to spend years, the young girls in my household outlined for me the exact sequence of events every bride went through in a Bedouin wedding. Over the years, I attended many weddings, all of which followed this outline, yet each of which was distinct. For each bride and groom, not to mention their families, the wedding would mark a moment of major life transformation, not just of status but of associations, daily life, experience, and the future. Each wedding was different in the kinds of families being brought together, the network of relations created and the goods exchanged, spent, and displayed.

[...] Events take different courses. That is the nature of "life as lived" (Riesman 1977), everywhere. Generalizations, by producing effects of timelessness and coherence to support the essentialized notion of "cultures" different from ours and peoples separate from us, make us forget this.

Conclusion: Tactical Humanism?

The critiques of anthropology that have emerged recently from various quarters have encouraged us to question what we work on, how we write, and for whom we write. I have been arguing that cultural difference, which has been both the ground and product of anthropological discourse, is a problematic construction and have proposed a number of strategies, most already taken up by others, for "writing against culture." I gave examples from my own work of the way in which one strategy – ethnography of the particular – might be an especially useful way to disturb the culture concept.

The special value of this strategy is that it brings out similarities in all our lives. To say that we all live in the particular is not to say that for any of us the particulars are the same. It could well be that even in looking at the everyday we might discover fundamental differences, such as those between everyday experience in a world set up to produce the effect of structures, institutions, or other abstractions (as Mitchell [1988] argues the modern West has been), and in worlds that have not. But the dailiness, in breaking coherence and introducing time, keeps us fixed on flux and contradiction. And the particulars suggest that others live as we perceive ourselves living, not as robots programmed with "cultural" rules, but as people going through life agonizing over decisions, making mistakes, trying to make themselves look good, enduring tragedies and personal losses, enjoying others, and finding moments of happiness.

The language of generalization cannot convey these sorts of experiences and activities. In our own lives, we balance the accounts of ourselves that social science purveys with the ordinary language we use in personal conversations to discuss and understand our lives, our friends and family, and our world. For those who live "outside" our world, however, we have no discourse of familiarity to counteract the distancing discourses of anthropology and other social sciences, discourses that also serve development experts, governments, journalists, and others who deal with the Third World.

Ethnographies of the particular could provide this discourse of familiarity, a familiarity that the humanist conventions favored by the unprofessional and devalued women ethnographers always encouraged. Why invoke humanism when it has become so discredited in poststructural and postmodernist circles.[22] There are certainly good reasons to be suspicious of a philosophy that has continually masked the persistence of systematic social differences by appealing to an allegedly universal individual as hero and autonomous subject; a philosophy that has allowed us to assume that the domination and exploitation of nature by man was justified by his place at the center of the universe; a philosophy that has failed to see that its essential human has culturally and socially specific characteristics and in fact excludes most humans; and a philosophy that refuses to understand how we as subjects are constructed in discourses attached to power.

Because humanism continues to be, in the West, the language of human equality with the most moral force, we cannot abandon it yet, if only as a convention of writing. In advocating new forms of writing – pastiche, dialogue, collage, and so forth – that break up narrative, subject identities, and identifications, antihumanists ask their readers to adopt sophisticated reading strategies along with social critique. Can anthropologists ask this? Already, complaints about boredom and resistance to being jarred have been leveled against experimental ethnographies. Humanism is a language with more speakers (and readers), even if it, too, is a local language rather than the universal one it pretends to be. To have an effect on people, perhaps we still need to speak this language, but to speak it knowing its limitations.

This might be called a tactical humanism, made both politically necessary and limited in its effects by anthropology's location on the side of domination in the context of a world organized by global inequality along lines of "cultural" difference. We should not have illusions that tactical humanism, whether in the form of ethnographies of the particular or other modes of writing against culture, contributes to some universal language or universal good. From our positions as anthropologists, however tenuous our identifications if we are feminists or "halfies," we work as Westerners, and what we contribute to is a Western discourse. As Mudimbe (1988: 19) writes in *The Invention of Africa*, "it seems impossible to imagine any anthropology without a Western epistemological link." I argued earlier that positionality could not be escaped. Nor can the fact, as Riesman (1982) bluntly puts it in his critical response to proposals for dialogic anthropology, "that we are using other people for our own purposes all the time" and "using the knowledge they give us for goals they would never imagine themselves." That does not mean that the goals are not worth pursuing or that working with Western discourse is not crucial. As Said (1989: 224) notes, "anthropological representations bear as much on the representer's world as on who or what is represented." The West still has tremendous discursive, military, and economic power. Our writing can either sustain it or work against its grain.

We must also be prepared, despite efforts directed at the West, to be confronted with the problems posed when even our most enlightened humanistic endeavors reach those in other contexts where the conventions may not be recognized and the power issues are read differently. Again I can illustrate from my work. Writing in the context of widespread Western antipathy towards the people of the Middle East has been in part a project to convey a sense of the common everyday humanity of an Arab community.[23] Yet although I can try to explain this context to the members of that community, the work cannot be received by them in the same way. My revelation of Bedouin individuals' attachments and vulnerabilities through their poetry, to create for Westerners a sense of recognition, not distance, has provoked several other responses in Egypt. When one woman heard someone read from the book a few of the poems she had recited years earlier, she exclaimed, half joking, "You've scandalized us!" For her, a book about particular people and everyday life in her community might seem only a public display of family secrets.

My presentation of the way ideals of personal autonomy and independence were manifested in men's lives also took on complex and different meanings in Egypt. A copy of a long review (in Arabic) of my book came to the attention of an Awlad 'Ali Bedouin who was a civil servant and aspiring official in the Egyptian government. He confronted my host with the article, angry that I had reported that they liked to carry guns, evade taxes, and guard their rights to settle their own disputes rather than let the government interfere. As my host told me, the man accusingly argued, "This is your girl who wrote this!" What happened then I will never know, since I was not there and heard only my host's version. He was, as

usual, defiant, retorting that he had taught me everything I knew. And wasn't it true? Didn't this man have unlicensed guns? Did he report all his sheep for tax purposes? My host had often told me he wanted my book translated into Arabic so that Egyptians would come to understand and appreciate the superior moral standards of his community – of which many Egyptians were contemptuous. Yet this incident showed that he was only one voice in the Bedouin community and his ideas about what would gain him respect were different from those of someone loyal to the government. My work, intended for a different audience, had entered a local political field where the relationship between Awlad 'Ali Bedouins and the Egyptian state was a contested issue.

Like all anthropological works these days, my writings will no doubt enter into a range of other debates. That is not cause for despair. Rather, in forcing us to reflect on dilemmas about anthropological practice that we can no longer ignore – because we live in times when the boundaries of "culture" are harder to keep in place and global politics less certain – such problems enable us to choose provisional strategies in line with our hopes but without self-righteous illusions about the larger value of our contributions.

NOTES

1 *Halfies* is a term I borrowed from Kirin Narayan (personal communication).
2 Likewise, Marcus and Clifford (1985) and Marcus and Fischer (1986) gesture toward feminists as important sources of cultural and anthropological critique but do not discuss their work. Fischer (1984, 1986, 1988), however, has long been interested in the phenomenon of biculturality.
3 It is still rare for anthropologists in this society or others to do what Laura Nader (1969) advocated many years ago – to "study up."
4 Its various strategies are based on this division and the series of oppositions (culture/nature, public/private, work/home,

transcendence/immediacies, abstract particular, objectivity/subjectivity, autonomy/connectedness, etc.) associated with it: (a) women should be allowed to join the valued men's world, to become like men or have their privileges, (b) women's values and work, even if different, should be as valued as men's, or (c) women and men should both change and enter each other's spheres so that gender differences are erased.

5   It does not, Harding adds, dissolve feminism as a political identity, but the most pressing issue in feminist circles now is how to develop a politics of solidarity, coalition, or affinity built on the recognition of difference rather than the solidarity of a unitary self defined by its opposition to an other which had formerly defined it as other. The most interesting thinking on this subject has been Haraway's (1985).

6   For a discussion of the convergence of anthropological and feminist critiques of objectivity, see Abu-Lughod (1990a).

7   In his 1988 address to the American Anthropological Association, Edward Said's central point was that anthropologists had to attend not just to "the anthropological site" but to the "cultural situation in which anthropological work is in fact done" (1989: 212).

8   Much of the literature on indigenous anthropology is taken up with the advantages and disadvantages of this identification. See Fahim (1982) and Altorki and El-Solh (1988).

9   See also my discussion of the study of gender in Middle East anthropology (L. Abu-Lughod 1989).

10   In parallel fashion, those who study the black experience are thought of as studying a marked form of experience. It could be pointed out, and has been by such figures as Adrienne Rich, that the universal unmarked form of experience from which it differs is itself partial. It is the experience of whiteness.

11   Crapanzano (1977) has written insightfully about the regular process of distancing from the fieldwork experience and

building identifications with the anthropological audience that all anthropologists go through when they return from the field.

12   This is happening, for example, in heated debates in the field of Middle East women's studies about who has the right to speak for Middle Eastern women.

13   Arens (1979), for example, has asked the provocative question of why anthropologists cling so tenaciously to the belief that in some cultures cannibalism is an accepted ritual practice, when the evidence (in the form of eye witness accounts) is so meager (if not, as he argues, absent).

14   In my own work on an Egyptian Bedouin community I began to think in terms of discourses rather than culture simply because I had to find ways to make sense of the fact that there seemed to be two contradictory discourses on interpersonal relations – the discourse of honor and modesty and the poetic discourse of vulnerability and attachment – which informed and were used by the same individuals in differing contexts (Abu-Lughod 1986). In a recent reflection on Bedouin responses to death (Abu-Lughod), I also had to make sense of the fact that there were multiple discourses on death in this community. Not only did people play with contradictory explanations of particular deaths (invoking, in one case of an accidental killing, stupidity, certain actions on the part of family members, the [evil] eye, fate, and God's will), but the two primary discourses – ritual funerary laments and the Islamic discourse of God's will – were attached to different social groups, men and women, and worked to sustain and justify the power differences between them.

15   Two new journals, *Public Culture: Bulletin of the Center for Transnational Cultural Studies* and *Diaspora: A Journal of Transnational Studies*, provide forums for discussion of these transnational issues.

16   For evidence of a "world system" in the thirteenth century, see J. Abu-Lughod (1989).

17 Dumont (1986) has recently reiterated this, declaring changes in social theory to be merely methodological changes.

18 For a more detailed and interesting discussion of Clifford's unease with feminism, see Gordon (1988).

19 To this list could be added many others, including most recently Friedl (1989).

20 This may also explain their neglect of Paul Riesman, whose experiment in ethnographic writing was published in French in 1974 and in English in 1977, making it one of the earliest.

21 See my own experiment in this sort of narrative ethnography (Abu-Lughod 1993a).

22 So damning is an association with humanism that Said's lapse into it is the crux of Clifford's (1980) critique of *Orientalism*.

23 The strength of anti-Arab racism in the West has sometimes seemed to make this a discouraging project. A recent article called "The Importance of Hugging" used a misrepresentation of my work as evidence for its argument that the natural violence and bloodthirstiness of Arabs are caused by their supposed failure to hug their children (Bloom 1989).

REFERENCES

Abu-Lughod, Janet. 1989. *Before European Hegemony*. New York: Oxford University Press.

Abu-Lughod, Lila. 1986. *Veiled Sentiments: Honor and Poetry in a Bedouin Society*. New York: Oxford University Press.

—— 1988. Constructions of Sexuality: Public and Private in Bedouin Weddings. Paper presented at the conference, "Feminist Perspectives on Women in the Arabo-Islamic Culture," Cornell University.

—— 1989. Zones of Theory in the Anthropology of the Arab World. *Annual Review of Anthropology*, 18: 276–306.

—— 1990a Can there be Feminist Ethnography? *Women and Performance: A Journal of Feminist Theory*, 5: 7–27.

—— 1990b Shifting Politics in Bedouin Love Poetry. In *Language and the Politics of Emotion*. C. Lutz and L. Abu-Lughod, eds. New York: Cambridge University Press.

—— 1993a *Writing Women's Worlds*. Berkeley: University of California Press.

—— 1993b Islam and the Gendered Discourses of Death. *International Journal of Middle East Studies*, 25/2: 187–205.

Abu-Lughod, Lila, and Catherine Lutz. 1990. Introduction. Discourse, Emotion, and the Politics of Everyday Life. In *Language and the Politics of Emotion*. New York: Cambridge University Press.

Altorki, Soraya, and Camillia El-Solh, eds. 1988. *Arab Women in the Field: Studying Your Own Society*. Syracuse, NY: Syracuse University Press.

Appadurai, Arjun. 1988. Putting Hierarchy in its Place. *Cultural Anthropology*, 3: 36–49.

Arens, William. 1979. *The Man-Eating Myth: Anthropology and Anthropophagy*. New York: Oxford University Press.

Asad, Talal. 1973. *Anthropology and the Colonial Encounter*. London: Ithaca Press.

—— 1983. Anthropological Conceptions of Religion: Reflections on Geertz. *Man*, 18: 237–59.

Bell, Diane. 1983. *Daughters of the Dreaming*. Melbourne: McPhee Gribble/N. Sydney: George Allen & Unwin.

Bloom, Howard. 1989. The Importance of Hugging. *Omni*, 11/5: 30, 116.

Bourdieu, Pierre. 1977. *Outline of a Theory of Practice*. Trans. R. Nice. Cambridge: Cambridge University Press.

Bowen, Elenore S. 1954. *Return to Laughter*. Reprint edition, 1964. Garden City, NY: Anchor Books.

Briggs, Jean. 1970. *Never in Anger*. Cambridge, MA: Harvard University Press.

Cesara, Manda. 1982. *Reflections of a Woman Anthropologist: No Hiding Place*. London and New york: Academic Press.

Clifford, James. 1980. Review of "Orientalism," by Edward Said. *History and Theory*, 19: 204–23.

—— 1983. Power in Dialogue in Ethnography. In *Observers Observed: Essays on Ethnographic Fieldwork*. G. W. Stocking, Jr., ed. pp. 121–56. Madison: University of Wisconsin Press.

Clifford, James. 1986. Introduction: Partial Truths. In *Writing Culture: The Poetics and Politics of Ethnography*. J. Clifford and G. Marcus, eds. pp. 1–26. Berkeley: University of California Press.

—— 1988a. On Collecting Art and Culture. In *The Predicament of Culture: Twentieth-Century Ethnography, Literature, and Art*. James Clifford, pp. 215–51. Cambridge, MA: Harvard University Press.

—— 1988b. On Ethnographic Self Fashioning. In *The Predicament of Culture: Twentieth-Century Ethnography, Literature, and Art*. James Clifford, pp. 92–113. Cambridge, MA: Harvard University Press.

Clifford, James, and George E. Marcus, eds. 1986. *Writing Culture: The Poetics and Politics of Ethnography*. Berkeley: University of California Press.

Crapanzano, Vincent. 1977. On the Writing of Ethnography. *Dialectical Anthropology*, 2: 69–73.

—— 1980. *Tuhami: Portrait of a Moroccan*. Chicago: University of Chicago Press.

Dumont, Jean-Paul. 1978. *The Headman and I*. Austin: University of Texas Press.

—— 1986. Prologue to Ethnography or Prolegomena to Anthropology. *Ethos*, 14: 344–67.

Dwyer, Kevin. 1982. *Moroccan Dialogues: Anthropology in Question*. Baltimore: Johns Hopkins University Press.

Echols, Alice. 1984. The Taming of the Id: Feminist Sexual Politics 1968–83. In *Pleasure and Danger*. C. Vance, ed. Boston: Routledge and Kegan Paul.

Fabian, Johannes. 1983. *Time and the Other: How Anthropology Makes Its Object*. New York: Columbia University Press.

Fahim, Hussein, ed. 1982. *Indigenous Anthropology in Non-Western Countries*. Durham: Carolina Academic Press.

Fernea, Elizabeth W. 1965. *Guests of the Sheik: An Ethnography of an Iraqi Village*. Reprint edition, 1969. Garden City, NY: Anchor Books.

Fischer, Michael M. J. 1984. Towards a Third World Poetics: Seeing through Short Stories and Films in the Iranian Culture Area. *Knowledge and Society*, 5: 171–241.

—— 1986. Ethnicity and the Post-modern Arts of Memory. In *Writing Culture: The Poetics and Politics of Ethnography*. J. Clifford and G. Marcus, eds. pp. 194–233. Berkeley: University of California Press.

—— 1988. Aestheticized Emotions and Critical Hermeneutics. *Culture, Medicine and Psychiatry*, 12: 31–42.

Foucault, Michel. 1978. *Discipline and Punish*. New York: Pantheon.

Fried, Erica. 1989. Women of Dehkoh: *Lives in an Iranian Village*. Washington DC: Smithsonian Institution Press.

Geertz, Clifford. 1973. The Impact of the Concept of Culture on the Concept of Man. In *The Interpretation of Cultures*. Clifford Geertz, pp. 33–54. New York: Basic Books.

—— 1975. Thick Description: Toward an Interpretive Theory of Culture. In *The Interpretation of Cultures*. Clifford Geertz, pp. 3–30. London: Hutchinson.

—— 1988. *Works and Lives: The Anthropologist as Author*. Stanford, CA: Stanford University Press.

Gordon, Deborah. 1988. Writing Culture, Writing Feminism: The Poetics and Politics of Experimental Ethnography. *Inscriptions*, 3/4: 7–24.

Haraway, Donna. 1985. A Manifesto for Cyborgs: Science, Technology and Socialist Feminism in the 1980s. *Socialist Review*, 80: 65–107.

Harding, Sandra. 1986. *The Science Question in Feminism*. Ithaca, NY: Cornell University Press.

Hymes, Dell, ed. 1969. *Reinventing Anthropology*. New York: Pantheon.

Joseph, Suad. 1988. Feminization, Familism, Self, and Politics: Research as a *Mughtaribi*. In *Arab Women in the Field: Studying Your Own Society*. S. Altorki and C. El-Solh, eds. pp. 25–47. Syracuse, NY: Syracuse University Press.

Kondo, Dorinne. 1986. Dissolution and Reconstitution of Self: Implications for Anthropological Epistemology. *Cultural Anthropology*, 1: 74–88.

Kuper, Adam. 1988. *The Invention of Primitive Society: Transformation of an Illusion*.

Boston and London: Routledge and Kegan
Paul.

Marcus, George E., and James Clifford. 1985.
The Making of Ethnographic Texts: Preliminary Report. *Current Anthropology*, 26:
267–71.

Marcus, George, and Michael M. J. Fischer.
1986. *Anthropology as Cultural Critique:
An Experimental Moment in the Human
Sciences*. Chicago: University of Chicago
Press.

Mitchell, Timothy. 1988. *Colonizing Egypt*.
Cambridge: Cambridge University Press.

Morsy, Soheir. 1988. Fieldwork in My Egyptian Homeland: Toward the Demise of
Anthropology's Distinctive-other Hegemonic Tradition. In *Arab Women in the
Field: Studying Your Own Society*. S. Altorki
and C. El-Solh, eds. pp. 69–90. Syracuse:
Syracuse University Press.

Mudimbe, Valentine Y. 1988. *The Invention of
Africa: Gnosis, Philosophy and the Order of
Knowledge*. Bloomington: Indiana Univer-
sity Press.

Nader, Laura. 1969. "Up the Anthropologist"
– Perspectives Gained from Studying Up. In
Reinventing Anthropology. D. Hymes, ed.
pp. 284–311. New York: Random House.

Narayan, Kirin. 1989. *Saints, Scoundrels, and
Storytellers*. Philadelphia: University of
Pennsylvania Press.

Ortner, Sherry B. 1984. Theory in Anthropology since the Sixties. *Comparative Studies
in Society and History*, 26: 126–66.

Rabinow, Paul. 1977. *Reflections on Fieldwork in Morocco*. Berkeley: University of
California Press.

Riesman, Paul. 1977. *Freedom in Fulani Social
Life*. Chicago: University of Chicago Press.

——1982. Fieldwork as Initiation and as
Therapy. Paper presented at the 81st annual
meeting of the American Anthropological
Association, Washington, DC.

Ruddick, Sara. 1980. Maternal Thinking.
Feminist Studies, 6/2: 342–67.

Said, Edward. 1978. *Orientalism*. New York:
Pantheon.

——1989. Representing the Colonized:
Anthropology's Interlocuters. *Critical Inquiry*, 15: 205–25.

Shostak, Marjorie. 1981. *Nisa: The Life and
Words of a !Kung Woman*. Cambridge, MA:
Harvard University Press.

Smith, Dorothy. 1987. *The Everyday World as
Problematic*. Boston: Northeastern University Press.

Strathern, Marilyn. 1985. Dislodging a World-
view: Challenge and Counter-challenge in
the Relationship Between Feminism and Anthropology. *Australian Feminist Studies*,
1: 1–25.

——1987. An Awkward Relationship: The
Case of Feminism and Anthropology. *Signs*,
12: 276–92.

Tedlock, Dennis. 1983. *The Spoken Word and
the Work of Interpretation*. Philadelphia:
University of Pennsylvania Press.

——1987. Questions Concerning Dialogical
Anthropology. *Journal of Anthropological
Research*, 43: 325–37.

Turner, Edith. 1987. *The Spirit and the Drum:
A Memoir of Africa*. Tucson: University of
Arizona Press.

Tyler, Stephen. 1986. Post-modern Ethnography: From Document of the Occult to
Occult Document. In *Writing Culture: The
Poetics and Politics of Ethnography*. J. Clifford and G. Marcus, eds. pp. 122–40. Berkeley: University of California Press.

Weiner, Annette. 1976. *Women of Value, Men
of Renown*. Austin: University of Texas
Press.

Wolf, Margery. 1968. *The House of Lim*. New
York: Appelton-Century-Crofts.

8

My Best Informant's Dress: The Erotic Equation in Fieldwork

Esther Newton

Malinowski's "Sex-Sickness"

"Aren't there any anthropologist jokes?" asked a doctor friend of my mother's who had just entertained a table of lunch buddies at their retirement community with a series of doctor gags. To my mother's disappointment, I couldn't think of even one. I do have a poor memory for jokes, but a quick survey of my peers revealed that we are not given to either wit or thigh-slapping when it comes to the practice of our trade. The only anthropologist to deliver was my friend and former mentor David Schneider, who came up with this one: "A postmodern anthropologist and his informant are talking; finally the informant says, 'Okay, enough about you, now let's talk about me.' "[1]

Retelling this joke I realized one reason that it struck me as funny was its similarity to a recent television advertisement. A young man and woman, postmodern looking in their tight black clothes and spiked hair, are chatting at a party, and she says to him, "Okay, now let's talk about you; what do you think of my dress?"

Not only did Schneider's joke suggest a certain absurdity in the so-called reflexivity discourse, but its kinship with the suggestive commercial also inspired me to wonder why the postmodern scrutiny of the relation between informant, researcher, and text is limited to who is talking or even what is said. What else is going on between fieldworker and informant? Is "the romance of anthropology" only a manner of speaking?

In their germinal article contrasting postmodernism and feminism in anthropology, Mascia-Lees, Sharpe, and Cohen see "a romantic yearning to know the 'other' " behind the reflexive "turn" (1989: 25–6). But rather than leading on to the obvious erotic possibilities, they circle back within the metaphor: "Traditionally, this romantic component has been linked to the heroic quests, by the single anthropologist, for 'his soul' through confrontation with the exotic 'other'. . . in turning inward, making himself, his motives, and his

From Esther Newton, "My Best Informant's Dress: The Erotic Equation in Fieldwork," pp. 212–35 in Ellen Lewin and William L. Leap, *Out in the Field: Reflections of Lesbian and Gay Anthropologists*. Urbana Il: University of Illinois Press, 1996. © 1993 University of California Press. Reproduced with permission of University of California Press via Copyright Clearance Center, and the author.

experience the thing to be confronted, the postmodernist anthropologist locates the 'other' in himself."

Following Mascia-Lees, Sharpe, and Cohen's suggestion to be "suspicious of relationships with 'others' that do not include a close and honest scrutiny of the motivations for research" (1989: 33), I am going to ask an embarrassing question. Is all this romance totally sublimated in fieldnotes and language learning only to emerge in texts as a metaphor for the "heroic quest by the single anthropologist," or does the erotic ever make a human gesture? If so, what might be the significance of the erotic equation in fieldwork and its representation or lack thereof in ethnographic texts?

Rarely is the erotic subjectivity or experience of the anthropologist discussed in public venues or written about for publication. If this omission is not due to any plot or conspiracy, neither is it incidental. In the dominant schematic that has set the terms of discourse the distanced neutral observer presented in traditional anthropological texts is at the opposite pole from the sexually aroused (repelled? ambivalent?) fieldworker. By not "problematizing" (dreadful word but none other works as well here) *his* own sexuality in his texts, the anthropologist makes *male* gender and *heterosexuality* the cultural givens, the unmarked categories. If straight men choose not to explore how their sexuality and gender may affect their perspective, privilege, and power in the field, women and gays, less credible by definition, are suspended between our urgent sense of difference and our justifiable fear of revealing it.

In graduate school during the early 1960s I learned – because it was never mentioned – that erotic interest between fieldworker and informant didn't exist, would be inappropriate, or couldn't be mentioned; I had no idea which. The anthropologist was pictured as a man who would ideally bring his wife to the field as company and helper. That she would absorb his sexual interests was, I suppose, understood. I knew that Margaret Mead and Ruth Benedict had done fieldwork, of course, but the former seemed to always be married to another anthropologist and the latter – whose

"private" life was opaque – to have spent little time there.[2] If single male fieldworkers were thought by our male professors to engage in, or even refrain from engaging in, sexual activities, these were never discussed in front of me. This being the case, how could the sexuality of female fieldworkers ever emerge as an issue?

The black hole enveloping this non-subject in most anthropological writing invites one of two conclusions. Either desire is to be firmly squelched – even though many anthropologists are (or were) young, unattached, and living in lonely, isolated situations for months at a time – or it should be satisfied away from the glare of the published account, cordoned off from legitimate ethnography. A comprehensive guide to conducting fieldwork (Ellen 1984) has no index heading under "sexuality." From Casagrande's groundbreaking collection *In the Company of Man* (1960) to *In the Field* (Smith and Kornblum, 1989), when a fieldworker writes in the first person, she or he thinks and sometimes feels but never actually lusts or loves. Most guides ward off desire with vague warnings against getting "too involved," hardly daring to admit that fieldworkers and informants do and must get involved emotionally.[3]

Between the lines lurk certain shadowy givens. The straight male anthropologist's "best informants" are likely to be, or at least to be represented as, male, presumably minimizing the danger of these key relationships becoming eroticized.[4] On the other hand, a veil of professional silence covers the face of indulgence toward men's casual sex with women in the field. For instance, the fieldwork guide mentioned earlier with no index heading for "sex" may allude to it coyly in a discussion of why anthropologists tend to "get so much more out of their first than out of subsequent fieldwork." Among other factors is the suggestion that "when anthropologists first go into the field they are often single" (Ellen 1984: 98).

Most reflexive anthropology, which explicitly spotlights how ethnographic knowledge is produced, has rendered sex and emotion between ethnographers and informants more abstract than before. The exceptions show a pattern: Briggs (1970) and Myerhoff (1978), who do make their subjectivity gendered and grounded, are women; of three men who come to mind, Murphy (1987) was disabled and Rosaldo (1989) is Chicano. So far the only white, able-bodied, and, one is led to infer, heterosexual male who writes as if he knows this affected his fieldwork is Michael Moffatt (1989).[5]

Generally, practitioners of "new ethnography" have used metaphors of emotion and sexuality to express their ethnographic angst. Vincent Crapanzano (1980: 134) likens his quest for knowledge of the Moroccans to a "belief in total sexual possession" and acknowledges that "passion" and "science" "are not in fact so easily separable" without grounding this observation in flesh.[6] And despite James Clifford's (1986: 13–14) observation that "excessive pleasures" and "desire" have been absent from traditional ethnography, these topics remain equally absent from the chapters in *Writing Culture* (Clifford and Marcus 1986). Why are emotion and sexuality less important or less implicated in what Clifford calls the "relations of production" of ethnography (Clifford 1986: 13) than are race or colonialism? And if the absence of odor, which played a large part in travel writing (Clifford 1986: 11), leaves ethnography at best stale and at worst deodorized, what does the absence of an erotic dimension do?

Historian John Boswell (1992) has advocated the contemplation of social margins both for their own beauty – he invoked the medieval manuscript page – and to advance our knowledge of the text. In anthropology, only the margins – marginal texts, the margins of more legitimate texts, or the work of socially marginal members of the profession – can tell us why we signify or squelch the erotics of fieldwork. By looking at who has written about sexuality in the field and how they have written about it, I will ask why the erotic dimension is absent from the anthropological canon and, after offering an example from my fieldwork, I will argue for its future inclusion.

As far as I know, only two white heterosexual men belonging to what Geertz (1988: 73–101) termed the "I-Witnessing" literary genre of ethnography have problematized themselves as "positioned [sexual] subjects" by writing

about sexual encounters with women in the field.[7] The revered ethnographer Bronislaw Malinowski was one of the few anthropologists to write about the sexuality of a non-Western people (1955), and in his private diary, in Polish (1967), he detailed his *own* sexual subjectivity, a persistent and painful struggle against "lewd" and "impure" fantasies about Trobriand and missionary women, whom he "pawed" and perhaps more (the *Diary* was censored by Malinowski's widow before publication).[8]

Not only was an exemplary "competent and experienced ethnographer" (Geertz 1988: 79) caught with his pants down, so to speak, but if anthropology's historic political agenda has been "to secure a recognition that the non-Western is as crucial an element of the human as the Western" (Mascia-Lees, Sharpe, and Cohen 1989: 8), why was Malinowski thinking of Trobrianders, including objects of his ambivalent lust, as "niggers"?

The anthropological honchos who reviewed the *Diary* defended, dismissed, or gloated over it within a common and familiar frame of reference: "These diaries do not add in any significant way to our knowledge of Malinowski as a social scientist. They do, however, tell us a good deal about Malinowski as a person" (Gorer 1967: 311).[9] Malinowski's sexuality, his physical health, his bigotry toward the Trobrianders, and his insecurity as a fieldworker were private matters subsumed in the concept "person," which had – or should have had – nothing to do with Malinowski the public social scientist. Underlying all the reviews is the belief that human beings can be sorted into "lower" and "higher" parts corresponding to self-consciousness and consciousness, emotions and intellect, body and soul. Of course Malinowski shared these same assumptions. Geertz (1967) noticed a resemblance between the *Diary* and a "Puritan tract," and Geoffrey Gorer (1967: 311) compared Malinowski to "the desert Fathers, [who are] tempted by devils" and likened the *Diary* to "spiritual confessions, with the same person being both the penitent and the priest." The hostile and dismissive reaction of the reviewers suggests even less tolerance in scientific dualism for the "lower" aspects of human experience than there had been in its Christian version. Ian Hogbin (1968) fumed that the *Diary* was concerned with nothing but "trivia" and should never have been published.

At the time, only Clifford Geertz realized the profound significance of the *Diary* for the anthropological enterprise.[10] The gap between Malinowski the "person" and Malinowski the "social scientist" revealed by the *Diary* was indeed "shattering" to the "self-congratulatory" image of anthropology (1967: 12). But for Geertz, Malinowski was all the more admirable because "through a mysterious transformation wrought by science" (1967: 13) he had heroically transcended his bad attitude and lack of empathy toward the Trobrianders to become a "great ethnographer."

Twenty years later Geertz looked backward and saw in the publication of this "backstage masterpiece" the first signs of the profound disquiet revealed in "new ethnography" and "the breakdown of epistemological (and moral) confidence" (1988: 75, 22) in postmodern anthropology. While Malinowski had turned his cultural pockets inside out in a diary he could bring himself neither to publish nor destroy, the postmodernists have made I-Witnessing central to their legitimate texts. But the unpleasantly corporeal body in Malinowski's diary has become, in deconstructionist thought, a more comfortable "metaphor of the body" (Bordo 1990). Admitting that there is no objective location outside the body from which to transcend culture, postmodernists in and out of anthropology have conceived the body as a "trickster" of "*indeterminate sex and changeable gender*" (Smith-Rosenberg 1985: 291, emphasis added) whose "unity has been shattered by the choreography of multiplicity.... Deconstructionist readings that enact this protean fantasy are continually 'slip-slidin' away'; through paradox, inversion, self-subversion, facile and intricate textual dance, they... *refuse to assume a shape for which they must take responsibility*" (Bordo 1990: 144, emphasis added).

Postmodern anthropologists are taking upon themselves one part of the white man's burden – the power to name the "other" – but they still do not want to shoulder the responsibility for

their erotic and social power in the field, possibly, as Mascia-Lees, Sharpe, and Cohen (1989) have argued, because they are not enthusiastic about the insights of feminism. Paul Rabinow, who has explicitly rejected a feminist perspective (Mascia-Lees, Sharpe, and Cohen 1989: 18) published – although not in his principal ethnography – an account of his one-night stand with a Moroccan woman thoughtfully provided by a male informant (1977: 63–9). Most of Rabinow's description is disingenuously off-handed and is made to seem – despite the unexplored admission that this was "the best single day I was to spend in Morocco" – primarily about validating his manhood to male Moroccans while fending off "haunting super-ego images of my anthropologist persona" (1977: 63–9).

Several women anthropologists have told me they read Rabinow's account as a boasting admission about what is really standard operating procedure for male fieldworkers. Very likely one of the models for the "haunting super-ego images" that interfered with Rabinow's pleasure was that of his mentor, Clifford Geertz. In his brilliant analysis of postmodern texts by (male) anthropologists Geertz specifically interprets the episode as part of Rabinow's literary strategy to show himself as a "pal, comrade, companion" type of fieldworker.[11] Just in case we might hope that Geertz's thinking had evolved beyond Malinowski's in the sexual department, he dismisses the woman involved as a "wanton" (1988: 93).

Progressives who want to transform the cruel, oppressive Judeo-Christian sexual system and the correlated "objectivist" power grid that both entraps and privileges white heterosexual men should not condemn Malinowski or Rabinow for writing explicitly about the sexual subjectivity they struggled against or indulged, because coercive silence regarding the unwritten rules of the sex and gender system makes changing them impossible. As the issues crystallize out of our history, anthropologists must begin to acknowledge eroticism, our own and that of others, if we are to reflect on its meaning for our work and perhaps help alter our cultural system for the better.

Changing the gender and/or sexual orientation and probably the race of either fieldworker or informant modifies the terms of the erotic equation.[12] The sexuality of heterosexual men – however much a puzzle or pain on a personal level – is the cultural "ego," the assumed subjectivity, and it is predictable that women and gays, for whom matters of sexuality and gender can never be unproblematic, have begun to address these issues for the discipline as a whole.[13]

Quite a few women anthropologists of undisclosed sexual orientation have written about *not* having sex with men where apparently even being seen as (hetero)sexual meant losing all credibility, risking personal danger and the catastrophic failure of their fieldwork projects. As Peggy Golde put it, women anthropologists have felt compelled to "surround [themselves] with symbolic 'chaperones' " (1970: 7). Working in South America, Mary Ellen Conaway restricted her freedom of movement and wore "odd-looking, loose-fitting clothing, no makeup, and flat-soled shoes" to prevent local men from getting any wrong ideas (1986: 59, 60). Maureen Giovannini warded off Sicilian men by "dressing conservatively and carrying a large notebook whenever I left the house" (1986: 110).

"Manda Cesara" [Karla O. Poewe] (1982) is the only woman I know about who has written for publication, although under a pseudonym and not in an ethnographic text, about having sex with male informants. Unlike the male anthropologists, she neither retreated into abstraction nor narrated her erotic experience as a casual notch on the bedpost: "To lay hold of a culture through one's love of one individual may be an illusion, but there can be no doubt that love became a fundamental relation of my thoughts and perceptions to both, the world of the Lenda and myself" (1982: 59); "Douglas opened for me the gate to Lenda. I don't mean that he introduced me to his friends. I mean that he opened my heart and mind" (1982: 61).

The male Africans' so-called natural attitude toward heterosexual intercourse and extramarital affairs buttressed Cesara's doubts about the Judeo-Christian system. And in the midst of a long reflection beginning with "sexuality is a cultural system" (1982: 146)

but veering off into a discussion of what is wrong with Western culture as measured by the prevalence of male homosexuality, she adds, "The Lenda, thank heaven, and I am speaking selfishly, are beautifully heterosexual" (1982: 147). While Cesara's homophobia upset me enough to write her an open letter (Newton 1984) – straights are still holding gays accountable for the decline of the Roman Empire – I do hope to read more bold papers and books like hers in which the erotic dimension of power and knowledge is acknowledged openly.

For years the pages of *SOLGAN*, formerly the *ARGOH Newsletter*, the quarterly publication of the Society of Lesbian and Gay Anthropologists, has been enlivened by accounts of (mostly) male homosexuality in far-flung parts of the world. Many of these brief accounts include a note on the fieldworker's sexual orientation, and a few have implied participation.[14] Walter Williams, in *The Spirit and the Flesh* (1986), was clear that his being gay gave him access to Plains Indian "berdaches" (1986: 105) and suggests that intimate relations enabled his knowledge (see especially p. 93).[15]

The anthropologist who has most lyrically expressed eroticism toward the "other" is Kenneth Read in his work on the Gahuku-Gama of New Guinea.[16] In *Return to the High Valley* (1986), Read, in hot pursuit of honesty about fieldwork and that illusive emotional dimension to ethnographic texts, scales the barbed wire fence between emotion and ethnography: "I have the greatest affection for... [the Gahuku-Gama]," he writes, adding, "I have never known why this admission generates suspicion" (1986: ix, x). That this attraction is or borders on homoerotic desire is signaled in code words that are understood by both gay and straight: "Lest anyone begin to feel uneasy at the possibility of being exposed to embarrassment, I assure the more sensitive members of my profession that I will not *flaunt this personal ingredient like a banner*" (p. x, emphasis added).[17]

Yet such is the intensity of Read's attachment, and so insistent, that he winds up doing a kind of literary striptease, first putting out disclaimers to alert the "more sensitive members of my profession" (1986: x), then revealing what had just been hidden. Read's "best informant," and the man who "may be said to have invited me there," was Makis, "an influential man in the tribe" (p. 11). Although Read reassures his readers that "propriety restrains me from revealing the full depth of my affective bond to him" (p. 12), he throws propriety to the winds, it seems to me, in his subsequent description of remembering, thirty years after the fact, Makis coming into his (Read's) room, "emerging with a marvelous physical solidity into the circle of light cast by my lamp, all the planes of his chest, his face, his abdomen and thighs chiseled from black and shining marble, his lips lifted upward with the natural pride of an aristocracy owing nothing to the accidents of birth, and his eyes holding mine with the implications of at least a partial understanding neither of us could express in words" (p. 75).[18]

Following in Read's footsteps (but with banners flying) I offer an account – perhaps the first to describe a relationship between a lesbian anthropologist and her female "best informant" – of the emotional and erotic equation in my recent fieldwork.[19]

Kay

My fieldwork experience has been fraught with sexual dangers and attractions that were much more like leitmotifs than light distractions. To begin with, the fact that I am a gay woman has disposed *me* – the great majority of gay anthropologists work with heterosexuals and avoid sexual topics – toward working with other gay people (a correspondence that heterosexuals observe more often than gays do, albeit with the unexamined privilege of the powerful).[20] I was not looking for sexual adventure in the field. Cultural, political, and psychological factors more than eroticism have determined my affinity for gays as research subjects – for one thing, I have worked more with gay men than women. Looking back, I used my first fieldwork among gay people, mostly male, to consolidate a fragile and imperiled gay identity. Prospective dissertation projects in East Africa and Fiji – again I stress I am not speaking *for* gay fieldworkers but *as* one – presented unknown dangers that scared me off. Most closeted gay people – as I then was – manage information and stress in America by retreating

Figure 8.1 *Kay at a costume party in the 1950s. (Collection of Esther Newton)*

to private or secret "gay zones" where, alone and with other gays, we can "be ourselves." No African or Fijian village would offer such refuge, I figured, and what if they found me out? Bringing my then-lover to an exotic field locale was never imaginable, and the prospect of living for months without physical and emotional intimacy was too bleak.[21]

So by the "erotic dimension," I mean, first, that my gay informants and I shared a very important background assumption that our social arrangements reflected – that women are attracted to women and men to men. Second, the very fact that I have worked with other gays means that some of the people who were objects of my research were also potential sexual partners. Partly because of this, my key informants and sponsors have usually been more to me than an expedient way of getting information and something different than "just" friends. Information has always flowed to me in a medium of emotion, ranging from passionate – although never consummated – erotic attachment through profound affection to lively interest, that empowers me in my projects, and, when it is reciprocated, helps motivate informants to put up with my questions and intrusions.

I had thought of writing an ethnohistory of the gay and lesbian community of Cherry Grove several months before I met Kay, having become attached to the place – a summer resort on Fire Island about forty-five miles from New York City – during the previous summer. Career pressures and political commitment were behind the initial decision. I needed a second big field experience and book to advance professionally. From the outset I also intended to write for New York's huge gay communities in whose evolution Cherry Grove had, I suspected, played a starring role.[22]

But not everyone who sets sail keeps afloat – or catches the wind. A great deal of the lift one needs in the field when one is becalmed or swamped came through my love for two elderly Grove women, and because of them the work was suffused with emotion and meaning. Two years after starting fieldwork I described them in my notes as "the sun and the moon of my love affair with Cherry Grove – without

them there would be neither heat nor light in me to pursue and embrace my subject." Peter [Ruth] Worth became my Grove cicerone, my close friend, and my confidant; I was in love with Kay.[23]

Kay was an old-timer I should meet, Grovers said. After several weeks I matched the name with a dignified and classy-looking old woman who rode around the boardwalks in an electric cart. Like most able-bodied people, I had looked through her out of misplaced politeness and because of her advanced age. When I did introduce myself, I received more than I hoped – a warm and impulsive invitation for a drink at her cottage. That evening I wrote about my first encounter:

Kay lives in a tiny charming white house, the deck full of potted flowers. I found her shuffling (she moves precariously by advancing each foot a few inches ahead of the other) to get me a drink of juice and complaining that her hair wasn't done – she hates that. Despite wrinkles and thinning hair, she still pulls off a look.

She told me unsentimentally how infirm she was: the hearing aid, the contact lenses, the inability to read, a slipped disk she was too old to have fused, and how she hated to be one of those complaining elderly.... Emphysema makes her wheeze painfully with every movement. (She still smokes: "I don't inhale, dear. Please – it's my only vice, the only one I have left.")

Was it because I liked her cottage which still had the diminutive charm of an earlier Cherry Grove, because I found her beautiful and her suffering poignant, or because her allusions to past vices intrigued me? Or was it because she called me "dear" that I came away enchanted?[24]

Several hours after writing my fieldnotes, too elated to sleep, I wrote to David Schneider: "The more I get into the history, the harder hold Cherry Grove has on my imagination… I'm embarking, and thrilled about it" (Newton 1986). And then I plunged on, far more confident and confiding than I had been as his closeted graduate student when I was doing fieldwork with female impersonators (Newton 1979) and my "best informant" was a gay man (whom I also adored).[25] "This morning I introduced myself to a woman of eighty plus whom I'd been wanting to meet, as she rolled toward me in her electric cart. Not only was she receptive, she clasped my arm in an intimate embrace and practically pulled me into her lap while we talked...and my heart quite turned over. Such are the perils of field-work."

After that I went by Kay's cottage every day, and as I talked to other community members, my fascination with her grew. I discovered her powers of seduction were legendary. As one Grove woman told me: "Kay was the first one to walk into the Waldorf and say, 'Send me a bottle and a blonde.' She's a law unto herself; don't think you can compare her to the average lesbian. She could walk into the Taj Mahal and people would think she was the owner." That triggered another reflection, only weeks after our first meeting: "Seeing Kay now, crippled and gasping for breath, I still can imagine it, remembering how her ex-lover Leslie came in and threw her arms around Kay saying, 'Oh Kay, we had some great times on this couch!' and Kay's enormous blue eyes light up to go with the smile – the expensive dentures gleaming – the gesture of a devilish flirt."

The work progressed around and through my crush on Kay. She helped me organize a group of old-timers to reminisce about the Grove, and I followed up in a burst of energy with individual interviews. And despite her often expressed fear that my book would re-veal to an unsuspecting world that the Grove was a gay haven, she became ever more help-ful. Six weeks later "we had an intense five minutes of smiling at each other. On my way out I gave her my number out here and said 'If there's ever a problem, don't hesitate to call me,' and she seemed very pleased, and asked if she could do anything for me. I said yes, 'Show me your pictures, tell me about the people.' She agreed."

That winter I returned to my teaching job. I spoke to Kay by telephone, and in April I picked her up at her Park Avenue apartment for a lunch date. By then our pattern of flirta-tion and teasing was established. "Back then Kay, did you get who you wanted?" I asked, as she was insisting on paying for our pricey meal with her American Express gold card. "Yes," she smiled, "and lots of them." She told me that she still got sexual urges but just waited for them to pass. We both flirted with the idea of making love. "Someday I'm going to sur-prise the hell out of you and really kiss you back," she said once gleefully.

Two summers after I met Kay the fieldwork project was cresting, and although it was tacitly settled that her physical pain and chronic illness precluded sex and we would not actually become lovers our daily visits were affectionate and full of erotic byplay. On July 11, 1988 I wrote, "I don't remember now when I used to sit *facing* Kay across the round coffee table. Probably even that first summer I began to sit next to her on the Nau-gahyde (so practical for the beach) orange couch, partly because she generally hears me if I speak about six inches from her right ear, and mostly just to get closer. In the last weeks my visits have taken a new pattern. I arrive, I kiss her quickly on the lips and find out what she needs from the store – then I return. Now comes the real visit."

During the "real visit," when she felt up to it, Kay repeated stories about her past life, her many lovers, her marriages, and about the major and minor characters in Cherry Grove's history. I sat enthralled as she recited verses from poems of Edna St. Vincent Millay – she had known the poet – which I guessed had been part of her seduction repertoire. And al-though I could never persuade her to leave her letters and papers to a university library, she did allow me to copy many valuable photo-graphs and newspaper clippings. She also continued to help me gain access to other old-timers. When I asked Kay to tell one Grover who had resisted an interview that I was a "good guy," she answered, smiling, "Oh, I tell that to everybody." I observed later, "Millions couldn't buy this goodwill. No one's word means more than Kay's to the old-timers here, and she has given me her trust freely. I know Kay's affection has never been com-pelled or bought. She just likes me, and the beauty of it is I adore her even though I need her and have ulterior professional motives."

Kay never had to say "now let's talk about me" because she rarely asked me about my life.

She was used to being the entertaining center of attention, even though she was acutely and painfully aware that her friends – me included – sometimes found her conversation boring because she didn't remember what she had told to whom, couldn't get out, didn't hear gossip, and was preoccupied with her physical problems. But even on days when Kay had no new story, no information or photograph to offer, I enjoyed being with her:

> What's deep about her is almost all non-verbal. It's her bodily presence, bearing – still – and that emotional force, crushing and liquid like an ocean wave...Kay once told me that driving out to the Grove with two other lesbians on a cloudy day she had raised her arms to the sky and intoned "Clouds Go Away, Sun Come Out" several times. Within minutes the clouds split and the sun came out. Kay showed me how the other two women turned around and looked at her incredulously from the front seat. In another culture Kay would have been some kind of priestess.

Her stories and our mutual pleasure in each other constantly led me back to the work:

> The more I think about Kay allowing herself to be seduced in the girls' school the more her life connection to the history I am helping to construct excites me. Kay's beauty and presence would have made me crazy in her younger days, but I wonder if – because she was a party girl rather than an intellectual – I could have loved her deeply. But now, instead of *having* ideas she *embodies* ideas. Kay spans almost the entire period from "smashing" and romantic friendship to the age of AIDS. When I kiss her I am kissing 1903.

My love affair with Kay and with Cherry Grove culminated in 1988 celebrations around her eighty-fifth birthday, which also marked her fiftieth summer as a Grover. At her small birthday party I was proud that her hand on my knee proved she could still attract women. I was her escort at a Cherry Grove theater performance dedicated to "Kay, our national institution." Until the day a year later when Kay had what quickly proved to be a fatal heart attack, our loving relationship continued. To Grovers, Kay's death symbolized the end of an era; for many of us her loss was also a personal one. My fieldwork suddenly felt more finished than it had before, and I decided not to return another summer.

"All Poems Are Love Poems"

This would have been a very different chapter had I set out to "decide" whether ethical and/ or strategic considerations should constrain anthropologists from having sexual relationships with informants. If we are to believe that only those who publicly confess to it are tempted, then, Manda Cesara aside, women fieldworkers' vulnerability as women rules out (hetero) sex. In print, and probably much more so in life, the men feel freer. Malinowski struggled to keep *himself* pure, and Rabinow saw no ethical difficulty in his sexual behavior in the field. Yet it is hard to see why, if our power as anthropologists to name the subordinated "other" poses an ethical problem, the power to screw them doesn't. Most of our English sexual vocabulary implies domination to begin with. I doubt that a way out of this problem will be found so long as it is posed in these terms. But if "the burden of authorship cannot be evaded," as Geertz suggests (1988: 140), then neither can the burden of being, and being seen as, an erotic creature.

In my case, there was no higher status to take advantage of to buy or attract sexual partners. Almost all my informants were, like me, American, white, and at least middle class. Although some Grovers were apprehensive about what I might write, few were impressed by my being a scholar, and many Grove men considered themselves my superior because of my gender. Far from my being above Kay, in Cherry Grove's lexicon she was a wealthy homeowner and longtime community icon whereas I was a passing blip, a newcomer and lowly renter. Unquestionably, her regard enhanced my status far more than the reverse. Because our loving relationship never became defined as an affair, my strategic anxieties about possible complications from becoming sexually involved with a beloved member of a small face-to-face community were never put to the test. Those fears did advise caution (as did the fact that we both had somewhat absent

Figure 8.2 *Kay and the author on Kay's deck, 1988. (Photo by Diane Quero; collection of Esther Newton)*

longtime companions – that is another story) but for Kay, too, the fact of sexual attraction was more compelling than "having sex" and much safer than "having an affair."

As a child who was more comfortable with adults than with other kids, I've often been attracted to older people as friends, advisors, and, in adulthood, as lovers, so it's predictable that the work of writing gay history seduced me and kept me enchanted through Kay, who had lived and created it. If Kay had not existed, I might have had to invent her. For me, intellectual and creative work, including fieldwork and the writing of ethnography, has always been inspired by and addressed to an interior audience of loved ones like informants and mentors. The most intense attractions have generated the most creative energy, as if the work were a form of courting and seduction.

What Kay got was an admirer forty years younger who could run errands, set up appointments, move garden furniture, bring friends by, flirt, and who genuinely wanted to know and hear who her friends had been and what their common experience had meant to her. Kay had other devoted friends who helped with some of the problems old age brings. Perhaps my unique gift was erotic admiration, which must have brought her vital powers back into focus amid the dissolution caused by failing mental and physical strength. Eroticism energized the project – which caught Kay's imagination – of giving her old age shape and meaning by recording the journey of her generation in Cherry Grove and seeing it as connected to my own life.[26]

This manner of working poses the danger of "uncritically adopting Kay's point of view," as one of the *Cultural Anthropology* readers and two colleagues who had read drafts of *Cherry Grove, Fire Island* (1993), my ethnohistory of the Grove, have warned. But until we are more honest about how we feel about informants we can't try to compensate for, incorporate, or acknowledge desire and repulsion into our analysis of subjects or in our discourse about text construction. We are also refusing to reproduce one of the mightiest vocabularies in the human language.

Philosophy, psychology, and literature have reflected on how creativity may be powered and shaped by Eros – I invoke both the glorious and the terrible powers of the winged god, not the debased sweetness of the cuddly Cupid – even if anthropology has not. "The lover is turned to the great sea of beauty," Diotima tells Socrates in that touchstone of Western meditation on Eros, the *Symposium* (Plato 1989: 58), "and, gazing upon this, he gives birth to many gloriously beautiful ideas and theories, in unstinting love of wisdom." Freud's theory of sublimation reinterprets Plato's encomium of Eros, albeit darkened by Judeo-Christian pessimism. And in a novel by May Sarton the lesbian protagonist declares, "When I said that all poems are love poems, I meant that the motor power, the electric cur-

rent is love of one kind or another. The subject may be something quite impersonal – a bird on a window sill, a cloud in the sky, a tree" (1965: 125).

The subject might also be a culture, a people, or a symbolic system. Of course, ethnographic texts are not poems, and neither are they diaries. Whatever motivates them, their purpose should be "enabling conversation over societal lines – of ethnicity, religion, class, gender, language, race – that have grown progressively more nuanced" (Geertz 1988: 147). The erotic dimension intersects with those lines. To follow Malinowski's lead by including the sexuality of "our" people among the topics worthy of publication, anthropologists will have to surpass him and describe not just in Polish but also in English – in I-Witnessing or any other authorial style of "being there" – where we anthropologists, as encultured individuals like all other humans, are coming from.[27] In the age of Anita Hill and AIDS, can we do less?

NOTES

1   One of my informants, Peter Worth, was shocked by reading here the word *informant* in reference to herself and her friends. I explained that in all my published work on Cherry Grove I intended to use the word *narrator* for those whom I had interviewed, but in this essay, I was addressing an anthropological audience for whom the historical importance of the word *informant* recommended its use.

    David Schneider said he had heard the postmodern anthropologist joke from Marshall Sahlins. Later Kath Weston pointed out that Judy Stacey (1990: 272) had quoted a slightly different version, attributing it to Sahlins (1991).

2   I think it was only in the later 1960s that I heard rumors that Mead lived with another woman who was thought to be her lover. Partly I doubted it because she had been so publicly and often married, and partly the news had less impact because being more confidently lesbian I needed

role models less. Much more important to my survival – I mean that quite literally – from high school on was the forceful advocacy for human variation, gender and otherwise, in both Mead and Benedict's work.

In the acceptance speech upon receiving the Margaret Mead Award at the 1991 annual meetings of the American Anthropological Association, Will Roscoe (1992) expressed the hope that if Benedict and Mead were still living they would not have to hide their sexuality to be credible public advocates for greater tolerance.

3 "Personal interactions and relationships are the stuff of field data collection," asserts sociologist Carol A. B. Warren (1977: 105) in an excellent article on fieldwork in the male gay world, but, she ends mysteriously, "They only become a problem when they block access to certain parts of the data." She astutely discusses how the researcher may be stigmatized as gay by "normals" and so lose credibility, how the fieldworker trying to establish trust may be grilled by informants about her own sexual orientation, and even the need for "reflective subjectivity" by the fieldworker (1977: 104) – all without ever tipping her own hand. This is the same illusiveness to which I resorted in my early work on gay men (Newton 1979).

4 Only one of the male anthropologists in *In the Company of Man* chose to write about a female informant – a prepubescent girl (Conklin 1960).

5 Jean Briggs (1970) made her own anger and frustration central to her Eskimo ethnography; Barbara Myerhoff's (1978) elderly Jewish informants got under her skin in a rich variety of ways; Robert Murphy's (1987) account of how becoming paralyzed changed his identity and propelled him toward studying the disabled moved me deeply; Renato Rosaldo (1989) explored how his wife Shelly's death helped him grasp the rage motivating Ilingot head-hunting; and Michael Moffatt (1989) constructs a narrative about college students with himself as a very pre-

sent participant-observer (whatever one thinks of his initial ethical lapse in fooling the students about his identity). All three of the men's texts do begin to construct the sexuality of the author as a subject, especially Moffatt's, perhaps because he writes extensively about the students' sexuality.

6 Quoted in Geertz (1988: 98).

7 Geertz (1988: 90) actually observes that in this genre the authorial voice is somehow configured as "an object of desire" but apparently only by readers and from afar. The term *positioned subject* is Rosaldo's (1989: 19), and I think he wouldn't mind my adding "sexual" because he alone, of the new ethnographers, includes sexual orientation as a meaningful axis of difference that can help dismantle "objectivism" and add richness to ethnographic accounts (see especially 1989: 190–3).

8 "Sex sickness" is Marvin Harris's (1967: 72) term from his review of Malinowski's *A Diary in the Strict Sense of the Term* (1967).

9 See also Geertz (1967), Greenway (1967), Harris (1967), and Hogbin (1968).

10 Recently, I was discussing the *Diary* in a class of undergraduates. One woman student said, indignantly, "Knowing about the *Diary*, why should I read Malinowski's ethnographies?" and another added, after thinking about it, "Maybe if you could put the *Diary* together with *Sex and Repression* you'd have good ethnography."

11 Of those who could be considered in the I-Witnessing school of ethnography, the only woman to rate a mention from Geertz is Barbara Myerhoff in a footnote (1988: 101–15). Not comparing Cesara's *Reflections of a Woman Anthropologist* (1982) to Rabinow's *Reflections on Fieldwork in Morocco* (1977) is disappointing to say the least. Note that Rabinow can just be in the field, but Cesara has chosen to accept and acknowledge being in the marked category.

12 For the perspective of an African American man working in the Caribbean see

T. Whitehead (1986). For the perspective of a black lesbian anthropologist working in Yemen see Delores M. Walters (1996).

13 Of course, the majority of gay and lesbian anthropologists are in the closet, which by definition precludes them from publicly acknowledging their orientation and generally from even writing about sexuality. And is it necessary to add that in the review of the literature that follows, the work done on gay *culture* is not mentioned unless it deals specifically with erotic issues and systems? An article about a gay community center, for instance, is not necessarily any more (or less) about sexuality than one on a small-town Elks Club.

14 For an interesting, odd (and perhaps fabricated) account that actually centers on the homoerotic relations between Amazonian Indians and a Western observer-adventurer see Schneebaum (1969).

15 In a conversation at the 1990 AAA convention in New Orleans, Walter Williams confirmed that this was the case and that, although he had written more explicitly about it in his manuscript, friends had advised him to "tone it down" before publication lest too much frankness jeopardize his tenure, which he has since gotten, although only after a struggle.

16 Perhaps emboldened by Read, other anthropologists have followed in his New Guinea trail with important (although less evocative) work on (homo)sexuality (Herdt 1981, 1984).

17 The authorial presence in Read's ethnography of a gay bar (1980) is far more tortured and dissembling than in the New Guinea work.

18 The diffuse homoeroticism, even in Read's first ethnography on the Gahuku-Gama (1965) *did* disturb at least one "sensitive" anthropologist – Clifford Geertz (1988: 86), who in an appreciation of Read's "brilliantly realized," I-Witnessing style can neither give his discomfort plain speech nor restrain a snide remark about Read's description of the farewell hug he shared with Makis.

19 After I began this chapter, Kath Weston sent me her "Requiem for a Street Fighter" (1996), which is about her relationship with a young woman who would have been an informant had she not committed suicide. The fieldwork was conducted in Cherry Grove, Long Island, New York, from the summer of 1985 through the summer of 1989 (Newton 1993).

20 A welcome exception is Serena Nanda's fascinating (1990) work on the gender variant Indian *hijras*, which received SOLGA's Ruth Benedict Prize in 1990.

21 Gay and lesbian anthropologists have discussed these problems in a series of recent panels at the annual meetings of the American Anthropological Association, and many of these ground-breaking and silence-breaking papers are in *Out in the Field* (Lewin and Leap, 1996).

22 I agree with Mascia-Lees, Sharpe, and Cohen (1989: 33) that the way anthropologists should work against power imbalance between themselves and their subjects is to make conscious choices to write for them too and to be attentive to research questions they want answered.

23 Kay asked me not to publish her last name. A different version of this narrative is embedded in Newton (1993: 3–7).

24 This and all subsequent quotes in this section are from my unpublished fieldnotes, except for the letter to Schneider.

25 The categories "gay" and "straight," no matter how fateful and socially real, cannot be taken literally to mean that people so identified are *never*, as individuals, sexually interested in whichever gender is supposed to be erotically null. Even at the time of my dissertation fieldwork with female impersonators in the mid-1960s, I recognized that, improbable as it seemed, my then "best informant's" considerable charms, which included his dresses, or rather his persona in dresses, had a certain erotic component for me. But here I allude to a complex subject far beyond the scope of this chapter.

26 Even when we gays are teachers, as many of us are, our identity is the one thing about which most of us can never teach

the young. Many gay people do not have children who could give them personal and intimate access to succeeding generations and cannot share their lives even with nieces and nephews. Kay, for instance, was childless, and in the name of "discretion" never discussed her homosexuality – all of her living, that is, that formed the substance and subject matter of our friendship and was the reason why she had lived in Cherry Grove for fifty summers – with any of her family. Because of the enforced secrecy in which we live, older gays have trouble transmitting our culture to younger ones.

27 Although our cupboard is bare, it isn't empty. In addition to the articles and books previously referred to, Gregersen (1983) has done a quirky follow-up of Ford and Beach's (1951) early cross-cultural work. For American culture, there is Rubin's (1984) article on the hierarchical stratification of sexual practices, Vance's (1983) witty essay on the Kinsey Institute, my effort to develop a more precise sexual vocabulary (Newton and Walton 1984), Thompson on teen girls (1984, 1990), and Davis and Kennedy's pioneering work on the sexuality of lesbians in Buffalo (1989). For non-Western cultures, there is the "berdache" controversy (Callender and Kochems 1983; Roscoe 1991; Whitehead 1981; Williams 1986), the essays in Blackwood (1985), and three monographs: Thomas Gregor's account of the heterosexual Mehanaku (1985), Gilbert Herdt and Robert Stoller's collaboration on the Sambia (1990), and Richard Parker's (1991) Brazilian work, the winner of SOLGA's 1991 Benedict Prize.

REFERENCES

Blackwood, Evelyn, ed. 1985. *Anthropology and Homosexual Behavior*. New York: Hawarth Press.

Bordo, Susan. 1990. Feminism, Postmodernism, and Gender-Scepticism. In *Feminism and Postmodernism*, ed. Linda J. Nicholson, pp. 133–56. New York: Routledge.

Boswell, John. 1992. Same Sex Marriages in Medieval Europe. Paper presented at State University of New York College at Purchase.

Briggs, Jean. 1970. *Never in Anger: Portrait of an Eskimo Family*. Cambridge, Mass.: Harvard University Press.

Callendar, Charles, and Lee M. Kochems. 1983. The North American Berdache. *Current Anthropology*, 24/4: 443–70.

Casagrande, Joseph, ed. 1960. *In the Company of Man: Twenty Portraits by Anthropologists*. New York: Harper and Brothers.

Cesara, Manda [Karla O. Poewe]. 1982. *Reflections of a Woman Anthropologist: No Hiding Place*. New York: Academic Press.

Clifford, James. 1986. Introduction. In *Writing Culture: The Poetics and Politics of Ethnography*. James Clifford and George E. Marcus, eds. pp. 1–26. Berkeley: University of California Press.

Clifford, James, and George E. Marcus, eds. 1986. *Writing Culture: The Poetics and Politics of Ethnography*. Berkeley: University of California Press.

Conaway, May Ellen. 1986. The Pretense of the Neutral Researcher. In *Self, Sex, and Gender in Cross-Cultural Fieldwork*. Tony Larry Whitehead and Mary Ellen Conaway, eds. pp. 52–63. Urbana: University of Illinois Press.

Conklin, Harold C. 1960. Maling, a Hanunoo Girl from the Philippines. In *In the Company of Man: Twenty Portraits by Anthropologists*. Joseph Casagrande, ed. New York: Harper and Brothers.

Crapanzano, Vincent. 1980. *Tuhami, Portrait of a Moroccan*. Chicago: University of Chicago Press.

Davis, Madeline, and Elizabeth Lapovsky Kennedy. 1989. Oral History and the Study of Sexuality in the Lesbian Community: Buffalo, NY, 1940–1960. In *Hidden from History: Reclaiming the Gay and Lesbian Past*. Martin Duberman, Martha Vicinus, and George Chauncey, eds. pp. 426–40. New York: New American Library.

Ellen, R. F., ed. 1984. *Ethnographic Research: A Guide to General Conduct*. London: Academic Press.

Ford, Clellan S., and Frank A. Beach. 1951. *Patterns of Sexual Behavior.* New York: Harper and Brothers.

Geertz, Clifford. 1967. Under the Mosquito Net. *New York Review of Books,* 14 September 12–13.

—— 1988. *Works and Lives: The Anthropologist as Author.* Stanford, Calif.: Stanford University Press.

Giovannini, Maureen. 1986. Female Anthropologist and Male Informant: Gender Conflict in a Sicilian Town. In *Self, Sex, and Gender in Cross-Cultural Fieldwork.* Tony Larry Whitehead and Mary Ellen Conaway, eds. pp. 103–16. Urbana: University of Illinois Press.

Golde, Peggy, ed. 1970. *Women in the Field: Anthropological Experiences.* Chicago: Aldine.

Gorer, Geoffrey. 1967. Island Exorcism. *The Listener,* 7 September: 311.

Greenway, John. 1967. Malinowski Unbuttoned. *World Journal Tribune,* 26 March.

Gregersen, Edgar. 1983. *Sexual Practices: The Story of Human Sexuality.* New York: Franklin Watts.

Gregor, Thomas. 1985. *Anxious Pleasures: The Sexual Lives of an Amazonian People.* Chicago: University of Chicago Press.

Harris, Marvin. 1967. Diary of an Anthropologist. *Natural History,* 76: 72–4.

Herdt, Gilbert H., ed. 1981. *The Sambia: Ritual and Gender in New Guinea.* New York: Holt, Rinehart and Winston.

—— 1984. *Ritualized Homosexuality in Melanesia.* Berkeley: University of California Press.

Hogbin, Ian. 1968. Review of *A Diary in the Strict Sense of the Term* by Bronislaw Malinowski. *American Anthropologist,* 70: 575.

Lewin, Ellen and William L. Leap. eds. 1996. *Out in the Field: Representations of Lesbian and Gay Anthropologists.* Urbana: University of Illinois Press.

Malinowski, Bronislaw. 1955. *Sex and Repression in Savage Society.* Cleveland, Ohio: World Publishing.

—— 1967. *A Diary in the Strict Sense of the Term.* London: Routledge.

Mascia-Lees, Frances E., Patricia Sharpe, and Colleen Ballerino Cohen. 1989. The Postmodernist Turn in Anthropology: Cautions From a Feminist Perspective. *Signs: Journal of Women in Culture and Society,* 15/1: 7–33.

Moffatt, Michael. 1989. *Coming of Age in New Jersey: College and American Culture.* New Brunswick, NJ: Rutgers University Press.

Murphy, Robert. 1987. *The Body Silent.* New York: Henry Holt.

Myerhoff, Barbara. 1978. *Number Our Days.* New York: Simon and Schuster.

Nanda, Serena. 1990. *Neither Man nor Woman: The* Hijras *of India.* Belmont, Calif.: Wadsworth Press.

Newton, Esther. 1979 [1972]. *Mother Camp: Female Impersonators in America.* Chicago: University of Chicago Press.

—— 1984. An Open Letter to "Manda Cesara." *Anthropology Research Group on Homosexuality Newsletter* (Spring).

—— 1993. *Cherry Grove, Fire Island: Sixty Years in America's First Gay and Lesbian Town.* Boston: Beacon Press.

Newton, Esther, and Shirley Walton. 1984. The Misunderstanding: Toward a More Precise Sexual Vocabulary. In *Pleasure and Danger: Exploring Female Sexuality.* Carole S. Vance, ed. pp. 242–50. Boston: Routledge.

Parker, Richard. 1991. *Bodies, Pleasures and Passions: Sexual Culture in Contemporary Brazil.* Boston: Beacon Press.

Plato. 1989. *Symposium.* Translated by Alexander Nehamas and Paul Woodruff. Indianapolis: Hackett.

Rabinow, Paul. 1977. *Reflections on Fieldwork in Morocco.* Berkeley: University of California Press.

Read, Kenneth. 1965. *The High Valley.* New York: Scribner's.

—— 1980. *Other Voices: The Style of a Male Homosexual Tavern.* Novato, Calif.: Chandler and Sharp.

—— 1986. *Return to the High Valley.* Berkeley: University of California Press.

Rosaldo, Renato. 1989. *Culture and Truth: The Remaking of Social Analysis.* Boston: Beacon Press.

Roscoe, Will. 1991. *The Zuni Man-Woman.* Albuquerque: University of New Mexico Press.

—— 1992. Comments on Receiving the Margaret Mead Award. *Society of Lesbian and Gay Anthropologists Newsletter*, 14/1: 11–12.

Rubin, Gayle. 1984. Thinking Sex: Notes for a Radical Theory of Politics in Sexuality. In *Pleasure and Danger: Exploring Female Sexuality*. Carole S. Vance, ed. pp. 267–319. Boston: Routledge.

Sahlins, Marshall. 1991. The Return of the Event, Again. In *Clio in Oceania*. Aletta Biersack, ed. Washington, DC: Smithsonian Institution Press.

Sarton, May. 1965. *Mrs. Stevens Hears the Mermaids Singing*. New York: W. W. Norton.

Schneebaum, Tobias. 1969. *Keep the River on Your Right*. New York: Grove Press.

Smith, Carolyn D., and William Kornblum, eds. 1989. *In the Field: Readings on the Field Research Experience*. New York: Praeger.

Smith-Rosenberg, Carroll. 1985. *Disorderly Conduct: Visions of Gender in Victorian America*. New York: Knopf.

Stacey, Judith. 1990. *Brave New Families*. New York: Basic Books.

Thompson, Sharon. 1984. Search for Tomorrow: On Feminism and the Reconstruction of Teen Romance. In *Pleasure and Danger: Exploring Female Sexuality*. Carole S. Vance, ed. pp. 350–84. Boston: Routledge.

—— 1990. Putting a Big Thing into a Little Hole: Teenage Girls' Accounts of Sexual Initiation. *Journal of Sex Research*, 27/3: 341–61.

Vance, Carole S. 1983. "Gender Systems, Ideology, and Sex Research." In *Powers of Desire: The Politics of Sexuality*. Ann Snitow, eds. Christine Stansell, and Sharon Thompson, eds. pp. 371–84. New York: Monthly Review Press.

Walters, Delores. 1996. Cast Among Outcasts: Interpreting Sexual Orientation, Racial and Gender Identity on the Yemen Arab Republic. In *Out in the Field: Reflections on Gay and Lesbian Anthropologists*, eds E. Lewin and W. L. Leap, pp. 58–69. Urbana: University of Illinois Press.

Warren, Carol A. B. 1977. Fieldwork in the Gay World: Issues in Phenomenological Research. *Journal of Social Issues*, 33/4: 93–107.

Weston, Kath. 1996. Requiem for a Street Fighter. In *Out in the Field: Reflections of Lesbian and Gay Anthropologists*, eds. E. Lewin and W. L. Leap, pp. 274–85. Urbana: University of Illinois Press.

Whitehead, Harriet. 1981. The Bow and the Burden Strap: A New Look at Institutionalized Homosexuality in Native North America. In *Sexual Meanings: The Cultural Construction of Gender and Sexuality*. Sherry B. Ortner and Harriet Whitehead, eds. pp. 80–115. Cambridge: Cambridge University Press.

Whitehead, Tony Larry. 1986. Breakdown, Resolution, and Coherence: The Fieldwork Experiences of a Big, Brown, Pretty-Talking Man in a West Indian Community. In *Self, Sex, and Gender in Cross-Cultural Fieldwork*. Tony Larry Whitehead and Mary Ellen Conaway, eds. pp. 213–39. Urbana: University of Illinois Press.

Williams, Walter. 1986. *The Spirit and the Flesh: Sexual Diversity in American Indian Culture*. Boston: Beacon Press.

9

Feminist Insider Dilemmas: Constructing Ethnic Identity with Chicana Informants

Patricia Zavella

What happens when the ethnographic "others" are from the same society and are members of the same race or ethnicity, gender, and class background as the ethnographer? This chapter articulates the dilemmas I faced as a member of the group I was studying – Chicana working mothers – particularly regarding the terms of ethnic identification. My purpose here is twofold: I will discuss how my status as a simultaneous cultural "insider" and Chicana feminist researcher reflected a conundrum. My sense of Chicana feminist identity, constructed through participation in the Chicano movement, ironically hindered my understanding of the nuances of the ethnic identity of the women I studied and regarded as historical actors. My status as insider also caused the dilemma of how to present the ethnographic "others" to my peers, Chicano/Latino scholars who privileged the term Chicano. (As a product of the movement, I will use Chicano and Mexican American interchangeably here, except when referring to Mexican Americans from New Mexico.) These dilemmas eventually provided insight into the power relations involved when women of Mexican origin identify themselves ethnically. My discussion will contextualize the meaning of ethnic identity for working-class Mexican American women workers in two field research settings with different historical contexts.

There is a debate among ethnographers about conducting fieldwork with subjects who are of the same gender or race or ethnicity as the researcher. Chicano scholars assert that insiders are more likely to be cognizant and accepting of complexity and internal variation, are better able to understand the nuances of language use, will avoid being duped by informants who create cultural performances for their own purposes, and are less apt to be distrusted by those they study. Some assert that ethnic insiders often have an easier time gaining access to a community similar to their own, and that they are more sensitive to framing

From Patricia Zavella, "Feminist Insider Dilemmas: Constructing Ethnic Identity with Chicana Informants," pp. 138–59 in Diane L. Wolf, *Feminist Dilemmas in Fieldwork*. Boulder, CO: Westview, 1996. Reprinted with permission of University of Nebraska Press, Lincoln, and the author.

INSIDER/OUTSIDER

questions in ways that respect community sensibilities (Aguilar 1988; Paredes 1977; Romano 1968).

Others, however, note that being a member of a subordinated group under study carries particular problems and creates personal and ethical dilemmas for social scientists on the basis of their race, ethnicity, gender, political sympathies, or even personal foibles. Maxine Baca Zinn found that being an insider woman conducting ethnographic research with Mexican Americans meant continually negotiating her status, since members of the community being studied often made assumptions about her intents, skills, and personal characteristics. She reminds us that insider researchers have the unique constraint of always being accountable to the community being studied. Along with the cooperation engendered by one's insider status comes the responsibility to construct analyses that are sympathetic to ethnic interests and that will somehow share whatever knowledge is generated with them: "These problems should serve to remind us of our political responsibility and compel us to carry out our research with ethical and intellectual integrity" (Zinn 1979: 218).

Women anthropologists and feminist fieldworkers have also long been concerned about relationships with informants and have grappled with the dilemmas of being insiders, particularly when they have important similarities with the population being studied (Fonow and Cook 1991; Golde 1986; Klein 1983; Reinharz 1992; Roberts 1981; Thorne 1979; Wax 1979; Weston 1991). Some have argued that ethnographic methods are ideally suited to research by women because of the contextual, involved, experiential approach to knowledge that includes the sharing of experiences with one's subjects, and which contrasts with the features of positivist approaches.[1] Ann Oakley, for example, in a widely cited article, argues that "in most cases, the goal of finding out about people through interviewing is best achieved when the relationship of interviewer and interviewee is non-hierarchical and when the interviewer is prepared to invest his or her own personal identity in the relationship"; and later asserts that "a feminist interviewing women is by definition both 'inside' the culture

and participating in that which she is observing" (1982: 41, 57). Susan Krieger (1987) discusses how being an insider in a lesbian community enabled her to see how interviews were reflections of community norms, and her personal interpretations are sources of sociological insight.

Increasingly, feminist and other fieldworkers realize that we need to be sensitive to differences between our subjects and ourselves as well, and aware of the possible power relations involved in doing research by, about, and for women, and that feminist studies must include a diversity of women's experiences based on race, class, and sexual preferences, among others. Lynn Weber Cannon and her colleagues (1988) critique the white, middle-class bias of much qualitative feminist research and suggest that feminists take extraordinary measures to recruit women of color so as to include a variety of perspectives. Catherine Kohler Riessman (1987) points out that white women must be careful about analyzing interviews with women of color using their own narrative forms, lest they miss important nuances in meaning.

Women fieldworkers do not agree, however, on what constitutes feminist ethnography, nor do they agree on the role of the feminist insider as researcher. Judith Stacey (1988: 21), for example, suggests that feminist ethnography draws upon "such traditionally female strengths as empathy and human concern, and allows for an egalitarian, reciprocal relationship between knower and known." She questions whether there can be a truly feminist ethnography, arguing that the personal and ethical dilemmas inevitably pose insurmountable problems. In contrast to the goals of mutuality, nonexploitation, and empathy that she hoped for with feminist field research, Stacey argues that ironically this approach places informants at greater risk in the power relations inherent to any field research. By being involved in closer friendships, Stacey claims, informants are subject to betrayal and abandonment by the researcher, and thus feminist ethnography "masks a deeper, more dangerous form of exploitation." Stacey's naïveté, which she claims is overstated, is nonetheless disturbing. Although she confirms that conflicting interests and emotions are inherent to field research, there is not enough context in her discussion of her own "inauthenticity, dissimilitude and potential, perhaps inevitable betrayal" to assess how she tried to deal with the dilemmas she faced. A discussion of how she negotiated with those involved, or whether she reciprocated the trust and openness that her informants shared, could have convinced us that a feminist dilemma, not her expectations and behavior, was at issue.

There are two implicit assumptions in Stacey's formulation (and that of others who think of feminist methodology in this way) that remain despite her critique of feminist ethnography: that all women share some authentic feminine selfhood – with characteristics like being more cooperative, empathetic, attentive to daily life, or relational than men – so that women can thus bond with one another across time and space; and that feminist ethnography can somehow transcend the inequalities between women researchers and their subjects. Clearly these assumptions are problematic, particularly when Western ethnographers are doing research in the Third World or in working-class and poor communities in the United States. Micaela di Leonardo (1991a: 235) labels this perspective, which assumes that all women share common experiences or interests, as "cultural feminism," and argues that these assumptions form a women's culture as "invented tradition." Without "marking" the social location of the ethnographer and informants (their status based on class, race or ethnicity, sexual preference, or other relevant attributes) and with little presentation of the negotiations of differences between feminist fieldworkers and their informants, we cannot judge whether and how the ethnographer indeed has more power and privilege than those being researched. This lack of context leaves us with the impression that researchers and subjects are more similar than they really are and leaves unchallenged the questionable assumptions embedded in "feminist ethnography" as previously formulated.

Similarly, Marilyn Strathern (1987: 290) asserts that there is a "particularly awkward dissonance between feminist practice and the practice of social anthropology," and she implies that feminist anthropology is virtually impossible, since the two fields "mock" one another on the basis of fundamental differences in how the ethnographic "other" is construed. According to Strathern, ideally anthropologists interpret the experiences of traditionally non-Western, preindustrial, or peasant cultures by respecting their own emic view of the world, and more recently by creating space for other voices; yet the ultimate purpose serves the discipline. On the other hand, feminists, Strathern argues, construe the ethnographic "other" as men and patriarchal institutions, and therefore there can be no shared experience between them and feminists. Within her framework, feminists and their informants "have no interests in common to be served" by collaborating on producing an ethnographic text. Those of us who consider ourselves feminist ethnographers wonder where we and our women informants fit into her schema.[2]

Stacey and Strathern are correct in noting the inevitable ambivalence involved in doing ethnographic work. Their particular feminist positions, however, beg the question when the ethnographers are conducting research in real field sites. Feminist ethnographers must move beyond posing simple dichotomous methodological approaches to discussing how we as individual "marked" researchers – contextualized in our own milieu of research goals, ethics, sensitivities, and academic affinities – have grappled with the contradictions of feminist research. In other words, rather than assume some type of panfemale solidarity (with inevitable betrayal) or a lack of shared experience between researchers and subjects, we should realize that we are almost always simultaneously insiders and outsiders and discuss what this means for our particular research projects.

I will argue that my Chicana feminist perspective itself was problematic. In the framework of larger historical forces and political struggles, identifying myself as a Chicana feminist meant contesting and simultaneously drawing from Chicano nationalist ideology and white feminism – being an insider and outsider within both movements and ideologies. It was only in retrospect, when I came to understand how Mexican American women informants from New Mexico constructed their ethnic identity in very different ways, that I realized I needed to deconstruct and problematize my own sense of Chicana feminism so that I could "see" the nuances of ethnic identity among my informants.

My experience was a form of what Micaela di Leonardo (1991b) suggests is a general feminist fieldwork conundrum: we simultaneously seek out women's experiences and critically analyze male domination in societies whose customs anthropology has defended under the stance of cultural relativism. Thus feminists now face the dilemma of seeing those customs as patriarchal, and rather than defend their existence, want to advocate change for women's benefit. There is growing acceptance in the field that feminist and other researchers, then, must self-consciously reflect upon their status within the field site, on how they are situated within social and power relations, and place their own work within the changing tides of academic discourse as well. José Limón (1989: 484) reminds us that "however 'liberating' a narrative discourse that we propose to write, it is one always intimate with power, and many of our 'informants,' 'subjects,' 'consultants,' 'teachers,' 'friends' know it.... We must always decenter our own narrative self-assurance lest it be saturated with dominating power." Such self-reflexive analysis of our own experience will push us to provide "provisional" analyses that are always incomplete, but which make clear whose viewpoint is being represented (Rosaldo 1989).

Constructing Chicana Identity

As part of my own process of becoming a Chicana feminist beginning in the early 1970s, I became conscious of the critical importance of ethnic identity. I and others of my generation who were involved in Chicano movement activities deliberately rejected the hyphenated term Mexican-American, which to us connoted assimilation. We adopted the highly politicized term "Chicano," which designated pride in our rich pre-Columbian heritage and the importance of celebrating our mestizo racial and cultural mixtures, and rejected the influence of the Spanish colonizers. The term "Chicano" also signaled the history of racism of North American society toward people of Mexican descent; it claimed the right to self-determination and control over institutions within the Chicano community, and called for spiritual and organizational unity of the Chicano people. An integral part of reclaiming our Mexican heritage was speaking Spanish and celebrating cultural values of communalism, the family, and brotherhood (*el pueblo, la familia y carnalismo*). Chicano movement ideology also had separatist leanings, suggested the importance of recognizing *Aztlan* – the mythical northern part of pre-Columbian society – as a symbolic celebration of our spiritual unity, and explicitly rejected white culture. The Marxists among us argued that Chicanos and Mexican immigrants were the same people, that is, we were a primarily working-class community *sin fronteras* (without borders) who held common interests as a racialized class. These activists pushed for political strategies and organizations that would encourage the development of class consciousness between Chicanos and Mexicanos (that is, Mexican immigrants), regardless of the U.S.–Mexican border (I. García, 1989; Gómez-Quiñones, 1990; Hammerback et al., 1985).

At the time, Chicana activists proudly embraced movement ideology, yet our identity as feminists was submerged. "Feminism" was seen as a white, middle-class term and itself a reason for dismissing women's views (Cortera 1977; Gonzalez 1977; Hernandez 1980; Nieto-Gómez 1974). Chicanos often tried to silence feminists by branding us "cultural betrayers," "white-identified," "man haters," and "lesbians." Despite these travails, many of us maintained our critiques of the Chicano movement, with its male-oriented organizational concerns, the outright sexism of some leaders, the lack of recognition of women, and the unquestioning acceptance of the patriarchy inherent in the ideology of *la familia*. I further embraced the feminist principles that household decision-making and the division of labor should be shared equally between partners, that women should feel good about their participation in the labor force, and that labor organizing should include women. Thus was my construction of Chicana feminism when I entered the field.

As I have discussed previously (1987), I started my field research in 1977–8 with the assumption that my identity would provide an entrée to women cannery workers. I assumed that being a woman from a working-class background myself would provide ready access to this community of informants. Although women were generous with their time and insights, I found that indeed there were important differences between us. In retrospect, my expectations were naïve, for these were predominantly middle-aged, seasonal cannery workers who were being displaced from cannery employment in the Santa Clara Valley.[3] These women (and men) were acutely conscious of my privileges as an educated woman and assumed I had resources that as a poverty-stricken graduate student I did not have. More important, the very research questions I posed alerted them to significant political differences between us. I asked about how women made decisions, how they organized the household division of labor, how they felt about being working mothers, and about racism and sexism on the job. Implicit in my questions were Chicana feminist notions. As I came to understand, these women struggled to live independent lives – working in strenuous jobs, participating in the decisions as to how their wages were spent, taking pride in enduring the demanding labor process, and finding meaning in constructing a work culture with other women workers. Like many North American women, my informants supported feminist notions like "equal pay for equal work" and affirmative action.

These women also had very "traditional" notions about family, however, having originally sought seasonal employment because it allowed them to fulfill their familial obligations, and they identified themselves as "homemakers" for most of the year. With a few notable exceptions, these were women who "happened to work," and whose seasonal employment did not challenge the traditional notions that their husbands should be the breadwinners and heads of the family and

that they should do most of the domestic work, although some did contest these notions somewhat. My feminist questions, then, pointed out the contradictions of their constructions of their selves and led to some awkward moments when women preferred silence to full discussions of problems in their families or with their husbands. It was at these times that my outsider status seemed glaring.

Furthermore, those who were politically involved in the attempts to reform the Teamsters Union from within were also aware of possible political differences between us. Thus my experience of "establishing rapport" often meant discussing my political sensibilities and commitments in great detail, and I worried about "contaminating the field" with my own biases.

Although my cannery worker informants identified themselves ethnically in varied terms, ranging from "Mexicana," "Mexican American," or "Chicana" to "Spanish," as a self-identified Chicana, I was not particularly concerned with variation in ethnic identification at the time I wrote the book, merely noting it in passing. I was more concerned with their political consciousness and activities and wrote a critique about how race and gender were incorporated into strategies for organizing cannery workers (Zavella, 1988). I did not explicitly analyze the connection between ethnic identity and politics, however, and I now see that that would have been an interesting relationship to pursue.

Reflecting back, I recall that most were of the second generation (their parents were born in Mexico, but they themselves were born in the United States). Among the second generation, those who identified themselves as Spanish or Mexican American were often the most conservative. Usually those cannery workers who were the most militant and most deeply involved in the Teamster reform movement explicitly called themselves "Chicanos" or "Mexicanos." Moreover, the ideological polarities that often erupted in organizational conflicts were present among the cannery worker activists with whom I did participant observation, and ethnic identification was central to ideological posturing. Some of the nationalist Chicanos advocated political strategies that focused on Chicano demands, whereas the more moderate or leftist Chicanos and Mexicanos pushed for multiethnic reformist strategies centered on bread-and-butter issues and downplayed ethnic differences among workers.

In sum, my cannery research experience challenged my Chicana feminist perspective, but more in terms of the gender politics within "the movement" and how class consciousness was framed in daily life. It was only in retrospect that I came to see the importance of ethnic identification with different political strategies. My shortsightedness was in tune with the field at the time.

Recognizing Heterogeneity

Writing in 1981, anthropologist José Limón pointed out that "Chicano" was a problematic term because it was rooted in folklore performances that were usually private (among fellow Mexican Americans), where it held both pejorative and positive connotations: To assimilated middle-class Mexican Americans, "Chicano" connotes the proletarian Mexican immigrant experience and later the militancy and celebration of the indigenous ancestry of the movement. When used by working-class Mexican Americans through customary nicknaming practices or in situations that are culturally ambiguous, "Chicano" can convey affection or intimacy or legitimize one's status as an authentic Mexican American. Thus, Limón argues, through the construction of a Chicano *public* ethnic identity (in discourse where English was used or in Anglo-dominated contexts), academics and activists drew upon its highly charged symbolic power that already held intraethnic tensions and "added political meanings to the term which did not meet with the approval of the larger community" (1981: 214).[4] Despite his cautions, the term "Chicano" – with its nationalist and gender-contested connotations that were added by the movement – is still the predominant term in the field of Chicano Studies.

It has only been within the past few years that we are seeing theoretical analyses that explicitly look for fine-tuned differences among Chicanos and distinguish Chicanos from Mexicanos and other Latinos. Re-

searchers have found variation in how Chicanos identify themselves, with regional differences being very important (García 1981; Hurtado and Arce 1987; Miller 1976). New Mexico, where there is a long-standing "ethnic sensitivity," has always posed a unique case in how Mexican Americans identify themselves. According to this analysis, Mexican Americans in New Mexico identified with their Spanish heritage and sought to dissociate themselves from racist sentiments directed at Mexican immigrants (Gonzalez 1969). Thus people preferred the terms "Spanish" or "Spanish Americans," and women especially rejected the term "Chicano."[5]

The term "Spanish" (or the synonymous "Spanish American") became hegemonic in New Mexican society after World War I, and clearly demarcated native-born Mexican Americans from those who had migrated from Mexico,[6] yet challenged racism and discrimination against the Mexican American working class in education, politics, and the economy (Gonzales 1986). This hegemony can be seen in the casual use of "Spanish" throughout the state today; it is a term that has become part of daily experience for Mexican Americans generally, and for our informants in particular. It wasn't until the 1980s that recent Mexican immigrants became a large presence in economically undeveloped northern New Mexican cities. Mexican migrants became integrated into a society where the major social categories of Anglo, Indian, and Spanish were already clearly established.

Constructing Hispana Ethnicity

In a second research project conducted during 1982–3, a time of national recession, Louise Lamphere, Felipe Gonzales, Peter B. Evans, and I (1993) studied the effects of industrialization in the Sun Belt on working-class families, comparing Mexican Americans and whites.[7] We found that women's work in apparel factories and electronics production facilities sometimes brought important changes in family life as women became coproviders, mainstay providers, or, in the case of single parents, sole economic providers for their families. We argue that these working-class families are changing as women deal with the contradictions of full-time work and family commitments. Our women informants were more committed to full-time work than their mothers were, while their spouses were doing more housework and child care than we expected. Without the economic resources of highly paid professional women, these women constructed varied strategies to help mediate the contradictions of daily life – dividing up economic upkeep, finding day care for their children, negotiating a division of household chores and child care with husbands, room-mates, or kin, and seeking emotional support and social exchange from relatives or friends. Mexican American and white women had similar experiences rooted in a common class status and family circumstances, yet within each group there was nuanced variation.

We were interested in ethnic differences and explicitly questioned our informants about their own sense of ethnicity and ethnic identity. As we began the analysis, in which ethnic differences were not as pronounced as we expected, we began to grapple directly with our informants' particular ethnic identity. We came to use the term "Mexican American" advisedly. The majority of our Mexican American informants identified themselves as Spanish or Spanish American, a custom at odds with my sense of ethnic identification.

Upon moving to Albuquerque before getting involved in this project, I became aware of the New Mexican prejudice toward Californians in general, and Californian Mexican Americans in particular, as being arrogant and assimilated, and I began to downplay my California connections. I had lived in Albuquerque for almost a year before embarking on research, so I had become accustomed to hearing the term "Spanish" in daily conversation and to hearing colleagues – aware of the ethnic sensitivity – referring to the local Mexican Americans with hyphenated terms like Chicano-Mexicano-Spanish community. When I found "Spanish" rather than "Chicano" or "Mexican American" on institutional forms where I was supposed to designate my ethnic identity, I even became accustomed (with only slight hesitation) to checking the "Spanish" box, even though that

seemed to deny my Chicana identity. As a feminist, I was aware of the possible offense of using this term and restricted it to contexts within higher education, where it was more acceptable.

As I began interviewing women, then, in the course of chatting informally before starting the interview, I let them know how aspects of our identities coincided: I was a working mother with a young child myself who struggled to find day care and juggle work and family, my partner had been reared in Albuquerque, and we lived in the predominantly Mexican American South Valley. Further, my great-grandparents had lived and farmed in the northern New Mexican village of Tierra Amarilla and were part of the migration northward to southern Colorado, considered by scholars and laypeople to be part of the northern New Mexico culture region. In short, my own experience seemed to parallel those of our informants. Although I only got a chance to discuss our common heritage on a few occasions, having kinship ties in "the north" on the face of it made me a *manita* – figuratively a cultural compatriot. (New Mexicans use the terms "Hispano" or "manito" [literally, little brother] interchangeably, and use "Mexicano" when speaking in Spanish.) I hoped that my brief disclosures about my own ethnic heritage would allow my informants to express their own sense of ethnicity openly.

We asked questions about ethnic identity toward the end of the second interview, presumably when rapport was established and informants were comfortable with the interview format. Our strategy was to evoke their own terms by first asking them to designate a term for the Spanish-surnamed or Spanish-speaking people in Albuquerque, ask if that was the term they used for themselves, and then to ask for clarification about the meaning of whatever term they had selected. We also asked how whatever group they had identified (usually "Spanish") differed from Mexicans, and what they thought of the term "Chicano." As in previous research on ethnic identification in New Mexico, about two-thirds of our informants found that responding to questions about ethnic identity was a very sensitive issue. People made comments like, "I was afraid that you'd ask that." One man explained: "I'd play it by ear. Some people get offended real easy, because if other people's Chicano, they get real upset – others, uh, Spanish American." One could argue that these respondents were aware that ethnic identification expresses power relations, where being labeled or "naming" oneself can be a reflection of opposing or acquiescing to the subordination of the ethnic group (Gutiérrez 1986). Or one could argue that since ethnic identification is so influenced by context, our informants were not aware of the norms within the interview situation and thus felt that choosing a term meant taking some risk.[8]

Yet when we asked further questions, they had difficulty articulating their meaning of "Spanish American," in part because their lives were so ethnically bounded. My first interview immediately signaled me that these informants were different from other Mexican Americans, and that they did not characterize their ethnicity in ways that were familiar. Geri Sandoval (all names are pseudonyms), a taciturn woman from the northern village of Mora, seemed reluctant to even discuss ethnicity. When I probed, however, she said that her family still owned a farm with a private *campo santo* (cemetery) that had been in her family for generations, that she was related to "everyone" in the general area, that her grandparents had been active members of the Catholic but renegade religious group *los penetentes*, and that they regularly celebrated Easter with traditional ethnic foods. She readily identified herself as Spanish American, but when asked how Mexicans and Spanish Americans differ, she said, "I don't know," and her tone of voice indicated she did not want to discuss it further. I let the matter drop.

In another interview, when asked about her ethnic identity, Delores Baca asked for clarification and then responded, "I don't know, I'm just me. I've never had that question asked of me." It turned out that this woman had the largest and most dense ethnic network of any informant, and she had participated in ethnic activities. Like Geri Sandoval, Delores Baca's grandparents had owned a small farm in a northern village but had sold it and settled the family on property in Bernalillo, near Albuquerque. Thus her parents lived across

the street, and her eight siblings and several other extended kin all lived within walking distance, some with their own families. Delores had rich social exchange with her relatives – her mother provided daily day care while she worked, and her relatives often borrowed and lent money and clothes or did car repairs – and they saw one another frequently. Her wedding had been "traditional," with three attempts at mock kidnapping and finally a collective "ransom" so the festivities could continue, and a *marcha*, in which the godparents led the bridesmaids and attendants in a ritualized dance. When asked to describe her ethnic heritage and special traditions in her family, Delores didn't know how to respond. After some probes she described an elaborate festival in honor of San Lorenzo, of which her parents had been sponsors, and told me she had participated in *matachines* – ritualized, costumed dances. When pressed about what ethnic term she would use, Delores responded, "I'd say I'm Spanish-Mexican, Mexican-Spanish, whatever. I'd tell them where I work, what I do, I guess." Despite being totally immersed in ethnic culture, Delores did not immediately see herself as having any special ethnic heritage or identity, and distanced herself from it by coupling ethnicity with occupational identity.

One of the final interviews, with Christina Espinosa, who was the child of a "mixed marriage," drove home these informants' points about the sensitivity of ethnic identity and added meaning that was new to me. On the basis of her looks, Christina's ethnicity was ambiguous, since she had fair skin but dark brown hair, and she had a Spanish surname from a former marriage (I initially thought she was white). It wasn't until the second interview, when we took information on extended kin, that I realized that Christina's German American father had left when she was young and that she was close to her Mexican American mother and maternal kin. When asked directly, Christina refused to provide a term for her own ethnic identity:

P. Z.: For the Spanish-surnamed population in Albuquerque, what word would you use to call them?

C. E.: I'd just call people by name. I don't like putting tags on people.

P. Z.: So if someone asked you what you are, what would you say?

C. E.: An Albuquerquian; I was born in Albuquerque, that's all I know. I don't know what my mom and dad did, that's their problem. You ask them what I am, that's not my problem. . . . I have a hard time 'cause I really don't see no difference. To me people are the same.

P. Z.: How are Spanish people here different from Mexicans?

C. E.: I don't really know. I don't really think they are. See I have a hard time when people say, you know, "Well look at that Mexican." I go, "How do you know they're not Spanish?" Because I really don't see no difference. To me they're the same. But now you can't tell them that 'cause they get angry. And I don't know why.

What was this, I wondered? Christina's kin network had a texture that seemed Mexican American, yet she refused to identify with any group and to characterize herself ethnically. Christina believed that Spanish and Mexicans, like all people, were "the same." Her defensive tone of voice and body language, however, indicated that this was difficult for her to discuss, for she had a "hard time" when people noticed Mexicans, who looked like the Spanish, who perhaps looked like her. Clearly she was trying to distance herself from claiming any ethnic identity.

Similarly, other informants emphasized the more neutral term "*New Mexican.*" One woman, who had lived in the northern city of Española through high school and who was close to her husband's extended kin from the same area, could only explain: "I am what I am and I'm Spanish."[9] In general, our research reinforced previous findings that women had more aversion to the use of Chicano than men did.

Part of our dilemma was to figure out how to convey the seemingly contradictory evidence: our informants did not necessarily characterize their ethnic identity in ways with which we were familiar – they did not convey explicit pride in their ethnic heritage, and their

use of the term "Spanish" seemed on the face of it to identify them with the colonizer part of their heritage. Yet our informants did not disclaim their ethnic heritage. They were mainly third generation, born in the United States, and their parents had migrated to Albuquerque from predominantly Spanish villages in northern New Mexico. Though they spoke English as their first language, they did not seem assimilated. They believed that maintaining the Spanish language was important and wished their children could learn it, but since they did not consider themselves fluent (often speaking to grandparents and elders in broken Spanish), this value could not be fully realized. They did not reject their ethnic heritage, but they also did not have strong views about its content.

Ethnic and gender subordination can be found in many forms in contemporary Albuquerque. Spanish Americans make up only about a third of the population. The city of Albuquerque historically was segregated by class and race/ethnicity so that predominantly Anglos lived in the Northeast Heights while the Spanish lived primarily in Old Town, and in the north and south valleys, with some pockets of Anglos in the two valleys. (There has been some recent residential dispersal, however, so that the southeast and north valley and central areas have integrated neighborhoods that include blacks and Navajos as well.) The electronics and garment work sites we studied have predominantly Spanish female work forces, although because of recruiting practices, only small numbers are Mexican immigrants. These women struggled daily on the shop floor to make their piece rates, cooperated with other workers, or engaged in collective struggle – including staging a strike for union recognition in one factory. Our informants, then, were located in working-class occupations where the majority of their coworkers were Spanish; their daily experiences and social worlds revolved around family and kin and at work and church activities where others were predominantly Spanish. Their lives were so immersed in ethnic social worlds that they had little information about others, so they did not know how their lives were ethnically distinct.

So when our informants used the terms "Spanish" or "Spanish American" in the early 1980s, the meaning included a sense of ethnic and class segmentation. We eventually realized that despite their apparent diffidence, they had a definite awareness of their membership in a distinct social category and their constructions of meaning were complex. We discuss the varied meanings of "Spanish" in detail elsewhere (Lamphere et al. 1993).

To some, "Spanish" meant an ethnic category that was distinct from "Mexican." One woman said, "Spanish American is born here in America.... Mexicans to me are different than what we are, 'cause our language is different." Another meaning was to differentiate Mexican Americans from other ethnic or racial groups, sometimes using racial features like skin color or notions of "Spanish blood." A third meaning centered on aspects of the Mexican American cultural heritage, where a family still owned land in the north, networks of relatives still lived in rural areas, or there was participation in regional cultural activities such as the *penitentes* religious rites or the *matachines*. In short, these informants were a particular segment of the Mexican American working class, who were ethnically distinct with important regional differences from other Chicanos, but who did not explicitly claim ethnic identity unless asked, as in our interviews. Although they did not explicitly express ethnic pride, their struggles to retain their way of life were inherently political, but did not include politicized terms like Chicano.

In contrast to the situation among our informants, more recent research on ethnic identity among Mexican Americans in other areas shows that generation as well as region are important.[10] Collectively, this research highlights the regional variation of our New Mexico sample. Through their rejection of the term "Chicano" and the straightforward (as opposed to strident) ways they described their lives, these informants pushed me to a new understanding of Mexican American ethnicity and the importance of contextualizing our informants' own terms of identity.

The Politics of Ethnic Identity in Academia

A second dilemma arose when I attempted to present our research findings to fellow Chicano or Latino colleagues in the late 1980s. On two occasions, I made presentations on our research findings in ways that respected our informants' construction of identity and tried to contextualize their meanings. Yet I was attacked and my integrity questioned when I used the term "Spanish." Puerto Rican scholars in particular strongly objected to the use of "Spanish." One colleague claimed – to general agreement – that he had never even heard of anyone using the term "Spanish American" "*in the community*," so he could not understand how I could use it. They grilled me about my motivations and purposes, questioned my relationships with informants, and demanded to know how I would use the data. Embedded in their questions was the assumption that I was using the term "Spanish" as a euphemistic way of identifying Mexican Americans, and they implied that I was identifying with the white power structure and would use the data in ways that would harm my informants. It was only after other Hispana colleagues who were from northern New Mexico rescued me, asserting that indeed "Spanish American" was widely used even by scholars, that they relented. To someone who saw herself as a feminist activist scholar, this felt ironic and unfair. Clearly I had violated the Chicano/ Latino academic cultural norms of ethnic identification.

I found myself in an ambivalent position: I was very sympathetic to their insistence that we scholars not buy into the racism and insensitivity involved in labeling a group by terms they would not claim, or in avoiding the mestizo racial content of the terms themselves, which "Spanish" seemed to imply. Chicano/Latino scholars are well aware of the pressures to be token spokespeople for "our people," and the importance of resisting any type of pejorative labeling and of perpetrating misconceptions about our communities. Yet I felt very uncomfortable about their assumption that by using "Spanish" I was somehow a "mainstream" scholar who would be insensitive to these issues.

In response to the critique, I cautioned my coauthors, and we self-consciously decided to use the term "Hispanic" instead, even though we felt uncomfortable with the Euro-centered sensibility it implied. "Hispanic" was a term agreed upon by an advisory committee formed from representatives of various Chicano and Latino political organizations, in response to efforts to sensitize the Census Bureau's accounting of people of "Spanish origin" in the 1970s census.[11] Yet because the Census Bureau then lumped together groups with very disparate histories, sociodemographic characteristics, political interests, and treatment upon immigration to the United States – notably Cubans, Puerto Ricans, and Mexicans (Portes and Bach 1985) – many activists and scholars (including us) found "Hispanic" problematic.[12] The preferred term by the late 1980s was "Latino," which carried connotations of community self-sufficiency and empowerment and leftist political leanings. Yet "Hispanic" was the term selected by our informants after "Spanish," and seemed to be the next-best approximation of their own sense of ethnic identity.

The last piece of evidence concerning this dilemma came more recently. In 1991 the National Association for Chicano Studies passed a student-initiated resolution that condemned the use of "Hispanic" (National Association for Chicano Studies 1991). (In the politics of the association, students have a political voice through a plenary session on student issues, so a student-initiated resolution carries a lot of weight.) We realized that we would be violating the Chicano/Latino academic norms once again if we continued using "Hispanic."

In retrospect, it is clear there were two contesting principles at work – the feminist notion that we should respect our women informants' constructions of their identity, and at the same time respecting Chicano/Latino academic norms regarding the public presentation of ourselves. A Chicana feminist approach to ethnography clearly would combine the two, fully aware that academic norms must include women's interests as well.

As a way of reconciling these competing dilemmas, and after much discussion, we eventually decided to use the terms "Mexican American" and "Hispana" (for women) interchangeably. "Hispano" (the generic male term) is a term indigenous to northern New Mexico and approximates the use of "Spanish," in that working-class people use it in daily life. But "Hispano" is also becoming politicized similarly to "Chicano." In a number of contexts in New Mexico, scholars and activists have begun using "Hispano" to signify Mexican American political interests (Sierra 1992).[13] We hope that by using "Mexican American" and "Hispano" interchangeably we can respect both sides in this dilemma, yet we realize that no one term will please everyone. It seemed as if the "danger" that Judith Stacey identifies in doing ethnographic research concerned my own integrity more than violating our informants' sense of self. They, after all, were shielded from political critique by anonymity and by having their lives placed in context. I (and my colleagues) were subject to verbal jostling without the benefit of presenting our personal concerns and agendas.

I should note that we also had a similar dilemma about how to label our white informants, since most of them did not identify with the term "Anglo," which is widely used in New Mexico. When asked about ethnic identity, working-class white informants used terms that specified their own mixed and varied ancestry: "I'm a little bit of everything – German, Scottish, Irish, Italian, Danish, Slavic." Or they used terms like "Heinz 57, 31 flavors," which conveys a sense of culture that is processed. One woman evoked racial features and responded, "freckled and fair-skinned."[14] After more discussion and soul-searching, we decided to use "white" and "Anglo" interchangeably as well. We have yet to receive criticisms from white academics or activists for using this term. The term "white," however, is clearly problematic for people of European descent as well.

More telling, and a dilemma I came to see only recently, is that my Chicano/Latino colleagues and I were operating with a rigid construction of ethnic identity. Although Chicano activists generally agreed on the necessity of using "Chicano," this in turn muted the internal political and theoretical differences among Chicana (and Chicano) scholars. Thus I realized that I needed to deconstruct the "Chicana" part of Chicana feminism with which I identified and reflect upon how Chicana feminism itself was framed.

Chicana feminists have long contested the male-centered intellectual and political traditions of the Chicano movement and the white middle-class focus of the second-wave feminist movement. Yet Chicana feminists have simultaneously used concepts from Chicano Studies for analyzing the intersection of class and race oppression and have drawn from feminist studies concepts of patriarchy and male dominance in analyzing the Chicana experience (Cortera 1980; A. García 1989). Chicana feminists also identify with our long history of labor and political activism, although again many activists did not use the term "feminist." Chicana studies was the product of a "mixed union," which has been problematic, and created the need for Chicana feminist institutions, organizations, and perspectives (Zavella 1989).[15]

In 1988 Beatriz Pesquera and Denise Segura did a survey of 101 Chicana faculty, students, and staff who belong to Mujeres Activas en Letras y Cambio Social (Activist Women in Letters and Social Change), an organization of Chicana/Latina activist academics; 83 percent of their respondents identified themselves as feminists. Pesquera and Segura argued that there have been internal differences since the late 1960s, but that these have become more noticeable in more recent years. They identified three types of Chicana feminists in their sample: Cultural nationalists emphasize the concerns of the Chicano movement, but want recognition of women's concerns and rights as well. Liberal Chicana feminists are oriented toward reform and hope to enhance the well-being of the Chicano community with a special emphasis on improving the status of women. Insurgent Chicana feminists, immersed in radical traditions, emphasize that Chicana inequality is the product of interrelated forms of stratification based on race-ethnicity, class, and gender – and for some, heterosexism. These women favor personal and institutional

change, and compared to the other groups, are more actively involved in political activities (Pesquera and Segura, 1998; Segura and Pesquera 1993).

Pesquera and Segura's analysis helped me realize that my own thinking had undergone changes. The whole field of Chicana/o Studies has become more self-reflexive and sophisticated in its analyses of the experiences of Chicanos, male and female. Insider research, then, is more complicated than we had anticipated in the early flush of nationalist fervor, and we are beginning to realize how we are insiders and outsiders within several constituencies, each with its own norms and responsibilities.

Reconfiguring Chicana Feminist Ethnography

To be sure, I will continue to honor some of the norms of Chicano academic discourse, some of which are critical and in some ways parallel the concerns of feminist scholars – such as the importance of activist scholarship. I believe that Chicano scholars, like feminists and others who aim to reconstruct the canon and the structure of the academy, should continue their self-critical reflections on ethical and research dilemmas. In contesting the dominant discourses about women, in this case giving voice to Chicanas, Mexican Americans, and Spanish women workers, we must not be seduced into thinking that our work is without its own contradictions.

In the service of Chicana – or Hispana – informants, I had unconsciously privileged the Chicano side of my identity and not listened to women carefully. After returning to our interview data and culling from our own experiences of living in Albuquerque and observing working-class Mexican Americans, we came to see that our Hispana informants were telling us something new about ethnic identification. That is, within the constraints of their lives, "Spanish" meant accommodation, resistance, and struggle to these informants. They helped me to realize that I should deconstruct my own Chicana feminist viewpoint. The critiques of our Chicano/Latino colleagues notwithstanding, we must respect our informants' own constructions of identity, however politically unpalatable they may appear to us.

In conclusion, I want to return to the notion of Chicana feminist ethnography. The dilemmas I raise here really have meaning only within the constraints of my own life. I have no delusions that our research was collaborative in some type of panfemale sense that was based on special bonding or that broke down status differences between us and our subjects. Although women were remarkably cooperative within the interview setting, in sometimes subtle ways they pointed out the differences between us, and showed me how I had stakes in understanding their lives in ways they did not. In the cannery research project, my informants' political ethnic senses seemed more familiar, more like mine. In the New Mexico project, our informants' sense of ethnicity and identity was so different that we were forced into rethinking in order to recognize its implicit political nature.

In both projects, as in most academic work, the self-defined interests of the research subjects were elsewhere. The researchers defined the problem to study; we asked questions about work, family, and ethnic identity that they found sensitive and even uncomfortable; and our analysis will probably have little direct effect on their daily lives. And however self-consciously provisional an account we provide, our analysis is aimed at a primarily academic community and will provide real benefits to us. In paying careful attention to our informants' sense of their selves, I came in time to see my own Chicana feminist blinders. As we are becoming all too aware, when one claims or has attributed a categorical difference based on ethnicity, the power relations involved are readily apparent. My status as Chicana feminist researcher, then, created two audiences that I should be sensitive and accountable to. Increasingly, I share our Spanish informants' sense of struggle and unease in grappling with this "name game," realizing that I too construct an ethnic identity depending on the context.

Feminist dilemmas begin at home, and we cannot take a cultural feminist stance in our approach to fieldwork. As we go through the process of talking with people like ourselves who are called "other," we should try to understand our own feminism and political struggles. Chicana feminist ethnography, then, would present more nuanced, fully contextualized, pluralistic self identities of women, both as informants and researchers.

NOTES

1 Shulamit Reinharz (1983) reviews the work of feminists who claim that feminist research has these and other characteristics, including "shar[ing] the fate of our subjects."

2 Shulamit Reinharz (1992) points out that contrasting perspectives on the relationship between the ethnographer and her subjects have a long history.

3 I spent fifteen months conducting field research during 1977–8. The bulk of my data was life histories with twenty-four cannery workers and labor organizers, but I also did historical research on the canning industry and unionization by the International Brotherhood of Teamsters, and did participant-observations in canneries and other public settings, such as union meetings. A few of the interviews were conducted in Spanish, in which my fluency is good but not excellent.

4 Limón provides a discussion of the origin of the term "Chicano," which has been traced to usage in 1911, and reports on surveys on ethnic identification where the majority of respondents preferred the terms "Mexicano" or "Mexican American," except in New Mexico.

5 Joseph V. Metzgar (1975) found that the use of "Spanish-American" had actually declined in use between 1962 and 1972, and that those who increased their use of "Chicano" were primarily aged twenty and younger.

6 Ramón A. Gutiérrez (1991) investigated ethnic categories and identity in northern New Mexico, beginning in the eighteenth century after Spanish frontier society was firmly established. He documents that the overwhelming majority of the elites could

not claim pure Spanish ancestry, yet they claimed an identity as Españoles to differentiate themselves from the Indians and claim honor. Mestizos, the ancestors of today's working-class Hispanos, socially constructed their self-designation as Spanish for their own ideological and material benefit. Even in Spain, there were so many interracial unions that it was impossible to reckon pure Spanish ancestry (Gutiérrez, personal communication).

7 Lamphere and Evans were the project directors, and Gonzáles and I were graduate student interviewers at the time, writing our own dissertations. We did a little participant-observation in public settings, but the research mainly drew from the interviews with eighty-nine people – thirty-eight worker couples and fifteen single mothers (in the end, two men were not interviewed) – of which I conducted many with the Mexican American women. Peter Evans interviewed plant managers as well.

8 Focusing on Chicago, Felix M. Padilla (1985) notes the importance of context for Mexican American identity: Encouraged by the division of labor in US industrial society, which created common experiences of social inequality among Mexican Americans and Puerto Ricans, Chicano activists forged coalitions with other Latino groups and constructed a situational ethnic identity of Latinos.

9 Similarly, José Limón (1981) found that some Texans of Mexican descent have used "tejano" as a public referent, in part to distinguish between a Mexicano from Mexico and one from Texas.

10 In a survey of 370 respondents, Keefe and Padilla (1987) found that 25% had high Mexican cultural awareness and ethnic loyalty and were most likely to identify themselves as Mexicans; 74% were bicultural individuals who retained moderate or high ethnic identity. Only a small percentage were highly Anglicized and preferred "Americans of Mexican descent." In a survey of people of Mexican origin, Hurtado (Hayes-Bautista et al., 1992; Hurtado et al., 1992:59) found that the

first-generation respondents preferred "Hispanic" (88%), "Latino" (86%), and "Mexican" (76%); the second generation preferred "Hispanic" (83%), "Californian" (81%), and "American of Mexican descent" (78%); and the third-generation respondents preferred "Mexican American" (85%), "Hispanic" (83%), and "American" (82%), as well as "American of Mexican descent" (82%).

11 Based on interviews with advisory committee participants and political leaders, Laura E. Gómez (1992) argues that Hispanic represents the more "mainstream" political viewpoints of the participants, and became popularized during the 1980s.

12 Beginning with the 1980 census, the term "Hispanic" is a specially designated ethnic term that includes four subcategories: Mexican, Mexican American, Chicano; Puerto Rican; Cuban; Other Spanish/Hispanic. For the state of New Mexico, there have been bipolar self-designations, with the Mexican, Mexican American, and Chicano and the Other Spanish/Hispanic making up the largest categories. Since it is unclear how many Iberians reside in New Mexico, and since unlike other cities (like Miami, San Francisco, Los Angeles, Washington, DC, or New York), Albuquerque (the largest New Mexican city) is not a major site of Latin American immigrant settlement, we can only conclude that some Mexican Americans are choosing "Other Spanish." Thus census data are particularly imprecise for counting the Mexican American population in New Mexico.

13 Metzgar (1975: 55) claims that in the 1970s "Hispano" was used almost exclusively by scholars and professional writers to describe Spanish-speaking New Mexicans and did not have widespread use in the barrios.

14 Ruth Frankenberg (1992) argues that the social construction of "white" carries several meanings – as distinct from "white ethnic," it means "spoiled by capitalism," so that brand names like Wonder Bread connote blandness or processing and

evocations of features of the body such as skin color. Micaela di Leonardo (1984) shows how late 1970s white Italian-American women socially constructed their own sense of ethnicity, sometimes in racist terms.

15 Actually I said "mixed marriage." Thanks to Emma Perez (1993), who reminded me that my use of a marriage analogy is a heterosexist formulation.

REFERENCES

Aguilar, John L. 1988. Insider Research: An Ethnography of a Debate. In *Anthropologists at Home in North America: Methods and Issues in the Study of One's Own Society*, edited by D. A. Messerschmidt, pp. 15–26. New York: Cambridge University Press.

Cannon, Lynn Weber, Elizabeth Higginbotham, and Marianne L. A. Leung. 1988. Race and Class Bias in Qualitative Research on Women. *Gender and Society*, 2/4: 449–62.

Cortera, Marta. 1977. *The Chicana Feminist*. Austin: Information Systems Development.

—— 1980. Feminism: The Chicana and the Anglo Versions, a Historical Analysis. In *Twice a Minority: Mexican American Women*, edited by M. B. Melville. St. Louis: C. V. Mosby.

di Leonardo, Micaela. 1984. *The Varieties of Ethnic Experience: Kinship, Class, and Gender Among California Italian-Americans*. Ithaca, NY: Cornell University Press.

—— 1991a. Habits of the Cumbered Heart: Ethnic Community and Women's Culture as American Invented Traditions. In *Imagining the Past in Anthropology and History*, edited by W. Roseberry and J. O'Brien. Berkeley: University of California Press.

—— 1991b. Introduction: Gender, Culture, and Political Economy: Feminist Anthropology in Historical Perspective. In *Gender at the Crossroads of Knowledge: Feminist Anthropology in the Postmodern Era*, edited by Micaela di Leonardo, pp. 1–48. Berkeley: University of California Press.

Fonow, Mary Margaret, and Judith A. Cook. 1991. *Beyond Methodology: Feminist Scholarship as Lived Research*. Bloomington: Indiana University Press.

Frankenberg, R. 1992. *White Women, Race Matters: The Social Construction of Whiteness*. Minneapolis: University of Minnesota Press.

García, Alma M. 1989. The Development of Chicana Feminist Discourse, 1970–1980. *Gender and Society*, 3: 217–38.

García, Ignacio M. 1989. *United We Win: The Rise and Fall of La Raza Unida Party*. Tucson: University of Arizona Press.

García, John A. 1981. "Yo Soy Mexicano."....: Self-Identity and Sociodemographic Correlates. *Social Science Quarterly*, 62/1: 88–98.

Golde, Peggy, ed. 1986. *Women in the Field: Anthropological Experiences*. Berkeley: University of California Press.

Gómez, Laura E. 1992. The Birth of the "Hispanic" Generation: Attitudes of Mexican-American Political Elites Toward the Hispanic Label. *Latin American Perspectives*, 19/4: 45–58.

Gómez-Quiñones, Juan. 1990. *Chicano Politics, Reality and Promise, 1940–1990*. Albuquerque: University of New Mexico Press.

Gonzales, Phillip B. 1986. Spanish Heritage and Ethnic Protest in New Mexico: The Anti-Fraternity Bill of 1933. *New Mexico Historical Review*, 61/4: 281–99.

—— 1993. The Political Construction of Latino Nomenclatures in Twentieth Century New Mexico. *Journal of the Southwest*, 35/3: 158–72.

—— 1997. The Categorical Meaning of Spanish American Identity among Blue Collar New Mexicans. *Hispanic Journal of Behavioral Sciences*: 123–36.

Gonzalez, Nancy. 1969. *Spanish Americans of New Mexico: A Heritage of Pride*. Albuquerque: University of New Mexico Press.

Gonzalez, Sylvia. 1977. The White Feminist Movement: The Chicana Perspective. *Social Science Journal*, 4: 65–74.

Gutiérrez, Ramon A. 1986. Unraveling America's Hispanic Past: Internal Stratification and Class Boundaries. *Aztlan*, 17/1: 79–101.

—— 1991. *When Jesus Came the Corn Mothers Went Away: Marriage, Sexuality,* and Power in New Mexico, 1500–1846. Stanford: Stanford University Press.

Hammerback, John C., Richard J. Jensen, andJosé Angel Gutiérrez. 1985. A War of Words: Chicano Protest in the 1960s and 1970s. Westport, Conn.: Greenwood Press.

Hayes-Bautista, David E., Aída Hurtado, R. Burciaga Valdez, and Anthony C. R. Hernández. 1992. No Longer a Minority: Latinos and Social Policy in California. Los Angeles: Chicano Studies Research Center.

Hernandez, Patricia. 1980. Lives of Chicana Activists: The Chicano Student Movement (A Case Study). In Mexican Women in the United States, Struggles Past and Present, edited by M. Mora and A. R. del Castillo. Los Angeles: Chicano Studies Research Center Publications.

Hurtado, Aída, and Carlos H. Arce. 1987. Mexicans, Chicano, Mexican Americans, or Pochos...¿Que Somos? The Impact of Language and Nativity on Ethnic Labeling. Aztlan, 17: 103–29.

Hurtado, Aída, David E. Hayes-Bautista, R. Burciaga Valdez, and Anthony C. R. Hernández. 1992. Redefining California: Latino Social Engagement in a Multicultural Society. Los Angeles: Chicano Studies Research Center.

Keefe, Susan E., and Amado M. Padilla. 1987. Chicano Ethnicity. Albuquerque: University of New Mexico Press.

Klein, Renate Duelli. 1983. How to Do What We Want to Do: Thoughts About Feminist Methodology. In Theories of Women's Studies, edited by G. Bowles and R. D. Klein. London: Routledge & Kegan Paul.

Krieger, Susan. 1987. Beyond "Subjectivity": The Use of the Self in Social Science. Qualitative Sociology, 8/4: 309–24.

Lamphere, Louise, Patricia Zavella, Felipe Gonzales, with Peter B. Evans. 1993. Sunbelt Working Mothers: Reconciling Family and Factory. Ithaca, NY: Cornell University Press.

Limón, José E. 1981. The Folk Performance of "Chicano" and the Cultural Limits of Political Ideology. In "And Other Neighborly Names": Social Process and Cultural Image in Texas Folklore, edited by R. Bauman and R. D. Abrahams. Austin: University of Texas Press.

—— 1989. Carne, Carnales, and the Carnivalesque: Bakhtinian Batos, Disorder, and Narrative Discourses. American Ethnologist, 16/3: 49–73.

Méndez Negrete, Josie. 1991. What Are You? What Can I Call You? A Study of Chicano and Chicana Ethnic Identity. Master's thesis, University of California, Santa Cruz.

Metzgar, Joseph V. 1975. The Ethnic Sensitivity of Spanish New Mexicans. New Mexico Historical Review, 49/1: 49–73.

Miller, Michael V. 1976. Mexican Americans, Chicanos, and Others: Ethnic Identification and Selected Social Attributes of Rural Texas Youth. Rural Sociology, 41: 234–47.

National Association for Chicano Studies. 1991. Noticias de NACS 9, 3.

Nieto-Gomez, Ana. 1974. La Femenista. Encuentro Femenil, 1/2: 34–9.

Oakley, A. 1982. Interviewing Women: A Contradiction in Terms. In Doing Feminist Research, edited by Helen Roberts. London: Routledge.

Padilla, Felix M. 1985. Latino Ethnic Consciousness: The Case of Mexican Americans and Puerto Ricans in Chicago. Notre Dame: University of Notre Dame Press.

Paredes, Américo. 1977. On Ethnographic Work among Minority Groups: A Folklorist's Perspective. New Scholar, 6/1/2: 1–32.

Pérez, Emma. 1993. Speaking from the Margin: Uninvited Discourse on Sexuality and Power. In With These Hands: Building Chicana Scholarship, edited by Beatriz M. Pesquera and Adela de la Torre. Berkeley: University of California Press.

Pesquera, Beatriz M., and Denise A. Segura. 1998. With Quill and Torch: A Chicana Perspective on the American Women's Movement and Feminist Theories. In The Third Wave: Feminist Perspectives on Racism, edited by M. J. Alexander and L. Albrecht. New York: Kitchen Table Press.

Portes, Alejandro, and Robert L. Bach. 1985. Latin Journey: Cuban and Mexican Immigrants in the United States. Berkeley: University of California Press.

Reinharz, Shulamit. 1983. Experiential Analysis: A Contribution to Feminist Research. In

Theories of Women's Studies, edited by Bowles and Klein, pp. 162–91. London: Routledge & Kegan Paul.

—— 1992. *Feminist Methods in Social Research*. New York: Oxford University Press.

Riessman, Catherine Kohler. 1987. When Gender Is Not Enough: Women Interviewing Women. *Gender and Society*, 1/2: 172–207.

Roberts, Helen, ed. 1981. *Doing Feminist Research*. London: Routledge & Kegan Paul.

Romano, Octavio I. 1968. The Anthropology and Sociology of the Mexican American. *El Grito*, 2: 13–26.

Rosaldo, Renato. 1989. *Culture and Truth: The Remaking of Social Analysis*. Boston: Beacon.

Segura, Denise A., and Beatriz M. Pesquera. 1992. Beyond Indifference and Antipathy: The Chicana Movement and Chicana Feminist Discourse. *Aztlan: International Journal of Chicano Studies Research*, 19: 69–92.

Sierra, Christine M. 1992. Hispanos and the 1988 General Election in New Mexico. In *From Rhetoric to Reality: Latinos and the 1988 Election*, edited by O. de la Garza and Luis de Cippio. Boulder, Colo.: Westview.

Stacey, Judith. 1988. Can There Be a Feminist Ethnography? *Women's Studies International Forum*, 11/1: 21–7.

Strathern, Marilyn. 1987. An Awkward Relationship: The Case of Feminism and Anthropology. *Signs*, 12/2.

Thorne, Barrie. 1979. Political Activist as Participant Observer: Conflicts of Commitment in a Study of the Draft Resistance Movement of the 1960s. *Symbolic Interaction*, 2/1: 73–88.

Wax, Rosalie H. 1979. Gender and Age in Fieldwork and Fieldwork Education: No Good Thing Is Done by Any Man Alone: *Social Problems*, 26/5: 509–22.

Weston, Kath. 1991. *Families We Choose: Lesbians, Gays, Kinship*. New York: Columbia University Press.

Zavella, Patricia. 1987. *Women's Work and Chicano Families: Cannery Workers of the Santa Clara Valley*. Ithaca, NY: Cornell University Press.

—— 1988. The Politics of Race and Gender: Organizing Chicana Cannery Workers in Northern California. *Women and the Politics of Empowerment*, edited by A. Bookman and S. Morgen, pp. 202–24. Philadelphia: Temple University Press.

—— 1989. The Problematic Relationship of Feminism and Chicana Studies. *Women's Studies*, 17/1–2: 23–34.

Zinn, Maxine B. 1979. Field Research in Minority Communities: Ethical, Methodological, and Political Observations by an Insider. *Social Problems*, 27/2: 209–19.

10

Contingent Stories of Anthropology, Race, and Feminism

Paulla A. Ebron

Beginnings

Deliberations, meditations: On the subject of anthropology and on the intersection of feminism, black feminism.

Suggested frame: "autoethnography," interpreted here as an exploration of the intersection of autobiography and anthropological practice.

Critical question: What are the terms under which one can proceed to address these subjects?

Through an intimate consideration of both form and content, I explore the topics of anthropology, feminism, black feminism, and autoethnography. It is my position that an autoethnographic approach must track back and forth between a personal sense of the way things were, the *memory* of events, on the one hand, and on the other, the institutional markers, texts, and features of public culture that provide guideposts and social referents of that experience. Autoethnography

raises questions surrounding personal memory and its relationship to social history. The intersections between the self and social history and the cultural artifact of institutional structures serve as the scaffolding for mapping a social history of anthropology and feminism.

A memory: At age thirteen I discovered Zora Neale Hurston's autobiography, *Dust Tracks on a Road*.[1] This book introduced me to anthropology and the importance of African American culture kept alive in folkways and stories. These stories were exotic to my Northern imagination – magical in their apparent Otherness. They created a world outside of the terrors of junior high school. I would visit the central library and order Hurston's books from Special Collections, for she had not yet become the popular icon we have known of late. Her writing raised new questions: What was the relationship of black women to creative writing? Who had permission to authorize and convey the experiences of the black community? For many, I know that the answer was simple: It was the men of the Harlem

Renaissance, who presented themselves, and were represented by scholars, as the legitimate voice for the race. Although I now have adopted a more critical stance toward Hurston's views, it is this memory, an embodied moment, that pointed me toward anthropology as a discipline. Hurston's work created a space for me to imagine black women as critical voices amid a world that dismissed black women's vision of community.

Yet Hurston, for all her guiding insight, could never have imagined the social, political, economic, and intellectual developments that allow us to speak of a black feminist anthropology today. My memory of her story cannot erase the texts, politics, and subjectivities of sixty years. Rather, my reflections upon the intellectual and social debates that have informed the context in which my own ideas developed provide a "partial truth" of this social history.[2] Yet the reflexive mode of presentation I use obliges a self-conscious effort that I also be attentive to details that get mobilized to recount the trajectory of my ideas: What is the process of my presentation, of selection, and the ordering of the "facts"? How are temporality and location integral to the story I convey?[3]

These concerns are present even as I introduce the general direction of the essay. Indeed, my commitment to interpreting the relationship of feminism(s) to anthropology is my contribution to the broad analysis of how ideas about feminism and race, and scholarship are always unfolding in relationship to larger historical processes and social events. Indeed, it is useful to note the shifting terms under which black feminism as a category can now be naturalized. The early efforts of cultural critics Barbara Smith, Hazel Carby, bell hooks, and Patricia Hill Collins, along with the countermove by others toward the use of the alternative term *womanist*, helped the notion of black feminism circulate in wide-ranging debates. In no way, however, should these uses of the term *black feminism* be collapsed into a single meaning or invocation. I trace this formation of black women's subjectivity in multiple ways that parallel this history of changes in our understanding of the social location of women, categories at once viewed only as

relations among women and men, to a more recent shift toward the use of the term *gender*. This later use finds the concept of gender to be an important analytic category. It allows one to see the intersection of gender with other power-laden social relations.

As an anthropologist, my research is sparked by an interest in representation (that is, the making of Otherness) and performance (or the enactment of self) as they relate to the social history of the African Diaspora. This interest also draws me toward issues that surround the politics of contemporary Africa. Thus, I chose The Gambia as the site for my research because of its significance for African Americans.[4] Like many, I was strongly influenced by Alex Haley's *Roots* journey in the seventies, which traced his history to a Gambian village.[5] But I have also resisted the hegemony of African American representations of the African continent.[6] As a result, a few of the research questions that have guided me are: How do we make sense of African political economies? How is The Gambia – one of the smallest countries – to survive economically without an agricultural or industrial base? How is culture turned into a commodity?

In my work I analyze representations of Africa from varied sources both in and beyond Africa. What do scholars, political leaders, African Americans, and Gambian cultural performers mean by African culture? After all, although Africa is the place of memory for those in the African Diaspora, it is also more than that – it is a place with its own varied histories and debates.

More recently, these concerns have taken me to explore the memory of Africa in the southeastern region of the United States. How have we imagined African influences in the most "African" of sites in North America? Here again, I am interested in the role of Africa in African American discourses of identity formation. But I also cannot forget the political position of sub-Saharan Africa in international debates over geopolitical relations. These interests were formed early in my intellectual trajectory through a particular political moment in which I learned the importance of an internationalist perspective that moves back and forth between particular sites of meaning, but with a sense of wide-ranging, transnational contests over power and meaning.

The privileging of race in the U.S. political arena, or the urging of one to choose a single identity over another – as if these social selves could be shed of the histories that created them – seems, in hindsight, reductive at the very least. We have now grown accustomed to the notion of multiple and shifting selves;[7] identities are now viewed as relational and situation-sensitive. As I chart my relationship to a political and social history in which feminism and race form central moments, both personally and institutionally, I use this history to illustrate the varied course of notions of blackness and feminism I have had to navigate. Feminism and black political movements figure critically in the kinds of questions that have emerged during this process and that now inform my professional practice as an anthropologist.

Emergent Forms

This reflexive account owes much to recent challenges by a number of constituencies that became critical of the objectifying gaze of social scientists.[8] Critics objected to a scholarship that presented itself as a transparent window of explanation that somehow magically, and apparently effortlessly, hid the conditions of knowledge production.[9] In particular, I argue, feminist anthropology, postcolonial studies, and minority discourses have been in the forefront of such critiques. They especially have been instrumental in stimulating an exploration of various literary forms that critique the objectivist stance and ethnographic authority. Without access to mainstream audiences, these discourses developed more self-consciously reflexive ways of articulating their perspectives: through autobiography, fiction, plays, poetry, and wives tales. They created counternarratives to stand alongside the accounts found in conventional anthropology. Now these forms, at one time considered of marginal status, are currently subsumed (and legitimated) under the rubric of reflexive anthropology. Minority discourses, along with feminism and postcolonial studies, are but a

few of the perspectives that are influential to my framing context; their importance signifies a particular era in the history of anthropology, during a time when the discipline formed new intersections with public discourses and events that have helped to simultaneously constitute theories of "the social" and subjectivities.

Geopolitical Imaginations

Any genealogy of subaltern-oriented theories and research projects (such as this one) is compelled to take into account shifts in world political events, and, in particular, the impact of anticolonial struggles after World War II. This is the context in which many North American anthropologists found themselves rethinking the discipline in the mid-1960s.[10] For anthropologists of the Atlantic rim, early moments in Pan-Africanism and the impact of anticolonial struggles informed a diasporic sense of connections among disadvantaged peoples. This was a moment of internationalism in which solidarity was imagined in relation to communities and nations. Its specificity becomes even clearer if we juxtapose it against contemporary concerns with global networking and the erasure of communal and national boundaries.[11] Indeed, global connections in this earlier moment drew a map of connections that imagined a critique of neocolonial relations. The postwar anticolonial struggles of the Third World were about building nations. Similarly, the social movements of the 1960s, both in the United States and in other parts of the world, depended on imaginings of nations and nation-like communal units.[12] It is in this context that progressive scholars and activists turned to counter-hegemonic nation building as a context for thinking about and participating in the elimination of inequality and oppression. Nationalism invigorated a counter-movement and provided a logic for political struggle.

During my first experience of college in the 1970s, like so many students at the time, I searched for a more meaningful set of options than what seemed to present itself at the small, overwhelmingly white, liberal arts college I attended. As members of the generation just after the Civil Rights and Vietnam era, my cohorts and I were inspired by the example of those slightly older than ourselves to work for social and political transformation. My path was involvement in black cultural politics.

Black cultural political groups drew inspiration from a range of sources, but a notable inclusion in most was the selective appropriation of Pan-African cultural artifacts. From Nigeria we borrowed Yoruban religious practice; from Ghana, initiation ceremonies; from Tanzania, a political vision based on scientific socialism. These elements were fused into a cultural stew that became for many African Americans "a bit of Africa" in the New World.[13] The interest in Africa, although having long roots among Africans of the Diaspora, was in this moment inspired by the move of many African nations toward independence from colonialism.[14] This fact served to facilitate a more politically engaged appreciation of Africa's significance to the identity of African Americans.

A memory: One of the striking aspects that framed my involvement in political work during this early phase of my life was the expected place of black women in organizations focused on community development. These organizations, like their white counterparts, placed women in the position of being expected to make coffee while, of course, the men talked over important ideas. I recall protesting one day, along with other women, this bourgeois notion of women's roles. We pointed out the apparent disjuncture between worlds that marked a domestic/political divide; this forced a heated debate. Although I was much younger than the other women, I understood the significance of the moment: coming to terms over our location within these social groups offered another moment of consciousness of what it meant to be black and a woman; ours was a dual identity recognized in private but erased in public debates, where the single category of importance was race. This collective action proved that the women were no longer willing to buy the prevailing justification commonly offered up by even these progressive black men: "when the Community becomes liberated, then we can deal with women's issues."

As I became more involved with political issues, I joined the activities of groups concerned with advancing African American self-determination. Again the influence of nationalisms from the Third World was ever present in that the rhetoric of many newly liberated countries stressed political and economic sovereignty. For African Americans, our move toward self-determination took various forms, including the development of independent black schools, seen as viable alternatives to the failures we associated with public schools; political theater groups that provided ways for us to use art as social commentary and thus provided a critique that might enable transformation; and adult literacy programs, inspired by Paulo Freire's work on literacy with Brazilian peasants.[15] These were projects that powerfully shaped my sense of politics and culture.

This was also a moment when progressive U.S. domestic politics drew strength from a number of internationalist movements to formulate a plurality of visions of social change. In the United States and Europe, Third World elite students joined forces in a cosmopolitan anticolonial enterprise whereby the national fates of various colonies and ex-colonies were viewed as intertwined; some of these students, who were "citizens of the world," became important nationalist leaders.[16] U.S. movements imagined themselves, too, within this nationalist cosmopolitanism. Inspired by Third World intellectuals, many U.S. black activists understood themselves to be part of a more cosmopolitan moment.

A memory: We walked the streets of a northeastern urban community as if we were in tropical Africa, yet it was in the cold of November: women in sandals and wearing long skirts and tops – bubbas and lappas – in "African" cotton fabric designed to mimic batiked cloth. Still, these "African" clothes would mark our distinctiveness as neither Black Muslim nor ordinary resident of the neighborhood. We were in the service of a political vision: "Who are we?" we asked rhetorically. And we answered ourselves, "African people." "What must we do? Make change." And the room, again filled with cosmopolitan cultural analysis, sat divided – men on one side and women on the other.

Inspired by these internationalist commitments, I enrolled in a program in Pan-African studies. Here, the desire for connections beyond the borders of the nation helped frame my intellectual agenda. I began to learn both about Africa and about the African Diaspora. Even in these emergent years of African and African American studies programs, a sometimes-productive tension existed between African intellectuals from the continent, who stressed historical difference, and scholars of the Diaspora, who, more often than not, generated static, albeit celebratory notions of Africa. The debate rippled outward as black intellectuals from the Caribbean raised the importance of a class analysis, interrupting the privileging of race as the primary political division in U.S. discussions. These tensions pointed to the lack of an easy affinity between peoples of the Diaspora and those throughout Africa, particularly once one acknowledged Africa as a place in historic time and not simply a symbol used to further African American political desires. On the one hand, as students, we began to appreciate the fact that Africa was a diverse continent, made up of several countries and not a singular place. Colonialism affected regions differently, and class and cultural differences did matter. On the other hand, we experienced the excitement of having intellectual and political conversations across these divides.

Pan-African studies gave me new ideas about the meaning of scholarship. Notions of the Diaspora were created in the dialogue among African, African American, and Caribbean scholars and usefully de-territorialized views of culture, allowing scholars to recognize connections between Africa and those dispersed in diaspora. This idea of diasporic connection continues to inform contemporary scholarship. The creative amalgam of scholars across the lines of tension formed an imagined constituency for dialogue and debate about the culture and history of Africa and its Diaspora. This constituency stretched the academy, allowing scholarship to flower outside historic Western genealogies. Indeed, although I have become critical of many of the original concepts and frameworks we used in this early period, I continue to write into this space of

multiple intersections, which invigorates me as a scholar despite the internal critical tensions, and I remain committed to merging political and intellectual questions.

Despite the radical astuteness of the political groups with which I worked at this time, none acknowledged feminism as an important social movement; nor was feminism mentioned in my academic classes. Instead, I first came to feminism through my own independent reading, a practice not uncommon among social activists who frequently formed their own eclectic reading groups to discuss certain issues. Perhaps because I first learned feminism through books, I have always been particularly appreciative of its critical force. That is, I have been captivated by feminism's ability to analyze and critique other forms of social mobilization. I also came to feminism at a time when women of color, both in the United States and around the world, were critically impacting feminist theories as well as feminist political actions. In the Third World, feminists were questioning the politics of postcolonial nationalisms.[17] In the United States, the influential women-of-color anthology *This Bridge Called My Back* was stirring up discussion of the inadequacy of white women's priorities as well as those of men of color for challenging the intersection of gender and race hierarchies.[18] Also important in this conversation was the collection *All the Women Are White, All the Blacks Are Men, but Some of Us Are Brave*.[19] In this context, I came to share a critical understanding of the kinds of nationalism that informed black cultural politics and Pan-African studies, as well as so many other social movements of those times.

Nationalism, as Benedict Anderson points out, creates a horizontal community of "brothers."[20] During the late 1960s and early 1970s, excitement at building a progressive community elided questions about who was excluded. When spokespeople for the community were put forward, they invariably were men who had the power and authority to command. It took women some time to figure out how to intervene. Although African American women were critical participants in black nationalist struggles, they were often relegated to the place of support staff with the promise that questions of gender equality would be addressed in time. With the advent of feminism, however, a powerful critique by Third World women of the limits of the nationalist political vision gradually trickled into the United States. In Africa, women who were part of national struggles in Namibia, Algeria, Mozambique, and Guinea Bissau raised questions about gender equity under postcolonial and socialist nationalisms. Women of color in North America and Europe as well began to describe their own positions within progressive social movements as problematic. Feminism intervened in African American struggles by asserting questions of gender over race; it also interrogated the place of other inequalities, such as those based on class and sexuality, within progressive contexts. All in all, feminist critique forged a new kind of scholarship composed of new ideas and frameworks, and a new constituency.

By the time I enrolled in graduate school in anthropology, feminist scholarship was an exciting, historically layered, and diverse intellectual movement. Guided by my commitments and research interests, I found myself particularly compelled by several strands in feminist scholarship: first, the sympathetic but critical analysis of oppositional nationalisms; second, the insistence on the simultaneity of multiple structures of power and difference in forging identities, both in everyday life and in social movements; and third, the importance of cultural differences in gender understandings and practices, but with tensions and disagreements characterizing the interaction of even similarly disadvantaged groups. Let me elaborate.

Given my background, I was especially excited by feminist analysis of the disjuncture between oppositional nationalism and feminism. I found myself examining the use of "Africa" in African American cultural politics, inspired by an essay by historian E. Frances White in which she analyzed the role Africa played in African American nationalist discourses and showed how imagined "African customs" were used to advocate subordinate, supportive positions for African American women.[21] So-called African ideals were assembled from a continent-wide sweep of cultural attributes, many of which, indeed, were mythic. Stressing "complementarity" between women and men, such ideals solidly reaffirmed the importance of male leadership for African American communities. White also introduced the concepts of "discourse" and "counter discourse" to interrogate the combination of progressive and conservative rhetorics that enlivened black nationalism. Her analysis allowed me to see the persuasive logics as well as the limits of oppositional discourses that develop their own regimes of truth.

These challenges posed by attention to gender by White and those critical of nationalism's exclusions and of difference were not merely confined to a re-examination of relations between men and women in the context of nationalist politics but extended beyond. Criticism was also levied against the kind of feminism that took gender as a singular, structuring principle of inequality but ignored the class and racial differences that critically shape women's relationship to each other.[22] An influential essay by Bonnie Thornton Dill incisively examined differences among women that positioned them as unequal partners in feminist struggles.[23] She highlighted the importance of race and class in the basic construction of gender differences and argued that we can only understand women's concerns if we pay attention to the multiple structures of inequality. According to Dill, these are differentially formed within certain historical contexts and impinge upon women in a myriad of ways; her analysis proved that the "feminist" concerns of black maids and their white employers were not parallel.

Cultural differences among women emerged as significant in a panoply of feminist critical discourses. By the late 1980s, feminist anthropologists had gathered a wealth of cross-cultural ethnographic data on women's roles and status. Contributions such as *Gender and Anthropology*, a compilation of feminist research results, curricula, and pedagogy edited by Sandra Morgen, marked a turning point in anthropology. This work made it obvious that anthropologists could no longer responsibly argue about culture and society without paying attention to gender as both a system of ideas and a system of inequalities that divided communities even as it sought to unite them. Similarly, the collection *Uncertain Terms:*

Negotiating Gender in American Culture, edited by Faye Ginsburg and Anna Tsing, explored the dimensions of differences among women in U.S. contexts.[24] What each of these seminal works attested to was that at the boundaries between communities, gender forms are a particularly important arena for coercion, conflict, and negotiation.

It is this concern with gender negotiation that has informed my own research into how disadvantaged groups often relate to each other – whether in solidarity or tension – through concerns about gender. For example, I have argued (together with Anna Tsing) that African American and Chinese American gender issues communicate awkwardly, forming dense misunderstandings.[25] Such "border zones," as Chicana feminists have shown, may be particularly creative and laden sites for the negotiation of gender.[26] It was precisely these feminist concerns – with critical understandings of nationalism, multiple bases of identity and difference, and complex cultural borders – that informed my research in The Gambia. My goal in this process was to locate and appreciate cultural tensions and interruptions rather than to assimilate them into a singular understanding of cultural communities or political causes. Yet, as is invariably the case, the contingencies of fieldwork brought me to new insights as well.

An Apprenticeship in Difference

Despite my immersion in feminist theory, I did not anticipate the degree to which gender would become important as I gathered data during my field research. I assumed I might draw upon the "honorary male privilege" that many Western women researchers have reported as contributing to their high status in non-Western settings. Indeed, in a preliminary, short visit to The Gambia, I had taken a male role; I had apprenticed with a Mandinka *jali* (praise-singer) to learn to play the *kora* (harp).[27]

Kora playing is restricted to Mandinka men, although women jali sing and play a metal bar called the *neo* or tap the side of the kora to keep rhythm. Like a male apprentice, I studied with a teacher six to eight hours every day. During this time, we sat in the company of his friends: men who generally went about their business and occasionally interrupted to comment on my practice. At the end of my initial visit, I traveled to my teacher's village and played for the village head and residents, who all graciously accepted the foreigner's feeble attempts to play the kora.

On a second visit to The Gambia, as a "proper" researcher, in a collaborative relation with the national Oral History and Antiquities Division of the Ministry of Youth, Sports and Culture, I wanted to abide by local understandings of the place of women. During this visit, it seemed inappropriate for me to spend hours in the company of men as I had done previously, following them to their performance events while rejecting the proper training of women. Indeed, this second visit led me to understand the centrality of gender in creating the kinds of access to knowledge that constituted the social, material, economic, and political difference between men and women. This became particularly evident as I listened to repeated stories about a previous woman researcher who had assumed male privilege to learn an instrument. I found it disconcerting to hear her described as pushy, aggressive, obnoxious, and inappropriate. It was said she would do anything to obtain her goal. To complicate matters, my work took place during a moment when foreign women were seen as having come to The Gambia to look for sexual partners.[28] People constantly spoke to me of women travelers from the North who, according to Gambian standards, had no sense of propriety and social decorum. With this input, I decided rather quickly that I could not present myself as a "male" apprentice. In actuality, to maintain my respect within the Gambian context, I chose to be a "proper" woman.

These discoveries about the politics of gender changed my research agenda. Instead of learning about jali training from the "inside," by learning how to play the kora through apprenticeship, I decided to work on jali interactions with others. I relinquished the prospects of the "intimate" portraits I had first imagined and instead focused on the rhetoric through which *jaliya* operated. Jali are professional performers whose job it is to make others perform. They must move their patrons to action – and in return, the patrons must perform as patrons. Similarly, in relation to the tourist trade, jali see their job as moving their audiences into an appreciation of African history and culture. But their audiences also must perform properly. The inter-caste and inter-group rhetoric of jaliya is thus a key aspect of its imagined effectiveness. Words are powerful vehicles that can both give and take away. The jali's message can either create or ruin a patron's reputation. In taking up this study, then, I found I did not have to relinquish my interest in the construction of social categories and processes; rather, I approached them from a new angle that proved, I am persuaded, more informative.

A memory: An African American woman traveled to The Gambia for a brief time. During her visit to the home of an important man, accompanied by her sponsor who was considerably younger, she entered into a debate with us about polygamy. This newly arrived visitor wondered why women were not allowed to pursue whomever they wished exactly as men did. I sat frozen in my seat, unable to do more than side with the older gentleman in my silence. He seemed taken aback by her forthright ability to comment on a place in which she had lived for three days. In retrospect, I wonder: Where was my feminism then? Could I have at least offered a mediating opinion? At the time, I was struck by the woman's efforts to talk about what every woman, according to her, should be able to pursue – "her own hopes, dreams, and aspirations." Even African American women are capable of espousing the unproblematic notion that "sisterhood is global." But at that moment in The Gambia, such a universalizing concept of feminism confronted its limits. And persuaded by this line of thought, the visitor moved beyond the expected rules of the family and challenged the codes of behavior that were more restrictive for women than men.

As I listened to the stories that surrounded her, her mythical reputation far surpassed her actions. Yet, I was enlisted by her sponsor to "speak with her." As he explained, his reputa-

tion was on the line: "What if something bad were to happen to her?" But rather than "speak with her," I tried to understand the issues from the points of view of both people involved. After all, from a societal perspective, she was a woman traveling around without the protection of a man; as such, she appeared to be someone without moral scruples. Yet from her point of view, she desired to learn as much about Africa as she could in the short time she had to visit The Gambia. To accomplish this meant moving about and meeting lots of people. Although I did not take up the role of interlocutor, the incident confirmed for me that my own practices during my stay needed to conform to the conventions. And I believe it was more than an issue of cowardliness and simply reproducing power differences between men and women. It was an issue informed by historical relationships between the West and Africa – which, at the very least, led me to proceed with caution, while being carefully attuned to geopolitical power and the realization that gender and national status created layers of complexities in any position one might take.

These moments of debates over the social and global status of men, women, caste and class, and professional performers and their interlocutors raise the importance of performance as more than an enactment; how might it be viewed, rather, as an analytic category? Performance, of late, is a topic that has captured the anthropological imagination, for it challenges the idea that there are foundational moments that fix identities in an immutable state. Judith Butler's deconstruction of the sex/gender system offers a critical intervention in dominant understandings of gender through her exploration of notions of male and female as givens.[29] Indeed, Butler argues that gender is performed, learned, and enacted in relationship to a social expectation. Similarly, Patricia Williams, among others, offers a critique of essentialized notions of race by showing the discursive construction of race and gender in social/legal arenas.[30] These critiques provided the foundation for me to analyze performance in two contexts: the official contexts of the jali artists with whom I worked, and the performance of status and identity in social interactions. Such key insights of feminist scholarship extend the earlier moment in the seventies, characterized as the study of the anthropology of women,[31] that analyzed the relationships between men and women but without necessarily challenging the biological basis of what is meant by male and female – that is, what these social locations might mean in themselves as performances.

My project required me to be self-conscious about my own performances of gender and status even as I was being retrained by the jali with whom I interacted. I was never able to take gender and status for granted, and I observed how gender and status were presumed givens for the jali. Many of the "intimate" insider accounts of jaliya told by male musicologists naturalize the travel and mobility of men.[32] Portraying their jali informants only as talented performers, they erase the making of insider and outsider – that is, those with access to specialized jali knowledge and those who, instead, must be moved to appropriate action. Yet this is the central premise of jaliya.

The conditions of my research also pressed me to appreciate the blurred border between formal performance and the performance of everyday life. Reminded daily of the lines that divide men and women, jali and patron, elite and commoner, young and old, and Gambian and foreigner, I did not imagine a "safe" homogeneous community in which the performance of difference became irrelevant. Instead, I saw how jali as professional performers taught their interlocutors how to perform gender, status, ethnicity, and national difference. These lessons occurred not only in formal performances and ceremonies but also in the interactions of everyday life.

One of the most striking arenas for thinking about this issue turned out to be my interviews with jali. Jali used interviews as performance spaces in which to tell not only of their professional talents but of the gender and caste considerations that gave them their status as jali. They prevailed upon me and my assistant to treat them as proper patrons should – with generosity and making opportunities. They made me self-conscious about my own performance as a researcher and, indeed, about the performative nature of describing cultural

difference. This became (and continues to be) a central theme of my research.

Gambians pressed me to reflect on race as well as gender and caste as performances. They had their own ideas about African Americans, and they performed them. I became the audience for a number of performances by my Gambian friends in which they portrayed African Americans as depicted in the Hollywood movies they had seen repeatedly. In both memorized lines and scripted gestures, they could reenact scenes that portrayed African American men as tough gangsters who would kill for what they wanted. Because of my immersion in critical, reflexive anthropology, I had thought a great deal about Western stereotypes of Africans; I had thought much less about African stereotypes of Americans. Of course these images would come from the endless circulation of Hollywood action films. Just as African Americans' sense of Africa is formed within powerful media-generated images, so, too, in The Gambia, African Americans are represented in media styles. But what was particularly striking was how Gambian "performers" performed the common role allotted African Americans by using their bodies and voices to mimic violent gun-slinging thugs and criminals.[33] In another representation, they mimicked pop music icons Michael and Janet Jackson, singing their songs and copying their styles. Performance was the medium through which cultural difference was assimilated and understood.

These experiences, by calling my attention to the importance of performance in communicating about cultural difference, enabled me to formulate a new understanding of the themes that have characterized reflexive and critical anticolonial anthropology. In this regard, an important work that I see in dialogue with mine is Carolyn Martin Shaw's *Colonial Inscriptions*.[34] She is attentive to issues of representation, but then she moves to trace the material effects of the interface between white African colonial presence and the making of Kenyan culture. This work is exceptional because in most discussions of colonialism's interface, representations of cultural difference have been seen mainly as textual and communicated in books.[35] Although texts have been important in creating stereotypes of difference, face-to-face interactions as well as formal ceremonies and scripted events are also key features of making difference. Attention to performance allows me to see how difference is negotiated and reformulated in context-specific enactments. It also makes it clear that representations need not be static and timeless.

Performance, then, is particularly relevant to my research because it is a central trope through which the continent of Africa is known in the rest of the world. Non-Africans imagine an Africa of performance. In turn, African performers, such as jali, build on this trope in presenting an "Africa" they want imagined through their performances. Everyday performances of difference augment and reformulate these understandings by making them part of personal repertoires. Thus, I came to appreciate that representations are always a performative issue. Today, performance critically informs my research not only in studying jali but also in studying the place of Africa in a global imagination.

From Research to Writing

When I returned to the United States to write about this research, I faced new challenges of navigating scholarly constituencies. One divide of particular concern for my research trajectory was the separation between African studies and African American studies. Historically these have been different worlds.[36] Until recently, African American students and scholars of African American studies have been actively discouraged from contributing to African studies. Researchers of European background have been considered more objective. Because of this history, many African American scholars have gone their own direction; indeed, they have emphasized the critique of objectivist standards of scholarship. Thus, somewhat different epistemological standards have come to characterize the two fields. African studies scholars have often imagined their challenge as impressing the European and North American historians and sociologists who still set disciplinary standards. They are particularly concerned, in this context, with "setting the

record straight" using rigorous standards of scholarship. In this light, archival records and demographic data appear solid, while oral history must be used very carefully to avoid its distortions. In contrast, African American studies has stressed the knowledge that can be gained outside of dominant conventions of scholarship. African American scholars find memory, oral history, and ritual performance particularly interesting sources of alternative knowledge. It is difficult to navigate across these differences. My solution has not been to evaluate each of these approaches but rather to show how each one contributes to cosmopolitan discourses of culture and, thus, to the making of contemporary history.

A feminist approach has also figured prominently in my work; I have come to appreciate the influences of gender analysis in allowing me to critique dichotomous categories of male and female and also to raise critical questions about the ease with which we sometimes rely on "the evidence of experience."[37] But there is one critical place where these, perhaps at times, abstract notions of feminist theory are able to speak to the world about the predicament of women in the throes of the global economy – my final retrospection.

A *memory*: Mariama, a Gambian friend, arrived in the Bronx, New York, and lived with family members. After she had been here for a few months, we talked on the phone. She said, "It's so dangerous here in New York. People are running around with guns. I hardly ever go outside; I only go just to get food at the store. It's so dangerous. I often wish I was at home." When I spoke with her after several more months, Mariama told me of her working conditions in a factory. The doors were locked all day. The women were stuck inside without any fresh air and it was so hot in there. "But Paulla," she said, "what can we immigrants do? No one can say anything. We're all just here." This is an issue of contemporary concern: the making of a United States citizen! The conditions of being a recent part of the African Diaspora are often times obscured from view by the hegemonic presence of African American dreams of homeland. Feminism is both a theory and a practice. This memory reminds me that all of the issues

I have discussed through this auto/ethnographic approach are more than academic issues; critical stakes were and are involved in our stories about global relations.

In bringing closure, I suggest that similar to the ways form and content are linked in my presentation, our lives as feminists, anthropologists, scientists, and social scientists are positioned in cross-cutting debates wherein public responsibility and intellectual pursuits critically interface. As Donna Haraway suggests in her essay "Situated Knowledges,"[38] acknowledging the conditions under which we produce our ideas only makes for a stronger sense of the research we conduct. In this respect, it has been important for me to show how my research draws critically on my background and training as a black feminist anthropologist. However, I am not simply satisfied with identifying "the power" in an unmediated way. Instead, my sense of gender, to paraphrase Joan Scott,[39] is to find gender a useful category of analysis important for examining power and difference. This notion helps disrupt the imagined homogeneity of women and men and communities of binary opposition. It allows us to notice power-laden cultural intersections at which standards of identity and proper behavior are being actively negotiated. As an analytic category, gender points to multiple intersecting and overlapping structures of identity and inequality. In my work, it allows me to see the *performance* of all kinds of difference, not just of gender but also of caste, class, ethnicity, and the continental representations that define the set of distinctions known as "Africa."

NOTES

1   Zora Neale Hurston, *Dust Tracks on a Road* (New York: Arno, 1942).
2   James Clifford's notion that ethnographies are "partial truths" is fitting here, for one includes yet also excludes many things when writing ethnographies. James Clifford, Introduction: Partial Truths, in *Writing Culture*, ed. George Marcus and James Clifford (Berkeley:

University of California Press, 1986), pp. 1–26.
3   Current interest in travel and displacement has contradictory effects. On the one hand, it can loosen up stable objects – places framed and situated in ethnographies; on the other hand, its presumed fluidity can leave questions about who has access and who can make claims around this imagined mobile community unattended. Theories have the same effect; they can seem to be "traveling," and yet they are also situated moments that need their location specified. See Janet Wolff, On the Road Again, in *Resident Alien* (New York: Routledge, 1997), pp. 115–34.
4   During Alex Haley's visit to The Gambia in the early seventies, he encountered a *jali*, a praise singer and oral historian, who provided a genealogy of the Kinte family. According to the jali, a distant relative of Haley's, Kunta Kinte, was reportedly captured, made a slave, and brought to the United States. Haley's account of the jali's narrative provided for many a moment of intimate (re)connection of African Americans to Africa. The village of Juffrey, where Kunta Kinte reportedly resided, has become the celebrated site in the quest for a homeland. For further discussion, see Paulla Ebron, *Performing Africa* (Princeton: Princeton University Press, 2001).
5   Alex Haley, *Roots* (New York: Doubleday, 1976). Also see *Roots: The Next Generation*, written by Alex Haley and produced by Stan Margulies and David Wolper in 1977 for Warner Brothers.
6   When one traces out the history of the African Diaspora, the more common set of references are made to those whose relatives departed from Africa long ago. Much more difficult to place in the history of Diaspora is the migration of Africans at the present moment. In may ways, we in the Diaspora feel we own this history of the continent, yet at the expense of intimate engagement with the present. A notable exception is the organization TransAfrica and its activities.

7 See, for example, Gayatri Spivak, *In Other Worlds* (New York: Routledge, 1987).

8 Notable among these are Sidonie Smith and Julia Watson, eds., *De/Colonizing the Subject: The Politics of Gender in Women's Autobiography* (Minneapolis: University of Minnesota Press, 1992); Carolyn Steedman, Writing the Self: The End of the Scholarship Girl, in *Cultural Methodologies*, ed. Jim McGuigan (London: Sage, 1992), pp. 106–25; Ann Gray, Learning from Experience: Cultural Studies and Feminism, in *Cultural Methodologies*, pp. 87–105; Deborah Reed-Danahay, *Auto/ethnography* (New York: Berg, 1997); and Frances Marcia-Lees, Patricia Sharp, and Colleen Ballerino Cohen, The Postmodernist Turn in Anthropology, *Signs*, 15/1 (1989): 7–33.

9 See, for example, Renato Rosaldo, *Culture and Truth* (Boston: Beacon Press, 1989).

10 Essays about these concerns have been published in two notable anthologies: Talad Asad, ed., *Anthropology and the Colonial Encounter* (New York: Humanities, 1973); and Dell Hymes, ed., *Reinventing Anthropology* (New York: Vintage, 1972).

11 I view the distinction here as one focused on the circulation of political visions and social moments in contrast to the globalism of today, which takes inspiration from the spread of corporate, primarily US culture.

12 Benedict Anderson, *Imagined Communities* (London: Verso, 1991).

13 Two influential texts of the period were Roger Bastide, *African Civilizations in the New World*, trans. Peter Green (New York: Harper and Row, 1971); and Julius Nyerere, *Ujamaa: Essays on Socialism* (Dar es Salaam: Oxford University Press, 1968).

14 Texts such as Amilcar Cabral, *Revolution in Guinea* (New York: Monthly Review, 1970), and the struggle in Mozambique against the US company Gulf Oil were of key interest to those involved in political struggles on the African continent during this period.

15 See Paulo Freire, *Pedagogy of the Oppressed* (New York: Seabury Press, 1970).

16 One important account among many is that of Aimé Césaire, who recounts his time in France with a number of Third World and French intellectuals and philosophers, including Jean-Paul Sartre. See Aimé Césaire, *Une voix pour l'histoire* (San Francisco: California Newsreel, 1994). These students would later return to their countries to become heads of state after the colonial regime. One of the features mentioned by a tour guide in London was a plaque left at the site of a former restaurant in which Ho Chi Minh had worked as a chef, "until he changed careers."

17 Some of these works included Gloria Joseph and Jill Lewis, *Common Differences* (New York: Anchor/Doubleday, 1981); Audre Lorde, *Zami: A New Spelling of My Name* (Trumansburg, NY: Crossing Press, 1983); Elly Bulkin, Minnie Bruce Pratt, and Barbara Smith, *Yours in Struggle* (Brooklyn, NY: Long Haul Press, 1984); and Michelle Cliff, *Claiming an Identity They Taught Me to Despise* (Watertown, Mass.: Persephone Press, 1980).

18 Cherrie Moraga and Gloria Anzuldúa, *This Bridge Called My Back* (New York: Kitchen Table Press, 1983).

19 Gloria Hull, Patricia Bell Scott, and Barbara Smith, *All the Women Are White, All the Blacks Are Men, but Some of Us Are Brave* (Old Westbury, NY: Feminist Press, 1987).

20 Anderson, *Imagined Communities*.

21 E. Frances White, Africa on My Mind: Gender, Counter Discourse and African American Nationalism, *Journal of Women's History*, 2/1 (1990): 73–97. Two collections of essays on African women that were less critical of nationalism as a discourse but that addressed the place of black women in Africa and the Diaspora are Rosalyn Terborg-Penn, Sharon Harley, and Andrea Benton Rushing, eds., *Women in Africa and the Diaspora* (Washington, DC: Howard University Press, 1987); and Filomina

Steady, ed., *Black Women Cross-Culturally* (Cambridge, Mass.: Schenkman Publications, 1981).

22 Linda Gordon, in a recent essay, frames these two moves as Difference I and Difference II, the former referring to differences between men and women and the latter to differences among women. See Gordon, The Trouble with Difference, *Dissent*, 46 (spring 1999): 41–7.

23 Bonnie Thornton Dill, Dialectics of Black Womanhood, *Signs* 4 (summer 1979): 543–55.

24 Sandra Morgen, ed., *Gender and Anthropology* (Washington, DC: American Anthropological Association, 1989); Faye Ginsburg and Anna Tsing, eds., *Uncertain Terms* (Boston: Beacon Press, 1990). See also Ann Bookman and Sandra Morgen, eds., *Women and the Politics of Empowerment* (Philadelphia: Temple University Press, 1990). For a parallel analysis of gender in history in non-Western contexts, see Margaret Strobel and Cheryl Johnson-Odum, eds., *Expanding the Boundaries of Women's History* (Bloomington, Ind.: *Journal of Women's History*, 1992).

25 Paulla Ebron and Anna Tsing, In Dialogue: Reading across Minority Discourse, in *Women Writing Culture*, eds. Ruth Behar and Deborah Gordon (Berkeley: University of California Press, 1995), 390–411.

26 Gloria Anzaldúa, *Borderlands/La Frontera* (San Francisco: Spinsters/Aunt Lute Books, 1987). See also Hull, Scott, and Smith, *All the Women Are White, All the Blacks Are Men, but Some of Us Are Brave.*

27 By suggesting that I could occupy male status, I mean that I was able to draw upon the privilege of status and mobility that many men can take for granted; of course class status and age-ranking systems temper some men's abilities to move about freely. This "harp" is one of the two key instruments associated with the jali tradition. The second instrument is the xylophone-like *balaphon*.

28 Paulla Ebron, Traffic in Men, in *Gendered Encounters*, eds. Maria Grosz-Ngate and Omari Kokole (New York: Routledge, 1997), 223–44.

29 Judith Butler, *Gender Trouble* (New York: Routledge, 1990).

30 Patricia Williams, *Alchemy of Race and Rights* (Cambridge, Mass.: Harvard University Press, 1991).

31 Anthologies relevant here include Rayna R. Reiter, ed., *Towards an Anthropology of Women* (New York: Monthly Review, 1975); and Michelle Rosaldo and Louise Lamphere, eds., *Women, Culture, and Society* (Stanford: Stanford University Press, 1974).

32 An early work on Gambian jali by musicologist Roderick Knight is one example. See Knight, Mandinka Jaliya: Professional Music of the Gambia, PhD dissertation, University of California, Los Angeles.

33 For a penetrating look at Hollywood's creation of stereotypic roles for African Americans, see Robert Townsend, *Hollywood Shuffle* (Los Angeles: Virgin Vision, 1987).

34 Carolyn Martin Shaw, *Colonial Inscriptions* (Minneapolis: University of Minnesota Press, 1995).

35 Edward Said, *Orientalism* (New York: Vintage, 1978), is a critical work in signaling the centrality of the Other in the Western imagination.

36 A thoughtful discussion of this history can be found in Deborah Amory, African Studies as an American Institution, in The Politics of Identity on Zanzibar, PhD dissertation, Stanford University, 1994.

37 Joan Wallach Scott, Evidence of Experience, *Critical Inquiry*, 17 (summer 1991): 773–97.

38 Donna Haraway, *Simians, Cyborgs, and Women* (New York: Routledge, 1991).

39 Joan Wallach Scott, Use of Gender as a Category of Analysis, in *Gender and the Politics of History* (New York: Columbia University Press, 1988), 28–50.

Part III

Confronting the USA

Introduction

Anthropological study of the United States and the West has a longer history than is usually believed, with early work by such scholars as Lloyd Warner demonstrating the power of applying anthropological methods and theories to the familiar. As I discussed in the Introduction to this volume, social critique has a long and honorable history in American anthropology; many contributions to this area have come from women anthropologists like Margaret Mead and Hortense Powdermaker who pioneered ethnographic research in the US and sought to apply their work to contemporary social problems.

But the field still possesses a mysterious myopia about its engagement with the culture its scholars come from. Anthropology has been firmly linked, therefore, not only in the public imagination but among practitioners of the discipline with the exotic, remote, and unfamiliar. Fieldwork has been assumed to be legitimate only if it is physically arduous and even life-threatening; anthropologists valorize primitive living conditions, the necessity to learn obscure languages, and other insignia of success in environments that are authoritatively not here. Despite, then, the continuous tradition of anthropological studies of the near-at-hand, anthropologists persist in framing such endeavors as "not really" anthropology.

When feminist anthropology burst on the scene in the early 1970s, debates about where fieldwork could properly be conducted had flared up over concerns with risks to vulnerable populations and possible ethical abuses. The possible use, for example, of ethnographic data to target groups for military intervention was intensely debated in the 1960s and 1970s as the Vietnam War became the focus of political conflict. Scholars were also concerned with the ethical demands of informed consent. Could impoverished, uneducated people actually "consent" to being studied or, more pointedly, could they refuse? What decision would they make if they knew that the anthropologist would achieve professional goals by telling their stories? How should anthropologists manage sensitive information that might be vital to their interpretations – evidence of criminal or insurgent activity, for example, or knowledge of behavior that might expose a group to ridicule or criticism in the West (Hymes 1972)?

It was in this context that feminist anthropologists began to discuss their obligations to study their own society, to subject the people around them, including the powerful, to othnographic inquiry. The work that emerged from this period, and that has continued into the present, has put study of the familiar on equal footing with examinations of the exotic, even as the anthropology establishment remains pro-foundly ambivalent about such efforts. A glance at the job listings in any issue of the *Anthropology Newsletter* will confirm that specializations in US cultures or non-Native populations of North America are virtually never the focus of faculty searches, and work in Western Europe is often regarded as equally unattractive. To be sure, scholars who have centered their work in the US do sometimes find positions, but it is likely to be their theoretical focus rather than their area specialization that makes employment possible. In other instances, turning one's attention to domestic populations that are arguably "exotic," such as recent immigrants or members of racial and ethnic minor-ities, allows their work to be perceived as acceptably "anthropological." In other words, the model of the exotic as the proper object of anthropological scrutiny continues to have considerable currency, even after many scholars – both feminists and others – have turned their attention inward.

The essays reprinted in this section offer some significant examples of how feminist anthropological interventions into local meanings and the seemingly familiar have offered radical new perspectives on gender and culture more generally. They also demonstrate variations in the ways feminists have approached their own society, corresponding to particular theoretical agendas and changing over time. Louise Lam-phere's article, for example, speaks to the central concern of many feminist anthropo-logists who sought to question rigid divisions between the domains of home and work, and also to make explicit the issues that face women in diverse workplaces. Her analysis demonstrates the artificiality of efforts to disengage work and home, with particularly vivid accounts of how women deploy their personal lives to create a social space at work. Thus the notion that these domains are contradictory and necessarily oppositional is effectively undermined, as she directs us to look instead at the creative ways women make these two parts of their lives mutually intelligible.

Faye Ginsburg's article is a now classic account of the narrative strategies of anti-abortion and pro-choice women locked in conflict over the opening of an abortion clinic. She skillfully mines the women's narratives for their underlying themes, finding that both groups of activists frame their stories in terms of themes embedded in accounts of their reproductive careers. Most notably, despite sharp divisions between the political philosophies that characterize the women, their narratives are framed in distinctively similar language. Stories of commitment to a cause are understood by both groups of women to proceed directly from their maternal identities and from the commitment to caring they see as integral to those identities. Both opposition to abortion and support for abortion rights, then, are justified in terms of a rhetoric of community responsibility and compassion. While such similarities may seem surprising because of the intensity of the debate between the two groups of activists, Ginsburg shows that their larger cultural experience, particularly with respect to fundamental categories of gender, are more formative of their positions than specific political differences.

In her article on ethnically correct dolls, Elizabeth Chin leaps into an area that might seem far from what anthropologists typically do. She takes on a discussion that has more usually been dominated by psychologists, who have argued for the psychological benefits to black children of playing with dolls that "resemble" themselves. She fully engages the now iconic work of Kenneth and Mamie Phipps Clark on racial self-image, work that has long supported the notion that children should play with ethnically correct dolls. But Chin shows that black girls in New Haven played with white dolls in ways that revealed far more complex constructions of race than those well-meaning toy makers may consider. The girls, all from low-income families, transformed their white dolls to make them fit into their worlds. She argues that their ability to shape the reality of their toys to fit their needs speaks to their understanding of their position in the hierarchy of race and class. The girls know that other significant attributes of their experience of gender are never represented in their dolls – fatness, pregnancy, abuse. Identification with their dolls is not a process, then, that is facilitated by any particular physical appearance, but rather is embedded in their ability to express their social understanding through play. In this paper, Chin both takes on the historically silent population of children, finding a way to make their words accessible, and asks how anthropologists can address persistent structures of class and racial inequality in the US.

The final contribution to this section, Charis Thompson's analysis of kinship discourse in a fertility clinic, represents a rapidly expanding area of application for feminist anthropology. In the constantly changing "gee-whiz" world of assisted reproductive technologies, fundamental ideas about the nature of kinship and relatedness must enter into conversation with technological methods unheard of just a few years ago. Thompson is among those anthropologists who have been drawn into this world, conducting ethnographic research in fertility clinics and other related facilities in a wide range of settings. In the US, questions of access loom large, given the uneven distribution of health care entitlement. Each new technology generates anxieties among patients as they seek to find a way to make that presumably most natural of quests – for parenthood – fit comfortably into a world of high-tech interventions. In particular, assisted reproduction involves a cast of characters beyond the hopeful parents in the process of achieving a pregnancy. Thompson uses the concept of "strategic normalizing" to convey the process prospective parents undertake, most notably in terms of their efforts to make the various contributors to the process "belong" as some kind of kin. Rather than undermining existing areas of kinship ideology, these parents reconfigure outsiders as insiders, thus finding a way to pre-serve family and reproduction as an enterprise based in kinship.

All of these studies, and others that take up similar issues, use anthropological theory and method to address current social issues of concern in the US – women's experience in the workplace, the fierce debates over abortion that have polarized many communities, the reproduction of race and class among children, and the expanding arena of assisted reproduction technologies. Like articles in the next sec-tion, they emerge from their authors' commitment to convey the cultural creativity with which women and girls address the challenges they face. They also reveal funda-mental concerns with allowing otherwise unrepresented constituencies to express their ideas and to demonstrate the active agency they take on their own behalf.

REFERENCE

Hymes, Dell ed. 1972. *Reinventing Anthropology*. New York: Pantheon.

11

Bringing the Family to Work: Women's Culture on the Shop Floor

Louise Lamphere

In the past several years, feminist anthropologists, sociologists, and social historians have produced a new literature on women's work outside the home. Inspired by Harry Braverman's *Labor and Monopoly Capital*,[1] many of us focused our attention on the labor process, examining the ways in which women workers responded to the demands of a particular production process, the process of deskilling, or a particular pay system in a given set of blue-collar or white-collar jobs.[2] Attempting to overcome the emphasis on management's use of technology to degrade and deskill work, which in Braverman's book seems to overwhelm an essentially passive work force, we isolated strategies of resistance and ways in which women workers actively dealt with their work situation.

This, in turn, led to the full examination of informal relationships on the shop floor, in the office, department store, or hospital, and to an analysis of women's work culture.[3] In some respects this was a rediscovery of the informal work group first studied by Elton Mayo and his colleagues in a series of experiments at the Hawthorne plant of the Western Electric Company in the 1930s.[4] But rather than viewing management/worker conflict as a result of miscommunication to be solved by more attention to universal aspects of human relations, the new feminist research has paid greater attention to the way in which work groups and management/worker relationships are shaped by the historical development of an individual industry or occupation and by the ways in which management policy has responded to a particular phase in the development of capitalism.

Although the Hawthorne studies and many subsequent analyses of the informal work group (such as those by Donald Roy and Michael Buroway[5]) focused almost completely on the shop floor and basically ignored the gender of the workers being studied, the fact that the workers we were studying were also women became something that demanded attention and analysis. Perhaps because our culture assumes that women are primarily daughters, wives, and mothers, researchers could not discount the impact of these family roles on

From Louise Lamphere, "Bringing the Family to Work: Women's Culture on the Shop Floor," pp. 519–40 in *Feminist Studies*, 11 (1985). Reprinted by permission of the publisher, Feminist Studies, Inc.

women employed outside the home. Women's employment seems inextricably linked to their position in the family,[6] and employment may not have had a liberating effect on women because of these family roles. Leslie Woodcock Tentler, for example, argues that workroom socializing (such as the sharing of oranges and chocolates in a turn-of-the-century garment shop) underwrote a romanticized dream that women would marry and leave the paid labor force.[7] Sallie Westwood makes a slightly different point in her study of a contemporary apparel plant in England.[8] She also examines women's informal socializing and describes the rituals surrounding weddings and engagements that take place at work or among work friends after hours. Westwood argues that women's work culture offers a context of resistance to management, but does so through celebrations that confirm a traditional vision of femininity (which is essentially patriarchal and assumes the subordination of women). Both these authors take the position that the informal work group was essentially conservative, fostering either complacency at work or traditional family and gender roles. On the other hand, Karen Sacks has argued that it is precisely a set of values and social connections forged in the working-class family that made it possible for a group of female black hospital workers to stage an effective walkout and begin a union drive in a southern city.[9]

My own research follows very much in the tradition of Sacks's analysis, emphasizing the nature of female resistance at work. In previous papers, I have focused primarily on women's strategies on the shop floor which relate most closely to the labor process itself, to the piece rate system of pay and to management's control of the work situation. In this article, however, I will explore a set of strategies that grow out of women's roles as wives and mothers and link work and family. I talk about these strategies as "bringing the family to work" or "humanizing the workplace." These are shorthand phrases for two processes: the first is the organization of informal activities often focusing on the female life cycle (such as birthday celebrations, baby and wedding showers, potlucks and retirement parties); and the second is the use of workers' common identities as women, wives, and mothers in interworker communication. Through both processes, women workers make friends of strangers and bridge cultural and age divisions within the work force.

Although Sacks's research highlights an example of family values and informal socializing feeding into resistance, I would argue that this does not always happen. Whether these strategies of "bringing the family to work" become part of a strong work culture "in resistance" depends on the entire work context. This includes workers' strategies generated directly out of the labor process or the system of pay on the one hand, and management's overall counterstrategies on the other. Where management is concerned to build a loyal work force, keep a union from gaining a foothold in a plant, or even co-opt the nature of the informal work group itself, women's informal activities may suit management's purposes rather than those of workers. In both cases (a resistant and a procompany work culture), these strategies building on women's family and gender roles provide some of the "glue" that holds participants in a work culture together. Because women workers are hired as individuals without regard to their age, marital status, and personal connection to other workers, women must build relationships between strangers into relations between coworkers who have common interests. Depending on the overall work context, these relationships can become part of an overall effort to counter a set of management policies, or they may feed into management's efforts to dampen down worker/management conflict.

The Complex Nature of Work Culture

In this article, I take the position, following the work of Nina Shapiro-Perl,[10] that although a work situation may generate resistance, it may also generate adaptation and consent. The formation of a work culture involves a complex set of relationships between cultural meanings or ideology on the one hand, and behavioral strategies or practice on the other. It also involves both management policies and worker responses to those tactics and strategies.

Susan P. Benson and Barbara Melosh have outlined these dual characteristics of work culture as follows. According to Benson and Melosh, work culture includes

the ideology and practice with which workers stake out a relatively autonomous sphere of action on the job.... A realm of informal, customary values and rules [work culture] mediates the formal authority structure of work places and distances workers from its impact. Work culture is created as workers confront the limitations and exploit the possibilities of their jobs. It is transmitted and enforced by oral tradition and social sanctions with the work group. Generated partly in response to specific working conditions, work culture includes both adaptation to and resistance to these structural constraints.[11]

In my own work, I have focused on "strategies" as a term to characterize the way in which women work at both an ideological and a behavioral level to actively cope with management policy.[12] In some strategies, women act to redefine management's view of a situation, primarily by manipulating cultural meanings, as for example, countering a floor lady's explanation of how easy it is to "make money" on the piece rate system. Other strategies, although communicated through a system of shared meanings, involve behavioral tactics such as keeping careful track of one's own output as a way of dealing with the piece rate system and management's manipulation of it. Usually, however, strategies involve an interaction between cultural meanings and behavior. For example, a system of informal work rules that helps workers to share work equally and dampen down competitiveness involves both a set of norms and purposive behavior actively sanctioning those who disregard the norms, bringing them into line. In outlining strategies that bring the family to work, I will examine behavior as well as cultural meanings. Both are important in creating ties between workers otherwise divided by age, marital status, and ethnicity.

Work culture is only relatively autonomous; it emerges in relation to management strategies. Management has a set of goals radically different from those of workers: increases in output for the same wage, reduction of turnover, the decrease of conflict between management and workers, or the creation of a work force loyal to the company. How plant managers, supervisors, floor ladies, and personnel managers implement these goals through a series of strategies depends on the industry, the production process, and the economic climate. However, management will probably manipulate cultural meanings or replace a work force's set of meanings with an alternative set. Or management may institute its own set of activities, particularly in the informal sphere, thus replacing the activities spontaneously organized by women. The relationship between worker strategies and management tactics can be seen in two contexts – one in a New England apparel plant studied in 1977 and the other in a series of apparel and electronics plants studied in the Southwest in 1982–3.

The data for the first part of this article are derived from my experiences as a worker in an apparel plant in New England in 1977 when I was engaged in a research project on "Women, Work, and Ethnicity in an Urban Setting."[13] During a period of five months (interrupted by a work stint in the plant's warehouse and by a two-month layoff), I was trained to "set sleeves" on little girls' dresses and toddlers' T-shirts. As a participant-observer, I was able to observe women's strategies for dealing with the piece rate system of pay, was socialized into a worker (rather than management) view of the production process, participated in the enforcement of informal work rules, and was a part of several informal work groups. In Rhode Island, most women worked in ethnically mixed, linguistically segregated workplaces in declining industries often located in old textile mills. In the unionized plant where I worked, "bringing the family to work" took place through informal friend-ship networks, union-sponsored activities (like the Christmas party and a weekly lottery), and management-condoned events (that is, those organized through the department with the help of the floor lady). The major function of these activities was to build ties between workers of diverse backgrounds.

In the Southwest, we have been studying women workers in newly built electronics and apparel plants, in a context where industry is relatively new to the economy and where wages for women are often higher than those available in the service sector where many working-class women are employed.[14] We gained our information through formal interviews with plant managers and women workers. Thus we did not participate in women's work culture, but only asked about it during interviews held in workers' homes. Although we were never able to observe birthday parties, showers, potlucks, or the exchange of pictures, we ascertained when such events were held and who organized them. They seemed to function, like such events in Rhode Island, to bring women of different backgrounds together. However, in several cases, these activities seemed orchestrated by the management for the purpose of building a loyal work force.

Due to the different natures of each project (one based on participant observation and the other on in-depth interviews), the data have led me to emphasize two different but related points. In Rhode Island, through working "on the shop floor," I was able to actually see women's strategies of resistance in action and to attend the occasions where women's life cycle events helped women to cross ethnic boundaries, particularly between Portuguese and non-Portuguese women of French Canadian, Polish, Italian, and other backgrounds. Elsewhere, I have published a fuller account of how strategies of "bringing the family to work" fit into an overall culture of resistance. Although I and other members of our research group in the Southwest were able to visit factories and get a "feel for the atmosphere of a particular plant," our data were gathered through in-depth interviews with working mothers. I have been placed in the position of inferring that much of the same "bridging" takes place through potlucks, birthdays, and showers that unite Hispanic, Anglo, Southeast Asian, and black women. But what is so striking about the data from the Southwest is how women's work culture is being shaped by management strategies, particularly in the context of an anti-union climate in two of the plants we studied. Further discussion of the New England and southwestern data will clarify the relationship between resistance and co-optation in these two contexts.

Celebrations on the Shop Floor in Rhode Island

The Rhode Island apparel plant where I worked in 1977 had been established in the 1930s by a manufacturer of children's wear who moved his production facilities from New York to New England to take advantage of the work force available from widespread mill closings in the textile industry. The plant was unionized in the 1950s and taken over by a large conglomerate in the 1970s. As the older women workers retired, rather than moving production facilities South, the management hired recent Portuguese and Latin American immigrants. The personnel manager described the sewing departments as "predominantly Portuguese." "They are the backbone of our sewing operation," he explained. In this plant, as in virtually all apparel plants, the work force was 80 percent female, and workers were paid by the piece. Beginning workers made the minimum wage of $2.35 an hour in 1977, those working at 100 percent efficiency made the base rate of $3.31 an hour, and experienced workers may have made as much as $4.00 an hour. Strategies for coping with the piece rate system and management's manipulation of it were an important part of women's work culture.

In addition to the Portuguese workers mentioned by the personnel manager, there were a number of women of other ethnic backgrounds: Polish, French Canadian, Italian, Irish, and English. Ethnic and age divisions were reflected in the informal and relatively stable groups of workers who met together during the lunch periods and the two breaks each day. For example, there were several clusters of Continental Portuguese, as opposed to those from the Azores, who clustered around their machines, drinking coffee and eating sweet rolls during the morning break. Also there were several groups of Polish workers, many of whom were first-generation immigrants. Women of second- and third-generation French, Italian, Irish, or English backgrounds often formed mixed groups. And finally there were clusters of young, unmarried high school graduates. (In our department, this group included two girls of French Canadian descent, a second-generation Portuguese, and a girl who said she was of several different ethnic backgrounds: "Heinz 57 Varieties," as she put it.)

In these groups, a fair amount of anti-Portuguese sentiment was often expressed, ranging from statements such as: "There are too many Portuguese being hired now," to an incident where a male warehouse worker complained that one of the Portuguese women "smelled bad." One Polish coworker, while riding to work with me, told a "Portuguese joke," which forty years ago would surely have been a "Polish joke" with the same story line, but with Polish immigrants portrayed as dumb and inept.

There were inter-ethnic tensions around the piece rate system as well. Employers hired Portuguese women because of their reputation as hard workers, but non-Portuguese workers often accused them of "rate busting." For example, one worker commented that the Azorean woman who sewed the elastic waistbands on dresses "ruined that job for everyone." In other words, she worked so fast that the piece rate was lowered, and workers had to increase their output to make the same pay. "She didn't miss a dime," and "she makes more money than anyone else on the floor," another worker commented. For their part, Portuguese workers often felt discriminated against and said that American workers did not work hard enough.

The divisions apparent in the structure of break groups and the attitudes expressed in them were crosscut when women gathered together to celebrate life cycle events that often focused on their family roles as wives and mothers. Marriages and the birth of children were celebrated with showers, usually organized by a group of friends. These women collected a small amount from members of the woman's department or other acquaintances. They then bought presents, wrapped them, and presented them as a surprise during the lunch break. Retirements were celebrated in a more extensive way with pastry for morning break and a special lunch at noon time. Retirements and sometimes showers were organized along department lines, often through the help

and certainly with the knowledge of management (such as the department floor lady). Especially in the department-organized functions, but also when friends initiated the activity, monetary contributions and the signing of a card cut across ethnic lines.

Leslie's baby shower provides a good example of how such non-work time events integrate workers of diverse ages and ethnic backgrounds. It was organized by her two friends, who collected the money from a wide range of women, as well as from her department coworkers. Later that week they bought the gifts – a car seat, a high chair, and a baby carriage. Then during one lunch break, the friends brought the huge, wrapped boxes down the center aisle and placed them by Leslie's machine, waiting until she returned from the ladies' room. Half way down the aisle, she realized what was happening. Perhaps a little embarrassed by all the attention, Leslie hesitated and was at a loss for words; one of her friends began helping her open the gifts. One of the Portuguese women picked up the yellow ribbon that came off the first package and pinned it on Leslie. She exclaimed, "Oh, Jesus," on opening the gifts, and finally pulled out the card to look at it. She thanked everyone, and newcomers to the crowd peered over others to see what the gifts were. "Let's see what we got you," the woman who served morning coffee said, while Leslie's floor lady looked on. More admirers came by as Leslie's two friends began to stuff the gifts back in their boxes. The buzzer rang, ending the lunch break and sending everyone scurrying back to their machines. Although organized by the clique of young high school graduates, Portuguese women in Leslie's department clearly had contributed to the gifts and stood by admiring them.

In our own department, Rose's retirement party was an all-day event, and our work was almost interspersed between the breaks, rather than the other way around. During the morning break, the floor lady presented Rose with a corsage, and we all had doughnuts and homemade coffee cakes. Rose also received a card with $60.00 from the department collection and another $60.00 from workers in other departments. Lunch brought another round of partying (including hamburgers ordered from a fast-food restaurant) and a visit from Angela, Rose's best friend who had retired several months earlier. After lunch Angela made the rounds of the department, stopping by each machine and talking to each of her ex-coworkers, whether English or Portuguese speaking. Her general comment on leaving was that she "missed all my girls." The mood of the whole day was one of departmental festivity. Despite the underlying tensions between Rose, Angela, and some of their Portuguese coworkers – which had surfaced several times over the spring and summer months – the retirement party was an occasion for crossing ethnic lines and expressing, despite a language barrier, feelings of solidarity.

On other occasions, women brought their family lives into the work situation by showing pictures of their families to those who worked at nearby machines, sharing news about an illness in the family, discussing vacation plans, and recounting an important event such as a wedding or confirmation. The showing of pictures, usually during morning or afternoon breaks, was one way in which women were able to communicate across ethnic lines. For example, several weeks after the summer vacation Vivian brought her wedding pictures to work. They were taken during her trip to Portugal where she married the man she had been engaged to for several years. During the morning break she showed them to our floor lady and her clique. Then she returned to her own Portuguese-speaking group and turned the pages for them, explaining who the godparents and various relatives were. Several Portuguese women came over from adjacent tables when Vivian opened the album, so she began her explanation over again. Sharing the wedding pictures gave non-Portuguese workers a glimpse of Portuguese culture and cemented relationships with Portuguese co-workers. It seemed an appropriate follow-up to the wedding present the department had given Vivian two weeks before.

When Lucille's sister died, we all heard immediately, guessing that something was wrong when she failed to show up for work one Tuesday morning. A sheet was circulated for each to sign and put down a contribution (usually $0.25 or $0.50). Then the money was collected to pay for flowers. When Lucille returned to work the following Monday, as she came around to each worker delivering their repairs, she thanked each one, greeting many with a kiss, even those who did not speak English well. Such department-wide expressions of support brought workers of different ethnic backgrounds together.

The celebration of special events and the sharing of family pictures were ways in which women workers "humanized" their workplace, bringing their family life into the industrial setting. Almost all the collections were for life cycle events (weddings, baby showers, retirements, and deaths), some of them specifically celebrating woman-centered activities (such as a marriage or the birth of a baby). These celebrations involved a concrete set of activities that brought women together during nonwork time (breaks and lunches) within the workday. In addition, the events created a set of shared cultural meanings centered on workers' experiences as women. In an ethnically diverse workplace, such shared meaning cannot be assumed. In fact, the meanings surrounding the roles of bride, wife, mother, or widow are very different for Azorean and Continental Portuguese women than for U.S.-born women of other ethnic backgrounds. Many Portuguese women probably had not participated in a baby shower before coming to the United States (and perhaps not before becoming involved in one at their place of work). Similarly, a village wedding in the Azores or on the Continent will be surrounded by a different set of rituals and customs than a wedding in a New England French Canadian parish. The sharing of pictures is perhaps the best example of the ways in which women make concrete these different versions of what it is to be a wife or mother and help build an expanded cross-cultural definition of these roles. In bringing family life into the workplace, at both a conceptual and behavioral level, women workers make connections with others. They make strangers into acquaintances and within the circle of one's break group, they make acquaintances into friends.

In a work setting where the piece rate system drove workers apart and where ethnic divisions were clear, with inter-ethnic tensions just beneath the surface, these events helped to consolidate relationships. On balance, I would argue, they fed into a women's work culture characterized by resistance, rather than one dominated by loyalty and consent. In the first place, the piece rate system and its manipulation by management generated an informal set of work rules and strategies for coping with the piece rates that were passed on to new workers. In the second place, the plant is unionized. Although the union in 1977 was not as active as it might have been in creating a cohesive body of workers through informal events, and although Portuguese participation in the union seemed low, the union's presence did provide a formal method for grievances and an arena for communicating company tactics to workers in other parts of the plant, warehouse, and knitting mill. Finally, the recent acquisition of the company by a conglomerate brought in a less paternalistic management, at the same time alienating many of the floor ladies, who perceived the new managers as "not knowing what they were doing." Thus, although many showers and retirement parties were organized through the departments and with the consent of the floor lady, these activities were not linked with any overall management/employee program, and a floor lady was often perceived as "one of the girls" rather than allied with the "bosses." Thus, the presence of the union and the identification of floor ladies with their subordinates, along with the "bridging function" of women's informal celebrations, supported a work culture in resistance.

Thus it was not surprising that, in 1979, women workers from the sewing plant participated in a wildcat strike. During the fall when the contract was being renegotiated, there were at least ninety local issues that remained unresolved, including a number of grievances concerning piece rates. Just three days before the vote on the contract, a wildcat strike erupted. Workers from the knitting mill and warehouse apparently spearheaded the strike, but a number of sewers who called in sick the first day participated in a picket line for the next two days and even defied a back-to-work court injunction on the last day of the wildcat.

Workers voted down the national contract by an overwhelming 834 to 118 votes, although it was accepted on a national level. Local members were disenchanted with the union, which since 1979 has worked hard to regain the support of the workers. However, worker resistance was also focused on the company that had been stepping up its tactics to squeeze workers' wages and employ more temporary workers, eroding union strength. Because I was not employed by the company at the time of the strike, I could not ascertain exactly how informal group structure related to militancy, but the participation of both Portuguese and non-Portuguese women sewers in the strike is consistent with the kinds of resistance and attempts to create solidarity across ethnic boundaries I witnessed two years earlier.

Women's Work Culture in the Southwest

My recent research on women workers in the Southwest demonstrates the place of the "family" aspects of women's work culture in a very different economic context, one of "Sunbelt Industrialization." The city's economy is based primarily on military and government jobs and the city's position as a commercial center. Within the last ten years, the city has begun to attract branch plants of large corporations, primarily in apparel and electronics. Recently, several plants have been built with modern equipment, richly carpeted offices, and the latest in computer technology. They seem very different places to work than small jewelry, textile, or apparel plants located in old textile mills. More importantly, several plants are involved in management experiments. These experiments range from introducing "quality circles" (where workers suggest changes in the production process), to the use of "flex-time" (where workers can opt to start work any time between 6:30 and 8:00 A.M.), to the reorganization of the plant work force into production teams that help make decisions about hiring, firing, shift schedules, and vacations.

There is a wide variety in the products produced in these plants with apparel workers producing surgical sutures, jeans, and leather jackets, and electronics workers engaged in the production of silicon wafers, computer terminals, digital phone equipment, home heating thermostats, and parts for jet engines. We interviewed women who were employed in semiskilled production jobs and who were also working mothers. Wages among the apparel workers we interviewed ranged from $4.00 to $7.00 an hour with an average wage of $5.50 an hour. Electronics workers earned an average of $5.75 an hour, with the exception of one unionized plant where women were earning between $9.00 and $11.00 an hour. The work force was composed predominantly of Hispanic women native to the Southwest, who spoke English as their first language. Anglos (white Americans of a variety of backgrounds) were the second largest group, and there were small numbers of blacks, Southeast Asians, and native Americans in the work force.

Although it has been difficult to obtain exact figures on each company, most plants seem to have a female labor force that is about 55 to 65 percent Hispanic. In apparel plants, where women are sewers or make surgical sutures, the labor force is 80 to 90 percent female; and in the electronic plants, the proportion of female workers may be as low as 60 percent, depending on the numbers of technicians, engineers, and other male-dominated jobs that are part of the production process. Only two of the electronics and apparel plants in the city are unionized. Examples from three companies will illustrate the ways in which management is seeking to penetrate the structure of the informal work group and co-opt the celebration of women's events. In all three settings "bringing the family to work" takes place in the context of management's efforts to build a loyal work force.

Women's Work Culture in the Context of Building a Loyal Work Force

In plant A, an electronics plant, women workers place components on boards as part of the assembly of electronically regulated thermo-stats. In a work force that is predominantly female, and with a substantial proportion of Hispanics, informal activities (such as potlucks and birthday parties) not only help to bridge ethnic differences, but also fit in well with management's attempt to build a loyal work force in the context of a philosophy of participation. In this plant, unique in the whole company, the management is fostering a climate of openness and trust, making as few distinctions as possible that would result in status differences. For example, there were no reserved parking spaces for management, no time clocks, and equal benefits for production and salaried employees. In the management philosophy, there were no "hourly" employees, only salaried workers, though production workers were paid on a weekly basis. The plant held quarterly "all-employees meetings" where managers presented information about the business and financial aspects of the company, what was happening in the plant, and what new products were being introduced. Employees were able to vote on the plant holiday schedule, the starting time for the day shift, and a number of other plant policies. Finally, the plant manager had monthly "coffee talks" with a dozen employees randomly selected from throughout the plant. These talks lasted a couple of hours and included an open-ended exchange of views on the work situation and management policy.

In the context of this experimental plant, the aspects of women's work culture that "humanize the work place" and bring family roles to work functioned not only to bind women together and break down ethnic boundaries, but also to blur distinctions between employees and management. In addition to structural changes in the organization of work, participative management involved organizing informal gatherings inside and outside work and sponsoring company picnics, dinners, sports teams, and nights at the baseball game. Thus birthdays, showers, and collections for hospitalizations became integrated into building a work force loyal to the company and to management philosophy. In the plant, we interviewed two women in a department with a supervisor particularly involved in creating strong relationships between himself and his women workers, as well as between the women themselves. Mary described how they had decided to deal with birthdays.

> Ya, we were talking about that today. We voted on that again. It depends on each individual department. And we were baking cakes before. But now we just voted on it today where we are all going to put in a dollar a month. And then that way this would be used for the birthdays. The birthdays of the month. We are just going to include everybody's birthday in one month. One birthday...and by putting in a dollar a month we'll have money left over for flowers if people are in the hospital. Or if we want to buy a gift for somebody that's getting married.

Juanita explained the supervisor's role:

> My supervisor's very nice to get along with...you don't find very many supervisors that come and sit down and eat lunch with you and act like he's not even a supervisor, you know...the other day he walked in and says, "Guess what, I'm going to get lunch for all of you tomorrow....My son got ordained Friday and we had so much food left....I'm taking food for my crew tomorrow."...And he brought all kinds of meats and potato salads for us and stuff like that.

The department potluck (where women serve different dishes at lunch in an area of the cafeteria) seemed to be the southwestern hallmark of women's family lives brought to work. Mary remarked that even the supervisor's birthday was an occasion for one potluck. "Sometimes if it's a supervisor's birthday or something, then we would try to have a potluck [for him] during lunch. Then we would bring stuff. Because we have the microwaves and we have plug-ins and refrigerators...we would all have potluck. And we would buy him a gift or we would just have a cake and potluck or something."

In this same plant, potlucks and showers are supplemented by activities planned by the "Company Team Committee." This committee, which included two representatives from each department, received funds from the company to plan the annual picnic and a yearly open house, as well as other events that took place off company time and involved women

and their families in social or recreational activities. At the time of our interviews, women workers were enthusiastic about their jobs, their relatively high wages, and job stability. Although we may have interviewed company loyalists (we were given names solicited by the personnel director through supervisors), nevertheless, these women saw no incompatibility between their informal relationships with other women, their supervisors, and their support of the company as well. The lack of resistance may have derived from the newness of the plant, careful screening of applicants to weed out potential union activists, relatively high wages for women workers, and management's efforts to create an atmosphere that emphasized informal activities, as well as the company's participative philosophy and strong benefit program.

Participative Management, Co-opting the Informal Group and Blocking a Union Drive

Plant B, a plant which manufactures surgical sutures and resembles apparel firms in terms of some aspects of the labor process, also had a "high-involvement" philosophy. Like plant A, benefits for production and nonproduction employees were equal, and all employees were guaranteed pay for a forty-hour week, even if they occasionally missed a day.[15] In addition, the plant manager maintained an "open door" policy where any worker could talk with him about issues of concern. However, unlike plant A where the structure of departments was traditional (such as a large group of workers directed by a supervisor), plant B has gone a long way toward co-opting the informal work group and integrating it into the labor process itself. The labor force in 1982 was 90 percent female and 65 percent Hispanic; beginning workers made $4.80 an hour, and more experienced workers made between $5.20 and $5.80 an hour. Each department was divided into "production teams" of twelve to fourteen workers. Each team had a facilitator (rather than a supervisor), and the facilitators met weekly with the team members to discuss shift schedules and productivity.

Team members were rotated on an individual basis between first and second shift – the exact scheduling worked out within the team. Two team members interviewed prospective employees and future team members, and if the evaluation they brought back to the team meeting was negative, the person usually would not be hired. "Team support" was an important aspect of employee evaluations, along with attendance and quality and quantity of production. After a two-month probationary period, and for each six-month period thereafter, team members were asked to evaluate the behavior of a team member on the job. The evaluations were discussed in the team meeting with weaknesses and deficiencies explored, and the worker was asked to deal with them more effectively. Team meetings were also a place where one's production figures were examined and where each worker talked about how well she was doing in relation to her expected efficiency percentage.

In Plant B, birthday celebrations and potlucks were organized either through a whole department or within a production team. In one department (composed of several teams), the Quality Control woman organized the birthday celebration or the potluck because she was not working on a production quota and was relatively free to walk around and talk to individual workers and collect money. In another department, the team organized these activities. One worker, Linda, said: "Not too long ago we had a birthday box and we all collected a dollar or two dollars and we bought them a cake and then somebody's responsible for buying him a gift and at the end of the team meeting then they cut the cake and open the gift." Because the plant is relatively new, a whole repertoire of company activities had not yet been established. However, the firm had sponsored a Christmas Dance, a summer picnic, and several safety banquets.

In 1982 and early 1983, employees in plant B were involved in a union campaign that raised the issue of whether management policy had steered women's work culture in the direction of company loyalty and in opposition to union membership. The local management was decidedly anti-union and would not have located in the city we studied if it had been a community

with a "strong union environment." The management felt that with a third party (that is, a union) the high-involvement design would lose flexibility. Work rule restrictions were "a big problem with unions," and management felt that relations with the labor force were too structured when there was a union. There is evidence that aspects of the high-involvement design were geared toward keeping the union out of the plant. For example, trainees were carefully screened for "attitude" when they were initially trained at the assessment center. Some workers were uncomfortable with the team meetings, feeling that they degenerated into discussions about personal problems. Others suggested that personality conflicts played a part in team evaluations. As Josie said: "I don't really care for the evaluation but... because there's a lot of... say somebody didn't like you; they would give you a bad evaluation and say that they didn't think you were doing your job... just so you'd get fired."

During the fall of 1982, after a union organizing committee was formed in the plant and after a number of union cards were signed, the personnel administrators began to use the teams as "union-busting tools." A sociologist conducting research on the team system for his Ph.D. dissertation made this charge at a public meeting called by a citizen's monitoring committee to hear complaints and concerns regarding the union drive. In a lengthy statement, he made a number of charges.

For this purpose, facilitators (supervisors) are expected to remain in control of their teams while employees are made to feel that the system is "open" to their suggestions and decisions... teams are used as part of a strategy to "isolate" pro-union employees from their fellow team members. The "isolated" individual can then be dealt with in some fashion: he or she can be fired for not having "team support" (one of the "objective criteria" for termination at [plant B], or for a poor "attitude" or other factors ostensibly unrelated to union support. Yet [the personnel administrator] plainly told me that union support is a factor in termination "although we can never admit it."

The sociologist cited two cases of workers being fired on absence-related reasons as "trial balloons" to see "what the union would do when their supporters were fired." In two other cases, workers were fired for punching into the computer for each other (equivalent to clocking in) while similar offenses by non-union supporters had gone unpunished. The plant manager was quoted as saying that "it would be a good symbolic gesture, a good way to scare other pro-union employees. Even if we have to give their jobs back, it would be worth the hassle to fire them to see what the union would do and to see if it has a desired effect on the work force." For some union supporters, the team meeting became a context in which workers began to ask questions of management and put forward pro-union views. One facilitator stopped meeting with a team because of the strong pro-union views of the members. This same team then organized its potlucks and birthday parties through a friendship network, without the facilitator's help or the team meeting as a context for organizing these events.

In some teams, workers were divided into pro-union and anti-union factions, and this often led to conflict when peers were evaluated in a team meeting and to a split in informal activities. As one pro-union worker explained her situation:

> And we all went into a meeting every Monday. And if you had a gripe, you know, you told everybody. If you didn't like somebody you told everybody.... Like say five people didn't like you 'cause you didn't go eat [at a local restaurant] with them. You know, they'll say that in the team. And forget it, you're on the worst list now, you know, not doing what they want you to do. You see, the majority rules. If you don't go along with them, you're not in a good standing anymore.

This same worker reported that all but one of her work friends with whom she ate and spent breaks were union supporters. "We're always divided, union and non-union." The union drive had an important effect on plant socializing. In the one or two teams that were pro-union, the team remained a strong informal group. For other pro-union workers who were more isolated in their teams, socializing took place outside the team. One woman who felt especially isolated said that "if you're

labeled union, you're no good. If you're non-union, you're good." Union members, she continued, were sometimes excluded from activities "unless you made your own thing, which we did...to show them that we could do it, too, you know. No matter what we believed in, we could still do it." Even so, the management made it difficult for union members to socialize informally with each other or to talk with other employees who had not yet made up their minds about the union. Facilitators often broke up informal conversation groups or went on break with union supporters so that they could overhear or prevent positive talk about the union.

As the union drive accelerated and as a date for an election was set, management stepped up its efforts to keep the union out of the plant. As one worker described it: "For a while there they took us into meetings everyday. For two weeks, to talk about the union. But it wasn't about good talk. They wouldn't let us talk on our behalf. They'd always show films like about strikes...like violence...and all bad things. They would scare the people. And they would never let us come in and show good things or talk about it, you know, what we could offer." Eventually, the union lost in a two-to-one vote. However, they filed over 300 charges with the National Labor Relations Board to protest unfair labor practices and reinstate workers who had been fired. In late December 1983, seven months after the election, a settlement was reached. The company agreed not to engage in unlawful surveillance of union supporters, not to threaten employees with discharge for engaging in union activities, and not to discriminate against union supporters in a number of areas. Discharged employees were to be awarded back pay.

In the case of plant B, management restructured production around small groups or production teams. Facilitators in many cases attempted to create a situation where the team became an informal work group, eating together, celebrating birthdays, and having potlucks. In team meetings, workers would be encouraged to evaluate each other's productivity and their participation within the group. As a supervisor put it:

In the ideal situation, the employees would know exactly what their job was. Their job was to get the product out the best way they could and if they had time to sit down and talk about things, they'd do it. But if they felt that a person was not pulling their weight and making the department look bad, you know, then they'd jump on him.... Like this new group that I've got.... They're coming to me and saying, "Hey, she's not pulling her weight. She's walking around, she's doing this. Hey let's talk about it in a meeting. Let's confront her with it."

In the context of the union drive, such peer group pressure was encouraged not just around production issues, but also to convince neutral workers not to support the union and to isolate pro-union employees from social support. In the context of the team structure in plant B, women's life cycle celebrations helped to reinforce a loyal company-oriented work group.

Women's Work Culture in Support of a Union

"Humanizing the work place" can, of course, be incorporated into a union's program and become part of building strong relations among workers in the context of union membership. This happened to some extent in the apparel plant where I worked in New England, but the possibilities for union use of women's informal celebrations to build stronger ties among workers is best illustrated in one of the unionized plants we studied. In this case, plant C, which produces jet engine parts, the union – rather than the company – had an entertainment committee and publications committee. The union sponsored picnics, retirees' dinners and other social functions, and put out a newsletter. Friendship networks within departments sponsored showers and birthdays. As one worker explained:

I'm getting ready to have a baby shower now. Every time someone dies or there's an illness in the family or, say, one of our people goes out on sick leave, or there's going to be a baby born...even if it's a guy we throw them a shower.... We threw this guy a shower not long ago and we have another one coming

up.... Usually a couple of the women organize it. We have potlucks at Christmas; every Christmas we exchange presents. We have potlucks for Thanksgiving. Sometimes we have potlucks for the heck of it.

To counter management's new emphasis on worker involvement, union members placed themselves on the new "quality circle committees" in order to make sure that the contract was not being violated and to urge workers to put suggestions in the suggestion box. In this way, workers would be paid for suggested changes that benefited the company, rather than the company getting them "free" through the "quality circle" mechanism. In this plant, recreational teams and company-sponsored events were mainly for salaried employees and the union-sponsored and union-controlled activities for production employees. Thus, baby showers, birthdays, and potlucks took place in the context of union membership which built relations between coworkers, rather than pulling workers into closer relations with management.

In conclusion, my research in Rhode Island revealed an important set of links between women's home lives and work situations. By bringing the family to work, women could make connections among themselves and mitigate the distance that age, marital status, and ethnic background created. In the Southwest, much the same process took place where divisions between Hispanic, Anglo, black, and some Asian workers characterized the work force. However, our interviews in the Southwest led me to see the functions of "bringing the family to work" in relation to management policy in general. In some cases, these aspects of women's work culture were "co-opted" by management in order to help build a community of loyal company employees. In other, rare cases, celebrations around family roles were still a part of women creating links with other women in order to "stake out an autonomous sphere of action on the job," distancing themselves from management policy. In this new era when participative management strategies are even being extolled on the pages of popular national magazines, it is important to carefully analyze the relationship between these new management tactics and the work lives of women who are affected by them.

NOTES

1 Harry Braverman, *Labor and Monopoly Capital: The Degradation of Work in the Twentieth Century* (New York: Monthly Review Press, 1974).

2 Louise Lamphere, Fighting the Piece-Rate System: New Dimensions of an Old Struggle in the Apparel Industry; Nina Shapiro-Perl, The Piece Rate: Class Struggle on the Shop Floor: Evidence from the Costume Jewelry Industry in Providence, Rhode Island; and Proletarianizing Clerical Work: Technology and Organizational Control in the Office, all in *Case Studies in the Labor Process*, ed. Andrew Zimbalist (New York: Monthly Review Press, 1977), pp. 257–76, 277–98, 51–72.

3 Susan P. Benson, "The Clerking Sisterhood": Saleswomen's Work Culture (PhD diss., Boston University, 1982); Barbara Melosh, *"The Physician's Hand": Work Culture and Conflict in American Nursing* (Philadelphia: Temple University Press, 1983); Nina Shapiro-Perl, Labor Process and Class Relations in the Costume Jewelry Industry: A Study in Women's Work (PhD diss., University of Connecticut, 1983); Ann Bookman, The Process of Political Socialization among Women and Immigrant Workers: A Case Study of Unionization in the Electronics Industry (PhD diss., Harvard University, 1977).

4 Elton Mayo, *The Human Problems of an Industrial Civilization* (New York: Macmillan, 1933); F. J. Roethlisberger and William Dickson, *Management and the Worker* (Cambridge, Mass.: Harvard University Press, 1939).

5 Donald Roy, Restriction of Output in a Piecework Machine Shop (PhD. diss., University of Chicago, 1952); Michael Buroway, *Manufacturing Consent: Changes in the Labor Process under Monopoly Capitalism* (Chicago: University of Chicago Press, 1979).

6 Louise Tilly and Joan Scott, *Women, Work, and Family* (New York: Holt, Rinehart & Winston, 1978).

7 Leslie Woodcock Tentler, *Wage-earning Women: Industrial Work and Family Life in the United States, 1900–1930* (New York: Oxford University Press, 1979).

8 Sallie Westwood, *All Day, Every Day* (Urbana-Champaign: University of Illinois Press, 1985).

9 Karen Sacks, Computers, Ward Secretaries, and a Walkout in a Southern Hospital, in *My Troubles are Going to Have Trouble with Me: Everyday Trials and Triumphs of Women Workers*, eds. Karen Brodkin Sacks and Dorothy Remy (New Brunswick, NJ: Rutgers University Press, 1984), pp. 173–92.

10 See Shapiro-Perl, Labor Process and Class Relations.

11 Benson, "Clerking Sisterhood."

12 In Fighting the Piece-Rate System, pp. 257–76, I focused on isolating strategies of resistance having to do with the piece rate, with informal work rules, and with "outguessing" management policy.

13 This project was funded by the Center for the Study of Problems, National Institute of Mental Health, Bethesda, Maryland. Grant No. 1 RO1 MH27363.

14 This project, Women's Work and Family Strategies in the Context of "Sunbelt" Industrialization, was funded by National Science Foundation, Grant No. BNS 8112726. Interviews with Anglo women were conducted by myself, while Gary Lemons interviewed their husbands. Patricia Zavella interviewed Hispanic single parents and Hispanic working wives, while Felipe Gonzales interviewed Hispanic husbands. Peter Evans conducted interviews with plant managers.

15 In plant B, however, workers must keep their absences below 4% or face disciplinary action. There are clear rules about calling in tardies and absences, and employees are expected to make up time missed during the same week of an absence in order to keep their absence rate below 4%. Attendance is also an important part of evaluations for pay raises.

12

Procreation Stories: Reproduction, Nurturance, and Procreation in Life Narratives of Abortion Activists

Faye Ginsburg

The residents of Fargo, North Dakota – a small metropolitan center providing commercial and service industries for the surrounding rural area – pride themselves on their clean air, regular church attendance, rich topsoil, and their actual and metaphorical distance from places like New York City. The orderly pace of Fargo's daily life was disrupted in the fall of 1981 when the Fargo Woman's Health Center – the first free-standing facility in the state to publicly offer abortions – opened for business. A right-to-life[1] coalition against the clinic formed immediately. Soon after, a pro-choice group emerged to respond to the antiabortion activities. Each side asked for support by presenting itself as under attack, yet simultaneously claimed to represent the "true" interests of the community. The groups have evolved and fissioned. There are approximately 1000 potentially active supporters on each side and a hard core of 10 to 20 activists.

Broadly sketched, two positions emerged. For the pro-life movement in Fargo, the availability of abortion in their own community represented the intrusion of secularism, narcissism, materialism, and anomie, and the reshaping of women into structural men. Pro-choice activists reacted to right-to-life protesters as the forces of narrow-minded intolerance who would deny women access to a choice that is seen as fundamental to women's freedom and ability to overcome sexual discrimination.

When pro-life forces failed to close the clinic through conventional political tactics,[2] they shifted their strategy. They currently are engaged in a battle for the clinic's clientele. Competition is focused increasingly on winning the minds, bodies, and power to define the women who might choose to violate a basic cultural script – the dominant American procreation story – in which pregnancy necessarily results

From Faye Ginsburg, "Procreation Stories: Reproduction, Nurturance, and Procreation in Life Narratives of Abortion Activists," pp. 623–36 in *American Ethnologist*, 14/4 (1987). © 1999 by University of California Press. Reprinted by permission of University of California Press via Copyright Clearance Center, and the author.

in childbirth and motherhood, preferably within marriage.

The local controversy over the clinic opening in Fargo revealed at close range how the struggle over abortion rights has become a contested domain for control over the constellation of meanings attached to reproduction in America. In the course of fieldwork,[3] it became clear to me that this conflict does not indicate two fixed and irreconcilable positions. Rather, the social movements organized around abortion provide arenas for innovation where cultural and social definitions of gender are in the process of material and semiotic reorganization.

In each movement, then, a particular understanding of reproduction is demonstrated through abortion activism. This was especially apparent in life stories[4] – narratively shaped fragments of more comprehensive life histories – I collected with female abortion activists.[5] Such narratives, which I am calling procreation stories, reveal the way in which women use their activism to frame and interpret their experiences – both historical and biographical. The stories create provisional solutions to disruptions in a coherent cultural model for the place of reproduction and motherhood in the female life course in contemporary America. They illuminate how those dimensions of experience considered "private" in American culture intersect with particular social and historical conditions that distinguish the memberships of each group. In the ways that the rhetoric and action of abortion activism are incorporated into life stories, one can see how cultural definitions of the female life course, and the social consequences implied, are selected, rejected, reordered, and reproduced in new form.

This paper is based on my own fieldwork with local women activists engaged in the Fargo abortion controversy from 1981 to 1983. I chose subjects who were most prominent in local activity at the time and who reflected, in my estimation, the range of diversity encompassed in the active memberships of both pro-life and pro-choice groups in terms of age, socioeconomic status, religious affiliation, household and marriage arrangements, style of activism, and the like. Altogether I collected 21

life stories from right-to-life activists and 14 from pro-choice activists. While most of these people are still active, each side continues to undergo rapid permutations both locally and nationally. Thus, the benefits of in-depth participant observation research must be balanced against the debits of a small sample bound by the conditions of a particular time and setting. In addition, because of space limitations, I can present only a few cases, which are illustrative of themes that are prominent in the narratives more generally. However, my conclusions are confirmed in other qualitative studies of abortion activists (for example, Luker 1984), which also find abortion activism linked to a more general integrative process. For example, in an article discussing the role abortion seems to play in activists' lives, authors Callahan and Callahan write:

> The general debate has seen an effort, on all sides, to make abortion fit into some overall coherent scheme of values, one that can combine personal convictions and consistency with more broadly held social values. Abortion poses a supreme test in trying to achieve that coherence. It stands at the juncture of a number of value systems, which continually joust with each other for dominance, but none of which by itself can do full justice to all the values that, with varying degrees of insistence and historical rootedness, clamor for attention and respect. (1984: 219)

On the basis of such findings, it seems appropriate to use life stories as texts in which abortion is a key symbol around which activists are interpreting and reorienting their lives. More generally, this suggests a model for understanding how female social activism in the American context operates to mediate the construction of self and gender with larger social, political, and cultural processes.

Reproduction, Generation, and Nurturance

Surveys of representative samples of pro-life and pro-choice activists have not established any clear correlations between such activity and conventional social categories. Activists span and divide religious, ethnic, and occupational lines. The core of membership on both sides is primarily white, middle class,[6] and female[7] (Granberg 1981). Ideologically, the connections drawn between abortion activism and other social issues are diverse (Ginsburg 1986: 76–81). Of the life stories I collected from abortion activists in Fargo, in almost all cases, pro-choice and pro-life alike, women described a coming to consciousness regarding abortion in relation to some critical realignment of personal and social identity, usually related to reproduction. Initially, this recognition only seemed to confound the problem of trying to understand the differences between the women on opposite sides of the issue. From accounts of the early histories of Fargo activists, up to the age of 18 or so, it would be hard to predict whether women would end up pro-choice or pro-life in their views. Devout Catholics became ardent feminists; middle-class, college-educated, liberal Protestants became staunch pro-lifers. As I puzzled over the seeming convergences in catalyzing experiences, social backgrounds, and even sentiments – most see themselves as working toward the reform of society as a whole – I began to notice a generational distinction.

The pro-choice activists cluster in a group born in the 1940s. For the most part, they had reached adulthood – which generally meant marriage and children – in the late 1960s and early 1970s. Their life stories indicate that contact with the social movements of that period, particularly the second wave of feminism, was a central experience for nearly all of them. They describe their encounter with these movements as a kind of awakening or passage from a world defined by motherhood into one seen as filled with broader possibilities. For most of these women, feminism offered new resources with which to understand and frame their lives; it provided an analysis, a community of others, and a means for engaging in social change that legitimated their own experience.

By contrast, the right-to-life women cluster in two groups. Those born in the 1920s were most active in pro-life work in the early 1970s. A second cohort, the one currently most active, was born in the 1950s. Typically, this latter group was made up of women who had worked prior to having children and left wage labor when they became mothers. This transition occurred in the late 1970s or even more recently, a period when feminism was on the wane as an active social movement and pro-life and anti-ERA activity were on the rise. This latter group claims to have been or even be feminist in many respects (that is, on issues such as comparable worth). Many describe their commitment to the right-to-life movement as a kind of conversion; it occurs most frequently around the birth of a first or second child when many women of this group decided to move out of the paid work force to stay home and raise children.

Let me clarify that I am not arguing that all abortion activists fall neatly into one or another historical cohort. As is the case in most anthropological studies in complex societies, my study is small and local, allowing for fine-grained, long-term study that can reveal new understandings but not necessarily support broad generalizations. In this case, the appearance of a generational shift, even in this small sample, is intended less as an explanation and more as a reminder of the importance of temporal factors in the dialectics of social movements. In other words, social activists may hold different positions due not only to social and ideological differences. Differing views may also be produced by historical changes, which include their experience of the opposition at different points over the life course. On the basis of my research, I would argue that this might be particularly relevant in conflicts tied so closely to life cycle events. In the narratives, *all* the women are struggling to come to terms with problematic life-cycle transitions, but in each group, the way they experience those as problematic is associated with very particular historical situations. Abortion activism seems to mediate between these two domains, as a frame for action and interpretation of the self in relation to the world. For most of these women, their procreation stories create harmonious narrative out of the dissonance of history, both personal and generational.

In his classic essay "The Problem of Generations," Karl Mannheim underscores the importance of this nexus between the individual life cycle and rapidly changing historical conditions in understanding generational shifts in the formation of political consciousness and social movements:

in the case of generations, the "fresh contact" with the social and cultural heritage is determined not by mere social change but by fundamental biological factors. We can accordingly differentiate between two types of "fresh contact": one based on a shift in social relations, and the other in vital factors. (1952: 383)

The *sociological* problem of generations... begins at that point where the sociological relevance of these biological factors is discovered. (1952: 381).

To use Mannheim's suggestion, one must consider the intersection of two unfolding processes in order to understand what attracts women to opposing movements in the abortion controversy. One is the "biological factors," the trajectory of a woman's sexual and reproductive experiences over her life course and her interpretation of those events. The second is the historical moment shaping the culture when these key transitional points occur. It is this moment of "fresh contact" that creates the conditions of "a changed relationship" and a "novel approach" to the culture that ensures its continual reorganization. Such "fresh contact" is manifest in the self-definition and social actions of women engaged in the abortion controversy, some of whose life stories are analyzed below. Their narratives reveal how the embracing of a pro-life or pro-choice position emerges specifically out of a confluence of reproductive and generational experiences. In the negotiation of critical moments in the female life course with an ever-shifting social environment, the contours of their own biographies and the larger cultural and historical landscape are measured, reformulated, and given new meaning.

Such reconstructing is most marked at critical transitional points in the life course. In situations of rapid change when the normative rules for an assumed life trajectory are in question, these life-cycle shifts are experienced as crises, revealing contention over cultural defin-

itions. In other words, when the interpretation of a particular life event – abortion or more generally the transition to motherhood, for example – becomes the object of political struggle, it indicates a larger disruption occurring in the social order as well. What emerges in the biographical narratives of these women is an apparent dissonance between cultural codes, social process, and individual transformation in the life course. Analytically, then, life stories can be seen as the effort of individuals to create continuity between subjective and social experience, the past and current action and belief.

These orientations provide a useful framework for interpreting the narratives of abortion activists in relation to the social movements that engage them. The battles they fight are loci for potential cultural and social transformation; in life stories, change is incorporated, ordered, and assigned meaning by and for the individual. This process is central to the "changed relationships" of many women to American culture that have generated struggles over conflicting views of the interpretation of gender in the last two decades. Thus, in the case of abortion, two mutually exclusive interpretations and arenas of action are formulated, which give the narrator symbolic control over problematic transitions in the female life cycle.

I am arguing that these transitions constitute life crises for women at this moment in American history because of the gap between experiences of discontinuous changes in their own biographies and the available cultural models for marking them, both cognitively and socially. As increasing numbers of women are entering the wage labor market and traditional marriage and familial arrangements seem to be in disarray, it is hardly surprising that the relationship of women to reproduction, and mothering in particular, has been thrown open to reinterpretation.

In the United States, where the culture and economy are underwritten by an ideal of individual autonomy and achievement and the separation of workplace and home, the fact of dependency over the life course has been hidden in the household. Assigned to the "private realm" – the domain of unpaid labor performed by women serving as emotional and often material providers for infants, children, the sick, the elderly – nurturance thus escapes consideration as a larger cultural concern. Rather, the general social problem of caring for dependent human beings is linked to biological reproduction and childrearing in heterosexually organized families, all of which are conflated with the category female.[8] When women vote with their bodies to eschew the imperatives of American domesticity by remaining single, childless, and/or entering wage labor in large numbers, both the conditions and native understandings of nurturance and reproduction necessarily change.

Such changes are central narrative themes in the procreation stories of abortion activists. While their "life scripts" are cast against each other, both provide ways for managing the structural opposition in America between work and parenthood that still shapes the lives of most women and men in this culture. Because contrasting definitions of the cultural and personal meaning of reproduction are being created in a contested domain, they are shaped dialectically. Each side attempts to both incorporate and repudiate the claims to truth of their opposition, casting as unnatural, immoral, or false other possible formulations. In the abortion debate, both positions serve to "naturalize" constructions regarding women's work, sexuality, and motherhood, and the relationships among them, thus claiming a particular view of American culture and the place of men and women in it in a way that accommodates discontinuities and contradictions.

The location of and responsibility for nurturance in relationship to biological reproduction is of critical concern, the salient value and contradiction for women on both sides of the debate. Nurturance is claimed by activists as a source of moral authority for female action. Yet, it is also understood as the culturally assigned attribute that puts women at a disadvantage socially, economically, and politically, confining them to the unappreciated tasks of caring for dependent people. These two views of the "proper" place of reproduction and nurturance in the female life course are the poles around which activists' life stories are constituted.

Activists' views on abortion are linked to a very diverse range of moral, ethical, and religious questions, which I discuss in more detail elsewhere (Ginsburg 1986).[9] In this paper, however, I have confined my analysis to the issues that emerge in their life stories. My goal here is an effort to understand how abortion activism and abstract notions tied to it mediate between historical experience, construction of self, and social action. What I think is striking about the emergence of nurturance as a central theme in these narratives is that it ties female life-cycle transitions to the central philosophical questions of each side: the pro-life concern with the protection of nascent life, and the pro-choice concern with the rights and obligations of women, those to whom the care of that nascent life is culturally assigned.

The life stories

The pro-choice narratives

The pro-choice narratives were drawn from women activists who organized to defend the Fargo abortion clinic; most were born between 1942–52. They represent a range of backgrounds in terms of their natal families, yet all were influenced as young adults by the social unrest of the late 1960s and early 1970s, and by the women's movement in particular. While their current household, conjugal, and work arrangements differ, for almost all, the strong commitment to pro-choice activism was connected to specific life-cycle events, generally having to do with experiences and choices around sexuality, pregnancy, and childbearing, including the choice not to have children.

A central figure of the current controversy in Fargo is Kay Bellevue, an abortion rights activist since 1972. Kay grew up in the Midwest, the oldest of seven children. Her father was a Baptist minister; her mother worked as a homemaker and part-time public school teacher. In her senior year of college, Kay got pregnant and married. Like almost *all* of the women activists, regardless of their position on abortion, Kay's transition to motherhood was surrounded by ambivalence.

"I enjoyed being home, but I could never stay home all the time. I have never done that in my life. After being home one year and taking care of a kid, I felt my mind was a wasteland. And [my husband and I] were so poor we could almost never go out together."

Although her *behavior* was not that different from that of many right-to-life women – that is, as a young mother she became involved in community associations – Kay's interpretation of her actions stresses the limitations of motherhood; by contrast, pro-life women faced with the same dilemma emphasize the drawbacks of the workplace. Not surprisingly, for both groups of women, voluntary work for a "cause" was an acceptable and satisfying way of managing to balance the pleasures and duties of motherhood with the structural isolation of that work as it is organized in America. La Leche League, for example, is a group where one stands an equal chance of running into a pro-life or pro-choice woman. In her early 20s, Kay became active in a local chapter of that organization, an international group promoting breast-feeding and natural childbirth. She marks this as a key event.

"My first child had not been a pleasant birth experience so I went [to a La Leche meeting] and I was really intrigued. There were people talking about this childbirth experience like it was the most fantastic thing you'd ever been through. I certainly didn't feel that way. I had a very long labor. I screamed, I moaned, my husband thought I was dying. So . . . this group introduced me to a whole different conception of childbirth and my second experience was so different I couldn't believe it.

And the way I came to feminism was that through all of this, I became acutely aware of how little physicians actually knew about women's bodies . . . So I became a real advocate for women to stand up for their rights, starting with breastfeeding."

Surprisingly, the concerns Kay voices are not so different from those articulated by her neighbors and fellow citizens who so vehemently oppose her work.

In 1972, Kay moved to Fargo; she remembers this transition as a time of crisis. Her parents were divorcing, one of her children was having problems, and Kay became pregnant for the fifth time.

"Then I ended up having an abortion myself. My youngest was 18 months old and I accidentally got pregnant. We had four small kids at the time and we decided if we were going to make it as a family unit, we had all the stress we could tolerate if we were going to survive."

In her more public role, as was the case in these personal decisions regarding abortion, Kay always linked her activism to a strong commitment to maintain family ties. As such, she was responding to accusations made by right-to-life opponents that abortion advocacy means an oppositional stance toward marriage, children, and community.

"I think it's easy for them to stereotype us as having values very different than theirs and that's not the case at all. Many of the people who get abortions have values very similar to the anti-abortion people. The Right-to-lifers don't know how deeply I care for my own family and how involved I am, since I have four children and spent the early years of my life working for a breast-feeding organization."

Kay particularly resents the casting of pro-choice activists by right-to-lifers as not only "antifamily" but "godless" as well. Although she stopped attending church services when she got married – something she feels could stigmatize her in a community noted for its church attendance – Kay nonetheless connects her activism to religious principles of social justice learned in her natal family.

"I have always acted on what to me are Judeo-Christian principles. The Ten Commandments, plus love thy neighbor. I was raised by my family to have a very strong sense of ethics and it's still with me. I have a strong concern about people and social issues. I've had a tough time stomaching what goes on in the churches in the name of Christianity. I've found my sense of community elsewhere. I think pro-choice people have a very strong basis in theology for their loving, caring perspective. . . . It's very distressing to me that, particularly the people opposed to abortion will attempt to say their moral beliefs are the only correct ones."

Such stereotypes, to which most of the pro-choice women in Fargo were extremely sensitive, are addressed implicitly or explicitly in the repeated connections these activists made between abortion rights and a larger claim to the cultural values of nurturance which, in their view, women represent.

These concerns are prominent, for example, in the narratives of other abortion rights advocates. Janice Sundstrom, like most of the pro-choice activists in Fargo, frames her story by emphasizing her differentiation from, rather than integration with, her childhood milieu.

"In 1945, shortly after I was born, my mom and dad moved here and brought me along and left all the other children with relations back in Illinois. I think I'm different from the rest of them because I had the experience of being the only child at a time when they had far too many children to deal with."

While the transformations Janice eventually experienced are cast, in her story, as almost predictable, they hardly seem the inevitable outcome of her youth and adolescence: 12 years in Catholic parochial school and marriage to her high-school sweetheart a year after graduation, followed immediately by two pregnancies.

"We were both 19 then and I didn't want to have another child. We were both in school and working and there we were with this kid. But I didn't have any choice. There was no option for me about birth control because I was still strongly committed to the Church's teaching. And then, three months later, I was pregnant again. After Jodie was born I started taking pills and that's what ended the Church for me."

For Janice, ambivalent encounters with reproduction – in this case the problem of birth control that made her question her church – are key events in her story. In this way, her interpretation of her experiences resembles the way that pregnancy and pro-life activism are linked in the right-to-life narratives discussed later on. It is a central pivotal moment in her life, which turned her toward alternative cultural models.

"Up to that time, I felt very strongly about abortion as my church had taught me to think and somehow between 1968 and 1971 – those years were crucial to the political development of a lot of people in my generation – I came to have different feelings about abortion. My feeling toward abortion grew out of my personal experiences with friends who had abortions and a sensitivity to the place of women in this society."

What is striking in the connections Janice goes on to make to her abortion rights position is not its *difference* from that of her opponents, but its similarities. She is disturbed by cultural currents that promote, in her view, narcissistic attitudes toward sexuality and personal fulfillment in which the individual denies any responsibility to kin, community, and the larger social order. Several pro-choice women referred to this constellation of concerns as "midwestern feminism." They are described as natural attributes possessed and represented by women. In Janice's words,

"It's important that we remember our place, that we remember we are the caregivers, that we remember that nurturing is important, that we maintain the value system that has been given to us and that has resided in us and that we bring it with us into that new structure.... It's important that we bring to that world the recognition that 80-hour work weeks aren't healthy for anyone – that children suffer if they miss relationships with their fathers and that fathers suffer from missing relationships with their children. This society has got to begin recognizing its responsibility for caring for its children."

Such concerns are emblematic of a broader goal of pro-choice women to improve conditions in a less than perfect world. More generally, the agenda of women on the pro-choice side is to use legal and political means to extend the boundaries of the domain of nurturance into the culture as a whole. They are attempting to reformulate the requirements of human reproduction and dependency as conditions to be met collectively. Their narratives reveal both an embracing of nurturance as a valued quality natural to women and the basis of their cultural authority, and their rejecting of it as an attribute that assigns women to childbearing, caretaking, and domesticity. These themes emerge in pro-choice stories as well as in action. In their view, nurturance is broadly defined. It includes the stated and actual preference for nonhierarchical relationships and group organization, and an insistence that their activism is not for personal gain or individual indulgence but in the interests of women and social justice. This utopian subtext of their position is rooted in their historical encounter with feminism. More directly, it is expressed as a desire to create a society more hospitable to the qualities and tasks they identify as female: the reproduction of generative, compassionate, or at least tolerant relationships between family, friends, members of the community, people in the workplace, and even the nation as a whole. In the narratives they construct, their desire to control their own reproduction is linked to a larger goal of (re)producing cultural values of nurturance on a larger social scale.

The right-to-life narratives

Right-to-life activists express a similar concern for the preservation of female nurturance. While it is linked directly to biological reproduction, nurturance in their narratives is not natural but achieved. In all the stories of pregnancy and birth told by right-to-life women, the ambivalance of the mother towards that condition – either through reference to the storyteller's own mother or children, or experience of motherhood herself – is invoked and then overcome through a narrative strategy that stresses continuities between generations, as the following quote illustrates. The speaker is Shirley, a 63-year-old widow, part-time nurse, mother of six, and a well-known member of Fargo's comfortable middle class.

"Our Senator, he's not pro-life, sent me a congratulations letter when [my son] John got a teacher of the year award in 1980. I wanted to take the letter back to him and say, 'It was very inconvenient to have this son. My husband was in school and I was working. We thought we needed other things besides a child. And had abortion been available to me, I might have aborted the boy who was

teacher of the year.' What a loss to society that would have been. What losses are we having in society now?"

The first wave of right-to-life activity in Fargo received much of its support from women of Shirley's cohort, many of whom had recently been widowed and were facing the loss of children from their immediate lives as well. At a moment in their life cycles when the household and kin context for a lifelong vocation of motherhood was diminishing, prolife work provided an arena for extending that work beyond the boundaries of home and family.

Another woman of that cohort, Helen, also drew cross-generational connections through her right-to-life commitment. Raised in one of Fargo's elite Lutheran families, Helen fulfilled her mother's dream by attending an eastern "seven sisters' school" and going on for a master's degree in social work. After World War II, she married, returned to Fargo, and had three children. There, she has led the life appropriate for the wife of a local retail magnate. She was, until recently, a pro-choice advocate, a position of which her mother disapproved.

"Years ago, as a social worker, even though I reverenced life, I can still see some of those families and how they lived. I was pro-choice because I thought of those little children and how they lived. And I remember my mother saying 'Helena,' (she always called me Helena when it was serious) 'That's murder...' And I said, 'Better those children were never born, mother. They live a hell on earth...' and she never talked about it to me after that but I'm sure it hurt."

When the clinic opened in 1981, Helen was asked by a member of one of her prayer groups to join the pro-life coalition against the clinic, which she did. She saw her "conversion" to the right-to-life movement as a repudiation of a prior sense of self that had separated her from her mother, who recently died. She links all of these to the circumstances of her own birth.

"I had a sister killed in a car accident before I was born and...I don't know if I ever would have been if she hadn't died...My mother was so sick when she was pregnant with me because she was still grieving. They wanted to abort her and she said, 'No way.'

So when she died last year and all these checks came in, I gave them to LIFE Coalition and as a thank you note to people, I told them about her story... It brought life to me that at her death this could go on.

You know there is one scripture in Isaiah 44 that I especially pray for my family and that says 'I knew you before you were formed in your mother's womb. Fear not, for you are my witness.' "

In this fragment, Helen establishes metaphorical continuity between her pro-life conviction and the opening story of her narrative, in which she reconstructs her own sojourn in her mother's womb, identifying herself simultaneously with her earliest moments of existence and with her mother's trauma as well. As in Shirley's story, the denial and acceptance of mother and child of each other's lives are merged, and then given larger significance as reproductive events are linked figuratively and materially to the right-to-life movement and given new meaning.

The connections of the right-to-life position with overcoming ambivalence toward pregnancy, and the merging of divergent generational identities in the act of recollection are present, though less prominent, in the procreation stories of younger pro-life women as well. Sally Nordsen is part of a cohort of women born between 1952–62 who make up the majority and most dedicated members of Fargo's antiabortion activists. Like most of the other pro-life women of this group, Sally went to college and married soon after her graduation; she worked for seven years as a social worker. In her late 20s, she got pregnant and decided to leave the work force in order to raise her children. Sally regards this decision as a positive one; nonetheless, it was marked by ambivalance.

"I had two days left of work before my resignation was official but Dick was born earlier than expected. So I left the work on my desk and never went back to it. There were so many things that were abrupt. When I went into the hospital it was raining, and when I came out it was snowing. A change of seasons, a change

of work habits, a new baby in my life. It was hard. I was so anxious to get home and show this baby off. And when I walked in the door, it was like the weight of the world and I thought, 'What am I going to do with him now?' Well, these fears faded.

So it was a change. When Ken would come home, I would practically meet him at the door with my coat and purse cause I wanted to get out of there. I couldn't stand it, you know. And that's still the case sometimes. But the joys outweigh the desire to go back to work."

For Sally and the other pro-life activists her age, the move from wage labor to motherhood occurred in the late 1970s or more recently. Feminism was identified, more often than not, with its distorted reconstruction in the popular media. Women like Sally, who have decided to leave the work force for a "reproductive phase" of their life cycle, are keenly aware that the choices they have made are at odds with the images they see in the popular media of young, single, upwardly mobile corporate women. Sally's colleague, Roberta makes the case succinctly.

"They paint the job world as so glamorous, as if women are all in executive positions. But really, what is the average women doing? Mostly office work, secretarial stuff. When you watch TV, there aren't women being pictured working at grocery store check-outs."

For Roberta, her decision to leave the workplace represents a critique of what she considers to be the materialism of the dominant culture. For example, she sees in abortion a reevaluation of biological reproduction in the cost-benefit language and mores of the marketplace, and an extension of a more pervasive condition, the increasing commercialization of human relations, especially those involving dependents.

"You know, reasons given for most abortions is how much kids cost. How much work kids are, how much they can change your lifestyle, how they interrupt the timing of your goals. What is ten years out of a 70-year life span? ...If you don't have your family, if you don't have your values, then what's money, you know?"

In this view, legal abortion represents the loss of a locus of unconditional nurturance in the social order and the steady penetration of the forces of the market. In concrete terms, the threat is constituted in the public endorsement of sexuality disengaged from motherhood. From the right-to-life perspective, this situation serves to weaken social pressure on men to take responsibility for the reproductive consequences of intercourse. Pro-life women are fully cognizant of the fragility of traditional marriage arrangements and recognize as well the lack of other social forms that might ensure the emotional and material support of women with children or other dependents. Nonetheless, the movement's supporters continue to be stereotyped as reactionary right-wing housewives unaware of alternative possibilities. Almost all of the Fargo pro-life activists were aware of these representations and addressed them in a dialectical fashion, using them to confirm their own position. As Roberta explained,

"The image that's presented of us as having a lot of kids hanging around and that's all you do at home and you don't get anything else done, that's really untrue. In fact, when we do mailings here, my little one stands between my legs and I use her tongue as a sponge. She loves it and that's the heart of grass-roots involvement. That's the bottom. That's the stuff and the substance that makes it all worth it. Kids are what it boils down to. My husband and I really prize them; they are our future and that is what we feel is the root of the whole pro-life thing."

The collective portrait that emerges from these stories, then, is much more complex than the media portrayals of right-to-life women as housewives and others passed by in the sweep of social change. It is not that they discovered an ideology that "fit" some prior sociological category (see notes 6 and 7). Their sense of identification evolves from their own changing experiences with motherhood and wage labor, and in the very process of voicing their views against abortion. In their narratives and the regular performance of their activism, they are, simultaneously, transforming themselves, projecting their vision of the culture onto their own past and future, both pragmatically and symbolically. Sally, for example, describes her former "liberated" ideas about sexuality as a repression of her true self:

"You're looking at somebody who used to think the opposite. I used to think that sex outside of marriage was fine. I think there was part of me that never fully agreed. It wasn't a complete turnaround. It was kind of like inside you know it's not right but you make yourself think it's OK."

Rather than simply defining themselves in opposition to what they understand feminist ideology and practice to be, many of the younger right-to-life women claim to have held that position and to have transcended it. For example, a popular lecture in Fargo in 1984 was entitled, "I Was A Pro-choice Feminist But Now I'm Pro-Life." Much in the same way that pro-choice women embraced feminism, right-to-life women find in *their* movement a particular symbolic frame that integrates their experiences of work, reproduction, and marriage with shifting ideas of gender and politics that they encounter around them.

In the pro-life view of the world, to subvert the fertile union of men and women, either by denying procreative sex or the differentiation of male and female character, is to destroy the bases of biological, cultural, and social reproduction. This chain of associations to reproductive, heterosexual sex is central to the organization of meaning in pro-life discourse. For most right-to-lifers, abortion is not simply the termination of an individual potential life, or even that act multiplied a million-fold. It represents an active denial of the reproductive consequences of sex and a rejection of female nurturance, and thus sets forth the possibility of women structurally becoming men. This prospect threatens the union of opposites on which the continuity of the social whole is presumed to rest. In the words of a national pro-life leader

"Abortion is of crucial importance because it negates the one irrefutable difference between men and women. It symbolically destroys the precious essence of womanliness – nurturance.... Pro-abortion feminists open themselves to charges of crass hypocrisy by indulging in the very same behavior for which they condemn men: the unethical use of power to usurp the rights of the less powerful."

For pro-life women, then, their work is a gesture against what they see as the final triumph of self-interest. In their image of the unborn child ripped from the womb, they have symbolized the final penetration and destruction of the last arena of women's domain thought to be exempt from the truncated relations identified with both male sexuality and commercial exchange: reproduction and motherhood. At a time when wombs can be rented and zygotes are commodities, abortion is understood by right-to-lifers as an emblematic symbol for the increasing commercialization of human dependency. Their perception of their opponents' gender identity as culturally male – sexual pleasure and individual ambition separated from procreation and nurturant social bonds – is set against their own identification of "true femininity" with the self-sacrificing traits our culture conflates with motherhood. The interpretation of gender that underpins pro-life arguments, however, is based not on a woman's possession of but in her *stance toward* her reproductive capacities. Nurturance is achieved rather than natural, as illustrated in the procreation stories in which the point of the narrative is to show that pregnancy and motherhood are accepted *despite* the ambivalent feelings they produce. In their view, a woman who endorses abortion stresses the other side of the ambivalence and thus is "like a man," regardless of the shape of her body. Conversely, pro-life men encourage and take on a nurturant stance culturally identified as female, often at the urging of their activist wives.

Conclusion

This paper examines how American concepts of gender are being redefined by female activists in life story narratives and collective movements. While the analysis is specific to the abortion controversy as it developed in one locale, it is part of two interrelated areas of research: the cultural and social meanings of gender, reproduction, and sexuality; and arenas of conflict in contemporary American culture.[10] The common theoretical assumption of such work (cf. Colen 1986; Harding 1981; Martin 1986; Rapp 1986; Vance 1986) is that understandings of gender and its attendant meanings in American culture are not unified but multiple, and most clearly visible in moments of social and cultural discord. Methodologically, those interested in such dialectical processes focus on contested domains in America in which the definitions and control of procreation, sexuality, family, and nurturance are in contention.

At such moments of reformulation of cultural definitions, models from other societies offer instructive (or deconstructive) counterpoints to our own arrangements. New Guinea and Australia provide notable cases in which a high valuation is placed on nurturance and reproduction, broadly defined, and the role of men as well as women in "growing up" the next generation. Writing on the Trobriand Islanders, Annette Weiner points out

all societies make commitments to the reproduction of their most valued resources, i.e. resources that encompass human reproduction as well as the regeneration of social, material, and cosmological phenomena. In our Western tradition, however, the cyclical process of the regeneration of elements is not of central concern. Even the value of biological reproduction remains a secondary order of events in terms of power and immortality achieved through male domains. Yet in other societies, reproduction, in its most inclusive form, may be a basic principle through which other major societal structures are linked. (Weiner 1979)

Similarly, the abortion struggle demonstrates how reproduction, so frequently reified in American categorizations as a biological domain of activity, is always given meaning and value within a historically specific set of cultural conditions. Looked at in this way, the conflict over abortion, regardless of its particular substance, presents a paradox. The claims of opponents to each represent "the truth" about

women are at odds with the fact of the controversy. The very existence of the contest that they
have created draws attention to reproduction as
an "open" signifier in contemporary America.
Yet, both pro-life and pro-choice women are
trying, in their activism and procreation stories,
to "naturalize" their proposed solutions to the
problems created by the differential consequences of biological reproduction for men
and women in American culture.

Activists, as narrators of their life stories,
create symbolic continuity between discontinuous transitions in the female life cycle, particularly between motherhood and wage work,
that, for larger reasons, are particularly problematic for specific cohorts in ways that mark
them as "generations." In the procreation stories, abortion not only provides a framework
for organizing "disorderly" life transitions and
extending a newly articulated sense of self in
both space and time, it also provides narrators
a means of symbolically controlling their opposition. The narratives show how these activists require the "other" in order to exist. This is
what gives these stories their dialectical quality; in them the two sides are, by definition, in
dialogue with each other, and thus must address the position of their opposition in constituting their own identities.

The signification attached to abortion provides each position with opposed but interrelated paradigms which reconstitute and
claim a possible vision of being female. Reformulated to mesh with different historical and
biographical experiences, the authority of nurturance remains prominent in both positions.
As historian Linda Gordon points out

> contemporary feminism, like feminism a cen-
> tury ago, contains an ambivalence between
> individualism and its critique. [Right-to-lifers]
> fear a completely individualized society with
> all services based on cash nexus relationships,
> without the influence of nurturing women
> counteracting the completely egoistic prin-
> ciples of the economy, and without any forms
> in which children can learn about lasting
> human commitments to other people. Many
> feminists have the same fear. (1982: 50–1)

Grassroots pro-life and pro-choice women
alike envision their work as a full-scale social
crusade to enhance rather than diminish
women's position in American culture. While
their solutions differ, both sides share a critique of a society that increasingly stresses
materialism and self-enhancement while denying the value of dependents and those who care
for them. These conditions are faced by all
parties to the debate. Nonetheless, the abortion issue persists as a contested domain in
which the struggle over the place and meaning
of work, reproduction, and nurturance, and
their relationship to the category female, are
being reorganized in oppositional terms. By
casting two possible interpretations of this
situation in opposition, the abortion debate
masks their common roots in, and circumvents
effective resistance to, problematic conditions
engendered by a central contradiction for
women living in a system in which motherhood and wage labor are continually placed
in conflict.

The procreation stories told by women on
each side – spun from the uneven threads of
women's daily experience and woven into life
stories – give compelling shape to the reproductive experiences of different generations,
which stress one side of the contradiction. It
is not surprising that the abortion contest
arouses such passion. Its effects, played out
on women's bodies and lives in particular, are
the evidence and substance on which activists
draw. Their verbal and political performances
are created to fix with irreversible meaning
events in the female life course that are inherently contingent, variable, and liminal. Yet, the
narrative and political actions of activists are
intended to close off other possible interpretations, as each side claims to speak the truth
regarding contemporary as well as past and
future generations of American women.

NOTES

1   There is considerable argument in the de-
    bate over abortion regarding the proper
    name for each position. Those advocating
    abortion rights prefer to call their oppos-
    ition "anti-choice" while those opposed to
    legal abortion refer to their opponents as

"pro-abortion." Following Malinowski's axiom that the anthropologist's task is, in part, to represent the world from the native's point of view, I have used the appellation each group chooses for itself.

2 For a description and analysis of the "social drama" that took place over the clinic opening, see Faye Ginsburg (1984), The Body Politic: The Defense of Sexual Restriction by Anti-Abortion Activists, in *Pleasure and Danger*, C. Vance, ed.; and (1986), Part III of Reconstructing Gender in America: Self-Definition and Social Action among Abortion Activists, PhD diss., City University of New York.

3 I carried out research in Fargo during 1981–2, as a producer for WCCD-TV Minneapolis, for a documentary on the clinic conflict, "Prairie Storm," broadcast in 1982. I returned for another eight months of participant observation fieldwork in 1983.

4 In a 1984 review article on life histories in the *Annual Review of Sociology*, Daniel Bertaux and Martin Kohli use the term "life story" to distinguish such oral autobiographical fragments from more comprehensive, fully developed narrative texts that would more properly be called life histories, such as Vincent Crapanzano's *Tuhami* (Chicago: University of Chicago Press, 1980); Sidney Mintz's *Worker in the Cane* (New York: Norton, 1974); or Marjorie Shostak's *Nisa* (New York: Vintage, 1983). See Daniel Bertaux and Martin Kohli, The Life Story Approach: A Continental View, *Annual Review of Sociology*, 10: 1984, 215–37.

5 In order to better understand the connections activists made between their sense of personal identity and their engagement in a social movement, I asked them to work with me in creating "life stories." People were already well known to me. I interviewed them (using a tape recorder) for four to five hours, sometimes twice, at a location of their choice where we knew we would not be interrupted. Simply put, I asked people to tell me how they saw their lives in relation to their current activ-

ism on the abortion issue. I explained that my interests were to understand why women were so divided on the abortion issue, and to provide a more accurate portrayal of grassroots abortion activists since they tend to be overlooked or misrepresented in both popular and scholarly discussions of the issue. In general, the activists shared these concerns. I chose subjects who had taken during 1981–3, the period of my fieldwork, the most prominent roles in local activity and who reflected, in my estimation, the range of diversity encompassed in the active memberships of each group in terms of age, socioeconomic status, religious affiliation, household and marriage arrangements, style of activism, and the like. While most of these people continue to be active, each side continues to undergo rapid permutations both locally and nationally. Most of my interviews were with women since the membership of both groups is primarily female, as is the case throughout the country. The men I worked with were either husbands of activists or pro-life clergy. Altogether, I collected 21 life stories from right-to-life activists and 14 life stories from pro-choice activists. In the presentation of the data in the thesis I have changed names and obvious identifying features as I agreed to do at the time of the interview.

6 As Rayna Rapp notes in her essay "Family and Class In Contemporary America" (1982: 170–1),

> If ever a concept carried a heavy weight of ideology, it is the concept of class in American social science. We have a huge and muddled literature that attempts to reconcile objective and subjective criteria, to sort people into lowers, uppers, and middles, to argue about the relation of consciousness to material reality.... "Social class" is a short-hand for a process, not a thing... by which different social relations to the means of production are inherited and reproduced under capitalism... there are shifting frontiers which separate poverty, stable wage-earning, affluent salaries, and inherited wealth.

Recognizing this, as well as the complicated questions raised by the sticky question of the relationship of "class" to
women's unpaid domestic labor, I use
Rapp's definitions for middle-class families and house-holds.

> Households among the middle class are
> obviously based on a stable resource
> base that allows for some amount of
> luxury and discretionary spending... -
> Middle-class households probably are
> able to rely on commodity forms rather
> than kinship processes to ease both eco-
> nomic and geographic transitions.
>
> The families that organize such house-
> holds are commonly thought to be char-
> acterized by egalitarian marriages. (p.
> 181)

(For egalitarian marriages, see Schneider
and Smith 1973.) This definition is consistent with those used in the studies I cite (see
note 7) as evidence for the middle-class
basis for the abortion movement as a
whole. It offers a good general description
of the households and families of activists I
worked with in Fargo. I do not mean to
dismiss class but rather want to underscore
the point that the opposing positions on
abortion are not isomorphic with distinctive groups of people situated differently in
the social relations of production. I use the
life histories in particular to show how
much more complicated the process is,
and the multiple settings from which identity is drawn.

7   See, for example, Daniel Granberg 1981;
Harding 1981; and Tatalovich and Daynes
1981: 116–37. Granberg's random sample
survey of members of the National Abortion Rights Action League (NARAL) and
National Right to Life Committee (NRLC),
which is the most thorough of all research
to date, gives a breakdown of selected
demographic and social status characteristics (see Granberg 1981, table 1, p. 158).

8   In an article on new anthropological
views of the family, authors Collier,
Rosaldo, and Yanagisako write:

> One of the central notions in the modern
> American construct of The Family is that

of nurturance... a relationship that en-
> tails affection and love, that is based on
> cooperation as opposed to competition,
> that is enduring rather than temporary,
> that is noncontingent rather than contin-
> gent upon performance, and that is gov-
> erned by feeling and morality instead of
> law and contract.... a symbolic oppos-
> ition to the market relations of capital-
> ism. (1982: 34)

9   In assessing the way that abortion opponents view the world in relation to their
ideology, authors Callahan and Callahan
write:

> Both sides are prepared to argue
> that abortion is undesirable, a crude so-
> lution to problems that would better be
> solved by other means. The crucial dif-
> ference, however is that those on the
> pro-choice side believe that the world
> must be acknowledged as it is and not
> just as it ought to be.
>
> By contrast, the pro-life group be-
> lieves that a better future cannot be
> achieved... unless we are prepared to
> make present sacrifices toward future
> goals and unless aggression toward the
> fetus is denied, however high the indi-
> vidual cost of denying it. The dichoto-
> mies are experienced in our ordinary
> language when "idealists" are con-
> trasted with "realists." (1984: 221)

10 Several sessions at professional anthropology meetings in 1986 were indicative of
this trend. A panel organized by the
author and Linda Girdner entitled "Contested Domains of Reproduction, Sexuality, Family and Gender in America" was
held at the American Ethnological Society meetings in April. At the December
meetings of the American Anthropological Association, a session entitled
"Speaking Women: Representations of
Contemporary American Femininity"
was organized by Joyce Canaan; at the
same event, Susan Harding organized a
panel on "Ethnographic America." Specific research presented at these sessions
included Rayna Rapp's study of amnio-

centesis, Carole Vance's investigation of the pornography debates, Susan Harding's research on the Moral Majority, Shellee Colen's work on domestic childcare workers, Emily Martin's study of conflicting metaphors for birth and the female body, Joyce Canaan's work on adolescent sexuality in America, Linda Girdner's study of contested child custody disputes, and Judy Modell's research on adoption.

REFERENCES

Callahan, Daniel, and Sidney Callahan. 1984. Abortion: Understanding Differences. *Family Planning Perspectives*, 16/5: 219–20.

Colen, Shellee. 1986. Stratified Reproduction: The Case of Domestic Workers in America. Paper presented at the American Ethnological Society Meetings, Wrightsville Beach, NC.

Collier, Jane, Michelle Rosaldo, and Sylvia Yanagisako. 1982. Is There a Family? New Anthropological Views. In *Rethinking the Family*. B. Thorne and M. Yalom, eds. New York: Longman.

Ginsburg, Faye. 1984. The Body Politic: The Defense of Sexual Restriction by Anti-Abortion Activists. In *Pleasure and Danger: Exploring Female Sexuality*. C. Vance, ed. Boston: Routledge and Kegan Paul.

—— 1986. Reconstructing Gender in America: Self-Definition and Social Action Among Abortion Activists. PhD dissertation, City University of New York.

Gordon, Linda. 1982. Why Nineteenth-Century Feminists Did Not Support "Birth Control" and Twentieth Century Feminists Do: Feminism, Reproduction and the Family. In *Rethinking the Family*. B. Thorne and M. Yalom, eds. New York: Longman.

Granberg, Daniel, 1981. The Abortion Activists. *Family Planning Perspectives*, 13/4.

Harding, Susan. 1981. Family Reform Movements: Recent Feminism and Its Opposition. *Feminist Studies*, 7/1.

Luker, Kristin. 1984. *Abortion and the Politics of Motherhood*. Berkeley: University of California Press.

Mannheim, Karl. 1952. The Problem of Generations. In *Essays on the Sociology of Knowledge*. P. Kecskemeti, ed. New York: Oxford University Press.

Martin, Emily. 1986. Mind, Body and Machine. Paper presented at the American Anthropological Association Meetings, Philadelphia, PA.

Rapp, Rayna. 1982. Family and Class In Contemporary America. In *Rethinking the Family*. B. Thorne and M. Yalom, eds. New York: Longman.

—— 1986 Constructing Amniocentesis: Medical and Maternal Voices. Paper presented at the American Anthropological Association Meetings, Philadelphia, PA.

Schneider, David M., and R. T. Smith. 1973. *Class Differences and Sex Roles in American Kinship and Family Structure*. Englewood Cliffs, NJ: Prentice-Hall.

Tatalovich, Raymond, and Byron W. Daynes. 1981. *The Politics of Abortion*. New York: Praeger.

Vance. Carole S. 1986. Of Sex and Women, Meese and Men: The 1986 Attorney General's Commission on Pornography. Paper presented at the American Ethnological Society Meetings, Wrightsville Beach, NC.

Weiner, Annette. 1979. Trobriand Kinship from Another View: The Reproductive Power of Women and Men. *Man*, 14/2: 328–48.

13

Ethnically Correct Dolls: Toying with the Race Industry

Elizabeth Chin

Entering the Race Market

A July afternoon in 1992, amidst prodigious swelter. A typical New Haven, Connecticut, summer day: hot, gluey air slowly being stirred by an unenthusiastic breeze. In Newhallville, a working-class and poor African American neighborhood, most had abandoned even shady porches for the cooler, darkened living rooms. By three in the afternoon, the air had stilled and the sky clogged with soggy, gray clouds. As I sat talking with ten-year-old Natalia and her cousin, an invigorated wind suddenly began twisting leaves off trees and the sky erupted downward, dumping marble-sized raindrops upon the streets and stoops and rooftops. Thunder overpowered our voices. Braving the rain and lightning, the girls rushed out to Natalia's stoop, hopping about like gazelles when the thunder shook the small wood-frame house: a thrill! I spied a frazzle-haired, white Barbie doll beneath Natalia's seat, and holding my tape recorder, asked the girls to tell me about her. With the thunder jolting them periodically from their chairs, Natalia and Asia commandeered the machine and began to speak:

ASIA: You never see a fat Barbie. You never see a pregnant Barbie. What about those things? They should make a Barbie that can have a baby.
NATALIA: Yeah...and make a fat Barbie. So when we play Barbie...you could be a fat Barbie.
ASIA: OK. What I was saying that Barbie...how can I say this? They make her like a stereotype. Barbie is a stereotype. When you think of Barbie you don't think of fat Barbie...you don't think of pregnant Barbie. You never, ever...think of an abused Barbie.

Speaking into the tape recorder, Natalia announced: "I would like to say that Barbie is *dope*. But y'all probably don't know what that means so I will say that Barbie is *nice*!" The tape recorder was the girls' conduit to an imaginary audience, one located outside their own neighborhood, and one that is not black. In substituting the bland and inoffensive word "nice" for the tastiness of "dope," Natalia demonstrated a devastating sensitivity to the gap between her own world and the one where the "y'all" whom she addressed live. In wondering why there wasn't a Barbie that is "fat," "pregnant," or "abused," Natalia and Asia also wondered why these dolls represent social and cultural worlds so foreign to them.

In 1991, a year before these girls spoke their minds, the makers of Barbie had introduced their first ethnically correct fashion dolls to the market. Ostensibly meant to address the problem of minority representation alluded to in Natalia and Asia's interchange, Shani and her friends Asha and Nichelle were unlike other black dolls Mattel had produced: they came in light, medium, and dark skin tones; they had newly sculpted facial features (purportedly based on real African American faces); and there were reports that their bodies had been changed to more accurately represent African American figures. These toys were designed and marketed specifically to reshape a territory dominated by an assumption of whiteness, but paradoxically, they have integrated the toy world while at the same time fixing racial boundaries more firmly. These boundaries are based upon racialized markers: hair type, facial features, and skin color; toymakers like Mattel assiduously avoid delving into the social issues that Natalia and Asia identified as being central from their perspective. Ethnically correct dolls do not address Natalia's and Asia's questions about abused, pregnant, fat, or dope Barbies any more than their white counterparts did.

In Newhallville, however, girls tended to have white dolls that they worked to bring into their own worlds, often through styling their hair. These interactions highlight children's understanding that racialized commodities like Shani can only incompletely embody the experiences of kids who are not simply racial beings, but also poor, working class, young, ghettoized, and gendered. Embodied in these children's activities is a profound recognition that race is not only socially constructed but has potential to be imaginatively reconstructed. The situation in Newhallville poses problems for the assertions of ethnically correct toymakers who argue that kids of color play better with dolls that "look like them." Girls in Newhallville worked on their dolls materially and symbolically, blurring racial absolutes by putting their hair into distinctively

African American styles using beads, braids, and foil. These approaches to the question of race and dolls suggest ways in which feminist notions of multiple subjectivity and queer theory ideas about the flexibility of designations such as "straight" or "gay," "girl" and "boy" are relevant to the study of race and racism. In looking at the interactions of Newhallville girls and their white dolls, ways of thinking between and outside of bounded racial categories emerge. However, the radical potential of these girls' playful efforts is just that: potential, since Asia and Natalia – like the other kids in their neighborhood – live lives constrained by the contingencies of social inequality.

The question of dolls became important after my fieldwork was over, when I realized that photographs I had taken showed, over and over again, black girls with white dolls whose hair had been elaborately braided, twisted, or styled in ways racially marked as black. Understanding what their implications were meant looking in several territories. On the one hand, white dolls with black hairdos required looking into the ethnically correct toy industry, since these toys have been manufactured for children like Natalia and Asia. In a portion of this paper, I look at the ethnically correct toy industry, taking Mattel's Shani dolls as a case study. But few children in Newhallville had such dolls, and their importance in these kids' lives was as much – if not more – in their absence as in their presence. The social, economic, historical, and political factors that have engineered the absence of ethnically correct toys from Newhallville children's rooms are the same forces that have helped to form poor, racially segregated, and embattled communities in urban areas across the nation. It is precisely in the context of encompassing and multiple social inequality that ethnically correct toys like Shani and Newhallville's racially transformed white dolls need to be understood. This is a context breeding silence, and kids like those I knew in Newhallville rarely speak or are heard beyond their sequestered sphere. I cannot claim that this paper is itself the speech of Newhallville children, or that it speaks for them. However, the engaged, culturally active, and at times critical experiences, observations, and talk of Newhallville children are the foundation for understanding why white dolls with braids have a profound and potentially radical meaning that confounds the commercial rhetoric of ethnically correct toys like the Shani doll.

Learning from Kids about Race, Consumption, and the Question of Queer

This paper moves at once outward to corporate and cultural politics and inward to children's personal territories. This dual focus serves first to stress the relationship between commodities and consumers, a relationship that has been somewhat neglected until recently in anthropology (Miller 1995). This approach also engages recent work on identity that emphasizes it as a process that is flexible, dynamic, and multifaceted.[1]

The relationship between commodities and consumers is particularly clear when it comes to the question of American children. Since the latter half of the nineteenth century children have been increasingly excluded from participation in productive activities and redefined as passive and dependent. Simultaneously, the range and perceived importance of equipment and technology for children's education and entertainment has proliferated (Ariès 1962; Cross 1997). Erik Erikson's work featuring psychotherapy with innocuous toys helped to instill a sort of awe and terror about children's play: dollhouses and dolls, blocks, cars have not been the same since (1964). Coupled with Maria Montessori's dictum that "play is a child's work" ([1912] 1964), toys and play have come to hold increasing importance in American children's lives and in their families' concerns. Part of the result: toys are now a $17-billion-a-year business.

Some psychological researchers are placing a growing importance on the transactional, or interactive, relationship between kids and their playthings (see Kelly-Byrne 1989 for a rare ethnographic example). The transactional point of view rarely emerges in the two most common approaches to the question of kids and toys. One such approach follows from Erikson's work and focuses on kids' play, casting toys as relatively static and transparent

(Caldera et al. 1989; Henry and Henry 1974). In these works, the authors do not investigate the historical, cultural, or political context of either the toys or the industries producing them, and rarely of the children playing with them (an exception is Sutton-Smith 1986). Another focuses almost exclusively upon the toys themselves, without systematically examining how children actually relate to and interact with them.[2] Although some have stressed the importance of studying children who are poor or from ethnic and racial minorities (Pellegrini and Jones 1994; Sutton-Smith 1986), studies that are not focused on white, middle-class children are few and far between.[3]

Queer, feminist, and cultural studies analyses have already yielded incisive critiques of Barbie and her ilk, ethnically correct and otherwise.[4] These analyses have moved well beyond the shopworn observation that Barbie, with her sadistically pointed breasts, waspy waist, and permanently high-heel prepared feet,[5] does not look much like any real woman who has not had extensive plastic surgery. This literature has limitations similar to those discussed above: in a social history of the American doll, Miriam Formanek-Brunell charges that "at best, feminist scholars (influenced by the Frankfurt School) have interpreted dolls as agents of a hegemonic patriarchal culture in which girls are passive consumers" (1993: 1). Like most studies of American consumption (consumer and marketing research excepted), the great majority of Barbie analyses proceed without talking to or observing children themselves, and skirt – so to speak – issues of race and class. Child-centered research is needed partly because what children do and say is largely unanticipated in current, adult-centric analyses or theoretical frameworks.[6] This applies as much to work focusing on children and their lives as to that examining society at large: the ethnography of children and childhood, like feminist ethnography, holds potential for transforming anthropological thinking.

In the Barbie realm, the work of Erica Rand is an important model for how to think critically about toys, children, and culture – even though she explicitly excludes children from the scope of her inquiry. In *Barbie's Queer Accessories* (1995), Rand has collected women's recollections of Barbie in their lives. Rand is explicit and clear that adults recalling their own childhoods are not the equivalent of observances of actual children. Her book demonstrates the power of adult remembrance while emphasizing that children's experiences cannot fully be recuperated through adult-centric approaches.

One of the centrally important aspects of Rand's analysis is the way she conceptualizes the notion of queer. In *Barbie's Queer Accessories*, making Barbie queer is not necessarily about sex or sexuality. Rand's notion of queering highlights the bending, twisting, or flipping of apparently real or natural or accepted social states, and she explores a variety of ways in which Barbie gets queered: consumer activists switch the voice boxes of talking G.I. Joe with talking Barbie, adult women remember crossdressing Barbie or making her fuck Midge, 'zines generate faux ads for such items as AIDS Barbie. The fundamental tension is between a commodity with a packaged identity and the consumers who put her to work in their own lives; the deliciousness of the images is their transgression of Mattel's carefully managed Barbie profile.

As radical as these queerings may be in a given cultural space and social moment, they also make use of and take place within powerful ideological discourses: transgression does not make up its own rules, or exist in a world apart from hegemonic influences, and the power of resistance should not be overstated (Brown 1996; Sholle 1990). As Abu-Lughod has argued, when we look at resistance and the sites where it emerges, we stand to learn more about structures of power than arenas of freedom (1990). Rand's description of one of her own Barbie queerings illustrates the ways in which the layered and multiple meanings of race, sexual identity, and gender can reflect back upon each other, creating a hall-of-mirrors effect in which the subversion suddenly is itself subverted. In positioning two dolls in a staged "top/bottom dyke sex scene" between her White Barbie and "Chicana" Barbie (which, according to the package was an "American Indian" Barbie) she writes:

I struggled with how to assign roles to my two Barbies. Putting Chicana Barbie on top reinforces racial stereotypes of the dark brute overpowering the less animalistic white girl; the hair contrast alone places my *Dream Loft* firmly within the hetero-generated tradition of lesbian representation, which often features an aggressive, dark-haired vixen seducing a blond innocent. Putting blond Barbie on top would have subverted these stereotypes but performed white supremacy. In terms of race, there was no way out of dominant discourse. (1995: 172–3)

In Newhallville, Natalia and Asia used a considerably more condensed vocabulary to articulate similar concerns about Barbie's limitations. They wondered why there is no fat, abused, or pregnant Barbie, questions that were shaped by their being young black girls living in a poor and working-class, racially segregated neighborhood. These multiple facets of kids' identities are fixed neither internally nor socially; elsewhere I have examined how different geographic sites reconfigure the relationship and relevance of gender, race, and class in children's experience (Chin 1998). These shifts are connected to the creation or restriction of spaces in which resistance can take place: in the privacy of their homes, girls are safe to indulge in childish play; in the neighborhood streets, such childish vulnerability is replaced with a vigilant bravado aimed at fending off sexual danger; in downtown stores, sexual danger is transmuted into romantic fantasy, and the vigilance moves onto racial ground.

Despite a growing literature examining hybridity or mixed-race ethnicity and identity, in the U.S., discussions and analyses of race tend to make use of a polarized black/white framework, as Harrison notes (1995). The problem is that studies of hybridity "reproduce the error of misplaced concreteness" in Brackette Williams' view (1995), basing notions of mixture on still-problematic "pure" categories. Similarly, Peter Wade has argued that the basic ideas of phenotype and difference have not yet been sufficiently recognized as being *themselves* historical, Western, and colonial concepts (1993).

Ethnically correct toys draw upon these notions of difference and phenotype, paradoxically making use of oppressive distinctions to create progressive change. The braided heads of white dolls in Newhallville at least make a dent in the concreteness of race boundaries. Neither hybrid nor multicultural, they are instead queer. Seeing these dolls as racially queered is appropriate not only because naturalized categories of race are being bent, but also because it is a notion which, unlike hybridity, is fundamentally playful. Play is conceptually complex and sophisticated: "How does a dog know a play bite from a real bite?" asked Gregory Bateson in a well-known essay ([1955] 1972). Instead of Bateson's playful bite, these children have made a play on whiteness. Race that has been queered in this way challenges "pure" forms by disconnecting racial markers from particular bodies, much in the way that queer and gender studies have recognized that gender and sexuality are not inherently, predictably, or inevitably rooted in physical "male" or "female" individuals. These playfully imagined, resistant realities are not separable, however, from the context of discrimination, segregation, and oppression in which they have been generated, to which they ultimately refer, and with which they remain enmeshed.

Negotiating Newhallville

A host of terrifying statistics can be employed to illustrate the harsh economic contrasts and racial tensions that characterize New Haven today. Located in the wealthiest of the fifty states in terms of per capita income, this city of 130,000 was in 1980 the seventh-poorest of its size in the nation (U.S. Bureau of the Census 1980). Despite the nearness of Yale-New Haven Hospital's internationally renowned infant and child facilities, some neighborhoods in the city have infant mortality rates in excess of 66 per 1,000 (Reguero and Crane 1994). Since the 1950s, New Haven has lost over 20,000 manufacturing jobs, and the Winchester Repeating Arms factory in Newhallville, which once had 12,000 workers working three daily shifts, now employs less than 500. Local commerce has shifted from being factory-based to being dominated by service jobs, the drug trade, and government aid.

Newhallville is almost completely segregated and has a 91.7% minority population, but it borders the richest (and whitest) neighborhood in town.

Newhallville kids' sense of danger and possibility – and the themes of their playfulness – changed depending on the location. Downtown, the atmosphere was charged with racial tensions, but girls' romantic fantasies took wing. In contrast, their neighborhood was a racially safe and sexually dangerous place, one where the proprietor of the corner store watched them with the critical eye of an irascible grandparent, and where teenage boys and older men were seen as threats but increasingly interesting. Not trusting in my ability to negotiate this territory with success, the girls took to escorting me out of the area, guiding me past stores, streets, and people. One summer afternoon when Natalia decided I had let an impromptu conversation with a man last too long, she deftly cut the interaction short. "He's probably a drug dealer," Natalia said with assurance as we walked away. "He probably rapes little girls." For Newhallville girls, the concerns about rape and pregnancy begin early. Rape and pregnancy are issues relevant to all females but actively negotiating them at the age of ten is less the impact of gender, perhaps, than it is of class, race, social, and economic issues.[7] These concerns, arising from actual experience of abuse, reports of friends and relatives, close brushes with older boys and men in the street, were and continue to be real. Although she was not raped, Natalia became pregnant two years after the Barbie incident and delivered a baby girl when she was scarcely 13 years old.

Sometimes, as they were about to enter their homes, the girls would pause by the back door or front stoop and pretend to terrify themselves with stories of "Peanut Butter Man," a mythical convict who had escaped prison with a gun his mother gave to him, slipping it past guards by hiding it in a jar of peanut butter. These tales emphasized that in contrast to the streets, their homes were places of safety where girls could still be like little kids. Doll play, as Natalia's cousin Asia pointed out, was a sign of being a little kid. "We might play with

Barbies like this," she said, miming the way kids bounce a doll along a tabletop to make it walk, "but we don't let anybody see us." At ten years old, these girls had limited childish vulnerability to the interiors of their houses, whose windows were shrouded by shades and curtains. Boys their age still gathered together outside on stoops to play with their action figures and vehicles. Whether or not the girls played with their dolls much, their families still gave them dolls, as if to underscore the girls' continuing status as children. In 1992, Natalia's big Christmas gift from her mother was a life-sized battery-powered doll that talked and sucked a bottle. "It cost $60," Natalia told me. Through much of the day, she held the peachy-skinned, platinum-blonde doll on her hip and called it her "brat." Though the whiteness of Natalia's "brat" was striking, she never mentioned it and was most impressed with its cost and the novelty of its voice recognition technology.

Only once during my fieldwork did a child make an issue out of her dolls' race. In early October, as Tionna's birthday approached, she told me that she wanted some black dolls. "Why?" I asked her. She explained that at the moment she had more white dolls than black dolls and she wanted to even out the numbers. "After that, I'll get another white doll, and then a black doll, like that," she explained. Why, I wondered, hadn't Tionna given an answer that was more in line with the marketing and advertising of ethnically correct dolls, which made such claims as "Kids have more fun with dolls that look like them"? Part of the explanation lies in the dangers of wishing. In Newhallville, kids learn early to express their wants and wishes carefully, rather than candidly. Kids are well aware that their family's resources are not limitless and keep their requests modest. Carlos, for example, explained that before Christmas each year he gives his mother a list of things he'd like, and knows that those are the things he will receive. The list he showed me consisted of five toys, none costing over $20. I regularly asked Newhallville children what they would do if they found $20, and nearly all of them said they would give some or all of it to their mothers to buy groceries, or pay the rent. As Devon said,

"They help you, why shouldn't you help them?" In group interviews with middle-class children at a private school, none said they would give any of the money to their families, opting instead to "Put it in the bank!" or "Buy toys!"

Whining, throwing temper tantrums, or other attempts at coercion were usually dealt with harshly, and in Newhallville child discipline was generally both swift and physical. On several occasions children returned home from a trip to the supermarket or downtown with tear-streaked faces, having been punished for "acting stupid in the store," as one mother said. In this and other settings, kids learned early and well that their own desires had serious effects upon their caretakers and other family members, that they were expensive to house and feed, and that whatever they got usually meant someone else had to do without. I spent endless hours in malls and in stores with children and never heard them say "I want that," unless they had money of their own in their pockets and could actually buy the thing they wanted. Their concerns even extended to my own finances, and when I would offer to buy a child a soda or ice cream cone, they often declined. As Tarelle explained, "I don't want to spend up all your money, Miss Chin."

Even getting to the stores in order to buy the toys was difficult and expensive. Nearly half of Newhallville households did not have a car; friends and relatives could provide rides, but often charged for "gas money." The nearest Toys "R" Us was all but inaccessible by public transport and could only be reached by taking a highway to the next town. Most kids I knew in Newhallville visited it at most only once or twice a year. Some had never been there. The downtown toy store, Kaybee, specialized in overstock and discontinued items. It had higher prices than Toys "R" Us, was a fraction of the size, and offered a small and unpredictable selection of toys. Other places to buy toys included the supermarket or discount chains such as Caldor's, and several children cited these as their favorite stores.

Tionna, like many of her peers, had nearly fully incorporated the lesson that she should harbor few expectations and make few demands. On Christmas morning, in 1992, Tionna got up early and ran to look under the tree. She didn't see any gifts. Thinking that there just weren't any gifts that year, she went back to bed. There *were* presents, she just hadn't seen them. But despite her fierce (if temporary) disappointment, Tionna accepted the possibility that there were no presents at all because the possibility was real.

The primary appeal toy makers offer with their ethnically correct playthings is the idea that such toys can help minority kids to feel more at home in the world through allowing them to play with toys – and especially dolls – that look like them. In a community where kids can accept the idea that Santa just didn't come this year, having ethnically correct toys on the shelves of Toys "R" Us seems unlikely to have much impact. By framing the representation problem as being one only of race, makers of ethnically correct toys miss issues that for Newhallville children were often more immediately pressing. Despite the overt physical changes that Mattel made when they produced Shani, she still inhabits a fantasy world remarkably similar to Barbie's, the world where the word "dope" must be replaced with "nice" as the product packaging shows:

> Shani, Asha, and Nichelle invite you into their glamorous world to share the fun and excitement of being a top model. Imagine appearing on magazine covers, starring in fashion shows, and going to Hollywood parties as you, Shani, Asha, and Nichelle live your dreams of beauty and success, loving every marvelous minute!

The Unbearable Whiteness of Barbie

Welcome to Our World of OLMEC Toys.
Almost seven years ago, my son sent shock waves through my body when he said he couldn't be a super hero because he wasn't white.

"What!" I thought. At the tender age of three, my boy was already limiting his fantasies because he thought some dreams didn't come in his skin color.

That was my inspiration to create Sun-Man, the world's greatest super hero. Since then we

at OLMEC have expanded into girls and pre-school toys. We've got one thing in mind with all our products – let's build self-esteem.

Our children gain a sense of self importance through toys. So we make them look like them.

Now that he's 10, my son's dreams and goals soar. Playing with toys that look like him makes him feel good.

I hope you'll buy something from us that will expand your child's dream. (product packaging, Olmec toys)

Stories like the one that Yla Eason, Olmec's founder, has printed onto the packaging of many of her company's products are pervasive among minority toy makers and emphasize the deeply personal motivation behind the corporate entity. Companies such as Olmec have a focused social and political agenda aimed at undermining the racism endemic to an industry that seemed to espouse the notion that all baby dolls and Barbies – and by implication, people – ought to be white. The genesis of these toys has been in the crucible of urban racial strife: the nation's first minority toy maker, Shindana, was founded in the wake of the Watts riots with Federal monies and a start-up grant from Mattel.

Olmec's statement that "Our children gain a sense of self-importance through toys. So we make them look like them" bears a heavy debt to the revelations that emerged from the groundbreaking "doll studies" conducted by psychologists Kenneth and Mamie Phipps Clark in the late 1930s and early 1940s. These studies used black and white dolls as a way to unearth black children's views about race, asking them to point out, for instance, which doll "looks nice." In a series of devastating publications, the Clark studies revealed that black children often thought the white doll "looks nice," while the black doll "looks bad" (Clark and Clark 1939, 1947).[8] The Clarks argued that black children preferring white dolls could be seen to be suffering from "self-rejection" or "self-hatred." However, the impetus for these feelings was not internally generated. Rather, the Clarks' view was that kids understood all too well that the larger society denigrated and devalued blacks. As a result, children's feelings about themselves were complicated by this knowledge. The doll studies gained additional clout when they became associated with the landmark civil rights case *Brown v. the Board of Education of Topeka, Kansas*, in which the Supreme Court ruled segregated schooling to be unconstitutional.[9]

Olmec's Sun-Man figure seems to be a direct response to the Clark studies, and upends racial hierarchy by making dark skin a source of power rather than one of oppression: he gets his super-hero abilities from the melanin in his skin. The central motivating moment that Eason recounts is when her son Menelik announced "some dreams did not come in his skin color." The wording of this statement, which is printed on most Olmec packaging, effectively marries Martin Luther King's civil rights oratory ("I Have a Dream") with the startling discoveries of the Clark doll studies (the Negro doll is ugly/bad) to provide a powerful argument for the need of dolls that accurately and positively portray blackness.

Olmec is not alone in attempting to connect their toys to the visceral power of the Clark studies and the moral force of the civil rights movement. Mattel recruited the psychologist Darlene Powell-Hopson as a consultant in designing the Shani dolls. Powell-Hopson, who had replicated the Clark studies in the early 1980s, found that children's perceptions of race had hardly improved since the 1930s (Powell-Hopson 1985). A key element of her replication of the Clark studies had been new: the study design included an intervention aimed at children (white or black) who did not have positive value assessments of the black dolls. In these cases, the researcher demonstrated that *she* valued the black doll and found it beautiful or good. Powell-Hopson's results showed that the intervention was largely effective (at least in the short run), and the Shani dolls were shaped by these results.

The involvement of Powell-Hopson in the development of Shani dolls provided a direct line of descent from the work of the Clarks, connecting these products to social movements and historical moments of national scope. Shani has been molded on a set of assumptions

harkening back to the Clark studies, but with a commercial twist: children who play with dolls that look like them will not suffer from self-hatred. The message that manufacturers offer is "Buy toys that represent racial diversity and your children will be empowered as racial beings, not overpowered by racism." With ethnically correct toys, the logic of the Clark studies is reversed: it is the *toys* that are responsible for children's perceptions, not the society that produces them.

With the introduction of Shani and her friends, even the makers of Barbie herself have recognized the unbearable whiteness of Barbie in minority children's experience. A more cynical assessment of both Olmec and Mattel, however, might question which the companies find more unbearable: the Eurocentric toy industry or untapped market segments. Moreover, the type of diversity that has developed in the toy industry's products is far from being unproblematic; while mounting a challenge to whiteness as a norm, the diversity currently under manufacture in the form of "ethnically correct" playthings does not significantly transform the understanding of race, or even racism. Rather, ethnically correct dolls refashion racist discourses and market them to minority buyers.

One of the problems with all these overt and covert references to the civil rights movement is that they ultimately appeal more to parents – or grandparents – than they do to kids themselves. In Newhallville, dolls did not seem to be a flashpoint of racial tension for kids, though themes of race were certainly present. One afternoon as I visited Takeina, a classmate of Tionna and Natalia, I asked her to tell me about the black Barbies that she had flung, naked and with matted hair, into her dollhouse. My request generated little interest from her either in talk or play. A little while later, however, her older brother and a friend had joined us. The subject of race came up again, and I asked them to tell me how white people talk. The children could hardly contain themselves, and practically fell over each other trying not only to imitate white people's talk, but their physicality. Adopting a gangling, uncoordinated swagger, her brother drawled, "Let's go to the mall and buy some *rags*."

For Newhallville kids the mall was a racially charged space where they felt embattled and unwelcome (Chin 1996, 1998). Takeina's brother identifies the mall as a place for white kids to go and buy "rags." New Haven's downtown mall is permeated by measures to discourage poor and minority shoppers (who are often viewed as being synonymous): bus stops have been moved away from the mall, Frank Sinatra dominates the sound system. Unlike mall management, manufacturers of ethnically correct toys have not made the mistake of assuming that all minority consumers are poor: the market for ethnically correct toys has been explicitly built upon the buying power of the black middle class. *Ebony* magazine press materials provided at a toy industry event in 1993 estimated that black consumers spent $745.6 million on toys the year before. While this strategy is sound business practice (marketing toys to the poor is unlikely to generate much revenue – although marketing cigarettes and malt liquor seems to pay off pretty well), it forces manufacturers into an uncomfortable position. Toy executives told me time and again that these toys are good because they serve an important social function, but it is not their responsibility to make these products available to economically disadvantaged kids.

Shani and the Marketing of Blackness

The signature aspects of ethnically correct dolls are resculpted faces, skin tones, hair types, and ethnic fashions. Until companies like Shindana and Olmec jump-started the mass production and marketing of ethnically correct toys, mass-produced black dolls were basically made by pouring brown plastic into the same molds used to make white dolls. This was and continues to be a powerful material demonstration of an assimilationist ethic, one that has been rejected with growing vehemence by ethnic groups who are, increasingly, no longer numerical minorities in their communities. While these toys do celebrate and enshrine difference in a way that preceding black dolls and toys do not, the emphasis on the visibility

of race as a collection of markers masks the complexity of race both as a social construct and as a social experience.

The Shani line of dolls introduced by Mattel in 1991 reduces race to a simulacrum consisting of phenotypical features: skin color, hair, and butt. Ann DuCille (1996) has discussed much of their complex and contradictory nature, highlighting two central issues: derriere and hair. According to DuCille's interviews with Shani designers, the dolls have been remanufactured to give the illusion of a higher, rounder butt than other Barbies. This has been accomplished, they told her, by pitching Shani's back at a different angle and changing some of the proportions of her hips. I had heard these and other rumors from students at the college where I teach: "Shani's butt is bigger than the other Barbies' butts," "Shani dolls have bigger breasts than Barbie", "Shani dolls have bigger thighs than Barbie."[10] DuCille rightly wonders why a bigger butt is necessarily an attribute of blackness, tying this obsession to turn-of-the-century strains of scientific racism.

Deciding I had to see for myself, I pulled my Shani doll off my office bookshelf, stripped her naked, and placed her on my desk next to a naked Barbie doll that had been cruelly mutilated by a colleague's dog (her arms were chewed off and her head had puncture wounds, but the rest was unharmed). Try as I might, manipulating the dolls in ways both painful and obscene, I could find no difference between them, even after prying their legs off and smashing their bodies apart. As far as I have been able to determine, Shani's bigger butt is an illusion (figure 13.1). The faces of Shani and Barbie dolls are more visibly different than their behinds, yet still, why these differences could be considered natural indicators of race is perplexing. As a friend of mine remarked acidly, "They still look like they've had plastic surgery." The most telling difference between Shani and Barbie is at the base of the cranium, where Shani bears a raised mark similar to a branding iron scar: © 1990 MATTEL INC. Barbie's head reads simply © MATTEL INC. Despite claims of redesign, both Barbie and Shani's torsos bear a 1966 copyright, and although DuCille asserts that Shani's legs are shaped differently than Barbie's, their legs are imprinted

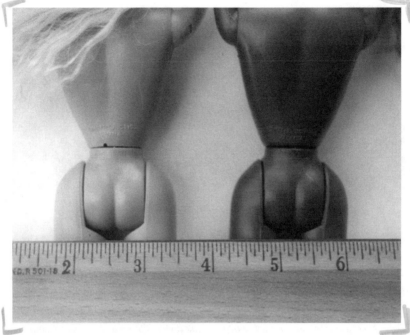

Figure 13.1   *Barbie and Shani from behind. (Photo by Elizabeth Chin, 1998)*

with the same part numbers. This all strongly suggests that despite claims and rumors to the contrary, Shani and Barbie are the same from the neck down.

These ethnically correct dolls demonstrate one of the abiding aspects of racism: that a stolid belief in racial difference can shape people's perceptions so profoundly that they will find difference and make something of it, no matter how imperceptible or irrelevant its physical manifestation might be. If I had to smash two dolls to bits in order to see if their butts were different sizes, the differences must be small indeed: holding them next to each other revealed no difference whatsoever – except color – regardless of the positioning (crack to crack or cheek to cheek). With the butt index so excruciatingly small, its meaning as a racial signifier becomes frighteningly problematic. Like the notion of race itself, Shani's derriere has a social meaning that is out of all proportion to its scientific measurement.

The Shani dolls, with their light, medium, and dark skin tones, were designed to signify different kinds of blackness (see figure 13.2). The progressive notion that black does not look just one way is not as progressive as it might appear when one looks closely at the Shani dolls, whose facial features seem to get more stereotypically "black" the darker the doll's skin color: Asha, the light-skinned doll, has the smallest nose and thinnest lips; meanwhile Nichelle, the darkest doll, has lips that are much wider than the outlines of her stamped-on pink lipstick, and her nose is the largest and widest of the Shani dolls. Light as Asha is, she is not so light that there is any danger that she might be able to "pass" as white.

In the mind of at least one Newhallville child, the meaning of the various skin colors was not kinds of blackness, but rather kinds of racial mixing. When Carlos and I were in Toys "R" Us, I pointed out to him that the dolls came in three skin tones. As I held one of each color in my hand, Carlos spontaneously began to describe them. "She's African American," he said, about Nichelle, the darkest-skinned doll. "She must be part Indian,"

Figure 13.2 *The Shani dolls are manufactured in three different face molds and skin tones. From left to right: Nichelle (dark), Shani (medium), and Asha (light). (Photo by Elizabeth Chin, 1998)*

he said, referring to Shani. "This one is like Puerto Rican or a light-colored black person," he finished, as he examined Asha. When Carlos describes Asha as being "Puerto Rican or a light-colored black person" he captures the difficulty in being able to know race simply by looking. His comment also highlights the logical inconsistencies in U.S. racial categories, which would in fact (according to the U.S. Census) classify Asha's human counterpart as being either "black – not of Hispanic Origin" or "Hispanic." That is, as far as the government is concerned, her race would be determined not by genetics or parentage, but by geography and history. This issue was close to home for Carlos, a curly-haired, medium-skinned Puerto Rican boy living in a primarily African American neighborhood. Racial distinctions are the products of history and legal mechanisms and do not conform to scientifically valid biological or genetic categories; Puerto Ricans with African ancestry are a case in point, both in terms of official definitions and in their daily lives.

What Carlos has also pinpointed is that in depicting kinds of blackness, Mattel has inadvertently roused the specter of miscegenation.[11] There is (of course) no interracial Barbie, no mulatto or quadroon Barbie, no Eurasian Barbie, nor a Barbie that like golf sensation Tiger Woods might be described as "Cablinasian" – caucasian, black, Indian and Asian – a mixture not of two races, but several. Tiger Woods' insistence on creating a name for what he is, like Carlos' description of the racial backgrounds of Shani, Asha, and Nichelle, speaks to the inability of our racial categories to capture the finely tuned perceptions of kids (or adults), who may not understand how to put the "one drop rule" to work in their everyday lives, especially when they may be the offspring of parents who are themselves of different races or multiracial. Racial identity, in other words, is complex and multifaceted experientially, socially, and historically. In the made-up world of Mattel, and much American public discourse, however, the current option is to check the boxes that apply: White, Black (not of Hispanic origin), Hispanic, Asian,

Native Hawaiian or Pacific Islander, American Indian or Alaska Native, or Other.[12]

Shani, like white Barbie, is deeply in need of the kind of racial queering that has been going on for years in relation to Barbie's gender. Even Erica Rand (1995), with her keen critical eye, couldn't see a way to queer the racial boundaries of her "Chicana" and "White" Barbies. Why did it not occur to her to switch the dolls' heads? It says a lot of things about minds and bodies, about perception and experience, and, in another form, this is precisely what the girls I knew in Newhallville were doing with their own dolls.

Braids and the Blonde Doll

I have a photograph of Cherelle's younger sister Clarice sitting on the front steps of their porch, next to her younger brother Joey (see figure 13.3). Clarice was the fourth of six children, all of whom looked almost exactly like their mother. The family, who lived across the street from me in Newhallville, was in a simmering chaotic state: the oldest son was in jail, writing long and lonely letters to his sisters at home; the children's mother was having trouble kicking a drug habit; and Clarice's older sister Cherelle spent much of her time caring for her younger siblings. Cherelle would often tell me, "I don't want to have no kids, I already raised all the kids I'm goin' to." Stubborn and sensitive to slights, Cherelle had been getting in fights in school and was on the verge of being expelled but she was also a patient and kind mother-sibling, often sitting her younger sister down on the front steps to grease and braid her hair, kissing boo-boos, and playing games with Clarice and Joey.

Joey seems to look out from the photo (at me) with a skeptical, almost belligerent glower. He holds a plastic toy in his hand as if to display it to me, the way you might display a weapon. Clarice, more at ease, has a doll snuggled on her lap. Against the dark color of Clarice's T-shirt, the doll's light skin and blonde hair are blazingly white. The front section of the doll's long, silky hair is done up in braids, each held at the end with a small plastic barette. Like the doll, Clarice has her hair in braids, and like the doll, the end of each braid is secured with a small plastic barette. The first thing one might notice about Clarice and her doll is that Clarice is black and her doll is white. But Clarice and her doll are also wearing their hair in almost identical ways. Several other Newhallville girls had dolls that, while white, had distinctly un-white hairdos.

When white baby dolls with cascades of long blonde hair have that hair heavy with beads and foil, or tucked up into a braid-upon-braid 'do, what has happened to the boundary between white and black? One obvious development is a sort of appropriation: the image that jumps to mind is Bo Derek in the movie *10* jogging along a Caribbean beach in slow motion, her hair braided and beaded, a vapid smile on her face, her sleek Barbie-doll body the main plot element in the film. Derek's hairstyle sparked a vociferous criticism from the black community for being yet another instance of white co-optation of black cultural forms. The film also spawned a beach-side cottage industry in the Caribbean, where (native) women and children scour vacation spots persistently trying to recruit people to get their hair braided as a sort of souvenir. In one surreal encounter, I came across a huddle of young, white Christian missionaries in the Port-au-Prince airport in Haiti, the women wearing fuzzed-up cornrows and singing Christian hymns in Kreyol. Clearly, the cornrows had hardly transformed these people or their beliefs.

The context in which heads get done matters tremendously, and what is happening between Newhallville kids and their dolls is not directly analogous to what happens to vacationers in St. Croix, to Bo Derek's hair, or to American teenagers on a religious mission. These situations are not analogous primarily because the power relationships and conceptual boundaries between white and black are destabilized as Newhallville girls braid their dolls' hair, in a way that they are not on a Bajan beach. This destabilization is delicate, fleeting even, and is likely to have little social impact beyond the realm of these children's own personal spheres, because it is undertaken in the context of far-reaching and multiple oppressions. What kids

Figure 13.3 *Clarice and Joey on their front stoop. Clarice and her doll wear similar hair styles. (Photo by Elizabeth Chin, 1992)*

are doing with dolls is limited much as I have asserted that the self-esteem angle is also limited. Such destabilization is not even likely to have any real or lasting impact on these kids' living relationships with either white people or the idea of whiteness: the elements of play and control present in doll hairstyling are markedly missing in kids' interactions with their white teachers, shopkeepers, police. Though fleeting and precarious, what these girls are doing subtly works away at the constricted and constricting notions of race that continue to dominate current discourse. It is a form of racial integration that has been largely unimagined by adult activists, scholars, politicians, or toy manufacturers.

Clarice does not appear to assume that just because her doll is white, she must treat her that way. When deciding to do her hair, she gives her very white, very blonde, and very blue-eyed doll a hairstyle that is worn by young black girls. She does not put her doll's hair into a pony tail, or brush it over and over again just for the pleasure of feeling the brush traveling the long strands.

Clarice was not alone in this: other girls' dolls had beads in their hair, braids held at the end with twists of tin foil, and series of braids that were themselves braided together. In some sense, by doing this, the girls bring their dolls into their own worlds, and whiteness here is not absolutely defined by skin and hair, but by style and way of life. The complexities of racial reference and racial politics have been much discussed in the case of black hair simulating the look of whiteness; what these girls are creating is quite the opposite: white hair that looks black.

The question of hair in African American culture is a particularly contentious one, especially for girls and women. Hair emerges as an almost living character in scores of novels, memoirs, magazine articles, and scholarly works by or about African American women.[13] As a primary racial marker, hair has become increasingly politicized as a medium through which racial identity potentially may be embraced or erased (Mercer 1990). Debates over whether black women and girls should do things to their hair that make it approximate the straight, silky, flowing hair associated with whiteness have been especially heated. At an extreme, curly, nappy hair has been judged "bad" hair, while flowing, silky hair is "good" hair.

Given this situation it is no wonder that Darlene Powell-Hopson encouraged Mattel to produce dolls that had a variety of hair textures. However, because hair play has become an increasingly central element of toy marketing to girls, Mattel did not comply. Each of the Shani dolls has what kids in Newhallville called "Barbie Doll Hair," styled in ways similar to those typical of white Barbie dolls: curls for Nichelle and Asha and a crimped style similar to that found on "Totally Hair Barbie" for Shani. In a somewhat half-hearted stab at African-Americanizing this hair, my "Beach Dazzle" Shani dolls come not with the brush that my white Barbie has, but wide-toothed implements that the company describes as "hair picks." Aside from facial features and skin tone, blackness seems to be signified more by accessories than anything else, at least in the hair department, a development that DuCille describes as "precious ready-to-ware difference" (1996: 43).

These girls' work on their dolls' heads, however, makes it seem as if the good hair/bad hair debate is not so simple as nappy versus silky, black versus white. Among Newhallville children, and among my own African American students at the college where I teach, the phrase "Barbie Doll Hair" denotes a specific phenomenon – long, long silky hair. There are at least three types of Barbie Doll Hair that kids referred to when they used this term: (1) the kind that grows out of the heads of "white" girls, (2) the kind implanted to the head of a Barbie Doll, and (3) the kind you buy at a beauty shop and add on to your own. The problem is complex: when purchased Barbie Doll Hair is used in distinctively black hairstyles, it is not just an exercise in reproducing whiteness upon black girls' heads. While actual White Girl Hair might be appropriate for use in styles that *do* replicate the head of whiteness, it does not serve at all for a whole range of other styles for which synthetic hair is perfect. Some call for melting the ends of synthetic hair, which would

be a disaster with White Girl Hair, yielding a lot of stink, but no fusion. While synthetic hair may be metaphorically white, it literally *is* Barbie Doll Hair: both are made from the same material known as Kanekalon (Jones 1990: 290). The now-common joke is when someone asks you if that's "your hair" to respond, "Sure it's mine. I bought it!" This reference alludes not only to plain old race but to good old consumerism, and elides the absolute difference between what is white and what is black. Ultimately, it may be the reference to consumerism that may be more important for the girls and women sporting Barbie Doll Hair on their heads. Can one reasonably argue, in the face of that kind of statement, that the braid-ins, extensions, or weaves are "really" white rather than black?[14]

Accepting stereotypical notions about black hair makes light of the fact that the "good" and "bad" hair debate would not be possible if black kids did not have hair that comes not just in tight, nappy curls, but also in straight or curly locks as silky, and even as blonde as Veronica Lake's famous eye-obscuring cascade. There are some indications that the absolute line between what constitutes "black" or "white" hair was originally enforced by whites who claimed long silky hair as a marker of their racial identity: there are accounts of slave-owning women, who, when faced with female slaves who had long, silky hair, would remove the offending tresses from the slave's head to enforce their blackness (White and White 1995).[15]

Underlying criticisms of Barbie Doll Hair is the assumption that white hair must be treated within the confines of the racial boundaries it is seen to represent. If one accepts that racial divisions are absolute and unbridgeable, what these girls are doing with their dolls makes little sense. Why put a black hairstyle on a white doll? And yet, if these dolls belong to these black girls, and live in the worlds they inhabit, how inflexibly white are they? Remember Asia and Natalia's ruminations on Barbie, which urgently pointed out that the main difference between them and the doll could be summarized with a nod to race, but really rested on the way they lived, the way they spoke. These criticisms apply as much to Shani as they do to any other white dolls. What these girls are doing seems to recognize in multiple ways the socially constructed nature of race, the ambiguity of a racialized existence, and the flexibility of racialized expression: it is not always or only the color of their dolls that makes them hard to relate to or identify with. Moreover, what these girls are doing emphasizes that they do not need to buy racial difference, or even to buy dolls that look like them; they can create dolls that look like them in fundamental ways through their own imaginative and material work.

The girls' refusal to accept racial boundaries as absolute and unbridgeable spilled over into my relationships with them, since from the very beginning they were fascinated with my own waist-length "Barbie Doll Hair." As I grew to know the girls better, they began to get their hands in my hair, styling it in ways that made me look better to them, while also demonstrating their nearness to me both physically and emotionally. Rather than my practical buns and messy ponytails, they'd yank and gel and twist my hair into sleek topknots with long, twirling curls just in front of each ear, or part my hair into five or six sections and braid each one. One rainy afternoon, Nyzerraye spent five hours meticulously putting my hair into over sixty braids, their ends sealed closed with bits of Reynold's Wrap that made a scratchy, musical sound when I shook my head. These girls were changing my head around on days like this, and when they'd finished their creations and sent me into the bathroom to look at their work, it seemed that it wasn't quite me in the mirror. Their work of transformation was not to rearrange my race or racial identity in some biological sense; nevertheless, they were working to make me more like them just as they did with their dolls. Their joy in being able to re-create me was tangible, and during the week that my braids stayed in kids greeted me with surprised glee: "Ooooh, Miss Chin, you got your hair braided! You look so nice!"

Conclusion

Our society can mobilize itself to wage a dramatic and successful war against racial preju-

dice and its effects upon human beings. In doing so it will eliminate the situation where the prejudiced individuals are the ones who have higher status, and where they compel others to conform to their prejudices. (Clark [1955] 1963: 139)

While making consistent references to the pioneering work of the Clarks, and in particular their "doll studies," ethnically correct dolls embody a fundamentally different social project than the one Kenneth Clark envisioned. The effort to manufacture racial diversity in the form of ethnically correct dolls is not in the end an effort to transform the assumptions and beliefs that dominate racial discourse. Consider, for instance, this comment by Yvonne Rubie, president of the International Black Toy Association: "If children grow up with things that are like themselves, they will tend to like themselves or at least identify themselves with that positive image" (Ebony 1993: 66). Ms. Rubie's assertion that it is children's relationships with things rather than people that is most critically important for their sense of self is utterly startling, and yet utterly in line with a consumerist ethic. This understanding fits in well with the emergence of an industry ready to supply the things kids need in order to have a "positive self image" but neatly sidesteps the question of fundamental social, political, and historical issues that also impinge on children's experiences and hence their perceptions of themselves as people in the world. This shift is typical of makers of ethnically correct toys, but these assumptions are belied by what can be seen and heard among children from places like Newhallville. Kids like Carlos, Asia, and Natalia are keenly aware of the complexity of race, seeing Native American ancestry in a Shani doll, and omissions in the personality of Barbie who must be described as "nice," not "dope."

What Newhallville girls said and thought about Barbie indicates that ethnically correct dolls may not provide a solution to the problems embodied in these toys, which address the issue of race, but little else. While diversifying the ethnic mix available at Toys "R" Us, Walmart, and Target, ethnically correct dolls and their producers do not redefine the market itself

Figure 13.4 *LaQuisha and her Cabbage Patch Kid. (Photo by Elizabeth Chin, 1992)*

as a sphere accessible to children of color who are also poor: despite any corporation's best intentions, it is unlikely that any of the 500,000 Kenya dolls sold by Tyco in 1992 ended up in Newhallville kids' homes. The notion that the toy box is or should be a democratic space mirrors the commonly held notion that the consumer world is similarly democratic – a place and sphere of equal opportunity for anyone with a few bucks to spend. Makers of ethnically correct dolls do little to discourage this notion of the democratic marketplace, emphasizing instead the growing power of minority consumers as part of the buying public. For poor minority children, the entry of minority toys and toymakers into the industry has made little, if any, impact on their own toy collections, or for that matter, their self-esteem.

It is perhaps because kids like those in Newhallville do not have a ready ability to buy the commodities being marketed to them that they are able to bend racial boundaries as readily as they do, and one wonders whether middle-class minority children, who are more likely to possess ethnically correct dolls, are fashioning the kinds of critical commentaries like those discussed here. From Cabbage Patch Kids with hair heavy with beads and foil (see figure 13.4) to long-haired blonde dolls sporting elaborately braided 'dos, white dolls in Newhallville were, over and over again, not quite recognized as such. They were still white, of course, and kids knew that, but the whiteness of the dolls did not stop girls from integrating them into their worlds, and girls did not seem compelled to treat them in ways that commemorate boundaries of racial difference. And yet, I have already noted that these transformations are probably fleeting, at best, even in the consciousness of the children who create them. This is what Fiske (1993) calls "weak power," a concept that recognizes the transformative *potential* of processes like those being undertaken by these Newhallville children, but that also places that potential within the larger, and oppressive, structure of the society within which these processes are generated.

The rigid understanding of race evidenced by toy makers is one based in notions of the fixity of genetics, an attempt to turn racism on its head but not an attempt to reimagine race itself. Toy makers have remolded their products, but not the parameters of the debate, ultimately perpetuating a vision of race that anthropologists, at least, have been endeavoring to dismantle since the time of Boas.[16] In confronting the market as an exclusionary sphere, describing Barbie as "nice," and then wondering why there is no abused or pregnant Barbie, Asia and Natalia reject the notion that their self-esteem can be boosted through consumer items that address issues of race but neglect other pressing issues. In making their white dolls live in black worlds, they similarly reconfigure the boundaries of race, which minority toy makers portray as being immutable. In so doing, these girls challenge the social construction not only of their own blackness, but of race itself as well.

NOTES

1   See Brewer 1997; Espiritu 1994; Harrison 1995. For an ethnographic study along these lines with youth, see Reynolds' (1995) work among Sikh youth in Great Britain.

2   See Kinder 1991; McLaren and Morris 1997; and Seiter 1993. These works, which are theoretically insightful with regard to toys, do not deal in depth with issues of theorizing children and childhood. These authors do make efforts to discuss race and class. However, each author's analysis is hampered by a prob-

lematic tendency to rely on anecdotal evidence gathered from their own (middle-class, white) children. Minority children are discussed, but not consulted, interviewed, or observed. This approach creates a hierarchy wherein middle-class white children are real and individual, while minority children are merely theoretical and generic.

3   Some exceptions are Hill 1992; and McLoyd 1982, 1983.

4   See DuCille 1996; Lord 1994; Rand 1995.

5   "Hula Hair Barbie" has flat feet, apparently so that she can swivel her hips, though the box warns that "Barbie cannot Hula alone." Analysis of the racial implications of this doll – which are nearly irresistible in their ridiculousness – must await another venue.

6   See Caputo 1995; Schwartzman 1978; Stephens 1995; Thorne 1987.

7   Bourgois has also documented similarly early concerns among Puerto Ricans in New York's East Harlem. One boy he knew "told us he hoped his mother would give birth to a boy 'because girls are too easy to rape' " (1995: 213).

8   The studies have provoked a large and still growing literature that has challenged the original research (Burnett 1995), argued for recognizing the importance of social history and gender (Fine and Bowers 1984), and examined cross-cultural validity problems (Gopaul-McNichol 1995). The Clarks' original ideas about self-hatred and self-rejection came under special criticism in the 1970s and 1980s (Banks 1976; McAdoo 1985; Porter and Washington 1979). It was the Clarks' own assessment that other methods they had used were more effective in exploring the complexities of children's racial identification (Clark and Clark 1940, Clark and Clark 1950), and yet the doll studies remain for the public the most compelling demonstration of the negative effects of racism on black children's self-concept or what is more often now called self-esteem.

9   It is a testament to the emotional power of the doll studies that it is often asserted

these very studies were responsible for convincing the Supreme Court justices that segregated schools caused unconscionable damage to black children (McAdoo 1985; Wallace 1990; Wilkinson 1979). Neither the doll studies nor psychological research by Kenneth Clark were mentioned in the text or footnotes of the court's decision. The famous reference in footnote 11 of the court's decision refers not to the doll studies, but to an overview of the social science literature assessing the impact of segregation on children. Kenneth Clark had prepared this summary report earlier for a national summit on youth. His own studies are mentioned, but the majority of the work reviews a variety of studies focused on children from a variety of ethnic groups, races, and cultures. Among the materials presented to the Supreme Court was an Amicus Brief detailing the social effects of enforced segregation signed by 33 social scientists, including Kenneth Clark.

10 Urla and Swedlund (1995) did find physical differences in an anthropometric comparison of Barbie and Shani, but because their measurements were recalculated on the assumption that Barbie is 5' 10", the absolute difference in the two dolls' sizes was not provided. None of these changes, DuCille (1996) notes, prevent the Shani dolls from being able to wear Barbie clothes. With Barbie setting the standard for the $11\frac{1}{2}$ inch fashion doll, Olmec's Imani doll also can wear Barbie's clothes, and this is mentioned on the front of Imani's package. Even the newly redesigned Barbie body, touted at the 1998 International Toy Fair as being more representative of something approaching a living human female, appears to be able to wear the old Barbie clothes.

11 DuCille (1996) writes that Colored Francie also raised the issue of miscegenation, since she was the black version of Barbie's cousin Francie. This is entirely possible, but there is little direct evidence that children or other consumers reacted this way to the doll.

12 In 1997 the Federal Government, after four years of contentious debate, decided to allow people to use more than one racial category when identifying themselves. For the first time, the estimated 2,000,000 mixed-race Americans will be able to approximate something like Woods' "Cablinasian" status when filling out census forms. The notion of separate races, however, remains unchanged in this new policy (*New York Times* 1997).

13 See DuCille 1996; Morrison 1970; Rooks 1996.

14 The black/white distinction about this hair is probably inappropriate in any case. Most human hair sold to the African American market comes from Asian countries, primarily China, India, and Thailand (Jones 1990).

15 Kobena Mercer's observation that no black hairstyle is inherently "natural" (Mercer 1990) applies equally to white hair. White Girl Hair, especially in the long and flowing form represented by Barbie, can be difficult to maintain. In the long and flowing version, this kind of hair is no more a natural or easy assertion of whiteness than the Afro or Dreadlocks are an easy or natural assertion of blackness. In any case, the tradition of long flowing hair is much more prevalent among Chicanas and Asians than it is among whites.

16 Lee D. Baker's work (1992) on this subject amply documents that this enterprise has been rife with complexity and contradiction and is historically not as rosy as many of us were taught even in left-leaning graduate institutions!

REFERENCES

Abu-Lughod, Lila. 1990. The Romance of Resistance: Tracing Transformations of Power through Bedouin Women. *American Ethnologist*, 17/1: 41–55.

Ariès, Philippe. 1962. *Centuries of Childhood: A Social History of Family Life*. New York: Vintage Books.

Baker, Lee David. 1992. The Role of Anthropology in the Social Construction of Race,

1896–1954. PhD dissertation, Anthropology Department, Temple University.

Banks, W. C. 1976. White Preference in Blacks: A Paradigm in Search of a Phenomenon. *Psychological Bulletin*, 83(b): 1179–86.

Bateson, Gregory. [1955] 1972. A Theory of Play and Fantasy. In *Steps Towards an Ecology of Mind*, pp. 177–93. San Francisco and Scranton: Chandler.

Bourgois, Philippe. 1995. *In Search of Respect*. New York: Cambridge University Press.

Brewer, Rose M. 1997. Theorizing Race, Class, and Gender: The New Scholarship or Black Feminist Intellectuals and Black Women's Labor. In *Materialist Feminism: A Reader in Class, Difference, and Women's Lives*. Rosemary Hennessy and Chrys Ingraham, eds. pp. 236–47. New York: Routledge.

Brown, Michael F. 1996. On Resisting Resistance. *American Anthropologist*, 98/4: 729–35.

Burnett, Myra N. 1995. Doll Studies Revisited: A Question of Validity. *Journal of Black Psychology*, 21/1: 19–29.

Caldera, Yvonne M., Aletha C. Huston, and Marion O'Brien, 1989. Social Interactions and Play Patterns of Parents and Toddlers with Feminine, Masculine, and Neutral Toys. Child Development 60: 70–6.

Caputo, Virginia. 1995. Anthropology's Silent "Others": A Consideration of Some Conceptual and Methodological Issues for the Study of Youth and Children's Cultures. In *Youth Cultures: A Cross-Cultural Perspective*. Vered Amit-Talai and Helena Wulff, eds. pp. 19–42. New York: Routledge.

Chin, Elizabeth. 1996. Fettered Desire: Consumption and Social Experience among Minority Children in New Haven, Connecticut. PhD dissertation, Anthropology Department, Graduate School of the City University of New York.

—— 1998. Social Inequality and Servicescape: Local Groceries and Downtown Stores in New Haven, Connecticut. In *Servicescapes: The Concept of Place in Contemporary Markets*. John F. Sherry, Jr., ed. pp. 591–617. Chicago: NTC Group.

Clark, Kenneth B. [1955] 1963. *Prejudice and Your Child*. Boston: Beacon Press.

Clark, Kenneth B., and Mamie P. Clark. 1939. The Development of Consciousness of Self and the Emergence of Racial Identification in Negro Preschool Children. *Journal of Social Psychology*, SPSSI Bulletin, 10: 591–9.

—— 1940 Skin Color as a Factor in Racial Identification of Negro Preschool Children. *Journal of Social Psychology*, SPSSI Bulletin, 11: 159–69.

Clark, Kenneth B., and Mamie Phipps Clark. 1947. Racial Identification and Preference in Negro Children. In *Readings in Social Psychology*. T. M. Newcomb and E. L. Hartley, eds. pp. 169–78. New York: Henry Holt.

—— 1950. Emotional Factors in Racial Identification and Preference in Negro Children. *Journal of Negro Education*, 19/3: 341–50.

Cross, Gary. 1997. *Kids' Stuff: Toys and the Changing World of American Childhood*. Cambridge, MA: Harvard University Press.

DuCille, Ann. 1996. *Skin Trade*. Cambridge, MA: Harvard University Press.

Ebony. 1993. New Boom in Ethnic Toys: Experts Say the Trend is More than Skin Deep. *Ebony*, November: 64–6.

Erikson, Erik. 1964. *Childhood and Society*. 2nd edition. New York: Norton.

Espiritu, Yen Le. 1994. The Intersection of Race, Ethnicity, and Class: The Multiple Identities of Second-Generation Filipinos. *Identities*, 1/2–3: 249–73.

Fine, Michelle, and Cheryl Bowers. 1984. Racial Self-Identification: The Effects of Social History and Gender. *Journal of Applied Social Psychology*, 14/2: 136– 46.

Fiske, John. 1993. *Power Plays, Power Works*. London and New York: Verso.

Formanek-Brunell, Miriam. 1993. *Made to Play House: Dolls and the Commercialization of American Girlhood, 1830–1930*. New Haven, CT: Yale University Press.

Gopaul-McNichol, Sharon-Ann. 1995. A Cross-Cultural Examination of Racial Identity and Racial Preference of Preschool Children in the West Indies. *Journal of Cross-Cultural Psychology*, 26/2: 141–52.

Harrison, Faye V. 1995. The Persistent Power of "Race" in the Cultural and Political Economy of Racism. *Annual Review of Anthropology*, 24: 47–74.

Henry, Jules, and Zunia Henry. 1974. *Doll Play of Pilagá Indian Children*. New York: Vintage Books.

Hill, Ronald Paul. 1992. Homeless Children: Coping with Material Losses. *Journal of Consumer Affairs*, 26/2: 274–87.

Jones, Lisa. 1990. *Bulletproof Diva*. New York: Doubleday.

Kelly-Byrne, Diana. 1989. *A Child's Play Life: An Ethnographic Study*. New York: Teacher's College Press.

Kinder, Marsha. 1991. *Playing with Power in Movies, Television, and Video Games: From Muppet Babies to Teenage Mutant Ninja Turtles*. Berkeley: University of California Press.

Lord, M. G. 1994. *Forever Barbie: The Unauthorized Biography of a Real Doll*. New York: William Morrow.

McAdoo, Harriette Pipes. 1985. Racial Attitude and Self-Concept of Black Children Over Time. In *Black Children: Social, Educational, and Parental Environments*. Harriette Pipes McAdoo and John Lewis McAdoo, eds. pp. 213–42. London: Sage.

McLaren, Peter, and Janet Morris. 1997. Mighty Morphin Power Rangers: The Aesthetics of Phallo-Militaristic Justice. In *Kinderculture: The Corporate Construction of Childhood*. Shirley R. Steinberg and Joe L. Kincheloe, eds. pp. 115–28. Boulder, CO: Westview Press.

McLoyd, V. 1982. Social Class Differences in Sociodramatic Play: A Critical Review. *Developmental Review*, 2: 1–30.

—— 1983. The Effects of the Structure of Play Objects on the Pretend Play of Low-Income Children. *Child Development*, 54: 626–35.

Mercer, Kobena. 1990. Black Hair/Style Politics. In *Out There: Marginalization in Contemporary Cultures*. Russell Ferguson, Martha Gever, Trinh T. Minh-ha, and Cornel West, eds. pp. 247–64. New York and Cambridge, MA: New Museum of Contemporary Art and MIT Press.

Miller, Daniel J. 1995. Consumption and Commodities. *Annual Reviews in Anthropology*, 24: 141–62.

Montessori, Maria. [1912] 1964. *The Montessori Method*. New York: Schocken.

Morrison, Toni. 1970. *The Bluest Eye*. New York: Holt, Rinehart and Winston.

New York Times. 1997. Multiracial Americans. Editorial, November 8: A14.

Pellegrini, Anthony D., and Ithel Jones. 1994. Play, Toys, and Language. In *Toys, Play, and Child Development*. Jeffrey H. Goldstein, ed. pp. 27–45. New York: Cambridge University Press.

Porter, J., and R. Washington. 1979. Black Identity and Self Esteem: A Review of Studies of Black Self-Concept. *Annual Review of Sociology*, 5: 53–4.

Powell-Hopson, Darlene. 1985. The Effects of Modeling, Reinforcement, and Color Meaning Word Associations on Doll Color Preferences of Black Preschool Children and White Preschool Children. PhD dissertation, Hofstra University.

Rand, Erica. 1995. *Barbie's Queer Accessories*. Durham, NC: Duke University Press.

Reguero, Wilfred, and Marilyn Crane. 1994. Project MotherCare: One Hospital's Response to the High Perinatal Death Rate in New Haven, CT. *Public Health Reports*, 109/5: 647–52.

Reynolds, Pamela. 1995. Youth and the Politics of Culture in South Africa. In *Children and the Politics of Culture*. Sharon Stephens, ed. pp. 218–40. Princeton, NJ: Princeton University Press.

Rooks, Noliwe, M. 1996. *Hair Raising: Beauty, Culture, and African American Women*. New Brunswick, NJ: Rutgers University Press.

Schwartzman, Helen B., ed. 1978. *Transformations: The Anthropology of Children's Play*. New York: Plenum.

Seiter, Ellen. 1993. *Sold Separately: Children and Parents in Consumer Culture*. New Brunswick, NJ: Rutgers University Press.

Sholle, David. 1990. Resistance: Pinning Down a Wandering Concept in Cultural Studies Discourse. *Journal of Urban and Cultural Studies*, 1/1: 87–105.

Stephens, Sharon. 1995. Children and the Politics of Culture in "Late Capitalism." In *Children and the Politics of Culture*. Sharon

Stephens, ed. pp. 3–48. Princeton, NJ: Princeton University Press.

Sutton-Smith, Brian. 1986. *Toys as Culture*. New York: Gardener.

Thorne, Barrie. 1987. Re-Visioning Women and Social Change: Where Are the Children? *Gender & Society*, 1/1: 85–109.

Urla, Jacqueline, and Alan C. Swedlund. 1995. The Anthropometry of Barbie: Unsettling Ideals of the Feminine Body in Popular Culture. In *Deviant Bodies: Critical Perspectives on Difference in Science and Popular Culture*. Jennifer Terry and Jaqueline Urla, eds. pp. 277–313. Bloomington: Indiana University Press.

US Bureau of the Census. 1980. *Census of Population and Housing*. Washington, DC: Government Printing Office.

Wade, Peter. 1993. 'Race', Nature and Culture. *Man*, 28: 17–34.

Wallace, Michele. 1990. Modernism, Postmodernism and the Problem of the Visual in Afro-American Culture. In *Out There: Marginalization and Contemporary Cultures*. Russell Ferguson, Martha Gever, Trinh T. Minh-ha, and Cornel West, eds. pp. 39–50. New York and Cambridge, MA: New Museum of Contemporary Art and MIT Press.

White, Shane, and Graham White. 1995. Slave Hair and African American Culture in the Eighteenth and Nineteenth Centuries. *Journal of Southern History*, 61/1: 45–76.

Wilkinson, J. Harvie, III. 1979. *From Brown to Bakke: The Supreme Court and School Integration: 1954–1978*. New York: Oxford University Press.

Williams, Brackette. 1995. Beaming Them Up: First Blood and Some Views on the Pleasures and Dangers of Fresh Blood in the Making of U.S. Americans. *Identities*, 1/4: 427–42.

14

Strategic Naturalizing: Kinship in an Infertility Clinic

Charis Thompson

What might California infertility clinics in the 1990s reveal about contemporary kinship? This essay raises that question by going inside clinics and analyzing the work done during gestational surrogacy and egg donation to establish and disambiguate kin relations. Patients, practitioners, and third-party reproducers (egg and sperm donors and surrogates), with the help of medical techniques, lab standards, body parts, psychological screening, and rapidly evolving laws, all take on part of this work. The examples below show that the clinic is a site where certain bases of kin differentiation are foregrounded and recrafted while others are minimized to make the couples who seek and pay for infertility treatment – the intended parents – come out through legitimate and intact chains of descent as the real parents. All other parties to the reproduction, human and nonhuman, are rendered sufficiently prosthetic in the reproduction as to prevent (if all goes well) contest over who the child's parents are. The alignment of procreative intent and biological kinship is achieved over time through a mixed bag of surprisingly everyday strategies for naturalizing and socializing particular traits, substances, precedents, and behaviors. The dynamics of this are described below.

This essay is inspired by the writings of Marilyn Strathern (1992), Sarah Franklin (1997), and their colleagues on the role of reproductive technologies in complicating naturalized linear cognatic descent, and in reinvigorating the study of Western kinship (Edwards et al. 1999; Franklin and Ragoné 1998; Ragoné 1994). The cases analyzed here elaborate Strathern's and Franklin's counterintuitive discovery of the underdeterminacy of biogenetic ways of determining kinship. I attempt to show that biology can nonetheless be mobilized to differentiate ambiguous kinship. In the process, the meaning of biological motherhood is somewhat transformed; in particular, biological motherhood is becoming something that can be partial. This work is thus about "doing" kinship, as opposed to simply "being" a particular and fixed kind of kin. I also draw on the literature in science and technology studies on the interconnections between, or coproduction of, politics and ontology, nature and culture. Rather than simply observing the dissolution of the boundary between nature and culture, I specify the means by which the facts and practices of biomedicine and the social meanings of kinship are used to generate and substantiate each other in specific cases. The analytic stress on naturalization is indebted to scholars who have pointed out the ubiquitous and multiple means by which identities get naturalized (Yanagisako and Delaney 1995). The emphasis on the strategies for enforcing procreative intent resonates with studies indicating that reproduction is always already stratified (Ginsburg and Rapp 1995; Rapp 1999). Again, I attempt to contribute to these exciting areas of analysis by providing an account of some of the processes whereby the ontology of naturalization and politics of stratification occur.

The Argument

Human reproduction is routinely "assisted" in infertility clinics, using many of the same techniques of modern biology that inform dominant systems of Western kinship reckoning, such as genetics and evolutionary biology. Paradoxically, in reproductive technology clinics there are both more explicit biological definitions of relatedness, on the one hand, and more precise social definitions of parenthood, on the other, but these are not always complementary. One might expect to find the connections enhanced between relatedness as determined by biological practice and socially meaningful answers to questions about who is related to whom. The science would help to hone or perfect an understanding of such terms as "mother," "father," and "child." Tracking biomedical interventions in infertility medicine from the perspective of kinship theory reveals something altogether different, however. Rather than finding the natural ground to social categories exposed at its most concrete level, one discovers a number of disruptions of the categories of relatedness (especially parent and child, but also sibling, aunt, uncle, and grandparent). In particular, one sees that the connec-

tions between the biological facts taken to be relevant to kinship and socially meaningful kinship categories are highly indeterminate. Keeping biological and social accounts aligned, and utilizing biology as a resource for understanding the latter, takes work. Norms governing the family; laws regulating reproductive technologies, custody, and descent; the medical technologies themselves; and the financial dynamics of third-party, medically assisted reproduction are the feedstocks and products of this kinship work.[1] Infertility patients, third parties, and practitioners routinely, and largely informally, do this kinship work; they are practical metaphysicians. In documenting kinship negotiations in infertility clinics, this essay is therefore an empirical argument about metaphysics.

The cases discussed below involve two technically identical procedures that lead to different kinds of kinship configurations – gestational surrogacy and in vitro fertilization (IVF) with ovum donation – as they arose in contemporary California infertility clinics. The two procedures draw on substance and genes as natural resources for making parents and children, but they distribute the elements of identity and personhood differently. It is possible to map out what is rendered relevant to establishing parenthood (what I call a "relational" stage in the process of conceiving and bearing a child because it can support claims of parenthood) and what is rendered irrelevant (what I label "custodial" because it is a stage of the procedure that involves caring for the gametes or embryos as ends, not means, yet it cannot sustain parental claims). From this mapping exercise, one can suggest some elements that underlie the various uses of biology to configure kinship. The examples chosen are all complicated cases, involving friendship egg donation, intergenerational though intrafamilial egg donation, and family member surrogates. Of the six cases, only one involves an egg donor or surrogate who is commercially contracted because I wanted to focus on instances where there is the greatest need to disambiguate kinship – namely, cases with close friends or family members as donors or surrogates. Here, the need to rule out the possibility of incest and adultery meant that the parties to the reproduction were very explicit about how the correct kinship relations were being created and maintained.

In attempting to show the choreography and innovativeness of processes of naturalization, I make three claims, which are taken up again in the conclusion. First, drawing on the different ways in which these gestational surrogacies and egg donations distribute what is natural, I argue against a fixed or unique natural base for the relevant categories of kinship.[2] I also contend that high-tech interventions in reproduction are not necessarily dehumanizing or antithetical to the production of kinship and identity, as some critics of the procedures – including, for example, mainstream Catholic theologians and some feminists – have maintained.[3] Indeed, in the clinical setting, gestational surrogacy and donor egg IVF are means through which patients exercise agency, and claim or disown bonds of ancestry and descent, blood and genes, nation and ethnicity.[4] Third, and for reasons that will turn out to be intricately related to the first two assertions, I maintain that the innovations offered by these technologies do not intrinsically provide only new ways of drawing these fundamental distinctions, nor do they simply reinforce old ways of claiming identity (see Farquhar 1996). The technologies contain both elements.

Substance vs. Genes

Most people are used to thinking of there being just two biological parents who both donate genetic material: what is termed a bilateral or cognatic kinship pattern is inscribed in the understanding of biogenetics. A baby is the product of the fusion of the mother's and father's genetic material. Kin are divided into blood relations and non-blood-relations, and it is usually assumed that blood relations share biological substance with one another in a manner that simply reflects the genetic relationship. By the end of the 1990s, however, it was already a commonplace that a woman can share bodily substance with a fetus to whom she is not genetically related. As a result of donor egg IVF and gestational surrogacy, the

overlapping biological idioms of shared bodily substance and genes come apart.[5] The maternal genetic material, including the determinants of the blood type and characteristics of the fetus, is contributed by the egg, which is derived from the ovaries of one woman. Nonetheless, the embryo grows in and out of the substance of another woman's body; the fetus is fed by and takes form from the gestational woman's blood, oxygen, and placenta. It is not unreasonable to accord the gestating mother a biological claim to motherhood. Indeed, some have suggested that shared substance is a much more intimate biological connection than shared genetics, and more uniquely characteristic of motherhood, as genes are shared between many different kinds of relations.[6] Where gestational motherhood arises from egg donation rather than surrogacy, and is thus backed up by procreative intent, financial transaction, laws sympathetic to a birth mother's claim to be a child's legal mother, and so on, the case for considering the woman who gestated the fetus as the "natural" mother can become almost unassailable. The examples from the field recounted below illustrate the in situ constructions of a case for natural motherhood as it arose in infertility clinics where I worked.

Gestational surrogacy means that eggs from one woman are fertilized with her partner's sperm in vitro (occasionally, donor eggs or sperm are used in place of the gametes of one partner from the paying patient couple) and then transferred to the uterus of a different woman who gestates the pregnancy. The woman who gestates the pregnancy is known as a gestational surrogate (see Ragoné 1994). In some states, the woman from whom the eggs were derived, and her partner, have custody of the child and are the parents at the child's birth. In other states, although the laws are rapidly changing, the genetic mother and her husband have to adopt the baby at birth, and the surrogate's name goes on the birth certificate. If donor eggs from a third woman were used, the woman from the paying couple is still the mother and she adopts the baby at birth, as in conventional surrogacy. A combination of intent, financial transaction, and genetics trace maternity through the various bodies producing the baby in commercial gestational surrogacy. In noncommercial gestational surrogacy, an emotional or familial commitment takes the place of a financial transaction.

Gestational surrogacy is procedurally identical to donor egg IVF: eggs from one woman are fertilized in vitro and then gestated in the uterus of another woman. Two things make donor egg IVF and gestational surrogacy different from each other. In the case of donor egg IVF, the sperm with which the eggs are fertilized comes from the gestational woman's partner (or a donor standing in for him and picked by that couple), whereas in gestational surrogacy, sperm comes from the partner of the provider of the eggs (or a donor standing in for him). From a lab perspective, there is no difference – sperm collected by masturbation is prepared and added to retrieved eggs, and the embryos are incubated and transferred identically in both cases. The sperm comes from the person standing in the right sociolegal relationship to whichever of the women is designated as the mother-to-be. The identity of the intended mother depends on who came into the clinic for treatment for infertility, the various parties' reproductive history, and in the case of private clinics, who is paying. Where additional donors are used, or where the egg donor or gestational surrogate is being contracted on a commercial basis, the importance of who is paying for the treatment in deciding who the designated parents are is reinforced.[7] In cases where motherhood is contested, one or more of these aspects breaks down or falls out of alignment with the others. Both gestational surrogacy and donor egg IVF separate shared bodily substance and genes, but whereas donor egg IVF traces motherhood through the substance half of this separation, gestational surrogacy traces it through the genetic half.[8]

Cases from the Field

IVF with donor egg

CASE 1: GIOVANNA *Summary: Giovanna will gestate embryos made from donor eggs from*

an Italian American friend and sperm from Giovanna's husband. Giovanna and her husband will be the parents if pregnancy ensues.

One afternoon, I was in an examination room getting ready for the next patient's ultrasound scan in preparation for a cycle of IVF. The patient, Giovanna, was already in the room, changed, and ready for her scan, so we talked as we awaited the physician's arrival. Giovanna described herself as an Italian American approaching forty years of age. She explained that she had tried but "failed" IVF before, using her own eggs and her husband's sperm. Her response to the superovulatory drugs and doctor's recommendation had persuaded Giovanna to try to get pregnant using donor eggs from a younger woman. Almost all clinics report better implantation rates in IVF using donor eggs, which are retrieved from women under thirty-five years old, than those obtained using an older patient's eggs.

Giovanna said that she had decided to use a donor who was a good friend, rather than an anonymous donor. Choosing a friend for a donor seemed to be an important part of reconfiguring the experience of pregnancy: if conception was not to occur inside her body or with her eggs, then it was preferable that she had emotional attachments of friendship to, and could make the corresponding demands on, the woman who was to be her donor. Giovanna described her friend as also Italian American, and said that she was excited and ready to help. She depicted the shared ethnic classification as being "enough genetic similarity." Further, Giovanna accorded her gestational role a rich biological significance: she said that the baby would grow inside her, nourished by her blood and made out of the very stuff of her body all the way from a four-celled embryo to a fully formed baby.

There is currently a gradual de-privatizing trend creeping further and further back in pregnancy, socializing gestation and opening the pregnant woman up to medical scrutiny as well as state regulation and intervention. Examples of the trend include fetal monitoring and surgery, right-to-life political movements, the improved survival rates of significantly premature infants, and a predominantly child-based perspective for discussing the social and ethical dimensions of human reproduction. In these arenas, gestation is increasingly assimilated to the care one provides to a child once it is born. When gestational surrogacy is uncontested (see below), everything except for fertilization is de-privatized and equated to child care, despite its biological nature. This makes genetics into the essential natural component that confers kinship and minimizes the role of gestation. In Giovanna's case, however, she cast her gestation as conferring kinship because of its biological nature, despite the absence of genetic connection. Against the de-privatizing and genetic essentialist cultural trend, she renaturalized gestation.

Giovanna pried apart the natural, biological basis for specifying mother/child relations into separable components. In addition, she complicated the natural status of the genetic component that would be derived from her friend by socializing genetics. She said that what mattered to her in genetic inheritance was that the donor share a similar history to her own. She said that because her friend was also Italian American, they both came from the same kind of home, and because they both had Italian mothers, they had grown up with the same cultural influences. So genes were coding for ethnicity, which Giovanna was expressing as a national/natural category of Italian Americanness. As in so many instances of contemporary biomedicine, it turns out, then, that genes have social categories built into them, without which they would not make sense or be relevant. This is a reversal of what is often presumed to be the unidirectionality of genealogy. Genes figure in Giovanna's kinship reckoning because there is a chain of transactions between the natural and cultural that not only grounds the cultural in the natural but gives the natural its explanatory power by its links to culturally relevant categories.

Giovanna's separation of biology into shared bodily substance and genetics, and her formulation of what matters to her about genetics in the context of her procedure, resists the scientistic impulse to assume that biology under-writes sociocultural potential and not the other way around, and that biology is sufficient to account for sociocultural reality. For

her, the reduction to genes is only meaningful because it codes back to sociocultural aspects of being Italian American (it is not unidirectional). Likewise, the ethnic category does not just perform a transitional function between nature and culture but is an elision, collecting disparate elements and linking them without any assumption that every one of the sociocultural aspects of having an Italian American mother, for example, needs to map back onto biology.

CASE 2: PAULA *Summary: Paula will gestate embryos made from donor eggs from either her sister or an African American friend and sperm from Paula's husband. Paula and her husband will be the parents if pregnancy ensues.*

In a related case, an African American patient, Paula, who I met at the clinic only once, spontaneously offered commentary on the kinship implications of her upcoming procedure. Paula had undergone "premature ovarian failure" and entered menopause in her early thirties before she had had any children. She and her husband had decided to try donor egg IVF, and she was hoping to be able to carry a pregnancy. They had not yet chosen an egg donor, and Paula said that she would first ask her sister and a friend, to see if either of them would be willing to be her egg donor. Paula expressed a strong preference for using a donor "from my community."[9] She said that using a donor was not as strange as it might at first seem, as it was like something "we've been doing all along." When I asked her what she meant, she explained that in African American communities, it was not unusual for women to "mother" or "second mother" their sister's or daughter's or friend's child(ren).

Paula's explanation suggests the possibility of legitimizing the natural "deviance" of her procedure by pointing to its social basis: it was OK to give birth to a child made with another woman's eggs, as sharing child raising was already a common social phenomenon. This is the reverse of the familiar strategy where naturalization can normalize social deviance, as for example, when behavior is explained by genetics or an underlying mental or medical problem. If using a donor to get pregnant is just one more way of doing something that is already a prevalent social phenomenon – dividing different aspects of mothering across generations, between friends and sisters – then it is not a radical departure from existing social practice. In presenting it like this, Paula was normalizing her reproductive options. Rather than being exploitative, using a donor is assimilated to other ways in which women help each other to lead livable lives.

Gestational surrogacy where the surrogate is a family member

CASE 3: RACHEL, KAY, AND MICHAEL *Summary: Rachel will gestate embryos made from Kay's eggs and sperm from Kay's husband, Michael. Rachel will give birth, but Kay and Michael will be the parents. In addition, Rachel is Michael's sister.*

Michael and Kay had a history of long-term infertility, including two unsuccessful attempts to get pregnant with IVF. They decided to maximize their chances on one last attempt at IVF by using a gestational surrogate, Michael's sister, Rachel. Rachel was referred to approvingly as an ideal surrogate by several staff members during the weeks of treatment. Her own family of three children was already complete. She was actively compliant, making explicit references to how she would organize her life so as to do whatever was in the treatment's best interests. She was good-humored about the long waits during appointments at the clinic. Her husband's job was lucrative enough that she could assume the risks associated with taking a leave of absence from work, and Rachel said she was glad of a break from work and a chance to spend more time at home with her children. The generic role of the "good patient," then, was masterfully deployed by Rachel to emphasize the fact that her part in this was subordinate to those whose procreative intent they were all working to realize. I followed Rachel's treatment as a case study of gestational surrogacy.

An important activity during their treatment involved ruling out Rachel as a parent and counting in Kay, because of the incest with her brother Michael that would be implied if Rachel were the mother. Such conventional strategies as distinguishing between medium and information, and between nature and nurture, were used by the parties involved in the pregnancy to rule out incest, and negotiate descent and heredity. During one appointment Rachel, the surrogate, turned to Kay, the mother-to-be, and said that it was lucky that she, Rachel, had had her tubes tied after her last child. Kay raised her eyebrows, seeming not to understand, and Rachel elaborated by saying that otherwise there might be a danger of one of her eggs being in her tubes or uterus and some spare sperm out of the petri dish from her brother fertilizing her egg. Kay understood, laughed, and agreed. I was struck at the time that this would be incest, but that gestating her brother's baby was obviously not, despite the fact that her brother's baby would grow inside her. If the procedure had utilized a donor egg, the gestating woman, that is, Rachel, would have been the mother; then this same medical procedure would have been incest, because Rachel would have been the mother and her brother the father.

Five embryos resulted from the egg retrieval from Kay and subsequent fertilization with Michael's sperm. On the day of the embryo transfer, the doctor tried to persuade Kay and Rachel to let him transfer three embryos into Rachel and two into Kay. The doctor was being quite insistent, reiterating "Are you sure you don't want to split the embryos?" several times, but Kay and Rachel stood firm. Later on in the staff room, the doctor expressed disappointment that Kay and Rachel would not both have an embryo transfer, thereby enabling him to "make history" as he called it. If they had both become pregnant, it would have been the first time that a single set of twins would have been born from different mothers.

Rachel's husband, referred to by the staff as an "awkward attorney," was not present for the embryo transfer and was conspicuously absent throughout the whole treatment cycle. Kay's husband (and Rachel's brother), Michael, was in the room, though, as the father-to-be. Rachel's prosthetic role was heightened during the embryo transfer by the presence of her brother while she was lying with her legs in stirrups. After the embryo transfer, Rachel had to remain in a prone position for two hours. Michael left soon after the embryo transfer, but Rachel and Kay were "in this together," as Kay expressed it, and so Kay stayed by Rachel's side.

During the two-hour wait, Kay and Rachel discussed what the baby would look like if Rachel became pregnant. Rachel began by flattering Kay, saying that if the baby looked like a combination of her brother, Michael, and Kay, it would be good-looking. This fit the normal genetic reckoning of half the characteristics coming from the egg (Kay's) and half from the sperm (Michael's). Kay responded, however, by saying that it might look more like Rachel, and that if it came out looking like her nephews and niece (Rachel's children), she would be happy. Perhaps Kay was just returning the compliment. But if the baby could look like Rachel, then Rachel was not merely as custodial in this pregnancy as the logic of gestational surrogacy seems to need her to be so as not to be incestuous. Rachel took up the thread, asking rhetorically whether the baby could get anything of her from growing inside her. They joked about dogs looking like their owners and mentioned that identical twins can have different birth weights depending on how they fare during pregnancy, both classic cases of the effect of "nurture" on "nature." They resolved the question by accepting that if Rachel had an effect on what the baby looked like, it would be because she had provided a certain environment for the baby to grow in, not because she was part of the baby's "nature." Rachel's role in the pregnancy was thus returned safely to the realm of caregiver and provider of a nurturing environment. Their narrow geneticization of incest prevented biological embodiment of her brother's child from being incest; the genetic discourse of naturalization worked in opposition to the discourse of biological kinship through embodiment by denaturalizing the latter. The threat of incest was again avoided, leaving the logic of the procedure and both compliments intact.

Ten days later, Rachel's pregnancy test was positive. The embryologist recounted the story that she had just been told by Rachel: Rachel didn't phone Kay straightaway but instead went out and bought a little teddy bear, to which she attached a note saying, "Your chil-

d(ren) are doing fine with Auntie Rachel – can't wait to meet you in eight and a half months." She took the teddy around to Kay's house, left it on the doorstep, rang the doorbell, and hid herself. Apparently Kay opened the door, found the bear, and burst into tears. It was not until Rachel came in for her final infertility clinic scan that her husband, the awkward attorney, was mentioned in connection with the pregnancy. Rachel told the doctor that her husband was happy about the twins that she was carrying. Apparently he had suggested naming the twins after the doctor – calling one by the doctor's first name and one by his last name. In choosing names and the male doctor for eponymy, Rachel's husband was able to contribute to the babies' lineage. In building in quasi-patrilineal kinship through naming practices, Rachel's husband also illustrated the manner in which people in this site routinely used tropes (including conservative ones like male eponymy) with which they were familiar from other contexts, extending them to cover and disambiguate kinship in this novel setting.

CASE 4: JANE *Summary: Jane will gestate embryos made from an infertile patient's eggs and sperm from that patient's husband. Jane will give birth, but the patient and her husband will be the parents. Jane is married to the infertile patient's brother, so she is the patient's sister-in-law by marriage.*

While Rachel's treatment cycle was in progress, another noncommercial surrogacy treatment was ongoing at the same clinic. In this case the surrogate, Jane, was related, but only by marriage, to the intended infertile couple. The surrogate was married to the brother of a woman and her husband who were providing the gametes and hoping to be parents. Staff members compared Jane unfavorably with Rachel from the beginning, complaining that her heart was not in it, and that Jane and her husband's sister (the mother-to-be) were "passive aggressive" toward each other. When Jane failed to get pregnant after two attempts, the clinic's psychologist went so far as to suggest at the weekly staff meeting that Jane's "unresolved feelings," deemed evident from her psychological evaluation, were getting in the way of implantation of the embryos. The psychologist felt, or at least presented a narrative constructed thus, that the demands of the emotional contract necessary to undertake a pregnancy on someone else's behalf could not be sustained unless the two had a very close relationship. She voiced a strong preference for close girlfriends or sisters over relations by marriage when a noncommercial surrogate was needed. In Jane's case, then, reproductive failure was blamed on a relationship that was insufficiently biologically or socially grounded to sustain the biological demands of this particular form of custodial care.

Intergenerational donor egg IVF

CASE 5: FLORA *Summary: Flora will gestate embryos made from her daughter's eggs and sperm from Flora's second husband. Flora will give birth, and her second husband will be the father. Flora's daughter will be the baby's half sister, not its mother.*

A fifty-one-year-old woman, Flora, came in for treatment. She was perimenopausal and had five grown-up children from a previous marriage. She didn't fit the typical patient profile of the elite, white, postponed-childbearing woman. Flora was Mexican and crossed the border from an affluent suburb of Tijuana, where she lived, to southern California for her treatment. With five children, she already had what many would probably consider "too many" offspring. She had recently been remarried to a man many years her junior who had not yet had children. Flora was quite explicit about the gender, age, and financial relations between herself and her new younger husband, and her desire to, as she put it, "give him a child."

Because of her age, it was suggested that if Flora wanted any significant chance of getting pregnant, she should find an egg donor. The donor eggs would be inseminated by Flora's husband's sperm, and the resulting embryos would either be transferred to Flora's uterus or frozen for use in subsequent cycles. Flora read widely in the medical and popular literature, and frequently made suggestions about or fine-tuned her own protocol. She also picked her own egg donor: one of her daughters in her early twenties, who herself already had chil-

dren.[10] The mother's and daughter's cycles were synchronized, and the daughter was given superovulatory drugs to stimulate the simultaneous maturation of several preovulatory follicles. The daughter responded dramatically to the drugs, and at the time of egg recovery, the physician and embryologist removed sixty-five eggs from her ovaries (ten, plus or minus five, is "normal"). The eggs were inseminated with Flora's husband's sperm, forty-five fertilized, and five fresh embryos were transferred to Flora's uterus that cycle. Flora did not get pregnant in the fresh cycle or in the first two frozen cycles, but did in the third.

Flora did not seem overly perturbed by the intergenerational confusion of a mother giving birth to her own "grandchildren" and to her daughter's "daughter/sister." Neither did I ever hear her mention the fact that her resulting child would be genetically related to her ex-husband as well as her current one. Instead, she discussed her daughter's genetic similarity to her. Like Paula, the African American woman mentioned earlier, Flora also assimilated her case to existing social practice, in this instance to the prevalence of generation-skipping parenting (where a grandparent parents a child socially and legally) in the communities with which she was familiar. Flora nonetheless signaled some ambivalence on the part of her daughter. When asked who her donor was, she replied, "My daughter," adding that her daughter was "not exactly excited but she doesn't mind doing it." The daughter herself said, when the mother was out of the room, that she didn't mind helping them have a single baby but that the huge number of embryos stored away was unsettling. After all, she added, her mother already had a family: "She doesn't need to start a whole new family – one baby is one thing, but ...!"

The daughter's reluctance to see her mother having "a whole new family" might have been due in part to a distrust or disapproval of her mother's relation to her new husband, or with a reluctance to have the grandmother (Flora) of her children back being a mother of babies again. The daughter's anxiety about the stock of embryos that were frozen, however, seemed to be at least partly an anxiety about the existence of unaccounted for embryos using her eggs and her stepfather's sperm. Using one of her eggs to help initiate a pregnancy that was clearly tied into a trajectory on which it was Flora's and her husband's child was all right. It placed Flora between the daughter and her stepfather. The embryos in the freezer, though, were in limbo. If they were not used to initiate a pregnancy in Flora, then they existed as the conjoined gametes of the daughter and stepfather. As in all the cases recounted here, the trajectory of treatment, as a proxy for procreative intent, was of paramount importance. Where one step of that trajectory led clearly to the next, keeping biologized notions of descent in line with that intent, and keeping incest and adultery at bay, was obviously possible in the world of the clinic, structured as it is around treatment trajectories. The status of the embryos in the freezer – even though technically owned by Flora and her husband – were off that trajectory, and provoked Flora's daughter to express anxiety about inappropriate kinship.

Intergenerational gestational surrogacy

CASE 6: VANESSA AND UTE   *Summary: Vanessa will be a surrogate for Ute and her husband, using donor eggs from Ute's daughter.*

A final case concerns Vanessa, who started up her own surrogacy agency shortly after herself being a commercial gestational surrogate and giving birth to a baby for another couple. Vanessa had seen a program on television in which she noticed the "joy in the mother's eyes" when the baby was handed over by the surrogate. Vanessa's family was in some financial difficulty at the time as their small-scale manufacturing operation had just closed, and the approximately twelve thousand dollars she might make as a successful surrogate was attractive. She expressed the decision to try surrogacy in a religious idiom, as a chance offered by God simultaneously to do good and make a fresh start. Vanessa was introduced to "her" couple, a "German woman of about forty" (Ute) and an "Asian man."

On the first treatment cycle, Ute ovulated before the physician took her to surgery for ovum pickup and they only got one egg at surgery. The one egg was successfully fertilized with Ute's husband's sperm and transferred to Vanessa, but Vanessa did not get pregnant. For the second treatment cycle, Ute and her husband decided to combine gestational surrogacy with donor egg IVF. Ute had an adult daughter from a previous marriage who agreed (as Flora's daughter had) to be her mother and stepfather's donor. It was decided that the use of the daughter as a donor would be kept secret by the daughter as well as Ute and her husband from everyone outside the clinic setting. Ute explained that using her daughter's eggs was the next best thing to using her own eggs because of their genetic similarity. The daughter was safeguarded from being considered the biological mother in the pregnancy by making the relevant fact be the genetic relation of her eggs to Ute. This reduction to the genetics of the eggs and protection it afforded the daughter were both reinforced by removing the daughter herself by keeping her role secret. The logic of gestational surrogacy, essentializing the genetic aspect of biological kin, and making the blood and shared bodily substance of gestation custodial rather than relational, was also maintained. Ute was providing the essential genetic component, even though that genetic material had traveled a circuitous route from her down a generation to her daughter and back up again. This required reversing the usual temporal direction of genealogy, but naturalizing kinship to genetics to a large extent removed the need to mark kinship by descent, and so removed the temporal direction from the kinship reckoning.

Vanessa did not get pregnant on the fresh IVF cycle using the daughter's eggs, but there had been sufficient embryos to freeze some for a subsequent attempt. On the frozen cycle, Ute's daughter and husband's remaining embryos were thawed, transferred to Vanessa's uterus, and Vanessa became pregnant with a singleton. The pregnancy, unlike her four previous ones, was not easy for Vanessa. Under her surrogacy contract, she was not allowed to make her own medical decisions while pregnant, and she had to consult with the recipient couple and the doctor before taking any medications or changing her agreed-on routine in any way. The recipient couple and the physicians took over jurisdiction of Vanessa's body for the twelve months of treatment and pregnancy, disciplining her body across class lines. Nonetheless, Vanessa described the pregnancy almost wistfully, explaining how exhilarating the intimacy with the couple was and how spoiled she had been. During the pregnancy, Ute and her husband took Vanessa out, bought her fancy maternity clothes, and temporarily conferred on her their privileged social status. Vanessa underlined the ambivalence of the "kin-or-not" relationship between the surrogate and recipient couple in commercial surrogacy arrangements with the oxymoronic observation that they are "the couple you're going to be a relative with for a year and a half."

Vanessa seemed surprised by the severing of the ties of relationship between herself and the recipient couple after the baby was born and handed over. She said that the couple stopped contacting her, and that when she called them to find out how they and the baby were, the couple made excuses and hung up quickly. Other commercial gestational surrogates have recounted similar experiences. Vanessa's relationship to the couple for the year and a half was enacted because she was prosthetically embodying their germ plasm and growing their child, but she was at no point related to the recipient couple or the baby in her own right. Unlike the cases described above, Vanessa was commercially contracted, and her reproduction was classically "alienated" labor. The commissioning couple honored the capitalist contract; they paid her and appropriated the surplus value of her reproductive labor – namely, the baby. The genius of capitalism is sometimes said to be that the fruits of one's labor can be exchanged for money, without setting up a chain of reciprocal obligation. Thus, once the baby was born, Vanessa was in many ways just like any other instrumental intermediary in establishing the pregnancy, such as the embryologist or even the petri dish. The fact that she cared for and had good reasons for continuing to feel connected to the couple and baby, and so did things like make phone calls, meant perhaps that she needed some postnatal management to be kept in the background. But because she had been commercially contracted, the logic of disconnection was the same as for other intermediaries in the recipient couples' reproduction. The irony was that this particular naturalization was heightened by the deeply entrenched conventions of capitalism.

Making Kinship: Relational and Custodial

I try here hypothetically to isolate some of the strategies that were used in the clinical setting in each case for delineating who the mother was for each child (or the children). These strategies are not exhaustive and cannot be expected to be invariant in different arenas of the patients' lives either. For example, legal and familial constraints bring their own sources of plasticity and relative invariance that are quite powerful in determining kin. But the clinic is one significant site of negotiation of kinship, and it is of particular interest because it articulates between the public and private, and because it illustrates flexibility in biological and scientific practice. I emphasize the mothers' relatedness because in the cases I have chosen, it is into motherhood in particular that the procedures raise a challenge to biological essentialism through the separability of egg, gestation, and biological mother. The cases also challenge biologically essentialist understandings of daughter, husband, father, grandmother, aunt, and child, however. For each case, I distinguish different key intermediaries in establishing the pregnancy. I then sort the intermediaries as to whether they are relational or custodial in the determination of who counts as the mother. I also ask where and under what conditions the ways of designating the mother are liable to breakdown or contestation.

In infertility clinics, clinicians, patients, family members, surrogates, and others together embody the intent and effort that is crucial to reproduction in these settings. Yet procreative intent only inscribes some of these parties (usually a paying patient couple) as kin of the anticipated child(ren). As noted earlier, I call any stage in the establishment of a pregnancy *relational* if it implicates kinship. I am primarily interested here in working out who the mother is, so a relational stage in this determination would be one that implicates a (or more than one) mother. As the cases showed, there are many resources for making a stage relational that are not necessarily well differentiated. Biology and nature are resources; so are a wide range of legal, socioeconomic, and familial factors that make up procreative intent, such as who is paying for treatment, who owns the gametes and embryos, who is providing the sperm, and who is projected to have future financial and "nuclear family" responsibility for the child. Depending on the kind of parenting in question, different kinds of coordination are appropriate. By contrast, I call a stage *custodial* if it enables relatedness, but does not itself thereby get configured in the web of kinship relations.[11] A women is custodial in conceiving and bearing a child if she is biologically involved in bringing the child into the world and yet is not (or not primarily) implicated as its mother. A custodial stage is somewhat like an instrumental intermediary, then, and yet custody is not merely instrumental. Both the custodial woman and the child(ren)-to-be are ends in themselves, not mere means.[12] There are degrees of custodianship, ranging from those that are strictly limited to those implying long-term commitment even if they don't confer parenthood. The cases described above exhibited different strategies for achieving kinship implication of some people and not others. Breakdown (from the point of view of clinics or designated recipient couples), contestation, and prohibition usually occur when an attempt by at least some of the actors to render one or more stage as custodial rather than relational is contested or fails.

Designating Motherhood

In the first case, that of Giovanna, the Italian American woman who was planning to undergo a donor egg procedure with the eggs of an Italian American friend of hers, the two potential candidates for motherhood were the donor friend and Giovanna herself. The friend was made appropriately custodial using three

strategies. First, the friend's contribution of the eggs was biologically minimized by stressing the small percentage of the pregnancy that would be spent at the gamete and embryo stage versus the length of time that the fetus would grow inside Giovanna. In addition, genetics were redeployed, so that the friend's genes were figured as deriving from a common ethnic gene pool (Italian American) of which Giovanna was a member and so also represented. Then, too, the friend was secured as a custodial intermediary in the pregnancy by emphasizing her other bonds to Giovanna of friendship and mutual obligation. Despite her custodial role in donating the eggs destined to make Giovanna's baby, her relation to the baby could be registered as enhancing her already significant cultural and personal connections to Giovanna. To further disambiguate who should be considered the mother, Giovanna put forward strategies through which she could assert her own relationality. Giovanna's claim to motherhood was to come from her gestation of the baby as well as the provision of the bodily substance and functioning out of which the baby would grow and be given life. Giovanna stressed the significance of the gestational component of reproduction along with the importance of the experiential aspects of being pregnant and giving birth in designating motherhood. Further, Giovanna was married to, and would parent with, the provider of the sperm.

In Paula's case (the African American woman who was going to use an African American friend or one of her sisters as her donor), the strategies of separating relationality and custodianship were similar to those employed by Giovanna, but there were also interesting differences. The most striking difference was that Paula drew the line between who was a kin relation and who a custodian more tenuously, being content to leave more ambiguity in the designation of motherhood. She took legitimacy for the procedure from the fact that shared parenting was commonplace among people she identified with racially, and she also commented on the natural, biological confirmation of these social patterns that her upcoming procedure would provide. Socially and biologically, her motherhood – including its ambiguity – would be recognizable and legitimate. Her motherhood would be sufficiently relational and her donor sufficiently custodial, without either needing to be wholly so. Like Giovanna, then, Paula gave an ethnic or racial interpretation to the genes such that, by getting genetic African Americanness from her donor, the baby would share genetic racial sameness with Paula. The familiar trope (underlying, for example, the Human Genome Diversity Project) that genes code for racial distinctions, group inclusion and exclusion, and ethnic purity, seemed to be readily available to patients like Giovanna, Paula, and Flora, where group racial or ethno-national identity was culturally significant. The equally prevalent trope (exemplified in the Human Genome Project) that genes provide the definitive mark of individuality, "the DNA fingerprint," that is passed down cognatically from a mother's and father's individual contributions was the template used by the patients of unmarked or hegemonic racial and ethnic origin. Depending on whether genetics was socialized or individualized, different naturalization strategies were available. The African American Paula seemed to be the most comfortable of the patients whose cases are discussed in this chapter with de-individualizing genetics. Giovanna, Flora, and Ute all also mobilized the idea of genetic ethnic or individual (depending on the case) similarity with their gamete donors to assert genetic connection to their off-spring, but unlike Paula, they were all reasonably strongly invested in making their claims to motherhood individual and exclusive.

Michael, Kay, and Rachel (the gestational surrogacy between a brother, his wife, and his sister, respectively) deployed yet other familiar resources for assuring the custodial role of Rachel and the relationality of Kay. Because of the need to protect Michael and Rachel from incest, the negotiations over custody versus relationality were explicit and repeated at different phases of the treatment. Although the opportunities for ambiguity were legion, there was a "zero-tolerance" standard for ambiguity in the designation of Kay, not Rachel, as the mother. Kay was the infertile paying patient, receiving treatment and hoping/intending to

parent. She also provided the eggs containing the genetic information, and was married to and intending to parent with the provider of the sperm. These elements of her claim to motherhood were stabilized by emphasizing the unidirectional individualized genetic basis of heredity along with the mirroring of biological kinship and this understanding of heredity. When a threat arose as to the uniqueness of this basis of heredity (when Kay said to Rachel that she wouldn't mind if the children looked like Rachel and the ensuing conversation), it was removed by assimilating that kind of acquisition of characteristics to environmental custodial factors. The provision by Rachel of the bodily substance and site for fetal development was made custodial, rather than parental or incestuous, through two strategies. First, Rachel was assimilated at all points by her active compliance and the kinds of boundary discussions she initiated, such as how lucky it was that her tubes were tied, to a model on which pregnancy and birth were instrumental phases of Kay and Michael's reproduction, with which she was helping. Second, Rachel's relatedness to Kay and Michael as well as the children she was carrying was used to make her custodial assistance exactly what would be expected of her social role. As Rachel put it, the children were fine with their auntie (whose social role would be expected to be custodial), but couldn't wait to be reunited with their parents. The natural relation of aunt underwrote a social role of custodianship, which in turn, helped denaturalize Rachel as a potential mother to the children.

In Flora's case (the perimenopausal woman from Mexico whose daughter was the donor, and from whom sixty-five eggs were retrieved), a significant strategy in making her daughter custodial was to see the daughter as custodian rather than origin of the genetic material. The eggs used were not the daughter's per se but were retraced to Flora by "rewinding" genealogical time, such that they contained genetic material sourced from Flora. The daughter's gamete contribution was expressed as a detour to her mother's genetic material, which could no longer be accessed directly from Flora. Flora, perhaps more closely than any of the other donor egg patients whose cases are described here, attempted to recapture in her own claims to motherhood the genetic idiom of linear descent. Flora's case was complicated by the intergenerational element, however, and her daughter's custodianship was threatened from at least two sources. Flora and her daughter discussed the similarity of what they were doing to other intergenerational parenting in which a grandparent can be the social and legal parent. Drawing an analogy with prevalent social practices, as Paula had done, Flora strengthened the legitimacy of the procedure and so stabilized her claim to being the mother of the child. In making this analogy, though, the daughter's role was in danger of being compromised, because grandparenting often allows for the "real" parent to reclaim his or her parental jurisdiction. Unlike for Paula, this analogy to social practices did not loosen the designation of who was to count as mother but was meant to disambiguate it even beyond the norm for the social practices with which she was drawing the analogy. Both Flora and her daughter were adamant that there was to be no ambiguity in who was to be the mother – Flora. Flora's marriage to the provider of the sperm and the incestuous implications of reckoning it otherwise reinforced the lack of an analogy with social grandparent parenting. The other threat to Flora's daughter's custodial role came from the unintended stockpiling of embryos formed from the daughter's eggs fertilized with her stepfather's sperm. The frozen embryos in the lab were only tenuously tied to the trajectory of Flora's reproduction and its social, legal, economic, and emotional umbrella of procreative intent. The embryos' quasi-independence left room for them to seem like the products of incest or agents of additional unintended pregnancies, both of which were troubling to the daughter.

In Vanessa's pregnancy (which she carried as a commercial surrogate for Ute and her husband, from an embryo formed with eggs donated by Ute's daughter), there were three potential candidates as to who should be designated as the mother. There was Vanessa herself, the commercial gestational surrogate; there was Ute, the intended mother, who was the wife in the paying patient couple; and there was Ute's daughter, the egg donor. As for

Rachel and Jane, Vanessa was made custodial by assimilating her role in gestating the fetus to the provision of a temporary caring environment. Unlike Rachel's and Jane's cases of gestational surrogacy, however, Vanessa's custodial role was not elicited by the obligations of a prior relationship to the recipient couple. Her services were instead contracted commercially, and Vanessa had no further claim on the child after the birth. This disconnection was underwritten by the assumption of contractual arrangements that both parties agree that recompense is satisfactory despite possible incommensurability of the things being exchanged. Furthermore, contracts assume that the transaction itself is limiting and does not set up any subsequent relationship or further obligation. Vanessa's custodial role was threatened when she experienced the sudden severing of relations after the birth of the baby as baffling and troubling. Like Flora's and Ute's daughters, Vanessa was "de-kinned," but whereas the former two desired this, Vanessa did not (or at least mourned the relationship). The contractual relation assured the temporary relation of shared bodily substance with the recipient couple, but insofar as it was uncontested, it sustained no further relationality.

Ute's daughter, who was acting as the egg donor, was excluded from being the baby's mother in two ways. First, the genetic contribution contained in her eggs was described as being closely similar to her mother's genetic material. This is not quite the same argument as that made by Flora and her daughter, where the daughter became a vehicle or detour through which genetic material originally from Flora had passed; in this case, the mother and daughter simply alluded to the similarity of the mother's and daughter's genes. The daughter was further spared from being implicated in parenthood by the recipient couple's commitment to keeping her role a secret. Ute sustained her claim as the intended mother not by wholly capturing either of the predominant biological idioms (genetics as represented by providing the egg, or blood and shared bodily substance as represented by gestation). Instead, the genetic component from the daughter was deemed similar enough to stand in for her genetic contribution, and the blood component was made custodial in the contracting out of the gestation. Neither natural base was sufficiently strong to overwhelm her claim to be the mother, which she asserted through being married to the person who supplied the sperm, through her daughter's compliance with her desires, and through having the buying power to contract Vanessa.

Prognosis

The genetic essentialism of gestational surrogacy in procedures such as Rachel's and Jane's seems to be faring very well, even as it extends and reconfigures preexisting ontologies. There have been gestational surrogates who have contested custody, but decisions have gone against them more often than for conventional surrogates who are genetically related to the child in question. Several of the patients coded genetics back to socioeconomic factors and thereby in some sense de-essentialized genetics in this setting just as they no doubt did in other areas of their lives. Eliding ethno-national, racial, and class-based categories with natural grounds for designating kinship is a strategy fundamental to bilateral, blood-based kinship systems. Nonetheless, developments in other contemporary U.S. sites over the same period as this fieldwork, such as decisions in legal custody disputes, have tended to favor genetic essentialism in determining motherhood, although this has not been universal. On the other hand, they have often followed procreative intent in determining legal custody, regardless of the decision on motherhood (see Seibel and Crockin 1996, 111–216).

The donor egg procedures seem to offer the potential somewhat to transform biological kinship in the directions indicated, for example, by Giovanna when she draws on the trope of blood connection and shared bodily substance without genetics. If an overwhelming predominance of nonclinical cultural contexts come down on the side of genetic essentialism, donor egg procedures might well become assimilated to adoption or artificial insemination with donor sperm. The bid to make gestation in donor egg procedures a means of conferring biological kinship would

have failed. A newer procedure, reports of which began to appear in journals and the press in 1997, uses the eggs of older patients, but "revivifies" them by injecting cytoplasmic material derived from the eggs of younger women into the older eggs before fertilization; this donor procedure preserves the genetic connection between the recipient mother and fetus, and so brings the genetic and blood idioms back into line. It thereby tightens up again the flexible ontological space for designating biological motherhood that had been opened up by donor egg procedures. The meritocratizing and commercializing of the donor egg market (much like the sperm market, only much more expensive) of the late 1990s has emphasized the extent to which egg donation is beginning to match the paternity template. On the one hand, motherhood, like fatherhood, is determined by the genes; on the other hand, if a proxy is used for the intended mother, the gametes should encode socioeconomic mobility in the way the sperm market does.

Paula used a more mixed ontology for motherhood than the other cases recorded here. For her, it was satisfactory if there was not an exclusive answer to who the mother was, and she was happy to accept that in some ways there might be more than one mother. Likewise, because she raised the possibility of biologically enacting what she described as already prevalent social practices (shared mothering), there was less at stake in having gestation without genetics confer motherhood biologically. Shared mothering was not presented as necessarily involving a natural kinship rift; indeed, it was presented as a practice that preserves racial identity and integrity. Conventional adoption has historically predominantly gone in one direction, with African American children being adopted into Caucasian families, arguably disrupting racial identification without disrupting racism. For Paula, having her procedure assimilated to some kinds of social parenting would still entitle her to make appeal to notions of biological sameness because of the group understanding of genetics offered paternalistically to, and taken up defensively by, minority groups. The option to individualize or personalize genetic generative agency is only differentially available.

The likely stability of Flora's and Ute's claims to motherhood is hard to gauge. Ute's claim could have been challenged by Vanessa's desire for contact with the child after its birth, set against the purchasing power of the contracting couple. Flora is likely to encounter social censure, just as she did in the clinic, for her desire to bear a child "for" her younger husband. If either Ute or Flora confess to using, or are found to have used, their daughters as donors, they may be condemned for coercion and putting their daughters through medical interventions so as to regain their own youth. If either daughter contests the circumstances of her role at a later date, the settlement of who is the designated mother might break down. Likewise, the relations of the daughters' own children to the ones born from their eggs may become complicated. But it is also possible that parenting with donor eggs for perimenopausal and postmenopausal women will play a part in dismantling some of the more oppressive aspects for women of the "biological clock." If Flora and Ute can maintain their claims to motherhood, they will be cases to hold against the elision of women's identities, femininity, youth, and ovulation. If Flora is buying into the cult of youth to keep her husband, as she claims, she may yet be subverting the wider essentialist identification of women's identities with their youthful biologies, as she also maintains.

Practical Metaphysics and the Dynamics of Naturalizing

It has become commonplace to talk of the implosion or collapse of nature and culture; to claim that all concepts of nature, including scientific ones, are always already shaped, marked, and interpenetrated with the imprimatur of culture, and (somewhat less frequently) that all concepts of culture invoke legitimizing natural grounds for their systems of classification. Critics of these postmodern sensibilities rightly distrust the looseness or voluntarism that this seems to imply. Ontologically, they decry the violation of common

sense: of course there is a real material world subject to more or less regular laws, and of course there is a distinction between truth and falsehood, science and myth. Politically, they disparage the loss of an Enlightenment platform, and the neglect of persistent stratification among people implied by the moral and ontological relativism of a nature/culture implosion. Talking about a nature/culture collapse in vague and programmatic terms is almost always counterproductive. And yet there is something extraordinarily important about the insight that nature and culture are coproduced, and that the explanatory relations between them are eminently revisable.

In an attempt to rescue and further this insight, I have tried to avoid hand-waving statements about the collapse or dissolution of nature and culture. I instead discussed small and detailed examples of productive (not deconstructive) negotiations of the boundaries and explanatory relations between cultural and natural concepts in one specific arena: the contemporary U.S. biomedical infertility clinic. The advantage of this, if it has been successful, is that it should make it clear that the coproductive thesis about nature and culture is no more a "culturalist" position than it is a "naturalist" one. It doesn't dismiss the reality of the realm of biology any more than it dismisses the realm of culture. Indeed, studying the strategies used to bring order to new reproductive and kinship situations convinced me that making distinctions between social and natural roles and facts, and then using natural roles and facts to ground cultural categories, is absolutely fundamental to meaning making in contemporary U.S. society. At the same time, however, the cases made a compelling argument for the absence of a unique biological ground for answering the question, "Who is the mother?" There was more than one possible answer here, and cultural dynamics – most predominantly the bundle of "factors" that make up procreative intent – propelled the sorting and classifying of some things and not others as the biological facts of relevance. The narratives of the trajectories of reproductive intent were choreographed between cultural and natural constraints at all points, and were neither biologically nor culturally voluntaristic. The ambivalence evident in feminist theory, for example, about the relative virtues of naturalism and social constructivism is entirely appropriate: sometimes important political and ontological work is done by denaturalizing what has previously been taken to be natural and deterministic; sometimes the reverse is necessary. What cases like these drawn from infertility medicine reveal is that it is not necessary for the theorist to champion one strategy rather than another. Modern medicine offers many cases where the choreography between the natural and cultural is managed flexibly by ordinary people (the practitioners and patients using the technologies in question).

In focusing on the dynamics of naturalization in the clinics, as just discussed, some aspects of the process of cultural change in the midst of technological innovation became evident. First, the cases suggested that high-tech interventions are not necessarily antithetical to the production of affiliation and identity, the claims of antimodern Luddites that technology is intrinsically dehumanizing notwithstanding. In this clinical setting, gestational surrogacy and donor egg IVF were means through which racial, ethno-national, familial, and individual desires and biologies were all promulgated. In the kinship innovation described here, the various naturalization strategies drew on deeply rooted and familiar ways of forming and claiming kin as well as simultaneously extending the reference of the kinship terms being disambiguated through the strategies. Given this slightly counterintuitive aspect of these high-tech sites that technological innovation and cultural history implicate each other so strongly, it is no wonder that progressive cultural critics cannot decide whether the new reproductive technologies are best judged as innovative ways of breaking free of bondage to old cultural categories of affiliation, or whether they are best denounced as part of a hegemonic reification of the same old stultifying ways of classifying and valuing human beings. The technologies are fundamentally both. Technological change and cultural conservatism go hand in hand; the famous lag between technological innovation and cultural reaction is nothing of the sort. The lag simply refers to the "catchup" requirements in social, legal, and ethical spheres to organize and calibrate the coemergence of entities and relations produced in these extended cultural and natural biologies.

NOTES

1   For discussions of the question of procreative intent relevant to this kinship work, see Dolgin 1995.
2   I take this not as antirealism but as attentiveness to the contingent realities of complex phenomena. See Latour 1999.
3   See Catholic Church 1987.
4   Bruno Latour expressed it as showing that "high-tech processes can be reemployed to provide powerful fetishes – in the good sense of the word – to produce affiliation and identity" (1999).
5   IVF involves the fertilization of an egg (or eggs) with sperm outside the body, usually in a petri dish in a lab. The egg (or eggs) is surgically removed from the ovaries of a woman who has (usually) taken hormones to induce the maturation of multiple follicles, and then the egg is inseminated in vitro with a partner's or donor's sperm. Any embryos that result are transferred back to the same woman's or a different woman's uterus, or else they are made available for research or donation. Anonymous eggs can either be purchased commercially or gifted as leftovers from other women's treatments. It is rare for eggs to be gifted during IVF, however, as it is standard practice to attempt to fertilize all the eggs retrieved, even for women with many eggs, so that they have some embryos in reserve for future attempts.
6   This lies behind the feminist claim that egg donors should be thought of as second fathers, while the gestating woman should be considered the mother.
7   At the start of the twenty-first century, demand for eggs far outstrips supply, as human eggs are a scarce commodity par excellence. There are several differences

between the meritocratization of commercial eggs and that of commercial sperm. Sperm does not vary widely in its price, but eggs do; the man is rewarded for his act of donation, not the quality of offspring he is promising the clients. Sperm banks handle the storage, marketing, and meritocratizing. Eggs, on the other hand, are stored in the body in immature form and are not routinely expelled, so they are difficult to harvest. Immature eggs are also hard to mature in vitro, and no human eggs freeze and thaw well yet. This means that the woman embodying the eggs becomes the market interface, and must be attracted according to the market value of her standardized and hierarchized qualities. The hunt for ideal egg donors with particular characteristics, the high prices (up to fifty thousand dollars at the time of this writing) being offered as recompense to chosen egg donors, and the competition among, for example, elite college students to be selected, have become something of a cultural phenomenon in the United States. There is an unspoken etiquette that one seek roughly to match the qualities and phenotype of the infertile partner in both donor egg and sperm, but it is nonetheless expected that this will be interpreted leniently enough to permit upward mobility or "maximization" in certain areas such as height or IQ.

8   As well as raising the specter of eugenics, commercial egg donation or surrogacy introduces other kinship prerogatives based in particular on class, as explored indepth for commercial conventional surrogacy in Ragoné 1994. When biological relationship is crosscut by class, the donor's or surrogate's reproduction can be temporarily purchased (see case 6, Vanessa). Ownership of the child and the donor's or surrogate's reproduction is a means of trumping biology and forging kinship in reproductive technologies. In slavery, rape, and so on, ownership of another's reproduction and offspring can be a means of the exact opposite: denying kinship.

9   This woman was what I would call upper-middle-class and living in an affluent neighborhood (like most – but by no means all – infertility patients); I think the relevant notion of community, given how she elaborated it in explaining to me the alternative kinds of mothering, was primarily one based on a shared African American identity.

10 In Britain, daughters are not allowed to be donors for their own mothers because the relationship is seen as necessarily involving a coercive element. Frances Price (Edwards et al. 1999: 36–7) recounts the British test case at the end of 1986 that resulted in what was then the Voluntary Licensing Authority declaring mother/daughter egg donations out of bounds.

11 Here, I am following the common usage of the word custody to mean "a guarding or keeping safe; care; protection, guardianship."

12 According to the Catholic Church, no part of human reproduction can be made instrumental and alienated. Every part of the process must be relational, tracing a trajectory of ownership and presence at all points. It is my contention that the difference between being custodial and instrumental is underappreciated, and that the former does not imply treating any person or potential person as a means rather than an end. In commercial surrogacy, the mother comes close to being merely instrumental at the moment of handover (see text on this point), but typically even if the surrogacy contract was entered into for economic gain, the infant is not treated as a means, for a moral discourse intervenes between the transaction and the gift of life.

REFERENCES

Catholic Church, Congregation for the Doctrine of the Faith. 1987. Instruction on Respect for Human Life in Its Origin and on the Dignity of Procreation. In *Gift of Life: Catholic Scholars Respond to the Vatican Instruction*, edited by Edmund Pellegrino, John

Collins Harvey, and John Langan. Washington, DC: Georgetown University Press.

Cussins, Charis. 1998. Quit Snivelling Cryo-Baby. We'll Work Out Which One's Your Mama! In *Cyborg Babies: From Techno-Sex to Techno-Tots*, edited by Robbie Davis-Floyd and Joseph Dumit. New York: Routledge.

Dolgin, Janet L. 1995. Family Law and the Facts of Family. In *Naturalizing Power: Essays in Feminist Cultural Analysis*, edited by Sylvia J. Yanagisako and Carol Delaney. New York: Routledge.

Edwards, Jeanette, Sarah Franklin, Eric Hirsch, Frances Price, and Marilyn Strathern. 1999. *Technologies of Procreation: Kinship in the Age of Assisted Conception*. 2nd edn. London: Routledge.

Farquhar, Dion. 1996. *The Other Machine: Discourse and Reproductive Technologies (Thinking Gender)*. London: Routledge.

Franklin, Sarah. 1997. *Embodied Progress: A Cultural Account of Assisted Conception*. London: Routledge.

Franklin, Sarah, and Helena Ragoné, eds. 1998. *Reproducing Reproduction: Kinship, Power, and Technological Innovation*. Philadelphia: University of Pennsylvania Press.

Ginsburg, Faye D., and Rayna Rapp, eds. 1995. *Conceiving the New World Order: The Global Politics of Reproduction*. Berkeley: University of California Press.

Latour, Bruno. 1999. Personal correspondence with the author.

Ragoné, Helena. 1994. *Surrogate Motherhood: Conception in the Heart*. Boulder, Colo.: Westview Press.

Rapp, Rayna. 1999. *Testing Women, Testing the Fetus: The Social Impact of Amniocentesis in America*. New York: Routledge.

Seibel, Machelle, and Susan Crockin, eds. 1996. *Family Building through Egg and Sperm Donation: Medical, Legal, and Ethical Issues*. Sudbury, Mass.: Jones and Bartlett.

Strathern, Marilyn. 1992. *Reproducing the Future: Anthropology, Kinship and the New Reproductive Technologies*. New York: Routledge.

Yanagisako, Sylvia J., and Carol Delaney, eds. 1995. *Naturalizing Power: Essays in Feminist Cultural Analysis*. New York: Routledge.

Part IV
Maintaining Commitments

Introduction

While the essays in Part III speak to US feminist scholars' insistence that anthropological methods and theories ought to be extended on a more regular basis to studies of their own society, the contributions in Part IV speak even more directly to the ongoing commitment of these scholars to addressing pressing social issues facing women around the world. In some instances their accounts of women's struggles for various sorts of freedoms speak directly to problems that also obtain in the US. But in other cases, they document processes that diverge sharply from our local understandings of political action, demonstrating the importance of taking cultures on their own terms and not prejudging how "feminism" should look elsewhere.

Begoña Aretxaga's article takes on conventional images of political protest that assume male agency and a secondary role for women. But she also confronts assumptions that bodily substances such as menstrual blood and feces are best viewed as abstract symbols of the social order, instead showing how they can be used to perform acts of violence in ways that are deeply embodied and personal. Individuals imprisoned in Northern Ireland during struggles with the British suffered from particularly humiliating privations having to do with food, sanitary needs, and direct invasions of their intimate body parts in the course of searches. Although both male and female prisoners began to protest against their treatment by smearing feces on the walls and making their cells and themselves too repulsive to be touched by guards, in the case of the women, these tactics also drew on the gendered meanings of menstrual blood. Observers found the exposure of menstrual blood to have escalated the horror of the Dirty Protest, somehow being more repulsive than the urine and feces that were also in the men's section. Aretxaga takes up the question of what this particular tactic meant for the women, arguing that while the larger Dirty Protest stood for a rejection of colonial authority, the women's amplification of the Protest with menstrual blood made gender a far more visible dimension of the struggle than it otherwise would have been. While women were, on the one hand, seeking to participate in actions against the British on the same basis as the men, they found themselves confronted by images of asexual motherhood and the national icon of Mother Ireland. Such symbols were useful for women who sought political engagement, but also constrained their full participation. In Aretxaga's analysis, the deployment of the most powerful reminder of sexual difference, menstrual blood, both allowed women to emphasize their particular claims as women and to disrupt notions of correct femininity. She shows that such embodied actions can simultaneously draw on conflicting meanings, both advancing and derailing women's efforts to be full partners in the struggle against British colonialism.

In her article on a mothers' organization in El Salvador, Lynn Stephen takes a very different approach to women's political participation. Using personal narratives generated by movement activists, Stephen seeks to understand how their involvement can both draw on and resist traditional ideas about motherhood. The group of mothers she studied focused its efforts on demanding accountability for their children who had "disappeared" during the country's civil war. Like other such organizations across Latin America, CO-MADRES confronted the atrocities that had been committed by the military, using their authority as mothers (though other persons were also involved) to support the legitimacy of their desire for information. But membership in the organization drew them into more complex political arenas than they could have anticipated. In some instances, abuses including rape and torture were used against them. But for others, political engagement led to invitations to meet with activists in other countries, a process that broadened their vision of the kinds of social change they should be concerned with. Stephen is careful to ground her study both in a thorough exploration of the political and economic context in which the organization developed, including an account of the kinds of injustices, beyond the disappearances, that CO-MADRE members found themselves confronting. At the same time, she situates her work in the words and experience of the women themselves, as related in their narratives. Thus, rather than imposing an interpretation on them, she makes clear that an understanding of how the women's political work operated as resistance and accommodation must emerge from their own accounts and understandings. Most importantly, Stephens challenges conventional divisions between women's rights and human rights, demonstrating that neither from the perspective of the observer nor from the inside subjectivity of the women can political struggle be so bifurcated.

Christine Walley takes on the issue of female genital operations, perhaps the most contentious women's rights issue that has come to the attention of feminist activists. Variously called female circumcision, genital mutilation, or by more specific medical descriptions, these practices are widespread in an area including parts of the Middle East and Islamic Africa. Walley carefully documents the debate that has followed discussion of this issue in the popular media, among feminist activists, and in academic discourse. Variously seen as an attack on female sexual autonomy, a public health risk, a form of torture, and as a culturally coherent custom that must be understood in context, the practices of female genital operations have particularly horrified feminists in the West, who see sexual pleasure – most definitively imagined as linked to clitoral orgasm – as a fundamental human right that transcends cultural relativism. Walley uses her own interactions with adolescent girls in Kenya to examine the issue, focusing on the instability of their responses to genital surgery. At times, the girls decried the practice as retrograde, while at other moments they embraced it as a coming-of-age ritual surrounded by excitement and celebration. Without taking a definitive stance, Walley's approach compels readers to consider how thoroughly their own assumptions about sexuality and the body color their responses. Questions of who speaks for women in areas where these procedures are routine, who should properly organize to abolish or change them, and how particular circumstances come to horrify Westerners – in this case, genital operations seems to excite more passion than hunger and other more pervasive privations – are all central to her analysis.

"Imagining the Unborn in the Ecuadoran Andes" by Lynn Morgan intervenes in the passionate debates about when life begins that have so absorbed Americans since abortion rights were granted by the Supreme Court. Like ideas about the importance of sexual response, activists have tended to assume that "life" is a stable category that can readily be translated across cultural boundaries. The result of these debates in the US has been the formation of a new social category, the "fetal person," understood to have legal and medical rights that often supersede those of its mother. Morgan's examination of how the unborn are imagined in rural Ecuador points to the cultural specificity of the US categorization and undermines the universal claims made about "fetal persons."

Morgan found sharp disparities in the construction of fetuses among the Ecuadorans she studied. Unlike the "radical individualism" that typifies the American approach, where medical technologies have intensified tendencies to define the fetus as a being ontologically separate from its mother, Ecuadorans imagined their unborn as not fully formed, not completely human until after birth. Even newborns, she found, were not yet thought to be fully human. Rather than developing inexorably because of their innate potential, newborns were thought to need their mothers to "form" them after they were born. In other words, notions of fetal and infant personhood were far more fluid and indistinct than they are in the current US environment. Personhood, in this construction, happens in a social context, not autonomously, and mothers are the people who must undertake it. Unlike the US situation, where some medical technologies such as ultrasound have fostered an image of mothers as almost incidental to fetal survival, mothers in Ecuador are absolutely central to the process and have considerable latitude in bringing an infant into full personhood.

All the essays in this section demonstrate what I argue is a key attribute of feminist anthropology, perhaps even more definitively than its concern with women and gender. Feminist anthropology came into being not only to document the varied conditions of women's lives, not only to reach more nuanced understandings of how gender operates, but to focus on how anthropological knowledge and methods can enhance struggles for social justice. This commitment comes through in all these essays, though each author pursues the mandate quite differently.

In Aretxaga's article, our attention is directed to the symbolic strategies that women's bodies and that uniquely female substance, menstrual blood, make possible in the violent circumstances of incarceration in Northern Ireland. While the women's actions in the Dirty Protest are seemingly no different from those of the men, the effect of using menstrual blood ratchets up the horror, enabling a more thorough subversion of the prison system. The article doesn't promote any particular political strategy, or call for women to organize in other struggles with colonial powers. Rather, it helps us see that no actions can be divorced from their gendered meanings, and that other protest tactics might be considered using a similar lens.

Stephen's article is far more explicitly concerned with the dynamics of political mobilization and with how women can make specific contributions to political struggles for justice. In the Salvadoran case, women's moral authority as mothers opened up a possibility for action, even as the wider meaning of that action quickly escalated. Not only did the women and their allies have a powerful effect on the political climate of their country, but their activism pulled them into a larger, even global activist community, profoundly changing each woman's understanding of her role in the movement. Stephen makes clear that women have particular resources to bring to struggles, even as the existence of rapid communication links between activists in various locations easily expands the scope of their actions. Her concern, then, is with the conditions that foster women's activism and the ways that mobilization can become even more powerful and influential.

Walley takes a different tack in her article, pointing to the movement against female genital surgery that has largely had its origins outside the areas where these procedures are commonly carried out. In her case, the activism under consideration is primarily that of Western feminists, variously viewed as noble or imperialistic, depending on one's stance. She urges her audience to consider how particular issues rise to the level of generating protest, and how we can situate those issues authentically in their cultural settings. While not urging radical relativism or action, Walley's article makes clear how unstable the practices we abhor may actually be, and how essential it is for women in the relevant societies to be in the forefront of actions opposing them. Considering concerns that Western feminism tends to erase indigenous movements, her caution must be central to how feminists in the West craft their politics.

Finally, Morgan interrogates a cultural icon in the US, the "fetal person," using cross-cultural comparison to undermine assumptions about its universality. Working in the best tradition of comparative method, Morgan turns the mirror away from the culture she examines in Ecuador toward the familiar and the taken-for-granted. If the fetus and even the newborn are so variously constructed elsewhere, how have we arrived at the particular definition that obtains in our society? Morgan demonstrates that the "fetal person" has little to do with biological processes, but rather is a creation of a culture that exalts and naturalizes individual autonomy.

15

Dirty Protest: Symbolic Overdetermination and Gender in Northern Ireland Ethnic Violence

Begoña Aretxaga

Introduction

In a personal interview a man arrested for Irish Republican Army (IRA) activity described a prison scene of the late 1970s that became known as the Dirty Protest. He recalled the first contact with his comrades – already immersed in the protest – shortly upon arrival to Long-Kesh prison:

> We went to Mass – it was Sunday. Afterwards I walk into the canteen and if you can imagine this yourself... there were about 150 people in the canteen and all that they were wearing was trousers. Other than that they were naked, and had nothing on their feet. They had matted long beards and long hair, and they were stinking, really filthy... can you imagine? I walked in there and I said to myself, "They are all mad!" Everybody had big staring eyes, and they were all talking fast, firing questions and very nervous... you know, all

this. And I was seeing fellows in the canteen I had known outside [prison] and they were all just ribs, very thin. I thought they were really crazy... mad. I was really taken aback.

From 1978 to 1981 IRA and Irish National Liberation Army (INLA) male prisoners in Northern Ireland undertook an extraordinary form of protest against prison authorities and the British government. They refused to leave their cells either to wash or to use the toilets, living instead in the midst of their own dirt and body waste. In 1980 they were joined by their female comrades, thus adding menstrual blood to the horrendous excretal imagery of the protest. Unlike the hunger strike on which the prisoners would embark in 1981, the Dirty Protest had no precedent in the existing political culture. This action, which resonated with notions of savagery, irrationality, and madness, was shocking and largely incomprehensible to the public in Ireland and Britain. Not only did relatives and supporters of the prisoners admit this popular incomprehensibility, but the main newspapers treated the protest as "a bizarre and foul exercise," to use the not uncommon words of the [London] *Times*. The striking form of this political action, coupled on the one hand with the strong emotional reactions that it provoked and on the other with its genderized character, makes the Dirty Protest a particularly suitable case for the exploration of how subjectivity, gender, and power are articulated in situations of heightened political violence.

Bodily violence has been extensively theorized as a disciplinary mechanism (Asad 1983; Feldman 1991; Foucault 1979; Scarry 1985). In *Discipline and Punish* Foucault powerfully analyzed punishment as a political technology of the body aimed at the production of submissive subjects. In the modern prison discipline and punishment are directed at the subjective transformation of individuals from dangerous criminals to docile citizens. In Foucault's analysis the body ceases to be the repository of signs to become the material through which subjectivities are molded (1979: 23). What Foucault has not addressed are the points at which the technology of normalization breaks down, the moments in which rational disciplines of the body fail to produce docile subjects, either because the subjects refuse to be normalized, even at the cost of death, or because the exercise of punishment indulges in an excess that betrays its rational aims, becoming a drama of its own rather than merely a political tactic, as recent work has well shown (Graziano 1992; Obeyesekere 1992; Suarez-Orozco 1992; Taussing 1987).

In his extensive study of the Dirty Protest, Allen Feldman (1991) has criticized the unidirectionality of Foucault's analysis. For Feldman, the prisoners themselves instrumentalized their bodies against the technologies of domination first applied to them. Feldman's critique of Foucault remains, however, inside the Foucaudian paradigm. In his analysis the body continues to be an artifact, an instrument subject to political technologies managed now by both the prisoners and the guards. Feldman, like Foucault, belies the question of subjectivity. Disciplines of the body are permeated by an emotional dynamic that includes powerful feelings of fear, desire, and hate that are crucial to the political operativity of the body. This emotional dynamic is entangled in cultural forms such as myth, religious images, stories, and the like. It is not only a product of the disciplines of the body used in the prison; it also plays an important part in the excess of violence characterizing those disciplines. Carceral violence has been used against political prisoners all over the world, including Ireland, yet there is no other case in which prisoners resisted with something like the Dirty Protest. The excreta and menstrual blood that characterized the protest exposes an excess of meaning that reveals the very character of violence as an intersubjective relation that must necessarily be interpreted. This interpretative approach does not negate, however, Foucault's important understanding of the body as political field. Instead, it invests such political field (the body) with the intersubjective dynamic through which power takes place. For Lacan (1977: 50–2), subjectivity is always grounded in history – a history that includes the scars left by forgotten episodes and hidden discourses as much as conscious narratives.

The Dirty Protest is a good case for an approach that combines a Foucaudian critique of power with an interpretative anthropology sensitive to the "deep play" of subjectivity. To develop this analysis I conceptualized the feces and menstrual blood that characterized the Dirty Protest not as artifacts but as overdetermined primordial symbols. I do not mean by *primordial* an ontological essence. I use *primordial symbols* here for lack of a better word to refer to those symbols that resort to physiological material of great psychological significance and that are elaborated in one form or another in all cultures. Following Sapir, Victor Turner (1967) called them "condensation symbols," Mary Douglas (1966), "natural symbols." I mean overdetermination in the Freudian sense of the term, as the condensation of different strands of meaning, none of which are in themselves necessarily determinant. Obeyesekere has noted that the power of symbols is derived from their capacity to tap into diverse areas of experience (1990: 280).

The prisoners' excreta and menstrual blood tap into the interconnected domains of prison violence, colonial history, unconscious motivation, and gender discourses.

Resisting Normalization

With the escalation of the political crisis that followed the riots of 1969 in Northern Ireland, large numbers of people in the working class Catholic communities of Belfast were arrested. Most of them were accused of crimes against the state, a general label that included a wide variety of actions ranging from the wearing of combat jackets to participation in demonstrations to the use of firearms. After a hunger strike in 1972, the British government agreed to give the prisoners "special category" status, regarding them as de facto political prisoners. These included members of Irish paramilitary organizations, both Republican and Loyalists.[1]

In 1976 the British government, as part of a more general counterinsurgency operation, withdrew "special category" status from Republican and Loyalist prisoners, who were then to be considered and treated as ODCs (Ordinary Decent Criminals), in British legal parlance. This entailed the use of prison uniforms instead of personal clothes and the cancellation of rights of association, internal organization, and free disposal of time. Republican prisoners resisted government regulations by refusing to wear the prison uniforms. Since other clothes were lacking, the prisoners covered themselves with blankets. The prison administration penalized their insubordination with an array of disciplinary measures: 24-hour cell confinement, inadequate food, lack of exercise and intellectual stimulation, curtailment of visits, frequent beatings, and recurrent body and cell searches. The prisoners (three-quarters of whom were between the ages of 17 and 21) left their cells only for trips to the toilet, weekly showers, Sunday mass, and monthly visits. Physiological necessities such as food and excretory functions became a focus of humiliating practices. The already inadequate diet was frequently spoiled with defiling substances such as spit, urine, roaches, or maggots. Access to the toilet was controlled by the permission of guards who would delay or deny it at will. After a year of this situation the prison administration forbade wearing blankets outside the cells. Prisoners had to leave their cells naked on their way to toilets and showers. Harassment increased at these times, leaving prisoners especially vulnerable to beatings, guards' mockery and sexual insults, as well as the hated body searches. These were described to me by an IRA ex-prisoner:

> They made you squat on the floor on your haunches. You wouldn't do that so they beat you, they sat over you and probed your back passage, and then with the same finger some would search your mouth, your nose, your hair, your beard, every part of your body, there was nothing private about your body.

According to prisoners, it was the increased harassment and heightened violence accompanying the use of toilets that sparked the Dirty Protest in 1978. In a coordinated action, prisoners refused to leave their cells except to go to mass and visits. At first they emptied the chamber pots through windows and peepholes of the doors. When the guards boarded them up prisoners began to dispose of feces by leaving them in a corner of their cells. This, however, allowed the guards to mess the mattresses and blankets of prisoners with the feces during cell searches. Finally, prisoners began to smear their excreta on the walls of their cells.

In 1980 the Republican women in Armagh prison joined their male comrades in the Dirty Protest. They had also been resisting the change of status from political prisoners to criminals since 1976 by refusing to do mandatory prison work and were also enduring similar disciplinary measures. But in contrast to the male prisoners in Long-Kesh, Republican women were allowed to use their own clothes – as were all female prisoners in Britain. Although harassment and tension had been rising inside the jail, what prompted women into the Dirty Protest was not humiliation accompanying use of the toilets but an assault by male officers – the second of its kind – followed by two days' lock-up in their cells. What justified this assault was the search of "subversive garments." If in Long-Kesh male prisoners

spurned the prison uniform to assert their political identity, in a similar metonymic move
Armagh women used their clothes to impro-
vise IRA uniforms. It was in search of those
small pieces of apparel – berets, black skirts,
trivial in themselves yet full of significance in
the encoded world of the prison – that military
men in full riot gear entered the cells of IRA
prisoners on February 7, 1980, kicking and
punching the women. The following quote
from a report smuggled out of jail by one of
the prisoners illustrates the sexual overtones of
the assault:

At around 3:45pm on Thursday Feb. 7th, numerous male and female screws [guards] in-
vaded my cell in order to get me down to the
governor. They charged in full riot gear
equipped with shields. I sat unprotected but
aware of what was going to happen as I had
heard my comrades screaming in pain. I was
suddenly pinned to the bed by a shield and the
weight of a male screw on top of me. Then my
shoes were dragged off my feet. I was bodily
assaulted, thumped, trailed and kicked. I was
then trailed out of my cell, and during the
course of my being dragged and hauled from
the wing both my breasts were exposed to the
jeering and mocking eyes of all the screws,
there must have been about twenty of them.
While being carried, I was also abused with
punches to the back of my head and my stomach. I was eventually carried into the governor, my breasts were still exposed. While I
was held by the screws the governor carried
out the adjudication, and I was then trailed
back and thrown into a cell.[2]

Sexual harassment by state forces has been a
systematic complaint during the last 20 years
that reappears in informal conversations with
women as well as in their narratives of encounters with security forces.[3] For the prisoners, the
assault was as much a political attempt to
discipline through punishment as a humiliating
assertion of male dominance. Moreover, at the
time of the assault, there was a lot of pain,
grief, and anger among women prisoners.
In addition to health problems and increasing
petty harassment, a high percentage of women
lost close relatives in shootings by Loyalist
paramilitaries or British army during their

time in jail. The devastating emotions of
mourning were repressed to preserve collective
morale and inner strength as well as to avoid
special targeting from guards. The assault and
enforced lock up in the cells provoked a strong
response. Shortly after the beginning of the
protest, Mairead Farrell, leader of the women
prisoners, described their situation in a letter
smuggled out of jail:

The stench of urine and excrement clings to
the cells and our bodies. No longer can we
empty the pots of urine and excrement out
the window, as the male screws [guards]
have boarded them up. Little light or air pen-
etrates the thick boarding. The electric light
has to be kept constantly on in the cells; the
other option is to sit in the dark. Regardless of
day or night, the cells are dark. Now we can't
even see out the window; our only view is the
wall of excreta. The spy holes are locked so
they can only be opened by the screws to
look in. Sanitary towels are thrown into us
without wrapping. We are not permitted
paper bags or such like so they lie in the dirt
until used. For twenty-three hours a day we lie
in these cells.[4]

The Dirty Protest was by any standard of
political culture, and certainly by that of Ireland, an unusual political action. The British
national press, upon visiting Long-Kesh for the
first time, called it "the most bizarre protest by
prisoners in revolt against their gaolers" and
"self-inflicted degradation" (*Guardian* and
Daily Telegraph, March 16, 1979). It was as
incomprehensible to the general public as it
was to prison officers and government administration. In the Catholic communities, massive
support for the prisoners was not reached, for
instance, until the end of the Dirty Protest
and the beginning of the hunger strike. The
Dirty Protest provoked an inexpressible horror
and a rising spiral of violence inside and outside the jails. If the men's Dirty Protest was
incomprehensible, the women's was unthinkable, generating in many men, even among
the ranks of supporting Republicans, reactions
of denial. It was no doubt a form of warfare, a violent contest of power, as Feldman
(1991) has noted. But why this form and not
another?

Humiliation and Violence:
The Deep Play of Subjectivity

Feces are a primordial symbol of revulsion as well as a primary mechanism for aggression and the assertion of will to power. As we know from Freud, they become especially significant in childhood during the period of sphincter training, an early systematic discipline applied on the body and a crucial step in socialization. The disciplines and ritual punishments enacted in jail were deliberately aimed at socializing the prisoners into the new social order of the prison. To that end the identity of the prisoner as a political militant had to be destroyed. The random beatings, scarce diet, constant visibility, body searches, and denial of control over their excretory functions were directed at defeating the will of autonomous individuals and transforming them into dependent infantilized subjects through physical pain and humiliating practices. This divestment of individual identity is, in more or less drastic forms, characteristic of what Goffman (1959) called "total institutions." Once the power battle was displaced to the psychological arena of childhood and the prisoners were left in a state of absolute powerlessness with nothing but their bodies to resist institutional assault, they resorted to the primordial mechanism of feces, at once a weapon and a symbol of utter rejection. Thus, an ex-prison officer admitted to anthropologist Allen Feldman that "[h]umiliation was a big weapon. Prisoners were constantly propelled into an infantile role. You could see the Dirty Protest as virtually resistance to toilet training in a bizarre way" (Feldman 1991: 192). That is to say, the Dirty Protest can be interpreted as simultaneously literal and symbolic resistance to prison socialization and the accompanying moral system that legitimized it. Feldman has suggested that the prisoners carried out this resistance by utilizing the excretory function as a detached weapon (1991: 178). The use of excreta as a weapon of resistance was not, however, the only bodily weapon available to the prisoners. The hunger strike, to which the prisoners resorted later on, was a more likely and socially understandable

form of political resistance. Neither was the Dirty Protest very effective in attracting international sympathy. Amnesty International, for example, concluded upon examination of the case that the prisoners' conditions were self-inflicted.[5] Any socialization process implies an emotional dynamic that Feldman does not analyze. After a year of close contact an IRA ex-prisoner man openly admitted the turmoil of emotions provoked by our lengthy conversation on the Dirty Protest:

> I feel funny now, my emotions are mixed. You suffer a lot in jail, some people more than others. Some people remember the good things about jail, the laughs. You don't want to remember the times you felt like crying. . . . It was just strange. You are on your own, you worry sick no matter how much you laugh or share, you have irrational fears. People cry in jail. A lot of strange things happen to you.

I would like to suggest that far from being a detached weapon, the Dirty Protest entailed a deep personal involvement, a process that was tremendously painful psychologically and physically.

Physical pain, insufficient diet, and constant humiliation evoked in the prisoners, in acute and extreme form, the vulnerability and powerlessness of childhood. The sense of permanent physical insecurity produced, as is frequently the case in these situations, anxieties about disfigurement (Goffman 1959: 21; Scarry 1985: 40–1). Fantasies of dismemberment, dislocation, and mutilation accompanied any venture outside the cells and were particularly present during body searches, forced baths, and wing shifts.[6] In a personal interview, an IRA ex-prisoner recalled the terror experienced at being suspended in the air held spread eagle by four officers who were pulling his arms and legs during a body search while another inspected his anus: "It was very, very frightening because there were times when you thought you were going to tear apart." Forced baths entailed heavy scrubbing with rough brushes that left the body bruised and scarred. They also involved forced shaving of beard and hair with the frequent result of skin cuts. Not only physical pain but the images of mutilation triggered by the hostility of warders made the baths terrifying experiences:

They used scrubbing brushes to wash you. The whole thing was very violent, a terrifying experience. After they finished they dragged me to the zinc and one cut my head with a razor and they cut my head in a whole lot of places while all the time they were making fun of me. Then they threw me to the floor, spread eagle. I had massive dark bruises all over my ribs and they painted them with a white stuff, I don't know what it was and they painted my face too.

The terror was augmented by the association of cleaning and death in other contexts. For example, another ex-prisoner of the same affiliation commented, apropos of the situation: "It just reminded me of the Jews in the concentration camps because every man in the [visiting] room was bald and we were all very thin and frightened" (see also Feldman 1991).

The prison dynamic of punishment and humiliation fueled feelings of hate and anger that threatened to overcome the psychological integrity of the prisoners. The following quotes from two prisoners interviewed by Feldman illustrate best the force of these feelings:

I hated the screws [prison officers]. I used to live for the day that I got out. I would have taken three day before I killed a screw. I was wrapped up in the hatred thing, and it wasn't political motivation at all. (1991: 196–7)

The hate, I found out what hatred was. I used to talk about hate on the outside, but it was superstitious, it was depersonalized. There were wee people you didn't like. But it was in jail that I came face to face with the naked hatred. It frighten the life out of me when I seen it for what it was. When you thought of getting your own back on the screw, how much you would enjoy it, it really frighten you. You just blacked those thoughts out of your mind. At the end of the day I knew I was smarter than the screws. But I knew the road of black hatred. I just got a glimpse of it. It scared the balls clean out of me. (1991: 197)

The Dirty Protest was simultaneously a sign of rejection and an instrument of power, but one that constituted also the symbolic articulation of dangerous feelings that could not be expressed in other forms without risking madness or serious physical injury. The feces constituted not so much the instrument of a mimetic violence, as Feldman has suggested, but the crystallization of a conflict between the desire of mimetic violence against prison officers and the need for restraint to preserve some physical and psychological integrity. In this sense, the feces appear as a compromise formation, a symptom in the Freudian sense of the term. However, unlike the hysterical symptom, the Dirty Protest had conscious meaning and political intentionality for the prisoners. Its significance was elaborated by them in the idiom of Republican resistance, which is part of Northern Ireland's nationalist culture. The prisoners' political beliefs arise out of a shared social experience of the working-class ghettos and are essential to the protest in that they provide its rationale and moral legitimation, as the ethnographies of Burton (1978) and Sluka (1989) have well shown. In other words, the prisoners knew why they were smearing their cells with excrement and under which conditions they would cease to do so. They were also aware that their political language made sense to an audience outside the jail, even when their action remained largely uncomprehended. Thus, if we consider the Dirty Protest as an emotionally loaded compromise formation meaningful to the actors yet not to the larger society, we can read it as a symptom of profound alienation midway between the elusive hysterical symptom and the graspable cultural symbol. Here is where Obeyesekere's concept of personal symbols (1981, 1990) becomes useful. Obeyesekere has defined personal symbols as symbols that have meaning at the personal and cultural levels. Yet while Obeyesekere's personal symbols arise out of unconscious motivation, the feces as symptom-symbol arise out of a situation of violent political conflict capable of triggering powerful unconscious associations. Republican consciousness, then, is crucial in understanding the experience of the Dirty Protest, yet it does not exhaust it. To understand the Dirty Protest we need to look beyond what is experienced "subjectively" by the individuals (Lacan 1977: 55; Scott 1991). This requires a deeper probing into the kind of relation in which prisoners and guards were engaged and the larger discourses in which such relation was embedded.

The prison experience since 1976 evoked for Republicans in extreme form the historical experience of neglect and the desire for social recognition that characterized the lives of working-class Catholics in Northern Ireland. The claim to political status was so important to them precisely because it implied a deep existential recognition, the acknowledgement that one's being-in-the-world mattered. Recognition can only come from an "other." At the closest level the significant "other" was represented by the Loyalist guards with whom prisoners interacted daily. Although in terms of profession the guards occupied the lower ranks of the social structure, as Protestants they occupied a position of social superiority vis-à-vis Catholics. Thus, the relation between prisoners and guards was mediated by a relation of social inequality larger and historically more significant than that existing in the prison universe. At a more removed level, however, the position of the "other" was occupied by the British government, which became the embodiment of the "Law of the Father." Britain became the absent presence whose law threatened to erase the prisoners by eliminating their political identity. The desire of recognition from Britain was implicit in the prisoners' and supporters' representation of the protest as a battle between Ireland and Britain. The prison disciplines, with their uniformity, the substitution of names for numbers, and extreme forms of humiliation, constituted an ultimate form of erasure.

If existential recognition was essential to the prisoners – literally a matter of life and death – the Dirty Protest must be understood as a violent attempt to force such recognition without succumbing to physical elimination, which could ultimately happen – as it did happen in 1981 – with a hunger strike. In this context, which links prison power relations with larger social-political arenas, the feces of the Dirty Protest tap into a whole new domain of meaning. They are not just a symbolic and material weapon against the prison regime, and a symptom of the alienation of the prisoners qua prisoners, but also a social symptom that must be understood in historical perspective.

The symptom appears initially as a trace, as a return of a repressed history. In the words of Slavoj Žižek, "[I]n working through the symptom we are precisely bringing about the past, producing the symbolic reality of the past" (1989: 57). In the case of the Dirty Protest what we have is the reelaboration of Anglo-Irish history. The excreta on the walls of the cells made visible the hidden history of prison violence; furthermore, it appeared to the world as *a* record of Irish history. The Catholic Primate of Ireland, Archbishop Tomas O'Fiaich, upon visiting the Long-Kesh jail, declared publicly that the situation of the prisoners was inhuman. He denounced the inflexibility of the British government that was violating the personal dignity of the prisoners and voiced concern about beatings and ill-treatment of the prisoners (*Times* and *Guardian*, August 2, 1978). Archbishop O'Fiaich's press declaration unleashed a polemic storm. The British government emphatically denied any liability for the protest as well as any mistreatment of the prisoners: "These criminals are totally responsible for the situation in which they find themselves. . . . There is no truth in those allegations [of mistreatment]" (*Times*, August 2, 1978). While unionist and conservative parties accused O'Fiaich of IRA sympathy (*Times*, August 3, 1978), Nationalist parties supported the Archbishop's concern. The Presbyterian church, on the other hand, attacked O'Fiaich for his "grave moral confusion" (*Guardian* and *Times*, August 5, 1978). The prison violence came to occupy an important place in public political discussions in Ireland and England, attracting also the attention of the international media. The connection between prison and colonial violence was drawn during the years of the Dirty Protest not only by the prisoners and their Republican supporters. The *Washington Post* compared the inflexibility of the British government with the "iron-fisted rule of Oliver Cromwell" (quoted in the *Times*, November 22, 1978). Even the European Court of Human Rights, while ruling that the prisoners were not entitled to political status, expressed its concern "at the inflexible approach of the State authorities which has been concerned more to punish offenders against prison discipline than to explore ways of resolving such a serious deadlock" (European Law Centre 1981: 201).

The rigidity of the British government, which held onto the banner of "The Law" with an intransigence highly evocative of paternal authority, as well as the refusal by prison officers to acknowledge any responsibility in the emergence of the Dirty Protest echoed the historical denial of British responsibility in the dynamics of violence in Ireland.

Historical amnesia, though common enough, is never trivial or accidental (De Certeau 1988). Such emphatic negation of any relation to the dirty prisoners, coupled with the inability to end the protest, reveals perhaps a stumbling block in the history of Britain and Ireland that remains to be explained. In this context the power of feces as a symptom of the political (dis)order of Northern Ireland may lie not so much in what it signified, but precisely in that which resisted symbolization: its capacity to tap into unconscious fears, desires, and fantasies that had come to form part of ethnic violence in Ireland through a colonial discourse of dirtiness. This discourse provided yet another arena, or another field of power, if you will, in which the Dirty Protest acquired a new set of cultural resonances appearing as a materialization of the buried "shit" of British colonization, a de-metaphorization of the "savage, dirty Irish."

Excrement and the Fiction of Civilization

Dirtiness has been a metaphor of barbarism in British anti-Irish discourse for centuries. From Elizabethan writings to Victorian accounts of Ireland there have been recurrent descriptions of the dirtiness, misery, and primitiveness of the country and its people. "Irish" and "primitive" soon implicated each other, and the image of the dirty, primitive Irish became familiar to the English imagination through jokes, cartoons, and other popular forms of representation. Such images have proliferated at times of political turmoil in Ireland, with the Irish frequently depicted with simian or pig-like fea-

tures (Curtis 1971; Darby 1983). After the partition of Ireland, "dirty" continued to be a favorite epithet to debase Catholics in Northern Ireland. My Nationalist informants were acutely aware of the operativity of this discourse, and many, like this middle-aged woman, recalled growing up hearing that they were dirty: "You would hear people saying that Catholics were dirty, and live like rats, and had too many children... and you suddenly realized that was you and your family."

The investment of excrement and dirt with intense feelings of disgust, which are then associated with aggression and fear of racial contamination, is well known and need not be underscored here. Notions of dirt and purity are crucial, as Mary Douglas (1966) noted, in organizing ideas of savagery and civilization and highly significant in establishing social boundaries and cultural differentiations. For many people in England and Ireland the prisoners living amid their own excreta constituted the image par excellence of the uncivilized, the erasure of categorical distinctions that structure human society, the regression to a presocial state, with its concomitant power of pollution and contagion. In the women's prison of Armagh officers wore masks, insulating suits, and rubber boots that shielded them from the polluting conditions of the prisoners' wing. Prisoners noted that the guards did not like to touch anything belonging to the prisoners even though they used gloves. Prison officers felt defiled coming in contact with the prisoners. As the women looked increasingly dirty, the guards tried to counteract defilement by increasing their care in making themselves up and having their hair done. Similarly, in Long-Kesh physical contact with the prisoners was abhorrent for guards.

The images of the prisoners surrounded by excreta seemed to reinforce stereotypes of Irish barbarism, yet the inability of government and administrators to handle the situation reveals other effects. Thus, I would argue that the fantasies of savagery projected onto Catholics were appropriated, literalized, and enacted by the prisoners. This materialization inevitably confronted the officers in an inescapable physical form with their own aggressive fantasies, which produced shock, horror, and the futile attempt to erase them by increasing violence, forced baths, and periodic steam cleaning of cells – acts of cleansing that, like the dirtying of the prisoners, were both literal and symbolic (Feldman 1991: 185). The "Dirty Irish" had became *really* shitty. In so doing they were transforming the closed universe of prison into an overflowing cloaca, exposing in the process a Boschian vision of the world, a scathing critique of Britain and, by association, of civilization. One cannot help but find a parallel of this critique in the writings of that polemic Irishman, Jonathan Swift.

Swift utilized the excretory function as a satiric weapon against the pretentiousness and self-righteousness of English civilization. His "excremental vision" (Brown 1959: 179) is sharply displayed in part 4 of *Gulliver's, Travels*. In "A Voyage to the Country of the Houyhnhnms," Gulliver encounters the Yahoo. Although Yahoos possess a human form, they are filthy and nasty, have a strong smell and bad eating habits, and use excrement as an instrument of self-expression and aggression (Swift 1967 [1726]: 270, 313). Immediately after their encounter the Yahoos shoot feces at Gulliver, who tries failingly to stay clear of them. If the Yahoo represents the archetype of human savagery, its juxtaposition with Gulliver's narrative of English life soon makes clear that the civilized human is nastier than the savage Yahoo. In other words, Swift made excremental aggression the hidden core of civilization, an insight hard to swallow.

In the context of the Anglo-Irish colonial relation in which it emerged, the Dirty Protest, like the Yahoo, acted as a mirror of colonial barbarism that reflected back to prison officers and British public an obscured image of themselves that challenged their identity as a civilized nation. This excremental image literally entered the center of gravity of British civilization when two supporters of the prisoners hurled horse dung to the startled members of Parliament (*Guardian*, July 7, 1978).

Guards and government alike responded to this image with absolute denial, voiced in the argument that "prisoners' condition was self-inflicted." Yet the guards' rising brutality reproduced on the incarcerated bodies the same barbarity attributed to the prisoners. Such mimesis seems inherent to the colonial production of reality, which frequently uses the fiction of the savage (or the terrorist) to create a culture of terror (Bhaba 1984; Taussig 1987). In Northern Ireland the fiction of criminality of Republican prisoners ultimately exposed and reproduced the savagery of state policies. Inside Long-Kesh positions had been reversed: from objects of a defiling power, the prisoners had come to be the subjects that controlled it (Feldman 1991). Yet the prisoners were inescapably locked in a political impasse characterized by a vicious cycle of projection-reflection that spilled the violence from the prison onto the wider society.[7] While the men's Dirty Protest was locked in its own violence, the women's provoked a movement of social transformation. The impulse of such transformation came from the articulation of menstrual blood as a symbol of sexual difference with ongoing feminist discourse.

Dirt and Blood: The Meaning of Sexual Difference

Inside the walls of Armagh prison filthiness was tainted with menstrual blood. An additional set of meanings resonated there. Journalist Tim Coogan, who visited the jail at that time, wrote:

I was taken to inspect "A" wing where the Dirty Protest is in full swing. This was sickening and appalling. Tissues, slops, consisting of tea and urine, some faeces, and clots of blood – obviously the detritus of menstruation – lay in the corridor between the two rows of cells....I found the smell in the girl's cells far worse than at Long-Kesh, and several times found myself having to control feelings of nausea. (1980: 215–16)

What can make 30 dirty women more revolting than 400 dirty men if not the exposure of menstrual blood – an element that cannot contribute much to the fetid odors of urine and feces but can turn the stomach. What Coogan expresses with his body – it literally makes him sick – is the horror and repulsion triggered by the sight of "that" which constitutes a linguistic and optic taboo, a horror that he cannot articulate linguistically. Through his own body Coogan also inscribes a crucial difference between men and women prisoners. Ironically, it was this difference that Armagh women were trying to eradicate by joining the Dirty Protest.

Women did not belong to prison in popular consciousness, even though they had participated in armed operations and had been imprisoned in rising numbers since 1972. Most Nationalists perceived women's presence in jail as a product of an idealistic youth and the freedom from family commitments. Through the course of my fieldwork, some women ex-prisoners acknowledged that Republican men still assumed that after marriage women would abandon political activities that entail a risk of death or imprisonment. Although this frequently happens it is by no means always the case. On the other hand, the image of male prisoners did not have an age reference. Although the majority of male prisoners were young, it was not rare for them to be married and have children. In contrast to male prisoners, female prisoners were permanently thought of as girls. Their cultural space was in this sense liminal. Neither men nor completely women, they were perceived at a general social level as gender neutral.

Women prisoners did not consider gender a significant element of differentiation either. Female members of the IRA had fought to be part of this organization rather than part of its feminine counterpart, Cumman na mBan. Thus, they had consciously rejected gender as a differential factor in political militancy. To prove that gender was irrelevant to military performance in a male organization de facto entailed downplaying women's difference and interiorizing men's standards. At the level of consciousness gender difference was at the beginning of the Dirty Protest completely accidental to its meaning. From the point of view of Armagh women their Dirty Protest was not different from that of the men's: it was the same struggle undertaken by equal comrades for political recognition. The emphatic reassertion of the sameness of prisoners' identity regardless of gender must be understood as an attempt to counteract the overshadowing of women prisoners under the focus of attention given to male prisoners. Such an eclipse was partly a consequence of the fact that women were not required to use prison uniforms and thus were not subjected to the dramatic conditions that the men were. That fact asserted from the start a gender difference that worked against their political visibility. At this level the Dirty Protest was for Armagh women an attempt to erase that gender difference introduced by the penal institution and to thus reassert their political visibility. Yet, unintentionally, the menstrual blood brought to the surface the contradictions involved in this process, shifting the meaning of the protest. It objectified a difference that women had carefully obliterated in other dimensions of their political life. That is, while their political identity as members of the IRA entailed at one level a cultural desexualization, and the Dirty Protest a personal defeminization, at a deeper level the exposure of menstrual blood subverted this process by radically transforming the asexual bodies of "girls" into the sexualized bodies of women. In so doing, the menstrual blood became a symbol through which gender identity was reflected upon, bringing to the surface what had been otherwise erased.

Menstruation as an elemental sign of womanhood also marks women's social vulnerability. At the level of representation it is a metonym linking sex and motherhood, a sign of the dangerously uncontrolled nature of women's flesh in Catholic ideology from which only the mother of god escaped (Warner 1983); a tabooed and polluting substance that must be hidden from discourse as it is from sight. In the context of arrest it is a sabotage of the body. The meaning of this sabotage has been forcefully expressed by Northern Ireland writer and Republican ex-prisoner Brenda Murphy in a short story entitled "A Curse." An arrested young woman gets her period in between interrogation shifts and is forced to talk about it to a male officer:

"I've taken my period" she said simply. "I need some sanitary napkins and a wash." He looked at her with disgust. "Have you no shame? I've been married twenty years and my wife wouldn't mention things like that." What is the color of shame? All she could see was red as it trickled down her legs. (1989: 226–7).

When it comes to women, impotence and shame have color, not name. Mary Cardinal, in the superb fictional account of her own madness (1983), calls the permanent flow of her menstrual blood "the thing." Her cure entailed a process of inscribing meaning in language, of finding "The Words To Say It." In choosing the theme of menstruation to talk about the experience of arrest, Brenda Murphy – who participated in the Dirty Protest – broke a taboo of silence that made Nationalist women's personal and political experience invisible. One can read her story as a commentary on the Armagh Dirty Protest. Indeed, on her release Maureen Gibson, one of the protesting prisoners, said:

I do get the impression that people outside [the prison] don't fully realize that there are actually women in Armagh. They don't understand what the women are going through both physically and psychologically. You go through a lot with your menstrual cycle. (*Republican News*, September 27, 1980)

The shocking character of the imagery that the words of released prisoners evoked was recalled to me by Mary, a middle-aged Republican woman:

I remember one rally in which a girl released from Armagh spoke about what it was for them during their periods. It was very hard for her to talk about menstruation, to say that even during that time they could not get a change of clothes, could not get washed. And some people, including Republican men, were saying "How can she talk about that?" They did not want to hear that women were being mistreated in Armagh jail during their menstruation. And so, the Republican movement did not talk about it. They only talked about the men, but they did not want to hear about girls. Some people just could not cope with that.

What the Nationalist community did not understand and could not cope with was *women's* pain. Not a mother's suffering, which ultimately roused the emotions of Nationalist people in support of the prisoners. Nor the suffering of incarcerated young men, whose image, naked and beaten, resembled that of Jesus Christ. Unintentionally, the women prisoners in Armagh brought to the fore a different kind of suffering, one systematically obscured in social life and in cultural constructions, devalued in Catholic religion and Nationalist ideologies: that women's pain of which menstruation is a sign and a symbol.

If the men's Dirty Protest represented the rejection of the civilizing mission of British colonialism, the Armagh women permeated that rejection with gender politics. At one level it encapsulated the negation of dominant models of femininity embedded in the idealized asexual Catholic mother and elaborated in Nationalist discourse around the image of Mother Ireland. This model provokes high ambivalence in many Nationalist women for whom motherhood is at once a source of comfort and support and a restrictive social role.[8] On the other hand, the women's Dirty Protest represented also a rejection of male violence fused, as noted below, with political dominance in colonial discourse and practice. In the prison context the visibility of menstrual blood can be read as a curse redirected from the bodies of women to the male "body politic" of colonialism.[9]

As symptom, symbol, and weapon, the Dirty Protest involved an enormous suffering. The young women in Armagh, like the men in Long-Kesh, conceptualized their physical and psychological pain within the parameters of a religious ethic of salvation acting in the political arena. At the level of conscious purpose it was for them a necessary requisite to save Ireland from colonization and reestablish a just and equal society in a reunited Irish land. This ethic of salvation acted as an interpretative language for pain that would otherwise be meaningless. Yet if a religious-political frame can provide meaning to the prisoners' pain, it cannot express it. Their suffering eludes language. Republican women could narrate the events of the Dirty Protest, but the emotional experience was encountered with painful silence and the explicit admission of lacking words to describe it.

For Elaine Scarry (1985), inexpressibility is what characterizes pain, which needs to be objectified in order to be comprehended. But pain does not operate in the same way for women and men. In Armagh, the prisoners' suffering became objectified in the menstrual blood, a complex symbol that inscribed their suffering inside the symbolic contours of what Gayatri Spivak has called "the space of what can only happen to a woman" (1988: 184). As this space had been actively silenced in the cultural logic of nationalism, tensions were bound to arise on the different shades of the political horizon.

Mimesis or the Power of Transgression: The Feminist Debate

The feminist movement in Ireland grew bitterly divided as the Dirty Protest went on.[10] Mainstream feminists were sharply critical of the male-dominated Republican movement, whose use of violence, they argued, divided women. At the head of these feminists was the Northern Ireland Women's Rights Movement (NIWRM), a broadly defined organization founded in 1975 and very hostile to nationalism in general and Republicanism in particular. The NIWRM refused any support to Armagh prisoners on the grounds that they were aping their male comrades. Other women's groups such as the Socialist Women's Group and the Belfast Women's Collective quite literally agonized over the meaning and degree of support to the prisoners. The Republican movement, on the other hand, was not less hostile to feminism, which they easily dismissed as being pro-British. Preoccupied with the large number of male prisoners, Republicans had largely ignored the existence of women in jail, seeing them at best as an appendix to the men's protest. Was the Armagh women's protest a mimetic enactment? I think so, but one that had important political implications. Drucilla Cornell has argued that mimesis constitutes not a simple repetition but a reappropriation entailing a process of refiguration (1991: 182). It is in this light that we must interpret the Armagh protest.

When the Armagh women demanded to be part of the IRA, rejecting its feminine branch, they were criticizing a genderized system that set them in the position of political subsidiaries. This critique already modified the terms of

the system. Similarly, by mimetically reappropriating the Dirty Protest, the Armagh women at first negated gender difference, stating that their struggle was the same as that of the men. Yet this attempt to transcend a genderized context by negating the feminine was negated in turn by the objectification of sexual difference that the menstrual blood represented. Thus, the mimetic appropriation of the Dirty Protest entailed a process of rewriting a (hi)story of resistance, a rewriting that specified the feminine in its most transgressive form. But it also entailed a refiguration of the feminine inasmuch as it was affirmed not as a shared essence but as existentially inseparable from class and ethnic positions.

The rising tensions exploded publicly when Nell McCafferty, a journalist from Derry City, wrote in the pages of the *Irish Times*, "There is menstrual blood in the walls of Armagh prison in Northern Ireland."[11] McCafferty shouted aloud in the main Irish newspaper what most people had been refusing to hear, that there was a specific women's pain, and that in Northern Ireland it was inextricably linked, but not reduced, to colonial oppression. Such a link was encapsulated in the menstrual blood as a symbol of an existence, of a being-in-the-world that could not be represented by dominant feminist and Nationalist discourses, even less by the discourse of the *law*. The menstrual blood stood as a symbol of that reality excluded from language. In so doing it acted as a catalyst of cultural change, a vehicle of reflection and discussion about the meanings of gender difference in Northern Ireland. The most public manifestation of such – often bitter – debate was McCafferty's article. As time went on, Armagh prisoners began to inscribe their difference in language, translating the dirt and menstrual blood into a critique of a ready-made feminist subject that failed to represent them. In a letter published in the *Irish Times* in 1980, Armagh prisoners answered the NIWRM, which had contended that the predicament of the prisoners did not concern feminists, with a demand for redefinition of feminism:

> It is our belief that not only is our plight a feminist issue, but a very fundamental social

and human issue. It is a feminist issue in so far as we are women, and the network of this jail is completely geared to male domination. The governor, the assistant governor, and the doctor are all males. We are subject to physical and mental abuse from male guards who patrol our wing daily, continually peeping into our cells.... If this is not a feminist issue then we feel that the word feminist needs to be redefined. (quoted in Loughran 1986: 64)

The articulation of the symbol of menstrual blood with ongoing political and feminist discourses forced a discussion among Nationalists and feminists alike on the exclusionary politics of the very categories of feminism and nationalism, which had a social effect.

By the end of 1980, a policy document on women's rights was approved for the first time in the Republican movement. Two years later, in 1982, a Women's Center was opened also for the first time in the working class Nationalist ghetto of Falls Road. It set to work amid the discomfort and protest of many Nationalist men. Women flowed in with a hitherto muted knowledge. A Republican woman recalled that "there were battered women, incest, rape, appalling poverty. We had been too busy with the war and didn't realize until the Women's Center that all those problems were there too." Another kind of shit had surfaced. As it gained social visibility, the stinking reality of male violence against women disputed both Catholic models of gender and Nationalist heroic epics. Since then the Nationalist community, and Republicanism in particular, have not been able to ignore easily gender politics. Neither have Irish feminists been able to ignore Nationalist politics. Yet the problem of defining a Nationalist-feminist subject is fraught with difficulties as Irish nationalism – like other postcolonial nationalisms – continues to use gender discourse to advance political claims. Nationalist-feminists have to contend in Northern Ireland with a permanent split between anti-imperialist positions and feminist positions that both exclude them. It is precisely this self-conscious, split political identity that may open the political field in Northern Ireland to new critical possibilities.

Conclusion

I have attempted to show that a Foucauldian notion of power as force relations is not incompatible with an interpretative anthropology sensitive to the "deep play" of subjectivity. Departing from the premise that the Dirty Protest was a violent contest of power, I have tried to elucidate the dynamics that organized it in that form and not others, as well as its social and political consequences in a shared universe of meaning. I have conceptualized the feces and blood characterizing the protest as primordial symbols. These symbols are invested with political power; contrary to Mary Douglas, though, they are not just an expression of the social order. Neither are they locked in unconscious motivation. They partake of both domains and are simultaneously instrumental in that, like speech acts, they have a performative character. The excreta and menstrual blood arose out of a situation of violent political conflict that became overdetermined by tapping into the interconnected domains of prison violence, colonial history, unconscious motivation (infantile fantasies, fears, and desires) and gender discourse, *all* of which constituted the political field at the particular historical moment of the Dirty Protest. It was precisely this overdetermination that gave the protest its shocking power, simultaneously allowing the prisoners to endure its suffering by crystallizing inexpressible and contradictory emotions. The meanings of the Dirty Protest were not fixed, but shifted with each domain of experience into which they tapped, acting simultaneously as weapon, symbol, and symptom. In so doing, they also revealed the gender organization of power.

I regard gender not just as a dimension of violence but as an intrinsic component of it, crucial to the understanding of its meanings, deployments, and ends. My analysis suggests that political violence performed on and from the body cannot escape the meaning of sexual difference. Despite the shared political consciousness and goals of men and women prisoners, their protests had different significance. While the men's protest was articulated through an intense dynamic of violence, the women's protest was crystallized around the meaning of sexual difference. Armagh women provoked, albeit unintentionally, a reformulation of feminine subjectivity. Inasmuch as sexual difference is, in Ireland as everywhere else, inseparable from class, ethnic, and even political positions, such reformulation in turn sparked a transformation of dominant discourses of feminism and nationalism.

I have suggested in this article that ethnic and political violence predicated on the bodies of women cannot be considered as an addendum to violence performed on men's bodies. As I have shown, it might have disparate meanings and effects that are crucial to both the construction of sexual difference and the construction of ethnic identity.

NOTES

1   Republicans favor Irish reunification and independence from Britain; they include IRA and INLA. Loyalists are pro-British and radically opposed to Irish reunification.
2   *Republican News*, February 16, 1980; McCafferty 1981; Women against Imperialism 1980. The sexual overtones of the assault were confirmed by personal interview.
3   In relation to colonialism and sexuality, see Chatterjee 1989, Kelly 1991, Sangari and Vaid 1990, and Stoler 1991, among others.
4   *Republican News*, February 23, 1980; Report by Women against Imperialism, April 9, 1980, p. 27.
5   Amnesty International Report on Long-Kesh 1977.
6   These images are characteristic of childhood aggressiveness and the formation of the image of one's body. They belong to the repertoire of the unconscious and thus appear frequently in dreams, myth, art, and so on. They are, however, easily triggered under special physical or psychological duress. See Lacan 1977: 10–11.

7   As the violence inside the prison augmented, so did IRA and Loyalist assassinations and military repression. The brutalization of the warders had a direct effect in isolating them from their own communities and increasing conflicts in their domestic life. See Coogan 1980 and Feldman 1991.
8   This ambivalence emerged in recurrent comments made by Nationalist women during my fieldwork. Particularly important were the discussions following the screening in the Nationalist districts of Belfast and Derry of the documentary *Mother Ireland*, directed by Anne Crilly and produced by the Derry Film and Video Company, and of the play about the Armagh women, *Now and at the Hour of Our Death*, produced by the theater group Trouble and Strife.
9   In this sense the Armagh women's Dirty Protest is reminiscent of the kind of symbolic warfare enacted by women in some parts of Africa. Ardener and Ifeka-Moller have documented women's exposure of genitals as a powerful sexual insult used against men violating their dignity and rights. This display publicly states disrespect, denial of dominance, and nonrecognition of authority. See Ardener 1975 and Ifeka-Moller 1975.
10 In relation to the history and composition of the feminist movement in Northern Ireland, see Evason 1991, Loughran 1986, and Ward 1987 and 1991.
11 Nell McCafferty, "It is my belief that Armagh is a feminist issue," *Irish Times*, June 17, 1980.

REFERENCES

Amnesty International. 1977. Report of an Amnesty International Mission to Northern Ireland. June.
Ardener, Shirley. 1975. Sexual Insult and Female Militancy. In *Perceiving Women*. Shirley Ardener, ed. pp. 29–54. London: Dent and Sons.
Asad, Talal. 1983. Notes on Body Pain and Truth in Medieval Christian Ritual. *Economy and Society*, 12: 1.

Bhabha, Homi. 1994. *The Location of Culture*. New York: Routledge.

Brown, Norman O. 1959. *Life against Death: The Psychoanalytical Meaning of History*. Middletown, CO: Wesleyan University Press.

Burton, Frank. 1978. *The Politics of Legitimacy: Struggles in a Belfast Community*. London: Routledge & Kegan Paul.

Cardinal, Marie. 1983. *The Words to Say It: An Autobiographical Novel*. Cambridge, MA: Van Vactor & Goodheart.

Chatterjee, Partha. 1989. Colonialism, Nationalism and Colonized Women: The Contest in India. *American Ethnologist*, 16/4: 622–33.

Coogan, Tim Pat. 1980. *On the Blanket: The H-Block Story*. Dublin: Ward River Press.

Cornell, Drucilla. 1991. *Beyond Accommodation: Ethical Feminism, Deconstruction and the Law*. New York: Routledge.

Curtis, L. Perry. 1997 [1971]. *Apes and Angels*. Washington, DC: Smithsonian Books.

Darby, John. 1983. *Dressed To Kill: Cartoonists and the Northern Ireland Conflict*. Belfast: Appletree.

De Certeau, Michel. 1988. *The Writing of History*. New York: Columbia University Press.

Douglas, Mary. 1966. *Purity and Danger: An Analysis of the Concepts of Pollution and Taboo*. London: Routledge & Kegan Paul.

European Law Centre. 1981. European Human Rights Reports, Part 10.

Evason, Eileen. 1991. *Against the Grain: The Contemporary Women's Movement in Northern Ireland*. Dublin: Attic Press.

Feldman, Allen. 1991. *Formations of Violence: The Narrative of the Body and Political Terror in Northern Ireland*. Chicago: University of Chicago Press.

Foucault, Michel. 1979. *Discipline and Punish: The Birth of the Prison*. New York: Vintage Books.

Goffman, Erving. 1959. *Asylums: Essays on the Social Situation of Mental Patients and Other Inmates*. New York: Anchor Books.

Graziano, Frank. 1992. *Divine Violence: Spectacle, Psychosexuality and Radical Christianity in the Argentine Dirty War*. Boulder, CO: Westview Press.

Ifeka-Moller, Caroline. 1975. Female Militancy and Colonial Revolt: The Women's War of 1929, Eastern Nigeria. In *Perceiving Women*. Shirley Ardener, ed. pp. 127–59. London: Dent and Sons.

Kelly, John. 1991. *A Politics of Virtue: Hinduism, Sexuality and Countercolonial Discourse in Fiji*. Chicago: University of Chicago Press.

Lacan, Jacques. 1977. Aggressivity in Psychoanalysis *and* Function and Field of Speech and Language. In *Écrits*, pp. 8–114. New York: Norton.

Loughran, Christine. 1986. Armagh and Feminist Strategy. *Feminist Review*, 23: 59–79.

McCafferty, Nell. 1981. *Armagh Women*. Dublin: Co-op Books.

Murphy, Brenda. 1989. A Curse. In *Territories of the Voice. Contemporary Stories by Irish Women Writers*. L. DeSalvo, K. W. D'Arcy, and K. Hogan, eds. pp. 226–7. Boston: Beacon Press.

Obeyesekere, Gananath. 1981. *Medusa's Hair: An Essay on Personal Symbols and Religious Experience*. Chicago: University of Chicago Press.

—— 1990. *The Work of Culture: Symbolic Transformation in Psychoanalysis and Anthropology*. Chicago: University of Chicago Press.

—— 1992. *The Apotheosis of Captain Cook: European Myth Making in the Pacific*. Princeton: Princeton University Press.

Sangari, K., and S. Vaid. 1990. *Recasting Women: Essays in Indian Colonial History*. New Brunswick, NJ: Rutgers University Press.

Scarry, Elaine. 1985. *The Body in Pain: The Making and Unmaking of the World*. New York: Oxford University Press.

Scott, Joan. 1991. The Evidence of Experience. *Critical Inquiry*, 17: 773–97.

Sluka, Jeffrey. 1989. *Hearts and Minds, Water and Fish: Support for the INLA in a Northern Irish Ghetto*. Greenwich, CT.: AI Press.

Spivak, Gayatri. 1988. Forward to "Draupadi" by Mahasweta Devi. In *In Other Worlds: Essays in Cultural Politics*. New York: Routledge.

Stoler, Ann L. 1991. Carnal Knowledge and Imperial Power: Gender, Race and Morality in Colonial Asia. In *Gender at the Cross-roads of Knowledge: Feminist Anthropology in the Postmodern Era*. Micaela di Leonardo, ed. pp. 51–101. Berkeley: University of California Press.

Suarez-Orozco, Marcelo. 1992. Dirty War and Post Dirty War in Argentina. In *The Paths of Domination Resistance and Terror*. C. Nordstrom and J. A. Martin, eds. pp. 219–60. Berkeley: University of California Press.

Swift, Jonathan. 1967 [1726]. *Gulliver's Travels*. London: Penguin.

Taussig, Michael. 1987. *Shamanism, Colonialism and the Wild Man*. Chicago: University of Chicago Press.

Turner, Victor. 1967. *The Forest of Symbols. Aspects of Ndembu Ritual*. Ithaca, NY: Cornell University Press.

Ward, Margaret. 1987. A Difficult, Dangerous Honesty. Ten Years of Feminism in Northern Ireland. A Discussion. Belfast.

——1991. The Women's Movement in the North of Ireland: Twenty Years On. In *Ireland's Histories: Aspects of State, Society and Ideology*. S. Hutton and P. Steward, eds. pp. 149–63. London: Routledge.

Warner, Marina. 1983. *Alone of All Her Sex: The Myth and the Cult of the Virgin Mary*. New York: Vintage.

Women against Imperialism. 1980. Women Protest for Political Status in Armagh Gaol. April 9.

Žižek, Slavoj. 1989. *The Sublime Object of Ideology*. New York: Verso.

16

Women's Rights are Human Rights: The Merging of Feminine and Feminist Interests among El Salvador's Mothers of the Disappeared (CO-MADRES)

Lynn Stephen

Women are the backbone of a wide range of social movements in Latin America, including rural and urban movements for improved living conditions, student movements, feminist movements, and movements for human rights, land reclamations, relatives of the disappeared, labor unions, abortion and reproductive rights, democratization of political systems, and more (Saporta Sternbach et al. 1992). Self-labeling by movement activists has resulted in the division of women's movements into feminist movements and *movimientos populares de mujeres* (grassroots women's movements). This dichotomy is frequently replicated by social scientists, who divide movements between feminist or strategically oriented movements that challenge women's gender oppression and feminine or practical movements that focus on helping women to fulfill their traditional gender roles.

This tendency to sort women's movements into one of two essentialist categories can be countered by some new theoretical insights from social-movements theory and anthropological studies of cultural resistance that stress the multiple subjectivity of women as movement participants and the blurred line between resistance and accommodation, respectively.[1] Recent discussions on women in Latin American social movements also considerably advance this analysis.[2] Perhaps more important, however, is the self-analysis and description offered by movement participants. As June Nash has pointed out (1992: 291–2), anthropologists must put more emphasis on the interpretations given by actors about their own situations than the anthropologist's own interpretations.

In this article I highlight the case of the CO-MADRES (Committee of Mothers and

Relatives of Political Prisoners, Disappeared and Assassinated of El Salvador "Monseñor Romero") of El Salvador, an organization that attracted members because of its pursuit of women's rights and the assumption of responsibilities as mothers and wives. CO-MADRES includes both rural and urban women from a mixture of the poor, working, and middle classes. An examination of the historical trajectory of the public demands and goals of the CO-MADRES, as well as of interviews with members, suggests that women's lives were changed because of their political activism but that such changes were not uniformly experienced. At first demanding that the government and various military and security forces provide information about disappeared, incarcerated, and assassinated family members, the CO-MADRES later moved into a political sphere from which they had previously been marginalized as women. They now demand that women's inclusion in formal political decision-making bodies comprise a fundamental element of the democratization process in El Salvador. With the encouragement of self-identified feminists, they have also brought issues of domestic violence, rape, and women's lack of control over their own sexuality into their political analysis and work. In the process they have clearly been transformed, but not all through the same experiences or interpretations of events. They have been able to act together in contingent moments of unity. Their experience of that unity remains, like them, diverse. Here I argue that labeling their movement as either feminine or feminist with corresponding private and public claims makes little sense and does not capture the richness and complexity of the political ideologies and agendas that they have developed.

Ideology of National Security and El Salvador's Civil War

El Salvador was locked in a civil war from 1979 until January 1992, when formal peace accords were signed by the Cristiani government and the FMLN (Farabundo Martí National Liberation Front) in Mexico City. In

the spring of 1994, El Salvador held national, state, and local elections in which the FMLN participated as an open political party with the Democratic Convergence (CD) as the CD-FMLN, headed by presidential candidate Ruben Zamora. While the FMLN did not fare well in the elections, its emergence as a legitimate political force has changed the political culture of El Salvador.

It is estimated that one out of every 100 Salvadorans either was murdered or disappeared during the civil war. As of late 1991, a total of 80,000 had died and 7,000 more had disappeared. Human rights organizations such as Amnesty International have linked the Salvadoran military to tens of thousands of cases of assassination, torture, rape, and imprisonment of peasants, union leaders, students, and others. The final report of the United Nations Truth Commission (Comisión de la Verdad) published in March 1993 found that the military and far-right death squads with ties to the army were responsible for 85 percent of the 25,000 civilian deaths that the Commission investigated (Naciones Unidas 1993). Thousands of men and women who disappeared were tortured and assassinated: they were sons, daughters, husbands, wives, brothers, sisters, aunts, uncles, and cousins. They were *comadres* and *compadres, ahijados* and *ahijadas* (godmothers and godfathers, godsons and goddaughters). They lived in the social world of family and kinship relations. They also had occupational and class identities as workers, peasants, intellectuals, lawyers, artists, musicians, priests, businessmen and businesswomen, nuns, doctors, nurses, librarians, shopkeepers, market vendors, and more. They had cultural and ethnic identities as Indians, part-Indians, and mestizos. Some also had political identities as members of political organizations, political parties, and grassroots organizations such as peasant cooperatives, human rights organizations, labor unions, student groups, consumer organizations, and teachers' unions.

To the military, various security police units, and many branches of the Salvadoran state, these people had one identity – that of subversives who were a threat to national security and to the capitalist modernization process of

El Salvador. In death, they were at best faceless numbers and, at worst, as nonexistent and as invisible as the disappeared. To their relatives, these thousands of people remained whole human beings, vibrant in all the aspects of their identities and social relations, and the fact of kinship was never severed from the class, occupational, political, and cultural aspects of the dead and disappeareds' identities. To understand how thousands of people came to be victims of the Salvadoran civil war, we must look at the emergence of doctrines of national security in Latin America and at their relationship to state ideologies promoting gender hierarchy.

A watershed event in the political history of El Salvador is known as the *matanza*, or massacre. In 1931, Arturo Araujo was elected president of El Salvador in what many called the country's only free elections. He was overthrown by the military at the end of the year and replaced by General Maximiliano Hernández Martínez. During 1932, Salvadoran Communist Party members who had expected to make significant electoral gains became dismayed when Hernández Martínez called off the elections. Party members headed by Augustín Farabundo Martí responded by trying to harness widespread insurrectionary actions into full-scale revolution. They planned to build on the widespread discontent in the country-side created by a drastic drop in world coffee prices and widespread layoffs and pay cuts instituted throughout El Salvador. A large trade union federation influenced by the clandestine Salvadoran Communist Party also figured importantly as a source of support.

The planned insurrection went awry when Martí and others were arrested and rendered incapable of providing coordination. The revolt happened anyway. Peasants armed with machetes attacked government offices and coffee warehouses and took over several towns in the heart of Sonsonate, El Salvador's coffee district. Government troops took the offensive and forced most of the rebels into the town of Sonzacate. The military quickly regained control of the country and unleashed a campaign of terror that killed between 10,000 and 30,000 people, mostly indigenous peasants (Anderson 1971).

The cultural and political effects of the matanza were enduring. Because the majority of those killed in the matanza were perceived as Indian, outward manifestations of Indian identity (language, dress, religious customs) were quickly abandoned. The region of Sonsonate also remained one of the few areas in El Salvador where grassroots organizations have since found only mediocre support. The matanza set a precedent in which the military established itself as the client of El Salvador's ruling class, with primary investments in the coffee and export sector; it established a political culture in which defense of Salvadoran national security focused on protecting the interests of El Salvador's agro-export elite. The involvement of the clandestine Salvadoran Communist Party in the revolt also provided a basis for later anticommunist ideology, with the exception of an antifascist movement during World War II that in 1944 succeeded in ousting Martínez (Ready 1994). The military regained control of the Salvadoran government within a year and continued to serve the interests of the country's elite.

The emerging Salvadoran culture of national security based on the experience of the matanza was reinforced and cultivated by U.S. anticommunism campaigns that solidified after the Cuban Revolution. After 1959, U.S. foreign policy makers became very worried about the spread of communism throughout Latin America. In 1961 the nationalist revolution in Cuba was attacked by counterrevolutionaries trained by U.S. Special Forces and flown in U.S. planes to the Bay of Pigs. That same year, President John F. Kennedy proposed the opening of a new stage of U.S.–Latin relations by forging the Alliance for Progress. The Alliance preached that certain reforms were necessary if Castro-style revolutions were to be contained. Tax, land, and labor reforms could help bridge the gap between rich and poor, and electoral contests could provide channels for discontent.

While the Alliance for Progress contained many economic proposals, it also espoused a military strategy. The armies and police forces of Latin America were trained in the latest techniques of counterinsurgency warfare to be used against current and expected guerrilla threats. Local police forces took courses in interrogation methods to be used in the extraction of information from potential subversives. They were also schooled in the use of kinship and social networks to manipulate torture victims into revealing the names and addresses of others to whom they were close. While national governments in Central America eagerly signed up for military training and assistance, the economic reforms proposed in the Alliance did not fare as well.

Land reform was proposed but never realized. Oligarchs and right-wing forces in the country did not accept the argument that agrarian reform was needed to prevent agrarian revolutions. They argued instead for more national security measures (Barry 1987: 109). Since the 1960s, a majority of the senior officers of El Salvador and some other countries have been – and continue to be – trained in the United States (at Fort Benning) and elsewhere (Panama and Honduras). In El Salvador the U.S. commitment went from training officers to helping the Salvadoran military grow.

The upward spiral of U.S. financing of the Salvadoran military corresponded with the 1979 victory of the Sandinistas in neighboring Nicaragua. The Salvadoran armed forces mushroomed from fewer than 10,000 in 1979 to close to 70,000 in 1991. During this same period, the United States sent nearly $6 billion to the Salvadoran government, a majority of which was designated for military aid. All of El Salvador's top-ranked officers received extensive U.S. training. U.S. advisers created the army's elite counterinsurgency units, including the Atlacatl Battalion – whose soldiers were responsible for shooting the Jesuits and murdering as many as 700 people in the 1981 El Mozote massacres (Danner 1994).

In El Salvador, as elsewhere, the doctrine of national security assigned to the armed forces and their allies "the role of safeguarding internal security and waging war against 'subversive elements' within their borders" (Fisher 1993: 10). Threats to national security include any type of idea, event, project, or organization that threatens the status quo politically, economically, or culturally.

A basic look at economic, health, and land distribution statistics compiled in the 1980s reveals the grave social and economic situation in which most Salvadorans lived. In 1980, the richest 20 percent of the Salvadoran population controlled 66 percent of the income. The poorest 20 percent controlled 2 percent of the income. In 1987 the per capita gross domestic product was $900.

Land distribution mirrored the distribution of wealth. In 1987, 1 percent of the farms comprised 71 percent of the farmland and 41 percent of the farms comprised 10 percent of the farmland. In 1988 life expectancy at birth was 58.8 years and the infant mortality rate was 86 per 1,000 live births. Finally, in 1988 urban unemployment was 50 percent while rural unemployment was 71 percent.[3]

These figures clearly represent the extended crisis of the civil war and demonstrate consistent patterns of extreme disparities in wealth distribution, widespread under- and unemployment, landlessness, and poor health found throughout this century in El Salvador. These marginal living conditions for the majority are linked to a consistent dependency on export agriculture (coffee is its major export) and a growing external public debt that went from $88 million in 1970 to $1.825 billion in 1989 (Barry 1990: 177). This debt has grown despite major infusions of aid from the United States and remittances from Salvadorans living in the United States to their families. These remittances are estimated to total from $500 million to over $1.3 billion annually (Barry 1990: 79).

Any group of people perceived to challenge the economic status quo represented in the preceding statistics was considered a threat to national security. Anyone questioning the political system that held the economic system in place was even more suspect. Many political analysts believe that the 1970s marked a breakdown of El Salvador's political order, a collapse marked by widespread electoral fraud, extreme repression, and violations of human rights (Central America Information Office 1982: 15; see also Arnson 1982: 15). The decade of the 1970s was also characterized by a resurgence of popular organizations and movements of peasants, the urban poor, students, and labor, which responded to a faltering economy and army repression by increasing their demands and public presence. The obvious electoral fraud of 1972, in which Napoleon Duarte and Guillermo Ungo were robbed of a clear victory, beaten, and exiled, called into question the process of building democracy in El Salvador (Arnson 1982: 27). The late 1970s were marked by a campaign of terror by death squads and the military against the grassroots organizations and the liberation theology sectors of the church. Every morning people in San Salvador and other urban areas were greeted by the sight of bodies exhibiting visible signs of torture and left lying on the streets. Areas on the outskirts of the city known as "body dumps" exhibited the evidence of the previous night's slaughter. And some of the people who were detained, the "disappeared," were simply never seen again.

The popular Catholic church, following liberation theology, was an important political actor during this period. In response to the Bishop's Conference in Medellìn in 1968, the progressive Salvadoran Catholic Church began to define poverty and oppression of the masses as a sin, the most profound contradiction to Christian faith (Berryman 1986). The organization of hundreds of Christian base communities that organized around and discussed the problems of poverty in relation to biblical teaching politicized both the rural and the urban poor. The late 1970s were marked by a campaign of terror by death squads and the military against the grassroots organizations and the liberation theology sectors of the church. Priests, along with peasant leaders, union leaders, and others labeled subversives, were arrested, tortured, and made to disappear.

During the 1970s, the armed left also began to emerge in El Salvador. Three important guerrilla groups dedicated to achieving profound socioeconomic and political transformations were formed in the first half of the decade. They include the Popular Forces for Liberation-"Farabundo Martí" (FPL-FM), formed in 1970 from a radical wing of the Salvadoran Communist Party (PCS); the People's Revolutionary Army (ERP), formed in 1971 by dissident Christian Democrats and other leftists; and the Armed Forces of National Resistance (FARN or RN), formed in

1975 from a fraction for the ERP (Central American Information Office 1982:124). The Salvadoran Communist Party (PCS), founded in 1930 and banned in 1932, did not support armed resistance until 1980. Another small armed group, the Revolutionary Party of Central American Workers (PRTC-El Salvador), was formed in 1979. In 1980, a coalition of four guerrilla groups and the Salvadoran Communist Party formed the Farabundo Martí National Liberation Front (FMLN). They became legalized as political parties in the Peace Accords of January 1992.

Gendered Aspects of National Security Doctrine

The status quo, which is projected as necessary to protect national security, possesses gendered as well as political, cultural, and economic aspects. Writers who have analyzed the "motherist" movements (Fisher 1989, 1993; Navarro 1989; Schirmer 1993a, 1993b) have all pointed out the links between Catholic images of femininity and their use by repressive states to control women. Images of the various incarnations of the Virgin Mary portray an idealized mother who is obedient and self-sacrificing. The Virgin Mary obeyed the wishes of Christ, her son, and of other males including the disciples, and of God himself. As summarized by Aquino, a feminist and advocate of liberation theology:

> First, there is the image of Mary as obedient and passive, resigned and suffering, humbly dedicated to domestic tasks in accordance with the role that is naturally hers in the private sphere. This figure of weakness and submission, of all the "typically feminine" virtues, becomes a symbol of the subordinate position women should occupy in the church and society. Second, there is the exalted and idealized image of Mary as the supreme symbol of purity and virginity, which neutralizes her human integrity and her sexuality as a woman. (1993: 173)

The counterpart to the image of the Virgin Mary is the whore, as manifested in the story of Mary Magdalene, the prostitute who is counseled by Christ. As the inverse of the Virgin Mary, the whore is seen as aggressive, impure, and disconnected from motherhood. Her sexuality is constructed to service men and her personhood (if she is granted any) is focused through this role.[4]

Women as citizens are viewed as being under the care and supervision of the state. This is consistent with their dependence on their fathers and, later, their husbands and sons. In this extension of Catholic imagery the various offices of the state serve as incarnated extensions of male family roles, whether they are heads of state, generals, or police authorities. Women who disobey state authority and assume active roles in society deviate from the characteristics associated with the Virgin Mary and can be cast into the opposing role of symbolic whore. As Schirmer notes, another aspect of Catholic views of women is that "women are naturally culpable for men's transgressions and those of their children" (1993a: 54). As family caretakers and citizens of El Salvador, Salvadoran women are responsible for ensuring that their family members do not become threats to national security, as are women in Argentina, Chile, Paraguay, Guatemala, and elsewhere.

When the Salvadoran government forged an ideology of national security and left its interpretation to various military and police units, an ideological contradiction was created in the state's discourse on gender. When in the 1970s large numbers of Salvadoran women – many of them mothers – began to move into the streets and actively confront state authorities as a part of grassroots movements, they invoked the images of mother, virgin, and whore simultaneously. The predominant imagery of women as self-sacrificing mothers and wives was shattered. After women established the street as their territory through participation in marches, sit-ins, hunger strikes, and public meetings, the members of El Salvador's security forces began to view all women in public places with suspicion and to treat them accordingly.

The following incident illustrates this. Sofía Aves Escamillas, a 58-year-old member of CO-MADRES, describes what it was like to go shopping at the central market in San Salvador in the late 1970s and early 1980s. Sofía's experiences in CO-MADRES are discussed in greater detail below.

When we went to the market, we would have to use see-through shopping bags so that the soldiers posted around the market could see what we had bought. If not, they would tell us that we had bombs in our shopping bags. One day I had bought a ball of soap wrapped in dark paper and they detained me for an entire day. The soldiers who detained me were little boys. They were only 16 years old, if that. They kept telling me I had a bomb in my shopping bag. I just kept telling them that it wasn't a bomb and finally they let me go at the end of the day. Imagine, boys making an old woman stand in the hot sun for hours and hours.

If Sofía met a 16-year-old boy out of uniform in her neighborhood, he would have been expected to help her carry her bag of groceries. Gender and age conventions would have required the young man to show deference and respect to Sofía because of her age and her clear parallel position to his mother and grandmother in kinship relations. If the identities of older woman, wife, mother, and poor female shopper are reread and collapsed into the frame of "potential subversive" by a 16-year-old soldier with a gun, power relations change instantly. Sofía can be absorbed into a homogeneous category and treated appropriately, losing her humanity and all her rights and privileges as a citizen, human being, and protected woman in a patriarchal state. Later, in 1989, Sofía was kidnapped and detained for 15 days during the FMLN's "final offensive." She was literally transformed into a guerrilla/subversive when a combined force of the National Police and the Treasury Police broke into the CO-MADRES office, destroyed its contents, photographed Sofía and others in front of an FMLN banner they had brought, and forced some of them to pose in Che Guevara T-shirts. As Schirmer (1993a: 55) points out, once a woman is perceived as a subversive or as having become political, regardless of whether or not she in fact is, another standard of gendered behavior is applied to her by her captors. If a woman has been reclassified by a male in the military or police from wife, mother, or daughter equivalent to subversive, then her femaleness is read as " 'tainted,' soiled, and by definition sexually aggressive and active – she becomes a whore" (1993a: 55). Women prisoners are then punished uniformly with rape, sexual brutality, and often death. If released, they are urged not to discuss their tainted condition and to return to their homes. Ideologies of national security fracture and redefine gender and kinship roles not only for women but also for men. While this subject is not pursued here, men who are read in the category of subversive and who assume a position of feminine equivalence with their captors are often called feminine names and treated as women, sexually and otherwise.

This discussion of the origins of national security ideology and its gendered implications sets the scene of hegemonic ideology in which the CO-MADRES began operating as an organization in the 1970s. What follows is a description of the development of CO-MADRES as an organization.

CO-MADRES: Committee of Mothers and Relatives of Political Prisoners, Disappeared and Assassinated of El Salvador "Monseñor Romero"

Founded in 1977 by a group of mothers, CO-MADRES was one of the first groups in El Salvador to denounce the atrocities of the Salvadoran government and military. The group was formally constituted as a committee on Christmas Eve in 1977 under the auspices of the Archdiocese of Monseñor Romero (Schirmer 1993b: 32). The initial group of mothers numbered approximately nine but grew to between 25 and 30 by early 1978 (Schirmer 1993b: 32, interviews). The first group of women and a few men who constituted CO-MADRES was quite heterogeneous in terms of class and occupation. This has been consistently true throughout the life of the organization. The initial group included teachers, workers, peasants, students, lawyers, market women, housewives, and small shopkeepers.

The group contained significant numbers of people who resided in Christian base communities and whose families had suffered severe repression because of their church activism (Schirmer 1993b; Stephen 1994). Following liberation theology, a philosophy that regarded poverty and exploitation as a sin, these women worked with priests and nuns to begin confronting the Salvadoran military and oligarchy and to demand an end to the gross inequalities that characterized El Salvador by the late 1960s. They brought this philosophy with them into CO-MADRES.

The CO-MADRES slowly pecked away at the shroud of silence surrounding the repression that had become normal in El Salvador in the 1970s. Armed with a small list of missing relatives they demanded to know who was in the jails, forced the excavation of clandestine cemeteries, and publicized the repressive tactics of the government in an international arena. Their first actions in 1978 included taking over the Salvadoran Red Cross Building and organizing a hunger strike and a peaceful takeover of the United Nations building in San Salvador. They then moved on to occupying Catholic churches and holding public demonstrations in parks and plazas.

For the first two years of their existence they had no office. They held their meetings in various locations and did not leave any of their materials in permanent locations. Three committees of the organization focused on finances, publicity, and organizing.

The year 1979 was a turning point for the organization in two significant ways. First, they acquired a permanent location and set up an office. This allowed the organization to have a more permanent structure and to set up archives and files. Second, they made their first trip abroad and began to develop their international recognition. Once they were settled into a new office, they set up a governance structure of four committees – publicity, finances, organizing, and exterior political relations (which related to foreign governments, the foreign press, and international solidarity organizations). Each committee has five full-time members. The organization as a whole holds assemblies as often as once a week or as needed. In the early 1980s an additional layer of organizational structure was added with a director and five representatives elected by the larger assembly. The director and representatives are responsible for the day-to-day planning and management of the organization.

Once they were invited outside of the country in 1979 to Costa Rica, the CO-MADRES began an extremely effective campaign of building international solidarity behind their work. In the 1980s the CO-MADRES traveled around the world to Europe, Australia, Canada, and the United States, and to other Latin American countries, bringing their demands for justice with them. They became one of the leading voices of FEDEFAM, the Federation of the Relatives of the Disappeared and Detained in Latin America, which includes organizations from 17 Latin American and Caribbean countries. In 1984 the CO-MADRES were the first recipients of the Robert F. Kennedy Human Rights Award. The Kennedy family has been a long-standing supporter of CO-MADRES, as has musician Bonnie Raitt. "Friends of CO-MADRES" solidarity organizations were established in the United States, Australia, Switzerland, Germany, Mexico, and Canada, beginning in the mid-1980s. These support groups carried out fundraising and acted as political watchdogs for human rights abuses in El Salvador. Nine chapters of Friends of CO-MADRES were established in the United States. During the 1980s, solidarity delegations from the United States, Europe, Australia, and New Zealand also came to visit the CO-MADRES in El Salvador.

Soon after the CO-MADRES began organizing in the late 1970s, they themselves became the victims of government repression. Their first office was bombed in 1980, and since then their offices have been bombed on four additional occasions, most recently in 1989 (shortly before the FMLN's November offensive). Each time they have regrouped and kept on working. In 1989 money donated by the Women's Section of the Norwegian Social Democratic Party was used to purchase a permanent office site.

A majority of the most active CO-MADRES have been detained, tortured, and raped. Forty-eight members of CO-MADRES have been detained since 1977; five have been assas-sinated for their activism; and three have disappeared (Stephen 1994; see also Schirmer 1993b). Even after the Peace Accords were signed in January 1992, harassment and disappearances have continued. In February 1993, the son and the nephew of one of the founders of CO-MADRES were assassinated in Usulutan. This woman had already lived through the experience of her own detention, the detention and gang rape of her daughter, and the disappearance and assassination of other family members. For many women the kind of human rights abuses they have suffered has fortified their determination and has resulted in a painful self-awareness and acknowledgment of their treatment as women at the hands of national security forces.

While the formal agenda of the CO-MADRES remained focused on confronting the sources of human rights abuses in El Salvador, in their private conversations and experience some women also began seriously questioning female gender roles. Many female activists were at best not supported by their husbands and at worst beaten by them. When members of CO-MADRES were raped as a routine part of torture, some were rejected by their husbands and families as damaged goods. Private, internal discussions about what kinds of rights they had as women, as workers, and as mothers slowly became part of their public agenda toward the end of the 1980s. Support for a questioning of oppressive gender roles for women came in part from a small feminist movement emerging in El Salvador at that time. As women's sections of other popular organizations began to question their subordinate position within their own organizations and homes, other Salvadoran women were beginning to take a public stand on issues often identified with feminism – rape, unequal work burdens in the home, the political marginalization of women, and women's lack of control over their own sexuality and bodies.

Methods of Analysis and Presentation

The growth and change of the organizational agenda of the CO-MADRES is the focus of the following ethnographic analysis. Rather than using tidbits of interviews from many different women, I have chosen to focus on three activists within the CO-MADRES and to use their histories and experiences to represent the diversity within the organization. Sofía Aves Escamillas and Alicia Panameño de García were interviewed at length during a field visit to El Salvador in 1991. During that time seven members of CO-MADRES were interviewed in depth, and meetings were observed. María Teresa Tula was interviewed periodically over a two-year period from 1991–3 for a total of 40 hours. Some of the material from those interviews is published as her testimonial (see Stephen 1994). Other sources of information included documents from the CO-MADRES offices in San Salvador and Washington, DC, and interviews I conducted in 1991 with women activists from seven other organizations with whom I discussed the CO-MADRES.

I chose to focus on María Teresa, Sofía, and Alicia because they represent the range of experience, political perspectives, and age found within the CO-MADRES. While María and Sofía come from poor, peasant, and rural worker backgrounds, Alicia grew up in a lower-middle-class urban family in San Salvador. María grew up in the town of Izalco, and Sofía grew up in a small community in the district of Guazapa. Alicia grew up in a neighborhood of San Salvador known as Santa Lucía. María and Sofía attended only the first two years of primary school; Alicia finished high school. María made a living taking in people's laundry. Sofía worked in the countryside and later made leather wallets and suitcases. Alicia was a maternity nurse in a large hospital. All three were married and had children.

While María came into CO-MADRES without prior political experience, Alicia had been active for some time in a Christian base community[5] in one of San Salvador's shantytowns before joining CO-MADRES. Like María, Sofía had little previous political involvement, but her children were heavily involved in labor and peasant movements. Alicia has been working with the CO-MADRES for the past 15 years and continues to live in San Salvador. María began working full-time for the CO-MADRES

in the mid-1980s. She now lives in Minneapolis, MN; she and her children received political asylum in 1994. Sofía continues to work making leather articles and attends CO-MADRES meetings. In the analysis that follows, interview questions are included in sections where the quotations from Alicia, Sofía, or María are in direct response to them.

On the Diverse Experiences and Meanings of Motherhood

A majority of women in CO-MADRES are mothers. While these women share the biological experience of giving birth and/or adoption and a general socialization of what it means to be a Salvadoran mother, this by no means ensures that they joined CO-MADRES with uniform interpretations about what motherhood meant. The diversity of class and occupational sectors represented and the varied political experiences of women when they joined CO-MADRES ensured a variety of perspectives on motherhood. Once they entered the organization the various paths of political work, which put CO-MADRES women into contact with everyone from lesbian feminists in Europe to the Archbishop of El Salvador, ensured a variety of political experiences.

A significant number of women in CO-MADRES came into the organization after having suffered repression in their families for their participation in Christian base communities. Alicia Panameño de García, one of the founding members of CO-MADRES, had followed this trajectory. She recalls that she and several other founding members came into CO-MADRES having already done some critical thinking about relationships between mothers and children and husbands and wives. Alicia is 49 years old and has been a CO-MADRES member since 1977; she became director in 1993. She started participating in Christian base communities in 1972 and first began to work in the area of human rights in 1975. She says of her participation in Christian base communities:

A lot of work was done in this time to change family relations. A lot of families had very bad relations between people. We learned about how to divide the housework. We taught that everyone had to share in the housework – husbands, wives, and children. Everyone was supposed to participate, not just mothers. We also talked about what went on between couples. So we had already started to discuss these issues. A lot of the original mothers were mothers of catechists. These were people who were active in the base communities and the cooperatives. A lot of them were captured or assassinated so it was logical that the mothers of these young people were part of the committee.

While leaders such as Alicia came into the organization already questioning their roles as wives and mothers responsible for all housework, childcare, and general reproductive maintenance, other members such as María Teresa Tula and Sofía Aves Escamillas did not. María Teresa Tula became a part of the CO-MADRES after her husband was incarcerated for his role in leading a sugar mill strike in Izalco in 1978. María was unaware of his union activism and had never been to any kind of political meeting or belonged to any grassroots organizations. Her original impetus for joining was to get her husband out of jail so that he could help support the children. At the time of his arrest, she was ironing other people's clothing to earn a living. In 1993 when she was 43 years old, she commented on that earlier part of her life:

> During that time I didn't really have an occupation that would allow me to work. I had no idea what Rafael was doing at the time. He never told me. What I did was to keep house. He would go to work and I would iron for other people. I couldn't do washing for money because it was hard to go down to the river with my kids. So I ironed for working people who didn't have time to press their clothes. They would bring me clothes to iron at home. I would iron with a steam iron and received ten cents for each piece of clothing. Sometimes I would be ironing from two o'clock in the afternoon until eleven o'clock at night just to earn about two dollars. It was hard work. I always had callouses on my hands from where I had grabbed the iron in the wrong place.

When María first began coming to CO-MADRES meetings at the initial suggestion of her husband, she was quite intimidated. Alicia recalls her first visits in 1978.

L.S.: How did you get to know María?
ALICIA: I got to know María after her husband was arrested in the sugar strike and she started to work with us. She attended some of our meetings and courses on how to help political prisoners, but she had never had any experience to develop herself before. She was very nervous.
L.S.: So CO-MADRES was the first political work she participated in?
ALICIA: Yes.
L.S.: So she had to learn everything?
ALICIA: Yes. It is where she started to discover herself as María Teresa Tula. It was where she started to feel important as a human being.

María went on to become one of the best known and most vocal leaders of CO-MADRES internationally. Her integration into the group raised issues for her that had never surfaced before. Her struggle to legitimize her work with CO-MADRES later conflicted with her husband's expectations of her as a wife, mother, and homemaker, once he got out of jail.

Sofía Aves Escamillas came into CO-MADRES from the countryside where her son and husband were killed for their participation in peasant and labor organizing. When I interviewed her and asked about CO-MADRES as a group of women, the question did not seem particularly meaningful to her even though I repeated it several times. What seemed significant to her was the role of suffering mothers that they all shared, mourning their lost husbands and children.

L.S.: So why do you think that people identified themselves so strongly as mothers when CO-MADRES started?
SOFÍA: We started out as a group of mothers who were asking for our children. I was trying to find out about my son. My husband had already died.... You see before there were cooperatives where the people who were poor got

together to plant rice, beans, and other food. The army thought that these coops were bad. So they threw everyone in the coops out of their houses, detained them, and then disappeared them. This caused us to join CO-MADRES. The reason we are all women is that we were looking for our children because we are mothers.

Sofía came into CO-MADRES identifying as a mother who has a legitimate right to know the whereabouts of her children. As she stayed with CO-MADRES over a 15-year period, she began to explore other issues such as female sexuality and the overall oppression of women. Her thinking on these issues, however, remained distinct from that of María and Alicia.

Redefining Human Rights to Include Those of Women

The trajectory of CO-MADRES' programmatic activities between 1977 and 1994 is a reflection of the personal and political experiences of the women in it. Rather than shifting from an initial focus on human rights abuses to issues more directly related to the oppression of women, CO-MADRES has expanded to embrace a much wider definition of human rights, one that incorporates the rights of women. This change has not been a shift from a "motherist" agenda to that of feminism, but a nuanced process in which women's detention, rape, and torture at the hands of police and military authorities, their domestic conflicts with their husbands and children, and their contact with other human rights organizations and self-identified feminists have combined to give human rights a new meaning for women in CO-MADRES. While most women in CO-MADRES have shared many experiences over the past 15 years their interpretations of the relationship between women's rights and human rights remains varied.

Rape is a well-documented method of terrorizing and torturing women in the name of maintaining national security (Schirmer 1993a). Salvadoran men and boys have also been victims of rape. The Salvadoran army, National Police, National Guard, and Treas-

ury Police have all been implicated in the use of rape as a systematic method of torture. All the active members of CO-MADRES have been detained, tortured, and raped. Rape as a routine part of torture has been a common experience not only for women in CO-MADRES, but also for many Salvadoran women in the course of the civil war, especially in the countryside. María Teresa Tula describes women she met in the women's prison while recovering from her own torture and rape. The horror of what she was telling was evident by the tears welling up in her eyes as she spoke and remembered:

We women would talk to each other about all of the horrible things that had happened to us. We had been tortured and raped by as many as eight or ten men and some women got pregnant when they were raped. That is where some of the children in the prison came from. Some of the women were refugees who had been captured by the army. I still remember one who was over 60 years old. They raped her with a flashlight over and over again. "Shove the flashlight in her vagina, in her vagina. See what she is hiding in there." That's what they shouted to her. We women suffered horrible things. It was terrible. Almost everyone had signs of torture. People had received electric shock on their breasts, in their ears, and in their private parts. They were treated like animals, not respected like human beings. I will never forget it.

María has been an organizer for CO-MADRES in the United States since 1987. In the course of her work she has traveled to most of the 50 states in the U.S. and recounted her story. She states that every time she tells it, however, discussing her own rape is always the most difficult aspect. What is most painful for her is the fact the some people seem to doubt her story:

We have to make people understand how men of power in El Salvador have turned into beasts who don't respect women of any age. Women from 13 to 70 have been systematically raped as part of their torture. This is the hardest thing to deal with. I feel deeply ashamed telling people that I was raped during my torture. The reality is that the majority of women who are detained are raped. They always think that rape is something that happens to someone else. Even in El Salvador. It's difficult to bring up. When other women would come to the office in El Salvador and talk about what happened to them in their torture, I would want to tell them, "It didn't just happen to you." Many women have been raped.

While the use of rape as an instrument of torture has been common knowledge among activists for the past ten years, the issue has only recently been openly discussed in a systematic manner. Alicia Panameño de García, herself a victim of rape, says that in El Salvador not a single one of the women who have been captured and detained escaped being raped. This is psychologically very difficult for women, especially in a culture that still requires women to be virgins when they are married:

Rape was one of those things we didn't really think about. We weren't really prepared for it happening to us. We didn't think that the military would systematically be using these practices. So the first few women were detained and they were raped and because we are taught that women are supposed to be pure, they didn't talk about that. They didn't say, "They did this to me."

L.S.:   They didn't talk about it?
ALICIA: Yes. But little by little we discovered it. The women started talking about it. They had to because it had consequences for their health. They needed medical assistance and when we would give people medical aid we started discovering that every one of the women had been raped.

With time, the CO-MADRES discovered that rape was used as a form of torture against men as well. Men are even more reluctant to talk about it. Alicia began to realize that men were raped because of her work as a nurse who provided people with medical assistance after their release from detention:

We began to realize that it wasn't just women who were raped by the military. It was happening to men too. First we saw it with one boy who had been badly beaten. Then I worked in the hospital where a lot of boys came after their detention. Many of them had been raped. It was happening to men

too. It was a form of torture used to lower people's morale, men and women. . . . The men would never talk about it. We knew because we were nurses. I had to take care of them.

The sexual brutalization of all women detainees helped to forward the issue of sexuality in CO-MADRES as women discovered that they needed a place to discuss their experiences. They also needed to talk about their fears that, if they told anyone, especially their husbands, they would be abandoned. Through their discussions and denunciations of torture and detention, CO-MADRES and other human rights groups composed primarily of women raised the issue of rape for public discussion. This has benefited women, who are now beginning to question legal codes that give rape victims no rights.

During 1991 CO-MADRES was discussing problems that are specific to women, with rape and sexuality at the top of the list. Many group members reported that they had never felt sexual pleasure, discussed sexual relationships, or spoken about their own rapes. This program of discussion, however, was not received equally well by all women. Some older women like Sofía, despite their own experiences of rape in detention, were very uncomfortable talking about the subject. Alicia continues on this topic:

At first when we tried to talk about rape and sexual relations among couples it was rejected by various women. They would say, "Oh, that is disgusting. How can we talk about this?" . . . There are a lot of women who have many children and they have never felt satisfied in a sexual relationship. They have never felt sexual pleasure. The man just arrived, did what he wanted, and then left. . . . We have discussed this here and how couples can be happy.

Eventually many women did join discussions on sexuality that went until all hours of the morning. Everyone was interested in the topic. In my interviews in 1991, however, some CO-MADRES members were still uneasy about the topic.

Another common experience women shared was the reluctance of their husbands, if they were still alive, to let them be active in CO-MADRES. Women's activism was often perceived as taking away from their time for domestic chores and childcare. After María's husband's release from jail, he pushed very hard to stop her from working with CO-MADRES. He persuaded her to stay away from the organization until members of CO-MADRES came looking for her. María describes what happened, leading up to her husband's confrontation with an older woman called *la abuela* (the grandmother). She relates what happened in the form of a conversation. The sequence begins with her husband Rafael talking:

"The truth is that I don't want you to keep working with CO-MADRES. I need you here at home. Sometimes I want to talk to you and you aren't here. Sometimes I get tired of taking care of the kids and they need you to be here more than I do. And sometimes I really ask myself, what is she doing with them? What is she doing fooling around in San Salvador?"

"Really?" I sighed, surprised. "You really think I go to San Salvador to fool around?" I was crying, embracing him, and kissing him. "You really think that I'm just wasting my time?"

"Yes," he said.

"Ok, then," I replied. "I will obey the man of the house. If he wants me to stay home, then I will. But if they come from CO-MADRES and ask what happened to me, then you will have to answer to them."

"No, they won't come here looking for you," he said. "They won't even remember you."

I felt very conflicted. I had an appointment that day and people were counting on me. But at the same time, I was still dominated by my love for my *compañero* [spouse] more than by my love for my work. Two days went by and he was very happy because I stayed at home the whole time. Then at five o'clock in the morning on the third day there was a loud knock on the door.

"It is the abuela. That's what they call her," I said.

"The CO-MADRES are looking for you," he said.

"No, they are looking for you." I answered and opened the door. There was the abuela staring angrily at me.

"What's going on? How come you haven't come to the CO-MADRES office?" she asked, glaring at me.

"Well," I said shouting so Rafael could hear. "You see, it seems that when I go I don't really do anything at all. I don't do anything in the office and I'm just going into San Salvador to hang around on the streets. My beloved husband doesn't want me to leave anymore. He wants me to stay here to take care of him and the kids, to clean the house."

The grandmother turned toward the bed where Rafael was lying down and raised her voice. "Mmmm. Compañero, I had pegged you for a more intelligent person. But look at the foolishness that has come out of your mouth."

Rafael got up. "Good morning, abuela," he said sleepily.

"Good morning," she said to him. "So now, answer my question."

"Look, abuela, it isn't like it seems. This woman is just fickle. I was just kidding when I said those things to her and she took me seriously. I don't keep her from going out."

"Listen," the abuela told him. "This woman has responsibility. People are counting on her. When she isn't there it is a problem."

"Why didn't you tell me that?" Rafael asked.

That day I got a change of clothes and left with the abuela to go off and do some work. But it was the beginning of a long struggle with Rafael about my work.

Sofía describes similar episodes that have occurred often in the 15 years she has worked with CO-MADRES:

We often would have women in the group who would say, "Look, my husband is beating me because he doesn't want me to come here." So what we would do is go to talk with the man and tell him, "Look, she is coming here to work with us." The problem is that the men misunderstand. They don't believe the women are coming here with us. My husband was already dead when I joined CO-MADRES so I didn't have this problem.

Sofía also stated that some women had to leave CO-MADRES because of pressure from their husbands, often in combination with economic distress.

To the men who questioned their participation, and to each other, the CO-MADRES explained the necessity of their work as a combination of struggling for the human rights of all Salvadorans, including the rights of women to work outside the house and control their own lives. They also told their husbands that their participation did not mean that they would never do domestic work; they would continue to do some – just not all. Alicia, who had been present at another visit to María's husband Rafael when he was questioning María's involvement with CO-MADRES, found his resistance difficult to understand:

ALICIA: When I went there he told me that he didn't want her to participate. He said that she was away from the house too much....So I told him that taking care of the house was as important as the work she was doing with us for human rights. I said what she needed to learn how to do was organize her time. She needed some time with us and some time at home. That would make them both feel better.

L.S.:   So you gave him a little marriage counseling? Talked with him about how couples could get along?

ALICIA: Yes. He wasn't paying much attention to her and she would come home and feel bad. He would accuse her of doing all kinds of things. So I told him that he was mistaken about what she was doing. I was really surprised by his attitude because of his education and involvement with the union.

When María described the treatment she got upon returning to work with CO-MADRES after staying home with her husband, she focused primarily on the kinds of rights she had as a woman. Sofía and several other women interviewed also followed up their discussions about women's repression by their husbands with remarks about the general oppression of women. Sofía commented:

Here in El Salvador we are exploited by the government. They behave as if they are our bosses. And women have been the most exploited. Because even when a woman goes to work in the countryside, she is paid less

than a man for the same work. She receives this same kind of exploitation from her husband. You know, we have to do the wash, and everything for our husbands. We are starting to realize that we are exploited as well.

The rationale that different women in CO-MADRES use to justify their work reflects the different political and ideological spheres in which they have been working. Several leaders of the CO-MADRES, including María and Alicia, have had wide exposure in the international human rights community as well as to feminism in varying forms. Others, such as Sofía, have not done as much traveling or been to feminist meetings or workshops. They hear reports on what went on from those who attended and then integrate what they hear with their own experience.

Most CO-MADRES have met with women from other organizations formed by relatives of the disappeared. In 1981, Alicia and several other CO-MADRES went to the first meeting of the Federation of the Relatives of the Disappeared and Detained in Latin America (FEDEFAM), where they met women from the Mothers of the Plaza de Mayo, an Argentine group formed in the early 1970s.

L.S.:   Was it important for you to meet the Mothers of the Plaza de Mayo?

ALICIA: Yes, because their work was very similar to ours and they had the same problems. The same methods are used by the military all over Latin America. The same repressive scheme is applied to all the countries.

In 1985, Alicia traveled to the international conference on Women and Development in Kenya. She has been to three international meetings (encuentros) of Latin American feminists and to meetings of European feminists. María went to Europe twice on tours organized by feminist women and has met with a wide variety of women's groups in the United States and Europe. Alicia and María both seem quite comfortable discussing feminism.

L.S.:   How did you feel at the Latin American Feminist Encuentros you attended?

ALICIA: Well, maybe it is because of the work that we do, but we have already been taking some courses on human rights work that incorporate the problems raised by feminists. This included the problems of feminist women as well as lesbian women. From our point of view we understand perfectly well the problems of feminist women and lesbian women. They are all discriminated against.

L.S.:   Do you see any of the struggles of feminists as struggles that are connected with what you are doing?

ALICIA: Well, I already mentioned that women have been the victims of men's machismo for centuries, right? So in this sense there is a need for women to create a movement which has women's rights as its principal struggles. I don't feel like a feminist because I need to learn more about it. But the general struggle for women, I understand that. I have to learn some more about the concept of feminism. That isn't entirely clear to me.

María's discussion of her first contact with feminists in Germany was laced with frustration about the difficulty she had in getting women to understand her need to talk with Salvadoran men with whom she came into contact. It was also her first contact with openly lesbian women. Since then she has refined her feminist discourse, which, like Alicia's, exhibits a mixture of influences.

This passage quoted from her testimonial captures the unique blend of Salvadoran feminism she has developed. While it cannot be construed as representative of the position of all women in CO-MADRES, as a whole it does contain many elements that have influenced their thinking:

In El Salvador we don't run around calling ourselves feminists, but we are feminists because we are fighting for our rights. The difference for us in El Salvador is that our struggle as women comes together with our struggle for change in El Salvador. Our feminism doesn't just involve fighting for ourselves, but for a change for all of us. We can't forget about the system that oppresses all of us. So we are doing two things at once. We are fighting for our rights as women and we are also fighting for

social change in our country. If there isn't drastic social change in our country, then we will always be oppressed even though we are fighting for our rights as women. For us our struggle as women includes many things. I think it's fine for the women in the groups we met to be talking about feminism and bring out the oppression that women have suffered for centuries and be working for change through a women's movement. Everyone has the right to wage their struggle as they see fit. I have heard a lot about women's decisions about abortion, "yes" or "no." I believe that I or any woman should have the right to decide what she wants to do. I am a mother of six children and I'm not going to criticize anyone's choice.

As women we all share some common history. We are all different colors, but I think that we share some common sentiments and our blood is all the same color. We all have red blood, not yellow or orange. We all share the same blood and some commonalities as women that make us identify with one another. I think the suffering that women have gone through everywhere helps to build international solidarity between women.

But the system that we live under in El Salvador gives feminism a different meaning. We see all women as feminists, whether they are workers, peasants, or professionals. In El Salvador and other Latin American countries there are big differences between bourgeois women who call themselves feminists and other women. Sometimes we see these women who call themselves feminists, but all they do is talk, roaring like lions, but not doing anything. They go on marches, but they don't really do anything, just march around in the name of feminism. To be that kind of feminist in El Salvador means that you are a member of the bourgeois, not an ordinary woman like a peasant or a housewife who has always been oppressed for years and years. These women don't call themselves feminists, but they are more oppressed than someone who is the wife of the president or a businessman. It's these humble women who have demonstrated in their practice that they have the political, ideological, and military capacity to help make change in El Salvador. If we don't change our government in El Salvador then we could all unite for women's rights, but we wouldn't get anywhere.

You know it isn't just being women that makes for change. There are women in positions of power, even presidents or prime ministers, who have the bodies of women, but they have the minds and hearts of oppressive men. It's a shame. It just goes to show that it isn't enough to have women in power, but we have to change the whole system in El Salvador, in the United States, and in Europe. If we don't, then we could die and another generation of feminists would be born with more ideas, but they would continue to be repressed.

The work of the CO-MADRES in the 1990s has focused on holding the state accountable for human rights violations committed during the war and, most recently, for making sure that the recommendations of the UN Truth Commission are followed. In addition, they have been confronting the legal system to provide better protection for political prisoners and assurances that human rights abuses will not be committed in the future; working against domestic violence and to some extent unequal gender relations in the home; educating women about political participation (specifically in the 1994 elections); and developing small economic projects such as sewing coops to help women support themselves. They are a part of a coalition of women's groups called Mujeres '94 (Women in the 1994 Election), which worked on a unified platform for women and gave it to all the political parties who participated in the 1994 elections. This coalition called for an end to incest, rape, and sexual harassment; for free and voluntary motherhood and sexual education for women; for land, credit, and technical assistance for women; for adequate housing with ownership for women; for economic development programs and job training for women; for more education for women and girls; for better medical attention for women; and for an end to the rising cost of wage goods. During 1993 the coalition held debates on the following topics for possible incorporation into the platform: domestic violence, women and the land reform process, the legal system, education, the environment, health, reproductive rights, sexuality, and political participation. As can be seen from the above description,

the political trajectory of CO-MADRES is not a unilateral move from the private/domestic/feminine into the public/political/feminist sphere. By way of conclusion, I will reflect on the tendency to compartmentalize women's movements such as that of the CO-MADRES and suggest an alternative model of analysis.

Conclusions: Dichotomies in Gender Theory, Anthropology, and Beyond

Initial theorizing about gender in anthropology was built around a series of dualisms that ultimately demonstrated the cultural difficulty Western social scientists, feminists, and others experienced in separating the categorization of reproductive organs known as biological sex from socially learned gender behavior. Formulations such as "male is to female as culture is to nature and public is to private" were ultimately discarded, but with more difficulty than had been anticipated. Reinterpretations of what was meant by public and private spheres sometimes came from the very theorists who first formulated these concepts. Michelle Rosaldo noted that a focus on universal dichotomies makes us "victims of a conceptual tradition that discovers 'essence' in the natural characteristics that distinguish the sexes and then declares that women's present lot derives from what, 'in essence,' women are" (1980: 401, cited in Yanagisako and Collier 1987: 19–20). Yanagisako and Collier have sought to avoid analytical dualisms by studying gender institutions as social wholes and by asking how all social inequalities are culturally constituted; they avoid treating sex or gender differences as universally given:

[O]ur problem of continually rediscovering gendered categories can be overcome by calling into question the universality of our cultural assumptions about the difference between males and females. Both gender and kinship studies, we suggest have foundered on the unquestioned assumption that the biologically given differences in the roles of men and women in sexual reproduction lies at the core of the cultural organization of gender.... Only by calling this assumption into question can we begin to ask how other cultures might understand the difference between women and men, and simultaneously make possible studies of how our own culture comes to focus on coitus and parturition as *the* moments constituting masculinity and femininity. (Yanagisako and Collier 1987: 49)

They go on to urge the construction of models that specify the dialectical relationship between practice and ideas in the constitution of social inequalities of all kinds, including those associated with gender.

The questioning of public/private and other gendered dichotomies is not confined to anthropology. New social movements are often described as taking place in societies where the separation between private and public life is fading away, thus requiring a redefinition of "the political." This redefinition is also required because the identity of social agents (that is, those who participate in social movements) is no longer related to fixed categories in the social structure. Laclau argues that since it is impossible to identify people with one stable political reference group, the notion of politics as the representation of interests loses its validity (1985: 29). The political thus ceases to comprise a distinct social level and is present in all social practice:

> The new social movements have been characterized by an increasing politicization of social life (remember the feminist slogan: "The personal is political"); but also it is precisely this which has shattered the vision of the political as a closed, homogeneous space. (Laclau 1985: 29–30)

While new social movements theorists such as Laclau (1985) and Melucci (1989) attribute the blurring of public/private spheres in politics and the incorporation of informal networks into political processes as the results of social movements in postmodern and postindustrial societies, feminist anthropologists who have worked with marginalized and disenfranchised societies or social groups have documented these trends for quite some time.[6] Another example is found in the vast literature in Latin America on civil-religious cargo systems

that describes the merging of civil-government hierarchies with cult religious ceremonies (sponsored by male/female pairs of household heads). This literature documents the changing history of merging household religion with civil government (see Chance 1990; Nash 1970; Stephen and Dow 1990). The institution of *compadrazgo* (ritual kinship) has served as a basis for extending family ties and influence within and between communities, for political and other ends (see Sault 1985a, 1985b; Stephen 1991; Stephen and Dow 1990).

While anthropologists (feminist and otherwise) and new social movements theorists have thoroughly discarded the dualism of public/private that for so long was offered as an explanation for why women's activities were directed to their roles as wives and mothers, feminist theories that analyze women's political participation according to its feminist or feminine characteristics indirectly reproduce this dichotomy to explain different types of women's activism. The basis of much current feminist theory on women's mobilization is found in the work of Maxine Molyneux (1986) and Temma Kaplan (1982, 1990).[7]

In an analysis of women's collective action in early-20th-century Barcelona, Kaplan (1982) elaborates a theory of "female consciousness." Kaplan states that when women who have internalized their designated roles as domestic providers and caretakers are unable to carry out their duties, they will be moved to take action in order to fulfill their social roles as females. This may even include taking on the state when it impedes their normal activities. She has also extended this analysis to women's participation in grassroots movements in contemporary Latin America (1990).

Kaplan's "female consciousness" is similar to what Molyneux (1986) terms "practical" gender interests – interests that emerge from an acceptance of cultural gender roles and the assertion of rights based on these roles. Practical gender interests do not directly challenge gender subordination. In contrast to "practical gender interests," Molyneux proposes that strategic gender interests are derived deductively and focus on strategic objectives to overcome women's subordination such as alleviation of the burden of domestic labor and childcare and the removal of institutionalized forms of discrimination (1986: 284).

One implication of practical/feminine movements is that they simply reinforce women's place in the domestic/private side of society. Feminist movements with strategic interests are seen as allowing women to break into public life and to gain access to arenas previously dominated by men. By breaking into the traditionally male sphere of public power, feminist movements are thus seen to challenge oppressive gender hierarchies and forge a new place for women. While such a progression may sound very desirable and convincing to Western feminists, it is built on the old assumption of a gendered public/private dichotomy. Nikki Craske, in an analysis of women's political participation in *colonias populares* in Guadalajara, proposes turning the dichotomy into a continuum to "allow for different degrees of participation between the two extremes and the unlikelihood that a woman is completely immersed in the private with no participation in the public" (1993: 114). Such a compromise still hinges, however, on the existence of public and private spheres between which women negotiate.

Other recent analyses of women's political participation in Latin America question the utility of the strategic versus practical gender interest dichotomy and, by implication of the categorization of social, economic, personal, and political relations, as either public or private. In an article on popular women's organizations in Ecuador, Amy Conger Lind suggests that although women's organizing projects may focus around procuring basic needs, "basic needs are not tied solely to survival, but rather to constructions of identity and relations of power." She criticizes Molyneux's paradigm based on its assumption that a "practical or survival strategy cannot simultaneously be a political strategy that challenges the social order" (1992: 137).

In an edited collection on women and popular protest in Latin America, Sallie Westwood and Sarah Radcliffe (1993) reject the strategic/practical dichotomy for two reasons. First, they suggest that such a dichotomy is founded on a linear view of progress rooted in a post-Enlightenment evolutionary perspective that posits a hierarchical relationship between feminine and feminist movements. Progress is made when a women's organization moves from practical to strategic interest. In addition, they state, such a perspective "tends to maintain the distinction between public and private, and between the personal and the political, the deconstruction of which has always been so central to feminist politics" (1993: 20). Instead of dichotomies of public and private and of practical and strategic interests, they propose understanding women as political subjects and actors in relation to "the multiplicity of sites wherein women are engaged in power struggles" (1993: 20). In the same volume, in an analysis of CO-MADRES and of the National Coordinator of Widows of Guatemala (CONAVIGUA), Schirmer raises the question of how we understand women who have multiple "strategic" and "pragmatic" interests that change over time and that "they themselves do not deem as separate" (1993b: 61). She proposes a dialectical understanding of how women gain gender consciousness, "dependent upon both what women bring to the struggle as well as how the state constructs them and their actions externally" (1993: 61–2). If we begin by assuming that political, economic, and social life never was and is not currently permeated by a public/private dichotomy confining women only to domestic space, then we must seriously reconsider how women's activism is described and analyzed.

To avoid another fundamental characteristic of dualistic theories, that of slotting people into all encompassing, essentialist categories of identity – women versus men in this case – we must reconceptualize women activists as having many different facets to their identities, facets that will influence their interpretation and experience of political, social, and cultural events. While people do act collectively on the basis of a partially shared experience or perspective – the torture, disappearance, and assassination of relatives, their own rape and detention, resistance to their political participation from their husbands, and exposure to a variety of human rights and feminist ideologies and organizations in the case of the CO-MADRES of El Salvador – they participate in many sets of social relations including gender, kinship, race, ethnicity, nationality, and vicinity (Mouffe 1988). Within CO-MADRES the varying identities with which each woman entered, as well as each woman's political experiences while in CO-MADRES, resulted in agreement around fighting for human rights, but also produced a multiplicity of interpretations of what that meant. We indeed must become more comfortable with the different perspectives most probably held by the members of a single movement. As June Nash points out, long before anthropologists and others were disturbed by the tendency toward unifying theories, Third World peoples living in a postmodern world were not "discomfited by the variety of claims to truth that sprout in any one social movement" (1992: 292).

The case of the CO-MADRES highlights the need to approach the analysis of women's organizations and movements with a model that allows for both accommodation and resistance to so-called traditional gender roles and a multiplicity of interpretations and truth claims within the same movement. If we want to understand how and why people act, we must deeply consider the synthetic effects of their own experience on their behavior. This prevents us from portraying women activists as flattened, uniform caricatures who either fall on one side or another of some universal feminist continuum. The CO-MADRES' understanding of their gendered position in the world did not emerge suddenly or in a uniform manner. It was not a transition from traditional ideas about women to a model of total liberation. CO-MADRES members' awareness of the gendered meanings of national security ideology and women's unequal treatment under the law and at home came sporadically and was integrated with other kinds of political experience. Government repression forced the integration of existent public and private spheres in women's lives – and the contradictions of women's treatment within these spheres – into the public eye. In turn this repression politicized existing gender and kinship relations. In many ways, CO-MADRES women retained some of their original and varied ideas about motherhood and added to them, incorporating ideas about women's rights within a discourse on human rights. To identify motherhood simultaneously with childrearing, personal sacrifice for one's children, persistent confrontation with military authorities, and campaigns to end rape and promote sexual education may appear contradictory to those outside the movement, but the experience of the women in CO-MADRES has made these ideas mutually consistent. The way in which they have framed their ideas has become part of the rich variety of discourses now found in El Salvador's feminisms and women's movements.

NOTES

1   See Laclau 1985, Laclau and Mouffe 1985, and Mouffe 1988 on discarding totalizing categories as the basis for understanding people's participation in social movements and on the meaning and use of multiple subjectivities. See Scott 1985 and Comaroff 1985 for insights on the blurry line between accommodation and resistance. Scott's treatise specifically challenges Gramsci's ideas on the totalizing effects of hegemony and the sources of counterhegemony. See also Joseph and Nugent 1994.

2   See the anthology *"Viva!": Women and Popular Protest in Latin America*, edited by Sallie Westwood and Sara Radcliffe, which I discuss in the conclusions of this article.

3   All figures in the preceding two paragraphs are from Barry 1990: 177–8.

4   Chicana writers Gloria Anzaldúa and Cherríe Moraga have commented at length about the power of this dual-gender image, not only in Mexico, but also among Chicanos/as (see Anzaldúa 1980, 1990; Anzaldúa and Moraga 1983; Moraga 1983, 1993). In popular Mexican historical accounts the figure of Malinche, a Maya noblewoman given to Cortés as a slave, is regarded as a whore and traitor for consorting with Cortés. She is also held responsible for the creation of the mestizo race. Her counterpart is the Virgen de Guadalupe, who is emblematic of all that is desirable in womanhood – obedience,

devotion, passivity, and motherhood. Anzaldúa, Moraga, and others have offered feminist reinterpretations of these two historical figures.

5   Christian base communities are neighborhoods and communities organized around the self-help, participatory model of liberation theology: "One of the key elements of the grassroots communities was the way they sought to involve lay people in church functions previously closed to them.... Delegates of the Word – men or women – were lay preachers who could do most of the tasks of the priest... although not the sacramental functions" (Pierce 1986: 113). The base communities provided a structural organization for the poor and facilitated the organization of collective production and consumption projects, agricultural cooperatives, and helped forge links between communities. Many of the lay church workers began to connect religious work with political work and became critical players in peasant and labor organizing.

6   See Bookman and Morgen 1988, Bourque and Warren 1981, Gailey 1987, Mathews 1985, Nash and Safa 1986, Sacks 1988, and Stephen 1991.

7   For examples of work that follow the tendencies of Molyneux and Kaplan, see Alvarez 1990, Jaquette 1989, Jelin 1990, and Logan 1990.

REFERENCES

Alvarez, Sonia E. 1990. *Engendering Democracy in Brazil: Women's Movements in Transition Politics*. Princeton: Princeton University Press.

Anderson, Thomas. 1971. *Matanza: El Salvador's First Communist Revolt of 1932*. Lincoln: University of Nebraska Press.

Anzaldúa, Gloria. 1980. *Borderlands*. San Francisco: Spinsters/Aunt Lute Book Company.

——1990. *Haciendo Caras*. San Francisco: Aunt Lute Foundation.

Anzaldúa, Gloria, and Cherríe Moraga, eds. 1983. *This Bridge Called My Back*. Watertown, MA: Persephone Press.

Aquino, María Pilar. 1993. *Our Cry for Life: Feminist Theology from Latin America*. Maryknoll, NY: Orbis Books.

Arnson, Cynthia. 1982. *El Salvador: A Revolution Confronts the United States*. Washington, DC: Institute for Policy Studies.

Barry, Tom. 1987. *Roots of Rebellion: Land and Hunger in Central America*. Boston: South End Press.

——1990. *El Salvador: A Country Guide*. Albuquerque, NM: Inter-Hemispheric Education Resource Center.

Berryman, Phillip. 1986. Religion, the Poor and Politics in Latin America Today. In *Religion and Political Conflict in Latin America*. Daniel Levine, ed. pp. 3–23. Chapel Hill: University of North Carolina Press.

Bookman, Ann, and Sandra Morgen. 1988. *Women and the Politics of Empowerment*. Philadelphia: Temple University Press.

Bourque, Susan C., and Kay B. Warren. 1981. *Women of the Andes*. Ann Arbor: University of Michigan Press.

Central America Information Office. 1982. *El Salvador: Background to the Crisis*. Cambridge, MA: Central America Information Office.

Chance, John. 1990. Changes in Twentieth-Century Mesoamerican Cargo Systems. In *Class, Politics, and Popular Religion: Religious Change in Mexico and Central America*. L. Stephen and J. Dow, eds. pp. 27–42. Arlington, VA: American Anthropological Association.

Comaroff, Jean. 1985. *Body of Power, Spirit of Resistance: The Culture and History of a South African People*. Chicago: University of Chicago Press.

Craske, Nikki. 1993. Women's Participation in Colonias Populares in Guadalajara, Mexico. In *"Viva!": Women and Popular Protest in Latin America*. Sarah A. Radcliffe and Sallie Westwood, eds. pp. 112–35. London: Routledge.

Danner, Mark. 1994. *The Massacre at El Mozote*. New York: Vintage Books.

Fisher, Jo. 1989. *Mothers of the Disappeared*. London: Zed Books.

——1993. *Out of the Shadows: Women, Resistance, and Politics in South America*. London: Latin American Bureau.

Gailey, Christine. 1987. *Kinship to Kingship: Gender Hierarchy and State Formation in the Tongan Islands*. Austin: University of Texas Press.

Jaquette, Jane, ed. 1989. *The Women's Movement in Latin America: Feminism and the Transition to Democracy*. Boston: Unwin Hyman.

Jelin, Elizabeth. 1990. Citizenship and Identity: Final Reflections. In *Women and Social Change in Latin America*. Elizabeth Jelin, ed. pp. 184–207. London: Zed Books.

Joseph, Gilbert, and Daniel Nugets, eds. 1994. *Everyday Forms of State Formation: Revolution and the Negotiation of Rule in Modern Mexico*. Durham, NC: Duke University Press.

Kaplan, Temma. 1982. Female Consciousness and Collective Action: The Case of Barcelona, 1910–1918. *Signs* 7: 545–60.

——1990. Community and Resistance in Women's Political Cultures. *Dialectical Anthropology*, 15: 259–64.

Laclau, Ernesto. 1985. New Social Movements and the Plurality of the Social. In *New Social Movements and the State in Latin America*. David Slater, ed. pp. 27–42. Dordrecht: Center for Latin American Research and Documentation.

Laclau, Ernesto, and Chantal Mouffe. 1985. *Hegemony and Socialist Strategy: Towards a Radical Democratic Politics*. London: Verso Books.

Lind, Amy. 1992. Power, Gender, and Development: Popular Women's Organizations and the Politics of Needs in Ecuador. In *The Making of Social Movements in Latin America: Identity, Strategy, and Democracy*. Arturo Escoblar and Sonia E. Alvarez, eds. pp. 134–49. Boulder, CO: Westview.

Logan, Kathleen. 1990. Women's Participation in Urban Protest. In *Popular Movements and Political Change in Mexico*. Joe Foweraker and Ann Craig, eds. pp. 150–9. Boulder, CO: Lynne Reinner.

Mathews, Holly. 1985. "We Are Mayordomo": A Reinterpretation of Women's Roles in the Mexican Cargo System. *American Ethnologist*, 17: 85–301.

Melucci, Alberto. 1989. *Nomads of the Present*. Philadelphia: Temple University Press.

Molyneux, Maxine. 1986. Mobilization without Emancipation? Women's Interests, State, and Revolution. In *Transition and Development: Problems of Third World Socialism*. Richard Fagen, Carmen Diana Deere, and José Luis Coraggio, eds. New York: Monthly Review Press; Berkeley, CA: Center for the Study of the Americas.

Moraga, Cherrie. 1983. *Loving in the War Years*. Boston: South End Press.

——1993. *The Last Generation*. Boston: South End Press.

Mouffe, Chantal. 1988. Hegemony and New Political Subjects: Toward a New Concept of Democracy. In *Marxism and the Interpretation of Culture*. Carl Nelson, ed. pp. 3–18. Urbana: University of Illinois Press.

Naciones Unidas [United Nations]. 1993. *De la locura a la esperanza: La guerra de 12 años en El Salvador*. (From Insanity to Hope: The 12-Year War in El Salvador.) Informe de la Comisión de la Verdad para El Salvador. (Report of the Truth Commission for El Salvador.) San Salvador, New York: United Nations.

Nash, June. 1970. *In the Eyes of the Ancestors: Belief and Behavior in a Maya Community*. New Haven, CT: Yale University Press.

——1992. Interpreting Social Movements: Bolivian Resistance to Economic Conditions Imposed by the International Monetary Fund. *American Ethnologist*, 19: 275–93.

Nash, June, and Helen Safa, eds. 1986. *Women and Change in Latin America*. South Hadley: Bergin & Garvey.

Navarro, Marysa. 1989. The Personal Is Political: Las Madres de Plaza de Mayo. In *Power and Popular Protest: Latin American Social Movements*. Susan Eckstein, ed. pp. 241–58. Los Angeles: University of California Press.

Pierce, Jenny. 1986. *Promised Land: Peasant Rebellion in Chalatenango El Salvador*. London: Latin American Bureau.

Ready, Kelly. 1994. It's a Hard Life: Women in El Salvador's Economic History. In *Hear My Testimony: María Teresa Tula, Human Rights Activist of El Salvador*. Lynn Stephen, ed. pp. 187–200. Boston: South End Press.

Rosaldo, Michelle Zimbalist. 1980. The Use and Abuse of Anthropology: Reflections on Feminism and Cross-Cultural Understanding. *Signs: Journal of Women in Culture and Society*, 5/3: 389–417.

Sacks, Karen Brodkin. 1988. *Caring by the Hour: Women, Work and Organizing at Duke Medical Center.* Urbana: University of Illinois Press.

Saporta Sternbach, Nancy, Marysa Navarro-Aranguren, Patricia Chuchryk, and Sonia E. Alvarez. 1992. Feminisms in Latin America: From Bogotá to San Bernadino. *Signs*, 17: 393–434.

Sault, Nicole. 1985a. Zapotec Godmothers: The Centrality of Women for Compadrazgo Groups in a Village of Oaxaca, Mexico. PhD dissertation, University of California, Los Angeles.

—— 1985b. Baptismal Sponsorship as a Source of Power for Zapotec Women in Oaxaca, Mexico. *Journal of Latin American Lore*, 11/2: 225–43.

Schirmer, Jennifer. 1993a. Those Who Die for Life Cannot Be Called Dead: Women and Human Rights Protest in Latin America. In *Surviving Beyond Fear: Women, Children and Human Rights in Latin America.* Marjorie Agosin, ed. pp. 31–57. Fredonia: White Pine Press.

—— 1993b. The Seeking of Truth and the Gendering of Consciousness: The CO-MADRES of El Salvador and the CONAVI-GUA Widows of Guatemala. In *"Viva!": Women and Popular Protest in Latin America.* Sarah A. Radcliffe and Sallie Westwood, eds. pp. 30–64. London: Routledge.

Scott, James. 1985. *Weapons of the Weak.* New Haven, CT: Yale University Press.

Stephen, Lynn. 1991. *Zapotec Women.* Austin: University of Texas Press.

—— 1994. *Hear My Testimony: María Teresa Tula, Human Rights Activist of El Salvador.* Boston: South End Press.

Stephen, Lynn, and James Dow. 1990. Introduction: Popular Religion in Mexico and Central America. In *Class, Politics, and Popular Religion: Religious Change in Mexico and Central America.* Lynn Stephen and James Dow, eds. pp. 1–24. Arlington, VA: American Anthropological Association.

Westwood, Sallie, and Sarah Radcliffe. 1993. Gender, Racism, and the Politics of Identities in Latin America. In *"Viva!": Women and Popular Protest in Latin America.* Sarah A. Radcliffe and Sallie Westwood, eds. pp. 1–29. London: Routledge.

Yanagisako, Sylvia Junko, and Jane Fishburne Collier. 1987. Toward a Unified Analysis of Kinship and Gender. In *Gender and Kinship: Essays Toward a Unified Analysis.* Jane Fishburne Collier and Junko Yanagisako, eds. pp. 14–52. Stanford, CA: Stanford University Press.

17

Searching for "Voices": Feminism, Anthropology, and the Global Debates over Female Genital Operations

Christine J. Walley

The issue of "female circumcision" has generated heated public debate in Europe and the United States over the last several years. The controversy has centered not only on the North African and sub-Saharan African countries where most clitoridectomies and infibulations have historically been performed, but increasingly on those Euro-American countries where immigrants who perform such practices now reside. Several legal cases in France in the early 1990s generated widespread publicity when African immigrant parents and a circumcisor were charged with child abuse and assault for performing clitoridectomies (Weil-Curiel 1994; Winter 1994). In 1994, a Nigerian woman residing in the United States, Lydia Oluloro, successfully contested her deportation by arguing that if she returned to Nigeria her daughters would be forced to undergo "circumcision" (Corbin 1994; Gregory 1994). The recent case of Fauziya Kasinga, a young Togolese woman who came to the United States seeking political asylum in an effort to escape a forced clitoridectomy and a forced marriage, has generated even greater media attention; a public outcry emerged when it was revealed that Kasinga had been incarcerated in a Pennsylvania prison for 16 months along with other asylum-seekers (Dugger 1996a, 1996b). In a more literary vein, Alice Walker's widely publicized novel, *Possessing the Secret of Joy* (1992), has strongly condemned the practice of female genital mutilation. More recently, she has collaborated with Pratibha Parmar to produce a documentary film and companion volume on the subject, both of which are entitled *Warrior Marks*, garnering still more media attention in Western countries (Parmar 1993b; Walker and Parmar 1993). Media accounts have included articles and op-ed pieces in *The New York Times*, *The Washington Post*, and *Time* magazine, and segments aired on TV and radio news programs including *ABC World News Tonight*, *Dateline NBC*, *ABC's Nightline*,

From Christine J. Walley, "Searching for 'Voices': Feminism, Anthropology, and the Global Debates over Female Genital Operations," pp. 405–38 in *Cultural Anthropology*, 12/3 (1997).

CNN's *Newsnight*, and National Public Radio's (NPR) *All Things Considered.*[1]

Despite, or perhaps because of the explosiveness of the topic, feminist anthropologists have paid relatively little attention to female genital operations.[2] Nevertheless, there is clearly a need for such analysis. The issue strikes numerous nerves, as it challenges fundamental understandings of body, self, sexuality, family, and morality, and as it plays upon tensions relating to cultural difference, the relationship between women and "tradition," and the legacy of colonial-era depictions of gender relations in non-Western countries. The public debates over female genital operations also raise pertinent questions about our contemporary social world. While an earlier international debate about female genital mutilation reflected the growing influence of feminist movements in the 1970s, the recent controversy bears a distinctly 1990s cast. As is now commonly acknowledged, the exponential growth of global communications and multinational corporations has been accompanied by increasingly migratory habits as immigrants, refugees, and tourists, among others, crisscross the globe. These transformations are breaking down what has been a pervasive, if always problematic assumption – namely, that internally homogeneous First and Third Worlds exist as radically separate "worlds."[3] The centrality of African immigrants in Europe and the United States to recent Western media accounts of female genital operations, as well as the role Africans have played on both sides of the debate, suggests the growing permeability of national and social boundaries in an increasingly "globalized" era. In short, the current controversy surrounding female genital operations is inextricably linked to other contemporary debates that concern the nature of universal "human rights" and the ways such rights include, or exclude, women; the cultural rights of minorities as immigration increases in Euro-American countries; and, ultimately, the meaning and viability of "multicultural" societies.

The issue of female genital operations poses particular challenges for feminist anthropologists in that the topic viscerally encapsulates the potential tension between feminism and anthropology. Marilyn Strathern (1987) once accurately characterized the relationship between the two as "awkward," and part of that awkwardness stems from a perennial conflict: when feminist political concerns challenge anthropology's trademark emphasis on cultural understanding, where should the allegiance of feminist anthropologists lie? This apparent awkwardness, however, may instead prove useful by challenging us to grapple with a central assumption underlying the debate. Namely, why is there a tendency to understand female genital operations in "either/or" terms, in other words, in terms of *either* cultural relativism *or* politically-informed outrage?

In this article, I attempt to address this issue by offering a dual perspective that looks at the practice of, and discourse surrounding, female genital operations. I will ground an analysis of the discursive politics surrounding genital operations by offering an ethnographic account of clitoridectomy within the context of daily life for a rural population in western Kenya's Kikhome village in 1988.[4] In doing so, I question whether either of the seemingly polar viewpoints commonly expressed toward female genital operations in Europe and the United States – moral opprobrium or relativistic tolerance – is sufficient to construct an adequate feminist and "humanist" political response to this issue.[5] I instead suggest that within the Euro-American debates, both sides – critics and relativists – often share an unacknowledged common thread. This commonality is a hardened view of "culture" based on a rigid essentialist notion of difference that can be historically linked to the colonial era (see also Koptiuch 1996). By addressing these issues, I hope to help lay the groundwork for a more productive feminist and anthropological debate capable of transcending the binary terms in which female genital operations are commonly discussed – binary terms that falsely suggest an insurmountable chasm between "us" and "them."

Circumcision, Mutilation, or Torture? The Politics of Naming

Female genital operations are known by a variety of names. In addition to the names found in the languages of those conducting the practices, there is an extensive terminology in English that includes female circumcision, clitoridectomies, excision, infibulation, genital mutilation, and, in the perspective of some Anglo-American observers, torture. The practices, like the names, are not monolithic; the severity of the procedure varies, as do the peoples and geographic regions involved. Female genital operations occur in a variety of places, from Indonesia to the Middle East to Europe and the United States; however, the vast majority of female genital operations occur on the African continent in countries as diverse as Sudan, Somalia, Ethiopia, Egypt, Kenya, Tanzania, Nigeria, Togo, Senegal, and Mali. Practitioners include Muslims, Christians, Falasha Jews, and followers of indigenous African religions. Although the reliability of such statistics is unclear, estimates suggest that up to 100 million women have presently undergone some form of genital operation (Toubia 1994).[6] The physical operation ranges from the removal of the tip of the clitoris (a procedure known as *sunna*) to the excision of the clitoris itself and potentially portions of the labia minora and majora (clitoridectomy or excision) to the most radical form, which includes clitoridectomy as well as the removal of the labia minora and majora and the sewing together of the remaining tissues (infibulation). These practices also have a history in Europe and the United States: ancient Romans pierced the genitalia of their female slaves with pins or fibula, hence the term *infibulation*, while some turn-of-the-century European and American doctors used clitoridectomy as a cure for masturbation and so-called nymphomania (Dawit 1994; Harcourt 1988; Lightfoot-Klein 1989).[7]

The act of naming these practices is controversial in and of itself. The generic use of the term *circumcision* in English treats the removal of the foreskin in males as equivalent to the removal of the clitoris in females, obscuring the permanent loss of sexual sensation in girls.[8] Similar usages often exist in the languages of those people engaging in such practices, suggesting the social and symbolic links that many practitioners make between "circumcision" for boys and girls. In this article I have sought to avoid this mystifying usage,

while I have also avoided the terms *female genital mutilation* and *female genital torture*, which carry the implicit assumption that parents and relatives deliberately intend to harm children. When referring to the full range of such practices, I have instead adopted the term *female genital operations*. My goal in doing so is not to coin a new phrase that purports to escape the problematic power relationships surrounding this topic, for clearly that is impossible. Nevertheless, existing usages are deeply embedded in the "either/or" perspectives characteristic of discussions of female genital operations, with *circumcision* signaling relativistic tolerance and *mutilation* implying moral outrage. Although I find the term *female genital operations* preferable to existing terminology, whenever possible I have preferred the more historically and geographically specific terms *clitoridectomy* and *infibulation*.

Contextualizing Clitoridectomy: Excision as Initiation in Western Kenya

By sketching the social context of clitoridectomies as performed by the people living around the village of Kikhome in western Kenya in 1988, I hope to encourage a reinfusion of humanity into a debate that has often been reduced to dehumanizing abstractions. However, by drawing on my own observations and experiences in the Kikhome region, I also run certain risks. In Kikhome I was an outsider, a young white female North American living in the community while on a teaching stint, and my knowledge of the practice of excision was limited.[9] My goal, however, is not to offer a generically applicable social scientific analysis of female genital operations – an impossible task given the diversity of practices and the plethora of meanings attributed to them. Nor is my intention to offer a definitive ethnographic account of clitoridectomies as performed in the Kikhome region. Instead, my purpose is to describe the quest to know, the desire to understand these practices as an "outsider," someone inevitably forced (as we all are) to draw upon her or his own resources for understanding the world. In Kikhome, I felt compelled to try to understand the ritual clitoridectomies performed there both because the practice deeply troubled me and because I sought some way of thinking about the issue that I could reconcile with my sense of myself as a feminist, as a student of anthropology, and as a friend of many in the community where I was staying.

While my account is written by someone on the cultural margins of life in Kikhome, such a location is perhaps ironically appropriate. The international controversy over female genital operations has largely occurred in human rights reports, health bulletins, international conferences, and media accounts across a variety of countries. In this international debate, I, along with many Euro-Americans, have been a privileged "insider" with greater access to the international flow of representations concerning female genital operations than most women in Kikhome, whose bodies carry such intimate knowledge of these practices. We are all to various degrees both "insiders" and "outsiders," and these statuses are deeply embedded in the power dynamics that structure our relationships with each other. In writing this, I hope to blur our sense of where the "problem" with female genital operations lies, at the same time blurring distinctions over who has the "right" to speak about such issues. To suggest that only those who have experienced a practice or those who can lay claim to it on the basis of racial or ethnic identity have the "right" to speak essentializes both practitioners and nonpractitioners by locating them in bounded groups assumed to share common beliefs – a reductionist view that ignores a far messier reality. In choosing to write on this topic, however, I do not justify the ways in which Euro-Americans have dominated international debates over female genital operations both historically and at present. Instead, by locating this controversy "interculturally," I intend to draw attention to the responsibility that Westerners hold for the terms of these debates – for interest in Europe and the United States stems not only from feminist or humanist concern, but also from the desire to sensationalize, to titillate, and to call attention to differences between "us" and "them" in ways that reaffirm notions of Western cultural superiority.

"Circumcision": The Ceremonies

Kikhome, a village that consists of a few small storefronts, is located amidst the dispersed mud-and-thatch homes and the subsistence farm plots that checker the foothills of Mount Elgon near the Ugandan border. For town- and city-dwellers in the heavily populated western province of Kenya, the village of Kikhome in 1988 was seen as a remote backwater, difficult to reach by transportation and almost inaccessible when the rainy season turned the dirt roads and paths into slippery, viscous mud. The high school compound where I stayed as an English teacher was located in the flat valley at the base of the foothills. While the Bukusu, a Bantu-speaking group, formed the majority of the people living in the valley, the Sabaot, a group of Kalenjin Nilotic ancestry who had historically been pastoralists, now farmed the hills overshadowing Kikhome. Although the majority of students at Kikhome were Bukusu, there was a sizeable minority of Sabaot. Immediately after I arrived, my high school students, both male and female, began telling me with a boisterous pride about their circumcision ceremonies. They informed me that while the Bukusu circumcised only boys, the Sabaot initiated both girls and boys. Unfortunately, they lamented, I had missed the Bukusu ceremonies, but assuredly I would be invited to Sabaot circumcisions over the December school holidays.

True to their word, and to my unacknowledged discomfort, several of my teenage students did invite me, months later, to their initiations. On the evening before one of the initiations I attended was to take place, Beatrice, a teenage student at Kikhome, led me and a fellow U.S. teacher along the winding paths criss-crossing the foothills of Mount Elgon to the family compound of her cousins. It was just before dusk when we entered the compound, which encompassed a series of round mud houses neatly roofed with thatch, and where we encountered a festive atmosphere that reminded me of graduation parties at home in the mid-western United States. The compound was crowded with people of all ages, and many of the older guests were sitting on the ground drinking homemade grain beer, or *buzaa*, brewed especially for the occasion. Near the main house, both male and female initiates "danced," or rather, paced strenuously back and forth, swinging their arms and loudly blowing whistles. The teenage girls wore skirts and the boys wore shorts of bright red fabric decorated with colored strips of cloth and white T-shirts emblazoned with "Datsun" or "Free Mandela" logos. Their arms and faces were painted with white, chalky designs; the girls wore colored knitted caps and the boys colobus monkey headdresses. Beatrice explained that when young people felt they were ready (generally between the ages of 14 and 16 for the Sabaot), they would request their parents' permission to be initiated. After training for several months to learn the necessary songs and dances under the guidance of their sponsors, the initiates would go around inviting friends and relatives to the ceremonies.[10]

As darkness fell, the increasingly drunken crowd surrounded the candidates and encouraged them by joining in the dancing and singing. The bright glow of pressure lamps cast a flickering light on the raucous, gyrating crowd as well as on the wooden faces of the initiates, which were masked with the expressionlessness expected of those awaiting circumcision. The dancing continued throughout the night; we were told that it would tire the novices and numb them for the pain to come. At dawn, the initiates were led by circuitous routes to a stream, and before being bathed in its water (a restricted part of the ceremony witnessed only by the initiated), they were harangued by their mothers and warned not to disgrace their relatives, living or dead, by showing cowardice. After being led back to the family compound, they were immediately circumcised. The cutting was public and demonstrated to the community the bravery of the initiated. The boys were cut by a male circumcisor while standing; the girls were excised by a woman as they sat with legs spread on the ground, their backs supported by their sponsors. The crucial test was for the initiate to show no pain, to neither change expression nor even blink, during the cutting. Remarkably enough to my friend and I, the initiates remained utterly stoic and expressionless throughout. We were told it is this ability to withstand the ordeal that confers adulthood, that allows one to marry and have children, and that binds one to one's age-mates.[11]

Mary, one of the students whose ceremony I had witnessed, later told me that she and her fellow initiates had recuperated for a month, boys and girls separately, in special huts. After both male and female initiates judged themselves sufficiently healed they informed the adults, and then the boys and girls rejoined and ceremonially climbed up into the lower hills of Mount Elgon to a large cave behind a small waterfall. After a ceremony at the cave during which the ancestors were invoked, the celebrating initiates were allowed to raid local gardens on their return, mischievously stealing bananas and pelting the houses of their owners without fear of punishment. In a final ceremony at the family compound, they were given new clothes and gifts, and they then reentered daily life as adults.

The Search for Voices

After witnessing these ceremonies, I had a better idea of what Sabaot initiation entailed.[12] Yet I had not come any closer to relieving my own inner distress about excision. I decided that if I could ascertain what these young people "really" thought about the practice, it would help me formulate a position of my own. But the question remained – how could I discover their "real" thoughts? Obviously, there was a great deal of public support for initiation. For them to criticize circumcision publicly or to reject it would have led to accusations of cowardice, to social ostracism, and perhaps to physical violence, as Beatrice acknowledged had happened in the past. Thus, pondering the relationship between the public voices of these young people and their "real" voices, I embarked on a search for an "authentic" perspective.

In my capacity as an English teacher at the secondary school where I taught, I gave the Form III students – the equivalent of U.S. high school juniors – the option of writing an essay about "female circumcision," and some of the Sabaot students chose to do so. Although clitoridectomies have been illegal in Kenya since 1982 and were denounced in the Social Education classes at the secondary school where I taught, the students who responded argued that the continuation of the practice was important on the grounds that it was, as they described it, "our custom." They stated that the primary purpose of the practice was to keep unmarried girls from getting "hot" – that is, from having sexual relations and getting pregnant before marriage or from having extramarital affairs later. Yet while the one essay written by a boy contained no objections to the practice, the essays by girls (who had already had clitoridectomies) did. These students argued that the practice was "bad" because it was forbidden by President Moi and by Christianity (most people in the area were syncretic in their religious beliefs, espousing both Christianity and indigenous African religions). One female student, who had enthusiastically invited me to her sister's initiation, stated that the practice was simply another way of "destroying" women's bodies, a use of language that seemed to mirror the Social Education curriculum more than the usual voices of my teenage students.

At the time, I was perplexed: Were the objections raised by these young women what they really thought or were they merely parroting what they had learned in school or in the sermons of local Christian leaders, who had a long history of deploring the practice? Were objections based on Christian teaching "authentic" or was this simply another way their voices had been colonized? What "authentic" voice might these young women use to object to the practice? Certainly they would not use the language of individual rights prominent in Euro-American feminism but which seemed selfish and antifamily to many East Africans. Perhaps these young women were simply strategically merging their voices with those of more powerful others, such as the Christian church or President Moi, and hence circuitously expressing their "real" thoughts?

I attempted to address these issues when several young female Sabaot students stopped by my house on the school compound one afternoon to see the pictures I had taken during their initiation. Trying to summon a neutral tone, I explained that I wanted to know more about the practice. I pleaded ignorance, stating that although baby boys are often circumcised in hospitals in the United States, we do not have public circumcision ceremonies.[13] The four young women assured me that their "custom," as they called it in English, was good. Lydia, who had recently been initiated and who had a look of religious ecstasy on her face that startled me, argued that it was something a person had to accept with her "whole being" and when one did so, one did not feel the pain. Laughing at my skepticism, they told me that the pain at the time of the ceremony was not very bad (due presumably to shock and fatigue), and that it was only later that the pain became intense. But, I asked carefully, women in my country would worry that they would "regret" the ceremony later. My innuendoes to the sexual consequences of excision met with boisterous laughter, and the young women replied in a light yet serious tone, "But we are already regretting it!" In other words, there was no delusion among these adolescent girls, some of whose married and unmarried peers were already pregnant, about how it would affect their sexual pleasure. I asked whether they wanted their daughters to be "circumcised." One said she would because it was an important custom to continue; a second, after some thought, said she would not; and Mary, whose initiation photos we were perusing, looked uncomfortable and declined to comment.

The interactions that I have narrated, a few among many, were complex and full of nuances. I began to recognize the naïveté of my search for "real" voices, for clearly the girls' voices shifted according to context depending on whether they were at the ceremonies, with adults or peers, in mixed-sex settings or among female friends, or, I surmised, alone. Given the legacy of both Freud and Erving Goffman, it seems evident that each self has a public as well as a private side and many more layers within it, from the conscious to the deeply unconscious. What happens, however, when these apparent layers of the self contradict each other? Do these young women, and indeed all of us, have straightforward "best interests" or are our interests, on the contrary, multiple and contradictory? And, where would one locate the "authentic" self? In Western thought, we tend to privilege that which is most interior or private. Yet obviously, as critics of Freud's universalism would emphasize, our unconscious is also a product of the times and places in which we exist, thus challenging the idea of a "layered" self that possesses an inner core untouched by our contemporary surroundings.

Another incident in Kikhome supported my later interpretation that the "best interests" of these young women were indeed contradictory. My responsibilities at the secondary school included organizing schoolwide debates. Before the main debate, students were allowed to publicly raise issues in front of their classmates. On one occasion, a young Sabaot woman who had recently been initiated demanded to know why Sabaot girls were forced into circumcision. In a mirror image of this challenge, a female Bukusu student at a later debate asked why Bukusu girls were not "allowed" to be initiated like Bukusu boys. Here, the Bukusu young men jeered, saying derisively that Bukusu girls were not allowed to be circumcised because circumcision of girls did not happen "in the Bible." The irony that at least some of the girls of both ethnic groups envied the position of the other reconfirmed for me that excision was both in *and* against the interests of the Sabaot young women. By undergoing the painful public ordeal of initiation, not only did they develop a personal sense of self-confidence and pride that made them feel like adults, they were awarded considerable public respect. But this respect came at a price – the price of decreased pleasure and the containment of their sexuality, even if in ways widely considered appropriate by both women and men.

Kikhome through the Anthropological Looking-Glass

Later during the course of my graduate studies, I combed the anthropological literature for help in understanding the clitoridectomies I had witnessed in Kikhome, hoping that other scholars could assist in untangling the complex questions these practices raised. As I searched for deeper insight into why Sabaot women and girls in Kikhome supported excision, I wanted to know how the significance of these practices extended beyond their ritual and psychological meanings and related to other forms of social life such as kinship groups, ethnic identity, and economic practices. Furthermore, I wondered how women's support for excision in Kikhome could be reconciled with the Western assumption that female genital operations are an expression of male dominance and, in a different vein, how women who have experienced these practices conceived of their sexuality.

There was, however, almost nothing in the anthropological literature that focused on excision in sub-Saharan Africa. Anthropologists and social theorists from Van Gennep to Victor Turner offered context for excision as a social ritual by discussing the meanings of rites of passage and adolescent initiation (for example, Gluckman 1963; Richards 1956; Turner 1970; Van Gennep 1909); none, however, focused specifically on clitoridectomies. Goldschmidt's (1976, 1986) fieldwork during the 1960s among the Sebei, a Ugandan subgroup of the Mount Elgon Sabaot, proved more pertinent, although his account of initiation rites was largely descriptive and touched upon differences between male and female circumcision only in passing. He did, however, briefly speculate that excision was less about controlling women's sexual desire than about offering Sebei women a source of collective strength as a counterweight to male dominance. Goldschmidt suggested that excision enhanced women's status by binding them together as a group in possession of ritual secrets revealed through initiation; men respected and feared these secrets, thereby offering women greater leverage in male/female interactions (1986: 110–11). While this insight was suggestive, his assumption that the practice was not about sexuality gave me pause: not only did it seem counterintuitive, but it also did not accord with the accounts from people I knew in Kikhome.

I later turned to the work of Rose Oldfield Hayes and Janice Boddy, who each had conducted research in northern Sudan during the 1970s and examined another type of female genital operation – the more severe infibula-tion, which involves both excision and the sewing together of the remaining tissues. This procedure was usually performed on small girls, often four to five years of age, and was not the test of endurance leading to adulthood that it was among the Sabaot. Many people in the area felt the practice to be an Islamic reli-gious duty, although most Muslim peoples do not engage in this practice and it is not re-quired by the Koran, as some contend. Despite the physical and social differences between in-fibulation and clitoridectomy, Hayes's and Boddy's analyses were relevant to Kikhome in that they further explored social settings in which it was widely considered desirable to "socialize" female sexuality or fertility through genital operations. In addition, both analyses focused on the motivations of women as par-ticipants in these practices, not simply as vic-tims.

In her 1975 article, Hayes argued that in order to understand why women, particularly older women, were the most vocal supporters of infibulation, it was necessary to consider their positioning within family groups. In northern Sudan, families were organized around lineages that traced descent solely through men, while women moved to join their husbands' lineages upon marriage. The importance of maintaining the integrity of patrilineages was paramount and served to determine the social status of individuals. As in many other Muslim societies (as well as in many Christian, circum-Mediterranean re-gions) strict sex-segregation prevailed, and the honor of families was intrinsically linked to the sexual purity of its female members and of the in-marrying women under its protec-tion. According to Hayes, proof of virginity remained a prerequisite for marriage, and in-fibulation was taken to index both physical and "social" virginity, as evidenced by the practice of reinfibulating women after child-birth or upon later marriages. If not properly channeled, female sexuality was considered to be the greatest possible source of disgrace to the patrilineage. As a consequence, women infibulated their daughters to protect them from the supposedly wanton sexuality believed intrinsic to women and which, if uncontrolled,

could lead to rape, illegitimate children, social disgrace, and retributive death. Given that family and social organization in this area was clearly male-dominant, the women who vigorously adhered to such practices were responding pragmatically to the exigencies of everyday life.

Hayes's analysis also helped illuminate the Sabaot context. While the Sabaot are not pre-occupied with chastity and virginity as are the northern Sudanese, kinship organization in both places is similar. Sabaot women experi-ence the characteristic ambiguity of women in patrilineal and patrilocal social orders. Al-though each Sabaot woman is a member of her father's patrilineage and thus an "outsider" in her husband's kin group, her hopes of in-creasing her social status are linked to produ-cing offspring for the husband's patrilineage.[14] As is true in other parts of the world, kinship arrangements have strong economic dimen-sions, and for the Sabaot, as largely sedentary former pastoralists, cattle remain symbolically and economically important. It is cattle that a circumcised, and thus marriageable, young woman's family receive from the groom and his family, thereby transferring rights in her reproductive potential; it is cattle (perhaps the very same cattle) that are used to pay the bridewealth for women's brothers' marriages, thus permitting those brothers to perpetuate the lineage for both living and dead relatives; and it is the reluctance to return cattle that may make a woman's father and brothers fail to support her claim for a divorce (Gold-schmidt 1976).

Janice Boddy's work (1982) has contributed a symbolic interpretation to the sociostructural explanation of infibulation offered by Hayes. Unlike the situation in Kikhome, Boddy noted that in the northern Sudanese village of Hofriyat, the ritual circumcision of little girls was only mildly celebrated, compared to the elaborate festivities associated with boys' cir-cumcisions. Nevertheless, infibulation held meaning for Hofriyatis as a source of purifica-tion. Boddy offered a richly detailed analysis linking infibulation, purification, and cleanli-ness to the symbolic properties of birds, ostrich eggs, warmth, moisture, enclosures, and wombs. She concluded that infibulation is actually an assertive symbolic act for Hofriyati women that serves to emphasize a type of femininity that focuses on fertility while deemphasizing their sexuality. She wrote, "By insisting on circumcision for their daughters, women assert their social indispensability, an importance that is not as the sexual partners of their husbands, nor, in this highly segregated male-authoritative society, as their servants, sexual or otherwise, but as the mothers of men" (1982: 687). The ability of women to reproduce or found lineages was the stuff on which the social careers of women were based, and it was older women, as mothers and grandmothers, who emerged as powerful forces within patrilineages through control over their offspring.

Boddy also noted that in this strictly sex-segregated society, women achieved social recognition not by becoming like men, but by emphasizing their differences. By removing that part of the external genitalia thought to most resemble that of the opposite sex, circumcision was believed to enhance the masculinity of boys and the femininity of girls (1982: 688). In an interesting parallel, this belief mirrors that of the Dogon of Mali, who also practice female genital operations (Griaule 1965), as well as that of some West African immigrants in France who have argued that to not circumcise a girl would leave her "not only 'unclean' but 'masculine,' in that she retains a vestige of a male sex organ" (Winter 1994: 941). A Kenyan teacher from a village neighboring Kikhome offered an argument about excision that echoed Boddy's interpretation that female genital operations served to emphasize differences between women and men. The female teacher argued that clitoridectomies were positive for women in that while men were enslaved to their sexuality, circumcised women were better able to resist their desires, thus affording them more control than men. This argument recalls the strategy of Victorian feminists in the United States who based claims to public authority on their alleged moral and sexual superiority to men (Epstein 1981; L. Gordon 1977). However, there is an important difference. In Sudan, while women's sexuality might be harshly "socialized," it was not repressed in the sense of encouraging prudish-

ness, as was common among the European and North American Victorian middle classes. Lightfoot-Klein (1989), an opponent of genital operations, noted the lustiness and bawdiness of older North African village women. To her surprise, some village women who had been infibulated gave detailed descriptions of orgasms, presumably because other areas of the body had become intensified erogenous zones. Lightfoot-Klein's account was confirmed by a Sudanese doctor, Nahid Toubia, who cautioned that little is known to medical practitioners about the sexual functioning of infibulated women or the processes by which women might compensate for loss of the clitoris through other sensory areas, emotion, or fantasy (1994:714).[15]

Among the Sebei Sabaots, Goldschmidt recorded an open interest in sexual matters and a concern with sexual prowess. He noted that a culturally sanctioned form of sexual petting in which orgasms were allowed but penetration prohibited had historically been permitted to both boys and girls prior to marriage and even circumcision (1976: 203).[16] Drawing on fieldwork observations from the 1960s, he expressed doubt as to whether "any normal boy or girl reaches circumcision a virgin..." although, he noted, it was still strongly disapproved of for an uncircumcised girl to be pregnant (1976: 204). He also described the initiation festivity itself as a time for open sexual license and that extramarital affairs were relatively common for both men and women, although women could be beaten on this account while wives held no sanctions over their husbands' behavior. On the basis of this apparent openness, Goldschmidt deemed implausible the view that clitoridectomies were intended to decrease women's sexual desire. He did, however, stress that sexual activity between men and women was tension-filled and that relationships between the sexes were generally characterized by hostility and mistrust (1976: 241). Thus, in this context, clitoridectomies might be best understood not as a simple attempt to eradicate the sexual desires of women, but as attempts to control, and appropriately channel, women's sexuality and fertility in a patrilineal and patrilocal context. The reality that most forms of clitoridectomies and infibulations originated and continue to be performed in patrilineal and patrilocal societies suggests the importance of such contexts.

After exploring these anthropological accounts of female genital operations, illuminating as the accounts were, I was frustrated by the numerous questions that remained unanswered. One crucial question concerned how these practices had changed over time. How, I wondered, had the ritual initiation of girls in Kikhome been transformed from the precolonial to the colonial and, ultimately, to the postcolonial era? Furthermore, was there room in existing anthropological accounts of female genital operations for the agency of individuals and for resistance to social norms? Goldschmidt noted that the refusal of girls or boys to be circumcised was called "crying the knife" (1976); had those who "cried the knife" always shared the dominant viewpoint that their actions were shameful? Did such actions ever take on connotations of active resistance, and were such actions ever more than individual? While sociostructural and symbolic interpretations of genital operations provided insight into the practice of female genital operations at a given moment in time, such interpretations also had their limitations. The theoretical legacy of functionalist and symbolic schools within anthropology has meant that many accounts have focused too narrowly on the present, on bounded social groups, and on cultural consensus.

What alternative understandings might historically-based accounts of female genital operations suggest? Historian Claire Robertson, who has looked at the relationship between clitoridectomies and collective social organization for Kikuyu women in Kenya, offers one attempt to consider female genital operations as historically malleable practices (1996). Robertson argues that women's age sets, a form of social organization originating in the precolonial era and characterized by gerontocracy and an emphasis on the ritual practices of initiation and excision, also historically served the little-known function of organizing women into collective work groups on farms. With the increased stratification of Kenyan society in the colonial and postcolonial periods, the im-

portance of women's collective efforts to organize their labor have, according to Robertson, not died out but been transformed. She argues that age sets have metamorphasized in the contemporary period into relatively egalitarian grassroots savings associations, environmental groups, and other cooperative labor and financial ventures that are being strategically used by Kikuyu women in their battle against poverty. Robertson writes,

> From the 1920s to 1990 women's collective efforts moved from a more specific form of patriarchally sanctioned organization concerned with controlling sexuality and fertility to a more class-based women's solidarity involved with promoting women's economic activities. (1996: 617)

As a result of this transformation, Robertson suggests that the importance and incidence of initiation and clitoridectomy have decreased (1996: 629–30). Theoretically, this account focuses on the agency of Kikuyu women and in doing so allows space for these women to either agree with or resist the valorization of excision, and thereby to potentially transform such practices. The possibility of resistance, for example, is suggested by colonial era accounts in which some Kikuyu women are reported to have run away to mission stations in apparent attempts to escape forced marriages and possibly clitoridectomies (1996: 624).

Presumably, female genital operations also play an important role as markers of social, ethnic, religious, and other forms of identity, an interpretation that has thus far gone largely unexplored in anthropological accounts. Even a brief consideration of the practice of male circumcision, which has both historically and at present served as a potent marker of group identity in European countries, would suggest the need to explore such a possibility (see Boon 1994; Boyarin 1996). Although excision appears to be on the wane among the Kikuyu (Robertson 1996), Goldschmidt's earlier account noted that the importance of the practice appeared to be on the rise among the Sabaot (1986: 111). Given the considerable violence that erupted between the Bukusu and the Sabaot in the years after I left Kikhome, one productive avenue for future research would

GLOBAL DEBATES OVER FEMALE GENITAL OPERATIONS   343

be to explore the potential relationship between ethnic identity and this increased support for clitoridectomies. In other words, how and to what extent do clitoridectomies serve as symbols of ethnic identity and "tradition" within the volatile politics of the Kenyan nation-state?[17]

Despite the insights provided by the literature on these practices, stumbling blocks remain for anthropologists in developing a politically-engaged feminist position on female genital operations. Anthropological accounts that focus on how such practices either function or provide meaning, without attendant focus on how practices are transformed and given new meaning, discourage activism by implying that if such practices ceased, a social "need," symbolic or material, would be left unfulfilled. The transformation of the role of female genital operations in initiation and age sets for Kikuyu women challenges any such rigid link between social "needs" and particular practices. If our analyses do not emphasize the potential for transformation in practices such as female genital operations, the result can be a dangerous perceived dichotomy between cultural "others" for whom cultural practices "function" (and thus should be respected) and Europe and the United States, where "traditions" are open to challenge. Alternatively, attempts to provide historically-based, nonessentialized accounts of such practices may offer one route to overcoming the widespread Euro-American tendency to view female genital operations solely in terms of either cultural relativism or moral outrage.

Beyond the Village: The International Controversy Surrounding Female Genital Operations

Clearly, the questions raised by female genital operations extend beyond Kikhome or Hofriyat in Sudan and even beyond the boundaries of the Kenyan, Sudanese, and other African nation-states. Even before arriving in western Kenya, my perceptions of "female circumcision" had already been shaped by the vocal international

controversy surrounding the issue; I had first learned of the practice from an article by Robin Morgan and Gloria Steinem (1983) that I had read in a women's studies class as an undergraduate. Obviously, I was operating in a particular social and cultural context as much as the villagers of Kikhome, and media accounts of female genital operations in places like Africa formed part of the background noise of the cultural world in which I was an "insider." As I followed the written and televised reports on female genital operations in the United States, I became increasingly intrigued by the cultural dynamics of the debate itself. After living in Kenya, the "commonsense" terms operative in Western accounts of such practices seemed increasingly peculiar and deserving of explanation in their own right. Consequently, I will now leave Kikhome to begin addressing the discourse of this international debate, its historical roots, and its relationship to preexisting Euro-American understandings of Africa and Africans.

Although opposition to female genital operations by Westerners has a long history extending back at least to the colonial era, it became an issue of concern to Second Wave feminists in the United States and Europe during the 1970s.[18] Influential articles by Gloria Steinem, Mary Daly, and others, including Third World activists such as Nawal El Saadawi (1980), condemned the practices, and international health organizations also took up the cause. In this depiction of female genital operations for an international audience, the practices became largely severed from their sociocultural context (with the exception of El Saadawi's article). While in Kikhome male and female initiations were performed side by side (albeit with very different consequences), in the Western-oriented literature opposing such practices there was an exclusive focus on the tormenting of girls, if not solely by men, then by a monolithic patriarchy.

During the United Nations Decade for Women (1975–85), female genital operations became a prominent and controversial issue. However, the response to the ensuing publicity was not what many First World feminists might have expected. Instead of being congratulated for their opposition to female circumcision, they were called to task by some African and Third World women, including a group that threatened to walk out of the mid-decade international women's conference in Copenhagen in 1980. While some of these women themselves opposed female genital operations, they objected to the way the issue was being handled by First World feminists and called attention to the troubling power dynamics that exist between the First and Third Worlds, as well as between First and Third World women.[19] This confrontation led by African women formed merely one segment of a broader challenge to mainstream Euro-American feminism by women of color, working-class women, lesbians, and many Third World women, who felt that their experiences and understandings had been excluded by white, middle-class formulations of feminism (Jayawardena 1986; Mohanty et al. 1991; Moraga and Anzaldua 1981; Tokarczyk and Fay 1993). This challenge to Euro-American feminism also resulted in a shift of attention toward issues of difference among women as well as toward a reformulation of feminist politics that focused on coalition-building and the recognition of diversity rather than an assumption of homogeneous interests (Butler and Scott 1992; Haraway 1989; Ramazanoglu 1989).

Despite these criticisms of the way Third World women had been represented, Alice Walker's novel (1992), the film *Warrior Marks*, and its companion volume (Parmar 1993b; Walker and Parmar 1993), as well as essays published by the National Organization for Women (see NOW 1994), have provoked a replay of debates over female genital operations in terms remarkably like those of the 1970s. This frustrating sense of déjà vu may be dismissed as Walker's and NOW's refusal to engage the productive aspects of earlier debates. However, more pertinent to understanding why these accounts have generated such a barrage of media attention is the way that Walker's and NOW's presentation of female genital operations have fed into powerful and value-laden understandings of differences between Africans and Euro-Americans – understandings that are being reemphasized with increased immigration from the Third

World to the First. Such understandings presume a radical difference, a binary opposition between First and Third Worlds that itself is built upon the historical belief in a chasm between "modern" Euro-Americans and "native" colonized others. Reading through much of the Western-based literature opposing female genital operations, the degree to which many of the arguments work to reproduce such beliefs is striking.

One common trope in much of the Euro-American-oriented literature opposing female genital operations has been the tendency to characterize African women as thoroughly oppressed victims of patriarchy, ignorance, or both, not as social actors in their own right. Sub-Saharan and North African women are alternately seen as not being allowed to express their voices, or as having defective or confused understandings if they speak in favor of genital operations. For example, Daly wrote that in relation to genital operations, "the apparently 'active' role of the women, themselves mutilated, is in fact a passive instrumental role.... Mentally castrated, these women participate in the destruction of their own kind" (1978: 164). Here women are blamed for their false consciousness and are seen as the mere pawns of men. More recently, in the case of African immigrants in France, Winter similarly argued that "one of the greatest problems facing feminists campaigning against excision is, in fact, women's complicity in their own oppression and in that of their children" (1994: 964). Hosken had attributed the apparent complicity of African women to their isolation from the "outside" world, stating, "Local women – who it is said should speak for themselves (the majority of whom are illiterate ...) – have no connection with the outside world and have no way to organize against the practice" (1981: 11). This position is particularly belied by the current organizing of African women's groups, both on and off the continent, in relation to female genital operations. Feminist scholars, particularly those from non-Western countries, are increasingly critiquing portrayals that presume Third World women to be dominated by an ahistorical patriarchal "tradition" that is assumed to be more severe than that in Europe or the

United States. The anthropological literature does support the view that gender inequality is widespread; nevertheless, the cultural and historical particulars of how gender relations are constructed differently in different places, and the alternate sources of power and authority that women often hold, are ignored in these generalized assumptions about the oppression of Third World women (Mohanty et al. 1991; Ong 1988; Spivak 1988).

Much of the Western-oriented literature opposing female genital operations also constructs "culture" and "tradition" in problematic ways. Rather than focusing on "culture" as historically changeable and broadly encompassing beliefs and practices characteristic of a social group, the discourse on genital operations understands culture as ahistorical "customs" or "traditions." Such "traditions" are simultaneously depicted as the meaningless hangovers of a premodern era and as the defining characteristic of the Third World. In this scenario, "traditions" in the Third World are hardened essences that can only be shed by modernization, while in the West, "backward" cultural traditions are conceived of as being steadily replaced by "rational" ways of life. To quote Hosken once again, "The myth about the importance of 'cultural traditions' must be laid to rest, considering that 'development' – the introduction of imported Western technology and living patterns – is the goal of every country where the operations are practiced today" (1981: 10). "Development," assumed to be the intrinsic property of Europe and the United States, rather than a cultural construct in its own right, emerges in this discourse as the antithesis of cultural traditions.

Culture and traditions are often coded as harmful, coercive, and superfluous. Pratibha Parmar proclaims that women who have undergone genital operations have "been irrevocably wounded by traditions" (1993a: 176), and she and Walker adopt the slogan "Culture is not Torture" in Warrior Marks (Walker and Parmar 1993). Linda Weil-Curiel, a lawyer prominent in legal battles against female genital operations in France, criticized the suspended sentences given to some African immigrant parents, stating, "the parents are the real culprits. They know they are going to hurt the child, and they nonetheless take the child to the excisors, to the knife ... there is no excuse, ever, for such a deed" (quoted in Walker and Parmar 1993: 265). Here, immigrant parents are condemned for not being able to think outside "culture," implying that the author feels herself capable of doing so. Forrest Sawyer, the anchor of ABC's Day One, emphasized the presumed weight of culture: "This is a brutal, disabling ritual so tied to culture and tradition that for thousands of years women have been powerless to stop it. In fact, the taboos are so strong that the women subjected to it will rarely talk about it at all" (1993).

A recent front-page article in the New York Times concerning Fauziya Kasinga highlights the assumption of the oppressive nature of "tradition" (Dugger 1996a). Despite information in the article suggesting Kasinga's elite and "modern" background (for example, Kasinga's father owned a successful trucking business in Togo, and she attended boarding school in Ghana), the language of the article stresses the exotic, relying on such terms as tribal law, bloody rite, banish[ment], and family patriarchs in their tribe (Dugger 1996a). Rhetorically, the article suggests the ironic parallels between the alleged fetters of "tribal customs" and actual fetters in a Pennsylvania prison, where Kasinga was detained while seeking political asylum; here, the irony emerges as Dugger challenges the assumption of "freedom" in the United States by suggesting parallels with the (unquestioned) oppression of "tradition" in African countries. Similarly, Kasinga's televised response to a surprised Ted Koppel, informing him that most young women in Togo are happy to have the procedure done and "think it is something very great," could not dislodge the program's implicit assumption that these women are coerced and would gladly flee their own countries to escape such practices (Nightline 1996). Thus, rather than acknowledging Kasinga as a young woman who had dared to resist social norms of which she disapproved (in part because she was raised in a liberal household that offered alternative life choices), the media accounts instead emphasized the allegedly coercive and oppressive nature of African cultures and societies as a whole.

In other accounts, collective "culture" is judged to be less relevant than "rights" premised on the individual. As Tilman Hasche, the lawyer for Lydia Oluloro, the Nigerian woman who legally petitioned to remain in the United States to prevent the excision of her daughters, stated in a *New York Times* article, "Frankly, I don't give a damn if opposing this is a violation of someone's culture. To me, female genital mutilation is a violation of the physical and spiritual integrity of a person" (Egan 1994). In some accounts, cultural beliefs are recognized only as "insanity." For example, A. M. Rosenthal of the *New York Times* called on the people and governments of the countries where genital operations are practiced "to revolt against the sexual and social insanities that allow the mutilation of half their population" (1992).

In contrast to this image of sub-Saharan and North African societies as tradition-bound and oppressed by culture, Euro-American institutions and values are depicted as exemplars of culture-free reason and rationality, as represented in particular by Western medicine. This binary distinction between a rational West and an overly traditional and cultured "rest" has been underscored in the oppositional literature by emphatic attention to the health problems associated with such practices. Health consequences *are* real and disturbing. For clitoridectomies, these include the possibility of hemorrhage and infection, and in the case of infibulation, they include difficulties with urination, intercourse, and childbirth; fluid retention; and cyst formation (Toubia 1994). Yet as a position statement issued by the Women's Caucus of the African Studies Association noted, these health consequences must be located within a larger context in which women's health may also be severely affected by malnutrition, lack of clean water, and inadequate health care (1984). Henry Louis Gates asks, "Is it, after all, unreasonable to be suspicious of Westerners who are exercised over female circumcision, but whose eyes glaze over when the same women are merely facing starvation?" (1994). The question of why these particular health issues generate such a barrage of interest deserves closer examination.

Clearly, popular interest in female genital operations stems in part from their sensational aspects, practices that simultaneously horrify and titillate Euro-American audiences. This tendency toward sensationalism draws on a long history in which sub-Saharan and North African women's bodies have been simultaneously exoticized and eroticized, as evidenced in the pickling of a "Bushman" woman's vulva and its display in France in the 19th century (Gould 1985) and erotic French colonial postcards that draw on sexually charged ideas about veiling and the alleged languorous harems of imprisoned Muslim women (Alloula 1986). Concerning the recent interest in female genital operations, Dawit noted the voyeurism implicit in a CNN newscast that spent nearly ten minutes graphically depicting the infibulation of an Egyptian girl (Dawit 1994). Modern medical discourse may in fact perform the dual role of using the "objective" language of science to construct the issue as outside of "culture," while simultaneously offering a sanitized way of continuing the preoccupation with the genitalia and sexuality of African women.

The privileging of Euro-American experience in the medical discourse surrounding genital operations is also apparent in the discussion of pain. Most of the literature lists pain at the forefront of the "medical" consequences or problems associated with genital operations (D. Gordon 1991; Kouba and Muasher 1985: 101). And it is pain that leads to accusations that genital operations are "torture." However, for the adolescent initiation rituals that I described for Kikhome, pain is an intrinsic part of the ritual and is socially meaningful – although it is not for infibulation and sunna operations, for which sometimes an anesthetic is used or which are done in the hospital. While all humans presumably have the same range of physiological responses to pain, barring individual differences and learned techniques for controlling pain, the meanings associated with pain and ideas about how one should respond to it vary situationally as well as cross-culturally. Within the context of sub-Saharan African initiation rituals (or for that matter, U.S. military boot camps or Indian ascetic rites), pain may be viewed not simply as something to be avoided but as something to be endured that can result in the positive transformation of the individual.

To summarize, much of the Western-oriented literature by Euro-Americans that opposes female genital operations invokes a series of binary oppositions, including:

First World
modernity
science
civilized
freedom
women as actors
medical knowledge

Third World
tradition
superstition
barbarous
torture/repression
women as oppressed
ignorance/disease

The cumulative effect of these binary oppositions is to perpetuate a dichotomous understanding of First and Third Worlds, an enduring division between "us" and "them." This division is strikingly apparent in Walker's *Possessing the Secret of Joy* (1992), where the dysfunctional sex life, intensely painful childbirth, deformed child, troubled marriage, and tortured soul of the main character, Tashi, are all attributed to "circumcision." Tashi is then contrasted with her U.S. husband's French lover, who emerges as the embodiment of female liberation and for whom birth is orgasmic. Perhaps the sense of a radical separation between First and Third Worlds, however, is most forcefully reproduced in accusations of "torture." Because clitoridectomies or infibulations are usually performed at the request of parents and relatives, those whom Weil-Curiel classifies as "the real culprits," this discourse implicitly suggests that even family members in such societies are callous or barbaric enough to "torture" their own.

Colonial History and the Debate over the Status of Women

A perusal of the Western-oriented literature opposing genital operations, much of which reproduces such disturbing power hierarchies, makes starkly apparent why gender is a fraught issue between so-called First and Third Worlds. It is also clear that understanding the tenacity of the discourse discussed above requires understanding its history; and in fact, much recent scholarship has focused on colonial discourses of gender and the uses to which such discourses were put. This scholarship has argued that the alleged overwhelming oppression of "native" women by "native" men was consistently used to justify colonial domination and that Euro-American feminism was itself used toward those ends.

The colonial discourse on female genital operations in Africa resembles that on other practices such as *sati* (widow-burning) in India, foot-binding in China, and veiling in Muslim societies. Numerous scholars have documented how representations of the domination of non-Western women by non-Western men were used to justify British and French imperialism (Ahmed 1992; Lazreg 1994; Liddle and Joshi 1989; Mani 1990). Colonial representations that reified male domination as "traditional" throughout the Third World ignored the ways in which colonialism, and the economic transformations that accompanied it, systematically oppressed both colonized women and men. It also ignored the ways that colonialism hurt women in particular by economically undermining what was an already vulnerable group and by subverting women's historical sources of power and autonomy. The symbolic importance of Algerian women's "oppression" in underpinning French colonialism was given physical form in a staged ceremony in which Algerian women were unveiled by French women in a symbolic enactment of the "enlightenment" of French rule. This ceremony was staged during the 1950s in response to the growing resistance to French rule by the Algerian nationalist party, the National Liberation Front (FLN), which itself included many women (Knauss 1987; Lazreg 1994). The reality of gender inequality in France – for instance, that French women were themselves not allowed to vote until after World War II – did not stop French women from being held up as the liberated ideal for Algerians.

Leila Ahmed argues that budding Euro-American feminist ideals were co-opted into the service of justifying colonial domination. She writes,

Even as the Victorian male establishment devised theories to contest the claims of feminism, and derided and rejected the ideas of feminism and the notion of men's oppressing women with respect to itself, it captured the language of feminism and redirected it, in the service of colonialism, toward Other men and the cultures of Other men. (1992: 151)

Ahmed addresses the ironies of this situation. She notes that Lord Cromer, the British consul general in Egypt at the turn of the century, wrote at length about the degraded status of Muslim women as epitomized by the veil and by sex segregation. It was this degradation that symbolized for him the cultural inferiority of Egyptian men and underscored the importance of the Western "civilizing" mission that could help Egyptians "develop" (Ahmed 1992: 153). Ahmed notes, however, that in England, Cromer was a founding member and even president of the Men's League for Opposing Women's Suffrage, and that in Egypt, he did little to implement educational policies that would help Egyptian women. Liddle and Joshi (1989) and Mani (1990) make similar arguments for colonial India. Mani argues that the debate over sati was less about women than about evaluating the worth of Hindu tradition in terms that would cast colonialism as a "civilizing" mission. Liddle and Joshi note that Katherine Mayo's 1927 book *Mother India*, which documented in detail male abuses of women, was used in England to justify the denial of self-rule to India (1989: 31).

What Ahmed labels "colonial feminism" was often replaced in the post-colonial era by "state feminism," in which many women's organizations were co-opted by national governments and staffed by female relatives of male politicians. For example, in Kenya the colonial government's women's organization, Maendeleo ya Wanawake, was later taken over by the national government (Robertson 1996: 633). Despite the centrality of women in many nationalist movements in the 1950s

and 1960s (and earlier in India), male nationalists were often ambivalent toward gender reform. In some cases, legal reforms affecting women were extremely limited as in Algeria and Egypt, or they were gestures offered by male politicians to demonstrate their countries' "modernity" (Hatem 1995; Kandiyoti 1991; Lazreg 1994). In the case of India, while male nationalists supported a women's movement that provided support for the nationalist cause, men were often hostile toward the reform of personal law that challenged the status quo within families (Liddle and Joshi 1989). As Kandiyoti suggests, in order to understand reactions to "feminism" in many Third World countries, it is necessary to understand the ways in which feminism has been co-opted and monopolized by ruling interests and elites in these countries (1991). Furthermore, focusing solely on formal "feminist" organizations obscures "indigenous" forms of feminism that do not necessarily accord with the middle-class Euro-American model (see also Ahmed 1989; Jayawardena 1986). For example, the activism of peasant, working-class, and minority women may be down-played when evaluated solely in terms of gender interests rather than the intersection of gender with ethnic and class issues. The reality that First and Third World women have different needs, concerns, and power bases, combined with the particular histories of feminism in former colonies (Kandiyoti 1991), has contributed to tensions in the midst of efforts to create an international women's movement (Moser 1991). Female genital operations have proven to be one of the most powerful fault lines along which such tensions erupt.

Gender and the Hardening of "Tradition"

Attention to colonial history reveals that cultural arguments can be a double-edged sword. While such arguments may be used to advocate tolerance in the face of difference, they may also be used to stifle change and impose or buttress particular culturally-defined power relationships. The conceptual fusing of women with culture and tradition has particular implications for women, who may become symbols in a battle to construct particular versions of "modern" or "traditional" society. This tendency is clear in the case of female genital operations. In Kenya in the late 1920s and early 1930s, missionaries of the Church of Scotland waged a campaign to stop the practice of clitoridectomy among the Kikuyu who lived in the area surrounding Nairobi. Clitoridectomy, which appeared to be on the wane despite its importance to the age-grade system, was revitalized and given new meaning not by "traditionalists," but by the young nationalists of the Kikuyu Central Association. As Pedersen notes,

As a defense of clitoridectomy became entangled with long-standing Kikuyu grievances about mission influence and access to land, clitoridectomy, always the sign of the "true Kikuyu," also came to be seen as a mark of loyalty to the incipient, as yet imaginary, nation. (1991: 651)

Although women's voices were largely unrecorded in this debate, Robertson suggests that the fight against the missionary ban on clitoridectomies was also related to the desire of Kikuyu elders and young militant men to control women's trading in Nairobi because it threatened male sexual and economic dominance (1996: 623). Jomo Kenyatta, leader of the Kikuyu Central Association and later the powerful first president of an independent Kenya, was himself a prominent cultural nationalist proponent of clitoridectomies. Kenyatta, who had been a student of the famous anthropologist Bronislaw Malinowski in England, positively portrayed and defended the practice in *Facing Mount Kenya*, an ethnographic study of his Kikuyu ethnic group (1959 [1938]).[20]

According to both Leila Ahmed (1992) and Lata Mani (1990), the association between women and tradition was in large part the result of the colonial legacy. Underlying much colonial thought (and much anthropology) has been the assumption that cultures are bounded, discrete units defined by ahistorical "traditions" or "customs" (Handler 1988). Ahmed argues that colonialist isolation of the veil as not simply the symbol, but the enactment par excellence, of Muslim cultural inferiority and degradation, positioned women as the ahistorical embodiment of that "tradition." She argues that this link between women and "tradition" was perpetuated by nationalists who in their fight for independence simply inverted the equation and instead championed the veil as the embodiment of religious and national identity (1992). Partha Chatterjee argues that Indian nationalists, operating under colonial control in public arenas, conceded Euro-American superiority in technological terms but came to view the "inner" world of domesticity and "tradition" associated with women as the sphere in which Indians could demonstrate their superiority, spiritually and culturally, over the West (1989, 1993; see also Kandiyoti 1991, Knauss 1987, and Lazreg 1994 for parallels in Middle Eastern and North African countries). Thus, while "tradition," codified in its most rigid and hierarchical form under British colonial law, was understood by the colonizers as both intrinsic to the character of the colonized and the embodiment of their inferiority, it was often inverted in its essentialist form by the colonized themselves to epitomize a cultural integrity and worth that was defined in highly gendered ways.

This association between women and culture-tradition has also meant that attempts to increase or maintain control over women are often argued in cultural terms, as demonstrated by a Kenyan legal case that attracted international attention in the 1980s (Cohen and Odhiambo 1992; Stamp 1991). This case pitted a socially prominent Kikuyu widow, Wambui Otieno, against her deceased husband's Luo patrilineage for the right to bury the body. This battle tapped deep tensions within Kenyan society, including the relations between Luo and Kikuyu ethnic groups, nuclear families versus patrilineages, and urban elites versus the rural poor. Nevertheless, the case was argued through an intertwined discourse of gender and "reified" tradition. The Otieno lawsuit encapsulated the same potentially contradictory meanings associated with "tradition," as have female genital operations, and it similarly pricked nationalist pride as the controversy circulated in the international media. Particularly when portrayed for international audiences, female genital operations have often been a symbol of "backwardness" and a source of "shame" to those in Third World countries who are concerned that their nations live up to Western-defined standards of "modernity."[21] At the same time, in a cultural nationalist tradition, defense of these practices has also served as a symbol of cultural integrity or resistance to Euro-American domination – ironically, a thoroughly "modern" position. What is disturbing to feminists, however, are the ways that attempts to create particular versions of cultural tradition may be translated into attempts to create, and thus control, particular kinds of women.

This association between women and hardened notions of "culture" and "tradition" is not limited to the so-called Third World. Kristin Koptiuch, for example, explores its implications in the use of "cultural defense" arguments in legal cases dealing with immigrants in the United States (1996). She cites a case in which a Chinese man living in Brooklyn murdered his wife for allegedly having an extramarital affair. His lawyers defended him on the grounds that his actions were dictated by his rural Chinese background, in which adultery brings great shame to a man and his ancestors – a position defended by an anthropologist brought in to offer expert testimony. The judge downgraded the charge from murder to manslaughter and gave him the lightest sentence possible – five years of probation, even though, as Koptiuch notes, he would have been sentenced for murder had he been living in China. Unfortunately, this case is not unusual; in the United States, many cases that make use of cultural defense arguments do so on behalf of men in instances of violence against women (Koptiuch 1996). To extrapolate from Koptiuch's argument, if cultural defense arguments are allowed to stand, the specter is also raised of a potential dismantling of protective legislation through the creation of innumerable exceptions. Such an escalation is possible because "cultural" arguments can be made not only for non-nationals, but also for numerous other racial, ethnic, religious, and other identity-based groups.

Koptiuch's argument carries implications for international debates over female genital oper-

ations. It suggests that the common responses to such practices – both the relativist argument, which privileges cultural tolerance, and the blatantly ethnocentric argument, which assumes the "backwardness" of African traditions and the inferiority of immigrants – carry male-dominant and colonial legacies based on hardened notions of tradition and culture. This raises difficult questions for feminist anthropologists: if we resort to cultural relativist arguments in the attempt to divert the racism embedded in much of the international outcry over female genital operations, do we end up undermining those African women who are themselves working to change these practices? Are we participating in leaving them exposed to charges that they are denigrating their own "traditions" and being culturally "inauthentic?" In using an uncritical notion of "culture," do we in fact create the same sense of difference, of estrangement from each other's lives and worlds, that is also generated in the flagrantly ethnocentric literature that opposes female genital operations?

Conclusion: Who Speaks?

Soon after the opening of the film *Warrior Marks* (1993), an op-ed piece appeared in the *New York Times* written by two African professional women, Seble Dawit and Salem Mekuria, with the named support of six others, all of whom oppose and have been working to abolish female genital operations. They wrote,

> We take great exception to the recent Western focus on female genital mutilation in Africa, most notably by the author Alice Walker.
>
> Ms. Walker's new film "Warrior Marks" portrays an African village where women and children are without personality, dancing and gazing blankly through some stranger's script of their lives. The respected elder women of the village's Secret Society turn into slit-eyed murderers wielding rusted weapons with which to butcher children.
>
> As is common in Western depictions of Africa, Ms. Walker and her collaborator, Pratibha Parmar, portray the continent as a monolith, African women and children are the props, and the village the background against which Alice

Walker, heroine-savior, comes to articulate their pain and condemn those who inflict it.

Like Ms. Walker's novel "Possessing the Secret of Joy," this film is emblematic of the Western feminist tendency to see female genital mutilation as the gender oppression to end all oppressions. Instead of being an issue worthy of attention in itself, it has become a powerfully emotive lens through which to view personal pain – a gauge by which to measure distance between the West and the rest of humanity. (1993)

They concluded by noting:

Neither Alice Walker nor any of us here can speak for them [African women on the continent]; but if we have the power and the resources, we can create the room for them to speak, and to speak with us as well. (1993)

Efua Dorkenoo, a woman of West African descent living in England, responded to Dawit and Mekuria's op-ed piece in an article that was signed as well by a number of other African professional women living in the West. The letter was printed in a special section of NOW's newsletter under the heading "African Women Speak Out on FGM [female genital mutilation]." Dorkenoo wrote,

The authors of . . . [the op-ed piece in the *New York Times*] made the mistake of presenting themselves as speaking on behalf of all African women. African women working on this problem come from different perspectives and different experiences. . . . If we Africans sincerely wish to see an end to this harmful practice, both in Africa and the West, we cannot rule out media coverage irrespective of how painful the memories of FGM might be. It is time that we stop blaming others and being hysterical whenever this subject is raised; rather we should focus on how to tap into international goodwill to stop this suffering of our girls. . . . Many may not care for Alice Walker's perspective on raising awareness of FGM, but at least we should be honest enough to acknowledge that her recent work is bringing the subject to the attention of a wider international audience. (1994)

That Dorkenoo and her supporters see Dawit and Mekuria as attempting to speak for *all* African women – despite their stated intention to the contrary – alerts us to the ongoing importance attached to "authentic voices" and the presumed ability of such voices to speak for others. This preoccupation with authentic voices stems from the recognition that such voices are widely considered persuasive in an Euro-American political discourse that focuses heavily on identity. At the same time, this exchange provides a graphic demonstration of the inadequacy of such a model. Obviously, there is no unified "voice" for African women, even among such a relatively distinct category of women as African professionals who oppose genital operations and live in Europe or the United States.

Poststructuralist feminist scholars like Judith Butler have criticized this preoccupation with identity politics (Butler 1990; Butler and Scott 1992). In a challenge similar to that posed against hardened understandings of "culture," Butler criticizes identity politics for building on and encouraging essentialism – that is, the reduction of complex human experiences and competing identities to static essences presumed to emanate from the unambiguous facts of gender, race, or nationality (1990). While historically, the concept of "culture" provided a space that allowed for respect and understanding of differences, "identity politics" has similarly provided dominated groups with an arena for organizing and demanding rights. If not problematized, however, the terms in which such claims are made can work to create new forms of oppression rather than greater liberation. Hardened conceptions of "culture" can suggest both insurmountable barriers between "us" and "them" and a predetermined "authenticity" to which individuals are pressured to conform. Similarly, a feminist politics based on identity can be reduced to a preoccupation with ever finer distinctions between categories of women, each presumed to be internally homogeneous. These questions are not theoretical niceties but reflect serious political concerns, particularly in this ever globalizing era. In the United States, where politics is often organized around identity and pleas for tolerance are made in the name of "multiculturalism," we need to know which understandings of "identity" and "culture" are at work. How, for example, do we interpret the calls being made for "cultural asylum" in cases like those of Oluloro and Kasinga? How can universalized conceptions of "human rights" be made to include "culture" and the particular situations that women find themselves in, without creating new cages for ourselves by reducing culture to coercion and identity to hardened essences?

In the effort to transcend "either/or" reactions to female genital operations that are limited to either moral outrage or cultural relativism, one initial step is to recognize that "female genital operations" – despite my own use of the phrase – do not exist as a category. To lump together the diverse forms of the practice into a bundle known as "female genital mutilation," "female circumcision," or "female genital operations" obscures the diverse geographic locations, meanings, and politics in which such practices are embedded, and rhetorically constitutes a generic "they" who conduct such practices and a generic "we" who do not. In offering an account of a particular place, Kikhome, my goal was not to provide a neatly argued social scientific account of the practice. Instead, my goal was to use this particular place at a particular point in time, as well as my encounters with some of the young women I knew there, as a means to explore the myriad issues surrounding female genital operations and to begin to phrase the kinds of questions that might help to elucidate these practices. Such questions range from symbolic meaning and individual psychology to the gendered politics of family organization, ethnic identity, colonial, and postcolonial states to the presumed links between women and culture-tradition.

The questions suggested by the situation in Kikhome, however, can just as productively illuminate the international controversies surrounding female genital operations. Just as we might explore the historical and political contexts in which clitoridectomies are embedded in Kikhome, and how such practices are both in and against the interests of young women there, we might ask related questions about the contexts in which international struggles around such practices occur. When and why do we exhibit relativistic tolerance toward female genital operations? In what contexts do we express moral outrage? How might our responses

hurt, as well as help, African women? How does the global politics of relationships between First and Third World countries, from the legacy of colonialism to contemporary global economics and population flows, shape our participation in these controversies? And, just as the young women in Kikhome might have strategically merged their "voices" with more powerful others like the church and state, so too can we ask how those of us participating in these international controversies are strategically merging our "voices" with one or more of the powerful discourses of feminism, cultural nationalism, relativism, humanism, and in some cases, to be blunt, racism. What are the histories of such discourses and to what ends are we using them?

Ultimately, however, the theoretical separation between clitoridectomy in Kikhome as ritual practice and the international controversy surrounding female genital operations as discourse is untenable. Discourse is also practice; it is not simply a way of understanding or thinking about the world, it is also a way of acting in it. Given that our discourse also signals a form of intervention, I would like to encourage feminists of whatever national origins, race, or gender to work against those assumptions being made in Western-oriented media accounts of female genital operations that reproduce colonial and neocolonial ideologies. Feminist anthropologists can also make a productive contribution by examining the social contexts of both ritual practices and international controversies and by exploring the power dynamics surrounding support and opposition to such practices, whether in rural African villages or urban France. For those interested in more hands-on styles of activism, critics of identity politics and hardened notions of culture are also pointing us in the direction of a feminist politics based on alliances and coalitions (Butler 1990; Haraway 1989; Mohanty 1991); hopefully, this brand of feminist politics will also be capable of critiquing practices such as clitoridectomy and infibulation without resorting to neocolonial ideologies of gender or denigrating the choices of women who support such practices. At the same time, Kenyan anthropologist Achola Pala-Okeyo cautions that "the role of [Western] feminists is not to be in front, leading the way for other women, but to be in the back *supporting* the other women's struggles to bring about change."[22] Here Pala-Okeyo forces us to recognize that all of us, along with the debates in which we are engaged, are products of tenacious power relationships with long histories. The hope is that we can bring this recognition to bear at the same time that we form alliances based on shared politics across boundaries of race, nationality, and gender.

NOTES

1   Dawit and Mekuria 1993; Dugger 1996a, 1996b; Raspberry 1993; Rosenthal 1992; Gregory 1994; *Nightline* 1996; *ABC World News Tonight* 1996; *Newsnight* 1994; *Dateline NBC* 1994; *All Things Considered* 1994. See also *CNN Specials* 1994a, 1994b; *Day One* 1993; *Morning Edition* 1993.

2   However, see Ellen Gruenbaum's article in the May 1995 edition of the *Anthropology Newsletter* of the American Anthropological Association. Panels were also held on "female circumcision" at the 1994 African Studies Association and American Anthropological Association meetings. Earlier research was done by Janice Boddy (1982) and Rose Oldfield Hayes (1975).

3   Despite the problematic aspects of the terms *First* and *Third* Worlds (problems include the assumption of hierarchy, the proclivity toward homogenization, and the attendant lack of specificity and historicity), I will nevertheless follow Mohanty et al. (1991) and retain this usage. Since this paper seeks to critique precisely these types of homogenizing and unhistorical tendencies, the continued use of *First* and *Third* Worlds here signals a desire to problematize rather than accept such assumptions.

4   Kikhome and all names mentioned herein are pseudonyms.

5   As Lila Abu-Lughod has argued, while the universalist presumptions of "humanism" must be problematized, the concept continues to hold value for anthropologists as

the "language of human equality with the most moral force..." (1991: 158).

6   Robertson notes that statistics may be based on the erroneous assumption that if some members of an ethnic group now practice genital operations or had in the past, then all members continue to do so today (1996: 61 n.2).

7   A recent *New York Times* article also described how some women in the United States, who at birth had their "abnormal" (often unusually large) clitorises surgically altered with detrimental effects on later sexual functioning, are protesting this medical practice (Angier 1997).

8   While some opponents of male circumcision also argue that removal of the foreskin decreases male sexual pleasure, the removal of the clitoris would be more equivalent to the amputation of the penis (for example, Toubia 1994: 712). It is not often discussed in the literature, however, how women who have had such procedures experience their sexuality. The more radical procedure of infibulation, which includes not only the removal of the clitoris and labia but the sewing together of the remaining tissues, commonly leads to painful sexual intercourse, and Boddy notes that many women she spoke to in the Sudan avoided intercourse for this reason (1982). On the other hand, Nahid Toubia, a Sudanese doctor who opposes the practice, cautions that "the assumption that all circumcised women have sexual problems or are unable to achieve orgasm is not substantiated by research or anecdotal evidence" (1994: 714). She notes that the "ability of women to compensate for it [infibulation] through other sensory areas or emotions and fantasy is not well understood" (1994: 714; see also Lightfoot-Klein 1989). Although there has been much concern by opponents of female genital operations with the psychological impact of genital operations (for example, Walker 1992; Walker and Parmar 1993), this impact would obviously depend heavily on the social context and meanings that individuals attribute to such practices. Toubia does state that in

her clinical experience in the Sudan many infibulated women seem to experience anxiety relating to their genitals. Presumably, the impact of such procedures would be very different for those women raised in Euro-American countries, where such practices are not prevalent and would be socially stigmatizing rather than valued. African women in France who have organized against the practices argue that "circumcised" adolescent girls living there experience "enormous psychosexual problems" (MODEFEN 1982, quoted in Winter 1994; Thiam 1978).

9 I was teaching under the auspices of the World Teach Program, a nongovernmental, US-based organization that helps college graduates find international teaching positions.

10 For a similar description among the Sebei, a subgroup of the Sabaot, see Goldschmidt 1976 and 1986.

11 See Goldschmidt 1986.

12 However, there were secret aspects of the initiation of which I would remain unaware. Goldschmidt (1986) describes a ceremony among the Sebei which parallels those of secret societies in other parts of Africa and which is closely guarded from the uninitiated or from the opposite sex. He states that at the end of the recuperation period, the night before the cave ceremony in the hills, initiates are taken out individually into the "bush" and frightened with a replica of an animal (a leopard for girls and a lion for boys), accompanied by noise produced by twirling a stick, one end of which is attached to the head of a drum or a bull-roarer. After receiving scratches from the animal that mark one as being initiated, they are "introduced" to the animal, learning its secret.

13 However, the public circumcision ceremony of the *bris* is performed on Jewish male babies in the United States.

14 Tellingly, Goldschmidt relates that women continue to hold the clan affiliation of their fathers, but Sebei men state that wives take the clan affiliation of their husband (1976: 87).

15 For further information, see note 8.

16 This practice bears a striking resemblance to that described for the Kikuyu, among whom young women were also excised. See Kenyatta 1959 [1938].

17 Also see Pedersen 1991.

18 The first wave of feminism emerged in the United States at roughly the turn of the century.

19 Author's interview with Dr Constance Sutton at New York University, May 10, 1995.

20 This issue is further explored by East African author Ngugi wa Thiong'o in his 1965 novel *The River Between*.

21 For example, in an interview with CNN in 1994, Egyptian President Hosni Mubarak attempted to dismiss the topic by stating (inaccurately) that female "circumcision" was rarely performed in Egypt. Similarly, a top Nigerian official in the United States described Lydia Oluloro's plea for asylum in 1994 as calculated to "denigrate the image of Nigeria," arguing that female "circumcision," "in the very few cases where it is still practiced," was done with the consent of those involved (Jaya Dayal, "Nigerian Official Calls Mother's Plea Calculated." Inter Press Third World News Agency, listserv message, March 26, 1994). Seble Dawit (1994) noted that the Nigerian Embassy submitted a protest to the US court that the practice of female genital mutilation was unheard of in Nigeria (although about half of Nigerian women undergo female genital operations) and that Oluloro was vilified and called a traitor by many Africans.

22 Dr Achola Pala-Okeyo was responding to recent media accounts of Euro-American feminist responses to female genital operations in an interview with Dr Constance Sutton at New York University, April 15, 1994.

REFERENCES

ABC World News Tonight. 1996. African Woman Seeks Asylum from Genital Mutilation. April 29.

Abu-Lughod, Lila. 1991. Writing against Culture. In *Recapturing Anthropology*. Richard

Fox, ed. pp. 137–62. Santa Fe, NM: School of American Research Press. [This volume, ch. 7.]

African Studies Association. 1984. Position Paper of the Women's Caucus on Clitoridectomy and Infibulation. October 30–November 2, Los Angeles.

Ahmed, Leila. 1989. Feminism and Cross-Cultural Inquiry: The Terms of Discourse in Islam. In *Coming to Terms: Feminism, Theory, Politics*. Elizabeth Weed, ed. pp. 143–51. New York: Routledge.

—— 1992. *Women and Gender in Islam: Roots of a Historical Debate*. New Haven, CT: Yale University Press.

Alloula, Malek. 1986. *The Colonial Harem*. Minneapolis: University of Minnesota Press.

All Things Considered. 1994. Activists Denounce Female Genital Mutilation. National Public Radio, March 23.

Angier, Natalie. 1997. New Debate Over Surgery on Genitals. *New York Times*, May 13: C1, C6.

Boddy, Janice. 1982. Womb as Oasis: The Symbolic Context of Pharaonic Circumcision in Rural Northern Sudan. *American Ethnologist*, 9: 682–98.

Boon, James A. 1994. Circumscribing Circumcision/Uncircumcision: An Essay amidst the History of Difficult Description. In *Implicit Understanding*. Stuart B. Schwartz, ed. pp. 556–85. Cambridge: Cambridge University Press.

Boyarin, Jonathan. 1996. Self-exposure as Theory: The Double Mark of the Male Jew. In *Thinking in Jewish* by Jonathan Boyarin. Chicago: University of Chicago Press.

Butler, Judith. 1990. *Gender Trouble: Feminism and the Subversion of Identity*. New York: Routledge.

Butler, Judith, and Joan Scott, eds. 1992. *Feminists Theorize the Political*. New York: Routledge.

CNN Specials. 1994a. Beyond the Numbers – Part 1. Female Circumcision. September 7.

—— 1994b Beyond the Numbers – Part 2. Egypt's Hosni Mubarak. September 9.

Chatterjee, Partha. 1989. Colonialism, Nationalism, and Colonialized Women: The Contest in India. *American Ethnologist*, 16: 622–33.

—— 1993. *The Nation and its Fragments: Colonial and Postcolonial Histories*. Princeton, NJ: Princeton University Press.

Cohen, David, and E. S. Atieno Odhiambo. 1992. *Burying SM: The Politics of Knowledge and the Sociology of Power in Africa*. Portsmouth, NH: Heinemann.

Corbin, Beth. 1994. Deportation vs. Female Genital Mutilation. *National NOW Times* Special Edition, June: 5.

Daly, Mary. 1978. African Genital Mutilation: The Unspeakable Atrocities. In *Gyn/Ecology: The Metaethics of Radical Feminism*. Boston: Beacon Press.

Dateline NBC. 1994. Lydia's Choice. March 22.

Dawit, Seble. 1994. African Women in the Diaspora and the Problem of Female Genital Mutilation. Address presented to the Women's Caucus, 37th Annual Meeting of the African Studies Association, November 19.

Dawit, Seble, and Salem Mekuria. 1993. The West Just Doesn't Get It. *New York Times*, December 7: A27.

Day One. 1993. Scarred for Life. ABC, September 20.

Dorkenoo, Efua. 1994. African Women Speak Out on FGM. *National NOW Times* Special Edition, June: 11.

Dugger, Celia W. 1996a. Women's Pleas for Asylum Puts Tribal Ritual on Trial. *New York Times*, April 15: A1, B4.

—— 1996b. U.S. Frees African Fleeing Ritual Mutilation. *New York Times*, April 25: A1, B7.

Egan, Timothy. 1994. An Ancient Ritual and a Mother's Asylum Plea. *New York Times*, March 4: A25 (Law Section).

El Saadawi, Nawal. 1980. *The Hidden Face of Eve*. London: Zed Books.

Epstein, Barbara. 1981. *The Politics of Domesticity*. Middletown, CT: Wesleyan University Press.

Gates, Henry Louis. 1994. A Liberalism of Heart and Spine. *New York Times*, March 27: D17.

Gluckman, Max. 1963. The Role of the Sexes in Wiko Circumcision Ceremonies. In *Social Structure Studies presented to A. R. Radcliffe-Brown*. M. Fortes, ed. pp. 145–67. New York: Russell and Russell, Inc.

Goldschmidt, Walter. 1976. *Culture and Behavior of the Sebei: A Study in Continuity and Adaptation*. Berkeley: University of California Press.

—— 1986. *The Sebei: A Study in Adaptation*. New York: Holt, Rinehart, and Winston.

Gordon, Daniel. 1991. Female Circumcision and Genital Operations in Egypt and the Sudan: A Dilemma for Medical Anthropology. *Medical Anthropology Quarterly*, 5: 3–14.

Gordon, Linda. 1977. *Woman's Body, Woman's Right: A Social History of Birth Control in America*. New York: Penguin.

Gould, Stephen Jay. 1985. The Hottentot Venus. In *The Flamingo's Smile: Reflections in Natural History* by Stephen Jay Gould. New York: Norton.

Gregory, Sophfronia Scott. 1994. At Risk of Mutilation. *Time*, March 21: 45–6.

Griaule, Marcel. 1965. *Conversations with Ogotommeli*. Oxford: Oxford University Press.

Gruenbaum, Ellen. 1995. Women's Rights and Cultural Self-Determination in the Female Genital Mutilation Controversy. *Anthropology Newsletter*, 36/5: 14–15.

Handler, Richard. 1988. *Nationalism and the Politics of Culture in Quebec*. Madison: University of Wisconsin Press.

Haraway, Donna. 1989. A Manifesto for Cyborgs. In *Coming to Terms*. Elizabeth Weed, ed. pp. 173–204. New York: Routledge.

Harcourt, Wendy. 1988. Gender, Culture and Reproduction: North–South. *Development*, 2/3: 66–8.

Hatem, Mervat. 1995. The Modernist Credentials of Egyptian Islamism. Paper presented at conference on "Women, Culture, Nation: Egyptian Moments." New York University, Kevorkian Center for Middle Eastern Studies, April 7.

Hayes, Rose Oldfield. 1975. Female Genital Mutilation, Fertility Control, Women's Roles, and the Patrilineage in Modern Sudan: A Functional Analysis. *American Ethnologist*, 2: 617–33.

Hosken, Fran P. 1981. Female Genital Mutilation and Human Rights. *Feminist Issues*, (summer): 3–23.

Jayawardena, Kumari. 1986. *Feminism and Nationalism in the Third World*. London: Zed Books.

Kandiyoti, Deniz, ed. 1991. *Women, Islam and the State*. Philadelphia: Temple University Press.

Kenyatta, Jomo. 1959 [1938]. *Facing Mount Kenya*. London: Secker and Warburg.

Knauss, Peter R. 1987. *The Persistence of Patriarchy: Class, Gender and Ideology in Twentieth Century Algeria*. New York: Praeger.

Koptiuch, Kristin. 1996. "Cultural Defense" and Criminological Displacements: Gender, Race and (Trans)Nation in the Legal Surveillance of U.S. Diaspora Asians. In *Displacement, Diaspora and Geographies of Identity*. Smadar Lavie and Ted Swedenburg, eds. pp. 215–33. Durham, NC: Duke University Press.

Kouba, Leonard J., and Judith Muasher. 1985. Female Circumcision in Africa: An Overview. *African Studies Review*, 28/1: 95–110.

Lazreg, Marnia. 1994. *The Eloquence of Silence: Algerian Women in Question*. New York: Routledge.

Liddle, Joanna, and Rama Joshi. 1989. *Daughters of Independence: Gender, Caste and Class in India*. New Brunswick, NJ: Rutgers University Press.

Lightfoot-Klein, Hanny. 1989. *Prisoners of Ritual: An Odyssey into Female Genital Circumcision in Africa*. New York: Haworth Press.

Mani, Lata. 1990. Contentious Traditions: The Debate on Sati in Colonial India. In *Recasting Women: Essays in Indian Colonial History*. Kumkum Sangari and Sudesh Vaid, eds. pp. 88–126. New Brunswick, NJ: Rutgers University Press.

Mayo, Katherine. 1927. *Mother India*. New York: Harcourt, Brace and Company.

MODEFEN (Mouvement pour la Défense des Droits de la Femme Noire). 1982. Sur l'infibulation et l'excision en Afrique. *Bulletin de l'Association Française des Anthropologues*, 9: 50–4.

Mohanty, Chandra Talpade. 1991. Introduction: Cartographies of Struggle: Third World Women and the Politics of Feminism.

In *Third World Women and the Politics of Feminism*. Chandra Talpade Mohanty, Ann Russo, and Lourdes Torres, eds. pp. 1–47. Bloomington: Indiana University Press.

Mohanty, Chandra Talpade, Ann Russo, and Lourdes Torres, eds. 1991. *Third World Women and the Politics of Feminism*. Bloomington: Indiana University Press.

Moraga, Cherrie, and Gloria Anzaldua. 1981. *This Bridge Called My Back: Writings by Radical Women of Color*. Watertown, MA: Persephone Press.

Morgan, Robin, and Gloria Steinem. 1983. The International Crime of Genital Mutilation. In *Outrageous Acts and Everyday Rebellions* by Gloria Steinem. New York: Holt, Rinehart, and Winston.

Morning Edition. 1993. New Book and Film Deals with Female Genital Mutilation. National Public Radio, December 7.

Moser, Caroline. 1991. Gender Planning in the Third World. In *Gender and International Relations*. Rebecca Grant and Kathleen Newland, eds. pp. 83–121. Bloomington: Indiana University Press.

National Organization for Women. 1994. Special Edition of the *National NOW Times*, June: 1–12.

Newsnight. 1994. Nigerian Says Daughters Face Mutilation if Deported. CNN, March 23.

Ngugi wa Thiong'o. 1965. *The River Between*. Nairobi and London: Heinemann.

Nightline. 1996. Female Genital Mutilation and Political Asylum. ABC, May 2.

Ong, Aihwa. 1988. Feminism and the Critique of Colonial Discourse. *Inscriptions*, 3/4: 79–93.

Parmar, Pratibha. 1993a. Pratibha's Journey. In *Warrior Marks*. Alice Walker and Pratibha Parmar, co-authors. pp. 99–238. New York: Harcourt Brace.

——, director and producer. 1993b. *Warrior Marks*. Debra Hauer and Alice Walker, executive producers. Our Daughters Have Mothers, Inc.

Pedersen, Susan. 1991. National Bodies, Unspeakable Acts: The Sexual Politics of Colonial Policy-making. *Journal of Modern History*, 63 (December): 647–80.

Ramazanoglu, Caroline. 1989. *Feminism and the Contradictions of Oppression*. London: Routledge.

Raspberry, William. 1993. Women and a Brutal Tradition. *Washington Post*, November 8: A21.

Richards, Audrey. 1956. *Chisungu: A Girl's Initiation Ceremony in Zambia*. London: Tavistock.

Robertson, Claire. 1996. Grassroots in Kenya: Women, Genital Mutilation, and Collective Action, 1920–1990. *Signs*, 21/31: 615–42.

Rosenthal, A. M. 1992. On My Mind: Female Genital Torture. *New York Times*, December 29: A15.

Spivak, Gayatri Chakravorty. 1988. Can the Subaltern Speak? In *Marxism and the Interpretation of Culture*. Cary Nelson and Lawrence Grossberg, eds. pp. 271–313. Basingstoke, England: Macmillan Education.

Stamp, Patricia. 1991. Burying Otieno: The Politics of Gender and Ethnicity in Kenya. *Signs*, 16/4: 808–45.

Strathern, Marilyn. 1987. An Awkward Relationship: The Case of Feminism and Anthropology. *Signs*, 12/2: 276–92.

Thiam, Awa. 1978. *La parole aux négresses*. Paris: Denoel/Conthier.

Tokarczyk, Michelle M., and Elizabeth A. Fay. 1993. *Working-Class Women in the Academy*. Amherst: University of Massachusetts Press.

Toubia, Nahid. 1994. Female Circumcision as a Public Health Issue. New England Journal of Medicine 331/11: 712–16.

Turner, Victor. 1970. *The Forest of Symbols*. Ithaca, NY: Cornell University Press.

Van Gennep, Arnold. 1909. *The Rites of Passage*. London: Routledge and Kegan Paul.

Walker, Alice. 1992. *Possessing the Secret of Joy*. New York: Harcourt Brace Jovanovich.

Walker, Alice, and Pratibha Parmar. 1993. *Warrior Marks: Female Genital Mutilation and the Sexual Blinding of Women*. New York: Harcourt, Brace and Company.

Weil-Curiel, Linda. 1994. Mali Woman Challenges International Law. *National NOW Times* Special Edition, June: 5.

Winter, Bronwyn. 1994. Women, the Law, and Cultural Relativism in France: The Case of Excision. *Signs*, 19/4: 939–74.

18

Imagining the Unborn in the Ecuadoran Andes

Lynn M. Morgan

> Fetal personhood is not a "property" that can or will be "discovered" with greater
> scientific knowledge or increased technological capabilities, but is produced in and
> through the very practices that claim merely to "reveal" it.
>
> Valerie Hartouni, "Fetal Exposures: Abortion Politics and the Optics of Allusion,"
> *Camera Obscura*, May 1992

Fetuses are rapidly being granted the status of cultural icons, present not only in the industrialized West but also as actors on the international reproductive rights scene.[1] It is useful, then, for feminists to attend to the diverse cultural, national, and political contexts within which persons are brought into social being. In the above epigraph, Valerie Hartouni argues that "fetal persons" are produced through social practices which themselves constitute and reify the category. This article looks at how women in highland Ecuador imagine and talk about the unborn and how their social practices might illuminate the processes through which fetuses are "naturalized" in the United States.

"Fetal persons" have for several years now been the subject of vigorous public debate in the United States, as physicians disagree over the wisdom of treating fetal "patients," lawyers struggle over the status of embryos fertilized in vitro and other fetal "plaintiffs" not recognized by the Constitution as legal persons, policymakers dispute the wisdom of mandatory prenatal testing and appropriate custody arrangements for offspring of multiple "parents," and the general public argues over whether fetuses can or should be treated as social subjects.[2] The discourses themselves are constitutive; in other words, the more we puzzle over fetuses, the more we legitimate the subject, and, by extension, the subjectivity, of the "fetal person." What is particularly striking about many of the U.S. debates is the extent to which popular appropriations of science help to constitute fetal subjects. Prolife activists in the United States often call upon the authority of science to support biologically deterministic models of when and how life begins. Rarely, however, do we recognize the

From Lynn M. Morgan, "Imagining the Unborn in the Ecuadoran Andes," pp. 323–50 in *Feminist Studies*, 23/2 (1997). Reprinted by permission of the publisher, Feminist Studies, Inc.

extent to which the popularization of science is manipulated to support a personification of fetuses, and rarely do we recognize how unique this is to American culture.

This article reflects on the uniqueness of U.S. abortion discourse by juxtaposing it against a landscape in which fetuses are generally *not* considered persons. In the Ecuadoran highlands where I have conducted anthropological fieldwork, women and men employ a variety of social practices that obscure and impede the possibility that fetuses will be granted personhood. This results not simply from differential access to sophisticated scientific or technological knowledge or equipment but also from a constellation of embedded social practices that render the contents of the womb as ambiguous and uncertain. In Ecuador, the course of pregnancy is governed by women themselves, who use overlapping and sometimes competing discourses to make sense of their own circumstances and the will of God. Even when the highland women use ultrasound screening, they do not personify or individualize fetuses the way people do in the United States; in fact, the women I interviewed rarely used the word *feto*, preferring *criatura* (creature) or *venidero* (the one to come). By looking more closely at constructions of pregnancy and the unborn in Ecuador, I hope to interrogate and destabilize certain scientized suppositions about what people take as the biological "nature" of fetuses in the United States.[3]

The Emergence of Fetal Persons

In the United States today, the right-to-life movement and right-wing cultural critics use popular understandings of science to invent and reinforce a unified "fetal subject" at multiple sites and at several levels of analysis: historical, rhetorical, visual, and cultural. They rely on the popular interpretation and widespread utilization of ultrasonography, intrauterine electron microscopy, and new reproductive technologies, for example, to support their contention that "life begins at conception" and that "the fetus" is a gradually emerging person endowed with genetic

uniqueness and biological facticity. To phrase the social relationship between the born and the unborn in biological terms, as they do, is "in effect an ideological mechanism to turn social facts into natural and therefore immutable facts."[4] The social practices that hitch scientific authority to the prolife cause have worked to keep the abortion debate focused on fetuses by emphasizing (and often literally illustrating) that "the fetus" is a miraculously complex biological entity. The success of this prolife political strategy, however, should not keep us from noticing that the practices that contribute to the social construction of the fetal subject are multiple, omnipresent, overlapping, and culturally particular.

Examples of the social practices that constitute fetuses come from the fields of medicine, ethics, religion, journalism, law, technology, entertainment, politics, and the academy. Some of them have global ambitions, as manifested, for example, in the work of the internationally oriented prolife organization, Human Life International. Some social practices associated with fetal personhood are nationally specific; for example, in Ireland where the contents of women's wombs have become implicated in debates over membership in the European community.[5] Some of the practices are large, public assertions of fetal personhood, such as Operation Rescue demonstrations (broadcast throughout the world on CNN) or anti-abortion bill-boards featuring ten-foot photographs of disembodied fetuses. Other constitutive practices occur in private: a pregnant woman thumbs through *What to Expect When You're Expecting* looking for a drawing that corresponds to the gestational age of the fetus she carries, so she can fit a visual image to the fluttering in her womb. Simple conversations among coworkers or friends can create fetal personhood, such as discussions among members of a medical team debating the ethics of intervening surgically given a diagnosis of fetal abnormality.[6] When physicians and midwives use ultrasound or fetal monitoring, for example, they enact the importance of fetal well-being. When pregnant women and their partners ascertain fetal sex and use that knowledge to name and personify an unborn child, they construct the fetus as a valued member of the family. When entertainment magazines print stories about unborn "celebrity children," they contribute to the personification of fetuses.[7] Over the past ten years, "fetal persons" have emerged from the realm of obstetricians' and ethicists' offices into popular culture, where they feature in film, print, and advertising.[8] Fetuses are depicted so regularly in everyday U.S. culture that their presence – outside the context of pregnant women's bodies – is scarcely remarkable anymore. Their presence has come to be accepted, by many, as natural.[9] The social value attributed to fetuses is accentuated in the United States by low fertility rates, which make each pregnancy and child seem more precious, and by access to contraception which insures that many U.S. women have less experience with unchecked fertility (and pregnancy losses) than their Ecuadoran counterparts.

The cumulative effect of these social circumstances is that North Americans have begun – in historically unprecedented ways – to individualize, personify, and sometimes even glorify and prize fetuses as "super-subjects."[10] Of course, the personification of the fetal subject is not uncritically endorsed by all segments of the U.S. population, and there is considerable disagreement about the status of fetal subjects, pregnancy, parenthood, and reproduction. U.S. reproductive ethics debates are too complex, diverse, and cross-cutting to be reduced to some monolithic "cultural norms." Nonetheless, the recent historical trend toward reification of the fetal subject is striking if the United States is compared even with other Western societies. It is my hope that the cross-cultural comparison I offer here can help us to realize the many ways in which "the fetus we know" is historically and culturally unique.

Methods

This study was motivated by my conviction that a comparative anthropological perspective on abortion and fetal personhood in non-Western societies might point out the culture-bound nature of U.S. reproductive rights debates. In particular, I was motivated by the obsession in my own country with the relationship between ideas about fetal personhood and the morality of abortion. But of course this link proved to be too tight, and too tightly American, because "abortion" is the end product of a long chain of social circumstances. In 1988 I spent two months in the Andean town of San Gabriel (pop. 10,000), Carchi Province, Ecuador, about four hours by car north of Quito, the capital. In San Gabriel and surrounding hamlets, I conducted semistructured interviews (tape-recorded, of one to two hours in duration) with thirty mestizo women. Interviews were arranged by my research assistant, Blanca, a twenty-year-old woman who had grown up in this blustery, potato-growing region (where people referred to themselves as borregos, or sheep, because they have a reputation as followers rather than leaders, and because warm woolen clothes help people to stay warm at 10,000 feet). Blanca and I ventured out each morning, sometimes trudging up and down the hills of town on foot, and sometimes hitching a ride into surrounding hamlets, to interview women in their homes. We took advantage of the midmorning lull in a woman's workday to ask her, indirectly, about her perceptions of the unborn by asking about her own fertility history; experience with pregnancy, birth, and child death; and her knowledge of local reproductive ethics. On our way back to the center of town, we would often stop in the cemetery, coffin-maker's shop, vital statistics registry, or health clinic. In 1992 I returned to Ecuador to spend six months in Quito, where I conducted an equal number of interviews with physicians, nurses, midwives and midwifery students, clergy, and members of local women's organizations. The research was designed to investigate the relationship between ideas about fetal identity, development, and personhood, and the morality and practice of induced abortion.

I had initially assumed that a country not polarized by public debate over abortion might endorse a cultural consensus about the moral status of the unborn. Unlike the United States, Ecuador has no history of public controversy over abortion. No public initiatives, past or present, have sought to liberalize church or state positions on abortion. I interpreted the lack of dissent as a reflection of unanimity and looked for the consensus I imagined must exist. My assumption, of course, implied a unified and coherent image of what a fetus is, and this assumption turned out to be highly problematic, as I show throughout this article. In San Gabriel, the fetus was never regarded separately from the pregnant woman, and women's stories about the events of pregnancy and the status of the unborn were as diverse as their experiences. In Quito I found a near-complete void on the subject of abortion and fetuses. I found no pictures of fetuses in magazines or newspapers, only one sensationalist episode of a television talk show focusing on women who had had abortions and the trauma and shame they had experienced. This focus highlighted the woman's ethical standing but not that of the fetus. There were no locally made movies about abortion or intrauterine development (although a dubbed version of *The Silent Scream* was occasionally aired on television). What I found, and what is described below, is that pregnant women are fused with and inseparable from the creatures they gestate. Consequently, responses to my questions about fetuses generated a great deal of incertitude and ambivalence. People often did not hold ready-formed opinions on these subjects, and they frequently disagreed among themselves. I quickly abandoned the search for a cultural consensus, even among the relatively homogeneous Catholic mestizo women in San Gabriel. The emphasis on consistency, I realized, was of course particular to the United States, where we privilege philosophies and narratives that can boast moral consistency. In the push to find consistency, scientific observations of fetal development are mustered to create representations of "the fetus" as a coherent biological "thing."

The focus on consistency is evident when anti-abortion activists who favor capital punishment – and prochoice proponents who oppose it – are criticized as hypocrites. Meanwhile, the moral high road is claimed by advocates of a "seamless web" philosophy, who preach respect for the right to life of all living things, including animals, murderers, and the unborn. In contrast, many of the Ecua-dorans I spoke with did not attempt to construct a consistent response in answer to my probing questions about fetal status. Their social and political milieu does not require that they strive for confident or coherent answers to such complex and vexing issues. Several people patiently explained that ambiguity and uncertainty made perfect sense when confronted with life's most profound mysteries. It led me to wonder why, in my country, we insist on erasing the mysterious, on knowing what is, perhaps, ultimately unknowable.

Ecuador and the Liminal Unborn

There are many reasons why North Americans might assume that Latin Americans respect the unborn. *Clandestine Abortion: A Latin American Reality* states that in "every country but Cuba, legal abortion is rarely available except for the strictest medical reasons."[11] The region has been dominated by Catholicism for 500 years, and the Vatican has become an increasingly ardent proponent of fetal personhood over the past twenty years.[12] Loyal Latin American Catholics are sometimes heard to say that they will bear "as many children as God will send" (*los que Dios me mande*). It would be a mistake, however, to conclude on the basis of these stereotypes that Latin Americans subscribe to the notion that fetuses are persons. Because "the fetus" is a culturally specific conceptual entity and not a biological "thing," and because "the fetus" is created in particular cultural circumstances, I realized that I would have to stop thinking and speaking about "the fetus" if I was to understand how the unborn are imagined in Ecuador.

In the rural highlands of northern Ecuador, the unborn are imagined as liminal, unripe, and unfinished creatures. Nascent persons are brought into being slowly, through processes rife with uncertainty and moral ambiguity. Adults are slow to assign individual identity and personhood to the not-yet-born and the newly born. These *criaturas*, as they are often called, bear little resemblance to disembodied, technologized, visualized, personified, and revered U.S. fetuses. These unknown, unknowable *criaturas* may teeter on the cusp of personhood for months before being fully welcomed into a human community. I will argue that in Ecuador social practices reinforce and perpetuate fetal liminality, insuring that personhood will not be easily attributed to the unborn. This article describes several of the social practices that encode, reaffirm, and perpetuate the notion that the unborn are not persons, that they remain ambiguous and liminal.

First, although abortion is illegal and rhetorically condemned by both church and state, there is little enforcement of anti-abortion laws (although the full extent of reliance on induced abortion is unknown). Second, there seems to be a large dose of social ambiguity built into determining "who counts" as the unborn come into social being. All Ecuadoran women do not count their children in the same ways nor employ the same conventions to number their babies. The civil registry does not have well-established or well-enforced procedures for counting live births, fetal deaths, or infant deaths. Third, there is no apparent social consensus for determining how to handle fetal death, including, for example, the baptismal, naming, and burial rites appropriate to miscarried, aborted, or stillborn fetuses. Indeed, a special category of liminal quasi-person (the *auca*) exists in the rural highlands to encompass unbaptized souls and other not-quite-persons. Fourth, induced abortion is characterized by many as a sin, but it is a sin of self-mutilation rather than murder. At issue is the mutilation of the pregnant woman's own body, not the personhood of the fetus. Fifth, beliefs about the course of fetal development range across a wide spectrum. Women contradict each other about when the fetus is "formed" and whether and how formation might affect the morality of abortion. The indeterminacy of the beginnings of life extend to the postpartum period; newborns are often described as still in the process of becoming, not yet fully human. Sixth, it seems that the work of "building personhood" at the beginnings of life is largely a female responsibility; women are predominantly responsible for bringing persons into being. As in the United States, each of these social practices has a particular context in which it is invoked, but the frames of discourse invariably overlap and reinforce each other. The cumulative effect of these social practices in Ecuador is that the unborn remain predominantly blurred, inchoate, and incipient.

An Open Secret: Illegal Abortion

Un secreto a voces (an open secret) is how many people in Ecuador describe the availability of abortion. Abortion is officially illegal but nonetheless widely available. Estimates of abortion rates are unreliable in Ecuador, as elsewhere in Latin America, for at least two reasons. First, most estimates are based on numbers of women hospitalized with complications resulting from a combination of both spontaneous and induced abortions. Of abortions registered by hospitals surveyed in Quito, 98 to 99 percent were classified as "type unspecified [i.e., spontaneous vs. induced] and others."[13] Second, hospital-based figures can capture only those women with access to health services, thus excluding much of the rural population, and do not reflect the numbers of women whose abortions are successful and safe. The few existing studies of abortion rates in Ecuador have concentrated on data collection and analysis techniques and do not attempt to estimate the rates per se.[14]

The Ecuadoran Constitution (Article 25) was changed in 1978 to specify that "a child will be protected from conception onward." Similarly, the Civil Code (Article 61) specifies that "the law protects the life of the unborn" (*del que está por nacer*), and the Penal Code (Articles 441 through 447) specifies the penalties for abortion. Ecuadoran law allows abortion under only two circumstances: to save the life of a woman, or when pregnancy is the result of the rape of a mentally ill woman (*mujer idiota o demente*).[15] In what seems a vestige from a more chivalrous era, the penalty for induced abortion can be reduced if a judge determines that the abortion was performed "to protect a woman's honor" (*aborto honoris causa*). The fact that abortion providers and clients are infrequently prosecuted in Ecuador suggests that the practice of abortion is tolerated by a state apparatus that protects the unborn only at the level of rhetoric.

Ecuadorans might continue to have abortion both illegal and widely available as long as the issue remains below the surface of public discourse.[16] Occasionally a newspaper article or television talk show will give journalists, politicians, or clergy an opportunity to condemn abortion, but their bluster is generally treated as requisite occupational rhetoric rather than a realistic recipe for action. (One thoughtful priest, for example, told me that Vatican doctrine is too rigid to apply to the complex circumstances faced by his parishioners.) Occasionally I noted an oblique reference to abortion in the sardonic, ephemeral graffiti found around Quito (such as *crece, crece, hombrecito, hay un aborto esperando por ti,* "grow, grow, little man, there's an abortion waiting for you"). Apart from these quixotic commentaries, however, there is no public debate over abortion in Ecuador. No one calls for more rigorous enforcement of antiabortion laws, and only a few Ecuadoran women's rights activists argue that abortion should be "decriminalized" (*descriminalizado* or *despenalizado,* as distinct from "legalized").

Those who do point out that decriminalization would stop people from profiting from women's misfortunes, prevent the complications that result from clandestine abortion, and reduce the maternal mortality rate and the hospital costs associated with treating abortion complications.[17] Once again, their focus is not on the fetus. Their views, however, are not representative of the public stance taken by many other Ecuadoran women's rights activists. The activists I spoke with in Quito said that the women's movement could not be advanced by making a public issue of abortion at this time. Such a strategy could easily backfire, they said, leaving women worse off than they currently are.

For the purposes of this article, the public and legal domains are significant for what they omit. Abortion is an issue in Ecuador, however covert; but fetal personhood is not. Fetuses are notoriously absent from the *sotto voce* conversations I had with Ecuadorans about abortion. There is virtually no mention of maternal-fetal conflict, nor of "fetal rights." The state's tacit acceptance of clandestine abortion could be viewed as society's pragmatic way of acknow-

ledging that circumstances sometimes compel women to terminate their pregnancies despite the legal and social stigma. The law purports to value and protect fetal life and personhood, but lack of enforcement of antiabortion laws belies the state's commitment. Fetuses may be theoretical persons by Ecuadoran law, but in social practice there are no fetal persons.

Numbering the Babies

One way to ascertain the social importance granted to fetuses and infants is to look at whether and how they are enumerated. In this section I argue that the distinction between fetuses and infants is blurred and imprecise in Ecuador, as manifested by how women in San Gabriel enumerate their own offspring and by how civil registration procedures both perpetuate and reinforce this uncertainty.

The women I interviewed in San Gabriel did not share among themselves a common method for enumerating their offspring. When I asked, *¿Cuántos hijos tiene usted?* ("How many children do you have?"), some women interpreted *hijos* to mean "pregnancies," in which case all pregnancies – including miscarriages – figured among a woman's "children." But to others *hijos* meant "children born alive" or "living children." The point always required clarification during an interview. When Doña Gabriela said, "Ten children, six living," I initially thought she meant that four children had died in childhood, until she explained that one of her ten pregnancies had resulted in a miscarriage at approximately two months' gestation. Similarly, Doña María, a seventy-year-old widow in San Gabriel, answered me by saying she had sixteen children. "Living?" I asked. "No," she said, "only five are living." The sixteen included four miscarriages (*arrojos,* literally "shedding blood"), four children who died in infancy, and three who died later in life.

The differences were significant to me because U.S. conventions mandate that people should distinguish among the *hijos* socially erased by miscarriage or induced abortion, the miscarried *hijos* who do not live to be born, the *hijos* born dead, and those born alive. Ecuadoran women make similar distinctions, of course, cognitively and at the level of lived experience, but in numbering their offspring they have a great deal of latitude in deciding how to classify and represent the differences among living, stillborn, live-born, miscarried, adopted, and deceased children.

The fact that women can count their *hijos* in so many different yet equally acceptable ways suggests two things. First, it suggests that every pregnancy can be – but is not necessarily – socially significant, no matter the result. The focus here is not on the baby, the "product," but on the woman's pregnancy and her social responsibility to reproduce. (This is a marked contrast to the U.S. "tentative pregnancy" in which some women postpone an announcement until they have completed the first trimester or until after receiving the results of amniocentesis.)[18] Second, it acknowledges that children emerge through a lengthy, gradual process that spans gestation and infancy and that any divisions imposed on the process (such as "trimesters," or "viability") are somewhat arbitrary.

The arbitrary nature of life-cycle divisions is evident, too, in national vital statistics and the registration standards as understood by the civil servant in San Gabriel. Birthrates and infant mortality rates are unreliable in Ecuador, in part because the state began to emphasize the importance of registering births and deaths only in the mid-1980s. For example, in 1982 only 4,627 live births were registered in the country of more than 9 million inhabitants, while by 1986 the number of live births registered was 205,797. "Live birth" figures are an inherently imprecise category as long as they continue to include all children registered that year, including older children. Underreporting continues to be a problem, in part because relatively few births are attended by professionals. In 1986, 85 percent of the 1,406 registered live births in urban areas of Carchi Province (which includes San Gabriel) were attended by a professional, but in the rural areas only 50 percent of the 1,699 registered live births were attended by a professional.[19] The reported infant mortality rate for the country as a whole in 1986 was 50.4/1,000 live births, while in Carchi Province it was 54.4/1,000. Actual rates are undoubtedly much higher, because parents have no particular incentive to register infant births or deaths, especially outside the cities.

Ecuador follows the World Health Organization in defining fetal death as "death prior to the complete expulsion or extraction from its mother of a product of conception, irrespective of the duration of the pregnancy; the death is indicated by the fact that after such separation the fetus does not breathe or show any other evidence of life, such as beating of the heart, pulsation of the umbilical cord, or definite movement of voluntary muscles."[20] The 1986 Vital Statistics Report makes it clear that the Ecuadoran state does not even try to enumerate fetal death or miscarriage:

> Fetal deaths: In Ecuador there is no special registry for reporting fetal deaths; when they occur and interested parties report them, an official of the Civil Registry should fill out a statistical report in duplicate, filing the original and sending the copy to the National Institute of Statistics and Census. In 1986 4,265 fetal deaths were registered [58 of which were in Carchi Province].[21]

Even if the state were more aggressive about collecting these vital statistics, compliance in the hinterlands could not be guaranteed. The law specifies that all live births must be registered, but when I spoke with the civil servant in San Gabriel, he was quite casual about the regulations. In his opinion, if an infant died within the first "four or six hours, or the first day" after birth, the parents did not need to register the birth, although they could if they wanted to. Although the lax registration standards could be regarded as a sign of bureaucratic inefficiency, they could also be interpreted as a codification of the imprecision described above. This particular official was reaffirming the liminality and arbitrariness that characterize the beginnings of life in the Ecuadoran Andes.

Fetal Death and the Amorphous *Auca*

The persistence of faith in the *auca* is perhaps the best evidence of the inherent ambiguity of the unborn in the rural highlands of Ecuador. The *auca* has long been a part of Andean ethnography, functioning as a master metaphor for the uncivilized and for several categories of quasi-person. Elsie Clews Parsons reported in 1945 that "[a]n infant (or anyone) dying unbaptized is called *auca*...and becomes a night-wandering spirit."[22] In Quito, said Parsons, any unbaptized person was referred to as *auca*, including all the indigenous, non-Christian residents of the Amazonian lowlands. The Ecuadoran *auca* includes savages, heathens, and other liminal beings. A celebrated national soccer team embodies fierceness and invincibility, calling itself "Los Aucas," and *Auca* is still in use as a pejorative name for the Huaorani Indians of the Amazonian low-lands (*oriente*). Michael Taussig explains:

Several modern Ecuadorian Quechua dictionaries clearly bring the various meanings together – savage, seditious, rebel, enemy – and in the Colombian Putumayo today *auca* also connotes, to my friends at least and with varying intensities, the unrepentantly "other" world of savagery down there in the jungles of the *oriente*, a world quintessentially pagan, without Christ, Spanish words, or salt, inhabited by naked, incestuous, violent, magical, and monstrous people.... [23]

The infant *aucas* described to me in San Gabriel, like the savage Indian *aucas* described to Taussig, were frightening and potentially dangerous; they could, by some accounts, turn themselves into ghosts or cannibals. As one woman told me, "An *auca* comes looking for its mother, to punish her for being irresponsible, for having sinned by not baptizing him." Yet when I repeated this interpretation to another woman, she rejected it as *falso, falso, falso*. Rather, she said, the *auca* makes itself into a big ghost, as tall as a tree, and looks for children to kill by eating their hearts. A third woman ridiculed this account, saying the *auca* does not pursue children, and no one can see it anyway, because it is just smoke. If there was any agreement about the nature of the *auca* in San Gabriel, most women agreed that it is the spirit of an aborted fetus, or still-born or murdered baby, which cries pitifully at night in sorrow (*por remordimiento*) at not having

been baptized. The cries emanate from the site where its body was supposedly discarded (*botado*) or thrown away without benefit of burial (*tirado no más, donde sea*). Four or five women told me of having heard the *auca* themselves, crying outside at night, and of their terror and prayers.

The existence of *aucas* was fairly widely recognized, but there was considerable disagreement about how properly to dispose of an unbaptized fetus or child to prevent it from becoming an *auca*. Luz María said that the *auca* can be prevented by baptizing a fetus or neonate even if it is dead; the mother or midwife can sprinkle holy water over its head and say, "In the name of Jesus Christ I baptize you, giving you the name of Jesus [for a boy] or María [for a girl]." But other women insisted that only living babies could receive baptism; the rite could not be posthumously conferred. Similar controversy arose over how and where to dispose of fetal remains.

The symbolism of burial space revealed a great deal about the ambiguous, wandering *auca*. Many women disapproved of discarding infant or fetal bodies without ceremony; however, some favored burial outside the cemetery for souls not destined to enter heaven. Others insisted that inside the cemetery was safer for both the living and the dead. Some suggested that fetal remains could be placed, above ground, along the inside of the cemetery fence, literally a liminal position on the outer margins of sacred ground. Another woman rejected burial altogether for the unbaptized: "To bury is bad (*enterrar es malo*). That child (*niño*) has been known to grow up by itself, to make itself into a ghost (*fantasma*). To keep it from becoming a ghost, it is better to put it in any little box and throw it into the river [because this is how Christ was baptized]. The priest said that way it can't do any harm." Although the river is a powerful salvation metaphor in Christian ideology, only one of the women I interviewed mentioned this method. There was little consensus about where the bodies belonged, where their souls would reside, or what their fate would be. The *auca* embodies uncertainty.

The inconsistent practice of other rituals that accompany birth and death, including naming, baptizing, and sitting with the body through a wake, further illustrate this ambiguity. I asked a sixty-five-year-old woman with six children to tell me, hypothetically, how a woman might feel and what she might do if she miscarried at six months' gestation.

Well, she would feel a little sad [un poco de pena] because she lost the child, without having known it, without having seen it, no? Then she would take it, because it is an object born of her [como es un objecto que nace de uno], with blood and everything, right? She would put it in a little box and bury it. Without a wake, they don't wake it [no lo velan]. Nor does she name it or baptize it.

Another woman had suffered two miscarriages: one at two months' gestation, another at eight months. The eight-month miscarriage was baptized, named, and buried in the cemetery. When the callous anthropologist inquired whether the fetus miscarried at two months would become an auca if deprived of baptism, I received a practical, if somewhat distressed, response: "But there's no way [to baptize it], it's just blood, how would you baptize it?" Unformed tissue cannot be properly baptized. But the women I interviewed seemed puzzled when I asked whether unformed tissue would, or could, become an auca; neither religion nor social practice offered any ready answer to this question. Thus the auca remains a relatively inchoate, subsocial being, a manifestation of discomfort with the prospect of unbaptized souls unable to gain entry into heaven. Its very iconography invokes murkiness: the auca is often described as cloudy or smoky or dark; as an auca, an unbaptized child "does not see the light [of heaven]" (no ve la claridad). The women of San Gabriel don't agree among themselves who becomes an auca, or under what circumstances, or what powers the auca might possess. Furthermore, they assert, there can be no satisfactory answer to these questions.

In Ecuadoran narratives of pregnancy, childbirth, and child death, the auca is invoked to signify the ever-present and inevitable ambiguity that accompanies the transitions into personhood. Interpreted in light of U.S. abortion debates, it appears that U.S. polemics have

reduced, indeed virtually eliminated, the space that might be allotted to not-yet-persons.[24] The auca, then, can be seen as an affirmation of a place for quasi-persons within the local cosmology. The auca accommodates those anomalous, liminal beings who exist somewhere between nothingness and full human personhood, and it reinforces the notion that mortal humans do not exercise complete control over the spiritual agency of the unborn. The auca, as part of the local practice of personhood, functions to remind Andean residents of the fragility and spiritual ambiguity of young human life and of the importance of baptism. The auca shapes the meanings attributed to the unborn and to babies who die prematurely or without church protection, and it wields a coercive power over those who believe in it by forcing them to think and act in accordance with local practices. To this extent, the auca could be considered a political actor with a bit part, influencing local reproductive ethics.

Because the social practices surrounding fetal and infant burial provided such insights into their status, I was interested to compare burial practices for fetal remains in San Gabriel with those in Quito. I asked the chief of perinatology at a Quito hospital what happens to the remains when a woman miscarries in his hospital. Do the parents ever claim the remains for burial?

Of the abortions [de los abortos], the parents never claim the remains. Yes, if it's a stillbirth, or if it dies of some disease, but even with these children many times parents don't claim [reclamar]. But with abortions, never, ever. And we don't give them the remains. Never. When it's a formed fetus, when it's already a child, then yes [cuando ya es un feto ya formado, cuando ya es un niño allí si].

His response was telling: in urban areas miscarried fetal tissue is not claimed or socially valued. But his response also complicates matters. He used the word aborto to refer to early miscarriages and induced abortions, apparently not distinguishing between them. But then he used feto and niño seemingly interchangeably to refer to the formed fetus/baby at a later stage of gestation. He thus made a distinction between "formed" and "unformed" tissue and granted to the former a moral and social identity (in death as in life?) not extended to the latter.

The same physician went on to tell me about the difficulty encountered by his staff in obtaining permission to perform autopsies on fetuses and babies. Many parents, he says, would rather pay a private physician to sign the death certificate than sign the hospital-issued death certificate which automatically authorizes autopsy. Parents are opposed, he said, to having autopsies performed, although he purported not to understand their reasoning: "I really don't understand them in this sense. The only thing I can think of is that they don't want the child dismembered (*despedazado*). But we don't dismember during an autopsy. And even if we *did* take the heart for study, the parents would never know because we stitch up the chest cavity." The traffic in body parts he seemed to condone[25] was probably as clear to bereaved parents as it was to me. His words, however, revealed something more than his willingness to deceive. Physical integrity and wholeness is important to the parents, because bodily mutilation is a sin.

Abortion: Self- Vs. Other-Mutilation

Most rural women answered my query with, "Yes, the fetus is a person from conception." By this they meant that God creates pregnancies and brings babies into being and that at some unspecifiable point during gestation God gives the fetus a soul. Because mortals do not know precisely when this happens, it is better to err on the generous side. Fetuses are "persons" from conception, then, because God made them but not because the community yet accepts them as such.

The women were equally adamant that it is (usually) wrong to induce abortion but not because abortion is "murder." They explained that induced abortion is a sin of self-mutilation. The horror of inducing abortion, I was told, was the blasphemous presumptuousness implied in taking one's bodily fate into one's own hands (*siendo rey de su propia sangre*).

God calls pregnancy into existence, they said, and we are not authorized to interfere with His divine plans. Abortion, then, is not about the mutilation or destruction of a person but about presuming to know God's will. The link between the personhood of the fetus and the morality of abortion – so omnipresent in contemporary North American culture – is largely absent in Ecuador.

Furthermore, several women told me that a decision to terminate a pregnancy could sometimes be morally defensible if women were in desperate straits. Moral justifications for abortion included abandonment by or abuse at the hands of a partner or husband; desperate poverty, hunger, or homelessness; life-threatening contraceptive failure (such as conceiving with an IUD in place); or the need to protect a family's honor. Even if the fetus is a person, I was told, this does not mean that abortion is *necessarily* wrong in all circumstances. Discussions about the morality of abortion tended to center around the social, economic, and health circumstances facing pregnant women, who were portrayed as the final moral arbiters in reproductive decisions. These discussions tended not to invoke church doctrine; nor were they framed in terms of fetal rights, fetal personhood, or maternal–fetal conflict. The rhetoric around abortion in Ecuador emphasizes the centrality of pregnant women's moral integrity and life circumstances, rather than fetal rights or personification of the unborn.

Gestational Development

Pregnant women in the United States have access to books, posters in physicians' offices, and even plastic models depicting an inexorable and cumulative process of gestational development through which an embryo turns into a fetus and then a baby. These visual models and books are part of a cultural iconography that helps to fix an image and create the meanings attached to particular gestational stages.[26] In the rural highlands of Ecuador there is no equivalent to this visual or technologically based information. Women learn about intrauterine fetal development from their own experiences, talking with other women, viewing their own or other women's miscarriages, and feeling fetal movement. The terminology the women use is revealing because it blurs the distinction between the unborn and the born: *criatura* (creature) or its diminutive, *criaturita*; also *nene* or *guagua* (baby), *niño* (child), or *venidero* (one to come), or, rarely, *bebe*. The unborn are not referred to in gendered terms, although, as we see below, the process of intrauterine development is considered different for girls and for boys.

The most significant marker of gestational development, women told me, is *formación*. In this context the word refers to the time when the fetus assumes a recognizably human form, but the word *formación* also, interestingly, means "education," drawing a parallel between gestational development and the socialization of children. When does *formación* happen? Accounts varied widely, implying that there is no cultural consensus or ready response apart from the gender differentiation many said was inherent in the process: males develop earlier than females. Doña Blanca washed her laundry while we talked. Thirty-three years old, she had six living children and one daughter who had died at age two. She explained, "Males, they say, form at one month [gestation]. In contrast, females still aren't formed at two months. Females form later (*la mujer se forma de más meses*)." Doña Teresa, a forty-nine-year-old illiterate woman with eight living and three deceased children, answered my question about *formación* by talking about quickening: "I usually felt them move at three months. And when it's female, around six months, it seems, no?" She smiled slyly and explained, "They say girls are lazy (*vaga*)." A fifty-nine-year-old mother of twenty-two, Doña Ileana said that boys begin to form at two weeks' gestational age, and girls begin to form at six months. Doña María, aged seventy, explained what her son looked like when she suffered a miscarriage at three months' gestation, because she had witnessed a woman slaughter a pig.

I arrived home. I began shivering and drooling. That night I started bleeding profusely. The little boy (*varoncito*) was born perfect. He was about this big [indicating about three inches]. He was born completely formed, with all the boy's parts. The miscarried female (*hembrita*) has nothing, she is just a chunk of flesh (*trozo de sangre*), and in the middle of the chunk of flesh there is a single eye. That's the female. Females form at six months. Males form by the first month. Females, no. The female comes out with a chicken's eye. Nothing more.

Doña Josefina, age sixty-two with six children, explained that *formación* took place at two months in boys, "just like Christ," and that girls remained "like chunks of meat" for a "long time." Observation and personal experience of miscarriage seemed not to affect the social perception that girls form more slowly than boys. The common wisdom about gender differentiation had little practical value, because a pregnant woman in the Ecuadoran highlands does not profess to know whether the fetus she carries is destined to be female or male. But *formación* can affect the morality of abortion, according to Doña Josefina, because an unformed conceptus can, if necessary, be aborted:

Here abortion is a crime. It's not a crime, though, when the child (*niño*) is not yet in flesh (*cuando todavía no esté en sangre*), when it is not yet formed with the blood of the mother, no? It's still just a few days [from conception], no? Then they say that it's made up of sex substances (*la naturaleza*) – from both sides – and that it's still in water (*todavía está en agua*), no? It's still not formed, nor is it made of flesh. Then they say that it [abortion] is permitted, that it is not a sin. But once it's formed, once it's formed of one's blood, then it [abortion] is a crime.

The "unformed fetus" might be the Ecuadoran equivalent of saying that a woman can be "a little bit pregnant." Because *formación* could happen so early, a woman who wants to terminate a pregnancy should do so as early as possible. Doña Teresa told me: "Of course earlier is better. Preferred, for example, in the case of unmarried women who find themselves pregnant, to do it at one month. At one month. That's like 'bringing down the period' (*bajando la regla*). There is not yet any fetus (*feto*), no one, nothing."[27]

The importance of *formación* was not shared by all the women I interviewed. Some said that abortion was always wrong, whenever it occurred. Doña Ileana disagreed about the emphasis on *formación*, explaining that the unborn "has a right to life" (*tiene derecho a la vida*; she was unique among the women I interviewed in San Gabriel in using this language) "by virtue of the fact that it is in the womb, even if it is only one or two months old it is already alive." This disagreement recalls debates ongoing elsewhere about the sanctity of life versus the social significance of personhood. Here, however, the disagreement occurs within a cultural repertoire that can accommodate a wide degree of variability on the question of when personhood might coalesce.

Not only does *formación* not happen all at once, but the physical and spiritual characteristics of newborns are still fluid and changing up until birth and well into the postpartum period. Newborns, like fetuses, were referred to by terms that indicated their unfinished quality: *tierno* means young or unripe, and is used also to describe green fruit.[28] Doña Josefina told me, "A newborn child (*guagua recién nacido*) is like a child of clay." She explained that the mother should carefully and frequently mold and shape its face and nose, its head and shoulders and legs to make them assume the desired shape. Women swaddle their babies, she said, to make their legs grow straight. Just as their bodies are unfinished and malleable, the spirits and souls of newborns are not yet firmly tethered to the social world. Babies are described as particularly vulnerable to collective social and supernatural forces that older children are toughened against. For example, babies are susceptible to fright (*susto*), evil eye (*mal ojo*), dew, night air, rainbows, inauspicious hours (*mala hora*), and traditionally dangerous places such as ravines. For this reason, said Doña María, it used to be the custom for new mothers to stay inside with their babies for forty days after birth (the traditional Latin American *cuarentena*, called the *dieta* in San Gabriel). Until recently, a postpartum mother would be enshrouded by a *toldo*, or screen, over the bed. "The *toldita* was a sheet that was put over the bed so that wind (*viento*) would not get in, is what they

used to say. Only this little tiny opening would be left so you could get into the bed, nothing more." The *toldo* prevented dangerous airs from reaching the child. It also served as the Ecuadoran variant of the "social womb" familiar to anthropologists. The social womb extends the physiological womb symbolically into social space, thus rendering biological birth as a necessary but insufficient condition for granting personhood. The infant and mother live inside the "social womb" for a time, until the infant is deemed "person enough," ripe enough or tough enough, to emerge. Sometimes the social womb was the bed where mother and newborn lay enshrouded, whereas sometimes the social womb was the entire house. Doña María said she kept her baby in the house for two months after it was born, to prevent harm from befalling the child. "Sometimes," she explained, "I would have to pass through a ravine (*quebra-da*) or overgrown area (*monte*). The child's spirit could get lost, stay behind in those places" (*que se queda el espíritu*). If she had to go out, she would leave the child behind in the house, where it would be safe even if unattended.

Building Persons is a Woman's Responsibility

The physical separation of the fetus from the mother at birth is one important step in the process of acquiring personhood, but newborns continue to be dependent on their parents to provide spiritual sustenance and physical strength. Fathers, as well as mothers, are held accountable for safeguarding fetuses and newborns in several ways. They must respond immediately to pregnant women's cravings (*antojos*), abstain from sexual relations for the forty-day postpartum period (*dieta*), and remain faithful to their wives (especially while children are at the breast). One of the most feared infant diseases in San Gabriel is *colerín*, which results when a father upsets his wife. Her anger or rage (*cólera*), passed immediately to the child through breastmilk, results in *colerín*, an acute, incurable disease which kills rapidly. "Don't you see that they're unripe (*tierni-tos*), and they can't take it (*no aguan-tan*), they can't withstand *colerín*." Because the consequences of rage can be so grave, the prospect of rage might well give pregnant women and nursing mothers some degree of control over inappropriate male behavior.[29] Apart from these rather limited responsibilities, however, men absent themselves from the sufferings of birth, miscarriage, and infant death. Here a Quito pathologist gradually reveals his conscious insensitivity to the death of his firstborn.

When a newborn dies, the most affected person is not the father, it's the mother. The person with whom you have to work – to console – is the mother, not the father. The father comes to accept his responsibilities gradually, as the child develops. I'm not the least bit afraid to say this, and I've always said it to my family, in my home. My first son died. I *did not feel* [his emphasis] what my wife felt. I think if the same thing happened right now to one of my [older] children, the calamity would fall hardest on me.

His honest confession illustrates a point made by Laurie Price in her discussion of Ecuadoran ideologies of the family. She writes that women are encouraged "to feel fully the anguish of a calamity that befalls a family member but [the ideologies do] not prepare men either psychologically or socially to acknowledge that kind of anguish."[30] For the purposes of our discussion, this gendered distinction illustrates the extent to which women are primarily responsible for the reproduction of the social order, for bringing children into social being.

Andie L. Knutson once concluded, with respect to the United States, that "people are made by people."[31] In the highlands of Ecuador, the work of making people, of constructing social persons, is specifically considered women's work. Women "serve as cultural mediators between the living and the dead"[32] but also between the world of the not-yet and the existing social community. Men do not feel the same degree of responsibility for ushering children into social existence, although, as noted above, women want their partners' support and work hard to recruit them to the task of

bringing babies into being. When women attempt to control men's behavior through devices such as *pena* (emotional pain and suffering)[33] and the prospect of children dying from *colerín*, they do so knowing that men would otherwise not readily concern themselves with assisting quasi-persons on the margins of life.[34]

Practicing Personhood

The ideologies and actions practiced by women in highland Ecuador militate against the radical individualization of fetuses currently underway in the United States. Yet much to the chagrin and consternation of U.S. feminists and prochoice activists, the abortion debate continues to revolve around the question of whether the fetus is a person. Devised by prolife activists to direct attention to their cause, the question is a trope in an era where definitions of personhood are increasingly based on popular appropriations of biology and genetics.[35] In other words, the answer must always be "yes" where personhood is defined with recourse to unified biological or genetic descriptions alleged to lie outside or prior to social attributes. The question reinforces the absolutist conviction that science can identify biological markers (such as the onset of brain stem activity) or invent medical interventions (such as lung surfactants to enable very premature babies to survive) that will influence decisions about when fetuses should be regarded as persons. Scientific investigation of this sort reinforces the presumption that biomedical insights are attainable, relevant, and consensual, even while the popular appropriations of science divert attention from the processes through which science is imbued with meaning and signification.

A focus on the onset of fetal personhood both presupposes and reasserts that the morality of abortion is and should be contingent on the status of the fetus. Of course many North Americans, including most feminists, reject the logic that links abortion to fetal personhood. Yet for the purposes of this article, it is useful to point out that even prochoice ideologies in the United States resist the notion of quasi-persons, semipersons, or incipient persons. U.S. ideologies favor a strict distinction between persons and nonpersons, with nothing in-between.[36] In this sense the Ecuadoran example presents an alternative view of the unborn and raises a series of questions about the U.S. context. What is the cultural basis for the absolutist assertion that fetuses must always be either full persons or nonpersons? When did this absolutist imperative emerge? Did the social and political effacement of pregnant women predate the introduction and widespread use of reproductive imaging technologies? Might some pregnancies involve fetal "persons" (if pregnant women and others involved grant them this status), but other pregnancies might not? Perhaps some pregnancies involve incipient or quasi-persons of indeterminate moral, spiritual, and physical status. Certainly the Ecuadoran women I interviewed would not suggest that any society could accurately or confidently pinpoint the beginning of the miraculous, mysterious process of social becoming.

Much of the U.S. debate over abortion has centered around identifying the most defensible moment at which personhood can or should be assigned. People often presume that personhood accrues cumulatively; fetuses and babies gradually acquire additional degrees of personhood, but persons generally do not come undone. Personhood is easily extended but rarely rescinded. It is thus difficult for North Americans to understand that the practices of personhood in the Ecuadoran highlands sometimes allow a degree of ebb and flow over the duration of pregnancy and infancy.[37] Women told me that the gradual process of intrauterine *formación*, for example, may be arrested or even reversed if a pregnant woman knowingly continues to breastfeed an older child. By showing inappropriate favoritism and diverting energy essential for fetal growth, she may "undo" the nascent personhood of the unborn. A *criatura* said to be formed (and thus *una persona*) by six months' gestation may be said at birth to be "little more than an animal" until it is baptized. The trajectory of personhood need not necessarily be linear, because people cannot predict the many influences that bring each person into being.

"God keeps certain secrets," people told me, and these things He does not tell us. Incipient personhood is understood as openly ambiguous and variable, its character perennially liminal, amorphous, and irresolvable.

Persons are everywhere the products of social action. In Ecuador at the early margins of life, social practices do not focus on personification of the unborn or reification of fetal subjects. The women I interviewed in San Gabriel have not been schooled, as I have, to imagine individualized, disembodied, animate, technicolor fetuses brought to consciousness through the popularization of science. Nor do their journalists constantly remind them, as mine do me, how contentious and violent abortion politics have become. The women I interviewed in San Gabriel were perplexed that I, or my compatriots, would expect to find a single or satisfactory answer to the question of when fetuses become persons. Why, they wondered, would we press so hard to know the unknowable? Through their eyes, I began to see their ways as sensible and my own as strange. These women imagine the unborn in a variety of ways, including as amorphous quasi-human entities with strong links to spiritual and social (as well as biological) domains. They bring the unborn into social being slowly and carefully, not by medical or legal fiat, but through a combination of overlapping personal, social, and religious actions. These include taking good care of pregnant women, baptizing children, respecting God's will and authority, working and hoping for prosperity, behaving responsibly and working together, protecting the incipient person from natural and supernatural threats and evil influences, and a good bit of luck. Women's stories about their miscarriages and children (both alive and dead) were interspersed with stories of *aucas* and cautionary remarks about the dangers of wind and night air, and the hardships posed by infidelity and poverty. All these examples serve to emphasize the radical disjunctures between their liminal unborn and "my fetus," the fetus I inadvertently reify myself, steeped as I am in my country's scientific images linked to abortion debates. This comparison thus denaturalizes the iconographic fetal subject in the United States and raises a question. Wouldn't

U.S. feminists do well to attend to the diverse social practices through which people create people, including the ways in which scientific images are mobilized politically to mask women's authority, responsibility, and moral integrity?

NOTES

1 Jodi L. Jacobson, *The Global Politics of Abortion* (Washington, DC: Worldwatch Paper no. 97, July 1990), 53; Faye D. Ginsburg and Rayna Rapp, eds., *Conceiving the New World Order: The Global Politics of Reproduction* (Berkeley: University of California Press, 1995).

2 Monica J. Casper, "Reframing and Grounding Nonhuman Agency: What Makes a Fetus an Agent?" *American Behavioral Scientist*, 37 (May 1994): 839–56; Rosalind Pollack Petchesky, "Fetal Images: The Power of Visual Culture in the Politics of Reproduction," *Feminist Studies*, 13 (summer 1987): 263–92, reprinted in *Reproductive Technologies*, ed. Michelle Stanworth (Minneapolis: University of Minnesota Press, 1987), 57–80; Janet Gallagher, "Collective Bad Faith: 'Protecting' the Fetus," in *Reproduction, Ethics, and the Law*, ed. Joan C. Callahan (Bloomington: Indiana University Press, 1995), 343–79; Carol A. Stabile, *Feminism and the Technological Fix* (New York: St Martin's Press, 1994).

3 A few caveats are warranted at the outset. Cross-cultural comparison can be a useful heuristic tool, but it carries certain risks. One is the danger of reifying "culture," of representing as uniform the views of "a people" which are more accurately depicted as divergent and highly contested. Another pitfall is a tendency to overemphasize similarities within groups while exaggerating contrasts between them. If I contrast "us" and "them" in this essay, I do so deliberately, aware of the representational problems I invoke, but equally convinced that comparison can be a powerful pedagogical and theoretical tool.

4 Verena Stolcke, "Women's Labours: The Naturalisation of Social Inequality and Women's Subordination," in *Of Marriage and the Market*, ed. Kate Young, Carol Wolkowitz, and Roslyn McCullagh (London: Routledge & Kegan Paul, 1981), 167.

5 Laury Oaks, "Irish Trans/National Politics and Locating Fetuses," in *Fetal Subjects, Feminist Positions*, ed. Lynn Morgan and Meredith Michaels (Philadelphia: University of Pennsylvania Press, 1999), 175–95. See also Barbara Duden, *Disembodying Women: Perspectives on Pregnancy and the Unborn* (Cambridge, MA: Harvard University Press, 1993).

6 Casper, "Reframing."

7 In March 1996, *New York Magazine* (11 Mar. 1996: p. 12) carried news of the wedding of Nicole Miller and Kim Taipale, noting, in a striking example of the personification of the fetal subject, "The couple is expecting a son, Palmer Taipale, in March." I thank Rachel Roth for bringing the clipping to my attention.

8 See Janelle S. Taylor, "The Public Fetus and the Family Car: From Abortion Politics to a Volvo Advertisement," *Public Culture* 4 (winter 1992): 67–79. Also Janelle S. Taylor, "Image of Contradiction: Obstetrical Ultrasound in American Culture," in *Reproducing Reproduction*, ed. Sarah Franklin and Helena Ragoné (Philadelphia: University of Pennsylvania Press, 1997), 15–45.

9 I might add that the multiple venues through which fetuses are created include the rhetoric that feminist scholars employ to remark on and to contest the emergence of fetal subjects.

10 Susan Bordo, *Unbearable Weight: Feminism, Western Culture, and the Body* (Berkeley: University of California Press, 1993), 80.

11 Alan Guttmacher Institute, *Clandestine Abortion: A Latin American Reality* (New York: Alan Guttmacher Institute, 1994), 3.

12 See Ana María Portugal, ed., *Mujeres e Iglesia: Sexualidad y Aborto en América*

Latina (Washington, DC: Catholics for a Free Choice/Mexico City: Distribuciones Fontamara, 1989), 114.

13 Centro de Estudios y Asesoría en Salud (CEAS), "La crisis, la mujer, y el aborto" (Quito, Ecuador: Centro de Estudios y Asesoría en Salud, 1985). See also Alan Guttmacher Institute.

14 See Didier Fassin, "El aborto en el Ecuador (1964–1988)," *Bulletin de l'Institut Français d'Études Andines*, 19 (1990): 215–31.

15 P. Ximena Costales, "El aborto: Repercusiones sociales de una drama individual" (Quito: Centro de Investigaciones y Apoyo a la Mujer, unpublished Ms).

16 Elsewhere I argue that the beginnings of an internationalization of the U.S. abortion debate are evident in Ecuador. See Lynn M. Morgan, "Ambiguities Lost: Fashioning the Fetus into a Child in Ecuador and the United States," in *Small Wars: The Cultural Politics of Childhood*, ed. Nancy Scheper-Hughes and Carolyn Sargent (Berkeley: University of California Press, 1998), 58–74.

17 Lilia Rodriguez, "Taller: Mujer y derechos reproductivos" (Quito: Casa Para la Mujer/United Nations Fund for Population Activities, 1989), 20. In May of 1992 I attended a seminar sponsored by the Corporación de Investigaciones Sociales y en Salud (COINSOS), International Projects Assistance Services, and the Prevention of Maternal Mortality Program at the Center for Population and Family Health at Columbia University entitled, "Impacto del aborto en el sistema de salud ecuatoriano" (Impact of abortion on the Ecuadoran health system) in Quito.

18 See Barbara Katz Rothman, *The Tentative Pregnancy* (New York: Penguin, 1986).

19 Instituto Nacional de Estadística y Censo, *Anuario de Estadísticas Vitales* (Quito, Ecuador: 1986), 3.

20 English version found in M. L. Chiswick, "Commentary on Current World Health Organization Definitions Used in Perinatal Statistics," *British Journal of Ob-*

stetrics and Gynaecology, 93 (Dec. 1986): 236–8. Spanish version found in *Anuario de Estadísticas Vitales*, v.

21 See *Anuario de Estadísticas Vitales*, iv.

22 Elsie Clews Parsons, *Peguche: Canton of Otavalo, Province of Imbabura, Ecuador* (Chicago: University of Chicago Press, 1945), 44.

23 Michael Taussig, *Shamanism, Colonialism, and the Wild Man: A Study in Terror and Healing* (Chicago: University of Chicago Press, 1987), 97. A physician in Quito reported that some people on the coast of Ecuador refer to unbaptized babies as *moritos*, or Moors, from the colonial Spanish equivalent for "heathen."

24 Perhaps the "not-yet-person" exists in the realm of infertility in the United States, where images abound of "our child" who is not yet conceived. See Margarete Sandelowski, *With Child in Mind: Studies of the Personal Encounter with Infertility* (Philadelphia: University of Pennsylvania Press, 1993).

25 See Nancy Scheper-Hughes, "Theft of Life: Organ Stealing Rumors," *Anthropology Today*, 12 (June 1996): 3–11.

26 Barbara Duden, *Disembodying Women: Perspectives on Pregnancy and the Unborn* (Cambridge, MA: Harvard University Press, 1993).

27 See also Susan C. M. Scrimshaw, "Bringing the Period Down: Government and Squatter Settlement Confront Induced Abortion in Ecuador," in *Micro- and Macro-Levels of Analysis in Anthropology: Issues in Theory and Research*, ed. Billie DeWalt and Pertti J. Pelto (Boulder, CO: Westview Press, 1985), 121–46.

28 See Lauris A. McKee, "Los cuerpos tiernos: Simbolismo y magia en las prácticas post-parto en Ecuador," *América Indígena* 42 (Oct.–Dec. 1982): 615–28.

29 Thanks to Rayna Rapp for suggesting this interpretation.

30 Laurie Price, "Ecuadorian Illness Stories: Cultural Knowledge in Natural Discourse," in *Cultural Models in Language and Thought*, ed. Dorothy Holland and Naomi Quinn (Cambridge: Cambridge University Press, 1987), 320.

31 Andie L. Knutson, "The Definition and Value of a New Human Life," *Social Science and Medicine*, 1 (1967): 7–29.

32 Mary M. Crain, "Poetics and Politics in the Ecuadorean Andes: Women's Narratives of Death and Devil Possession," *American Ethnologist*, 18 (Feb. 1991): 85.

33 Michel Tousignant, "*Pena* in the Ecuadorian Sierra: A Psychoanthropological Analysis of Sadness," *Culture, Medicine, and Psychiatry*, 8 (Dec. 1984): 381–98.

34 That the work of creating persons is stratified according to gender can also explain why *aucas* weigh so heavily on a *mother's* conscience, because mothers hold themselves principally responsible for having their children baptized. Women often said that newborns are not full persons prior to baptism: "Not children of God," said one Ecuadoran woman; "More like puppies than persons," said another. A newborn baby, the women told me, does not become a full person until it is welcomed into the Christian community through baptism.

35 Celeste Michelle Condit, *Decoding Abortion Rhetoric* (Urbana: University of Illinois Press, 1991); Sarah Franklin, "Fetal Fascinations: New Dimensions to the Medical-Scientific Construction of Fetal Personhood," in *Off-Centre: Feminism and Cultural Studies*, ed. Sarah Franklin, Celia Lury, and Jackie Stacey (New York: HarperCollins, 1991), 190–205; Clifford Grobstein, *Science and the Unborn: Choosing Human Futures* (New York: Basic Books, 1988).

36 For an alternative view, see Linda Layne, " 'I Remember the Day I Shopped for Your Layette': Consumer Goods, Fetuses, and Feminism in the Context of Pregnancy," in *Fetal Subjects, Feminist Positions.* (n. 5 above).

37 See Beth A. Conklin and Lynn M. Morgan, "Babies, Bodies, and the Production of Personhood in North America and a Native Amazonian Society," *Ethos*, 24 (Dec. 1996): 657–94.

Part V

Interpreting Instability and Fluidity

Introduction

The readings in this volume have demonstrated the shift that feminist anthropology – and anthropology in general – have made toward questioning cultural processes that were once held to be universal and essential to the operation of societies. Across cultural anthropology, divisions between the "primitive" and the "modern" have been thoroughly interrogated. Previously rigid notions about social boundaries, for example, between tribes and communities, have been challenged and left in disarray. The search for perfectly congruent cultural systems has been discarded in favor of a new fascination with the incongruent, resistant, and shifting nature of social life. Even the notion of "us" and "them" has crumbled, with anthropologists questioning whether they are insiders or outsiders to their research sites, and even asking whether any such categories can meaningfully exist. The focus on studying closed social systems has yielded to a concern with the rapid movements of transnational and global flows of labor, capital, and population, and with these shifts notions of place, community, and identity have had to be reconfigured.

In like fashion, feminist anthropology came to question its earliest mission – the documentation of women's lives and the exposition of their stories – a quest that was overwhelmingly recuperative. It moved decisively toward an analysis of "gender" as a cultural system, and away from essentialist notions about what was understood to be biological, "sex." But in recent years, it has had to change in other ways as well. First, in accordance with the new realities of global processes, feminists have turned their attention away from women or gender as it is played out in a specific place and time toward a more fluid focus on change. The articles in this section that deal with how transnational corporate practices shape the experience of women in particular localities speak most directly to these concerns.

Second, feminist anthropologists, like feminist scholars in other disciplines, have begun to consider the radical questioning of gender categories as natural or inevitable. To some extent, this rethinking has been spurred by the direction of some recent feminist theory that has focused on the performative dimensions of gender, and the ways in which such performances may reflect strategy more than nature. Here, the work of such scholars as Judith Butler has been central, as discussed in the Introduction to this volume. But feminist scholars have not only been inspired by postmodern questioning of essential categories, but by the behavior and beliefs of the people with whom we work. The two essays in this section that take up questions of sexual identity speak to elements of this larger shift in understanding as it applies not only to gender categories but to sexualities.

The growth in lesbian and gay rights movements that has paralleled the development of feminist scholarship has called our attention to the existence of sexual minorities across a wide spectrum of cultures. In moves that recall feminism's early effort to allow muted voices to be heard, gay rights activists and proponents of queer political agendas have sought to reveal the widespread existence of sexual variations, including some settings in which such variant identities and behaviors are respected and even celebrated. But such ventures also can suffer from the tendency to universalize Western understandings of sexuality, particularly to see sexuality as a fundamental attribute of the person, a key element of identity, that like gender is often seen to be immovable. Lesbian and gay anthropologists thus have drawn on feminist approaches to craft a study of sexual variation across cultures, and to overcome tendencies to naturalize particular constructions of sexual identities and behaviors.

Shellee Colen's paper on West Indian nannies working in New York City demands that we reconsider definitions of motherhood, situating that presumably obvious category in the political economic context of transnational migration. The women Colen describes have typically left their biological children at home in the West Indies while they migrate to the US in order to provide better for those children. Ironically, they find work in New York caring for the children of well-off families. Their experience exemplifies the concept of *stratified reproduction* whereby the tasks that conventionally amount to motherhood – physical reproduction and childcare – are reorganized and shaped by the exigencies of class and race inequalities as well as by forces derived from global population movements and economic patterns. The system in which these women operate is one that demands that they deploy their maternal labors for the benefit of children not their own, though this very labor enables them to provide for their faraway children and perhaps eventually to bring them to the United States as well. At the same time as they perform all of the physical and emotional work that growing children require, their contribution is disparaged as "work" rather than "real" motherhood. The biological mothers of the children are defined as "real" mothers regardless of what childrearing activities they perform, while labor is understood as inauthentic and readily replaceable.

Carla Freeman offers a compelling account of the ways that class has been refashioned by the "flexible labor" performed by women in a Barbados workplace. Situating the company as an outpost of the global assembly line, Freeman highlights the contradictions that obtain between the low-paid work performed by the women employees and the paradoxically high status that attaches to that work. While women have long been contributors to the labor force in Barbados, typically through work in informal trade and production, labor in the informatics industry is carried out in an office and demands an investment in a kind of professional demeanor that is seen as glamorous and highly desirable. Besides positioning women workers as producers in a transnational economy, then, the new requirements of status also make them consumers of goods that would otherwise be outside their orbits. In other words, the global setting of their work allows for a seemingly greater range of choices, even as the fundamental facts of the workers' positions remain very much the same.

These two articles tell differing stories of the impact of transnational economic trends on the lives of women workers from the Caribbean. They reveal the strategic elements of women's adaptation to global opportunities and constraints, showing the women to be agents rather than victims. But at the same time, the work of Colen and Freeman can be understood as part of a larger exploration by feminist and other anthropologists to document the limitations imposed by the very flexibility that offers them choices.

In her examination of *tombois* in West Sumatra, Evelyn Blackwood approaches a different area of flexibility and instability that feminist anthropologists have taken up in recent years. The so-called lesbians whom Blackwood came to know revealed not only divergent meanings for categories like "lesbian," but fundamental differences in definitions of masculinity and femininity. Sexual and gender identities taken up by *tombois* in West Sumatra cannot be fully understood apart from their dialogue with narratives of identity that prevail in local, national, and global arenas. On the one hand, *tombois* can draw on meanings they glean from transnational communications to situate their lives in a global context. But on the other hand, sexual transgression in West Sumatra cannot be divided from support for traditional gender roles, including motherhood and marriage. Masculine women, who in the West would be probably be read as butch lesbians, see themselves as "men," while others may interpret their behaviors as deviant less because of their gender presentation than because of their failure to perform expected roles of wife and mother. The existence of the *tombois,* however, poses no real threat to the continuity of more traditional femininity as practiced by their partners, understood to be unproblematically "women." These gender-based identities persist even as categories promoted by the international lesbian and gay rights movement have also begun to circulate and to offer different options for crafting individual identities.

Gloria Wekker's article on *mati* work in Suriname brings a different angle to bear on so-called lesbian relationships. Wekker questions the primacy of identity as a way of understanding how homosexuality is mapped onto persons. For low-income women in Suriname, who may form lifelong connections with other women, relationships are indistinguishable from matters of daily survival. Even when *mati* have long-term bonds with women, they also engage in a range of flexible relationships, bearing children with men, receiving support from both men and women, and understanding their situations as rooted in transactions that make survival possible. Such transactions are particularly characteristic of their relationships with men, since *mati* need men to give them children. Though economic exchanges also characterize their relationships with women, those exchanges are more diffuse and reciprocal, and are understood to be undertaken in a deeper set of loyalties. These are women whose preferences would mark them as "lesbian" elsewhere, but for whom such identifications have virtually no relevance. Identity seems, in Wekker's analysis, to be a luxury associated with a very different economic system than that in which *mati* are situated. Western conceptions of sexual identity and gender are also far more fixed and essentialized than behaviors associated with *mati*. For *mati*, not only sexual liaisons but gender attributes are understood to be malleable and flexible, with both feminine and masculine attributes coexisting within single individuals.

Both these articles, though explicitly concerned with phenomena that fall under the rubric of homosexuality, point to questions that promise to be central to feminist anthropology as it moves into its future. Like the first two papers in the section, which deal with the effects of global economic shifts on women's choices and constraints, these two papers speak to the ways in which Western definitions, and especially conceptualizations of the individual, travel and mutate, but also can be resisted. Will hegemonic Western categories finally supplant the ways that people in other settings understand themselves and try to make the best choices they can? All the contributions to this section interrogate whether the formation of an autonomous identity should be understood as a fundamental endeavor common to all persons. Can such identities – whether they be organized around nation, place, work, or sexuality – ever be stable or unambiguous? An even more basic question returns us to the categories that launched feminist anthropology – women and men – and the papers in this section suggest that we may know as little about these as we did when our field began in the early 1970s.

19

"Like a Mother to Them": Stratified Reproduction and West Indian Childcare Workers and Employers in New York

Shellee Colen

You have these kids sometimes from . . . seven in the morning to seven at night. Twelve hours of a day. You feed them. You clothe them. You take them out. You play with them. You're like a mother to them.

A Guyanese mother of four, speaking of her childcare work in New York City

The experiences of West Indian childcare workers in New York and their white U.S.-born employers reveal the operation of a transnational, highly stratified system of reproduction.[1] By *stratified reproduction* I mean that physical and social reproductive tasks are accomplished differentially according to inequalities that are based on hierarchies of class, race, ethnicity, gender, place in a global economy, and migration status and that are structured by social, economic, and political forces. The reproductive labor – physical, mental, and emotional – of bearing, raising, and socializing children and of creating and maintaining households and

people (from infancy to old age) is differentially experienced, valued, and rewarded according to inequalities of access to material and social resources in particular historical and cultural contexts. Stratified reproduction, particularly with the increasing commodification of reproductive labor, itself reproduces stratification by reflecting, reinforcing, and intensifying the inequalities on which it is based. (See Colen 1986a, 1986b, 1989, 1990; Colen and Sanjek 1990a; Rollins 1985, 1990.) The hiring of West Indian childcare labor in the United States, which linked New York City and the English-speaking Caribbean in the 1970s and 1980s,

From Shellee Colen, " 'Like a Mother to Them': Stratified Reproduction and West Indian Childcare Workers and Employers in New York," pp. 78–102 in Faye D. Ginsburg and Rayna Rapp, *Conceiving the New World Order: The Global Politics of Reproduction*. Berkeley, CA: University of California Press, 1995. © Shellee Colen. Reprinted with kind permission of the author.

opened up a window on a transnational system of stratified reproduction in which global processes are evident in local, intimate, daily events, and in which stratification itself is reproduced, as childcare occurs across class lines, kin lines, and oceans.[2]

From 1984 to 1986 I conducted research in New York through participant observation, extended interviews, and gathering life histories from twenty-five English-speaking Afro-Caribbean women who had performed household and childcare work at some point since migrating to New York City after 1965.[3] Brief fieldwork in St. Vincent and Barbados, West Indies, in 1986 centered on migrants' return visits, childcare and fostering, and migration processes. In 1988–9, I conducted twenty interviews with white U.S.-born employers of West Indian childcare workers in the New York area.[4] Elsewhere, I have discussed such aspects of stratified reproduction as the relationship among labor markets, immigration policy, and reproductive labor for West Indian women; undocumented West Indian women's experiences of exploitation while working in private households, especially when they live in; the asymmetrical power, material, and respect relations between household workers and employers and workers' juggling of paid reproductive work and their family responsibilities (Colen 1986a, 1989, 1990). Here, I concentrate on the differential experiences of stratified reproduction for West Indian childcare workers and their employers, focusing narrowly on parenting and childcare.

In this chapter, I outline some of the economic, social, and legal factors shaping West Indian women's migration to New York and their work as household childcare givers for white U.S.-born employers. Discussion of West Indian experiences and meanings of motherhood and fostering localizes the transnational experience of stratified reproduction. Employers' ideas about motherhood and childcare are influenced by changing socioeconomic realities and ideologies about reproductive labor and by media representations of motherhood. I draw on the daily, lived experiences of stratified reproduction and the reproduction of stratification, highlighting and contrasting workers' and employers' perspectives on childcare.

Mothers, Migration, and Reproductive Labor: Transnational Contexts

The differential experiences of reproduction, particularly of parenting and childcare, for West Indian workers and New York employers are framed by a transnational stratified system. In this system, West Indian women confront the legacies of slavery, colonialism, underdevelopment, and Caribbean articulation into a world capitalist system and the constraints these place on fulfilling their gender-defined obligations. They face, on the one hand, un- and underemployment, rising costs of living, and limited educational and occupational opportunities, and, on the other, gender expectations that they bear, raise, and carry the bulk of the financial responsibility for children and for other kin. Bolles (1981, 1983, 1986) and D'Amico-Samuels (1986, 1993) have shown the direct relationship between worsening economic conditions, including those induced by International Monetary Fund policies, and women's productive and reproductive strategies in Jamaica in the 1970s and 1980s. For many, migration is an "alternative employment strategy" (Bolles 1981: 62).

The West Indian women in my study viewed migration to New York as a means of constituting their families. While all were employed in the Caribbean in working- or middle-class jobs (as locally defined), economic conditions severely limited their financial capabilities, standards of living, and educational and employment opportunities. Mothers migrated to support themselves, their families, and others in the short run and to secure better opportunities (through obtaining legal residence in the United States) for themselves and their kin in the long run.

U.S. immigration policies mediated migration in two crucial ways (Colen 1990). First, if West Indian women were without permanent resident status (that is, with temporary tourist visas or without documents), they had to migrate alone, leaving children behind. Some of those few who migrated with legal status were prevented by immigration policy from bringing their children (and a few chose to spare their children some of the trauma of migration until they themselves were settled into jobs and homes). Second, women seeking legal status were directed by immigration policies (informed by labor needs and a class- and race-stratified division of labor) to private household work as a way to gain employer sponsorship for legal permanent-resident status (the green card).

Even migrants with green cards confronting this system of a racially stratified division of labor had difficulty translating their skills and job histories from home into comparable employment in New York yet found household childcare work with relative ease. This system of reproduction assigns paid reproductive labor to working-class women of color, and the system itself reproduces such stratification. For undocumented, live-in workers, specially those seeking legal status, this often meant exploitative, indenture-like conditions. For those with green cards working full-time, increased autonomy was accompanied by low wages without medical, retirement, or other benefits, which exacerbated their own household difficulties. While some women left household work after obtaining legal status through employer sponsorship, stratification created labor-market conditions often unfavorable to finding the kinds of higher-paying nonhousehold jobs with benefits and better conditions that they sought. Some found childcare preferable to the alternatives, at least temporarily.

Workers perceived a hierarchy of household reproductive labor in which live-in jobs with responsibility for all of a household's maintenance and childcare occupy the bottom, especially for undocumented workers needing sponsorship. On the next rungs, daywork housecleaning is followed by full-time, live-out household maintenance and childcare jobs. Childcare jobs with minimal or no housework are at the top. Most workers interviewed had worked at each level at some point. With green cards, workers enjoyed the relative power to set the parameters of private household work that their undocumented sisters lacked in their indenture-like positions, which they often compared to slavery. Whereas undocumented workers often had to "do every-thing" in the household to get their green cards and reunite with their children, those with legal status had more power to define their job responsibilities, to limit or eliminate housecleaning, and to devote themselves to childcare.

Social and economic shifts in the United States in the 1970s and 1980s created an acute need for childcare across classes. Such factors as the baby boomers' own baby boom coupled with the rising labor-force participation of mothers and continued expectations of female responsibility for reproductive labor left more families confronting inadequate options for childcare. In the United States, labor-force participation of women with children under eighteen increased from 42 percent in 1970 to 63 percent in 1986; by 1986 more than 70 percent of mothers of school-age children were in the work force; 54 percent of all mothers with children under six and 51 percent of all mothers with children under three were employed in 1986 (Kahn and Kamerman 1987: 11). In 1987, "50.8% of all new mothers remained in the job market," while "63% of new mothers with college degrees" did so (Working Mother Is Now the Norm 1988).

In the nation as a whole, because of the ideology of privatized childcare, the virtual absence of state- or employer-sponsored childcare, and severely limited day-care options, the stratification of childcare solutions intensified. From 1965 to 1985 national figures indicated declines in care by a relative (including parents) and by a nonrelative in the child's home (sitter) and increases in care by a nonrelative in that person's home (family day care) and in day-care centers or nurseries (Hofferth 1987: 3). Parents chose among these limited options on the basis of purchasing power, availability, and cost, as well as the age and number of children and beliefs about child development. Working-class and most middle-class parents could not afford in-home childcare and utilized other services. Kahn and Kamerman estimate that in 1986 most infants and toddlers were in family day care (1987: 6–7). The U.S. Bureau of the Census (1990: 7) reported that in fall 1987, 47.1 percent of employed mothers used relatives as their primary childcare provider for children under five; 24.3 percent used organized childcare facilities; 28.5 percent used care by nonrelatives, of which 22.3 percent was family day care in another home and only 6.2 percent was in-home care.

During this time, New York was a global city with an expanding, increasingly polarized service sector employing increasing numbers of women of all classes and races (Sassen Koob 1984, Waldinger 1989). As upper-middle- and upper-class women found higher-end positions, more women, especially women of color, including new immigrants, found positions on lower rungs. As in other areas of the country, the demand for childcare across classes in New York City became acute. Limited options, the ideology of privatized childcare, and the valuing of in-home infant care created a demand for reproductive laborers in upper-middle- and upper-class households at the same time as the pool of native-born workers willing to work in private households shrank and as a large pool of West Indian and other immigrant workers sought employment. Many New York parents with the means hired West Indian (and other immigrant) childcare workers on a full-time or live-in basis (Colen 1990).[5] In contrast, most middle- and working-class parents used family day care, day-care centers, care by relatives in New York, or, for migrants, care by fosterers in home countries.

While parenting and childcare activity may have been central in the lives of both the West Indian childcare workers and their employers, they were experienced and valued differently in a highly stratified system that reproduced and intensified the gender, class, and race inequalities on which they are based. Both childcare workers and their employers faced difficult choices and tenuous childcare arrangements. While they were undocumented and until their children's sponsorship was completed (minimally eighteen months), workers with children at the time of migration were forced to leave them in foster care in the home country. Workers living with infants and toddlers in New York used family day care or relative care when available. The majority of employers in my sample chose in-home sitters' care from the outset. A few with less household income initially chose other op-

tions until a second child's arrival made an in-home sitter a less costly alternative. Of these, one employer was committed to a parent-cooperative day-care center for four years of her first child's care before turning to the services of a West Indian sitter with her second child's birth. Another preferred her son's day-care center in Manhattan to a sitter's care but was unable to find an acceptable, convenient center when she moved to Brooklyn and had a second child. A third, who had used family day care in her old Bronx neighborhood, found that arrangement unmanageable on a full-time basis with the birth of her second child in her new Manhattan home. She patched together part-time family day care, part-time nursery school, and a West Indian sitter's care two days a week (sharing her services with a neighbor). For all the employers, West Indian women's labor formed the core of their children's care.

Paying for reproductive labor frees up members of employing households for other preferred activities. Remunerative and more prestigious work allows employers to maintain life-styles or class positions that they could not otherwise maintain. Leisure pursuits and investment in social relations (including participation in organizations) are also underwritten by waged reproductive labor (Colen 1990, Colen and Sanjek 1990b). In addition to employers' larger income, their medical and other benefits aid in household reproduction and are unavailable to workers. Consider the following cases. At the birth of their second child, a Brooklyn couple contemplated having one parent leave the work force to do childcare. They concluded that both enjoyed their jobs and that living on $30,000 (half their current income) would be difficult in New York, so they hired an in-home caregiver. A Manhattan couple with a combined household income of $150,000 would have to give up their fashionable, conveniently located condominium and the life-style it provided without a full-time worker to care for their three-year-old daughter while they worked. While employers of childcare workers took limited maternity leaves from full-time work (many preferring to return to work part-time for the first few months but few being able to do so), most employers did not entertain the possibility of either partner "giving up a career" to do childcare.

Ideologies of private and female responsibility for childcare meant that day-care options were few and fragile, and most reproductive labor fell to women – mothers, female kin, or low-waged service providers – who, according to a racial division of reproductive labor, are often women of color. Within employing households, workers interacted primarily with female employers who managed the tasks they did not themselves perform and who calculated childcare expenses in relation to their individual not their household incomes. Although several female employers stated that their husbands shared or "helped" with household or childcare work, workers in homes rarely reported male employers' doing so. Employing households seeking parenting help rarely challenged gender divisions of labor. Instead they crossed class, race, and national lines and hired West Indian caregivers whose own, often transnational, household reproduction was accomplished on low wages, in part with help from kin and family day-care arrangements.

"These are my Riches": West Indian Motherhood and Fostering

Motherhood is a major organizing principle of West Indian women's identities and the marker of adult status in West Indian communities (Durant-Gonzalez 1976, 1982; Powell 1984; Smith 1956). Children provide access to material and social resources from the father, kin, and community. "Baby fathers" and their kin are expected to provide some material support for the child. However, nonelite West Indian men's limited access to resources often means that nonelite women (with less access) bear most of the responsibility for children (Bolles 1986; D'Amico-Samuels 1986, 1993). Children link their mothers to the broader community, creating networks of economic, social, and emotional support that expand over time. As they reach adulthood, children (especially daughters) are expected to provide and care for their parents.

For women regardless of class, childbearing and child rearing are major sources of respect – a crucial component of West Indian social relations. Stigma is attached to childlessness (Durant-Gonzalez 1982). Raising more than one generation of children increases the respect earned. Entry into the "big-woman" role is signaled by becoming a grandmother and having adult children who provide goods and services. Both the grandmother role and fostering prolong mothering over a woman's life (Durant-Gonzalez 1982, Smith 1956). This role is marked linguistically as grandmothers are often called "mommy" by the grandchildren they raise. For example, Ms. S. in St. Vincent raised her daughter, two granddaughters, and her dead sister's children. When she was in her early sixties, a year after her granddaughters joined their mother in Brooklyn, Ms. S. was asked by another woman to raise an infant boy. In spite of the physical and financial hardship involved, she delightedly took him on.

Childcare tasks may be shared by a community of West Indian women rather than left to the mother or specified caregiver in both the West Indies and New York, as the common practice of fostering makes clear. Older children and adults look out for children in homes and public or semipublic spaces (the street, shared yards), and caregivers in New York watch and caution other women's charges as well as their own.

Children are considered women's wealth in West Indian cultures (Colen 1987, Lazarus-Black 1990). A woman in New York spoke of her mother in rural St. Vincent who had nine children, forty grandchildren, and twelve great-grandchildren and who cared for many of the "grands" and "great-grands." Her mother said of the children, "These are my riches." Children resemble a kind of social capital that yields benefits both immediately and over time.[6]

In New York the valuing of motherhood is expressed in many forms. Not only are baby showers important West Indian women's gatherings, but christenings are often marked by an elaborateness of preparation and presentation (in dress, food) that parallels that of weddings in dominant North American culture. Several women reported that the three days they attend church (whether or not they go at other times) are Christmas, their wedding day, and Mothers' Day.

Fostering is an extension of the activities, relationships, and values associated with motherhood in West Indian culture. It carries rich meanings and creates webs of interdependent ties in which social and economic resources are shared across time and space through the temporary transferral of parental rights in children. Fostering is central to the experience of migration and reproduction for the West Indian mothers working in New York homes.

Fostering has a long history in the Caribbean and in the families in my sample.[7] Many of the women had themselves been fostered while their mothers migrated for work. Children are also fostered when parents cannot afford to raise them. Generally female maternal kin such as grandmothers or aunts or, less often, paternal kin, fathers, or close friends foster children. Through fostering, childless women have the opportunity to parent and to gain emotional satisfaction as well as ties to growing children and increased status and respect. Fostering may also provide households with additional child helpers. For those with few or grown children, it extends the benefits of parenting. It intensifies emotional and economic ties between fosterers and fostered, as well as between fosterers and migrants, and it generally provides fosterers with access to material goods from migrant parents and from adults whom they have fostered.

West Indian women migrate to New York to provide for their families as a normative aspect of motherhood. Immigration restrictions force them to leave children behind in foster care, which is considered temporary until mothers can legally and financially sponsor children to join them. West Indian mothers in New York support their children, the fosterers, and other kin with remittances of as much as one-half of their income. Remittances take the form of barrels filled with soap, oil, rice, flour, sugar, toothpaste, clothing, and other items unavailable or unaffordable at home. Money is also remitted for school fees and uniforms, medical care, home improvements, and other expenses.

Fostering can create complicated relationships over the life cycle. It is not without emotional costs to parents, children, fosterers, and other family members. Parents and children may endure a variety of negative effects because of their separations. Children may feel like second-class citizens in fostering households, while fosterers complain of insufficient remittances from parents abroad. While close attachments to fostering adults may develop, children may feel confusion, loss, or resentment on account of their mothers' absence. These feelings complicate their already difficult adjustment to life in New York when they eventually join their mothers.

The costs of the social reproduction of West Indian children are borne in the West Indies. The prolonged, legally dictated sponsorship process ensures that the responsibility for socialization and education of children remains with the home community after the mother migrates since many children remain there through most of primary school. However, while workers' wages pay school fees, workers cannot claim children they support at home as tax deductions. While the majority of mothers sent for their children as soon as legally possible, a few made painful but strategic choices to keep their children at home a bit longer. Home provided a safer environment with more people to look out for young children than the hazardous neighborhoods in which mothers could afford housing in New York. The long hours workers devoted to childcare jobs and commuting left little time for their own children. Childcare income does not easily stretch to cover childcare costs, and newly mobilized, local support networks may not accommodate young children. The quality of education itself was a significant factor in decision making. The alien values, physical danger, and poor scholarship that characterize local New York public schools shocked some mothers into keeping their children at home, where primary education takes place in a safe environment steeped in West Indian values. Mothers tended to send for children by adolescence to ensure that they earned a high school diploma in the United States and thus could ease their way into employment and further education. In these and other ways, West

Indian mothers strategized for their children in their struggle in a stratified transnational system of reproduction.

Ideological and Socioeconomic Contexts of Reproductive Labor

Childcare workers' and employers' differential experiences of stratified reproduction are contextualized, in part, in the complex, shifting, and conflicting ideologies and behaviors surrounding reproductive labor in dominant North American culture since the 1950s. A central strand of 1950s gender ideology, which masked women's waged work (Kessler-Harris and Sacks 1987: 72–4, Ryan 1983: 278–80), continued to be influential in the 1970s and 1980s. It assigned reproductive labor to women, held motherhood and waged work in opposition, and prescribed that mothers "stay home" to raise their children. Reproductive labor was devalued and trivialized as unskilled, unwaged women's work in homes (even though many working-class women, especially of color, performed it in other women's homes for minimal wages).

However, economic realities, social behaviors, and changing beliefs and expectations increasingly contradicted this ideology. Motivated by economic necessity, by the pursuit of financial security and personal fulfillment, and, eventually, by feminism, mothers of young children increasingly joined the labor force (Hartmann 1987, Ryan 1983). Household survival or the maintenance of living standards or both (in the face of a decline in real income, husbands' unemployment, and the increases in female-headed households) were key economic factors in women's entrance into the labor market (Hartmann 1987: 50–1). Pursuing financial security, however ephemeral, was crucial to both single and married mothers given the doubling of divorce rates from 1965 to the mid-1980s, the prediction that one-half of first marriages in the mid-eighties would end in divorce (Hartmann 1987: 30), and the increasing "tendency for women to form and head households on their own" (Hartmann 1987: 41). Women's labor-force participation itself and contemporary

feminist ideas changed attitudes about working mothers. Mothers increasingly needed and felt entitled to work outside the home more or less continuously.

However, no corresponding reconceptualization of responsibility for reproductive labor occurred: it was still women's "nonwork" (Kessler-Harris and Sacks 1987: 76) with little or no state, corporate, or community support for childcare, poor parental leave policies, inflexible job schedules, and minimal cross-gender sharing of reproductive tasks. This continuing responsibility for household and children resulted in what Hartmann called a "speed up" for women working for wages (1987: 51) and the reinforcement of the devaluation of reproductive labor.

In 1980s, as more household functions moved to the marketplace, households, according to their means, could buy increasingly commodified reproductive services.[8] With increasing casualization as well, households could hire a variety of waged workers directly or buy services from various for-profit businesses (Colen and Sanjek 1990b). According to Ryan, "In 1980, one in every two food dollars was being spent in a restaurant" (1983: 325). Newspaper articles described businesses with names like "Rent-a-Wife" and "At Your Command" and the catering, childcare, dry-cleaning pick-up and delivery, housecleaning, and grocery-shopping services they offered (Brooks 1987). Such businesses generally relied on a pool of low-paid workers, often of color or migrant or both. Commodification of reproductive tasks reflected and reproduced a racialized class stratification – with, at one level, McDonald's and overcrowded family day care, in which a large number of workers and purchasers are working-class and of color, and, at another level, gourmet meals and in-home childcare supplemented by "prep" pre-school programs with a variety of workers catering to the needs of the wealthy and disproportionately white.

Under these rapidly shifting conditions, the views of female employers with whom I spoke often seemed contradictory and tension-filled. Before the birth of their first child, many believed they would immediately return to work and felt superior to stay-at-home mothers. But the realities of newborns sent many I interviewed to negotiate part-time or less demanding working conditions, often unsuccessfully.

One employing mother of two indicated that she had not intended to work until her children started school (replicating the conditions of her own upbringing), but financial necessity drove her back to teaching nursing: "I never imagined that I would be working – want to be working, need to be working – when I had little kids. And in fact I do want to work because I do feel like there's just so much your brain can take of sitting on the floor and playing, making farmyard noises. Although it's great, but to do it all day, every day, it's too much. There are some women that do it and probably do it well. But I think it's important also to know what you can manage, and I know I need to do something else – and not like go out for lunch with my friends either – the thing that's going to make the brain cells fire up occasionally." Like others she experienced this ambivalence in daily ways: "Even when I'm thinking 'I can't wait to get rid of these kids, they're driving me crazy,' when I actually turn around and walk out of the door, I always feel ambivalent."

Unlike the West Indian women, who were extremely articulate about children being women's wealth, the employers I interviewed had a hard time articulating what having children meant to them. Clearly, becoming parents in the 1980s, as many baby boomers did, meant being drawn into an expanding market in which children and the products and services for them became increasingly commodified. I often speculated about the relationship between this rapidly shifting cultural milieu and employers' inability to give an account of why they had children.

Shifting media images of motherhood and children in New York in the 1980s provide a backdrop for employers' conceptions of having children. In the early 1980s, mothering and reproductive labor were devalued, while overflowing datebooks and "dressing for success" were in vogue and careers were valorized. By the mid-1980s babies surfaced in television, movies, and advertisements as commodities that people collected. Babies became the "cuisinarts of the 1980s" (Heimel 1987), high-

status commodities. Print media, from the *New York Times* to *Self* to *Ms.* and *Working Mother*, published a plethora of articles on motherhood, juggling work and family, and dealing with nannies. This trend was given a major boost when, in 1986 and 1987, the Baby M case turned the focus squarely on the meanings of motherhood as a surrogate mother and the couple who hired her struggled over the custody of a baby conceived by artificial insemination. By 1987 a *New York Times* headline could proclaim that "In TV and Films, as in Life, Babies Are in Fashion Again" (Hirsch 1987). Television and film screens were flooded with images of babies, birth, children, and parents: for example, *Baby Boom* (1987), *Three Men and a Baby* (1987), *Parenthood* (1989). The message was that children were a valuable commodity and could fill a void that work and other activities could not.

By the late 1980s the "mommy track" replaced women's sixty-hour workweeks in media attention, as the focus shifted from women as workers to women as mothers and secondarily as jugglers of family and work. Pregnancy, birth, and having babies were presented as the defining and most meaningful women's experiences. Images of pregnant women, ultrasound fetal images, and birth scenes showed up everywhere, often to sell products not directly related to children – from automobile tires to telephone services. The discourse around new, assisted reproductive technologies and adoption suggested other forms of the commodification of children. In a 1989 American Express television advertisement, a pregnant woman learns during a sonogram that she is carrying twins. In the next scene she counts off the children's furnishings, of which she plans to buy two each, then orders two hamburgers and two milkshakes with her credit card.

Shifts in dominant representations meant that, by 1990, babies and children were firmly entrenched as possessions that necessitated the acquisition of other commodities (and that became more valuable with further investment in goods and services). Children were increasingly represented as those who gave true meaning to life. The impact of these changes and representations has yet to be fully analyzed for either the women who employ childcare workers or for the workers themselves. However, the daily tasks of childcare (except for breastfeeding) remained unglorified in the dominant representations in the midst of changing ideologies, discourses, and behaviors. In reality, reproductive tasks were and are accomplished in a highly stratified way.

West Indian Caregivers' Perspectives on their Work

For West Indian women, paid childcare work entailed complex and contradictory experiences. They generally valued childcare activity, were proud of their knowledge and skills, and were comfortable caring for children. However, inadequate pay, the lack of health, pension, and other benefits, and the lack of respect from employers offended them. Workers expected respect from parents who entrusted them with children. Yet every worker (including those with the "best" employers) related incidents in which they experienced profoundly disrespectful attitudes or behaviors. Doing childcare for money in New York was different from doing it in the kin network at home for love.

Workers had difficulty reconciling employers' dependence on them for care of their children with behavior that they felt denied them status as adult human beings with thoughts, feelings, and families of their own. This contradiction was especially powerful for undocumented workers who were living in and dependent on employers for sponsorship because of the complex interdependence and such structural aspects of live-in work as isolation; relationships that are at once waged, hierarchical, and personal; twenty-four-hour on-call status; and the intimacies of sharing household space. Workers endured exploitation and indignities only to obtain green cards and to allow their children to join them. Ms. T. expressed the sentiments of many when she responded to her employers' humiliating behavior this way: "I want to be treated as a full adult.... Once I had a husband and kids and had the same responsibility as you all,... but now I am in this situation."

Despite the crucial contributions caregivers made to employing households, they frequently felt invisible (as female, working-class reproductive workers of color often are made to feel), particularly when employers regularly failed to inquire about them or their families or to note work that they had accomplished. As one worker put it, they expect you to "give extra to these children" and yet they "treat you as if you were part of the furniture." With more autonomy, full-time live-out workers still contended with long, often erratic hours, low wages, a lack of benefits, the asymmetrical relations of waged work in homes, and employers' lack of consideration for workers' family lives and responsibilities. While many workers regularly worked from 7:30 or 8:00 A.M. to 6:30 or 7:00 P.M., several worked twelve or more hours and a few worked less. In fact, some live-in and full-time workers questioned why some employers had had children when they were too busy to care for them, even morning and night. Nearly two-hour commutes each way to and from work were not unusual, so it is no surprise that workers strongly resented employers' tendency to stay out late without warning or to call in just as they were preparing to leave and ask them to stay later than the usual or agreed time. Workers wondered whether employers saw that they too had lives and families: "It's O.K. for them to ask me to stay extra time because they have their family together, but what about me?... They don't think that I have my family waiting for me."

Differential notions of appropriate behavior for and discipline of children disturbed many West Indian workers whose expectations that children act "respectfully" toward adults were often unmet, particularly when they started a job with older (posttoddler) children who treated them "rudely." Many workers criticized employers' lax discipline and attempted to teach children "manners." One worker voiced her frustration at trying to teach a seven-year-old boy not to drink from a juice pitcher at the refrigerator when he repeatedly retorted, "Why not? My father does." Workers were given the responsibility for socializing children without being accorded the authority to discipline them.

Countless other contradictions arose out of the emotional fallout from caring for children as waged work. The daily work of childcare itself – the caring, the socializing, the investment of physical and emotional labor – promoted affective ties between workers and children. Twelve- or twenty-four-hour childcare responsibility forged bonds between workers and children, especially when workers had raised their charges since infancy. The emotional devastation of separation from their own children often intensified bonds. As one worker told her employer, "I really love my job and I really love [the employer's son].... I never raised my own kids, and I'm raising him." However, emotional involvement with children can make workers vulnerable. Although Ms. H. resented her employer's behavior, she stayed on because she loved the child. Her tolerance eventually ran out, and she left saying, "It's still just a job." The crucial aspect of workers' relations with children is controlled by employers: they have the power to hire, fire, and change the conditions of employment. Even after employment ended, many workers maintained informal contact with their charges, and some attended graduations and other events years later. Ms. M., who moved back to Barbados after several years in the States, made a point of seeing the last child she cared for when she visited New York.

Workers reported that children often called them "mommy." One worker said her employers told their daughter that she was "lucky to have two mommies who love her," and another worker received Mothers' Day presents from employers in the name of the infant for whom she cared. Nevertheless, many workers were aware that employers harbored jealousy toward them. A Barbadian woman told of the jealousy she sensed in her employer, whose little boy "cried 'mommy' behind" her every night when she left work: "Every evening he'd cry, 'I need mommy.' He did it many times. But that particular evening... I was going home, and he cried to get in the elevator with me. And she would say, 'That's not your mommy! I'm your mommy!' And she said [with forced calm], ... 'But I don't mind you calling her mommy because she's nice to you.' ... Prob-

ably when I went home, she said, 'That's not your mommy. That's not your mommy. Don't call her mommy!' "

Employers' Perspectives on Caregivers

Employers depended on caregivers to take responsibility for children for eight to twenty-four hours a day and to stabilize and make possible their busy lives. They acknowledged that "your life depends on your childcare person." One mother who employed a valued caregiver since her son's birth said, "I want her to stay at least until [my son] goes to college." I concentrate here on employers' conceptualizations of childcare, the qualities sought in workers, notions of appropriate age-specific care, and cultural discord between employers and caregivers in these arenas.

Even when most of the child's waking hours were spent in the worker's care, most employing mothers felt that they were still the primary caretakers. Employers wanted substitute caregivers who would provide daily care, nurturance, and socialization. As one employer (a special education teacher with shorter work hours than most) said when questioned about whether she had considered a live-in situation, "I don't need somebody to take over taking care of my children. I need somebody to help me take care of my children. And that's an important distinction to me.... I'm the person who does primary childcare here. And our sitter is the person who fills in for us. Even though she's here eight hours a day, I'm the one."

The majority of employers in my sample hired caregivers on a full-time basis. In most of these cases, childcare and associated tasks such as doing children's laundry, tidying their rooms, and preparing their meals were considered the workers' primary responsibility. Workers often performed more general housekeeping tasks as well, which a few employers expected to be done during naptime so as not to distract workers from children's needs. In addition, workers took children to parks, play dates, and programs. Most employers also indicated that workers did household errands at the post office, dry cleaners, and grocery store. A few employers in my sample hired childcare workers on a live-in basis with responsibility for all housekeeping and childcare. A couple of employers shared their childcare workers' services with another household, either with joint care of children or with the caregiver splitting her workweek between two households.

Employers' profound dependence on caregivers determined the qualities they most valued in them: trustworthiness and reliability. Employers wanted workers they could count on to handle any eventuality responsibly. As one mother of two noted, "You're relinquishing control of your children." They sought workers who would arrive punctually every day – "never sick and never late" – and provide their households with the security of steady, stable childcare. One employer said that in the interest of reliability she would not hire a worker whose life appeared to be "chaotic." Behind this word lurked a set of assumptions about the complicated family lives of immigrant workers as well as a need to deny workers' lives and family responsibilities outside of the job. This denial allowed employers to focus only on their own dependence on workers' labor and not on the interdependence of worker and employer for both their households. In fact, employers generally remained ignorant of their workers' family situations, a strategy that may have enabled them to make demands such as working extra hours.

Many employers felt strongly that they wanted to know what their children did every day in order to feel part of the milestones of child development. As one employer phrased it, when parents aren't there, they want to know "all the idiot details" of their children's activities. Yet a line of inquiry directed toward that end might have insulted a worker by making her feel she was not trusted.

Most employers cited "warmth" and "love for children" as crucial qualities they found in West Indian caregivers. They favored workers who "connected" with children during initial interviews. One employer spoke of what she called West Indian caregivers' "naturalness and warmth" with children and of her preference for hiring them because they "do not see it as inherently degrading work." Although her

use of the term *naturalness* is problematic for its overtones of racial/ethnic and gender stereotyping, her perception of West Indian women's feelings about childcare was valid for most of the workers in my sample.

While discipline was often a sore spot for workers, employers tended to be pleased with West Indian women's care in this arena (as long as they perceived no verbal, emotional, or physical abuse). One employer liked that her sitter was "loving and firm." Another appreciated the worker's setting limits. A third was pleased when the child's grandmother approved of the child's new habit of wiping her mouth after eating or drinking, a behavior taught by her sitter. Few were aware of the potential negative effects that their own more relaxed standards of discipline and acceptable children's behavior might have on workers.

Beyond basic characteristics – all employers sought competent, trustworthy, patient, intelligent workers to provide physical and affective care – what employers sought in caregivers was age-specific. For infants and toddlers they especially desired physical warmth and affection and expressed gratitude that West Indian workers seemed to "love" babies, held them, and gave them what one called "warm, laidback nurturing."

However, in discussions of what constituted appropriate childcare for older, preschool children, employers focused on particular kinds of child-rearing practices and enculturation. Many echoed the mother who said, "What you want for infancy tends to be different from what you want later, as opposed to a play partner or something like that." As children grew, many wanted workers to read to and provide other intellectual stimulation for children; take them to parks, playgrounds, and play dates where they could socialize with other children; engage in interactive play; and enculturate them in particular ways. Although employers appreciated when workers read to children and provided sociability, often through sitters' networks, several thought West Indian sitters might not engage "enough" in interactive play or "get down on the floor and play with" children at home or at playgrounds. As one teacher noted, "I didn't see a lot of caretakers getting their butts in the sand.

I didn't see a lot of women up on the slide." One academic employer reacted negatively to the difference in cultural styles she saw: "Watching the style of the West Indian babysitters in one corner sitting, and by my, I'll admit, my white middle-class standards... doing nothing. Or not intervening enough in the play.... The white middle-class mothers are just running in and intervening and settling disputes, or helping with disputes is how we see it, and there will be a tendency for the West Indian babysitters to let go.... It's just a very different head set. And even though I understand that intellectually, emotionally I find that I disapprove often of the things I see in the playground." Employers who remarked on this sought to hire workers who were more interactive with children. This couple had hired a young West Indian woman whom they described as "unusual." "She was always with the children in the sandbox and stuff like that."

Differential notions of appropriate childcare practices resulted in a clash of cultural styles between West Indian workers and their employers. Employers' expectations that sitters hold babies fit with the workers' cultural codes. But workers were likely to sit on the floor entertaining three-year-olds less than employers desired because of norms of behavior for grown women and their own beliefs about raising children. West Indian women, who do not play on the floor (especially as they age), believe that children should learn independence through play as well as in other ways. Thus, the play dates or park gatherings of sitters and children share elements with West Indian patterns of childcaring. When children play in these situations, West Indian sitters look out for the well-being of all the children in the group but may not continuously intervene in their activity. As in West Indian settings, children play together under adults' protective gaze with infrequent adult involvement; when intervention occurs, it might be by any of the adults present, not only the specified care-giver.

One employer couple appreciated their Barbadian worker's affectionate caring, "great" skill with babies, fierce protectiveness, and teaching of manners, but voiced uncertainty about her capacity to provide other appropri-

ate enculturation for their daughter. Like several parents, they expressed concern that their sitter did not speak "standard English" with the children. One said, "My reservations about [my sitter] increase as [my daughter – then three] gets older.... It would certainly be nice to have a nice well-educated nanny at this point, and we don't. But... school hopefully makes up for that." Like other parents with similar concerns, they enrolled their daughter in a part-time preschool program. They were delighted when they thought a female college student who sat for them at night might work days. They assumed the college student would pick the child up from school and take her to museums and so on, which their West Indian sitter did not do.

While more employers resembled that couple, the veterinarian mother of two children (aged three years and eight months) was an unusual exception. She expressed complete confidence in the competent child rearing of her Jamaican worker and was pleased when the children stayed over with the worker's family in Brooklyn from time to time. While she valued the reading and other learning activities her worker did regularly with the children, she quite clearly stated that nurturance was the key element she sought from caregivers: "I like the Caribbean women who take care of children. There's love there and there's care for the kids. I think children should have a childhood. I don't need to do flash cards with them."

Many employers chose to enroll children in preschool programs (at eighteen to thirty-six months old), supplementing the care of West Indian workers with additional stimulation, educational activity, and interaction with other children and adults. With these expanded services parents could shepherd children from the "nurturance" of West Indian caregivers to preschool programs geared toward Ivy League futures.

Employers' discourse about age-specific childcare expectations reflected a separation between a domain of love and nurturance and one of achievement and "obtaining culture," and stereotyped West Indian caregivers as warm, loving nurturers with questionable educational abilities. In fact, West Indian workers share with their employers a highly developed achievement orientation that motivated their difficult transnational move to New York and their struggles to support, educate, and empower their own kin. Both workers and employers sought to provide their children with what they considered "the best." But employers could afford to buy a range of reproductive services beyond the reach of workers. Such differences and similarities in values were open to massive cultural misunderstanding.

Communication in Employer/ Worker Relations

Communication, crucial in private childcare, was one of the most significant problems for West Indian childcare workers and their employers. Such structural aspects of private childcare work as the relationships that are simultaneously hierarchical and personal, isolation, and lack of formal contracts and grievance procedures as well as the interdependence of worker and employer intensify the importance of communication. Communication was stressful for both worker and employer. Each operated from different sets of assumptions about appropriate behavior, communication, and conflict resolution, yet each often entered into relationships thinking that the other shared basic attitudes and behaviors.

Fear and tension constrained some employers' relationships with childcare providers. Several pointed to the same fear: the potential negative consequences of indicating anger toward or criticizing a worker. One expressed her reluctance to criticize her sitter out of fear that the sitter would "take it out on the children." She didn't think that would ever happen, "but there's always that fear." As she put it, "[These are] employer–employee relationship[s] except these are dealing with something very precious to you – as opposed to just your job." A related concern is what one employer called the "Jamaican babysitter syndrome" – an offended worker walks out the door on Friday and does not return on Monday – which few had experienced but of which many had heard. Dependence on caregivers underlies most employers' fears.

Employers tended toward models of conflict resolution in which people express their grievances verbally and work them through to resolution by talking. Although some were fearful of expressing themselves, some, when they sensed worker dissatisfaction, attempted to probe and coax workers into conversations to identify and talk out problems. However, this model of conflict resolution was not part of the cultural repertoire of most of the West Indian women. While some expressed grievances verbally, most did not expect talking to resolve problems but feared it might lead to potentially explosive conflicts, jeopardizing relationships with employers, job security, and more. Avoidance of conflict was especially crucial to childcare workers who depended on employer sponsorship for legal residence, as their jobs were the means to reunite their families. Without green cards, West Indian workers felt silenced by their powerlessness, subordinate roles, and dependence. And all workers felt that engaging in angry discussion also could erode West Indian women's respectability.

West Indian women also brought assumptions about appropriate attitudes and behavior to interactions with employers. First, they assumed that employers shared a model of reciprocal respect; if one gives respect, one gets it back. Second, they assumed that employers shared their basic conceptions of appropriate behavior. They were taken aback when employers exhibited what they perceived as disrespectful behavior, which they felt was knowingly offensive. This perceived breach in employer conduct made the kind of communication that some employers sought all the more unlikely. Why engage in risky verbal conflict with people who had already offended and insulted them? Many remained silent.[9] Employers found the silence troubling and perhaps threatening.

For employers' models of conflict resolution to be effective, participants must share values and relevant interpersonal skills. However, initiating this kind of conversation, with its veneer of equality and friendliness, masks the power relations of employer and employee. Such conversations are especially problematic when the workplace is the employer's home and workers are isolated from one another.

But silence and other nonverbal communication can result in greater miscommunication and dissatisfaction on both sides.

Conclusion

Examining the cultural construction of parenting and childcare for West Indian workers and their U.S.-born employers illustrates some of the many ways in which reproduction is stratified. Although parenthood and reproductive labor are central in the lives of both West Indian childcare workers and their employers, they are valued and experienced differently. Both groups are caught in the squeeze of reproduction – both try "to do the best for" their children, sharing similar aspirations for them, while maintaining different notions about children and appropriate childcare. However, in a transnational system in which households have vastly disparate access to resources (according to class, race/ethnicity, gender, and place in a global economy), inequalities (themselves historically structured by social, economic, and political forces) shape and stratify experiences of reproduction for workers and employers. Moreover, this very stratification tends to reproduce itself by reinforcing the inequalities on which it is based.

Workers and employers constituted their families and accomplished reproductive tasks in different ways. Employers could, to some extent, buy their way out of their squeeze: their solutions were predicated on the availability of low-waged reproductive labor. In order to raise their own children, workers migrated for jobs and other opportunities, enduring separations from their children. In New York, they faced the devaluation of reproductive labor and class and racial hierarchies that were reflected in available jobs and wages, in the behavior of some employing household members, and in a dearth of affordable, high-quality services for their own children. Although they tried to mobilize local networks for childcare similar to the well-developed ones that they left at home, most struggled with profoundly inadequate care over whose quality they had little control, with limited or nonexistent maternity leave,

and with cramped, costly housing. While a few women in my sample gave birth in New York (those in their late twenties to early forties), many women spoke of not having more children under these conditions. As one woman said, comparing raising children in Jamaica (where she had a lot of help), in London (where her sister has access to government childcare assistance), and in New York, "You need a third hand here." The growing commodification of reproduction and reproductive labor, in the context of continued privatized, female responsibility for reproduction, intensifies stratified reproduction. What is increasingly evident, then, is not only the stratification of reproduction but the reproduction of stratification in the conditions and relations I have described.

A deeper understanding of stratified reproduction will be gained from further examination of the experiences of both workers' and employers' children. Research should also address the reproduction of stratification – the ways in which the inequalities of class, race, and gender are reinforced and intensified through stratified systems of reproduction (Colen and Sanjek 1990a; Rollins 1985, 1990; Rubbo and Taussig 1978). Future work might also inform policy, which assumes social responsibility for raising the next generation through the provision of such supports as parental leave, high-quality childcare and education, and other reproductive services across classes and neighborhoods.

Stratified reproduction permeates many aspects of contemporary world culture. Unpacking the cultural construction of parenting and childcare with attention to gender, class, race/ethnicity, and articulation into a global economy will help us to comprehend the parameters of parenting. Such attention also opens up such issues as entitlement to parenthood, domestic and international adoption, and the uses and consequences of new reproductive technologies, birth control, abortion, and population control. In this system of stratified reproduction, parenting is transnational, interracial, intercultural, cross-class, and informed by a variety of state policies. These complex, world-scale social relations are all around us – on the park benches and in the school pick-ups – inscribed in the daily ways in which West Indian women help raise the next generation of middle- and upper-class New Yorkers.

NOTES

1   By reproduction I refer to the recent conception of social reproduction as "the creation and recreation of people as cultural and social, as well as physical human beings" (Glenn 1992: 4) and as "the array of activities and relationships involved in maintaining people both on a daily basis and intergenerationally" (Glenn 1992: 1). See also Ginsburg and Rapp (1991) and Colen and Sanjek (1990a).

2   Other instances of stratified reproduction include enslaved African women laboring as "mammies" in the antebellum US South, Salvadoran nannies now in wealthy Los Angeles households, and Filipina workers in Kuwait City households. See Sanjek and Colen (1990).

3   Women in my sample migrated from several English-speaking Caribbean countries that broadly share a West Indian culture (see Mintz 1971). Research was conducted in workers' homes and workplaces and at family and community social activities. Attorneys, immigrants' rights organizations, and household-employment agencies were also contacted. For references on various aspects of Caribbean migration, see Colen (1990).

4   They were not employers of the workers interviewed. Seventeen interviews were with mothers only and three included fathers. All of the employers in this urban and suburban sample had attended college and had annual household incomes ranging from $40,000 to over $200,000, with most falling between $50,000 and $120,000. All were married to or living with men except for one single, lesbian mother.

5   Employers' advertisements in newspapers like the *New York Times* and the *Irish Echo* drew an overwhelmingly West Indian response, although other ethnic groups did respond. Employers generally preferred English-speaking West Indian women to

non-English speakers or to other African-diaspora women (who had previously dominated private household work in New York). Many employers perceived West Indians as better educated, more achievement-oriented, and less threatening than working-class African American women.

6   "Children are evidence of women's capacity to love, of having been loved, of adulthood, and of their ability to form and perpetuate alliances. Children are essential to women's identity and power in the common order.... Men also desire children and rarely deny paternity. Yet their children become most important to them later in life when they are themselves adults upon whom a 'big man' can call" (Lazarus-Black 1990: 327, 271).

7   On Caribbean fostering, see Clarke (1957) and Durant-Gonzalez (1976, 1982). For a comparison of fostering and migration for the English-speaking and Hispanic Caribbean, see Soto (1987).

8   This commodification of reproductive labor was distinct from the 1950s' corporate focus on female domesticity, which was aimed at expanding consumer markets (Ryan 1983: 269).

9   Compare Silvera (1983) on silence as a metaphor for the powerlessness of West Indian household workers in Canada. My discussion of silence in employer/worker communication emerges from my fieldwork, as I found no references to West Indian uses of silence in the literature.

REFERENCES

Bolles, A. Lynn. 1981. "Goin' Abroad": Working Class Jamaican Women and Migration. In *Female Immigrants to the United States: Caribbean, Latin American, and African Experiences*, edited by Delores M. Mortimer and Roy S. Bryce-Laporte. Research Institute on Immigration and Ethnic Studies, Occasional Paper 2. Washington, DC: Smithsonian Institution.
—— 1983. *IMF Destabilization: The Impact on Working Class Jamaican Women*. New York: Women's International Resource Exchange Service.

—— 1986. Economic Crisis and Female-Headed Households in Urban Jamaica. In *Women and Change in Latin America*, edited by June Nash and Helen Safa. South Hadley, Mass.: Bergin and Garvey.

Brooks, Andree. 1987. No Time to Do Tasks? Agencies Can Help. *New York Times*, 29 January, C1, C10.

Clarke, Edith. 1957. *My Mother Who Fathered Me: A Study of the Family in Selected Communities in Jamaica*. London: Allen & Unwin.

Colen, Shellee. 1986a. "With Respect and Feelings": Voices of West Indian Child Care and Domestic Workers in New York City. In *All American Women: Lines That Divide, Ties That Bind*, edited by Johnnetta B. Cole. New York: Free Press.

—— 1986b. Stratified Reproduction: The Case of Domestic Workers in New York City. Paper presented at the American Ethnological Society meetings. Wrightsville Beach, NC.

—— 1987. "Like a Mother to Them": Meanings of Child Care and Motherhood for West Indian Child Care Workers in New York. Paper presented at the American Anthropological Association annual meetings. Chicago.

—— 1989. "Just a Little Respect": West Indian Domestic Workers in New York City. In *Muchachas No More: Household Workers in Latin America and the Caribbean*, edited by Elsa M. Chaney and Mary Garcia Castro. Philadelphia: Temple University Press.

—— 1990. "Housekeeping" for the Green Card: West Indian Household Workers, the State, and Stratified Reproduction in New York. In *At Work in Homes: Household Workers in World Perspective*, edited by Roger Sanjek and Shellee Colen. American Ethnological Society Monograph 3. Washington, DC: American Anthropological Association.

Colen, Shellee, and Roger Sanjek. 1990a. At Work in Homes I: Orientations. In *At Work in Homes: Household Workers in World Perspective*, edited by Roger Sanjek and Shellee Colen. American Ethnological Society Monograph 3. Washington, DC: American Anthropological Association.

—— 1990b. At Work in Homes II: Directions. In *At Work in Homes: Household Workers in World Perspective*, edited by Roger Sanjek and Shellee Colen. American Ethnological Society Monograph 3. Washington, DC: American Anthropological Association.

D'Amico-Samuels, Deborah. 1986. "You Can't Get Me Out of the Race": Women and Economic Development in Negril, Jamaica, West Indies. PhD diss., Graduate Center of the City University of New York.

—— 1993. A Way Out of No Way: Female Headed Households in Jamaica Reconsidered. In *Where Did All the Men Go? Female Headed/Female Supported Households: Cross-Cultural Comparisons*, edited by Joan Mencher and Anne Okongwu. Boulder, Colo.: Westview Press.

Durant-Gonzalez, Victoria. 1976. Role and Status of Rural Jamaican Women: Higglering and Mothering. PhD diss., Anthropology Department, University of California, Berkeley.

—— 1982. The Realm of Female Familial Responsibility. In *Women and the Family*, edited by Joycelin Massiah. Women in the Caribbean Project, vol. 2. Cave Hill, Barbados: Institute for Social and Economic Research, University of the West Indies.

Ginsburg, Faye D., and Rayna Rapp. 1991. The Politics of Reproduction. *Annual Review of Anthropology*, 20: 311–43.

Glenn, Evelyn Nakano. 1992. From Servitude to Service Work: Historical Continuities in the Racial Division of Paid Reproductive Work. *Signs: Journal of Women in Culture and Society*, 18/1: 1–43.

Hartmann, Heidi I. 1987. Changes in Women's Economic and Family Roles in Post-World War II United States. In *Women, Households, and the Economy*, edited by Lourdes Beneria and Catherine R. Stimpson. New Brunswick, NJ: Rutgers University Press.

Heimel, Cynthia. 1987. Problem Lady. *Village Voice*, 10 March.

Hirsch, James. 1987. In TV and Films, as in Life, Babies Are in Fashion Again. *New York Times*, 12 October, B5.

Hofferth, Sandra L. 1987. Child Care in the U.S. Statement before the House Select

Committee on Children, Youth and Families, 1 July.

Kahn, Alfred J., and Sheila B. Kamerman. 1987. *Child Care: Facing the Hard Choices.* Dover, Mass.: Auburn House.

Kessler-Harris, Alice, and Karen Brodkin Sacks. 1987. The Demise of Domesticity in America. In *Women, Households, and the Economy,* edited by Lourdes Beneria and Catherine R. Stimpson. New Brunswick, NJ: Rutgers University Press.

Lazarus-Black, Mindie. 1990. Legitimate Acts and Illegal Encounters: The Development of Family Ideology and Structure in Antigua and Barbuda, West Indies. PhD diss., Department of Anthropology, University of Chicago.

Mintz, Sidney W. 1971. The Caribbean as a Sociocultural Area. In *Peoples and Cultures of the Caribbean,* edited by Michael M. Horowitz. Garden City, NY: Natural History Publishers.

Powell, Dorian. 1984. The Role of Women in the Caribbean. *Social and Economic Studies,* 33/2: 97–122.

Rollins, Judith. 1985. *Between Women: Domestics and their Employers.* Philadelphia: Temple University Press.

—— 1990. Ideology and Servitude. In *At Work in Homes: Household Workers in World Perspective,* edited by Roger Sanjek and Shellee Colen. American Ethnological Society Monograph 3. Washington, DC: American Anthropological Association.

Rubbo, Anna, and Michael Taussig. 1978. *Up Off Their Knees: Servanthood in Southwest Colombia.* Michigan Discussions in Anthropology 3. Ann Arbor, Mich.

Ryan, Mary P. 1983. *Womanhood in America: From Colonial Times to the Present.* New York: Watts.

Sanjek, Roger, and Shellee Colen, eds. 1990. *At Work in Homes: Household Workers in World Perspective.* American Ethnological Society Monograph 3. Washington, DC: American Anthropological Association.

Sassen Koob, Saskia. 1984. The New Labor Demand in Global Cities. In *Cities in Transformation,* edited by Michael P. Smith. Beverly Hills, Calif.: Sage.

Silvera, Makeda. 1983. *Silenced.* Toronto: Williams-Wallace.

Smith, Raymond T. 1956. *The Negro Family in British Guiana.* London: Routledge & Kegan Paul.

Soto, Isa Maria. 1987. West Indian Child Fostering: Its Role in Migrant Exchanges. In *Caribbean Life in New York City: Sociocultural Dimensions,* edited by Constance R. Sutton and Elsa M. Chaney. Staten Island, NY: Center for Migration Studies of New York.

US Bureau of the Census. 1990. *Who's Minding the Kids? Child Care Arrangements: Winter 1986–1987.* Series P-70, no. 20. Washington, DC: US Government Printing Office.

Waldinger, Roger. 1989. Immigration and Urban Change. *Annual Review of Sociology,* 15: 211–32.

Working Mother Is Now the Norm, Study Shows. 1988. *New York Times,* 16 June, A19.

20

Femininity and Flexible Labor: Fashioning Class through Gender on the Global Assembly Line

Carla Freeman

Inside Data Air, one of Barbados's largest and long-standing informatics companies (started in 1983), hundreds of women sit in clustered computer stations, entering diagnostic codes and coverage rates for by-pass surgery and appendectomies for one of America's largest insurance companies now performing its claims adjusting 'offshore'. In another of the company's divisions, data from over 300,000 ticket stubs from a single American airline's 2000 daily flights are entered by another hundred operators. One of roughly a dozen companies performing information processing in Barbados, Data Air employs close to 1,000 workers, almost all of whom are women.[1] It is the glamorous adornment of the office-like setting and of the well dressed operators more than the predominance of women alone, however, that sets this workplace apart from other offshore industries (e.g. garments, textiles and electronics assembly plants). The data processing companies are the newest members of a tightly concentrated circle of economic enterprises which encompass the entire 300-year history of this legendary sugar isle. Just west

of the data processing firms are aging factory shells dating from the 1960s and 1970s when enclave manufacturing was thought to be the cornerstone of economic diversification. Beyond them is a new cruise ship terminal, the latest enhancement to the tourism industry which has driven the island's economy since independence in 1966. And at the water's edge, looming large and unbowed is the sugar terminal, a steel rhomboid with a capacity for over 200,000 tonnes of sugar – but under foreign management today, and lucky to see the fruits of a once unimaginably small 50,000 tonne crop.

In the last 15 years, the Caribbean, and Barbados in particular, has become the locus of a new high-tech service industry called 'offshore informatics'. Clerical services are increasingly moving from North American offices to the Caribbean, where women process and edit texts (from Shakespeare to pornography, academic journals to airline tickets and health insurance claims) via satellite hook-ups and sophisticated computer technologies. In many ways, the industry bears

From Carla Freeman, "Femininity and Flexible Labor: Fashioning Class through Gender on the Global Assembly Line," pp. 245–62 in *Critique of Anthropology*, 18/3 (1998). © 1998 by Sage Publications. Reproduced by the kind permission of the author and Sage Publications Ltd, UK.

unmistakable marks of factory-like production, based on the export processing model of development widely adopted in the Caribbean following Puerto Rico's Operation Bootstrap in the 1950s. Much along the lines spelled out by Braverman (1974), as well as his feminist critics (Carter, 1987; Davies, 1982; McNeil, 1987; Pringle, 1988), work is increasingly fragmented, deskilled and feminized in the race by multinational capital to increase its profits.

In the 'post-industrial' US we are by now well aware of the movement of labor-intensive manufacturing industries. We have watched the flight of factories first from northeastern metropolitan centers to southern, mid-western or simply suburban parts of the country, and ultimately to developing countries 'offshore' in Asia, Central and South America and the Caribbean. While the labels on our clothes have for decades announced the global loci of production, the recent NAFTA debates brought this intensifying phenomenon to the consciousness of Americans, Mexicans and Canadians across class and regional divides. What has seldom been mentioned, however, is that computer-based service work – frequently presented as the panacea to economic restructuring, is also amenable to offshore flight. Information-centered office work that was once skilled or semi-skilled and involved the performance of varied tasks from bookkeeping to filing, typing to receiving, now faces increasing rationalization and deskilling in what some have hailed as the 'paperless office'. Today, 'pools' of data entry operators, word processors, and other information workers perform their jobs on anonymous 'typing floors'. Businesses facing exponential increases in the production and management of information have been experimenting with a number of alternative strategies for 'streamlining' data flows, and reducing their costs. Some companies, for example, have centralized secretarial work into large and impersonal data processing floors; others have moved labor-intensive information work out of the workplace altogether and into the arena of suburban homes, paying operators to process insurance claims and credit card applications at 'piece rates'.

At the core of these transformations are women workers – on *both* 'sides' of the international division of labor. Those in the US face job losses or restructuring. 'Homeworkers' or 'temporary workers' are offered low pay with no benefits under the banner of flexibility, which purportedly allows women to juggle wage work with childcare and other domestic obligations. Those 'offshore' in the 'developing world' are promised a clean, cool, comfortable job – and, most importantly, access to the linchpin of modernity – computers. Indeed, critics have described informatics as an electronic sweatshop, where once-skilled white-collar workers have been reduced to production-line automatons, demoted and proletarianized. Supporters of the industry, on the other hand, emphasize its clean and clerical, 'professional' white-collar setting, and take pains to disassociate it from traditional factory work.

However, with different ends in mind, women, local officials and the transnational management all sustain a veil of ambiguity around the informatics industry and its job categories. Each group points to its office-like nature including fashionable and professional-looking workers to hail different measures of local/transnational success: from the transfer of technology to the developing world, to the promotion of a new growth industry and foreign exchange for the ailing sugar and tourism-based economy, and the creation of avenues for the advancement of women in Barbados.

Herein lies a clue to the unique stature of the industry and its offshore workers that sets it/them apart from their manufacturing counterparts, and, to a great extent, ensure that these unorganized working women will remain so. Informatics' novelty and its widely touted links to the 'information revolution' have created a rhetorical space of invention outside the conventional occupational categories. This space is filled with ambiguous but powerful notions of a computer age where new kinds of literacy and practice represent the promise of modernity, and, in effect, where those associated with informatics have been able to define a workplace identity almost from scratch.[2]

By choosing to work in the large 'open offices' of the offshore informatics zone, Barbadian women can break with socially constructed constraints in several (perhaps ironic) ways. In such workplaces, they sever the symbolic 'over-lordship' of the white 'massa', for their remote (sometimes overseas) foreign white employers, who are not seen as carrying the burden of an association with slavery and racial hierarchy. Second, in the cool, clean realm of informatics, production supersedes all else, and little in the way of family connections, village origin, political affiliation let alone seniority affects pay scales or promotions. Generally, informatics workers have little direct contact with managers. Supervisors hand out work but even they rely on computers to calibrate operators' absences, performance and bi-weekly progress – a process largely immune to personal animus. While women clearly express resentment and stress associated with electronic monitoring, they *also* prefer it to the capriciousness and favoritism of the traditional supervisor.[3]

On the other hand, some of the advantages of local paternalism are not missed by workers even in this super-high-tech arena, and by lobbying energetically, data entry operators have succeeded in forcing transnational firms, much against their will, to bend and 'harmonize' with the local scene. For example, workers on the night shift of Data Air convinced management of the need for a privately operated transportation system to supplement the local bus service in the evenings, to ensure their safe journeys home. This costs Data Air $100,000 a year, and through intra-industry pressure has become a standard perk within the informatics sector at large.

Strong pressure from female employees has also forced foreign companies locating in the West Indies to rethink their standard worker profile (typically defined as young, single, well educated and childless females) abandoning, for example, the usual pregnancy tests which elsewhere in the world have been a commonplace in recruitment policy. Instead, in Barbados, one can now find foreign managers extolling the commitment and superior labor of self-sacrificing mothers, as opposed to mercenary and 'consumer-obsessed' young girls reflecting the simple reality of child bearing in young women's lives, and the fact that motherhood has never precluded wage work

for West Indian women.[4] Within this dialectic between local and global forces, other foreign transnational management practices have also been resisted. When 'Total Quality Management' (or TQM)[5] was introduced, the inter-hierarchical 'teams' and attempts at Japanese styled participatory 'work circles' were met with suspicion and unease. Some women complained that meeting together with managers 'just wasn't right', and that the mandatory use of first-names, designed to enhance familiarity and a 'corporate family' ethic, was 'awkward' and even 'disrespectful'. At the other extreme, workers' attempts to preserve some familiar aspects of local capitalist paternalism, such as company health coverage, have been uniformly resisted – along with any pressure toward unionization – by foreign transnationals.

While much of the literature about transnationals and women's labor has portrayed internationally consistent hegemonic measures to 'tap into' and 'use up' global female workforces, the Barbadian informatics zone reveals striking examples in which women workers have been deeply involved in the establishment of unique images and practices integral to the formation of the informatics industry. As such, they counter the assumption that multinational corporations simply scour the globe availing themselves of systematically cheap and docile pools of female labor, and demonstrate that these are active processes in which corporations, state administrators, local elites *and local women workers all* participate in the process of defining – indeed, creating – these female labor forces and the work they perform in particular, locally specific ways.

Because of its new and highly valued status within the rubric of 'off-shore industries' informatics has opened up the possibility for new definitions, new associations and, indeed, new identities. It is this space of invention that helps to explain one of the most striking phenomena surrounding the informatics sector in the Barbadian economy – the simultaneous lack of interest in unionization, and the degree to which women are willing to work long hours performing demanding and tedious work for a lower wage than that offered in a number of other sectors.[6]

Informatics has introduced a workplace discipline wholly unprecedented in the Barbadian context. Operators working on rotating shifts undergo constant surveillance by supervisors in their glass-enclosed offices and even more persistently, by the electronic panopticon of the computer itself. Their pay is determined by their ability to meet production quotas measured by keystrokes per hour, and demands of 99 percent accuracy. Lateness, absences and bathroom breaks are recorded and calibrated along with speed, accuracy and longitudinal progress. High unemployment (24 percent in general and estimated at 30 percent for women) is undeniably an important factor in the appeal of these jobs, but it is not the only one.[7] In many cases data processors pass up better-paying jobs in other sectors of the economy.[8] Among these are not only low-prestige jobs in agriculture and domestic work but also jobs in other service areas like retail sales, where the minimum wage rate is higher than data entry's unregulated base pay, and where job demands are clearly less arduous.[9]

Informatics remains a unique and elusive arena not only because of its slippery place between white- and blue-collar labor processes. 'Professionalism' and in particular 'professional looks' are noted by workers, management and state officials as distinguishing this industry from other sectors, particularly assembly-line manufacturing. High-tech modernity, as embodied most powerfully in the emblem of the computer and a distinct style of office-worker dress, lie at the heart of this image, and each of these three groups are distinctly invested with its importance – the corporate managers who count on a disciplined and flexible workforce, the government officials who anxiously hail informatics as a new cornerstone of national development and women workers, whose reasons are the most complex and interesting of all.

Disputing Appearances: Fashioning the Gender of Class

One hot afternoon at the crowded Lower Green bus stand in Bridgetown, Barbados, children in neat school uniforms and shoppers laden with heavy parcels hiding from the baking sun found their own hushed conversations punctuated by sudden shouting and defensive retorts. The morning shift at Global Informatics Ltd[10] had been busy, and the women workers looked eager to leave when the clock struck 3:30. Five of the 60 young women workers on the shift emerged from the glass doors animated as they compared their daily work rates and resultant pay. At the shift's end, they changed from slippers to patent leather and well polished high heels and headed toward the bus stand. The commotion that erupted there centered around one of the data processors, boldly adorned in a floral skirt suit and donning an elaborately braided hair style with great aplomb. Suddenly she noticed her ex-boyfriend who had been waiting for her under a shady breadfruit tree. 'You see *she*? You *see* she?' he shouted to all around, motioning wildly for everyone to look closely. 'Don' mind she dress so, when Friday come, she only carryin' home $98!' What his outburst conveyed was, 'in case you people might mistake her for a middle-class woman with a good office job, let me tell you, she is really just a village girl with a factory wage'. Onlookers shifted on their feet, some showed signs of disdain for the public airing of a domestic dispute; a group of schoolgirls laughed. The taunts so disturbed another group of data processors at the bus stand that some beckoned a manager inside to come and 'stop the palava'.

The threat posed by mocking the image of prosperity and professionalism of the data processors is conveyed in a Barbadian adage that warns, 'Gold teet(h) don'(t) suit hog mout(h)', and implies that even extravagant adornments can't hide one's true station in life. What the adage and story together reveal is a deep tradition of propriety and expected conformity between class status and appearance. For 'Little England', the once prized sugar isle of the British empire, conformity and respectability lie at the heart of cultural tradition, and 'knowing one's place' is an admonition well known to Bajans of all generations. By exposing the realities of her meager wage in contradistinction to her impressive appearance, the disgruntled exboyfriend threatened to undermine a powerful set of images created and enforced by women workers and the informatics industry that employs them. His public outcry cautions against the dangers of masquerade. As Bourdieu so aptly put it, 'These calls to order ("Who does she think she is" or "not for the likes of us"), reaffirm the principle of conformity...They contain a warning against the ambition to distinguish oneself by identifying with other groups, that is, they are a reminder of the need for class solidarity' (1984: 380–1).[11] While dress may seem a minor issue within a study of women workers in multinational industries, here amidst the high-tech glow of computer terminals within this new niche of the 'office-factory', dress and appearance become vital embodiments of the informatics sector and of new feminine identities for working women as members of a new pink-collar service class.[12] As such, dress and appearance become central to the maintenance of ambiguous boundaries of class status, the diminution of class consciousness and to the frank absence of interest in unionization.

Despite a long history of trade unionism in Barbados and the well known strength of the Barbados Workers' Union (BWU), the largest industrial workers' union representing a number of public and private sector trades and occupations, foreign-owned data entry companies are uniformly non-unionized. The Industrial Development Corporation claims that within the industrial relations context of the island, 'collective bargaining is the accepted practice for the agreement of employment terms and conditions, but union membership is not compulsory' (IDC, n.d.: 14). However, 'there is a sort of unwritten understanding that we [the unions] are not to go in there', as one labor unionist from the Barbados Workers Union described the relationship between labor and the offshore sector. While several union representatives expressed both annoyance at being kept out of these offshore industries, and keen interest in recruiting within this expanding new sector, during the Democratic Labour Party-led years of the fieldwork (1989–92) they avoided any strong efforts to unionize. The BWU stated matter of factly that in the face of rising un-

employment, and the government's strong push to recruit foreign investment, there was little point in making waves within established offshore operations. And not surprisingly, from the management standpoint, the consensus was quietly but clearly against unionization. As one foreign general manager said:

> I'm not against unions; I used to be a union man. Unions have a role to play, but obviously as a manager of a company I would prefer to work without them. I can respond to problems without the interference of a middleman who is motivated by political ends.

His comment reflected a widely held sentiment toward the Barbados Workers' Union around whom frequent charges of 'conflict of interest' revolved. Three senior union officers were members of parliament for the governing DLP, including the General Secretary, Leroy Trotman. Another Deputy General Secretary actually served on the DLP cabinet. The quiet agreement by the unions to keep out of the offshore enterprises reflects, to a large degree, their compliance with the export-led economic development plan as articulated by the state and clearly espoused by the then-ruling DLP. Interestingly, since 1993 when the Democratic Labour Party government lost office, the leadership of the Union, no longer serving simultaneously as members of government, turned the organizing of the offshore sector into a high-profile campaign. However, even now, with unemployment rates lower, the state of the economy more stable than in the previous period and greater activism on the part of the BWU, the informatics workers in both local and foreign owned companies are resistant to organizing.

Women are not drawn to labor organization not because they are naturally 'docile' and 'submissive' as multinational corporations have claimed for female workers across the global assembly line, but because their work in informatics offers them *symbolic* as well as economic capital that they are deeply interested in securing. The trade unions are seen as offering nothing that the human resources and employee relations departments of the firms do not already provide. The unions in Barbados, like other national institutions in the political–economic arena, have, according to an active female trade unionist, been a patriarchal stronghold not merely in allowing little participation of women within the movement itself, but also in its limited interest in predominantly female sectors of employment.

For the women workers in informatics, the emphasis on appearances and dress simultaneously comes to represent another medium of discipline (through corporate dress codes, peer pressure and pure expense) as well as an aperture of creative expression and a source of identification and pride. An identifiable *look* is both individually defined and collectively fostered. Both industry managers and operators themselves articulate standards for appropriate work attire – on one hand the official dress code specifies 'professional' appearance and deportment; on the other, operators and supervisors have honed and refined their own expectations that surpass those established by management. In one case, a group of employees started a campaign to introduce a company uniform in the colors of the company logo.

More generally, the level of surveillance and scrutiny operators and supervisors impose upon each other (more through gossip than formal reprimands) has introduced a self-awareness and self-discipline surrounding dress, hairstyles and general appearance that has reinforced this unmistakable image. The women's professional appearance is admired by industry affiliates[13] as well as daily passers-by. New styles copied from foreign pattern books and boutiques, embellished with individualized details like a pocket handkerchief in matching fabric, a sash, belt or covered buttons to accent a bold color, carry enormous symbolic importance in the informatics scene in ways which defy socially prescribed identities linking class, job titles and appearances. The 'pink collar' then, with its ubiquitous 'skirt suit', represents a sort of feminine/professional disguise. The data entry operator essentially performs a repetitive, tedious, semi-skilled sort of 'blue-collar' work but in place of the dust and fumes of garment and electronics houses, she is situated within a cleaner, cooler 'white-collar' setting. As part of the trade, she is expected to appear distinctly feminine and 'professional'.

As the earlier vignette implies, preoccupation with appearances, deportment and 'respectability' is a well known and much discussed phenomenon in the West Indies, associated particularly with women aspiring to the norms of white European society.[14] However, the lines between respectability and 'show-offiness' or 'dibby dibby styles' (whorish or sexually 'loose' appearances) are crucial. Admonishments in the employee-written newsletter echo the old Bajan adage 'a pick fowl en' got nuh pedigree ...' or, 'since one's feathers speak loudly of one's station in life, one should take care to dress in an appropriate manner'. One manager noted to me:

> Women are expected to dress professionally here. This is not a production mentality like jeans and tee shirts. When you see a group of the young ladies like the ones from Data Air, you see that they're much better dressed than the ones from the assembly plants ... They're probably not getting paid much better but their work environment is a cleaner one, a purer one, and they in fact live out that environment. The Data Air office is very plush so the young ladies working in there perceive that they are working in an office and they dress like it and they live like it ... it only got started when the data entry business got started – this new breed of office-type workers. They equate themselves with ... clerical staff in an office and they carry themselves in that way.

Like multinationals in other parts of the world, these high-tech service enterprises have shrewdly tapped into a strong Barbadian concern with appearance and have turned this set of cultural values to the advantage of international capital, by encouraging workers to identify with a well defined corporate image. By setting standards for appearance that give workers pride, the companies enhance the operators' commitment and sense of obligation to their employer. And, by creating a professional-looking working environment through decor and office ergonomics ($200 swivel chairs and custom designed work spaces), corporate managers expect in return, not only professional-*looking* workers but ones who are also willing to put in overtime on demand, as this is what professionals are expected to do. Corporate imperatives such as meeting deadlines, accommodating rush orders, or processing heavy batches of tickets or encyclopedia chapters on tight schedules, demand a great deal of overtime and flexible scheduling on the part of the workforce (e.g. staying late, coming in on weekends and working double shifts). One way of encouraging a willingness to put in 'the extra mile' is to make employees feel that it is to their benefit as well to see these goals met.[15]

What we are witnessing in Barbados is the emergence of a new West Indian woman who moves within a transnational arena, both as a producer, through the data she processes, and even more literally as a consumer, as she increasingly seeks out imported goods and invents new styles to mark her status. In light of the low wages of informatics workers, maintenance of this requisite 'professional' appearance is only made possible through additional economic activities – some of which closely resemble traditional market exchanges or home-based services, and others which are much more radically transformative transnational movements involving air travel.[16]

As an incentive scheme to promote high levels of production and reliability at work, highly productive informatics operators are rewarded with bonus pay and special 'thank you cards', redeemable for airline travel (compliments of Data Air's parent company). With such vouchers, women fly between Barbados, San Juan, Miami and New York on weekend or week-long shopping sprees, sometimes specifically orchestrated by local travel agents, and including inexpensive motels and ground transport to convenient shopping malls. In their travel, they are both generating income through the re-sale of goods, and 'checking styles' as they scour department stores and fashion books. Through the purchase and informal marketing of imported clothes, accessories and household goods, these new 'suitcase traders' add another dimension to their position and identity as workers in the transnational economy.[17]

Traditionally Barbadians have always supplemented their wages in the formal economy with income from informal trade and production. This practice is common among all classes. Doctors and members of parliament, white and black, will keep chickens, pigs or Barbadian black-belly sheep for occasional sale. Working-class men might cut hair or fish in their free time to earn extra money, and since the days of slavery, female country higglers have been the primary actors in vibrant produce markets across the West Indies. In addition to sewing clothes and school uniforms, women typically bake cakes, prepare traditional foods or braid hair for friends and acquaintances. What is different about the informatics sector is the degree to which it intensifies this cultural tradition by increasing both the demand for and the supply of new goods. By cultivating workers' identity in terms of a professional style, the informatics sector has become a site of display – a showcase of not only new age technology but also of new age femininity, and the latter has become entwined with fashion and 'accessorizing' in ways that deliberately distinguish them as a group from women workers in similar income brackets (hence the demand side of the equation). Informatics workers, therefore, not only subsidize low wages through their extra informal labor, but also sustain the mirage of professional prosperity and upward mobility for women that the Barbadian government and the international corporate sector so anxiously assert. At the same time the travel vouchers help to stimulate the supply of new and imported fashions and styles. Recently, among the data processors, fashion design and sewing courses have become popular after-work 'improvement' activities, and the installment purchase of sewing machines is a frequent expenditure. Home-based needle working (seamstressing), and the new 'suitcase trading' have become central arenas through which data processors not only supplement their formal income, but also refine their own 'professional look'.

The informal sector is important not simply for supplementing women's formal wage and increasing their purchasing power, but also in terms of the enjoyment and satisfaction women derive from creating and supplying new consumer goods and styles for their friends, family, fellow workers and themselves. The role played by the informal needleworker and suitcase trader is significant, therefore, not simply in providing a cheaper alternative to the machine-made clothes in the boutiques mushrooming around the island, and enabling fashion to play such a large role in the lives of working-class women, but they appear as well to be bound up in a growing globalization of consumption and aesthetics.

The links between women's practices as producers and consumers challenges what has for the past decade seemed to be a useful way of formulating the gendered contours of the international division of labor. Mies (1986) argued that the international division of labor 'worked' only when the following two conditions were fulfilled: production costs were dramatically lowered by export-oriented enterprises which depended on the cheap labor of docile and malleable Third World women; and consumer-housewives in rich industrialized countries were mobilized to purchase goods produced in the Third World. Both of these strategies, she argued, depended largely on women – Third World women as producers, First World women as consumers. Her analysis of the silent relationship between women on 'both sides' of the international division of labor was ground-breaking. However; Mies's model misses the complexities of transnationalism as these young Bajan data processors now experience it. What Mies could not have expected was the increasing rate at which Third World women too become consumers. Specifically, what the informatics workers demonstrate is the integral relationship between their experience as producers and the form and context in which they increasingly consume transnational goods, styles and culture. What makes mass consumption possible among these Barbadian women, however, is not simply their employment in the transnational arena, but their involvement in newly expanded practices of informal marketing and trade. Women's wage-earning employment as data processors becomes closely intertwined with informal economic activities that simultaneously place them within an international sphere where they are both the producers and consumers of services, commodities and styles. Women in developing countries who just a short while ago may have provided

only the labor behind these consumer goods that Mies depicts as the very life-blood of suburban housewives of the industrialized West, now *themselves* demand many such items of adornment and convenience.[18]

A number of recent writings about consumption, and fashion in particular (e.g. Craik 1994; de Certeau 1984; Miller 1987; Pringle 1988; Willis 1991; E. Wilson 1985), have challenged the notion that consumption essentially implies extravagance, waste and false consciousness. Others (e.g. Lee 1993; Rutz and Orlove 1989; Wilk 1990, etc.) have reminded us that consumption is as central to exchange as production. I take up these arguments in order to suggest that we explore the ways in which production and consumption are integrally connected – not simply as economic activities but in creating feminine identities – in this case, among a new category of workers. This entails a view of consumption not simply as a passive act – or worse, of consumers as uncritical dupes of multinational advertising. Rather, consumption becomes a process with creative possibilities and multiple meanings. For the data processors, consumption provides a means for social differentiation – for *making oneself* through the expression of taste, where taste is a signifier of class (Bourdieu 1984). New forms of consumption do not, in and of themselves, transform people into different sorts of human beings. However, as Mintz recently remarked about the working classes in late 18th-century Britain, 'consuming exotic products purchased with their own labor – which allowed them to see themselves as *being* different because they were able to choose to consume differently – surely helped to *make* them different' (1996: 78). The suggestive power of consumption that allows people to *imagine themselves otherwise* by participating in such practices embodies both creative as well as potentially transformative qualities.[19]

Elements of danger (as exhibited by the bus stand episode) and pleasure, embodied in the professional image-making of the informatics zone, lie in the blurring between this symbolic work and its economic underpinnings, indeed, in the delineation of class itself. The informatics operators in Barbados cannot concoct their jobs per se – they earn factory wages and have no *organized* effect on the use or structure of either the economic capital or the political order in the society in which they live. These companies may, as many others have done, suddenly decide to leave Barbados in search of more profitable conditions elsewhere in the developing world. However, the status women derive from their work (even if more 'symbolic' than economically 'real') has enabled them to contribute to the definition of a new occupational category whose mystery allows them some power of invention, and this in turn, extends beyond the realm of informatics.

At the same time, the concern about appearance and the desire to look professional has as much to do with demarcating a line which separates them from factory workers as it does with identifying with their foreign bosses. It has little or nothing in fact to do with the actual service aspect of their job, as their clients are by definition overseas and invisible. But it has everything to do with the public persona they and their employer wish to cultivate in their own communities.

Part of the intriguing nature of this emphasis on professional demeanor and deportment is precisely related to the hidden nature of the work. Others (Hochschild 1983; Leidner 1993; Paules 1991) have noted the importance of emotional labor and the gendered dimensions of service work in other occupations (e.g. restaurant waitresses, airline flight attendants). For a job performed not only in the 'back office' but thousands of miles away from its clients' gaze, the importance of appearances is notably ironic. In fact, professional dress is as important for the workers' *commute* as for the workplace itself. While most informatics companies are located in a centralized information processing zone in the capital city of Bridgetown, one company recently set up an operation in the countryside to save women the commute, and save themselves transportation costs demanded by women on the night shift. The experiment failed miserably, however, as the lackluster building, surrounding cane fields and view of the plantation yard held little appeal. Despite the early hours and often long bus rides demanded by shift work, women prefer to go to town. Indeed, unlike their urban American counterparts who don smart suits with running shoes en route to the office, the Bajan data operators display shiny patent leather or well polished shoes and bags on their commute to work or fast food lunch break. In the chilly recesses *inside*, however, high heels are often kicked under desks, in favor of stocking feet, plastic slippers or 'software' as sneakers are commonly called.

By escaping the paternalism of the traditional Barbadian workplace for a comparatively meritocratic, impersonal informatics company, and simultaneously challenging foreign management to localize their practices and workplaces with selected components of that same paternalism, Barbadian women have created a hybrid space between the transnational and the local. In this space, they are freer than at any time in Barbadians' living memory to construct a gendered occupational identity that marks itself with valued emblems of middle-class status, and through their patterns of consumption and their unique 'pink-collar' production, they are engaged in blurring class distinctions themselves. On the other hand, with the emphasis on distinguishing themselves from the ranks of their factory-working neighbors, class solidarity is clearly de-emphasized.

Of course, the mystery is not only liberating but burdensome as well, and both the freedom and the weight falls heaviest upon the shoulders of the women themselves – as they are pushed into a double or even triple day[20] to make ends meet, *and* sustain the 'professionalism' mirage. Their efforts to achieve middle-class status converge but are not identical with corporate and government efforts to convince them of the 'professional' nature of their work, and it bears repeating that at every turn the informatics workers are confronted with surveillance, discipline and their structurally subordinate status. By trying on fashions, adopting a new look and publicly obscuring the labor process of informatics in favor of its office appearance, I am not arguing that women are convinced that they are indeed 'professionals'. However, they are adamant that they are not factory workers, and, as such, become less interested and even hostile to movements towards class solidarity through unionization, since this would require an identification with occupational categories they precisely wish to deny. Their self-concepts (as revealed in taste, style and practices) have changed along with the distinct fashioning of informatics in ways that mark new identities along the transnational continuum of gender and class. At the heart of this lies disjuncture and contestation between material realities and symbolic appearances, between local paternalism and transnational anonymity, between compliance and resistance, and between alienation and pleasure.

NOTES

1 Many analyses of global industrialization have grappled with the question of why *women* have constituted the preponderant labor force along the global assembly line. Most attribute this phenomenon to the clear-cut prescriptions by transnational corporations for young, single, childless women who are construed as docile, dexterous, malleable and ultimately an ideal low-wage pool of available workers. Others have proposed that women's marginality in local labor forces leaves them few alternatives to the offshore sector. A number of key works about young women workers in Malaysia, Mexico, the Philippines and South Korea, have emphasized the point that patriarchal forces within women's families, under the local state and within multinational industries have reinforced each other and have contributed to women's vulnerability (e.g. Fernandez-Kelly 1983; Kim 1997; Ong 1987; Pearson 1993). The context of the Afro-West Indies, where stereotypes of women as strong and independent matriarchs have competed with those of docile and submissive 'girls' stands to challenge the apparently universal profile of the 'ideal' offshore worker (see Bolles 1983 on Jamaica; Kelly 1987 on St Lucia).

2 While surely women's notions of modernity transcend the realm of computers and informatics (e.g. through the tourism sector, the intensity of imported commodity goods,

media, etc.) the importance of the computer here is emphasized because this tool is a special modernist icon. It feeds into a long tradition privileging education as the source of upward mobility, and heightens this ethic with the hyperbolic sense of technological advancement – and the threat that developing nations might find themselves marginalized from the high-tech fast track. For these women, then, the computer is a powerful sign connoting progress and the future – distinct from agriculture and, to some extent, from manufacturing, which have come to be associated with the colonial and early independence periods. The computer is linked to white-collar services such as finance and accounting (the most frequently cited career goal among the women I interviewed) and to professional work in general. Among the data processors, correspondence courses in computer fields (from programming to various sorts of 'literacy' courses) are very popular, as are evening and part-time courses at the Community College and Polytechnic.

3 'Stress' is defined in a variety of ways by the women in these jobs. For some, stress involves physical pain and suffering from the sedentary and repetitive labor of keyboard work (i.e. a range of musculo-skeletal discomfort including back aches, neck pain, wrist, hand and finger pain). For others 'stress' is experienced as headaches and vision problems, and for many is equated with the experience of 'tension' and 'pressure' associated with piece rate work in which wages are determined by the number of keystrokes per hour and accuracy rates.

4 See Freeman (2000) for a more detailed discussion of these competing paradigms of femininity and their operation in the informatics industry and national context more generally.

5 The now popular management approach credited to W. E. Deming, who introduced the quality revolution in Japan's automotive industry in the 1950s.

6 Announcements in the local newspapers for jobs in informatics create a frenzy of interest unmatched by any other industry. One recent ad for 15 employees generated

3,000 applications, nearly all of whom were women. In contrast to the pattern of volatility and high turnover within transnational industries across the world, attrition rates are as low as 2%.

7   These rates of unemployment reflect the period of fieldwork (1989–91) and have declined somewhat in the past five years; however the attraction of these jobs for women has not waned.

8   The only established minimum wage rate is set for domestic workers and shop assistants – at BDS $30 (US $15)/per day or US $75/week. While this is roughly the same base wage as that offered to the data entry workers, many are not assured full work weeks, and therefore risk a lower weekly pay packet.

9   In a recent paper, Roger Rouse (1991) noted that Mexican migrants without papers in California are known to opt for lower-paid and marginal jobs at night vs. jobs during the day in order to preserve their tradition that they refer to as 'andar libre' or to travel and move about freely. In both cases, the Bajan data operators and the Mexican migrants are making choices that reflect not only individual strategies but cultural priorities – one of masculine freedom to engage in a social world precluded by many wage-earning daytime jobs and the surveillance of the INS, and the other of feminine desire to work in a 'professional' arena where they are not subject to paternalistic relations that often involve sexual harassment, and where the nature of the job itself is still imbued with the mystery and appeal of computer technology. For both of these groups, the compromise involves the choice of a low-paying job in order to preserve the tradition of, or invent a new space for, certain liberties. In the data processing zone, one woman quit her job and took a position in a neighboring cigar factory. Her decision was met with disdain and shock on the part of her fellow data entry co-workers which revealed a deep sense of betrayal – both personally, and perhaps more importantly of their shared identity they believed to be superior to that of a cigar assembly worker.

10   All names of companies and individuals are pseudonyms.

11   See Chandra Jayawardena's classic work *Conflict and Solidarity in a Guianese Plantation* (1963), which demonstrates another era's expression of subtle challenges among the 'middle strata' to a rigid class structure, elsewhere in the Anglophone West Indies. In this discussion of the position occupied by clerks, members of the 'Junior Staff' on the plantation, and their attempts to distinguish themselves from laborers, and ally themselves in lifestyle and habits with the 'Senior Staff' (managers, overseers, professional staff) several key themes emerge as parallels to the experience and expressions of the data entry workers in late 20th-century Barbados. Despite the clerks' efforts to demarcate themselves, however, Jayawardena notes that status differentiation is never complete, since clerks were typically bound by kinship, religious affiliation, marriage and/or residential proximity to laborers. As such, the perceptions by clerks of laborers and by laborers of clerks were somewhat fraught, in a manner not unlike that of the neighboring factory and data entry workers.

12   I develop the discussion of class in its dual economic and social dimensions and its relationship to multiple forms of capital (Bourdieu 1983, 1987).

13   The state offices that initially characterized informatics as a branch of offshore production, are now keen on its 'clerical services' label and have readily adopted the industry's language of 'open offices'. Through re-casting the internal workings of the industry to localize them in certain ways, and through sustaining a clearly demarcated high-tech clerical image, a new work category is in the making.

14   The paradigm of 'respectability' and 'reputation' was introduced by Peter Wilson (1969) and has been discussed and debated by several others (Abrahams 1979; Besson 1993; Miller 1994; Sutton 1974; Yelvington 1995). Essentially the duality refers to one set of values associated with stratification and inequality

that, Wilson claims, represents a specific-ally female tendency to adopt the values of the dominant social order – colonial white society – and another, more Afro-Caribbean in nature, which emphasizes equality and resists the hierarchical order of respectability through the mode of 'reputation'. Reputation, associated more with males, embodies a sense of 'comuni-tas' across those of a low social status (Sutton, 1974: 96).

The preoccupation with appearance is reflected as well in other practices such as diet and fitness. Indeed, 'Fit for Life', a popular American diet/lifestyle program, became popular among many of these women, particularly those who had gained a significant amount of weight (often up to 50 lbs) following marriage and childbirth. The interest in fitness is part of a changing aesthetic valuing slimness over the once-esteemed full and voluptuous figure.

15 This is where the rhetoric of being 'part of the corporate family' is frequently employed.

16 Several other recent works addressing the expansion of mass consumption in the developing world illustrate that we cannot assume that transnational consumption implies hegemony over taste and cultural practice. Daniel Miller, writing about modernity in Trinidad, argues that it is precisely through the acts and experience of consumption that Trinidadians come to engage in local cultural practices that de-fine and maintain their Trinidadianness (1994: 206). Hannerz and Lofgren, in a recent article (1994), make clear that what seemed to be an Americanization of marketing strategies and culture in Swe-den led instead to a sharpening of a dis-tinctly Swedish culture. My research indicates that data entry operators in Bar-bados appropriate and adapt trans-national symbols – including dress, workplace nomenclature, the computer – not in ways that foster national identity, but in ways that subvert both the repres-sive paternalism of domestic capitalism, and the discipline and homogenizing

forces of transnational capitalism, and allow them creative room to define them-selves in a society that has historically em-phasized a conservative conformity and condemned conspicuous display. This, incidentally, marks some intriguing con-trasts with the Trinidadian case Miller describes (1994). See Freeman (1997 and 2000) for a discussion of women's multiple forms of informal labor and their connec-tions to changing patterns of consumption.

17 See Freeman (1997) for a fuller discus-sion of this form of transnational 'higgler-ing' and its significance in these women's lives.

18 It bears mentioning that the depiction of the Western consumer housewife also re-quires reformulation, as women in the industrialized or 'post-industrial' West are also more and more likely to be sim-ultaneously producer/consumers.

19 Where Bourdieu (1984) saw distinction as pernicious and repressive, de Certeau (1984) presents consumption as poten-tially creative. Contemporary debates about mass consumption can be roughly characterized as emphasizing either its possibilities for creative and even rebelli-ous expression, or its reflection of the constraining, dehumanizing, homogeniz-ing forces of an ever expanding and ever exploitative global capitalism. My effort here is to emphasize the simultaneously disciplining and pleasurable, prescriptive and creative qualities of women's con-sumption through this medium of 'profes-sional appearance'.

20 By 'triple shift' I refer to women's formal wage-earning informatics jobs, informal economic activities, and domestic respon-sibilities (see Freeman 1997 for a discus-sion of the interrelationships between these 'shifts').

REFERENCES

Abrahams, Roger D. 1979. Reputation vs. Re-spectability: A Review of Peter J. Wilson's Concept. *Revista/Review Interamericana*, 9/3: 374–53.

Besson, Jean. 1993. Reputation and Respectability Reconsidered: A New Perspective on Afro-Caribbean Peasant Women. In *Women and Change in the Caribbean*. J. Momsen, ed. Bloomington: Indiana University Press.

Bolles, A. Lynn. 1983. Kitchens Hit by Priorities: Employed Working-Class Jamaican Women confront the IMF. In *Women, Men and the International Division of Labor*. J. Nash and M. Fernandez-Kelly, eds. Albany: State University of New York Press.

Bourdieu, Pierre. 1983. 'The Forms of Capital'. In *Handbook of Theory and Research for the Sociology of Education*. J. Richardson, ed. pp. 241–58. New York: Greenwood Press.

—— 1984 [1979]. *Distinction: A Social Critique of the Judgment of Taste*. Cambridge, MA: Harvard University Press. (Orig. 1979.)

—— 1987. What Makes a Social Class? *Berkeley Journal of Sociology*, 22: 1–18.

Braverman, Harry. 1974. *Labor and Monopoly Capitalism*. New York: Monthly Review Press.

Carter, Valerie J. 1987. Office Technology and Relations of Control in Clerical Work Organizations. In *Women, Work and Technology: Transformations*. Barbara D. Wright, ed. Ann Arbor: University of Michigan Press.

Craik, Jennifer. 1994. *The Face of Fashion: Cultural Studies in Fashion*. New York: Routledge.,

Davies, Margery W. 1982. *Woman's Place is at the Typewriter: Office Work and Office Workers 1870–1930*. Philadelphia: Temple University Press.

de Certeau, Michel. 1984. *The Practice of Everyday Life*. Berkeley: University of California Press.

Fernandez-Kelly, Maria Patricia. 1983. *For We are Sold, I and My People: Women and Industry in Mexico's Frontier*. Albany: State University of New York Press.

Freeman, Carla. 1997. Reinventing Higglering in Transnational Zones: Barbadian Women Juggle the Triple Shift. In *Daughters of Caliban: Caribbean Women in the Twentieth Century*. Consuelo Lopez-Springfield, ed. Bloomington: Indiana University Press.

—— 2000. *High Tech and High Heels in the Global Economy*. Durham, NC: Duke University Press.

Hannerz, Ulf and Orvar Lofgren. 1994. 'The Nation in the Global Village', *Cultural Studies*, 8/2: 198–207.

Hochschild, Arlie R. 1983. *The Managed Heart: Commercialization of Human Feeling*. Berkeley: University of California Press.

IDC (Industrial Development Corporation) n.d. *Doing Business in Barbados*. Promotional brochure.

Jayawardena, Chandra 1963. *Conflict and Solidarity in a Guianese Plantation*. London: University of London, Athlone Press.

Kelly, Deirdre. 1987. *Hard Work, Hard Choices: A Survey of Women in St Lucia's Export-Oriented Electronics Factories*. Occasional Paper 20, Institute of Social and Economic Research. Cave Hill, Barbados: University of the West Indies.

Kim, Seung Kyung. 1997. *Class Struggle or Family Struggle? The Lives of Women Factory Workers in South Korea*. Cambridge: Cambridge University Press.

Lee, Martyn J. 1993. *Consumer Culture Reborn: The Cultural Politics of Consumption*. New York: Routledge.

Leidner, Robin. 1993. *Fast Food, Fast Talk: Service Work and the Routinization of Everyday Life*. Berkeley: University of California Press.

McNeil, Maureen. 1987. *Gender and Expertise*. London: Free Association Books.

Mies, Maria. 1986. *Patriarchy and Accumulation on a World Scale: Women in the International Division of Labor*. London: Zed Books.

Miller, Daniel. 1987. *Material Culture and Mass Consumption*. Oxford: Basil Blackwell.

—— 1990. Fashion and Ontology in Trinidad. *Culture and History*, 7: 49–77.

—— 1994. *Modernity: An Ethnographic Approach: Dualism and Mass Consumption in Trinidad*. Oxford: Berg.

—— 1995. Consumption Studies as the Transformation of Anthropology. In *Acknowledging Consumption: A Review of New Studies*. D. Miller, ed. London and New York: Routledge.

Mills, C. Wright. 1956. *White Collar: The American Middle Classes*. New York: Oxford University Press.

Mintz, Sidney. 1985. *Sweetness and Power: The Place of Sugar in Modern History*. New York: Viking.

—— 1996. *Tasting Food, Tasting Freedom*. Boston: Beacon Press.

Ong, Aihwa. 1987. *Spirits of Resistance and Capitalist Discipline: Factory Women in Malaysia*. Albany: State University of New York Press.

Paules, Greta Foff. 1991. *Dishing it Out: Power and Resistance among Waitresses in a New Jersey Restaurant*. Philadelphia: Temple University Press.

Pearson, Ruth. 1993. Gender and New Technology in the Caribbean: New Work for Women? In *Women and Change in the Caribbean*. J. Momsen, ed. London/Kingston, Jamaica and Bloomington: James Curry/Ian Randle/and Indiana University Press.

Pringle, Rosemary. 1988. *Secretaries Talk: Sexuality, Power and Work*. London: Verso.

Rouse, Roger. 1991. Mexican Migration and the Social Space of Postmodernism. *Diaspora* (Spring).

Rutz, Henry J., and Benjamin S. Orlove. 1989. *The Social Economy of Consumption: Monographs in Economic Anthropology*. Lanham, MD: University Press of America.

Sutton, Constance. 1974. Cultural Duality in the Caribbean. *Caribbean Studies*, 14/2: 96–101.

Wilk, Richard. 1990. Consumer Goods as Dialogue about Development. *Culture and History*, 7: 79–100.

Willis, Susan. 1991. *A Primer for Daily Life*. New York: Routledge.

Wilson, Elizabeth. 1985. *Adorned in Dreams: Fashion and Modernity*. Berkeley: University of California Press.

Wilson, Peter H. 1969. Reputation and Respectability: A Suggestion for Caribbean Ethnography. *Man*, 4/1: 70–84.

Yelvington, Kevin. 1995. *Producing Power: Ethnicity, Gender and Class in a Caribbean Workplace*. Philadelphia: Temple University Press.

21

Tombois in West Sumatra: Constructing Masculinity and Erotic Desire

Evelyn Blackwood

During anthropological fieldwork on gender and agricultural development in West Sumatra, Indonesia, in 1989–90, I pursued a secondary research goal of investigating the situation of "lesbians" in the area. I met a small number of "women" who seemed butch in the way that term was used in the United States at the time.[1] In West Sumatra these individuals are called *lesbi* or *tomboi* (derived from the English words *lesbian* and *tomboy*). Although there are similarities, a tomboi in West Sumatra is different from a butch in the United States, not surprisingly, for social constructionists have shown that sexual practices reflect particular historical and cultural contexts (Elliston 1995; Weston 1993). The term *tomboi* is used for a female acting in the manner of men (*gaya laki-laki*). Through my relationship with a tomboi in West Sumatra, I learned some of the ways in which my concept of "lesbian" was not the same as my partner's, even though we were both, I thought, women-loving women.

This article explores how tombois in West Sumatra both shape their identities from and resist local, national, and transnational narratives of gender and sexuality.[2] By focusing on West Sumatra, I provide an in-depth analysis of the complexities of tomboi identity for individuals from one ethnic group in Indonesia, the Minangkabau. This piece is not a general explication of tombois across Indonesia, although there may be considerable overlap (see Wieringa 1998). Much excellent work on postcolonial states explores the interplay of national and transnational narratives in the production of genders and sexualities. This article provides a cultural location for tombois oriented to Minangkabau culture as well as national and transnational discourses.

Theories concerning the intersection of genders and sexualities provide considerable insights into, and a variety of labels for, gendered practices cross-culturally (see, for example, Bullough, Bullough, and Elias 1997; Devor 1989; Epstein and Straub 1991; Herdt 1994; Jacobs, Thomas, and Lang 1997; Ramet 1996; Roscoe 1991). In opposition to biological determinism, social constructionists argue that gender is not an essence preceding social expression but an identity that is constructed and fluid.[3] The multiplication of "gender" categories in cross-cultural studies, however, suggests that gender remains a problematic concept. Part of the problem, I would argue, comes from the conflation of two distinct but interacting processes, gender as cultural category and gender as subjective experience.

Viewing gender as a cultural category foregrounds the social structural and ideological processes that make it seem bounded – all the more so in a "scientific" age replete with minute diagnostics of human experience. Studying gender as a cultural category highlights normative representations of gender and the ways they are legitimated, privileged, and hegemonic. It allows one to identify so-called traditional gender systems, or "everyday categories of gender" (Poole 1996), as ideological discourses and to establish which gender representations are dominant or acceptable, and thereby which are transgressive. By highlighting gender as a cultural category, I can delineate normative gender through an analysis of dominant ideological discourses at the local and state levels.

Viewing gender as subjective experience exposes all the processes of negotiation, resistance, manipulation, and displacement possible by human subjects. Gender in this sense constitutes a set of social identities multiply shaped from and through cultural contexts and representations (see also Bourdieu 1977; Poole 1996; Yanagisako and Collier 1987). Viewing gender as a subset of possible social identities allows one to do two things: remove gender as a fundamental aspect of sexed bodies and investigate the way culturally constituted categories shape, inflect, and infuse gender identities. Learning, piecing together, adopting, or shaping identities (such as race, class, gender, or sexuality) is an on-going social process through which individuals negotiate, produce, and stabilize a sense of who they are. These identities are shaped and redefined in relation to dominant gender ideologies that claim constancy and immutability.

Because tombois are enmeshed in several discursive domains of gender and sexual identity,

I argue that they produce a complex identity not reducible to a single model. I show how the gender and kinship ideologies of the Minangkabau, the dominant ethnic group in West Sumatra, construct a system of oppositional genders ("man"–"woman") that persuades tombois to see themselves as masculine. The discourses of a modernizing Minangkabau society, the Indonesian state, and Islam reinforce this system through their representations of femininity and "female" nature. At another level, tomboi identity incorporates new models of sexuality and gender made available by the transnational flow of lesbian and gay discourse from Europe and North America.

This essay also explores the relation between gender ideology and the production of gender transgression. *Webster's College Dictionary* (1991) defines *transgression* as a violation of a law, command, or moral code; an offense or sin; or more neutrally, passing over or going beyond (a limit, boundary, et cetera). I use the term *gender transgression* to provide a new angle on a range of cultural practices not usually lumped under it. I include within it any gender identities – such as transgendered, reversed, mixed, crossed, cross-dressed, two-spirited, or liminal – that go beyond, or violate, gender-"appropriate" norms enshrined in dominant cultural ideologies. By defining gender transgression in this way, I want to highlight the way that various social structures and cultural ideologies interconnect to produce gender transgression.

Central to this analysis is the concept of hegemony as developed and used by Gramsci (1971), R. Williams (1977), and Ortner (1989). Hegemonic or dominant gender ideologies define what is permissible, even thinkable; they serve as the standard against which actions are measured, producing codes, regulations, and laws that perpetuate a particular ideology. Dominant ideologies generate discourses that stabilize, normalize, and naturalize gender (Yanagisako and Delaney 1995); yet within any dominant ideology there are emergent meanings, processes, and identities vying for legitimacy, authority, and recognition (R. Williams 1977).

Work on gender transgression has prompted some preliminary, and in most cases implicit, formulations about the conditions that produce it. The growing literature on "female-bodied" gender transgressors tends to cast the transgression as resistance to an oppressive gender ideology, usually identified as male dominance or patriarchy.[4] For instance, U.S. gender ideology has produced at various junctures butch-femme (Kennedy and Davis 1993), camp and drag (Newton 1972, 1993), and transgendered people (Bolin 1994; Garber 1991; Stone 1991). Some scholars argue that these identities result from a hierarchical gender system of compulsory heterosexuality and oppositional genders.

Evidence from Island Southeast Asia raises questions about the relationship between oppressive gender ideology and gender transgression. In her overview of gender in Island Southeast Asia, Errington (1990) suggested that gender is less salient than other categories, such as rank and age, in determining access to status or power. According to Errington, in the central islands of Southeast Asia "male and female are viewed as complementary or even identical beings in many respects" (1990:39). The "paucity of symbolic expressions of gender difference" suggests that gender is not highly marked in those areas (Errington 1990:4)[5] Despite an apparent lack of oppositional genders, gender transgressors are well known throughout the islands (Atkinson 1990; Chabot 1960; Oetomo 1991; Peacock 1978; Van der Kroef 1954; Yengoyan 1983).

The Minangkabau tomboi poses a further challenge concerning the relationship between oppressive gender ideology and gender transgression. The Minangkabau are a hierarchical, kin-based society in which both women and men lineage elders have access to power. Because Minangkabau gender relations do not fit the usual criteria for male dominance, the presence of tombois in West Sumatra forces a deeper analysis of the conditions that produce gender transgression. Whether a dominant ideology produces gender transgressors, and in what form, depends, I argue, on a number of processes, only one of which may be an oppressive gender hierarchy. A closer reading of cultural processes circulating in West Sumatra suggests the interrelation of kinship, capitalism, religion, and the state in producing gender transgressions.

Misreading Identities

In the following I first provide a brief description of West Sumatra to set the stage for the story of my introduction to tomboi identity. This narrative of misreadings and negotiations of tomboi identity shows the moments that moved me beyond my own culture-bound interpretations and led me to realize that different identities were in operation.

West Sumatra is the home of the Minangkabau people, one of the many ethnic groups that have been incorporated into the state of Indonesia. The Minangkabau, with a population over 4 million people, are rural agriculturalists, urban merchants, traders, migrants, and wage laborers. They are also Muslim and matrilineal. Being matrilineal means that, despite the fact that they are devout Muslims, inheritance and property pass from mother to daughter. I conducted research in the province of Lima Puluh Kota near the district capital of Payakumbuh. In 1990, the province had a population of 86,000; the large majority were Minangkabau.

Far from being an isolated region, the province is well integrated into global trade networks. Rice and other agricultural products produced in the region are traded well beyond Sumatra. Many Minangkabau men and women work for years in cities outside West Sumatra, providing further connections to the national and international scene. Villages have anywhere from 15 percent to 25 percent of their residents on temporary out-migration. Despite out-migration, many villages maintain a rich cultural life based on kinship ties; most social and economic activities are centered in and organized by matrilineally related groups. Other villages are more urban oriented, particularly where migration has led to reliance on outside sources of income.

I had no trouble locating males in West Sumatra who were *bancis*, a term that is defined in Echols and Shadily's Indonesian–English dictionary (1989) as "effeminate or transvestite homosexual[s]" (see also Oetomo 1991). This

definition links bancis' gender identity (effeminate or transvestite) and sexuality (homosexual). In the district capital I met several bancis
or *bencong*, as they are referred to in West
Sumatra. Bancis are obvious to local people,
who comment on their appearance or taunt
them when they walk down the street. Although bancis do not carry themselves as men
do, they do not carry themselves exactly like
women, either; rather, they behave in the exaggerated style of fashion models, a style that in
itself is a caricature of femininity, one they have
been exposed to through fashion magazines
and televised beauty pageants. Their sexual
partners are indistinguishable from other men
and are generally thought to be bisexual, or
biseks in local parlance, as these men might
also have relationships with women.

My search for "lesbians" was more difficult.
I asked some high school-aged acquaintances
of mine,[6] who had friends who were bancis,
whether they knew any lesbis – the term they
used with me – in the area. I was told that there
were several but that those women were worried about being found out. I was given the
impression that such women were very coarse
and tough, more like men than women. After
several months in West Sumatra, one of my
young friends introduced me to Dayan.[7] S/he,
however, did not fit the stereotype.[8] In hir
midtwenties, s/he appeared to me to be boy-
ish-looking in hir T-shirt, shorts, and short
hair, but s/he did not seem masculine or
tough in any way that I could perceive. I consequently felt quite certain that I had met another "lesbian." The term *lesbi* that my friends
used also offered familiar footing to an outsider from the United States.

Negotiating our identities was a perplexing
process in which we each tried to position the
other within different cultural categories:
butch–femme and *cowok–cewek*. *Butch–
femme* is an American term that refers to a
masculine-acting woman and her feminine
partner.[9] *Cowok–cewek* are Indonesian words
that mean "man" and "woman" but have the
connotation of "guy" and "girl." It is the practice of female couples to refer to a tomboi and
hir feminine partner as cowok and cewek.
(Most Indonesians are unfamiliar with this
use of the two terms.) In both the United States

and West Sumatra, female couples rely on and
draw from dominant cultural images of masculinity and femininity to make sense of their
relationships. These similarities were enough
to cause both my partner and myself to assume
that we fell within each other's cultural model,
an assumption I was forced to give up.

Dayan operated under the assumption that
I was cewek, despite the inconsistencies of my
behavior, because that fit with hir understanding of hirself in relation to hir lovers, who had
all been cewek. For instance, my failure to
cook for hir or organize hir birthday party
were quite disappointing to Dayan. On another occasion, when I visited an American
friend of mine at his hotel, s/he accused me of
sleeping with him. In hir experience, ceweks
are attracted to men and also like sex better
with men. Yet, as the one with the cash in the
relationship, I was allowed to pay for things
despite it not being proper cewek behavior. In
rural Minangkabau households, men are
expected to give their wives their cash earnings. Expectations about the husband's responsibility to provide income are even greater for
middle-class Indonesians, for men are represented as the sole breadwinners. Perhaps
Dayan justified my actions on the grounds
that I was an American with considerably
more income than s/he. Certainly s/he was
willing to entertain the possibility of my difference from hir understanding of ceweks.

One day I overheard the following exchange
between Dayan and a tomboi friend. Dayan's
friend asked if I was cewek, to which Dayan
replied, "Of course."

"Can she cook?"

"Well, not really."

The friend exclaimed, "How can that be, a
woman who can't cook? What are you going
to do?"

I was surprised to find that my gender identity was so critical to this (macho) tomboi. The
fact that I had a relationship with Dayan
said very little to me about what kind of
woman I was. I interpreted my relationship
with Dayan as reflective of my sexual identity
(a desire for other women).

For my part, I assumed that Dayan was a
butch, more or less in congruence with the way
I understood butches to be in the United States

in the 1980s, that is, as masculine-acting women who desired feminine partners.[10] S/he always dressed in jeans or shorts and T- or polo shirts, a style that was not at odds with the casual wear of many lesbians in the United States. One day, however, I heard a friend call hir "co," short for cowok. I knew what *cowok* meant in that context; it meant s/he was seen as a "guy" by hir close friends, which did not fit my notion of butch. I heard another female couple use the terms *mami* (mom) and *papi* (pop) for each other, so I started calling Dayan papi in private, which made hir very pleased. But when I told Dayan s/he was pretty, s/he looked hurt. Then I realized my mistake: "pretty" (*cantik*) is what a woman is called, not a man. Dayan wanted to be called "handsome" (*gagah*), as befits a masculine self.

Dayan's personal history underscored hir feelings that s/he was a man. S/he said s/he felt extremely isolated and "deviant" when s/he was growing up and acted more like a boy. People in hir town called hir *bujang gadis*, an Indonesian term meaning boy-girl (*bujang* means bachelor or unmarried young man, and *gadis* means unmarried young woman) that used to refer to an effeminate male or a masculine female (although not much in use currently). As a teenager, s/he only had desire for girls. S/he bound hir breasts because s/he did not want them to be noticeable. They did not fit with hir self-image. As a young adult, s/he hung out with young men, smoking and drinking with them. S/he said s/he felt like a man and wanted to be one. I finally had to admit to myself that tombois were not the Indonesian version of butches. They were men.

Cowok–Cewek

I met two other tombois in West Sumatra, Agus and Bujang, who were both friends of Dayan. The first time I met Agus, s/he was wearing a big khaki shirt and jeans; even I could not mistake the masculine attitude s/he projected. S/he wore short hair that was swept back on the sides. S/he carried herself like a "man," smoked cigarettes all the time, played cards, and made crude jokes. S/he struck me as coarse and tough like cowoks

were said to be. Dayan admired Agus and thought hir the more handsome of the two.

Dayan told me that Agus, who was approximately thirty years old, had only been with women, never with a man. S/he had had several lovers, all beautiful and very feminine, according to Dayan. One former lover married and had two children, but Dayan thought Agus probably still saw her occasionally. Agus spent much of hir time with hir lover, Yul, who lived in a large house only a few minutes by bus outside of Payakumbuh. Yul, who was in her early fifties, was a widow with grown children, some of whom were still living at home. After Agus started living with her, Yul wanted her children to call Agus papi. She said she did not care if her children disapproved of her relationship. If her children did not act respectfully toward Agus, Yul would get angry with them and not give them spending money when they asked for it. But one of Yul's daughters argued that because Agus is not married to her mother, s/he should not be part of the family and be treated better than her own father had been. The frequent squabbling and lack of privacy at Yul's house was too much for Agus, who spent less and less time with Yul and finally moved back to hir sister's house nearby.

The other tomboi I met, Bujang, was at that time living at hir mother's in a rural village. Bujang seemed quiet and somber. Boyish features and oversized clothes that hid hir breasts made it impossible for me to tell if s/he was male or female. We talked very little because hir mother was there. Later Dayan told me Bujang's story. Hir mother had forced hir to marry; s/he had had a son but then left hir husband. S/he had a lover (who, Dayan said, was feminine) and moved with her to Jakarta, where they lived for some time to avoid the prying eyes of relatives. Under continued pressure from hir family, however, and lacking adequate income, Bujang finally returned home with hir son, leaving hir lover temporarily in hopes of finding a better way to support hir family. Hir cewek lover, however, eventually married a man.[11]

Partners of tombois fit within the norms of femininity and maintain a "feminine" gender identity. Their sexual relationships with tombois do not mark them as different; their gender is not in question.[12] Like an earlier generation of femmes in the United States, tombois' partners are nearly invisible (see Nestle 1992). Yul, Agus's lover, was feminine in appearance. She had shoulder-length permed hair, wore makeup and lipstick, and had long fingernails. Yul had never been with a tomboi before she met Agus. She had not even thought about sleeping with one before. Although she sometimes wore slacks and smoked, even hung out at the local coffee shop with Agus to play cards, she was called *ibu* (mother) by men and mami by Agus. No one would think she was a tomboi just because she was partners with one; she was cewek. As a cewek, she adhered to the hegemonic standards of femininity in her appearance and behavior.

Although the fact that they sleep with tombois makes them "bad" women in the eyes of local people, for premarital sex and adultery are disapproved of for women, ceweks are still women. Even tombois expect ceweks to have greater desire for men because that is seen as natural for their sex. Dayan once said, "Unfortunately, they will leave you for a man if one comes along they like. It's our fate that we love women who leave us." No one seems to consider a cewek's desire for tombois problematic; she remains a woman who desires men.

Performing Masculinity

Tombois model masculinity in their behavior, attitudes, interests, and desires. Dayan often spoke of being *berani* (brave), a trait commonly associated with men, as an important part of who s/he was. S/he attributed the ability to be a tomboi to being berani; it meant, among other things, that one could withstand family pressures to get married. S/he said the ones that are berani become cowok. In talking about Agus's situation with hir lover Yul, Dayan commented that Agus was not brave enough to sleep at Yul's house anymore. S/he thought that Agus should not let Yul's children force hir to move out. Agus was not being as brave as Dayan thought a person should be in order to live up to the cowok identity.

Tombois pride themselves on doing things like men. They know how to play *koa*, a card game like poker, which is thought to be a men's game. They smoke as men do; rural women rarely take up smoking. They go out alone, especially at night, which is a prerogative of men. Like men, they drive motorcycles; women ride behind (women do drive motorcycles, but in mixed couples men always drive). Dayan arrived at my house on a motorcycle one time with a man friend riding behind. Like Minangkabau husbands, they move into and out of their partners' houses. Dayan said s/he often gets taken for a man if someone only sees hir walking from behind. Sometimes in public spaces, particularly in urban areas, s/he is called *mas*, a contemporary Indonesian term of address for a man. The thought that a tomboi might marry a man or bear a child like a woman seemed unconscionable to Dayan. S/he had little sympathy for Bujang, who was forced to marry, saying, "This person is cowok! How could s/he have done that, especially having a baby. That's wrong."

The taunting and joking between Agus and Dayan reflect one way in which their masculinity is negotiated. Agus's teasing questions to Dayan about whether I was a proper cewek is one example. Another incident occurred one evening when we were hanging out with Agus at a coffee shop. S/he had been playing cards (koa) with some men for awhile and it was getting late. Dayan told Agus s/he wanted to leave. Agus said tauntingly, "You're a guy [laki-laki]! How come you're afraid of the night?" I knew Dayan wanted to get back to the privacy of hir own place, a 45-minute drive by motorcycle. Agus ignored that fact and implied that Dayan was acting like a woman, for women are supposed to be more timid than men and stay indoors at night.

Another time Agus heard me call Dayan by hir first name. S/he gave Dayan a disparaging look, letting Dayan know that s/he was not demanding enough respect from me as hir cewek. Minangkabau usually do not call their spouses by their first names. Women generally use the term of address for older brother (*udah*), while *papi* is more common in urban areas or among those who live elsewhere in Indonesia.

Dayan also commented to me about a story circulating in West Sumatra concerning a female who passed as a man. This individual was rumored to have married his partner by going to another district where no one knew he was female. He (the cowok) runs a store, it was related; he wears loose clothes and straps his breasts down so they are not apparent. His wife (the cewek) is said to be very pretty. Dayan's response to this story was, "Oh, that cowok must really be a cowok," signifying that he had become the ultimate tomboi, one who passes as a man.

The sparring and comparing of masculine selves reveal one of the ways tombois create, confirm, and naturalize their identities as men. The teasing helps to reinforce and interrogate the masculine code of behavior. Their actions suggest that being cowok is an identity one can be better or worse at, more or less of; it is something that must be practiced and claimed – which is not to say that it is inauthentic, for no gender identity is more or less authentic than another, but, rather, is more or less an approximation of the hegemonic ideological domain accorded to that gender (see Butler 1991). As any man does, they are negotiating their culture's ideology of masculinity.

Tombois construct their desire for and relationships with women on the model of masculinity. The oft-repeated statement that their lovers are all feminine underscores their position as men who attract the "opposite sex." Because I was Dayan's partner, hir friend assumed that I was a particular gender, in this case the feminine woman. Their use of gendered terms of endearment, *mami* and *papi*, and the terms *cowok* and *cewek* reflect tombois' understanding of themselves as situated within the category "men" (laki-laki). Tombois' adherence to the model of masculinity and their insistence on replicating the heterosexuality of a man-woman couple point to the dominance of the normative model of gender and heterosexuality.

Gender Ideology and Gender Transgression

In constructing themselves as masculine and their relationships as heterosexual, tombois

are gender transgressors who nevertheless reflect the dominant ideology. Tombois' transgressions raise the issue of the relation between gender ideology and the production of gender transgression. What social conditions produce transgression of the dominant ideology? As I noted in the introduction, some preliminary attempts have been made to identify the conditions that produce gender transgression. Several scholars argue that oppressive gender ideologies (male dominance) force gender transgression.[13] According to Kennedy and Davis, "butch-fem" identities in the United States developed in a period in which "elaborate hierarchical distinctions were made between the sexes" (1992: 63).[14] Because men and women were culturally constructed as polar opposites ("the opposite sex" being a typical folk designation for the two genders in the United States), behaviors and privileges associated with men, including erotic attraction to women, were restricted to those with male genitalia. Male dominance and an ideology of oppositional genders created resistance to and subversion of the dominant paradigm by butches and femmes.

Some gender theorists argue that "women" become "men" (including female "berdache," female soldiers, and passing "women") because of sexual desire for other women (Newton 1984; Raymond 1979; Rich 1980; Rubin 1975; Trumbach 1994; Wieringa 1989). In this view, because "women" are not allowed freedom of sexual expression, they are forced to pass as men (with great caution, however) in order to be with women. Thus, the constraints on their sexual desire, which arise from an ideology of male dominance and men's control of women's sexuality, forces women to transgress. Although this interpretation may work in some cultural locations, it is problematic because it assumes the essentiality of sex. These individuals are claimed as "real" women whose desire for women forces them to take on a man's identity.[15] This explanation is implausible for tombois. As Dayan's story indicates, it was not sexual desire for women that "drove" hir to produce a masculine identity (a problematic construction anyway because being "driven" suggests a biological drive). S/he had already established a masculine identity before s/he was aware of hir sexual desires for women. Having identified hirself as masculine, s/he also laid claim to a desire for women.

Cross-cultural evidence, predominantly from societies with strict gender polarity, seems to support a strong connection between male dominance and gender transgression. On the one hand, Wikan (1977), who studied the highly sex-segregated patriarchal culture of the Omani, found that the *xanith*, a cross-dressing male prostitute, moves in the women's world. By providing men with an alternative to sex with women, the xanith preserves the gender dichotomy and protects women's virtue, Wikan argued. The gender dichotomy, she claimed, is the "precondition" for a male trans-sexual. In my analysis of genderstratified, patriarchal class societies, I argued that "women" in these societies were not allowed to take on a cross-gender role because such behavior was viewed as a threat to men's privilege (Blackwood 1986a). They did so, however, even at the risk of severe sanctions if they were discovered (see Crompton 1981; Cromwell 1997). On the other hand, so-called sworn virgins in the patriarchal Balkans are allowed to renounce their womanhood publicly, usually at puberty, and become social men (Dickemann 1997). Each of these cases supports the conclusion that male dominance and strict gender polarity produce individuals who reject or resist being slotted into normative gender categories. In these instances, it appears that the disadvantages of a normative feminine gender, such as the lack of access to men's privileges and the constraints against desiring women as a woman, produce gender transgressors.

Other instances of gender transgression, however, suggest that it is not always produced under oppressive conditions, nor is it always rejection of, or resistance to, normative gender. Although it goes beyond the limits or reverses cultural norms, gender transgression in some cases (in Indonesia and other cultures) is a culturally legitimated behavior believed to effect healing or give greater access to the spirit world. Examples include transformed shamans, clowns, and ritual specialists (Balzer 1996; Bogoras 1901; Jacobs, Thomas, and Lang 1997; Peacock 1978). In such cases, gender transgression is not the result of oppressive conditions but of the ritual power associated with gender. These examples suggest that transgressions can take many forms; different systems produce different types of transgressions.[16]

Another reason to ask what conditions produce gender transgressions has to do with essentialist claims about human "nature." Many scholars resort to essentialist explanations for gender transgression. For instance, a discredited theory of "berdache" gender argued that males became "berdache" because they were naturally effeminate and could not live up to the warrior role for males. Their refusal to become warriors was taken as an indication of the connection between physical nature and social identity; they were born that way. Although I do not deny the possibility of biophysical influences on human behavior, I want to pursue a social analysis further.

I use for comparison an example of the transgression of ethnic identity. In Stoler's (1996) work on colonial–indigenous relations, she found that ethnic transgressions were the subject of much concern in Dutch colonies. Colonial officials who hired indigenous women to care for their children found, to their chagrin, that their young children identified with the indigenous culture rather than that of the parents. Although every effort was made to instill in the children the language, manners, and behavior of their European parents, they often chose to speak Malay and associate with local children in ways not deemed proper for people of a "superior" race (Stoler 1996). Their behavior, a transgression of European norms of behavior, was the result not of an inborn desire to be Malay but of the conflicting identities with which they were presented. That the children chose to speak the maid's language first attests to what was most comfortable for them.

Culture works by applying social categories to bodies, but when individuals or groups reject particular categories designed for their bodies, such actions should not be deemed to result from "natural" desires. Rather, rejection or violation of cultural norms may arise from contradictory social processes and subaltern desires present in or produced by the culture itself. Thus, like ethnic transgressions, gender transgression is a rejection of social definitions that one finds intolerable or undesirable because other definitions are available that provide greater rewards or fit better with one's sense of self. In the case of tombois, certain ideologies of masculinity fit better.

Rejection is often read as "resistance" because the power of the dominant ideology and the daily practice of that ideology forces on-going resistance. The actions of Dayan's mother are a good example of a daily practice to slot Dayan back into the normative category of gender. Her efforts to have Dayan marry a man meant that Dayan was forced repeatedly to confront, question, and reassert hir own violation and reconstruction of gender. *Rejection*, which implies a onetime act, is too simplistic a term to describe an on-going struggle to maintain the identity one produces. Thus, gender transgression can be both a resistance to and rejection of cultural norms.

What social conditions produce the tomboi identity? Are tombois forced into a transgendered role by an oppressive, male-dominant society? To answer this question I turn now to social processes (cultural ideologies) in West Sumatra and the Indonesian state, looking first at the interrelations of Minangkabau kinship, gender, and economics in the production of oppositional genders.

Minangkabau Ideology and Oppositional Genders

Although the Minangkabau people are considered a single ethnic group, there are many Minangkabaus – many "fantasies" of Minangkabau ethnic identity, to borrow Sears's term (1996a). Minangkabau people are urban, rural, educated, and devout; they are civil servants, migrants, and farmers. Their identities vary according to their exposure to media, state ideology, Western-oriented education, and religious fundamentalism. The multiplicity of identities attests to the complex processes at work in contemporary Indonesia as individuals and ethnic groups situate themselves within the postcolonial state.[17]

The construction of gender in West Sumatra is equally complex. There are marked gender differences attached to male and female bodies, but these differences are produced within a matrilineal system that privileges women. Minangkabau women draw from and constantly rework several models of womanhood based on the ideologies of *adat* (local customs, beliefs, and prescriptions for behavior), Islam, and the state (Blackwood 1993, 1995b). The Minangkabau gender ideology I describe here has its basis in rural, rather than urban or nonfarming, life in West Sumatra.

Through its very commonness, something as simple as the segregation of girls and boys enculturates and reinforces ideas about sex difference. As is typical of many Islamic cultures, there is lifelong physical segregation of the sexes in most public spaces and events. Girls and boys socialize in predominantly single-sex groups. Teenaged girls and women are expected to stay in at night; going out alone after dark is frowned on. In contrast, adolescent boys and men can be outside in the evenings and often hang out in predominantly male-only spaces, such as coffee shops. These gender differences reflect the Minangkabau (and Islamic) view that men and women have different natures.[18] Men are said to be more aggressive and brave than women. Boys are admonished not to cry – crying is what girls do. Women are expected to be modest, respectful, and humble (all contained in the word *malu*), especially young unmarried women.

All ritual ceremonies – such as marriage, engagement, or death – are conducted by the sexes separately. During ceremonies women have control of the house space while men cluster outside until it is time to deliver speeches. I was told that men and women each have their own part of the ceremony and neither is more important than the other. Men make speeches, but women oversee the whole process and see it to its conclusion (see also Pak 1986). Ceremonial practices reflect the different rights and obligations of women and men but not their place in a gender hierarchy.

These gendered notions encode difference and men's privilege, yet they coexist with practices and discourses that encode women's privilege and power (Blackwood 1993, 2000).

Women lineage elders are powerful figures who, if they are wealthy, control land, labor, and kin. Economically, women control the distribution of land and its produce. Men figure peripherally in their wives' houses, but they maintain important relations with both natal and affinal houses. Husbands are treated with respect and even deference by their wives (in certain matters); some elite men hold important family titles and are considered the protectors of lineage property. Elite men and women carry out kinship affairs in democratic fashion, with neither women nor men able to enforce decisions without the agreement of the other side. Although gender ideology signifies differences in rights and privileges, it does not encode men's hegemonic superiority.

Minangkabau kinship and marriage practices provide deeper insights into the construction of gender and sexuality. Individuals, whether male or female, are not considered adult until they have married heterosexually. Everyone is expected and strongly encouraged (in some cases forced) to marry, an expectation generally true throughout Indonesia and Southeast Asia as a whole. While this expectation is commonplace in most cultures, its significance goes beyond the mere requirement to reproduce. Marriage constructs an extended network of kin and affines that forms the basis of social life in the village. For Minangkabau women, the continuation of the matrilineal kinship network through marriage and children is critical to their own standing and influence both in the kin group and in the community. An unmarried or childless daughter denies the lineage any offspring through her and risks the future status of the lineage, not only in terms of heirs but in terms of rank.[19] A man's marriage does not produce lineage heirs, making men peripheral to lineage reproduction. In contrast, a woman's marriage to a lower-ranked husband can effectively decrease their lineage standing in future generations. Women lineage heads exert control over young women to avoid the risk of a bad marriage or no marriage at all. Thus, in this matrilineal system, men are not the primary ones controlling women through marriage; senior elite women control young women through their desires to maintain and strengthen their own lineage standing (Blackwood 1993).

In the context of this rural kin-based society, heterosexual marriage is a paramount feature of Minangkabau kinship ideology. Within the terms of the kinship ideology, women are producers and reproducers of the lineage. There are no acceptable fantasies of femininity or female bodies in rural villages that do not include marriage and motherhood. This ideology remains hegemonic at the same time that emerging discourses of modernity and capitalism have opened up possibilities of resistance to marriage restrictions (Blackwood 1993).

Minangkabau culture produces gender transgression, I argue, because of restrictive definitions and expectations of masculinity and femininity attached to male and female bodies. In this case, male dominance is not an adequate reason for gender transgression because the Minangkabau do not fit any standard criteria for male dominance. It is not "men" (patriarchy) or their oppressive gender hierarchy that creates transgressions but, rather, a gender and kinship ideology that privileges women and men, yet insists on oppositional genders.

How does this sex/gender system induce the tomboi to claim a masculine identity? Why is (or was) this the form that transgression took? I am assuming here the temporal precedence of gender-based identities (cowok–cewek) relative to more recent identities available through the lesbian and gay movement internationally. To answer these questions, one needs to look at the way tombois are treated within the dominant culture. Tombois imagine themselves masculine, and as such are tolerated to a certain extent,[20] but there is a contradiction between the way tombois define themselves and the way others define them. Tombois are under great pressure to carry out family obligations, to marry a man and be reproductive. Dayan said that every time s/he saw hir mother, she asked when s/he was getting married. Hir mother worried that a woman could not support herself alone; she needs a husband. Hir mother's statement was a clear refusal of Dayan's self-definition as a man, a refusal that typifies the attitude of others within the local community.

The constant pressure to get married and the threat of forcible marriage reveal the way a person's body determines a person's gender. In this system the hegemonic, legitimate gender is based on one's sex; gender is not considered an "identity," performed or otherwise. In many ways this ideological rendering is similar to the dominant sex/gender paradigm in European and U.S. societies: gender is believed to derive naturally from physiological sex; a "real" woman possesses female genitalia, desires men, bears children, and acts like a woman.[21] A tomboi, according to the Minangkabau sex/gender system, is a "woman" even though s/he enacts a masculine gender, hence the refusal to legitimate that enactment and the insistence on the fulfillment of hir reproductive duties. Denying the female body is impermissible. Although tombois insist on being treated as men by their partners, their masculinity lacks cultural validation. Society insists on the priority of the body in determining gender.

Dayan said s/he played too rough and enjoyed boys' activities when s/he was little, so people called hir bujang gadis, a label that meant others perceived hir as masculine. At that time s/he had no other recourse but to assume s/he was a boy. Without other options available, and seeing that hir behavior falls outside the bounds of proper femininity, the tomboi denies hir female body, binding hir breasts so that the physical evidence will not betray hir. S/he produces the only other gender recognizable in the sex/gender system, the masculine gender. That interpretation would accord with the hegemonic cultural ideology, in which masculinity is male – with a twist, a twist that s/he continually has to substantiate and rectify in hir own mind and to others. Dominant ideologies, as noted by Poole, are "enshrined in prominent, powerful and pervasive stereotypes...and deployed in centrally institutionalized or otherwise significantly marked arenas of social action" (1996: 198). The hegemonic persuasiveness of such ideologies means that other forms of identity are unimaginable.[22] Consequently, some masculine females appropriate the masculine gender because it is the most persuasive model available.

The Promotion of Motherhood and Heterosexuality

Given the importance of the state and other institutions in the production and control of gender and sexuality, as attested to by a number of recent studies,[23] what messages about gender at the national level lead to the production of tomboi identity? The Indonesian state, particularly since the inception of the New Order in 1965, has avidly pursued a policy promoting nuclear families and motherhood.[24] This state ideology emphasizes the importance of women's role as mothers and consciously purveys the idea that women are primarily responsible for their children and their family's health, care, and education (Djajadiningrat-Nieuwenhuis 1987; Manderson 1980; Sullivan 1983; Suryakusuma 1996). In fact, the state argues that motherhood has been the traditional role for women in Indonesia since before the coming of the Dutch. According to Gayatri (1995), this line of argument has been used by state officials to fend off feminist efforts to change perceptions about women. All state family policies are oriented around a nuclear family defined as a husband, wife, and children in disregard of the many forms of family found within the borders of Indonesia.

Several state organizations for women perpetuate the belief that women are nurturing and selfless, if emotional, creatures who need to be married to be happy, productive citizens. The national dress code emphasizes femininity for women, with dresses, skirts, jewelry, and makeup the only acceptable attire for work. Dharma Wanita, the state organization for wives of government officials, heavily promotes cosmetics to its members and sponsors what it assumes to be important activities for women, such as knitting and cooking.

Television and magazines are replete with images of soft, pretty, domestic women. Advertisements bombard women with the most fashionable clothes, skin care, and health care products necessary to make them successful women. Avon, Revlon, and Pond's are some of the non-Indonesian companies promoting this vision of femininity. Women characters on popular television series are primarily domestic, irrational, emotional, and obedient – and incapable of solving their own problems (Aripurnami 1996). This emphasis on hyperfemininity and the importance of motherhood reinforces restrictive gender boundaries. The message for women is that it is a national and religious duty to marry heterosexually and be feminine.

Minangkabau newspapers published in West Sumatra for local readers reflect state propaganda on femininity. The women's section in *Singgalang* is devoted to health, beauty tips, and heterosexuality. One columnist advises women not to worry if they are not beautiful; there are other characteristics they can develop that will still be attractive to men. Another column claims that men and women need each other; each sex is incomplete without the other. "Although it's not impossible for a woman to find meaning without a man," advises Fadlillah, "it gives women's lives new meaning when a man is there" (1996: 3, my translation). Other articles admonish women to be modest (*malu*) and warn against too modern an attitude, *modern* here referring to the "loosened" values and attitudes of those in the cities.

Other representations of motherhood come from fundamentalist Islam, which claims that motherhood is the natural role for women and their destiny because they are female. Islamic fundamentalists idealize women as mothers and wives under the supervision of husbands (Blackwood 1995b). In regard to sexual practices, many Muslims believe same-sex sexuality is immoral, and this was Dayan's understanding of hir faith. Further, Islamic leaders teach that not being "true" to one's own sex by acting like the other is a sin and an offense to Allah because it is a rejection of the way one was made (which underscores the belief that biological sex and gender are one and the same).

The emphasis on heterosexual marriage and the nuclear family suggests that compulsory heterosexuality and women's subordination are actively being produced at the national level by religion, the state, media, and multinational corporations. This heterosexual imperative threatens to reproduce a limiting and ultimately coercive form of gender, marriage, and sexuality predicated on male control and desire. Dominant state ideology offers no options to females other than marriage and motherhood, which in this case is a male-dominant vision of gender, further substantiating the dictates of sex/gender congruence enunciated by Minangkabau gender and kinship ideology. For those who do not fit the normative model of gender, or find it limiting and oppressive, such a model persuades them of their masculinity, producing gender transgression.

Despite the dominance of the ideology of femininity and motherhood at the state level, there are cracks within it – unintended consequences that ironically open a space for imagining other gender and sexual possibilities. In its efforts to create modern nuclear families, state discourse undermines the influence of lineage elders in several ways. First, whereas rural life in many areas of Indonesia customarily centers around kin, state discourse emphasizes the priority of the nuclear (male-headed) family over the larger kin group. State support for nuclear families allows a daughter to contest her mother's authority (Blackwood 2000). Second, the discourse of modernity, with its emphasis on individualism and consumerism, provides a model of self-earned income for the earner's use alone. Finally, the availability of nonagricultural labor for women in a global economy also models alternatives to life in a rural household. All these processes undermine extended families and their power to require a daughter's marriage and support of the lineage (Blackwood 1995b). These imaginable alternatives help to question the ideology of oppositional genders, creating the possibility of gender and sexual identities not predicated on sexed bodies. For tombois these alternatives raise the possibility that their masculinity does not have to make them men.

Cewek Resistance to Marriage and Heterosexuality

The hegemonic heterosexuality of the state and the Minangkabau kinship system produce not only the tomboi as gender transgressor but also a different form of transgression. Some women participate in compulsory heterosexuality, marrying men and bearing children, but then quietly claim the right to choose a tomboi partner.[25] For some women, the pressure to marry a man makes refusal nearly unthinkable and marriage inevitable. For other women who marry heterosexually, their action fulfills a sense of duty to their mothers, their lineage, and themselves. Whatever the reason, women who have married and borne children are in a better position to resist both state dictates and local sanctions concerning women's sexuality. As there are few private spaces where young unmarried women can safely pursue erotic relationships, marriage allows them to establish their own households apart from their mothers'.

Initial compliance with the dictates of heterosexual reproductivity creates new possibilities for sexual relationships. Once they have fulfilled their obligations, these women can establish relationships with female partners in the interstices of an apparently heterosexual household. Some women divorce their husbands, but others make use of the tradition of frequent separation between spouses – for instance, a husband often may be away on business or living with a second wife – to maintain the facade of marriage and carry on a relationship with a tomboi. At that point neither the state nor the local community can closely control a woman's sexuality, as long as she manages her household and attends to the care of her children adequately. Family and local officials are apparently much more willing to ignore a relationship with a tomboi once a woman has fulfilled the duties accorded to her gender, as long as such relationships are hidden. At the national level, there is a good model for such benign collusion: In the patriarchal New Order, adultery is very prominent among men who are high-ranking government officials despite its official condemnation (Suryakusuma 1996).

A "normative" woman, that is, one who has the appearance of fitting gender norms, can pursue her desire for and sexual relations with a tomboi without becoming marked as a gender transgressor. This fact points to the privilege associated with the dominant gender ideology. Enacting the gender that is appropriate for one's sex fits with the heterosexual paradigm and is less problematic than enacting the "wrong" gender.[26]

Transnational Lesbian and Gay Discourse

In addition to local and state discourses, tomboi identity is situated within a transnational lesbian and gay discourse circulating in Indonesia primarily through national gay organizations and their newsletters. First organized in the early 1980s, these groups have nurtured a small but growing nationwide community of gays and lesbians (Boellstorff 1995), thereby developing a consciously new gay identity for Indonesians. *Gaya Nusantara*, a national magazine for gay men and lesbians that began publication in 1987, has been the leading edge of the movement. *Gaya Nusantara* is produced by a working group of gay men; their chief editor is Dede Oetomo, a Cornell-educated Indonesian gay man. Articles in *Gaya Nusantara* cover topics such as gay and lesbian identity, events on the international scene, and issues of local concern. *Gaya Nusantara* also carries stories about and advice on relationships and how to make them work, as well as personal ads for those seeking to get in touch with others within and beyond Indonesia. *Gaya Nusantara* articles assume a readership "out there" who, once they understand what being gay really is, will become part of the community and identify themselves as gay. Some of the contributors to the magazine urge readers to be out as much as possible while recognizing that such a position is extremely difficult for Indonesians.

Oetomo is one of the most visible members of the *Gaya Nusantara* work group. He has published several of his own articles in the newsletter as well as in national magazines and international journals. Oetomo himself uses the terms *gay* and *lesbi* "more or less as they are in the contemporary West; they refer to people who identify themselves as homosexuals, belong to delineated communities, and lead distinct subcultural lifestyles" (1996:

259 n. 1). His work has been influential in constructing an Indonesian lesbian and gay identity. Although this identity is different from the lesbian and gay identity dominant in the "West" (see also Boelstorff 1995), both are constructed primarily as sexual identities and not gender identities.

Because *Gaya Nusantara* reaches primarily a gay male audience, a few politically active lesbians have made efforts to build a nationwide network of their own. These efforts were spearheaded by Gayatri, a well-travelled activist with a college education. Gayatri briefly helped publish a newsletter called "Gaya Lestari" as a section of *Gaya Nusantara*. One author writing anonymously in "Gaya Lestari" admonished lesbians to come out, bemoaning their invisibility and their preference for GTM (Gerakan Tutup Mulut, the close-mouthed movement).

References to "our lesbians" and "the lesbian world" in the article suggest that the author imagines the existence of a group of women who hold a common identity (quoted in Boellstorff 2000: 31, 42, his translation). This new lesbian identity she envisions demands outward resistance to the heterosexual paradigm.

The new lesbian and gay movement in Indonesia is creating an identity distinct from the gender-marked banci and tomboi identities. Much as the post-Stonewall (post-1969) American lesbian and gay movement separated itself from butches, femmes, and drag queens (Kennedy and Davis 1993), gay and lesbian activists in Indonesia distinguish themselves from both bancis and tombois. Gay and lesbian identity is associated with a "modern," educated middle class, while banci is a "lower-class construction" distinct from the gay and lesbian community, although the distinction between the two is not that neat (Oetomo 1996: 263). Similarly, cowok–cewek are thought to be predominantly from the working class and not like lesbians of the middle and upper middle classes (Gayatri 1994). Gayatri (1993) specifically excluded cowok or "female-transvestites," as she called them then, from her early work on lesbians in Indonesia because she felt that their identification as men separated them from lesbians. In the emerging lesbian movement, tombois were perceived as imitating men, and hence in need of modernization and education (see also Murray 1998), although this stance has softened over time (see Gayatri 1997).

Print media in Indonesia since the early 1980s have also been a major source of information on gays and lesbians (Gayatri 1997). Media attention to an increasingly international gay and lesbian movement has brought into common use the terms *lesbi* and *tomboi*, transformations of the English terms *lesbian* and *tomboy*. These terms coexist somewhat uneasily with older terms, such as *bujang gadis* and *banci*, which are associated with a "nonconforming" gender identity (see also Oetomo 1991). Even in urban areas in Indonesia, bancis are seen as asexual, gender nonconforming (cross-dressing) males, although bancis consider themselves to be a third gender and are sexually active with men who occupy the normative category for males in Indonesian society (Oetomo 1996). The terms *tomboi* and *lesbi* are now synonymous for many people, although *tomboi* is more consistent with the older gender identity. The media perpetuates the image that lesbis are masculine women whose partners are feminine. This usage is inconsistent, however, with the term as used by activists, who define a lesbi as a woman who is sexually active with another woman.

Despite sometimes negative and sensationalizing coverage, newspapers carry stories about gay liberation and gay couples living together in Europe and the United States. They also avidly report stories about Indonesian lesbians who try to marry (Gayatri 1997). Such stories broadcast nationally a lesbi desire to live together despite resistance from "concerned" parents, for the first time portraying an alternative (if negatively construed) lifestyle for same-sex couples.

The transnational discourse on gender and sexuality is complicated by media coverage of transgendered individuals in Indonesia and other parts of the world. Indonesians know of both American and Indonesian transgendered people who have had sex-congruence surgery (bringing their sex into congruence with their gender). In fact Dayan's sister was so worried that s/he might want surgery that she specifically warned hir against it, at the same time pleading with hir to get married. Consequently, transnational narratives produce yet another possibility, that of surgically bringing one's body into conformity with one's gender, a model that fits with older indigenous notions of the primacy of bodies in determining gender.

The infusion of transnational gay discourse into the lives of tombois and their partners presents new cultural models of sexuality. In discussing gay culture in Indonesia's urban centers, Oetomo suggests that "whoever joins the metropolitan superculture adopts the going construction there, although traces of a local construction still may color the way s/he…construes gender and sexual orientation" (1996: 260). Movement between urban and rural areas means that local and urban identities confront each other and must be negotiated and claimed in hybrid ways. "The going construction" is brought back "home" to be remarked on with others, reworked, and then updated with each new trip to the metropolis. (Oetomo's gay subjects are most likely permanent residents of metropolises.) Tombois and their partners have heard of Western lesbian and gay couples living together. From their urban cohort they have been told of a "lesbian" identity that is an unchanging part of self and have been urged to claim that identity. These new models are being incorporated into older gender-based models (cowok–cewek) in contradictory ways.

Plural Identities

I want to pull together the various threads of my argument to reveal how one particular tomboi is situated within these narratives of gender, sexuality, and culture. Many representations of femininity circulate in Indonesia (Sears 1996a). In like manner, female subjects who are masculine, erotically attracted to women, or both are represented in many different ways. They are seen as "deviants" from the model of mother and wife so central to Indonesian state ideology, as the stereotypically masculine lesbian portrayed by the media, as women who love each other (the model favored by some activists), and as men (the identity claimed by tombois).

Dayan is positioned within all these possibilities. A product of the post-colonial Indonesian school system, s/he graduated from a technical high school with ambitions for a career. But, like many others in the working class, s/he struggles to find work. S/he is a member of hir mother's lineage but lives with hir older sister on their deceased father's land in a community that is only 15 minutes from the district capital, where some of hir brothers work. A large number of migrants in the community work in other areas. Not a vibrant adat community, this village is moving into the margins of urban life in Indonesia.

Dayan's location on the fringes of urban culture helps to explain hir rejection of Minangkabau womanhood. Raised in a family with little matrilineal money or land and thus dependent on the father's family to provide land and house, s/he, hir mother, and hir sister have lost some of the crucial connections that authorize women's power. Further, because not all daughters benefit equally or are treated favorably by their mothers, some, like Dayan, may never attain the power of a senior woman. Beyond that, the family's marginal position between rural and urban means that their desires are directed toward urban opportunities not village and matrilineal relations. The Minangkabau world Dayan knows is that of a struggling, urban-oriented family.

Like many youth growing up, Dayan has been influenced by divergent ideologies of womanhood. Educated in the "modern" school system, Minangkabau youth have received little state validation for the importance of Minangkabau women. Recent local efforts to provide more education about Minangkabau culture have only highlighted the role of men as "traditional" leaders (see Blackwood 1995b). Schoolgirls learn "proper" gender roles and are indoctrinated in the importance of becoming wives who serve their husbands' needs. They are inundated through media with representations of urban, middle-class, docile women. Yet with the increased availability of education, civil service, and other wage-labor jobs in the last 30 years, young women now have the right to choose their spouses or to pursue higher education and careers in urban areas. Many villagers believe that the potential economic benefits of higher education or urban careers may enhance lineage status, especially when successful educated daughters use their income to remodel or build new lineage houses. Many young women grow up believing that they are better off today under the patriarchal New Order because they can seek their own jobs and choose their own husbands. To these young women, the Minangkabau world of powerful elite women, wrapped up in the "esoteric" adat of ritual ceremonies and hard work in the rice fields, seems distant and old fashioned. Thus, the images of womanhood with which Dayan is familiar underscore the burden of privilege – of marriage, children, and lineage priorities – and the fear of dependence – of being a wife under the husband's control. Within this context the Minangkabau kinship ideology that requires daughters' obedience in marrying heterosexually may seem oppressive, but only in the context of postcolonial transformations that have weakened lineage priorities and promoted other images of family and happiness.

The masculinities that tombois construct reflect their different locations in the global market as well as the local community. Hegemonic masculinity is represented and enacted differently in the village, in urban areas, and on movie screens. It also is a hybrid of local, national, and transnational representations. In rural villages a young man may smoke, drink, gamble, and use coarse language, but he is also admonished to be strong, industrious, respectful of his elders, and responsible to his lineage and his wife's family. The bravado and coarseness of young urban (poor, working-class) men in Indonesia is far from the politeness and respectfulness of rural men. While Dayan's masculinity reflects more of the village, Agus's interpretation reflects a combination of the coarse masculinity and male privilege of urban areas. Dayan told me that when Agus is at Yul's house, "s/he expects to be served and won't do anything for hir wife except give her money." This interpretation of a man's role could be drawn from middle-class Indonesian images of manhood but also seems to selectively draw on older representations of high-ranking Minangkabau husbands who, as

guests in their wives' houses (male duolocal residence), were served by their wives. Agus's "macho" behavior, like the banci's performance of a fashion model persona, presents an extreme style of masculinity, one that is easily read as masculine by others.

Dayan's experience of lesbian and gay discourse creates another distinction between herself and Agus. Dayan described Agus as an old-fashioned tomboi, one who "is like a man and won't be any other way." Hir statement implies that s/he sees Agus as holding onto certain normative ideas of gender that contemporary Indonesian lesbians no longer find satisfying. S/he said further that "Agus has never been out of the kampung [village]," implying that had s/he been, Agus might see other models of lesbian relations and quit trying to be so much like a man.

In the past few years, Dayan has lived in Jakarta for one to two years at a time. Both at home and in Jakarta hir friends are cowok–cewek, but these friends also know about the Euro-American model of lesbian identity. At different times Dayan claimed both a masculine identity and a lesbi identity. S/he told me s/he has always been the way s/he is, meaning s/he has always been a tomboi, but s/he also calls hirself a lesbi. Hir statements imply that despite feeling like a man, the availability of other models makes it possible to interpolate the tomboi identity with a lesbian identity. Oetomo (1996) notes a similar shift occurring between the banci and gay male identities for some Indonesian men. As with the proliferation of transgendered identities in the United States (Bolin 1994; Cromwell 1999), tomboi identity is constantly being negotiated and redefined in response to local, national, and transnational processes.

Conclusion

Identity for tombois in West Sumatra at this point in time is a bricolage, a mix of local, national, and transnational identities. If their identity growing up was shaped by local cultural forces that emphasized oppositional genders, their movement between cities and rural areas means that they have been exposed to other models of sexuality and gender identity that they have used to construct a new sense of themselves. The complexities of their gender identity make it impossible to align tombois with any one category, whether "woman," "lesbian," or "transgendered person."

Tomboi identity refracts and transgresses normative gender constructs. While some theorists identify gender transgression as resistance to male-dominant hegemonic order, tombois in West Sumatra suggest a more complicated cultural production of gender transgression. They cannot be read simply as the product of male dominance. The tomboi identity in Minangkabau culture speaks to the significance of a hegemonic kinship ideology – in which each gender is rigidly distinct and based on two sexes but not male dominant – in producing particular forms of gender transgression. For the tomboi, processes of postcolonialism, capitalism, and modernity also converge to produce and reinforce gender transgression.

At the national level the tomboi can be read as resisting the constraints of state ibuism in much the same manner as European and North American lesbians, gay men, and transgendered people are said to resist dominant gender ideology. Although the Indonesian state enforces heterosexuality, wage labor and capitalism create a space for the tomboi to live as a single female. The discourse of modernity – the importance of education, careers, and middle-class status – legitimates models other than motherhood and femininity for females. Though the tomboi remains a deviant, s/he is also finding more room to negotiate a future.

At the same time, other models of sexuality and gender are becoming visible in a globalized world, multiplying, collapsing, and refracting social identities in new ways. Where sexuality was embedded in the ideology of oppositional genders (man–woman, cowok–cewek, banci–laki asli [real man]), sexual "identity" and the possibility of sexuality between two women or two men are emergent cultural practices. Desiring women is being rewritten for some as a product of the variability of human sexuality rather than the "natural" urge of the male body and the prerogative of "men."

NOTES

1 I put *women* in quotes to problematize the use of "woman" for individuals who are female bodied but do not identify as women. As I use it, *female* refers to physical sex characteristics, and *woman* refers to a set of social behaviors and characteristics that are culturally constructed and attributed to female bodies. I use "women" in this instance because at the time of first meeting, I assumed these individuals were women.

2 In Indonesian, the plural is formed by doubling the noun. I choose to use a hybrid form to represent the plural, attaching the English "s" to Indonesian terms. Sears (1996b) also employs this construction.

3 For relevant literature arguing and refining the social construction perspective on gender and sexuality, see Blackwood 1986a, 1986b; Caplan 1987; Carrier 1980; D'Emilio 1983; Ortner and Whitehead 1981; Padgug 1979; Plummer 1981; Ross and Rapp 1981; Vance 1989.

4 The term *female-bodied* is Cromwell's (1997) and refers to physiological sex.

5 Recent work on Javanese culture, however, argues that the dominant ideology poses greater constraints on gender than previously thought (Brenner 1995).

6 This age group seemed to be experimenting in a range of sexual practices.

7 I use fictitious names for the individuals mentioned in this article. Dayan (pronounced "Dai-yon") lived with an older married sister in a small town about an hour from where I lived. I visited Dayan mostly on weekends at the sister's house.

8 Although I have used the pronoun *she* in the past to refer to a tomboi (Blackwood 1995a), at this point in my thinking "she" and "her/him" seem inadequate to represent the complexity of the tomboi identity, particularly because of the connotations an English-speaking reader brings to them. The Indonesian language provides no guidance in this matter because its pronouns are gender neutral. The third-person pronoun for both women and men

is *dia*. I have chosen to use the pronominal constructions *s/he* (for "she/he"), *hir* (for "her/his" and "her/him"), and *hirself* (for "herself/himself"). These pronouns are gaining currency within the transgender movement in the United States (see Wilchins 1997). By doing so, I am not making any claims about the "gender" of tombois. These terms should not be read as suggesting that the tomboi is a transgendered person or some combination of masculine/feminine or not-masculine/not-feminine. Rather, by using these terms I want to unsettle the reader's assumptions about gender and gender binaries.

9   Nestle describes butches more eloquently as follows: "a butch lesbian wearing men's clothes in the 1950s was not a man wearing men's clothes; she was a woman creating an original style to signal to other women what she was capable of doing – taking erotic responsibility" (1992: 141).

10 This attribution is no longer so clear cut. Jeff Dickemann (letter to the author, November 30, 1997) argues that butches, who can be found in England as early as the 1820s, are degrees of transsexuals; there is no line between butch and female-to-male transsexual. See also for comparison, Nestle 1992 and Halberstam 1994.

11 I heard this news when I was in West Sumatra in 1996, but whether she was forced to marry or not, I do not know.

12 This practice is similar to one found in some Latin American cultures in which men who take the dominant (insertor) role in sex with another man are not marked as different because of their sexual behavior. They are seen as normatively masculine (see Carrier 1995; Parker 1986). I thank Jason Cromwell for making this connection.

13 The relevant literature includes Dickemann 1997; Frye 1983; Grimm 1987; Katz 1976; Kennedy and Davis 1992, 1993; Newton 1984; Rubin 1992; Shapiro 1991; Wikan 1977.

14 They use the spelling "butch–fem" in their book because it was the way women in

the community they studied spelled the term.

15 See Cromwell's (1999) critique of the way this interpretation erases transgendered females (female-to-males [FTMs]).

16 I thank Daniel Segal for making this point.

17 For relevant literature on the postcolonial state and ethnic identities, see Bentley 1987; Friedman 1992; Gupta and Ferguson 1992; Kipp 1993; Olwig and Hastrup 1997; B. Williams 1989, 1995.

18 Islam in West Sumatra is part of the everyday life of the Minangkabau, who generally see no conflict between adat and Islam. The two have come to be mutually constructed. For further discussion of this point, see Ellen 1983, Delaney 1991, Whalley 1993.

19 This is not an insignificant concern because prestige, status, and property are all at risk. One young married woman I knew was in turmoil over whether to have another child because her only daughter is not strong. Although she already has two children, a number that the Indonesian state says is sufficient for a family, she thinks that she should have another daughter to ensure the perpetuation of her lineage.

20 During my stay one young banci I knew in West Sumatra was forced to go to a *dukun* (shaman) by hir sister in an effort to "cure" hir of hir desire for men.

21 Building on Schneider's (1968) formative work on kinship, feminist anthropologists and others have argued forcefully for the conceptual separation between sex and gender. See Ortner 1974; Ortner and Whitehead 1981; Shapiro 1991; Yanagisako and Collier 1987.

22 I thank Deborah Elliston for suggesting the phrase "hegemonic persuasiveness" to describe the power of dominant models to reproduce themselves.

23 Some of the relevant literature on women and the state includes Alexander 1994; Alexander and Mohanty 1997; Delaney 1995; Kandiyoti 1991; Ong 1987; Ong and Peletz 1995; Parker et al. 1992; Sears 1996b; and B. Williams 1996.

24 The New Order refers to the postwar regime of General Suharto, who became acting head of state in 1966 and remained president until 1998.
25 The action of Chinese marriage resistors, which was not veiled but public resistance, was explicitly interpreted as resistance to a patriarchal oppressive marriage system both by the women themselves and by outside observers (Sankar 1986; Topley 1975).
26 I thank Jason Cromwell (e-mail to the author, March 1, 1998) for his comments on this point. Cromwell notes a similar pattern in the United States. The female partners of FTM transmen are not marked nor are male partners of MTFs (male-to-females) (see also Cromwell 1999).

REFERENCES

Alexander, M. Jacqui. 1994. Not Just (Any)body Can Be a Citizen: The Politics of Law, Sexuality and Post-Coloniality in Trinidad and Tobago and the Bahamas. *Feminist Review*, 48: 5–23.

Alexander, M. Jacqui, and Chandra Mohanty, eds. 1997. *Feminist Genealogies, Colonial Legacies, Democratic Futures*. New York: Routledge.

Aripurnami, Sita. 1996. A Feminist Comment on the Sinetron Presentation of Indonesian Women. In *Fantasizing the Feminine in Indonesia*. Laurie Sears, ed. pp. 249–58. Durham, NC: Duke University Press.

Atkinson, Jane M. 1990. How Gender Makes a Difference in Wana Society. In *Power and Difference: Gender in Island Southeast Asia*. Jane M. Atkinson and Shelly Errington, eds. pp. 59–93. Stanford, CA: Stanford University Press.

Balzer, Marjorie M. 1996. Sacred Genders in Siberia: Shamans, Bear Festivals and Androgyny. In *Gender Reversals and Gender Cultures: Anthropological and Historical Perspectives*. Sabrina Ramet, ed. pp. 164–82. London: Routledge.

Bentley, G. Carter. 1987. Ethnicity and Practice. *Comparative Study of Society and History*, 29/1: 24–55.

Blackwood, Evelyn. 1986a. Breaking the Mirror: The Construction of Lesbianism and the Anthropological Discourse on Homosexuality. In *The Many Faces of Homosexuality: Anthropological Approaches to Homosexual Behavior*. Evelyn Blackwood, ed. pp. 1–17. New York: Harrington Park Press.

——ed. 1986b. *The Many Faces of Homosexuality: Anthropological Approaches to Homosexual Behavior*. New York: Harrington Park Press.

——1993. The Politics of Daily Life: Gender, Kinship and Identity in a Minangkabau Village, West Sumatra, Indonesia. PhD dissertation, Stanford University.

——1995a. Falling in Love with An-Other Lesbian: Reflections on Identity in Fieldwork. In *Taboo: Sex, Identity and Erotic Subjectivity in Anthropological Fieldwork*. Don Kulick and Margaret Willson, eds. pp. 51–75. London: Routledge.

——1995b. Senior Women, Model Mothers, and Dutiful Wives: Managing Gender Contradictions in a Minangkabau Village. In *Bewitching Women, Pious Men: Gender and Body Politics in Southeast Asia*. Aihwa Ong and Michael Peletz, eds. pp. 124–58. Berkeley: University of California Press.

——2000. *Webs of Power: Women, Kin and Community in a Sumatran Village*. Lanham, MD: Rowman & Littlefield.

Boellstorff, Thomas David. 2000. The Gay Archipelago: Postcolonial Sexual Subjectivities in Indonesia. PhD diss., Stanford University.

Bogoras, Waldemar. 1901. The Chukchi of Northeastern Asia. *American Anthropologist*, 3: 80–108.

Bolin, Anne. 1994. Transcending and Transgendering: Male-to-Female Transsexuals, Dichotomy and Diversity. In *Third Sex, Third Gender: Beyond Sexual Dimorphism in Culture and History*. Gilbert Herdt, ed. pp. 447–85. New York: Zone Books.

Bourdieu, Pierre. 1977. *Outline of a Theory of Practice*. Cambridge: Cambridge University Press.

Brenner, Suzanne A. 1995. Why Women Rule the Roost: Rethinking Javanese Ideologies of Gender and Self-Control. In *Bewitching Women, Pious Men: Gender and Body*

Politics in Southeast Asia. Aihwa Ong and Michael Peletz, eds. pp. 19–50. Berkeley: University of California Press.

Bullough, Bonnie, Vern Bullough, and John Elias, eds. 1997. *Gender Blending.* Amherst, NY: Prometheus.

Butler, Judith. 1991. Imitation and Gender Insubordination. In *Inside/Out: Lesbian Theories, Gay Theories.* Diana Fuss, ed. pp. 13–31. New York: Routledge.

Caplan, Pat. 1987. *The Cultural Construction of Sexuality.* London: Tavistock.

Carrier, Joseph M. 1980. Homosexual Behavior in Cross-Cultural Perspective. In *Homosexual Behavior: A Modern Reappraisal.* Judd Marmor, ed. pp. 100–22. New York: Basic Books.

——1995. *De Los Otros: Intimacy and Homosexuality among Mexican Men.* New York: Columbia University Press.

Chabot, Hendrick Theodorus. 1960. *Kinship, Status and Sex in the South Celebes.* Richard Neuse, trans. New Haven, CT: Human Relations Area File.

Crompton, Louis. 1981. The Myth of Lesbian Impunity: Capital Laws from 1270 to 1791. *Journal of Homosexuality,* 6(½): 11–25.

Cromwell, Jason. 1997. Traditions of Gender Diversity and Sexualities: A Female-to-Male Transgendered Perspective. In *Two-Spirit People: Native American Gender Identity, Sexuality, and Spirituality.* Sue-Ellen Jacobs, Wesley Thomas, and Sabine Lang, eds. pp. 119–42. Urbana: University of Illinois Press.

——1999. *Transmen and FTMs: Identities, Bodies, and Sexualities.* Urbana: University of Illinois Press.

Delaney, Carol. 1991. *The Seed and the Soil: Gender and Cosmology in Turkish Village Society.* Berkeley: University of California Press.

——1995. Father State, Motherland, and the Birth of Modern Turkey. In *Naturalizing Power: Essays in Feminist Cultural Analysis.* Sylvia Yanagisako and Carol Delaney, eds. pp. 177–99. New York: Routledge.

D'Emilio, John. 1983. *Sexual Politics, Sexual Communities: The Making of a Homosexual Minority in the United States,* 1940–1970. Chicago: University of Chicago Press.

Devor, Holly. 1989. *Gender Blending: Confronting the Limits of Duality.* Bloomington: Indiana University Press.

Dickemann, Mildred. 1997. The Balkan Sworn Virgin: A Traditional European Transperson. In *Gender Blending.* Bonnie Bullough, Vern Bullough, and John Elias, eds. pp. 248–55. Amherst, NY: Prometheus.

Djajadiningrat-Nieuwenhuis, Madelon. 1987. Ibuism and Priyayization: Path to Power? In *Indonesian Women in Focus: Past and Present Notions.* Elsbeth Locher-Scholten and Anke Niehof, eds. pp. 43–51. Dordrecht, Holland: Foris Publications.

Echols, John M., and Hassan Shadily. 1989. *Kamus Indonesia Inggris: An Indonesian–English Dictionary,* 3rd edn. Jakarta: PT Gramedia.

Ellen, Roy F. 1983. Social Theory, Ethnography and the Understanding of Practical Islam in South-East Asia. In *Islam in South-East Asia.* M. B. Hooker, ed. pp. 50–91. Leiden: E. J. Brill.

Elliston, Deborah. 1995. Erotic Anthropology: "Ritualized Homosexuality" in Melanesia and Beyond. *American Ethnologist,* 22: 848–67.

Epstein, Julia, and Kristina Straub, eds. 1991. *Body/Guards: The Cultural Politics of Gender Ambiguity.* New York: Routledge.

Errington, Shelly. 1990. Recasting Sex, Gender, and Power: A Theoretical and Regional Overview. In *Power and Difference: Gender in Island Southeast Asia.* Jane M. Atkinson and Shelly Errington, eds. pp. 1–58. Stanford, CA: Stanford University Press.

Fadlillah. 1996. Wanita, Malin Kundang, dan Feminisme. *Singgalang,* June 30: 3.

Friedman, Jonathan. 1992. The Past in the Future: History and the Politics of Identity. *American Anthropologist,* 94: 837–59.

Frye, Marilyn. 1983. *The Politics of Reality: Essays in Feminist Theory.* Trumansberg, NY: Crossing Press.

Garber, Marjorie. 1991. The Chic of Araby: Transvestism, Transsexualism and the Erotics of Cultural Appropriation. In *Body/Guards: The Cultural Politics of Gender Ambiguity.* Julia Epstein and Kristina

Straub, eds. pp. 223–47. New York: Routledge.

Gayatri, BJD. 1993. Coming Out but Remaining Hidden: A Portrait of Lesbians in Java. Paper presented at the International Congress of Anthropological and Ethnological Sciences, Mexico City, Mexico.

—— 1994. Sentul-Kantil, Not Just Another Term. Jakarta, unpublished MS.

—— 1995. Indonesian Lesbians Writing Their Own Script: Issues of Feminism and Sexuality. In *From Amazon to Zami: Towards a Global Lesbian Feminism*. Monika Reinfelder, ed. pp. 86–98. London: Cassell.

—— 1997 [Come] Outed but Remaining Invisible: A Portrait of Lesbians in Java. Jakarta, unpublished MS.

Gramsci, Antonio. 1971. *Selections from the Prison Notebooks of Antonio Gramsci*. Quintin Hoare and Geoffrey N. Smith, trans. New York: International Publishers.

Grimm, David E. 1987. Toward a Theory of Gender: Transsexualism, Gender, Sexuality, and Relationships. *American Behavioral Scientist*, 31/1: 66–85.

Gupta, Akhil, and James Ferguson. 1992. Beyond "Culture": Space, Identity, and the Politics of Difference. *Cultural Anthropology*, 7: 6–23.

Halberstam, Judith. 1994. F2M: The Making of Female Masculinity. In *The Lesbian Postmodern*. Laura Doan, ed. pp. 210–28. New York: Columbia University Press.

Herdt, Gilbert, ed. 1994. *Third Sex, Third Gender: Beyond Sexual Dimorphism in Culture and History*. New York: Zone Books.

Jacobs, Sue-Ellen, Wesley Thomas, and Sabine Lang, eds. 1997. *Two-Spirit People: Native American Gender Identity, Sexuality, and Spirituality*. Urbana: University of Illinois Press.

Kandiyoti, Deniz, ed. 1991. *Women, Islam and the State*. Philadelphia: Temple University Press.

Katz, Jonathan Ned. 1976. *Gay American History: Lesbians and Gay Men in the U.S.A.* New York: Crowell.

Kennedy, Elizabeth, and Madeline Davis. 1992. "They Was No One to Mess With": The Construction of the Butch Role in the Lesbian Community of the 1940s and 1950s. In *The Persistent Desire: A Femme–Butch Reader*. Joan Nestle, ed. pp. 62–79. Boston: Alyson Publications.

—— 1993. *Boots of Leather, Slippers of Gold: The History of a Lesbian Community*. New York: Penguin Books.

Kipp, Rita Smith. 1993. *Dissociated Identities: Ethnicity, Religion and Class in an Indonesian Society*. Ann Arbor: University of Michigan Press.

Manderson, Lenore. 1980. Rights and Responsibilities, Power and Privilege: Women's Role in Contemporary Indonesia. In *Kartini Centenary: Indonesian Women Then and Now*, pp. 69–92. Melbourne: Monash University Press.

Murray, Alison. 1998. Let Them Take Ecstasy: Class and Jakarta Lesbians. In *Female Desires: Same-Sex Relations and Transgender Practices across Cultures*. Evelyn Blackwood and Saskia Wieringa, eds. New York: Columbia University Press.

Nestle, Joan. 1992. The Femme Question. In *The Persistent Desire: A Femme–Butch Reader*. Joan Nestle, ed. pp. 138–46. Boston: Alyson Publications.

Newton, Esther. 1972. *Mother Camp: Female Impersonators in America*. Chicago: University of Chicago Press.

—— 1984. The Mythic Mannish Lesbian: Radclyffe Hall and the New Woman. *Signs: Journal of Women in Culture and Society*, 9/4: 557–75.

—— 1993. *Cherry Grove, Fire Island: Sixty Years in America's First Gay and Lesbian Town*. Boston: Beacon.

Oetomo, Dede. 1991. Patterns of Bisexuality in Indonesia. In *Bisexuality and HIV/AIDS: A Global Perspective*. Rob Tielman, Manuel Carballo, and Aart Hendriks, eds. pp. 119–26. Buffalo, NY: Prometheus Books.

—— 1996. Gender and Sexual Orientation in Indonesia. In *Fantasizing the Feminine in Indonesia*. Laurie Sears, ed. pp. 259–69. Durham, NC: Duke University Press.

Olwig, Karen, and Kirsten Hastrup, eds. 1997. *Siting Culture: The Shifting Anthropological Object*. London: Routledge.

Ong, Aihwa. 1987. *Spirits of Resistance and Capitalist Discipline: Factory Women in*

Malaysia. Albany: State University of New York.

Ong, Aihwa, and Michael Peletz, eds. 1995. *Bewitching Women, Pious Men: Gender and Body Politics in Southeast Asia.* Berkeley: University of California Press.

Ortner, Sherry B. 1974. Is Female to Male as Nature Is to Culture? In *Woman, Culture, and Society.* Michelle Zimbalist Rosaldo and Louise Lamphere, eds. pp. 67–88. Stanford, CA: Stanford University Press. [This volume ch. 3.]

—— 1989 Gender Hegemonies. *Cultural Critique,* 14: 35–80.

Ortner, Sherry B., and Harriet Whitehead, eds. 1981. *Sexual Meanings: The Cultural Construction of Gender and Sexuality.* Cambridge: Cambridge University Press.

Padgug, Robert A. 1979. Sexual Matters: On Conceptualizing Sexuality in History. *Radical History Review,* 20: 3–23.

Pak, Ok-Kyung. 1986. Lowering the High, Raising the Low: The Gender Alliance and Property Relations in a Minangkabau Peasant Community of West Sumatra, Indonesia. PhD dissertation, Laval University.

Parker, Andrew, Mary Russo, Doris Sommer, and Patricia Yaeger, eds. 1992. *Nationalisms and Sexualities.* New York: Routledge.

Parker, Richard. 1986. Masculinity, Femininity and Homosexuality: On the Anthropological Interpretation of Sexual Meanings in Brazil. In *The Many Faces of Homosexuality: Anthropological Approaches to Homosexual Behavior.* Evelyn Blackwood, ed. pp. 155–63. New York: Harrington Park Press.

Peacock, James L. 1978. Symbolic Reversal and Social History: Transvestites and Clowns of Java. In *The Reversible World: Symbolic Inversion in Art and Society.* Barbara Babcock, ed. pp. 209–24. Ithaca, NY: Cornell University Press.

Plummer, Kenneth. 1981. *The Making of the Modern Homosexual.* Totowa, NJ: Barnes and Noble.

Poole, John Fitz Porter. 1996. The Procreative and Ritual Constitution of Female, Male and Other: Androgynous Beings in the Cultural Imagination of the Bimin-Kuskusmin

of Papua New Guinea. In *Gender Reversals and Gender Cultures: Anthropological and Historical Perspectives.* Sabrina Ramet, ed. pp. 197–218. London: Routledge.

Ramet, Sabrina Petra, ed. 1996. *Gender Reversals and Gender Cultures: Anthropological and Historical Perspectives.* London: Routledge.

Raymond, Janice. 1979. *The Transsexual Empire: The Making of the She-Male.* Boston: Beacon Press.

Rich, Adrienne. 1980. Compulsory Heterosexuality and Lesbian Existence. *Signs: Journal of Women in Culture and Society,* 5/4: 631–60.

Roscoe, Will. 1991. *The Zuni Man-Woman.* Albuquerque: University of New Mexico Press.

Ross, Ellen, and Rayna Rapp. 1981. Sex and Society: A Research Note from Social History and Anthropology. *Comparative Study of Society and History,* 23: 51–72.

Rubin, Gayle. 1975. The Traffic in Women: Notes on the "Political Economy" of Sex. In *Towards an Anthropology of Women.* Rayna R. Reiter, ed. pp. 157–210. New York: Monthly Review Press.

—— 1992. Of Catamites and Kings: Reflections on Butch, Gender and Boundaries. In *The Persistent Desire: A Femme–Butch Reader.* Joan Nestle, ed. pp. 466–82. Boston: Alyson Publications.

Sankar, Andrea. 1986. Sisters and Brothers, Lovers and Enemies: Marriage Resistance in Southern Kwangtung. In *The Many Faces of Homosexuality: Anthropological Approaches to Homosexual Behavior.* Evelyn Blackwood, ed. pp. 69–81. New York: Harrington Park Press.

Schneider, David. 1968. *American Kinship: A Cultural Account.* Englewood Cliffs, NJ: Prentice-Hall.

Sears, Laurie J. 1996a. Fragile Identities: Deconstructing Women and Indonesia. In *Fantasizing the Feminine in Indonesia.* Laurie Sears, ed. pp. 1–44. Durham, NC: Duke University Press.

—— ed. 1996b. *Fantasizing the Feminine in Indonesia.* Durham, NC: Duke University Press.

Shapiro, Judith. 1991. Transsexualism: Reflections on the Persistence of Gender and the Mutability of Sex. In *Body/Guards: The Cultural Politics of Gender Ambiguity.* Julia Epstein and Kristina Straub, eds. pp. 248–79. New York: Routledge.

Stoler, Ann. 1996. A Sentimental Education: Native Servants and the Cultivation of European Children in the Netherlands Indies. In *Fantasizing the Feminine in Indonesia.* Laurie Sears, ed. pp. 71–91. Durham, NC: Duke University Press.

Stone, Sandy. 1991. The "Empire" Strikes Back: A Posttranssexual Manifesto. In *Body/Guards: The Cultural Politics of Gender Ambiguity.* Julia Epstein and Kristina Straub, eds. pp. 280–304. New York: Routledge.

Sullivan, Norma. 1983. Indonesian Women in Development: State Theory and Urban Kampung Practice. In *Women's Work and Women's Roles: Economics and Everyday Life in Indonesia, Malaysia and Singapore.* Lenore Manderson, ed. pp. 147–71. Canberra: Australian National University.

Suryakusuma, Julia. 1996. The State and Sexuality in New Order Indonesia. In *Fantasizing the Feminine in Indonesia.* Laurie Sears, ed. pp. 92–119. Durham, NC: Duke University Press.

Topley, Marjorie. 1975. Marriage Resistance in Rural Kwangtung. In *Women in Chinese Society.* Margery Wolf and Roxane Witke, eds. pp. 57–88. Stanford, CA: Stanford University Press.

Trumbach, Randolph. 1994. London's Sapphists: From Three Sexes to Four Genders in the Making of Modern Culture. In *Third Sex, Third Gender: Beyond Sexual Dimorphism in Culture and History.* Gilbert Herdt, ed. pp. 111–36. New York: Zone Books.

Van der Kroef, Justus M. 1954. Transvestitism and the Religious Hermaphrodite in Indonesia. *Journal of East Asiatic Studies,* 3/3: 257–65.

Vance, Carole. 1989. Social Construction Theory: Problems in the History of Sexuality. In *Homosexuality, Which Homosexuality?* Dennis Altman et al., eds. pp. 13–35. Amsterdam: An Dekker/Schorer/London: GMP Publishers.

Weston, Kath. 1993. Lesbian/Gay Studies in the House of Anthropology. *Annual Review of Anthropology,* 22: 339–67.

Whalley, Lucy. 1993. Virtuous Women, Productive Citizens: Negotiating Tradition, Islam, and Modernity in Minangkabau, Indonesia. PhD dissertation, University of Illinois.

Wieringa, Saskia. 1989. An Anthropological Critique of Constructionism: Berdaches and Butches. In *Homosexuality, Which Homosexuality?* Dennis Altman et al., eds. pp. 215–38. Amsterdam: An Dekker/Schorer/London: GMP Publishers.

——1998. Desiring Bodies or Defiant Cultures. Butch–Femme Lesbians in Jakarta and Lima. In *Female Desires: Same-Sex Relations and Transgender Practices across Cultures.* Evelyn Blackwood and Saskia Wieringa, eds. New York: Columbia University Press.

Wikan, Unni. 1977. Man Becomes Woman: Transsexualism in Oman as a Key to Gender Roles. *Man,* ns 12: 304–19.

Wilchins, Riki Anne. 1997. *Read My Lips: Sexual Subversion and the End of Gender.* Ithaca, NY: Firebrand Books.

Williams, Brackette. 1989. A Class Act: Anthropology and the Race to Nation across Ethnic Terrain. *Annual Review of Anthropology,* 18: 401–44.

——1995. Classification Systems Revisited: Kinship, Caste, Race, and Nationality as the Flow of Blood and the Spread of Rights. In *Naturalizing Power: Essays in Feminist Cultural Analysis.* Sylvia Yanagisako and Carol Delaney, eds. pp. 201–36. New York: Routledge.

——ed. 1996. *Women out of Place: The Gender of Agency and the Race of Nationality.* New York: Routledge.

Williams, Raymond. 1977. *Marxism and Literature.* Oxford: Oxford University Press.

Yanagisako, Sylvia, and Jane F. Collier. 1987. Toward a Unified Analysis of Gender and Kinship. In *Gender and Kinship: Toward a Unified Analysis.* Jane Collier and Sylvia Yanagisako, eds. pp. 14–50. Stanford, CA: Stanford University Press.

Yanagisako, Sylvia, and Carol Delaney. 1995. Naturalizing Power. In *Naturalizing Power: Essays in Feminist Cultural Analysis*. Sylvia Yanagisako and Carol Delaney, eds. pp. 1–22. New York: Routledge.

Yengoyan, Aram. 1983. Transvestism and the Ideology of Gender: Southeast Asia and Beyond. In *Feminist Re-visions: What Has Been and Might Be*. Vivian Patraka and Louise A. Tilly, eds. pp. 135–48. Ann Arbor: Women's Studies Program, University of Michigan.

22

"What's Identity Got to Do with It?": Rethinking Identity in Light of the *Mati* Work in Suriname

Gloria Wekker

At minimum, all social construction approaches adopt the view that physically identical sexual acts may have varying social significance and subjective meaning depending on how they are defined and understood in different cultures and historical periods. Because a sexual act does not carry with it a universal social meaning, it follows that *the relationship between sexual acts and sexual identities is not a fixed one*, and it is projected from the observer's time and place to others at great peril.

Vance 1989: 18; emphasis mine

The concept of "homosexual identity" plays a privileged and tenacious part in discussions about homosexual behavior (cf. D'Emilio 1984; Vance 1989; De Cecco and Elia 1993). The concept is used as a particularly powerful mediator of gay and lesbian behaviors. Sometimes these discussions are limited to the Western world, but the concept is also, apparently without much hesitation, used in cross-cultural contexts. Even though in constructionist approaches the relationship between sexual acts and sexual identities is thought to be variable, scholars often do not question the notion of homosexual (or homoerotic) identity in itself

nor its ubiquitousness (cf. Vance's statement quoted above; Newton and Walton 1984; Lewin 1995). Whether "homosexual identity" is conceived of as an essentialist category, with biological and physiological influences preceding cultural ones and setting limits on the latter, or as a constructionist concept privileging social and cultural experiences, it is striking that a concept used with such frequency in the literature is not subjected to more reflection. However the concept is conceived, it apparently speaks to deeply ingrained, ethnopsychological notions in Western subjects that the core of our being, our essence, the privileged site in which the truth about ourselves and our social relationships is to be found, corresponds to something that we call (homo-)sexual identity (Foucault 1981; Kulick 1995). What has generally been lacking is an exploration of the implication and embeddedness of "identity" in hegemonic, Western thought, even if in feminist and "queer" versions. While it is not my intention here to give a thorough "reading" of the history of this concept in either Western folk wisdom or in various disciplinary domains, I think it generally will be agreed upon that "identity" carries heavy connotations of stasis, "core, unitary character," that which is immutable about a person, whether this core is ascribed to inborn or to learned characteristics (Geertz 1984; Weedon 1987; Kondo 1990). It will be my contention in this article that students of sexuality should problematize the notion of "identity" in order to avoid circuitous reasoning and premature closure.

By way of focusing on a widespread institution among Creole[1] working-class women in Paramaribo, Suriname, called the *mati* work, I want to present a differently conceived sexual configuration that does not posit a fixed notion of "sexual identity." Mati, although by no means a monolithic category, are women who engage in sexual relationships with men and with women, either simultaneously or consecutively, and who conceive of their sexual acts in terms of behavior. In focusing on female mati, I embark on a much overdue project in a Caribbean context: "to theorize from the point of view and contexts of marginalized women not in terms of victim status or an essentialized identity but in terms that push us to place women's agency, their subjectivities and collective consciousness, at the center of our understandings of power and resistance" (Alexander 1991: 148).

First, I will describe the mati work within its historical and sociocultural setting, and I will consider how this "unruly sexuality" relates to dominant, heterosexual patterns in the same context. Second, I want to defend the claim that conceptualizing homosocial bonding and homoerotic behavior among women in this Third World context as "identity" inscribes and reproduces hegemonic Western analytical categories. Third, and more generally, I will address the question of how to proceed fruitfully in theorizing homoerotic behavior cross-culturally, without radically distorting emic realities. It is vital to put the genesis of "homosexual identity under capitalism" (D'Emilio 1984) into cultural and historical perspective as just one possible configuration among many, without universal validity. Thinking about homosexuality should start from the realization that "homosexualities"[2] cross-culturally have in common sexual acts between same-gendered people, but these acts are also and importantly different and contextually conceived in multiple ways.

The Mati Work

I was alerted to the mati work by the literature while doing research for my master's thesis in the early 1980s. The institution is first mentioned in 1912, when a high Dutch government official, Schimmelpenninck van der Oye, on a fact-finding mission concerning the health situation of the population in the colony of Suriname, deplores the widespread occurrence of the "sexual communion between women, the *mati play*" (Ambacht 1912). Another observer in the 1930s remarks upon the fact that "the unusual relationships among women in Suriname...were not dependent on social rank, intellectual development, race or country of origin" (Comvalius 1935). In the course of this century, several studies – mostly by men, occasionally by white women – have dealt with "the unusual relationships between women" (Herskovits 1936; Buschkens 1974; Janssens and van Wetering 1985; van Lier 1986). My curiosity about the phenomenon was piqued by these descriptions, and I decided to devote my doctoral research to the mati work.

From January 1990 through July 1991, I explored how working-class Creole women construct themselves sexually in Paramaribo, Suriname.[3] As a black sociocultural anthropologist, born in Suriname and trained in the Netherlands and the United States, my interest in local constructions of subjectivity, gender, and sexuality clearly bespeaks issues in my own situated life (Wekker 1992b). In the course of my sexually coming-of-age in Amsterdam, the Netherlands, during the seventies, I noticed that there were at least two models available to me on how to be a woman who loved other women. There was a dominant model, mostly engaged in by white, middle-class women, in which the rhetoric of "political choice," feminist chauvinism, conformity between partners along a number of dimensions, including socioeconomic status and age, and predominantly childlessness, played central parts. And there was a subjugated model, of which I discerned merely the contours at the time but which I later learned to identify as the mati work. The latter was lived by working-class Afro-Surinamese women, who often differed greatly in age from their women partners, typically had children, and apparently maintained their ties with men, either as husbands, lovers, friends, or sons. My awareness of these two models, which did not seem to come together on any shared ground, made me increasingly aware of the situatedness and sociocultural construction of my own (Eurocentric) sexuality and its axioms, which I had taken for granted. When at a later stage I chose to occupy various sexual sites that are distinguished within a Western universe, it became clear that significant amounts of mental, psychological, and social work were necessary, both within myself and within the predominantly middle-class (white and black) circles in which I moved to obtain any kind of credibility for those choices. My periodically returning structural malaise in applying Western sexual labels (hetero-, homo-, and bisexuality) to myself while failing to "identify" with them was a major impetus to engage in this particular research. As Reinharz, among others, has noted "in feminist research 'the problem' frequently is a blend of an intellectual question and a personal trouble" (1992: 258).

Most of the authors, who have dealt with the mati work, locate its emergence at the beginning of this century, when men were frequently absent from the city due to migrant labor as gold diggers and balata bleeders in the interior of Suriname. Ironically, these authors explain the widespread occurrence of the mati work among women by the absence of men, either in a strict numerical sense or in a psychological or emotional sense. I have interpreted Creole working-class women's sexual behaviors by focusing on the accounts women themselves give of them, while locating them within an African-American diasporic framework. It should be clear that when talking about the mati work, I am not referring to a recent or a marginal phenomenon. In contradistinction to the periodization most students of the mati work give, I have argued that there is no good reason to assume that it was not already present from, possibly, the time of the Middle Passage and the beginning of the colony in the seventeenth century. Although it is, of course, impossible to obtain reliable quantitative data on the occurrence of the mati work in Paramaribo in the past or today, it is clear for those who have eyes to see (the symbolic behaviors) and ears to hear (the powerful, metaphorical language mati speak to each other) that it is widespread in the working class. I have suggested that three out of four working-class Creole women will be engaged in it at some point in their lives. There is no significant stigma attached to the mati work in a working-class environment. The longevity, tenacity, and vitality of the mati work are striking, given the fact that I first "saw" the mati work in Amsterdam – after large communities of Surinamese had migrated to the metropolis at the time of independence (1975) – without being fully cognizant of what it was I saw.

Although there is a comparable, yet less institutionalized, less visible, and less widely accepted, phenomenon also called mati work among Creole men, in this contribution I will focus exclusively on Creole, working-class women. While some mati, especially older women who have borne and raised their children, do not have sex with men anymore, other, younger mati have a variety of arrangements with men, such as marriage, concubinage, or a visiting relationship. Women's relationships with women mostly take the form of visiting relationships, although a minority of female partners with their children shares a household. These varied arrangements are made possible by the circumstance that most Creole working-class women own or rent their own houses and are single heads of households. Mati thus form part of and actually continually "cross over" in a dual sexual system, which comprises an opposite-gendered and a same-gendered arena. I will come back to this sexual system in more detail later.

I Am a Gold Coin

The most frequent response working-class women gave me when I asked them to name a proverb that most closely expressed how they saw themselves, was "I am a gold coin." Creole culture, like other Black cultures in the diaspora, abounds with verbal arts: *odo* (proverbs), riddles, stories, word games, and songs. Blacks formulated odo during slavery as a running commentary on their everyday experience, and many odo bespeak a woman's everyday reality (Wekker 1997). "I am a gold coin" is a clipped version of an odo, used by insiders who often only need the first three or four words to understand what is being referred to. The entire odo goes like this: *"Mi na gowt' monni, m'e waka na alasma anu, ma mi n'e las' mi waarde"* ("I am a gold coin, I pass through all hands, but I do not lose my value"). It expresses with precision, yet characteristic indirection, some important features of the (sexual) universe Creole working-class women inhabit. An analysis of the odo gives important insights into this universe, while it simultaneously contradicts some of the most frequent, hegemonic explanations of social and gender patterns in the Caribbean.

The entire odo points to working-class women's adherence to a value structure in which middle-class values like legal marriage, monogamy, the heterosexual contract, one man fathering all one's children are designated as irrelevant to their reality. In effect, working-class women (whether exclusively involved with men, women, or both) are saying: It does not matter how many relationships I have had, whether with men or with women. What counts is how I carry myself through life, as a mother, with dignity, (self-) respect, and savvy, all of which characterize a *dyaya uma* (a mature woman, who knows how to take care of business). This autonomous set of values, found in the working class, runs counter to

such a concept as "the lower-class value stretch" (Rodman 1971), which implies that working-class black people stretch middle-class values like monogamy and marriage, until their own practices can be said to fall within middle-class parameters.

My (African-American) understanding of the mati work and the alternative value structure in which it is embedded also flies in the face of Wilson's "respectability and reputation" paradigm (1969). Wilson stipulates that Afro-Caribbean working-class women are the bearers and perpetuators of inegalitarian, Eurocentric "respectability" due to their closer association with the master class during slavery as concubines and domestic slaves. Afro-Caribbean men, on the other hand, are said to subscribe to the egalitarian value system of "reputation," an indigenous counterculture based on the ethos of equality and rooted in personal as opposed to social worth. As I have shown elsewhere, Creole women participate fully in the local reputation system through their leadership roles in Winti, spirit possession, prophecy and healing, the significance and desirability of motherhood, their oral skills, and their entrepreneurial, political, and organizational roles (Wekker 1992b, 1997). Creole women have been and are central to cultures rooted in the tradition of slave resistance, which emerged in response to colonialism and the plantation system and which continued later in opposition to hegemonic, middle-class value patterns. My understanding of the frequency and openness of the phenomenon builds on West African heritage, the "grammatical principles" (Mintz and Price 1992) surrounding selfhood, gender, and sexuality, which Surinamese slaves elaborated upon under a specific constellation of historical, demographic, and cultural-political circumstances (Wekker 1992b). In addition, there are strong reasons to believe that slave women in other parts of the Caribbean developed comparable forms of relating to each other (Lorde 1983; Silvera 1992), pointing to the resiliency of the West African cultural heritage.

On a final note, the odo flatly denies the heterosexist representations of Caribbean women, encapsulated in the concept most widely used (and abused) to explain Caribbean family patterns and gender relations: matrifocality. The gendered sexual images that can be culled from the prolific literature on matrifocality is that men are sexually hyperactive, high performers, while women wait around patiently and pitifully for the hunter to bestow his favors upon them. So far, it has apparently been extremely difficult for (mostly male, heterosexual?) anthropologists to conceive that women did not wait around but took responsibility for orchestrating their own sexual pleasures.

Multiplicitous Subjectivities

Analyzing the parts of the odo "I am a gold coin," we first find an identification with *gold*. By inserting this adjective, women indicate that they consider themselves inherently worthy and valuable, which is symbolized by the allusion to the most desirable, durable, and precious good available in Surinamese society. Furthermore, gold is wanted to adorn and placate instantiations of the multiplicitous self as it is envisioned within the framework of the Afro-Surinamese Winti folk religion. Unlike the Western version of the subject as "unitary, authentic, bounded, static, trans-situational" (Geertz 1984), the self in an Afro-Surinamese working-class universe is conceptualized as multiplicitous, malleable, dynamic, contextually salient. Winti builds deeply upon West African "grammatical principles" (Mintz and Price 1992) and pervades virtually all aspects of life, from before birth to beyond death. Within this framework there is a relatively egalitarian gender ideology, in which both men and women are thought to be composed of male and female *winti*, gods. Also, importantly, both men and women are deemed to be full sexual subjects, with their own desires and own possibilities to act on these desires. Sexual fulfillment per se is considered important, healthy, and joyous, while the gender of one's object choice is regarded as less important. The following quote comes from an eighty-four-year-old mati, Misi Juliette Cummings, a retired market woman, who has had a variety of relationships with men in her life. She bore twelve children, seven of whom are alive

today. The "apples of her eye," throughout her long life, were definitely women:

Mi, noit' mi ben wan' trow, ef' mek' ver-bontu nanga man[4] [I never wanted to marry or "be in association with a man"]. *Mi yeye no ben wan' de ondro man* [My "soul"/"I" did not want to be under a man]. Some women are like that. I am somebody who was not *hebzuchtig* [greedy] on a man, *mi yeye ben wan' de nanga umasma* [my "soul," "I," wanted to be with women]. It is your "soul" that makes you so. It is more equal when you are with a woman; the same rights you have, I have too. (Wekker 1992b: 284)

In this quote Misi Juliette demonstrates some of the different instantiations of "I": in referring to herself she talks about *mi* (I) and *mi yeye* (my "soul"/I) wanting to be with women. *Yeye* refers to a decisive component of "I," made up of a male and a female God, both of which accompany the individual from birth (Wekker 1992b). An emic explanation of the mati work takes into account that one of the Gods, making up the *yeye*, is a male God, an Apuku, who desires women. This God, who is strong and jealous, cannot bear to see his child, the woman, involved on a long-term basis with a real flesh-and-blood male. Thus a mati is conceptualized as a woman, part of whose "I" desires and is sexually active with other women. Since the "I" is conceived as multiple and open, it is not necessary to claim a "truest, most authentic kernel of the self," a fixed "identity" that is attracted to other women. Rather, mati work is seen as a particularly pleasing and joyous activity, not as an identity. Linguistically, this conceptualization of sex as behavior is apparent in the phrase mati use to describe themselves. When pressed about the issue, as I often did in my role of "outsider within" (Hill Collins 1990) asking most impertinent, direct questions, they would say: *M'e mati*, using a verb ("I mati"), instead of: "*Mi na wan mati*" ("I am a mati").

A Dual Sexual System

In a further analysis of the odo "I am a gold coin" the identification with a coin is striking.

First, this elicits the obvious connotation of a coin, passing from hand to hand, with its counterpart of women going from one relationship to the next, "trying to find their happiness," as they themselves explain. The analogy between money and women having multiple relationships is made without attaching negative value to it, as the third part of the odo – "but I do not lose my value" – shows.

But there is a second, relatively hidden, meaning to the allusion to money. Far from sovereignly imagining oneself above money, it is the standard by which women measure the seriousness of intent of their male partners: women envision a relatively straightforward exchange relationship between sex and money in their connections with men. As one woman told me, when she was describing an imaginary but, in her eyes, most undesirable and ludicrous outcome of such a cross-gender connection: "*A koṅ sidon na mi tapu, dan e n'e tya mi sensi koṅ . . . dan m'e law*" ("Then he comes, sits down in my house and doesn't bring me my money, then I must be crazy") (Wekker 1992b: 178).

The transactional nature of opposite-gender relationships is by no means an exclusively Afro-Surinamese phenomenon. It is a connection found in divergent urban working-class settings, such as nineteenth- and early twentieth-century white New York (Peiss 1984, 1986), contemporary white American (Rubin 1976), African-American (Liebow 1967; Stack 1974), Nairobian (Nelson 1979), and Jamaican working-class cultures (Harrison 1988). It has, furthermore, been found in white middle-class settings that women tend to make more "pragmatic" choices regarding their mates, "knowing . . . that economic security is more important than passion" (Peplau and Gordon 1985: 264). Working-class women, both mati and women who are exclusively involved with men, by their own accounts, need men to make them children in a system where the epitome of womanhood is motherhood, and they need men's financial contributions to keep their households afloat (Wekker 1992b). Demonstrating one's fertility, by having a large *bere* (literally, belly: children and grandchildren) used to be important to both men and women in a working-class culture that leaves few other avenues for distinguishing oneself. Younger women, in general, do not want to raise large families anymore, but motherhood remains vital. In accounting for their relationships with men, some women, who are embedded in the Afro-Surinamese Winti religion, argue that it is unhealthy for your "insides" not to have sexual communion with men at least once in a while. This argument, again, needs to be understood in the framework of an outlook on subjectivity, embedded within Winti, that stresses the importance of balancing the multiple aspects of the self; male and female "instantiations" of the person need to be satisfied and kept in harmony.

In their relationships with women, mati deploy money in a much less direct way. Although female lovers do exchange money and help each other cope financially, this aspect of the relationship is embedded in a rich flow of reciprocal obligations, which include the sharing of everyday concerns, the raising of children, nurturing, emotional support, and sexual pleasure. Money, as an exchange object for sex, thus plays an independent and outspoken role in relationships with men, but it is part of a more elaborate, a "thicker" stream of exchanges and reciprocal obligations in relationships with women. In fact, the term *work* in mati work implies that there are mutual obligations involved between two female partners. Mati contrast mati work with another modality they call *didon gewoon*, i.e., "just lying down"/"sleeping around," a sexual connection that does not imply rights and obligations toward another woman. *Didon gewoon* is not part of an ongoing relationship but marks an unencumbered, incidental sexual encounter. The rights and obligations in mati work generally involve the (social, psychological, economic) activities that are needed to help one's partner weather life. This may be by going to the doctor with her when she is ill, helping her finance a "crown" year celebration (when she reaches an important, five-yearly birthday), or, as the younger partner in the relationship, by showing one's mati the appropriate, respectful behavior. Most important, mati have sexual obligations toward each other: when one partner feels sexual desire, the other is obliged to satisfy her. It is generally agreed by mati that when a woman's desire is consistently denied by her partner, she may go and seek sexual pleasures with someone else. This may very well spell the demise of the relationship, since few women will tolerate it when their partner openly engages in sex with another woman.

During my research period, I asked several women to reflect on what some of the differences were between being in a sexual relationship with a man or with a woman. My landlady Misi Juliette, the eighty-four-year-old market woman, often explained to me that, "I really did not mind much, when that man [Dorus, the man she had five children with] went to visit other women. Frankly, I often thought: Well, it is better that he goes and harasses them instead of me. I also didn't mind when Coba [her mati] lay down with a man. If she could find a little money with him, why not? But if she slept with another woman, now that was different business!! I did not tolerate it."

In this and other conversations we had, it was abundantly clear that the intensity of Juliette's feelings was entirely focused on Coba, not Dorus, and that jealousy was channeled toward Coba's encounters with other women, not men. It made the socially constructed nature of such "natural" feelings as jealousy vividly clear to me.

The following quote from Lydia de Vrede, a thirty-seven-year-old nurse's aide, mother of five, who is currently married to the father of her last two children, helps to further illustrate these differences:

I see it like this: love between two women is stronger than between a man and a woman. Maybe emancipated women will tell a man what they like in the bedroom, or tell him: do this or do that! But to satisfy that man, most women will pretend that they have come. But with a woman, you know what you like sexually and so does she, *dus a san' kan law yu ede zodanig, a kan tya' yu go na Kolera* [so the thing can make you so crazy, it may carry you into a mental hospital]. (Wekker, 1992b:283)

Before she was married, Lydia had several relationships with women, but given the jealous nature of her husband, she presently misses

having a female lover but finds it impossible to accommodate a woman in her situation.[5] The quote reveals the existence of a dual sexual system, in which different power dynamics between partners obtain. There is an opposite-gendered arena in which masculine values and men are hegemonic. This arena within the working class is fed by an array of societal forces and influences, including inegalitarian middle-class gender arrangements and values, government regulations producing inequalities between men and women in the area of, among others, income,[6] and media and educational institutions transmitting homogenizing, normative, nuclear family contents. Men, because of their stronger economic positions and because they mostly do not carry the exclusive or main financial burden of having to bring up children, have more free-floating capital. As elsewhere in the Caribbean, we find in Suriname an overall picture of a dually segmented labor market, where men are found in the heavier and more profitable sectors of the formal and informal economy, working under better conditions and with higher salaries; women, on the other hand, work in the softer sectors of the economy, for the government, where wages are notoriously low, and in the informal sector (Tjoa 1990; Wekker 1992b). It is through their economically stronger position, however tenuous it may in itself be at times, that men get the upper hand in defining the proceedings of opposite-gender sexual encounters. Within this opposite-gender exchange system, women have less room to maneuver, and even less so within a steadily declining economy and following the adoption of Structural Adjustment Programs. The following account by forty-three-year-old Mildred Jozefzoon, a hairdresser and mother of four children, illustrates some features of her visiting relationship with Johnny Samuel, who is the father of three of her children and who lives with another woman:

I get 100 or 125 Surinamese guilders from him, a week.[7] Mostly he comes around 11:30 A.M. and needs to be out of my house by 1:00 P.M. He wants it to be quick-quick. The way I feel about it is that somebody has come to take something away from me and then he leaves.

I feel misused, taken in, even though he gives me the money. It goes like this: he takes off his shirt and his trousers, lies down on my bed. Then he wants me to come lie down beside him. Sometimes I sabotage the whole business by being agonizingly slow in taking off my clothes. Sometimes I say I don't feel like it. Then he says: I will make you feel like it. What can I do? He wants it so often and I need the money. (Wekker 1992b: 224)

Pertinent in this segment of the sexual system is also that women tend to see each other as competitors for men's favors, and they do not exchange sexual information. Women consistently report an unfavorably skewed sex ratio, i.e., that the number of women far exceeds the number of men, yet what seems more likely to be the case is that the number of men whom women consider *eligible* – i.e., economically viable partners – is rather limited. Yet women still refuse, to varying degrees, to give up their subject status and agency. By elaborating on the concept of *kamraprekti*, chamber (i.e., sexual) obligations, women, whether they are in a permanent or in a more incidental relationship with a man, assert their own standards of fairness concerning the exchange of sexual favors for money; from unfavorable positions women try to adjust and manage the unequal balance of economic power with men (Wekker 1992b).

In the other domain of the dual sexual system, the same-gendered one, women are able to define what their sexual and emotional pleasures are. Life in society as a whole, but most markedly in the working class, is constituted along distinctly homosocial lines; men spend most of their time with other men, while women, whether mati or not, are more likely to share time, work, attention, nurturing and, possibly, sexual encounters with other women. Since most women spend the greater part of their time in the company of other women, this means that there is no marked difference in the daily, social environments of mati and women who are sexually active only with men. On the contrary, working-class women, regardless of the gender of their sexual partners, frequently mingle and share the same environments. Among older mati we find relationships that have sometimes lasted thirty,

forty, or more years. They raise their children together, share everyday concerns and ritual obligations and celebrations: "*Let' anu e was' krukt' anu*" ("the right hand washes the left"), is how older women typically conceive of their bonds with their mati. Traditionally, older women who were in a mati relationship used to wear dresses made out of the same material, *parweri*, but nowadays that is seen less often. Among younger mati there is a lively, sexual culture enacted at parties at people's homes and at *Winti Prey*, out-door ritual gatherings in the framework of the Winti religion. Flirting and seeking each other out by linguistic, symbolic, and behavioral means have been made into an art form in this universe. By all accounts, sex with women is an important feature of women's lives, and they talk about it, often indirectly and metaphorically, but with obvious gusto (Wekker 1992a, 1992b). One such narrative, which illustrates the joy inherent in sex with women, is told by Milly Pinas, a fifty-six-year-old street sweeper, mother of three children:

I had this lady that I was really infatuated with, Ingrid. She had a steady relationship with Lucia and I was living with a man at the time. One Saturday afternoon, I took the bus to her place, bringing a bag of groceries and some ice-cold beers. She was expecting her lover that afternoon, too, however, so she told me to lock the door from the outside and climb through a window. Pretty soon we were upstairs in bed. We were "stealing," so it had to be fast work. We were almost hitting, when *pam-pam-pam*, who comes knocking at the door? I was not afraid, I wanted to go on, but Ingrid was shaking. She jumped from the bedroom window unto her neighbor's roof. It turns out that Lucia had a spare key to the house, so she came upstairs. I was sitting on the bed, wearing only a black slip. She said: "Good afternoon." I said: "good afternoon to you, too." Ingrid stayed outside, did not dare to come in. Lucia had been after me for a long time, so we hit on each other right away. (Wekker 1992b: 275)

Women friends actively exchange sexual information and young girls are often initiated into the mati world by older women, sometimes explicitly in the form of an apprentice relationship (Wekker 1992a, 1992b). Women often structure their relationships erotically into a "male" and a "female" role, with the male role having more prerogatives, just as in the world out there. These sexual roles are not carved in stone, however, and many women can and do change roles, either in the same relationship or in another one. Economically, mati relationships are more egalitarian than those between men and women. I have also concluded that sexually and emotionally they are more satisfying to many women than their cross-gendered relationships.

If the foregoing analysis of a dual sexual system in the Afro-Surinamese working class, namely an opposite-gendered and a same-gendered arena, holds any validity, it is to be expected that there will be "leakage" between these two domains. There is considerable overlap in the personnel moving from one part of the system to the other, notably in the persons of mati, and it thus should not be surprising that several features of sexual culture, in the form of shared practices, are held in common in both parts of the system. The importance of motherhood; the polarization of roles within relationships, in a "male" and a "female" counterpart with accompanying role expectations; the existence of patterns of jealousy and violence between partners; the existence of sometimes wide age gaps between partners; and the underlying cosmology as it pertains to personhood and sexual being are all part of mati culture as well as of opposite-gender sexual arrangements. Thus the notion that the same-gendered arena proceeds according to a specific set of ideas, rules, and practices, which is totally distinct and insulated from what takes place in the opposite-gendered domain, cannot be held up.

While it is true that in many Western gay and lesbian sexual arrangements elements of dominant heterosexual culture are evoked, the point I am making here is a different one. From an emic point of view, mati and women exclusively involved with men have more in common with each other than is different between them. Being sexually active and fulfilled is more important than the object of one's passion. Mati are not singled out or stigmatized in a working-class environment nor do they feel the necessity to fight for their liberation or to "come out." Thus to the extent that I have stressed the differences between mati and women relating to men only, I may paradoxically and involuntarily have been highlighting the pernicious tendency of Western, bounded, fixed categories to insert and reproduce themselves in radically different constructions of being a (sexual) person.

What's Identity Got to Do with It?

It is clear that within this Afro-Surinamese working-class setting there is a radically different conceptualization of personhood and same-gender desire than is customarily the case within a Western frame of reference. I will first briefly address the latter configuration. The troubled Western relationship with homosexuality, naturalized, compartmentalized, medicalized, consecutively made into sin and into the "deepest, truest" expression of the self, of one's identity, is historically and culturally embedded (Foucault 1981; De Cecco and Elia 1993). Whether a homosexual identity is understood as the pure sediment of biological or physiological processes, or whether some kind of interaction between the biological and the cultural is envisioned, or whether primacy is given to sociocultural experiences, the notion of a sexual identity in itself carries deep strands of permanency, stability, fixity, and near-impermeability to change. Furthermore, the mere existence of a sexual identity is usually taken for granted. The static nature of sexual identity is in line with the ways personhood in general is envisioned within a Western universe. Despite much evidence to the contrary, this culture stubbornly persists in the fictive notion that a person has a stable "core" character (Shweder and Bourne 1984): "a bounded, unique, more or less integrated motivational and cognitive universe... organized in a distinctive whole and set contrastively... against other such wholes" (Geertz 1984: 126).

It is noteworthy that in most Indo-European languages there is only one way to make statements about the self: the personal pronoun "I." This particular understanding of a person as a bounded, fixed, rational, and self-determining agent is produced and reproduced in and by modern political, legal, social, and aesthetic discourses. Subjectivity has, until recently, implicitly been envisaged along masculine lines, thus leaving femininity no conceptual space but the nonmasculine; femininity is not just different, but in a hierarchically subordinate position to the masculine (Weedon 1987; Haraway 1991). While male sexuality is seen as aggressive and potent, female sexuality is conceptualized as passive and weak, needing to be awakened by a stronger force. Furthermore, one is either heterosexual or homosexual, with bisexuality muddying these clear waters. Dichotomous, either/or, hierarchical thinking characterizes this system.

A Creole universe is characterized by additive, inclusive, both/and thinking (cf. Hill Collins 1990). A person is conceived of as multiple, malleable, dynamic, and possessing male and female elements. Furthermore, all persons are inherently conceived of as sexual beings. A linguistic reflection and construction of this multiple, dynamic conceptualization of personhood is that in Sranantongo, the local creole, there are infinite possibilities to refer to "I" (Wekker 1992b). It is possible to talk about the self in masculine and in feminine terms, in singular and in plural forms, and in terms of third person construction, regardless of the gender of the speaker. All of these different terms refer to different instantiations of "I."

A human being in this universe is understood to be made up of human and "godly" elements. From conception until death, a person is "carried" and protected by Winti, gods. These gods are very near to a person's experience, and they are conceptualized like human beings, possessing the same virtues and vices. A person who is carried by Mama Aisa, the Uppergoddess of the Earth, for example, likes beautiful clothes and jewelry and is caring and nurturing. Both men and women can be carried by Aisa. Some characteristics of a person, such as those that she gets from the gods who accompany her throughout her life, or traits inherited from a biological parent, are seen as permanent, while others are temporary and contextually realized.

Women who engage in the mati work are, as we have seen, thought to be carried by a strong, male god, an Apuku, who is jealous of his "child," the woman, engaging in permanent sexual relationships with flesh-and-blood males. The Apuku is believed to be so strong and demanding that his child will have difficulty relating to men and will be more attracted to other women. An emic explanation of the mati work does not claim a core homosexual identity; rather, the behavior is conceived of as engagement in a pleasant activity, desired and instigated by one particular instantiation of the "I." It is the Apuku who is sexually attracted to women, and there is no emic reason to privilege this instantiation of the "I" above others by making him the decisive, "truest" element of the self. Likewise, when women state that it is good for your "insides" to have sex with men at least once in a while, they are building on an understanding of multiplicitous personhood that temporarily privileges a female instantiation of "I," which desires a man.

It is in keeping with the multiplicity of the "I" that a multiplicitous sexual repertoire was realized in the Creole working-class. There is no significant stigma attached to parts of this repertoire. Girls growing up in Creole working-class neighborhoods are confronted with different sexual choices and engaging in one variety – e.g., the same-gendered one – does not expose the girl to disapproval nor does it predispose her to stay in that part of the sexual system forever. Thus we see women who are alternately or simultaneously active in either part of the system. There are clear economic coordinates associated with their behavior (Wekker 1992b). Conceiving of same-gender sexual behavior embodied in the mati work in terms of "identity" inscribes and reproduces Western thought categories with their legacy of dichotomy, hierarchy, and permanency, thus distorting a phenomenon that is emically experienced in quite different terms.

Theorizing Same-Gender Sexual Behavior Cross-Culturally

Finally, what does all of this mean in light of our ongoing efforts to theorize same-gender sexual behavior cross-culturally? First of all,

I hope to have made a case for the critical investigation and bracketing of the concept "homosexual identity." The deeply essentialist strand it often unwittingly introduces hampers rather than facilitates our understanding of the behavior we are trying to understand cross-culturally.

In the second place, emic constructions and explanations of same-gender sexual behavior need to be taken seriously. There is no reason to assume that the Western folk knowledge about sex, which has been elevated into academic knowledge (cf. Lutz 1985), should have any more validity than folk knowledge anywhere else. Feminist anthropology has proven not to be immune against problems that have haunted the discipline from its inception: the exclusion, erasure, or negation of the subjectivity and the critical agency of the colonized, especially women (cf. Mohanty 1991; Harrison 1993).

Third, the cross-cultural study of same-gender sexual behavior should proceed from the realization that "homosexualities" are multiple and manifold, realized in different contexts and charged with different meanings. Clearly, there are some institutional domains within every society that seem crucial in understanding the local constructions of the phenomenon – such as notions of personhood, gender systems – in their ideological and practical dimensions and their crosscutting ties with other domains, such as the economy and religion. It is misleading and self-defeating to talk of same-gender sexual behavior as one single, cross-cultural institution. The use of seemingly innocuous concepts, such as "homosexual identity," contributes to the export of Western categories of thought.

Finally, if in participant observation it is the person of the researcher that serves as the most central and sensitive instrument of research, it behooves those of us who do (cross-cultural) sex research to be transparent, accountable, and reflective about our own sexualities (cf. Kulick and Willson 1995). Awareness of the situatedness and sociocultural construction of our own sexuality and about the different modalities in which we engage with others are only some of the minimal requirements we ought to place on ourselves.

NOTES

1 Creoles, the second largest population group in Suriname, are the descendants of slaves and are a mainly urban group. I will alternately call them Creoles, the local designation, and Afro-Surinamese. They distinguish themselves culturally, psychologically, and ethnically and are recognized by others to be distinct from other blacks, Maroons. The latter are the descendants of fugitive slaves who fled the plantations starting in the beginning of the seventeenth century.

2 In the rest of this article I will, sometimes at great and laborious length, avoid speaking of hetero-, homo-, and bisexuality. Because of their embeddedness within radically specific theological, medical, and social discourses, these concepts cast a distorted light on the phenomena I want to analyze here. As I have argued elsewhere (Wekker 1993), the mati work differs from bisexuality in sociohistorical background and embeddedness and in emic understanding.

3 This fieldwork was made possible through grants of the Inter-American Foundation (Washington, DC) and the Institute of American Cultures (UCLA).

4 *Mek' verbontu nanga man*, to make an association with a man, can be used in two ways: (1) It refers to a ritual oath a man and a woman may take not to have other sexual partners. If people do not keep this oath, it is believed that punishment, in the form of sickness or death, will follow. Women also can take this oath together. (2) It refers to the institution, initiated by the Evangelical Brethren Society during slavery when slaves were not allowed to marry, that men and women state publicly in church that they will be faithful to each other.

5 This particular husband's reaction is not the only imaginable one, nor, I would say, the most typical. Working-class men, who are also embedded within Winti and share its weltanschauung, display a variety of reactions toward their wives or lovers engaging in relationships with women. If

they, too, understand the need of the woman's "I" to be with other women, many men know and accept it.

6 Functioning as an economic safety net, the government is the largest employer in Suriname, employing about 45% of the total labor force. Of the female labor force (an estimated 40% of the total), 67% work for the government, mostly as cleaners, streetssweepers, and lower office personnel, thus in the lowest salary scales (Tjoa 1990). Furthermore, due to the flagrantly invalid, patriarchal notion that men are heads of households and that women earn merely additional income and have a breadwinner at home, women earn consistently less than men for the same labor.

7 Price index middle of 1991. Since then, inflation has risen rapidly.

REFERENCES

Alexander, Jacqui. 1991. Redrafting Morality: The Postcolonial State and the Sexual Offences Bill of Trinidad and Tobago. In Chandra Mohanty, Ann Russo, and Lourdes Torres, eds., *Third World Women and the Politics of Feminism*, pp. 133–52. Bloomington: Indiana University Press.

Ambacht. 1912. *Het Ambacht in Suriname.* Rapport van de Commissie Benoemd bij Goevernementsresolutie van 13 januarie 1910, no. 13. Paramaribo.

Buschkens, Willem. 1974. *The Family System of the Paramaribo Creoles.* Verhandelingen van het Koninklijk Instituut voor Taal-, Land-, en Volkenkunde, no. 71. The Hague: Martinus Nijhoff.

Comvalius, Th. 1935. Het Surinaamsch Negerlied: De Banja en de Doe. *West-Indische Gids*, 17: 213–20.

De Cecco, John, and John Elia. 1993. A Critique and Synthesis of Biological Essentialism and Social Constructionist Views of Sexuality and Gender. In John De Cecco and John Elia, eds., *If You Seduce a Straight Person, Can You Make them Gay? Issues in Biological Essentialism and Social Constructionism in Gay and Lesbian Identities*, pp. 1–26. New York: Haworth Press.

D'Emilio, John. 1984. Capitalism and Gay Identity. In Anne Snitow, Christine Stansell, and Sharon Thompson, eds., *Powers of Desire: The Politics of Sexuality*, pp. 100–13. London: Virago.

Foucault, Michel. 1981. *The History of Sexuality*, vol. 1: *An Introduction.* Harmondsworth: Pelican.

Geertz, Clifford. 1984. From the Native's Point of View: On the Nature of Anthropological Understanding. In Richard A. Shweder and Robert A. LeVine, eds., *Culture Theory: Essays on Mind, Self, and Emotion*, pp. 123–36. Cambridge: Cambridge University Press.

Haraway, Donna J. 1991. *Simians, Cyborgs, and Women: The Reinvention of Nature.* London: Free Association Books.

Harrison, Faye. 1988. Women in Jamaica's Informal Economy: Insights from a Kingston Slum. *Nieuwe West-Indische Gids*, 62/3 & 4: 103–28.

—— 1993. Writing against the Grain: Cultural Politics of Difference in the Work of Alice Walker. *Critique of Anthropology*, 13/4: 401–27.

Herskovits, Melville J., and Frances Herskovits. 1936. *Suriname Folk-Lore.* New York: Columbia University Press.

Hill Collins, Patricia. 1990. *Black Feminist Thought: Knowledge, Consciousness, and the Politics of Empowerment.* London: HarperCollins Academic.

Janssens, Mari-José and Wilhelmina van Wetering. 1985. Mati en Lesbiennes, Homoseksualiteit, en Etnische Identiteit bij Creools-Surinaamse Vrouwen in Nederland. *Sociologische Gids*, 54/6: 394–415.

Kondo, Dorinne. 1990. *Crafting Selves: Power, Gender, and Discourses of Identity in a Japanese Workplace.* Chicago: University of Chicago Press.

Kulick, Don. 1995. Introduction: The Sexual Life of Anthropologists: Erotic Subjectivity and Ethnographic Work. In Don Kulick and Margaret Willson, eds., *Taboo: Sex, Identity, and Erotic Subjectivity in Anthropological Fieldwork*, pp. 1–28. London: Routledge.

Kulick, Don and Margaret Willson, eds. 1995. *Taboo: Sex, Identity, and Erotic Subjectivity in Anthropological Fieldwork*. London: Routledge.

Lewin, Ellen. 1995. Writing Lesbian Ethnography. In Ruth Behar and Deborah Gordon, eds., *Women Writing Culture*, pp. 322–35. Berkeley: University of California Press.

Liebow, Elliot. 1967. *Tally's Corner: A Study of Negro Streetcorner Men*. Boston: Little, Brown.

Lorde, Audre. 1983. *Zami: A New Spelling of My Name*. New York: Crossing Press.

Lutz, Catherine. 1985. Ethnopsychology Compared to What? Explaining Behavior and Consciousness among the Ifaluk. In Geoffrey White and John Kirkpatrick, eds., *Person, Self and Experience: Exploring Pacific Ethnopsychologies*, pp. 35–79. Berkeley: University of California Press.

Mintz, Sidney, and Richard Price. 1992. *The Birth of African-American Culture: An Anthropological Perspective*. Boston: Beacon Press.

Mohanty, Chandra Talpade. 1991. Under Western Eyes: Feminist Scholarship and Colonial Discourses. In Chandra Mohanty, Ann Russo, and Lourdes Torres, eds., *Third World Women and the Politics of Feminism*, pp. 51–80. Chicago: University of Chicago Press.

Nelson, N. 1979. How Women and Men Get By: The Sexual Division of Labour in the Informal Sector of a Nairobi Squatter Settlement. In R. Bromley and C. Gerry, eds., *Casual Work and Poverty in Third World Cities*, pp. 283–302. Chichester, NY: John Wiley.

Newton, Esther, and Shirley Walton. 1984. The Misunderstanding: Toward a More Precise Sexual Vocabulary. In Carol Vance, ed., *Pleasure and Danger: Exploring Female Sexuality*, pp. 242–50. Boston: Routledge and Kegan Paul.

Peiss, Kathy. 1984. "Charity Girls" and City Pleasures: Historical Notes on Working-Class Sexuality, 1880–1920. In Ann Snitow, Christine Stansell, and Sharon Thompson, eds., *Powers of Desire: The Politics of Sexuality*, pp. 74–87. London: Virago.

—— 1986. *Cheap Amusements: Working Women and Leisure in Turn-of-the-Century New York*. Philadelphia: Temple University Press.

Peplau, Letitia, and Stephen Gordon. 1985. Women and Men in Love: Gender Differences in Close Heterosexual Relationships. In Virginia E. O'Leary et al., eds., *Women, Gender, and Social Psychology*. Hillsdale, NJ: Lawrence Erlbaum Associates.

Reinharz, Shulamit. 1992. *Feminist Methods in Social Research*. Oxford: Oxford University Press.

Rodman, Hyman. 1971. *Lower-Class Families: The Culture of Poverty in Negro Trinidad*. London: Oxford University Press.

Rubin, Lillian. 1976. *Worlds of Pain: Life in the Working-Class Family*. New York: Basic Books.

Shweder, Richard, and Edmund Bourne. 1984. Does the Concept of the Person Vary Cross-Culturally? In Richard A. Shweder and Robert A. LeVine, eds., *Culture Theory: Essays on Mind, Self, and Emotion*. Cambridge: Cambridge University Press.

Silvera, Makeda. 1992. Man Royals and Sodomites: Some Thoughts on the Invisibility of Afro-Caribbean Lesbians. *Feminist Studies*, 18/3: 521–32.

Stack, Carol. 1974. *All our Kin*. New York: Harper and Row.

Tjoa, Twie. 1990. *Vrouw Zijn in Suriname: Inleiding in het Kader van de Vierde Lustrumviering van de Vereniging van Medici in Suriname*. Paramaribo: ms.

Vance, Carole. 1989. Social Construction Theory: Problems in the History of Sexuality. In Dennis Altman et al., eds., *Homosexuality, Which Homosexuality?*, pp. 13–34. Amsterdam: An Dekker/Schorer/London: GMP Publishers.

Van Lier, Rudolf. 1986. *Tropische Tribaden: Een Verhandeling over Homoseksualiteit en Homoseksuele Vrouwen in Suriname*. Dordrecht: Foris Publications.

Weedon, Chris. 1987. *Feminist Practice and Poststructuralist Theory*. Oxford: Basil Blackwell.

Wekker, Gloria. 1992a. "Girl, It's Boobies You're Getting, No?" Creole Women in Suriname and Erotic Relationships with Children and Adolescents: Some Impressions. *Paidika: The Journal of Paedophilia*, 2/4: 43–8.

Wekker, Gloria. 1992b. I Am Gold Money (I Pass Through All Hands, But I Do Not Lose My Value): The Construction of Selves, Gender, and Sexualities in a Female, Working-Class, Afro-Surinamese Setting. PhD diss., University of California, Los Angeles.

—— 1993. Mati-ism and Black Lesbianism: Two Idealtypical Expressions of Female Homosexuality in Black Communities of the Diaspora. *Journal of Homosexuality*, 24/3–4: 145–58.

—— 1997. One Finger Does not Drink Okra Soup: Afro-Surinamese Women and Critical Agency. In M. Jacqui Alexander and Chandra Mohanty, eds., *Feminist Genealogies, Colonial Legacies, Democratic Futures*, pp. 330–52. London: Routledge.

Wilson, Peter. 1969. Reputation and Respectability: A Suggestion for Caribbean Ethnology. *Man*, NS 4/1: 70–84.

Index